Anonymous

Depositions From the Castle of York

Relating to Offenses Committed in the Northern Counties in the Seventeenth

Century

Anonymous

Depositions From the Castle of York
Relating to Offenses Committed in the Northern Counties in the Seventeenth Century

ISBN/EAN: 9783744732703

Printed in Europe, USA, Canada, Australia, Japan

Cover: Foto ©ninafisch / pixelio.de

More available books at **www.hansebooks.com**

THE PUBLICATIONS

OF THE

SURTEES SOCIETY.

ESTABLISHED IN THE YEAR

MDCCCXXXIV.

VOL. XL.

FOR THE YEAR MDCCCLXI.

WESTMINSTER:

PRINTED BY JOHN BOWYER NICHOLS AND SONS,

25, PARLIAMENT STREET.

DEPOSITIONS

FROM

THE CASTLE OF YORK,

RELATING TO OFFENCES COMMITTED IN

THE NORTHERN COUNTIES

IN THE SEVENTEENTH CENTURY.

Published for the Society

BY FRANCES ANDREWS, DURHAM;

WHITTAKER & Co., 13, AVE MARIA LANE; T. & W. BOONE,
29, NEW BOND STREET; BERNARD QUARITCH, 15, PICCADILLY,
LONDON.

AT a General Meeting of the Surtees Society held in the Castle of Durham on the 18th of June, 1860,

It was ordered, that a volume of the Depositions preserved in York Castle should be prepared for the Society, to be edited by the Secretary, as one of the publications for the year 1861.

JAMES RAINE,
Secretary.

PREFACE.

In the present work a class of documents is laid before the members of the Surtees Society, of which no one, up to this time, has made any use. In the many volumes of State Trials that have been published those cases only are to be found which are generally interesting, and almost everything of a local character has been necessarily omitted. The robberies and murders that once paralysed the village or the city have been forgotten, with the exception of a few startling crimes that are chronicled in the fugitive literature of the period or in the unwritten pages of tradition.

In the castle of York is preserved a large mass of documentary evidence, which illustrates the annals of crime in the North of England. It relates to four out of the six counties, Durham and Lancashire being the exceptions, and they had separate jurisdictions of their own. I have not been able to discover many papers at York anterior to 1640, but between that year and the arrival of William III. they exist in great numbers. During the reigns of William III. and Anne there is a hiatus in the series of records, and on that account it has been thought desirable to confine the period embraced by the present volume to the central portion of the seventeenth century.

The earliest papers that are preserved in York Castle are very similar to those which are still annually deposited there, and with which every one who is "learned in the law" is so perfectly familiar. They consist of calendars, lists of magistrates and jurors, recognisances, the presentments of parish constables, writs, petitions of various descriptions, and especially of the depositions taken before the magistrates, which exhibit many features of a striking and interesting kind. The series of minute-books is unfortunately imperfect, so that it is impossible to ascertain what was the fate of every criminal, and there are so many gaps among the files of depositions that I am unable to draw up any accurate statistical account of the crime of the district to which they relate. In every public repository of records there are many serious deficiencies, and York Castle is no exception to the general rule; but the remainder, in this instance, is so large, that the Council of the Surtees Society has determined, with the kind permission of the authorities, to select the material for one of its volumes out of this vast storehouse, which has been hitherto unexplored.

On the value of the depositions that are now given to the world there can be no controversy or difference of opinion. They give us a picture, which is drawn no where else, not only of the political feeling, but of the every-day life, of the inhabitants of the provinces. We see how the great movements and movers in the state were criticised in the cottage and the market-place. We can gauge the sentiments of the religious parties of the day. We can trace the origin and progress of great crimes, which arose and disappeared with the suddenness and the violence of an epidemic. We can put our finger upon the pulses of fanatics and politicians. We can trace vice to its haunts. We can see it festering in the alley and the court, or polluting by an unexpected and unwelcome visit the secluded village and the solitary homestead. There is much also to interest us in the style and composition of the depositions. Some good old Saxon English breaks every now and then through the stiff legal phraseology in which many of them are unfortunately drawn up. It would be an amusing sight could we place before us the justices of that day, when the depositions were being taken. In the town there would be the mayor, with an alderman or two, upon the bench, in all the pomp of civic grandeur, with a clerk to write down what was necessary, and the wish to awe both criminals and spectators with the " circumstance " and dignity of their position and their little smattering of law. Here and there in the country there would be a gentleman who had spent a few years at one of the Inns of Court. He would quote Bracton at the quarter-sessions, and know something of Coke and his erudition. How keenly would he try to puzzle the criminal that was brought before him! But in another place, and how frequently would this occur, the functionary was called to the judgment-seat from his farm-yard or his laith, unable to spell the words that he was to perpetuate, and scrawling what he heard upon the back of some letter, as there was no paper in the house. There were many Justice Shallows at that time, and it is impossible to read Roger North's description of the magistrates of Northumberland without a smile at the humour that is manifested in the picture.

The assizes were held twice a year, in March and August. Of their duration it is not easy to speak with certainty, but there seems to have been quite as much business to transact as there is at the present time. The circuit always commenced with York, and never with Lancaster or Appleby. The journeys of the dispensers of the law in many respects resembled the progresses of royalty. The sheriffs always escorted them with a gallant train of gentlemen. Within living memory the high-sheriff of Yorkshire has been attended by a large cavalcade of horsemen when he went to meet the judges. In the 16th century James Metcalfe, Esq. of Nappa, was accompanied by three hundred members of his clan, all bearing his livery and his name. Some of the old families in Northumberland, especially the Fenwicks and the Forsters, could bring an equally numerous retinue of kinsmen when the shrievalty was in their house. The judges were everywhere received with hospitality and respect. At Durham they were the guests of the Prince Palatine, who empowered them to act in his behalf. He drove them from his castle to the court in his coach and six, and sat between them on the bench, for a while, in his robes of Parliament. At Newcastle they were welcomed with great ceremony and state. They were feasted by the Corporation in the mansion-house. They sailed upon the Tyne in the mayor's barge, a pleasant custom, that was discontinued for a while, in consequence of the chief-magistrate of that ancient town having threatened, in the heat of passion, to commit one of his potent guests to prison, as the water of the Tyne was under his own jurisdiction! The sheriff of Northumberland escorted the judges to the boundaries of Cumberland, to guard them from the freebooters with whom the district was infested. When he returned homewards they passed on, under a similar protection, to trace their path among the sheep-walks across the hills and moors to Carlisle and Appleby. There were no regular roads in that country till they were laid down by General Wade in his progress against the rebels in the North. Some grateful poet has handed down the efforts of this military engineer in a characteristic couplet—

> If you'd ever been here when these roads were not made,
> You would lift up your hands and bless General Wade!

The number of cases that was brought under the cognisance of the judges at each assize was a very considerable one. Some of them were sent up from the country sessions, at which all minor offences were generally tried; but the prisoners, for the most part, were committed by the magistrates in their own authority. There were, however, many districts and places in which the judges were merely private individuals. The old prerogative of *ingfangtheof* was not yet extinct. Several baronies still retained it, and it was most jealously preserved. The justices of assize could not enter into the bishopric of Durham, which included at that time parts of Northumberland and Yorkshire, without the consent of the Prince-Bishop. There were several towns in the North that still possessed the right of trying their own offenders. The terrors of Halifax and Hull were known long before they became the chief article in the beggar's litany of deprecations. At the former town the guillotine was still in use, and at Hull the authorities had the reputation of shipping off, every now and then, a cargo of offenders and impostors, and consigning them—

Εἰς Ἔχετον βασιλῆα, βροτῶν δηλήμονα πάντων.

The labours of the judges in Northumberland and Cumberland were very materially lightened by the existence of a standing commission for the suppression of freebooters. Some of the principal gentlemen in the two counties sat upon it and dealt out justice with a relentless hand. Roger North tells us that "at one sessions they hanged eighteen for not reading *sicut clerici.*" And, in truth, there was very great need of the adoption of energetic measures. It was not from Scotland only that the moss-troopers made their depredations. An English commander, in a despatch written at the close of the 16th century, declared that there was more plundering and bloodshed by English thieves than by all the Scots in Scotland! And so it was. Every village had its party of thieves; every family had its own feuds and wrongs to avenge. No one could go to rest with the certainty of finding his cattle in his fold when he arose in the morning. The effects of such a system were most disastrous. Agriculture was necessarily neglected. Refinement there was none, and all the gentler arts were uncultivated and unknown. The husbandman tilled his fields with his arms by his side, meditating, perhaps, all the while a descent upon some neighbouring herd—

> Armati terram exercent, semperque recentes
> Convectare juvat prædas, et vivere rapto.

The landed proprietor, also, was but little in advance of his tenant in the social scale. He occasionally assisted him in his raids. At all times he was willing to cast a cloak over his offences. There are several startling pictures in the present volume of the evil influence that was exerted by the gentlemen of Northumberland and Cumberland. How lamentable is that state of society in which the fountain of justice is itself polluted! On every side there was rapine and bloodshed, and the inhabitants of the district, gentle as well as simple, were Ishmaelites indeed. An interesting account of the measures that were taken to repress the turbulence and the violence of the times is to be found in Mr. Hodgson Hinde's introductory volume to the History of Northumberland.*

* There is at York a thin volume containing the proceedings of the Border Commissioners for a few years. I take from it a code of rules upon which they acted:—

Morpeth, October the 5th, 1665. Articles of agreement made and concluded between the right honourable Charles Earle of Carlisle, William Lord Widdrington, and the rest of the commissioners for this generall gaole delivery, and justices on the part and behalfe of the Borders of England, with Henry Mackdougall of Mackerston, John Rotherfoord of Egerston, and Robert Pringle of Stitchill, for and on behalfe of the Borders of the kingdome of Scotland, commissioners for the said Borders for the suppressing of theft of both the Borders.

1. First, that the acts of Parliament shalbe put in execution, made for that purpose, and that the Act of the 7th of King James for re-demandinge shalbe duely observed, and that the manner for the demanding and delivering of felons shalbe soe often as conveniently it can according to the direction of that statute. That is to say, at the generall quarter sessions of the commissioners for the gaole delivery, and in the intervalls upon the information given to the neighbouring justices or commissioners of either kingdome of any person or persons that have committed any theft or other offence punishable by them, they shall, upon fourteen dayes notice, doe their endeavour to apprehend the said persons and bring them to some convenient place upon the Borders, where four commissioners or justices of each kingdome shalbe present to informe themselves touching the truth of such accusations; and, being satisfyed of the truth thereof, shall deliver the said persons soe demanded to be prosecuted according to the law for their offences.

2. It is further agreed, in case any Englishman shall committ any of the aforesaid offences in the kingdome of Scotland and fly into England, that, if any Scottish man shall have information whereto the said person is fled, if he doe pursue him and apprehend him and bring him before the next magistrate, he shalbe committed to the next immediate assizes, generall gaole delivery, quarter-sessions, or other meeting of commissioners which shall first happen, or come there to be tryed or re-demanded as the case shall require.

3. It is also agreed that at any assize or gaole delivery where any person or persons are brought to his or their tryalls for any of the offences aforesaid, that then noe person nor persons that shalbe produced as witnesses against such offender or offenders, or shalbe otherwise concerned in the management or prosecution of any evidence tendinge to the conviction of him or them, shall, and at that time, be questioned for any offence or offences

Of the social position and character of the people of the North during the 17th century it is impossible

of his or their owne, dureing that time of assizes or generall gaole delivery, but that he or they may safely returne againe to his or their respective kingdome and place of aboade.

4. It is also agreed that, in all the particulars herein expressed, that the same method and care shalbe used by the ministers of justice within the kingdome of Scotland for the attainement of the ends aforesaid.

5. It is also agreed that the commissioners of the kingdome of Scotland authorized for the suppression of theft, shalbe carefull to apprehend all such persons as shall endeavour to escape from us through that kingdome into Ireland.

6. It is further agreed that the commissioners of either kingdome, upon application to them made and satisfaction given that such person or persons as they shall then nominate to be suspected guilty of theft, or any other offences punishable by them, and thereupon declared demandable, that then it shall and may be lawfull for the commissioners of that kingdome to whom the persons suspected doe belong, to apprehend, or cause to be apprehended, the said persons, giveing notice to some magistrate of that kingdome after they are apprehended of such their apprehension.

HEN. MACKDOUGALL.   J. RUTHERFOORD.   ROB. PRINGLE.

The names of those that were remanded by the commissioners of the Borders of Scotland.

Roger Hangingshaw of Harehaugh, Gyles Hall of Woodhall, Alexander Rotherfoord of Peeles, John Chaiters of Woodhouses, William Hall of Wilkewood, William Hall of Eardhope, Anthony Pott of Eashop, Isack Hall of Woodhall, Adam Browne of Leerne, Roger Hall soldier in Berwicke, Alexander Hall of Woodhall, Parcivell Pott of Arnehouse, Andrew Bell called the chief Bell, Thomas Hedley of Elsden.

HEN. MACKDOUGALL.   J. RUTHERFOORD.   RO. PRINGLE.

Carlisle, 29 Augusti, 1674. Additionall articles of agreement (to those concluded at Morpeth, the 5th of October, 1665) made and concluded by and between the right hon^ble the commissioners of gaole delivery and justices on the part and behalfe of the Borders of England and Scotland, for the suppressing of theft and rapine upon the Borders of both the said kingdomes.

First, that every constable and proper officer in every constable-wicke, parish, or barony, within the counties of Northumberland, Cumberland, Westmorland, or any parts or members of the same, and within the parts and places lying on the north side of the river Tyne, commonly called and known by the names of Bedlingtonshire, Norhamshire, and Islandshire, the towne and county of Newcastle-upon-Tyne, and the towne of Barwick-

to speak with commendation. These depositions give us a very unvarnished tale. It is painful to find an Earl, the head of one of the noblest families in Scotland, killing his companion at the gaming-table in a drunken brawl. How often do we see gentlemen of the highest consideration drinking and stabbing one another in a country pot-house! Party-spirit seems to have raged with all the acrimony of later times unattended by their generosity. Treason, in one form or another, was not unfrequent. The convulsions in the state had shattered the foundations of society, and many vices had sprung up which were congenial to the period, and which the rulers treated with that unequal justice that is so detrimental to the morals and happiness of the people. Informers were far too busy

upon-Tweed, with the bounds and liberties thereof, in the kingdome of England, and within the shires and villages of Roxborough, Selkrigge, and Drumfreize, and stewartry of Annandale, within the kingdome of Scotland, shalbe authorised, by the persons haveing power for that end, to make diligent search in all suspected places, or wheresoever they shalbe desired, within their respective jurisdictions, by any person or persons haveing a warrant under the hand of any one commissioner or justice of the peace dwelling within either of the said kingdomes, for any goods stolen, or for any suspected person, and to convey the same before a commissioner or a justice of the peace of that kingdome where such person or goods shalbe apprehended or found, to be proceeded against as the case shall require.

2ly. That every person dwelling within any of the places abovesaid that shall receive againe any of his owne goods after they have been stolen, shall give account to any commissioner or justice of the peace how they came by the same.

3ly. That the commissioners or justices of the peace, or any one of them, within the places aforesaid, shall, with all expedition, binde over by recognizance or bond all such persons as shalbe suspected to be guilty of felony, or shalbe of known evill fame within their respective jurisdictions.

WILLIAM SCOTT, TARRAS, WALTER SCOTT, JON. SCOTT, F. ELIOTT, JA JOHNSTONN, J. RUTHERFURD.

with their calumnies and lies, and men had not yet learned to look upon them with contempt. There could be but little security either at home or abroad when freedom of speech and liberty of conscience were hampered or denied. Restrictions are too frequently the nurses of discontent and crime. What way could education have made among the people when superstition was still so rampant, and when they listened with such implicit belief to every tale of witchcraft and spiritual manifestations ? Religion, also, I fear, had but little hold upon the masses. They were obliged, indeed, to attend the services of the church, but there are few things more detrimental to true piety than such compulsory worship. It bore some very evil fruits. That this was the case the frequency of the crime of sacrilege is a sufficient proof. When the spirit of devotion is strong no unholy hand is laid upon a church. The painful scene that occurred in York Minster at the funeral of Lady Strafford cannot easily be forgotten.

The haunts of vice in the 17th and the 19th centuries are pretty nearly identical. In many of the agricultural and mountainous districts, in the East Riding of Yorkshire, in Craven and Westmerland, there was a general freedom from crime. It was principally to be found in the towns. The vapours that cannot contaminate the pure clear airs among the hills nestle over the crowded city. There are, however, far fewer heinous offences recorded among the depositions at York than any one could reasonably have expected. It is, perhaps, true that many crimes were undetected and even unknown, but it is pretty evident that the cases recorded in the pamphlet-literature of the day, and by men like Aubrey and Glanville, have no foundation in fact. They were written, in the first instance, merely to gratify the morbid taste of purchasers and readers. Murders were less numerous than might have been expected. Rape was almost unknown. There were, however, robbers of every description and degree, from the famous Nevinson to the ordinary cut-purse. Horse-stealing was a very frequent offence, especially in the time of the civil wars and among the disbanded soldiery. Cattle-stealing, which is now so rare, was one of the common vices both of town and country. But, perhaps, the most serious and frequent crime was the clipping and deterioration of the coin. No one can have any idea of the extent to which this infamous trade was carried on. I have seen the confessions of several culprits, each of whom inculpates twenty or thirty others. The offence, which was high-treason, was repressed by the severest punishments, but the temptation was greater than many would resist. There were few silversmiths in the North who had not purchased the proscribed filings, or clipped them off themselves.

The offences against the state, during the period embraced by the present volume, were many both in variety and number. The reader will be struck with the frequent occurrence of seditious speeches. Unimportant, for the most part, in themselves, they are still significant. They shew how freely public men and public acts were criticized in the country. We see in them the progress of popular opinion, and with what jealousy it was watched by the government in those unsettled times. The rulers, however, were generally satisfied with the mere vindication of the supremacy of the law, and a reprimand was usually the punishment with which the offenders were visited. Many, however, were not content with whispering or speaking treason. Whilst there were insurgents on land there were pirates on the seas. The adventure of Captain Denton at the market-cross at Malton will be read with great interest. The exploits of Colonel Morris at Pontefract Castle possess all the charms of a romance. One man startles us with an account of a visit that Prince Charles is said to have paid to Yorkshire during the usurpation. Another witness throws some light upon the origin of the great fire in London. Most of the leading events of the day elicit the remarks of some critic in the country. Nor were the people of the North unacquainted with the scandal of the court and capital. They would have us believe that Charles I. was a parricide, and Charles II. a Roman Catholic, and something worse. They make James II. into a murderer, and deny the death of Monmouth, whom they loved so well.

The most striking political offence recorded in this volume is the great Presbyterian rising in October, 1663. That powerful party had many real or imaginary grievances to arouse it. The neglect of that sovereign whom they had placed upon the throne—the vices that he countenanced and practised—the black Bartholomew act that emptied so many pulpits—generated much bitterness and discontent. They broke out at last in open rebellion. A conspiracy was organized at Harrogate and Knaresbrough, which spread its ramifications through the whole of the Northern counties. Liberty of conscience was the chief watchword of the insurgents. But, although there was much energy and determination evinced, they had neither system nor plan. There was no leader of any name to give his authority to the movement, for men like Fairfax and Wharton held themselves cautiously aloof. There were too many masters, with no presiding genius to direct them. The house, therefore, whilst it was in the builder's hands, crumbled to the ground. The night of the 12th of October witnessed the beginning and the ending of the Westmerland plot. The Bishopric men arose at the same time and with a similar result. In Yorkshire, however, some large preparations had been made. Farneley Wood, near Leeds, was the rendezvous of the insurgents, who assembled there on the night of the 12th in some force, and actually threw up entrenchments, which were abandoned at the approach of day. Concealment was impossible, and the Cavaliers were at once upon them. Numerous arrests were made throughout the North of England, and in the winter a special assize was held, at which the offenders were brought to the bar. Twenty-two were executed in Yorkshire, and four at Appleby. Many others were kept in prison for a long time; and so severe an example was made that the flames of treason were thoroughly stamped out. A list of the Yorkshire prisoners, which is quite new, will be read with interest. The offenders, it will be seen, were principally West Riding men, and many of them were engaged in the manufactures for which that part of England was even then renowned.

Jan. 7, 1663-4. Before Sir Christopher Turner, kt. Baron of the Exchequer, and Sir John Keeling and Sir John Archer, kts. Justices of the Common Pleas.

To be hanged, drawn, and quartered. Captain Thomas Oates of Morley, Samuel Ellis, John Ellis of Morley, John Nettleton, sen. and jun. of Dunningley, Robert Scott, of Alverthorp, Wm. Tolson, John Fossard, Robert Oldroyd of Dewsbury, Joshua Askwith, alias Sparling, of Morley, Peregrine Corney, John Sowden, John Smith, Wm. Ash, John Errington, exequendus apud Leeds, Robert Atkins, exequendus apud Leeds, Wm. Cotton, George Denham, Henry Watson, exequendus apud Leeds, Richard Wilson, Ralph Rymer, sen.

Richard Oldroyd, (the devil of Dewsbury,) sentenced to death in July, 1664.

Charles Carr, reprieved before judgment. Released from gaol in March, 1665.

Acquitted. To find sureties for their good behaviour, and to take the oath of allegiance.—William Towers and Robert Redshaw of Leeds, cloth-workers, Robert Cooke, James Newton of Leeds, locksmith, Samuel Ward of Morley, labourer, William Sparling of Woodchurch, cloth-worker, John Smirfitt of Morley, Ralph and John Wade of Leeds, cloth-workers.

To remain in gaol, without bail, till the delivery of the gaol, for

xx   PREFACE.

high-treason.—Leonard Flesher of Otley, yeoman, Richard Nelson of Helperby, yeoman, John Sergeant of Harrogate, yeo., John Hodgson, Theodore Parkinson, Walter Merry, William Stockdale of Bilton park, Esq., Joseph Oddy, James Oddy of Leeds, clothier, William Flesher, Daniel Lupton of Holbeck, Robert Fletcher, Henry Pownall of Hawnby, gen. Thomas Pickells of Beckwithshaw, George Robinson of Burrowby, yeo., John Pease of Leeds, cloth-worker, Robert Lucas, Ralph Robinson of Cockerton, co. Durham, Matthew Thackwray, Thomas Lascells of Mountgrace, gen., James Fisher of Sheffield, gen., Ralph Rymer, jun , John Joblin of Newhouse, gen., Robert Hutton, John Tayler, William Hogg of Leeds, cordwainer, George Fawcett, Henry Hanson of Broughton, yeo., Benjamin Lucas of Broughton, yeo.

Freed by proclamation, but to find securities, and to take the oath of allegiance.—David Hamond of Bolton, yeo., William Hamond of Bolton near Bradford, John Staveley of Calenton, yeo , Samuel Sparling, alias Askwith, of Woodchurch, linen-weaver, James Sparling, alias Askwith, of Earles Heaton, weaver, Robert Harrison, Robert Raine of Ripon, yeo., William Adkins, alias Atkinson, cloth-worker, William Day of Skipton, cloth-worker, John Wiseman, of Leeds, cloth-dresser, John Dickinson, of Gildersome, yeo., John Acey, David Leake of Ripon, malster, Percival Robinson of Northallerton, inn-holder, Francis White of Olton, yeo., John Dennison of Morley, yeo., Henry Laidman of Hunslet, clothier, Dennis Walker of Leeds, cloth-dresser, John Lascells of Little Siddall, gen., Miles Dawson of Beeston, clothier, William Dixon of Leeds, cloth-worker, Thomas Lobley, Edward Sheppardson, Timothy Crowther of Gildersome, yeo , Thomas Woollas of Glaipwell, co. Derby, gen., Ralph Rountree of Stokesley, yeo., Christopher Witton of Eaton, yeo., John Hill of York, grocer.

Thomas Benson, acquitted by proclamation and released.

To find bail to appear at the next assizes, and in the mean time to be of good behaviour.—Ralph Oates of Morley, gen., Timothy Idle of Holbeck, Enock Sincler of Burneby, John Hunter of Leeds, cloth-worker, Nathaniel Shrigley of Halifax, Robert Nicholson, Thomas Walker, Christopher Brogden of Holbeck, cloth-maker, William Bussy, William Flesher of Leeds, shoemaker, William Childrey, Henry Bradshaw of Manningham, and Peter Pattison of Bubwith, yeoman.

To remain in gaol without bail.—John Acy, Robert Hutton, John Joblin, William Fisher, Percival Robinson, Alexander Horner, Francis White, Dennis Walker, William Hamond and Robert Cooke.*

Among the political offenders of the day the Quakers must undoubtedly be enumerated. That peculiar sect had only recently sprung into existence, and, through its luminaries, Fox and Naylor, it was very closely connected with the North of England. The infancy of this religious party was more fiery than its age. The Quakers were concerned more or less in all the plots of the time. It was their delight to abuse the minister in the pulpit and the judge upon the bench. They were continually violating public order and decency in the grossest manner. They prophesied. They walked about the streets in the unadorned simplicity of our first parents. They howled and bellowed as if an evil spirit was within them. They professed to use earthly weapons, as the sword of the Lord and of Gideon. Madness like this was of

---

* Several others were in gaol for some years, including Parkinson and Merry. On July 25, 1664, Ralph Rymer and John Hodgson were ordered to be imprisoned for life, and all their goods and lands to be forfeited for their lives. Hodgson was pardoned, and released in March following.

course intolerable. The Yorkshire justices clapped the deluded creatures into prison. They suppressed their conventicles. They forced upon them the oath of allegiance, and cooled their religious ardour in the gaol. The Cumberland grand jury made a special presentment against these misguided men, for in that district they were more than usually numerous and obnoxious.* Francis Higginson, the vicar of Kirkby

---

* Aug. 17, 1655. Cumberland. The humble presentment of the grand jurie to the honorable the judges of the Notherin circuett.

Our duty to God and our country doth in our apprehenson oblige us as followeth, viz., to sett forth and represent to your lordshipp our sadd and deplorable condicion, occasioned by the multiplicity and irregularity of the deluded sect called the Quakers, as namly,

1. Their horride blasphemies and violations of the cleere and knowne fundamentall truthes of the Gospell.

2. Their notorious affronts to magistrates and ministers, whom they labour uncessantly by their scandalous speeches and pamphletts to expose to most infamous scorne and contempt, and consequently the whole nation to confusion.

3. Their apparent designe and common practise is to seduce and misleade the poore, ignorant, ungrounded, and unsetled people of these Northeren partes, and to involve them in most dangerous and detestable principles, worse then the Egiptian darknes, wherein they resemble the old serpent, who first applied his assaults against the weaker vessell.

4. They are growne numerous, and meete frequently to the number of diverse hundred together; and some of them have given out that their opposers should repent their withstandinge them before Michaelmas next, as was proved by oath att the last quarter sessions holden in July last for this county.

Hereupon yt is our most humble peticon to your Lordshipps, for the glory of God, the reducement of those misguided people themselves, and the prevention of mischiefe and destruction to the soules of others, that some speedie course be forwith taken, whereby pietie may be preserved in purity, and the people of this county in safty. And wee most humbly conceive that the restraint of strangers from coming into this county, and all others of them from meeting in soe great numbers together, may much conduce to the ends abovesaid, which wee most humbly submitt to your Lordshipps' order and direction.

Stephen, undertook to vanquish them in print, but it will be seen from a deposition that he could not silence them. His pamphlets, for he shot at them with light artillery, are most amusing and are full of curious information. An extract will suffice. Speaking of the excesses of the Quakers, he says, " They railed at the judges sitting upon the bench, calling them scarlet-coloured beasts. The justices of the peace they styled 'justices *so called;*' and said there would be Quakers in England when there should be no justices of the peace. They made it a constant practice to enter into the churches with their hats on during divine service, and to rail openly and exclaim aloud against the ministers with reproachful words, calling them liars, deluders of the people, Baal's priests, Babylon's merchants selling beastly ware, and bidding them come down from the high places. One instance of this kind (ludicrous enough) happened at Orton. Mr. Fothergill, vicar there, one Sunday exchanged pulpits with Mr. Dalton of Shap, *who had but one eye*. A Quaker stalking as usual into the church of Orton, whilst Mr. Dalton is preaching, says, ' Come down, thou false Fothergill ?' 'Who told thee,' says Mr. Dalton, 'that my name was Fothergill ?' 'The Spirit,' quoth the Quaker. 'That spirit of thine is a lying spirit,' says the other; 'for it is well

William Musgrave. John Aglionby. Richard Helton. Will. Hutton. John Whelpdall. Edmund Harrington. Robert Thomlinson. Hugh Askew. John Rawbancks. John Simson. Ar. Forster. Cuth. Studholme. George Graham. Thomas Stanwix. William Latus. Thomas Laythes. Roger Sleddall. Lawr. Parke. Joseph Dalston.

known I am not Fothergill, but *peed* Dalton of Shap!'"

Another religious body that must be noticed are the Roman Catholics. Although they are not to be mentioned in the same breath with the fanatics who have just been spoken of, they were treated with even greater harshness and severity. Ever since the Reformation they had been looked upon with suspicion. Doubtless there was in them the longing wish to recover the spiritual control over the province that they had lost—and could they be blamed for it? but the zeal of some of their more unscrupulous members had seemingly wrapped around the whole party, innocent as well as guilty, the garb of treason. There is something very touching in the devotion of the missionaries to England. Year after year did a number of English youths steal across the seas to the college of Douay, which was founded for the winning back of their fatherland to the bosom of their church. Year after year did they return in various disguises, heedless altogether of the laws which denounced them as traitors, and eager to spend their life-blood for their religion. There are many mournful chapters in the annals of their sufferings, and the adventures and fate of several of them will be disclosed in the pages of this volume. The fear of detection made them adepts in the art of deception. Who could fence more deftly with a question? They were ready for everything that occurred. Some of them were schoolmasters; others could labour, if necessary, with their hands, whilst in some secret recess were the vestments of their office concealed alike from the inquisitive and the incurious eye. In many old manor-houses there was an asylum for them, and some quiet hiding-place to which they could retire when the searchers were abroad. But the lash of authority was laid upon the laymen as well as upon the priests. During the reigns of Elizabeth and James I. a great number of the Yorkshire Roman Catholics were in prison for their faith. Many of them died in gaol. They were dragged to the service at the minster, where the archbishop preached at them. When his chaplain, Mr. Bunney, aspersed them from the pulpit with what Anthony a' Wood calls his " Divinity squirt," they cried out in indignation, and they were actually gagged ! Could intolerance go further than this ? In the following reign they met with some little consideration, but Charles I. was obliged to make them compound for their estates. This, however, did not damp their loyalty, for the Roman Catholic gentry were found among the ranks of the Cavaliers. After the Restoration, when religious parties became every day more divided, the Roman Catholics were looked upon with increased dislike. Those who had laid at the door of Henrietta-Maria more than half the evil deeds of Charles I., looked with dread upon the advent of Catherine of Braganza. Towards the close of Charles the Second's reign, the prospect of a Roman Catholic succession raised the fears of the one party and the hopes of the other. When the public mind was thus excited, the well known plots struggled into light. The outcry against the Roman Catholics was now immense. The old penal laws were put into full force, and more stringent enactments were devised. In 1675 there came down into the North an order of council desiring the justices of the peace to be more strict in reporting and punishing recusants. In 1678 and 1679 the oaths of allegiance were offered to many of the leading Roman Catholics in the district, and those who declined fell under the statute of præmunire and were thrown into prison. All suspicious persons were arrested. The sea-ports were watched, and every disaffected neighbourhood was put under the strictest surveillance.* In this crisis there arose

* The presentment of the grand jury for the county of Northumberland, at the assizes holden at the high castle of Newcastle the 7th day of August, anno Domini 1683.

We doe humbly present that the surest and most effectuall meanes to establish our happiness both in church and state, to preserve our King, and make us live a happie people under a great and glorious Prince, is to se the lawes made against the disturbers of our peace impartially and duly put in execution, especially against the teachers and ringleaders of that seditious crew.

Wee beleive recusants of all sorts are now growen equally dangerous in our established government; and, therefore, wee here present them as they come to our knowledge. Wee did the same last assises, and doe really beleive that, had the lawes against them been duly executed, wee should have had but a very few of them to have troubled you with again.

Wee humbly beg that certificates for the conformity of dissenters may not be allowed, except such certificate be under the hand of the minister of the parish where such dissenter dwelleth, wee being informed that it is their practice to goe from their owen parish church to others, where they come in for scrapps of sermons at the latter end or after divine service, and soe procure certificates for their comeing to church, and, in the meane tyme, the divine service and their owen parish church are utterly neglected, and their minister dispised.

Wee alsoe doe present that all persons who shall presume to speake

in the North two mischievous informers of the names of Bolron and Mowbray. Of their proceedings the present volume will supply much novel and interesting information. The first person that they struck at was Sir Thomas Gascoigne of Barnbrough, but this blow was unsuccessful They were equally unfortunate in their attack upon Sir Miles Stapleton of Carlton. At another time they laid an information against Anne Lady Tempest, the daughter of Sir Thomas Gascoigne, Charles Ingleby of Lawkland, a barrister of Gray's Inn, Thomas Thweng of Heworth, clerk, and Mary wife of Thomas Pressick, for subscribing money to bring about the murder of the King. In this instance Thweng was convicted on their testimony, and died upon the scaffold. The rest escaped, and Mr. Ingleby lived to become a Baron of the Exchequer in the reign of James II. In the following year Bol-

reflectively on the government, or shall dare to extenuate or excuse the horror of this late execrable plot, are dangerous and of evill example, debauching the loyall hearts of many of the ignorant sort, and ought to be disarm'd, that honnest men may be secured from the wicked effects of their inveteratly rebellious spirits.

Wee alsoe doe present that all persons who keep ale-houses, or other publicke-houses within this county, shall bring a certificate under the hand of the parson of the parish where hee or she dwelleth at the same tyme they come to renue their lycences, that they have duly repaired to their parish churches and received the Sacrament accordeing to law.

And whereas John Pigg hath lately been removed from the office of surveyor of the high-wayes for this county, cheifly upon the account of his nonconformity, wee doe here present George Barkass of Quarry house as a loyall person, a good churchman, and very fit to doe this county good service in that office. R. Bates, Will. Orde, Hen. Ogle, Willm. Ogle, Na. Whitehead, Surtes Swinburne, T. Swinho, Geo. De-lavall, John Clennell, Ephraim Reied, Nath. Salkeld, J. Irwin, Mark Errington, Wm. Bonner, Lan. Strother, Ed. Charleton, Ed. Parke.

ron and his companion accused Mr. Gascoigne, Mr. Stephen Tempest, and Mr. York, but no reliance was placed upon their evidence, and the three gentlemen escaped. In their disinclination to credit the statements of informers, the Yorkshire juries have set an example to the whole of England. On the accession of James II. the Roman Catholic prisoners were released. They became sheriffs and justices of peace, and honours were showered upon them which were in no small degree the cause of that revulsion of feeling which in the end removed the misguided monarch from his throne.

It is impossible, of course, to notice every kind of offence that will be placed before the reader in the present volume, but there is one which it is impossible to pass over; I mean that of witchcraft. The North of England has always been noted for its superstition, and in the seventeenth century it was peculiarly rampant. People, to a great extent, take their tone from the district in which they live, and we cannot therefore be surprised at finding that the inhabitants of the wilder parts of the North especially cherished that strange belief in possession and evil influences that was suggested by the scenery around them. Fearful stories of fancied sights and sounds would pass from lip to lip, far beyond the boundaries of the savage district that originated them; they would spread into the lowlands, till every heart trembled at the recital, and owned its own subjection to the influence that appalled it. In the earlier part of the seventeenth century there were several noted cases of witchcraft in the North. The first is the well-known tale of Janet Preston, of Gisburne, in 1612, which has been printed more than once. After this there were the very remarkable experiences of Edward Fairfax, the poet, which have just been brought to light by the Philobiblon Society. During the Commonwealth there were published two little volumes of great rarity and curiosity; one of them gives an account of some very singular occurrences that took place in the family of Mr. George Muschance, or Muschamp, of Barmoor, in Northumberland, the other relates the sufferings of Miss Martha Hatfield, of Laughton-en-le-Morthing, and is well known from the graphic notice of it in the pages of the historian of South Yorkshire. These four cases in themselves were enough to terrify the North of England for several generations. But there were many others. In the midst of the dismay that was generated by these strange stories, there sprung up several impostors, who professed to be able to detect witches, and to them the credulous public too frequently applied. In 1650 one of these fellows visited Newcastle, and fifteen persons were executed on the Moor in consequence of his impudent assertions! The disease, however, was not cured by examples like these, as will be shewn by the present volume. I have given a number of depositions which illustrate the history of this remarkable superstition. The great Northumbrian case of 1673 will almost rival the exploits of Mother Demdyke and her crew. It is striking, also, to observe what a range of victims the torturers select. They begin with the daughter of a knight, and end with cows and pigs! I am happy to say that in no instance have I discovered the record of the conviction of a reputed witch. All honour to the Northern juries for discrediting these absurd tales! And yet some of these weak and silly women had themselves only to thank for the position they were placed in. They made a trade of their evil reputation. They were the wise women of the day. They professed some knowledge of medicine, and could recover stolen property. People gave them money for their services. Their very threats brought silver into their coffers. It was to their interest to gain the ill name for which they suffered. They were certainly uniformly acquitted at the assizes, but no judge, or jury, or minister, could make the people generally believe that they were innocent. The superstition was too deeply rooted to be easily eradicated. I shall finish the paragraph with a story that is given by Sir John Reresby, who gives it as if he was nearly convinced of its truth. "I would venture to take notice of a private occurrence which made some noise at York. The assizes being there held on the 7th of March, 1686-7, an old woman was condemned for a witch. Those who were more credulous in points of this nature than myself, conceived the evidence to be very strong against her. The boy she was said to have bewitched fell down on a sudden before all the court, when he saw her, and would then as suddenly return to himself again, and very distinctly relate the several injuries she had done him: but in all this it was observed the boy was free from any distortion; that he did not foam at the mouth, and that his fits did not leave him gradually, but all at once; so that, upon the whole, the judge thought it proper to reprieve her, in which he seemed to act the part of a wise man. But, though such is my own private opinion, I cannot help continuing my story. One of my soldiers being upon guard about eleven in the night, at the gate of Clifford Tower, the very night after the witch was arraigned, he heard a great noise at the castle, and going to the porch, he there saw a scroll of paper creep from under the door, which, as he imagined by the moonshine, turned first into the shape of a monkey, and thence assumed the form of a turkey-cock, which passed to and fro by him. Surprised at this, he went to the prison, and called the under-keeper, who came and saw the scroll dance up and down, and creep under the door, where there was scarce an opening of the thickness of half-a-crown. This extraordinary story I had from the mouth of both the one and the other: and now leave it to be believed or disbelieved, as the reader may be inclined this way or that."

It is impossible to speak in terms of too strong reprobation of the state of the Northern prisons in the seventeenth century, and of the conduct of their keepers. They were dens of iniquity and horror, in which men and women herded together indiscriminately. The dungeons of the Inquisition themselves were scarcely worse. Some of them had no light and no ventilation; several were partly under water whenever there was a flood! The number of prisoners who died in gaol during this century is positively startling. And how could they live in such places, where they were treated worse than savages themselves? The ordinary conveniences and necessaries of life were denied to them. They were at the mercy of the gaolers for their food and for everything they possessed. They had the meanest fare at the most exorbitant price.* If they resisted there were irons and screws that compelled them to be silent. There was also the greatest inequality and injustice in the treatment of the prisoners. Those that had money had many indulgences. They were allowed to go to places

---

* The following papers will illustrate my remarks, and show the state of York Castle in the 17th century:—

My Lord,—It had bene fitter for me to have wayted on you myselfe, then to have presented my respects to you this way; but, my Lord, I have bene soe desperatly ill these six weekes, I have hardly bene able to stirr out of my bedd. My humble suite to your Lordshipp is, in the behalfe of a great many poore distressed people that are now prisoners within the Castle of Yorke, that have noethinge to subsist withall, but the charity of well disposed persons; and, as the case stands with them, the benifitt of what they have is very small, for they are not suffered to buy a bitt of bread or a dropp of drinke, nor so much as a halfe penny worth of milke, or a little fyreing in the wynter, but what they are compelled to buy of the keepers of the prison, where they pay 2d. or 3d. for that which is not sometymes worth a penny. My Lord, my lodginge being not farr from the Castle gate, the neighbours have made a great request to me to be a suiter to your Lordshippe, that at this Assizes your Lordshippe would be pleased to make an order that these poore people, as formerly they have done, may send into the towne for such provision as they are able to compasse, where they may have it at the best hand. I hope your Lordshipp will pardon the

of amusement without the walls of the gaol, and some were even permitted to lodge beyond the precincts, bouldnes of your most humble servant,—Jo. WORTHAM. From my lodginge this 9th of August, 1642.

In dorso.—To the honorable Sir Robert Heath, knt. his Ma^{tis} Judge of Assize for the county of Yorke, with my humble service, these present.

1654. A petition from the prisoners in York Castle, complaining of the gaolers.—They have hindred divers prisoners from haveinge theire meate and drinke at the best hand, and, to compell them to come to the high table, did lye some in dubble irons. That some prisoners sendinge for theire drinke within the castle, where they can have more for sixpence then they can have in the sellers for neenpence, the gaolers did abuse the prisoners and tooke theire drinke from them, and gave it to the low gaole prisoners. The gaolers' servant gets a share of the charities given to the prisoners. On July 10 last divers prisoners going to the sessions at Malton, the gaolers refused to devide the Cottrell bread till they were gone, and got their share. The gaolers doth refuse to hange up the stablishment of fees in a publique place, etc.

For the worshipfull William Bethell, Esqr., foreman of the grand jury for the county of Yorke.

The humble petecion of the prisoners in the castle of Yorke, complaining of the severall abuses committed and don by Thomas Core and William Crooke, jailors.

Sheweth, that, contry to a table of severall fees and acts of Parlement, the aforesaid jailors hath demaunded and taken severall sums of money for chamber-rent, and likewise for our owne bedds and bedding, and doth compell us to pay for ease of irons (being in execution), although wee have paid the same to the former jailors to whom wee was committed, lodgeing fellons and debtors together in one roome or chamber, takeing more fees then one, viz. for every accion one fee, althowgh wee are discharged from all such accions by the shirriffe, takeing unjust fees from the prisoners when discharged, receiveing 16*l*. and 8*s*. from 6 men committed and indicted for high treason at the last assizes, as fees due to them, besides 6*l*. for ease of irons, they or there servants takeing or receiveing money at severall times from 3 persons indicted for murther at Lent assizes last, promissing that the jury should acquitt and discharge, and alloweing weekly out of the county bread a greater share to fellons and condemd persons then they doe to debtors. Alloweing condemd persons not onely to dispose of it, but of most of the concernes in the jaiol. Tollerateing persons condemned for high treason, for murther, for fellony in execution, excommunication, besides 180 Quakers, at the least, to goe into the citty and county of Yorke,

subjected only to some trifling surveillance. Escapes were very frequently made.* The prisons also were too few in number, and were frequently out of repair. In 1684 there was no common gaol at all in Cumberland. In July 1658 the county of York was presented at the assizes for not renovating the common prison. In 1677 it was almost in ruins. In a later century those distinguished philanthropists Howard and Neild give most distressing pictures of the state of the Northern gaols. Peter prison, in York, and the hold on Ouse Bridge, were a disgrace to any civilized country. The cells in the latter place would almost have rivalled the notorious Black-hole. Air, light, and ventilation were absent, and the waters of the river rushed in when they were above their usual level. The castle of Newcastle-upon-Tyne was a

but to play-houses, taverns, coffee-houses, &c. not lodgeing in the jaiol above the number of 90 Quakers att any one time, from March last to July instant, takeing severall sums of money besides bond and judgement not onely from men committed as misdemeanors, but from all sorts of fellons for ease of there irons.

Wee distressed petecioners humbly craue to take the premises into consideration, moveing the judges and justices of peace nott onely that the abuses may be regulated, but that a table of fees may be settled; and wee shall be ever bound to pray, &c.

* I give one instance among many:

March 9, 1653-4. The affidavit of John Thackeray, Miles Fawcett, Wm. Hopkinson, and John Tomlinson, concerninge the escape of six prisoners out of the Castle of Yorke. The said prisoners were laid in the place called the low gaole, being supposed to be the safest place, and double-ironed according to law. That the goale being now knowne to be weake, in regard the said prisoners did worke through the stone wall in one night, the weakenesse whereof was presented to the grand jury the last assizes. That the kayes belonging to the backe gates (soe called) of the said goale were in the custody of the souldiery in Clifford's Tower, which obstructed the present pursuite of the saide prisoners, being in the night time.

dreadful den, but it was far eclipsed by the Bishop's prison in the palatinate city of Durham. It seems to have consisted of a succession of dungeons, one below the other, descending far into the ground!

The punishments of these times were as barbarous as the places of confinement. The pillory was occasionally used for political offenders. Burning in the hand was not unfrequent. Imprisonment was the usual penalty that prisoners paid for their misdemeanors, and, remembering what the gaols were, it was a very severe one. They were never sentenced for any specific period, but the list of those who were under confinement seems to have been revised and lessened by the judges at each assize. Occasionally a batch of criminals seems to have been sold to the best bidder, if they were not given away. I believe that this was the custom at Hull. After the fight on Seacroft Moor a number of the prisoners were confined in the Merchants'-hall in York, and came into the possession of a Mr. Clay. The remnant of the Scots, who after the battle of Dunbar were shut up in the cathedral of Durham, was sold *en masse* to an officer who is said to have sent them to the Plantations. Transportation was occasionally awarded, and the culprits were generally draughted into any portion of the army that was on foreign service. The well-known Nevinson was sent to Tangiers. The annual number of executions at York between 1650 and 1670 varied between six and twenty. Whenever there was a want of an executioner, a condemned criminal was reprieved if he would accept the odious office. The Border Commissioners, probably, put more to death in a year than were condemned on the whole Northern circuit. Theirs was, indeed, at many times, a very summary process. A little evidence, however incomplete, and after it the culprit was dangling on the limb of a neighbouring oak. How different was this from the long procession, with the cart and rope, that accompanied the wretched criminal to Tyburn! The vehicle conveyed the coffin in which his lifeless body was to be laid, and at the foot of the gallows, before his eyes, was the hole into which he was to be buried like a dog, if his bones were not to bleach near the scene of the atrocity that ruined him, or if he had no kinsman to procure for his remains the rites of sepulture at home. On the same unhallowed spot might occasionally be seen the faggots and the flames which consumed some miserable creature who had broken the most sacred tie that can be bound on earth, by murdering her husband. These are painful pictures, but happily they represent scenes which are no longer to be witnessed.

In conclusion, the Editor, on behalf of the Society, has to thank Sir John Bayley, for allowing the records under his charge to be inspected and made use of, and he has also to express his sincere obligations to Mr. Holtby, the deputy-custodier, and his son for the courtesy and attention which he has uniformly experienced at their hands.

J. R.

York, October 17. 1861.

DEPOSITIONS, ETC. FROM YORK CASTLE.

I. JOHN RERESBY, ESQ. FOR AN ASSAULT.

Oct. 1, 1640. Before Sir Wm. Allenson, Kt. *John Briggs*, servant to John Reasbie esquire, serjeant-major, saith that upon Tuesdaie was sevenight the said Mr. Reasbie went to a taverne att Castlegate-end,* to drinck a pint or quart of wyne; and that ther went with his said m^r to the said taverne his corronell, Sir Georg Wentworth, and diverse other gentlemen. And, afterwards, this informant, going into the roome where his said m^r was, found sitting with him one Captaine Wombwell, who had on him a buffe coat and britches; Captaine Darcie Wentworth, who also had a buffe coat on; also one John Brittane, ancient-bearer to Coronell Wentworth, having on a cloth sute mingled culler; Mr. Thomas Malliverer, ancient-bearer to the said Mr. Reasbie, having on a read coat, who dwelleth at Letwell; also one Mr. Bradley,†

---

* A description of a scene which occurred at a tavern in Castlegate in York. Charles I. was then in York, preparing for an expedition against Lesley and the Scots, and fifteen thousand men were quartered in and around the city. Many of the gentlemen of Yorkshire were in arms or in attendance upon the court, and the great council of peers was sitting in York.

The gentlemen mentioned in the deposition were all of them people of distinction in the county. Mr. Reresby was the father of Sir John Reresby, *armis togaque insignis*, who was afterwards Governor of York, and a well-known author. Sir George Wentworth was brother to the Earl of Strafford, and Darcy Wentworth of Brodsworth was gentleman usher of the black rod to the same nobleman when he was Viceroy of Ireland. The pedigree of the Mauleverers of Letwell is well known. It is not my intention to trouble my readers with many genealogical details in a work of this nature, save where they throw light upon any deposition, or its leading character.

The inn was probably the Blue Boar. It was situated between Castlegate House and the parish church. It is now a private dwelling, and was the residence of the late Mrs Campbell. It was to this inn that the well known Turpin resorted. In 1640, as we see, it was fitted up with boxes of wood for carousing parties, after the fashion of many old taverns at the present day.

† In "Mr. Bradley" I recognize an old friend. He was, I believe, Thomas Bradley, the eccentric rector of Castleford and Ackworth, which were given to him by Charles I. whom he was now attending in York in the capacity of chaplain. In the Rebellion he lost all, and was reduced to some straits; but his sun rose again at the Restoration. In addition to his other preferments he then became a prebendary of York. He pub-

a minister; and also an other minister, whose name this informant knowes not; also one Wheatley, lewetennant to Corronell Went-

lished ten or eleven sermons, seven of which I possess: I could wish that they were better known. Marred by few of the eccentricities of the period, they are remarkable for a boldness of diction and an eloquence and ease of expression which few divines of that period possessed. I shall give fuller specimens of his style in another place.

In a sermon preached before the judges of assize at York, in 1663, Bradley was bold enough to censure some of the public and private vices of the day in terms so strong that he was obliged to recant them publicly in another discourse which he delivered at the next assize. It ends with the following words: "I will conclude with one word which his Majesty spake to me himselfe at the Councell-table, and it was *close and home*, and did more to silence me then all that was spoken to me besides, and it was this, *That his Majestie thought it was my duty to preach conscience unto the people, and not to meddle with State affaires.*"

When Bradley was seventy-two years of age he actually preached and printed his own funeral sermons! Their style is more sober than that of his earlier productions, but it is striking, and there are some passages which will remind the reader of the *De Senectute*. The writer was evidently a person who had read and thought much.

"And although there be nothing in this world so desireable as that it should make a man in love with it in any state of his life and in his best years; yet much more, when his best dayes are gone and past, when he is entring into that state of life which David saith *It is but labour and sorrow*, and those years approach of which he shall say *I have no pleasure in them*, may he with good reason be content to leave the world and make it his request *That the Lord would take away his soule*. Then for an old Barzillai, *to refuse the pleasures of the court;* or an old Simeon, to sing his *Nunc dimittis;* or an aged Paul, *to desire to be dissolved;* or an old Elijah, to beseech the Lord *to take away his soule;* is no wonder. And all this as old age meerly considered in itself, without any other grievances added to it to make it burdensome and irksome, it is a burden to itself. But who ever saw it come but attended with a world of infirmities to make it more tedious, catarrhs, rheumes, aches, palsies, akings in the bones, gouts, dropsies, and, in all these, the inability to help itself. *Senex bis puer*, it is a second childhood, and 'tis a question whether the second be not worse than the first. Upon these and some other considerations it hath often been my prayer to the Lord God, and it is at this instant, that he would not detain this soule of mine in this tabernacle of clay, wherein it hath now lodged these seventy years and upward unto extremity of old age. But farther, if to all these there shall be added any externall grievances, poverty and want, discontent in the family, disobedience in prodigality of children, divisions among brethren, vexatious suits, or the like; these were enough, not only to make an old man desire dissolution, but to hasten it, *and to bring his gray haires with sorrow to the grave*.

"But what need I preach mortality to mortalls, whose very bodies that they carry about them dayly preach unto them the same thing; and the spectacles of mortality, which we dayly see, preach it more powerfully to our eyes then funerall sermons can doe unto our eares? Dayly we heare the tollings of the passing bells calling us to our long home. Dayly we see the bones and skulls of our friends deceased rak't out of the grave; dayly we see others following after them, and the mourners about the streets. It strikes me deeply into the meditation of mortality, when I doe but look over the register book, to see in the turning over of how few leaves I finde the same man baptized, married, buried. Thus one generation passeth away, and another succeedeth and hasteth after it, as we after them, till we all lye down in the dust of death, *for we are no better then our fathers*."

Bradley married a daughter of John Lord Savile. Thoresby tells us that she was "very memorable for constantly wearing a veil day and night, having made a vow no Englishman should see her face, and which she observed till within six weeks of her death." Of Savile Bradley, their son, there is a curious story in the Life of Anthony à Wood.

worth, who had on him a read coat; who, having drunck ther wyne and paid ther shott, were coming forth. And, in passage to the barr, ther were coming in a soldier and a weoman with him. And some of the company, his m^r being one, as this informant thincketh, did jeast with the weoman merrilie; whereupon the soldier did peremptorilie and saucecelie replie. Wherupon his said m^r gave him a blowe on the eare with his hand, and threwe him downe. And, in the interim, there came into the howse a gentleman of the name of Orrick, who, upon his coming in, justled upon this informant's m^r, and asked him why he did strike the boy, with other wordes of coller; but what they were he remembreth not. And, after this, the first thing that this informant did see was that his said m^r and the said gentleman had hold one of an other's haire, and was strugling. And in ther strugling drewe one and other into the said box or seat, where some blowes past betweene them. They parted, and his said m^r went into an other roome. And he further saith that, desireing to see the head of the said Orrick, hee wold not suffer him. And, presentlie after, a constable comeing in caried his said m^r, and all the rest of the gentlemen aforenamed, before Alderman Hodgson, to be examined. And there, after some passages and questions, the Lord Wharton, being ther present, said unto Orrick these wordes: " Robbin, it's but a broken head, let it alone."

II. THOMAS STAFFORD.   FOR SEDITIOUS WORDS.

Jan. 25, 1640-1.   Before Edward Payler, Esq.   *George Puryer* saith, that last Sonday being in George Dickson howse of Youlthorpe, beinge an ale howse, Thomas Stafford * revilled the informait, and said that the souldgeares weere all roges that came against the Scotes, and if it had not beene for the Scotes, thirtye thowsand Ireish had rissen all in armes, and cutt all our throtes, and that the Kinge and Queene was at masse together, and that hee would prove it uppon recorde, and that hee is fitter to be hangd then to be a Kinge, and that he hopte ere longe that

---

* Youlthorpe is a little village near the Wolds, not far from Bishop-Wilton. A great part of it is now the property of the parish of All Saints, Pavement, in York. The incident shows how jealous the executive was of any seditious language. A poor tipsy man is the culprit, and he denies everything, having, probably, forgotten all. Another witness, describing the scene, says that Stafford, " beinge hie flowne in drinke, takinge a kopp, drunke a health to the old prest, and, God a marcye, good Scot. And, withall, saeinge the Kinge and Queene was at masse together, and that such a Kinge was wourthye to be hanged."

Lashlaye* would be a Kinge, for he was a better man then any was in England.

III. RICHARD PENROSE. FOR SACRILEGE.

May 23, 1642. Before Sir Arthur Robinson, Kt. *John Penrose, of Wheldrake*, sayth, that, about 7 yeares since, he missed two iron crooks which used to be in the middle roome of the steeple of Wheldrake church,† in the fanones of the doore, and Richard Penrose confessed he puld them out. About 4 yeares since the sayd church was broken, and there was taken out one silver challice, twoo pewther plates, a carpett, a communion table cloth, a pulpitt clothe, and twoo searpleses, which did usually lye in the vestrie, of which Richard Penrose hadd the keeping of the keyes. The sayd Richard confessed before Doctor Stanhope, then parson of the sayd church, that he took away a piece of a pipe of lead which conveyed water from the sayd church, beinge about one ell longe. He also confessed hee tooke the serples out of the church, and carryed yt home to his owne house, and cutt it shorter.

IV. JOHN TROUTBECK. FOR SEDITIOUS WORDS.

June 9, 1642. Before Sir John Goodricke. *Thomas Waikefeild*, on the 5th instant, at the house of Marmaduke Bullocke, in Knasebrough, hard John Troutbeck say that the King was halfe French, halfe Germaine,‡ and that he could live as well without

---

* A great compliment to Sir David Lesley, who had much to do with the civil war in the North of England. At Marston Moor he was so roughly handled that he fled from the field, thinking that all was lost. His troops followed him,—

"Cursing the day when zeal or meed
"First lured their Lesley o'er the Tweed."

The supposed leaning of Charles I. towards the religion of his wife has been commented on by several writers.

† An account of some peculations in the church of Wheldrake. The culprit was a tailor in the village who appears to have been parish clerk or sexton. It is amusing to read of the mishap of the surplice which the sinning official would cut, as David did the skirts of Saul, *secundum artem*. The rector, Dr. George Stanhope, was the grandfather of the well-known Dean of Canterbury. He was Precentor of York and chaplain in ordinary to James I. and Charles I.

‡ The speaker was probably alluding to the King's wife and mother, but he could not properly call Anne of Denmark a German. Public men and public acts were now being canvassed pretty freely, and punishment generally had no lame foot in pursuing them. Troutbeck pleaded intoxication as his excuse.

Mr. Gifford lived at Scotton. His family, of Staffordshire extraction, had some cona King as with a King.   And Mr. Francis Gifford saying, "What did tye the King to observe and keepe the lawes?" the said Troutebecke answered "By his oath."   And Mr. Gifford asking further, "Howe, if the King did not keepe the lawes and his oath, how stoode the case then?" the said Troutebecke answered, "He might be deposed for ought he knew."

V. ROGER HOLLINGS.   FOR SLANDEROUS WORDS.

A true bill against Roger Hollings of Methley, for saying on Apr. 16, 1643, to John Savile,* Esq., "Traytor," and that he hoped to see him hanged, and that many honester men then he had beene hanged.

VI. THOMAS NEWTON AND OTHERS.   FOR FIRING INTO A DWELLING HOUSE.

Sep. 28, 1646.   Before Wm. West, Esq.   *Anne, the wife of Thomas Warter, of the Brushes, in the parishe of Ecclesfeld,† yeoman*, saithe, that upon Saturday the 13th of June last, aboute eleven of the clocke in the night, there came some unknowne persons, and attempted to breake into this informer's husbande's house, and discharged a muskitt with two bulletts throughe the doore into the said house towardes the fyer, where this informer Richard Burrose and Elizabeth Parkin, theire servantes, were sittinge.   One of the bulletts light upon the fyer hudde. And, likewise, upon the night followinge, there came some unknowne persons and attempted to breake into the said house, and discharged a muskitt in at a parloure windowe against a bedde, where this informer did usually lye, and broke the curtine rodde with a bullett, and so runne into the walle. And, upon the 20th of June, some unknowne persons attempted to breake into the said house, and discharged a muskitt with two bulletts in at another

---

nection with Darlington in the county of Durham.   Mr. William Dearlove, a native of Knaresbro', was also present on this occasion.   He came to the house, as he says himself, singularly enough, " to visitte one ancient Prior."

* The head of the great house of Savile, son of Sir John Savile, a Baron of the Exchequer, and nephew of the celebrated Provost of Eton.   He took the side of the Parliament, and was vigorously engaged in the siege of Pontefract Castle.   This extract is taken from the original presentment of the grand jury.

† A deposition which shows the lawless state of society in the wild country in Hallamshire.   Ecclesfield is in one of the principal parishes in that district, and the church is called the cathedral of the moors.

window, into another parloure, on the same side of the house, the first parloure window beinge walled up that they before shotte in at. And, likewise, they came the 25th of June, and discharged a little gunne with two bulletts in at a windowe on the other side of the house into the first parloure; which two bulletts light in the walle in the windowe that was walled up. And upon the 3d, 4th, and 18th of July last came some persons in the night-time and attempted to breake into the saide house: and this informer and the said Burrose and others in the house sawe five men some nightes which picked theire lockes. And one night this informer hearde one saye, "Newton, lay thy heade to the windowe, but not against the windowe, for I thinke they wente to bedde aboute a quarter of an houre since." And one night they left a lighted match in the fould; and one night they broke into a butterie next unto a parloure where a dore was made betweene the butterie and the parloure, and one of the said men gott in his arme and shoulder in to the said dore and strucke at the said Burrowes, and Burrowes haveinge a sworde in his hande thrust at the said man in the dore stead, and pricked him in the thighe, as he thought; so the man felle backe, and Burrowes gott the doore made againe. Then this informer sawe three men in the butterie, whereof she knewe two of them, the one to be Thomas Newton and the other Lawrence Wade.

VII. THOMAS BEEVERS. FOR SEDITIOUS WORDS.

Oct. 22, 1646. Before Thos. Jopson, Darcy Wentworth, and John Hewley, Esquires. *James Losh of Barnsley*, about Michaelmas last was a twelve month, heard Thomas Beevers of Thurleston, dyer, say he wold lay this informant tenn poundes the Kinge's cares was stowled * of within a month, and that the Queene was gone over into Holland to play the whore.

VIII. ELIZABETH CROSLEY AND OTHERS. FOR WITCHCRAFT.

Dec. 31, 1646. Before Charles Fairfax and Thos. Thornhill, Esqrs. *Henry Cockcrofte, of Heptenstall, clothier*, saith, that,

---

* Another indictment for seditious language. The charge against the Queen has been made by others. John Ellis of Burnsall, yeoman, was indicted at York for saying, on the 20th of June, 1677, "The old Queen had severall children in the absence of her husband: one att Pontefract, when her husband had not been with her of a twelve moneth. The King mynds nothing but women."

the weeke before Michaellmas last, Elizabeth Crosley of Heptenstall came to this informer's house, begginge an almes, shee beinge in an evill report for witchinge.* And (as it seemed, by his wive's relacon) displeased with her reward, departed thence, and, the next night after but one, William, a childe of this informer's, of the age of one yeare and three quarters, being att that tyme in very good health, fell sicke by fitts, bendinge backward, changinge his coulor and scrichinge, and soe continued one night, and then recovered. About seaven or eight weekes after, the said childe, not being soe perfectly in health as formerly, but more dull and stupid, did fall sicke in the same manner, as aforesaid, and soe continued for aboute a fortnight or three weeks, and then grew better, till aboute the tenth day of December, who, after hee hadd languished nyne or tenn dayes, dyed. And this informer concceiveinge that his childe was bewitched, wente unto Mary Midgley, who, as he suspected, was confederate with the said Elizabeth, and then urging that shee the said Mary was one that was the cause of the death of his said child, she, the said Mary, then confessed that shee could witch a litle, but said that Elizabeth Crosley, Sarah her daughter, and Mary Kitchinge were witches, and hadd bewitched the said childe, and the said Mary tould this informer that shee would bee sworne of it before any justice in England.

Samuel Midgeley, of Heptenstall, saith, that hee, together with Jonas Utley and Lawrence Hay, did accompany the said Henry Cockcrofte to the house of Mary Midgley, and the said Henry meetinge with the said Mary did both threaten and strike her, who thereupon confessed that shee herselfe was a witch, but that it was not shee but Mary Kitchin and Elizabeth Crosley that hadd bewitched the aforesaid childe.

Daniell Briggs, of Waddsworth, saith, that aboute Michaellmas was two yeares, one John Shackleton, an infante of aboute the age of two yeares and an halfe, beinge sore taken and held with paynes and convulcions, the head and knees beinge drawne

---

* The first of the many cases of witchcraft that the present volume will contain. They are a painful record of the ignorance and credulity of the age. The scene, in the present instance, is laid in the wild parish of Halifax, the very place, of all others, at that time for superstition. Good Vicar Favour had done a good deal to civilize his flock, but his voice was now silent and there was no one to oppose popular errors. And if a reformer had arisen, who would have listened to him? He would have been a bold man who ventured to decry the potency of ghosts and witches in the Yorkshire Highlands.

In the Journal of the Archæological Institute I have printed a very remarkable case which bears witness to the superstition prevalent in the parish of Halifax shortly before the Reformation. No one point in the charter of credulity had been lost when these depositions were written down.

neare together, and, haveinge soe remained for aboute a quarter of a yeare, was removed to a neighbor's house; whereunto William Whaley, clarke, minister of Croston chappell, came to see the said childe, who tould this informer and a maide servant that attended upon the said infante, that if they mett any by the way as they were to goe homewards, they would longe or desyer to mawle them on the heade; and they, shortly after, settinge forwards, did meete Elizabeth Crossley, and the maide that carryed the childe, perceiveinge it to bee her, shunned the way; notwithstand- inge, the said Elizabeth asked how the said childe did, but this informer suspectinge her to bee a witch did not tell her how ill it was, but said it was indifferent well, att which shee seemed very angry. And beinge shortly after in the next house where the said childe was, whether the maide came and strooke her with a candlesticke;* after which the said childe was reasonable well till about the breake of the day in the morneinge, att which tyme hee begun with his ill fitts againe, and, after hee hadd languished aboute eleaven weeks, dyed. And this informer further saith that the morneinge it was buryed hee mett with the sayd Elizabeth Crosley, who said "Have you brought this witched childe to towne?" To whom hee answered that hee was perswaded hee was not witched. Shee swore by —— it was witched; and, further, saith that Mary Briggs, this informer's mother, upon her death bedd, aboute seaven yeares agoe, said that shee feared shee hadd hurte done by Elizabeth Crosley, who hadd gone in an evill reporte for witchinge.

Richard Wood, of Heptenstall, saith, that aboute fower dayes before Midsomer last (as this informer's wife tould him) Mary Midgeley came to her and begged wooll; whereupon shee tould her shee hadd given her a good almes of wooll three weeks before, and would give her noe more, for they bought it, but did give her an almes of milke, with which shee departed very angry: and the day after six of this informer's milch kyne fell sicke. This informer's wife, feareinge shee hadd done them some hurte, tould her shee hadd made the faulte, and desired her to remedie it if she could. Longe it was before shee would take too that shee had done it, but at last tooke six pence of her, and wished her to goe home, for the kyne should mende, and desired her to take for every cow a handfull of salte and an old sickle, and lay under- neath them, and, if they amended not, then to come to her againe. The next day this informer comeinge home was informed by his

---

* The common belief was that if blood could be drawn from a witch the victim would recover.

wife of all the passages aforesaid, and hee, shortly after, meetinge with the said Mary in the house of one Ingham, an alehouse keeper in Heptenstall, tould her there hadd beene some litle fault made by her since hee wente from home, but hee did not mention any particuler wherein. Shee thereupon gave him an apple, and confessed shee hadd done him hurte diverse tymes, but never would doe more.*

IX. ROBERT JOHNSON, CLERK. FOR PUBLISHING UNLAWFUL BOOKS.

Aug. 14, 1647. Before Luke Robinson, Esq. *Ralph Walker, of New Malton,* saith, that upon Sonday last, being the 8th instant, Robert Johnson of New Malton did publish two bookes in the church at Old Malton, the contents of which publicacions hee saith to bee as follows, viz. To forbid the payment of tythes; and that any might refuse tythes as they would answere it afterwards.† Abraham Medd, of Old Malton, asked the said Johnson who should beare them harmelesse. Hee answered, " The King and Sir Thomas Fairfax."

X. RICHARD DUNWELL, CLERK. FOR USING THE PRAYER BOOK.

Aug. 16, 1647. Before Thomas Dickinson, Lord-mayor of York. *John Stones, tayler,* saith that on Saturday last about fower of the clock in the afternoone, Mr. Dunwell, the minister, did baptize‡ a childe in the parishe church of Bishophill the newer;

---

* The accused persons deny the charge altogether. Mary Midgeley, however, says that Martha Wood " did aske her advise touchinge one of her kyne whose mylke earned in the gallin, but said shee knew not which of them it was. Whereupon this ex¹ tould her that shee hadd learned of one Issabell Robinson who hadd good skill (if anythinge were gone) and shee wished her to take a litle salte and old yron, lay it under the cow, and pray to God for mend." The other two women deny all.

† Two of the ephemeral publications of the time, written, probably, by Puritans. It was a bold act to announce them for sale in a church. In those days, in the North of England, it was customary to proclaim from the pulpit any stolen goods, and other matters of interest to the congregation were also announced. One rich rector in the county of Durham, who sat in Barnard Gilpin's chair within the present century, used regularly to announce from the rostrum the sale of the hay off his glebe !

Johnson was a clergyman and a member of the Assembly of Divines. He was a graduate of Cambridge, and published the following sermon : " Lux et Lex, or the Light and the Law of Jacob's house : held forth in a Sermon before the honourable house of Commons at St. Margaret's Westminster, March 31, 1647, being the day of publike humiliation. By Robert Johnson, Eboraicus, one of the Assembly of Divines. London, 1647," 4to. pp. 38.

‡ The Liturgy of the Church of England was now voted down by Act of Parliament.

and, after he had prayed, he tooke the childe, and said " I baptize the in the name of the Father, and of the Son, and of the Holy Ghost, and doe signe the with the signe of the crosse;" and soe proceeded with other words in the booke of Comon Prayer. And the said Mr. Dunwell, imediately before he baptized the said childe, said that he would baptize none but such as he would baptize with the signe of the crosse; and that there was noe act against it, it was but an ordinance.

XI. HERBERT COOK. FOR SCANDALOUS BEHAVIOUR.

Aug. 24, 1647. At York Castle. *John Garthwayt, clerk,* deposeth, that one Herbert Cook,* being churchwarden of Heslington, detayneth the register book belonging to the sayd towne, insomuch as this ex^t, the minister, cannot therein record the names of such persons as are baptized and buryed within that parish. And the sayd Herbert Cook sayd that he would burne the sayd register before he would deliver it unto him. The sayd Cook is an ordinary frequenter of alehouses upon the Sabaoths and Fasting dayes, and he hath seen him drunk severall times on those dayes. He is by common fame a brabler and quareller. He is a man of such a vexatious and contentious disposition that his neighbors stand in awe of him in respect of suites, and he hath nowe a dosen suites on foot, and he actually saw him bunching an old man, and he hath often seen him distempered with drinck. The said Cook did undertake for 20s. to keep all the Company of Weavers within the Citty of York seaven yeares in suite.

The sign of the cross in baptism was peculiarly offensive to the Puritans. Mr. Dunwell was charged with baptizing another child after the proscribed form at St. Hellen's, the Directory being in both instances neglected. Mr. Dunwell pleads guilty to both charges.

On Feb. 1, 1649-50, Robert Hendley, of Snainton, clerk, was charged with marrying people " without the consent of their parents, nor doth in any publique manner make known the intencion of theire marriadge, according to the lawes of the land, but in private places, and at unlawfull houres doeth make itt his practise to joyne any men and women together in wedlocke, not of his parrish."

On Jan. 31, 1666-7, before Sir Joseph Cradock and James Darcy, Esq., Anne, wife of Henry Kilburne, late of Thorpe and now of Reeth, says that she and Henry Kilburne " were married togetber by one Mr. John Ladler, parson of Gateside, without license or banes askeing, in Mr. Ladler's parler, after 8 of the clock at night."

* A refractory churchwarden with whom, no doubt, Master Garthwaite was sorely troubled. I have not ventured to print all the misdemeanours of this dangerous official.

XII. GEORGE CLAY. AN ATTEMPT TO POISON.

March 10, 1647-8. Before Sir Robert Barwicke, Kt., at York. *Joseph Bannister, of Hallifax, locksmith,* saith that hee, being a souldier under command of the right honorable the Lord Fairefax, was, at the late battle upon Seacroft more,* taken prisoner with many others and brought into the Cittie of Yorke, and imprisoned in the Marchants' hall there; where he and the other prisoners had not continued many days before the said George Clay† (then one who bore armes with the enimie against the Parliament, but whether listed as a souldier or no he knoweth not), did come, and tooke a list of the names of all the said prisoners, beinge 700 in number. And, within few dayes after, came againe, and tould this informer and the rest of the prisoners that they were all his prisoners, and at his disposinge, by grant from the Lord Gowring, a comander in the then Earle of Newcastle's armie, and demanded of every prisoner severall somes of money, which sommes if they would not pay, they should rott in prison, as he then said.

The said Mr. Clay forced one Jonathan Tattersall, a prisoner, to pay him 60*l.* for his release, which he did pay, as many others did; and, likewise, he demanded of this deponent 10*l.* for his release, which he not beinge able to pay, the said Clay did deteine this deponent in prison nineteene weeks and 3 days, duringe which time (through his cruell usage) hee was almost famished for want of food; and many died by reason of his crueltie and hard usage in prison. Hee further saith that hee, havinge a

---

* The fight on Seacroft Moor, near Bramham, took place in April, 1643. It was between Lord Goring, with a portion of the Earl of Newcastle's army, and Sir Thomas Fairfax. Sir Thomas's troops were caught at a disadvantage and were terribly handled by Goring's cavalry. Fairfax says of this combat, in his Memorials, " This was one of the greatest losses we ever received."

A vast number of prisoners, principally countrymen, were taken by the Royalists. Many of them, as it will be seen, were shut up in the Merchants' Hall at York, where some died from confinement and neglect. Prisoners in those days were treated like slaves, and were bought and sold. The Scottish prisoners who were captured at Dunbar were brought to Durham and shut up in the cathedral. There is an account of their sufferings in a letter from Sir Arthur Haslerigg, which is printed in the first edition of the Memoirs of Sir Henry Slingsby. Mickleton, the Durham antiquary, in his MS. diary, tells us that 4,500 were imprisoned in that sacred building. In eight months all had died except 500, who were taken away by Captain Rokeby, having been probably bought by him. What a frightful desecration!

† I have reason to believe that this gentleman was a kinsman, if not a son, of Robert Clay, vicar of Halifax, who was a singular character. The vicar ends his will in the following manner : " As a father I leave this last chardge to my sonnes: to avoide drunkenes, tobaccho, and swearing, and profaneing of the Saboth." There is much about Dr. Clay in Watson's History of Halifax.

warrant from Col. Generall Lambert, dated 3rd of March instant, to apprehend the said Clay to answere his misdemeanor, the said Clay beinge apprehended accordingly, and brought to Leedes, did in the house of widow Droninge there, upon the 8th day of March instant, indeavour to poyson this deponent, and to that end did secretly put into a cupp of ale quicksilver, and came to him and offered him the said cupp to drinke, telling him he should drinke it, for it was the Queen's health; which this deponent after much and importunate intreatie did drinke, thinkinge noe harme, till he found some of the quicksilver in his mouth at th'end of his drinke, some of which he hath yet to shew. Whereupon he sent for an apothecarie and did drinke a cup of sacke, whereupon he did purge. And he deposeth that the said Mr. Clay, upon his apprehension, did promis to give presently to this deponent 20s. if he would lett him escape; and he would also give bond to answere Col. Lambert: which this deponent refused to doe, and brought him to Yorke, where he now is comitted by Col. Lambert * to the provost-marshall his custodie.

XIII. ROBERT KAY AND OTHERS. FOR A RIOT.

Oct. 20, 1648. At Doncaster, before Wm. Armitage and Darcy Wentworth, Esqrs. *Mark Vanvaulcouburghe*,† *of Midlins, Esqr.*, saith, that upon Wednesday the 11th, about nyne of the clock in the morning, Robert Kay, together with 16 or 18 men, unknowne to this informant, came to this informant's father house at Midlins in a warlike manner, with musketts and swords drawne, and broke open the outgate and fower other doores within the

---

* The tables were now turned, and the prisoner was able to pay off an old score. Lambert, who was now almost paramount in the North, would give Clay no quarter.

† The Van Valkenburghs were a Dutch family of distinction, some members of which came over with Sir Cornelius Vermuyden to assist him in the draining of Hatfield Chase. The difficulties they experienced in this task would have driven any English settlers insane, but the Dutch were more cold-blooded and went through them all. By the inhabitants of the district they were regarded as intruders, their system of drainage interfered with old rights, and they were being continually robbed and maltreated. These depositions disclose an appalling adventure.

Midlins, or Middle Ing, on the Don, was a large hall erected by Sir Matthew Von Valkenburgh, which continued after his decease in the possession of his family. In later times it was the abode of what Mr. Hunter calls *a striking spirit*, which drove every one in terror from the house, and it was on that account for a long period without a tenant.

The Valkenburghs were the owners, at one time, of above 3,000 acres of Hatfield Chase. They were a family of wealth and consequence.

Robert Kay, the person alluded to in the deposition, was a Doncaster "gentleman." That town was deeply interested in the drainage of the levels.

said house, and did beat, cutt, and wound three servants within the said howse; and afterwards tooke divers parcells of goods out of the same howse. And he did heare the said Kay say to the rest with him, " Goe on, for I will beare you out in it whatsoever you doe."

Elizabeth Hargrave, of Midlins, spinster, heard the said Kay say that hee would fyre the howse if Mr. Vanvaulconburgh came not out presently to him, for hee would have him quicke or dead. And Kay and the men turned her master's servaunts out of the said howse, and threatned to pistoll her with a brace of bulletts.

John Warunn saith, that Robert Kay, together with 16 or 18 men, came in a vyolent and outragious manner to his master's howse at Midlins, with their musketts cockt, light matches, and swords drawne; and did breake open the outgates of the said howse, and the kitchin doore, and other chamber doores wheere his said master was. And one of them with his muskett knockt his master downe, and forced him out of the house, and afterwards this examinate. And the said Kay stroke this informant with his tuck. And, about a quarter of an hower after, there came two captaines thither, and was very angry with the soldiers that came alonge with Kay, and clensed the howse of Kay and the rest with him, and put his said master into possession againe. But, within a quarter of an hower after the captaines weere gone, the said Kay, together with six men more, came againe to the howse and broke open the out doores againe, and a chamber doore in which there was a cupboard that had wrytings. And took his master by force away with them againe, a quarter of a myle from his howse; who was againe sett at libertye by the soldiers and putt into possession of the said howse.

XIV. COLONEL MORRIS AND CORNET BLACKBURN. FOR HIGH TREASON.

July 30, 1649. Before Edward Feild, Mayor of Pontefract, and John Scurr, Mathew Franck, and John Cowper, Aldermen and Justices of the Peace. *William Foster, of Pontefract*, saith, that he knoweth John Morrice;* and that the said Morrice, im-

---

* An important addition to Nathan Drake's account of the siege of Pontefract Castle that has been recently published by this Society. I now give the depositions against Colonel Morris for his successful surprisal of the castle in June 1648, one of the most daring exploits of that eventful period.

John Morris was a Yorkshire gentleman, of some little consequence and estate, who had followed the profession of arms. His first patron was the great Earl of Strafford,

mediately after surprizall of the castle, tooke upon him to be governor and commander in cheife of the said castle; and that,

to whom he was deeply attached. He served under him among the King's troops in Ireland, and saw some fighting in that country and in England. After a while he entered into the employment of the Parliament; but, taking offence at some slight which had been shewn him, he threw up his connection with that party and retired to his own estate at Elmsall in Yorkshire.

In 1648 he shewed his discontent at the new *régime* by entering into the plans of Sir Marmaduke Langdale, who was fomenting a rising in the North. The surprisal of the key of the North, Pontefract Castle, was then mooted, and Morris, who had been thinking of such a scheme for some time, threw himself at once into that difficult and perilous enterprise. Great caution as well as daring were requisite for the attempt, and in both Morris shewed himself an adept. He nursed a close intimacy with the governor and his soldiers, who never thought of suspecting him of treachery. He gathered together many associates. In May 1648, he made an unsuccessful attempt to scale the walls of the castle in the night time. The failure, and the increased precautions adopted by Major Cotterill, the governor, precipitated a second adventure, which was more fortunate than its predecessor. Morris with eight or nine associates entered the castle in disguise on the 3rd of June as the purveyors of some beds which were being brought in from the country. They were dressed like ordinary villagers, but each one was secretly armed with a pistol and a dagger. When they were within the gates, the drawbridge was thrown up, the astonished guards were hastily tumbled into the dungeon, the governor was surprised in his bed, and the castle was won. The Royalists flocked into the fortress and placed themselves under the command of Morris, who acted with wise forethought in victualling the castle and preparing it for a siege.

Morris was the master of the stronghold till the end of March 1649, when after a vehement resistance it was surrendered to Cromwell himself. Six persons were specially excepted in the conditions. They were Morris, the governor, Lieutenant Austwick, and Cornet Blackburn, who were suspected of being concerned in the death of Colonel Rainsbrough at Doncaster; Major Ashby, Ensign Smyth, and Serjeant Floyd, who were charged with a treasonable correspondence with the surprisers of the castle, having been a portion of the garrison. The gallant defenders of the fortress refused to surrender it if they were required to give up their friends. The reply was that they might escape if they could. With the daring of despair the six rode right at the guard; one, Smyth, was killed upon the spot, Morris and Blackburn cut their way through; the other three were obliged to retire within the castle. But even then they did not fall into the hands of the enemy. The surrendering garrison walled them up within the castle, giving them provisions for a month, and these three gallant soldiers actually made their escape.

Morris and Blackburn went into Lancashire, and were arrested ten days after they had broken away from Pontefract. Lambert had promised them their lives if they could escape, but Cromwell ordered them to York, where they were tried in August 1649. Thorpe and Puleston were the judges; George Eure, Esq., was foreman of the grand jury, and Sir William St. Quintin, sheriff.

The following gentlemen acted on the jury: Richard Brooke, of Birstall, gen., Thomas Reynolds, of Thorpe, gen., Thomas Thomlynson, gen., Sampson Darnebrough, gen., John Yonge, of Rocliffe, gen., William Robinson, gen., Henry Peele, gen., John Rookesby, gen., John Clerke, gen., William Johnson, gen., William Oldridge, gen., John Hewan, gen.

Morris challenged Brooke, as his enemy, but his objection was overruled. His defence and the account of the proceedings may be seen in the State Trials. The object of the prosecution was to shew that Morris had acted as governor; this he did not deny, but produced his commission for that post signed by Prince Charles, as Captain-general under his father. This was not allowed, and irons were actually put upon the prisoner before the verdict was found. He and his companion were convicted and died upon the scaffold on the 22nd.

within one weeke after the castle was taken, the said Morrice sent musketteirs to take this informant, and carried him downe and imprisoned him in the dungeon six weeks. In which time the said Morrice, in this informant's presence and hearing, said that if he had 1,000*l*. in gold he could not tell itt, he was soe overjoyed, for he had now brought the worke to passe that he had beene about two yeares, meaneing takeing of the castle. He further sayth that diverse of the lord generall's forces and souldiers being taken att Ollerton, and brought prisoners into the castle, and one of them being stripped and to be putt into the dungeon, the said souldier being unwilling to goe into the dungeon, the said Morrice did sticke the said souldier in the backe, and said that he must goe in, and if the Parliament were there themselves they should have no better place nor usage. The said Morrice did make out commissions and appointed officers and souldiers under him; and he saw a draught of a commission wherein one Ashby was made a captaine under Morrice, and it did mencion that the said Morrice derived his power from the Prince. He hath heard him say to the men that assisted him, and were att takeing and surprizeing of the said castle, that every one of them should have and weare a gold chaine that they might be knowne from others, for that their noble and gallant act of takeing the castle.

The night before they died the two prisoners very nearly made their escape. Morris let himself down from the wall, but his companion, in descending, fell and broke his leg. Morris, like a gallant gentleman, would not desert his friend, and the two were easily re-captured.

On the morrow they were executed, and Morris's last words were a prayer for his King and a grateful expression of thanks to his late master, the Earl of Strafford. His body was afterwards laid by his side in the little chapel at Wentworth.

At Sledmere there are several relics connected with the siege of Pontefract. Among them there is a large bundle of papers once belonging to the family of Drake, including a curious list of the watches in the castle. Colonel Rainsbrough's sword is also preserved there. But the most interesting memorial is a half-length portrait of Colonel Morris. It shews a dark-complexioned young man in armour, with a rich lace collar, and long hair hanging over it. I am indebted for this information to my friend Mr. C. Sykes.

Castilian Morris, the Colonel's son, was town-clerk of Leeds, and drew up for the press an account of Pontefract Castle, in which his father's exploits were duly chronicled. What became of it, I do not know. Castilian Morris, who was born in Pontefract Castle when his father was there, had a son John, who was famous not for military skill or legal and historical research, but, as Thoresby tells us, "not only as an eminent dancer, but peculiarly noted for his admirable dexterity, whereby he can put his body into so various shapes as is very surprising ; he has also so much of the art of insinuation from his grandfather, Colonel John Morris, who surprised Pontefract Castle for King Charles I., that he thereby discovered the cheat of Walter Freazer, who, pretending his tongue was cut out by the Turks, had imposed upon a great part of the nation, by a trick he learned in Holland of drawing so much of his tongue into the throat, that there seemed to be only the root remaining."

Richard Lile of Pontefract, grocer, saith, that he heard Morrice saie that, the Wednesdaie before the castle was surprized, being the fast daie, the said Morrice was in a chamber in the house of Mr. John Tatham in Pontefract, and intended to have surprized the castle that night, but that a regiment of the lord generall's foot being to quarter in the towne that night caused him to deferre it.

Richard Tailor saith, that Major Morrice before the surprizeing of the castle was an officer in service for the Parliament against the King's partie, and did duty as other officers did. He saith also that Major Morrice ledd forth the forces that went against Ferrybridge against the Parliament's forces soe farre as the Newhall, and then gave order and command to Major Bonnyvant, an officer under him, to march and lead on the said forces to Ferribriggs. He saith that Major Morrice did direct and issue forth warrants for listing of men, levying of monies and provicion for the said castle, and likewise sent out warrants to fetch in severall persons as prisoners, and there detained them untill they lent moneys; and commaunded the gunners and other officers and souldiers under him to dischardge their gunnes and muskitts against the Parliament's forces then before the castle.

Thomas Acaster, of Pontefract, being with others upon the guard, Morrice came to them, and did incourage them, and said, "Stand to it, ladds, against our enimies (the Parliament's soldiors then approaching neare the castle), for if wee be taken, I myselfe shal bee pulled in peeces before any of yow."

Richard Clement, of Pontefract, saith that Major Morrice did cause him to be taken prisoner into the castle, and forced him to pay 5l. for his libertie; and he did see the said Morrice lead upp a partie of horse with his pistoll in his hand against Leiftenant Generall Cromwell's forces being to enter the towne of Pontefract.

Mary Metcalfe, of Pontefract, saith that Michaell Blackburne was a souldier in the castle, and coronett to Captaine William Paulden.* She knew that the said Blackburne was one of that party at Doncaster when Coll. Rainsbrough † was slaine, and she

---

* Captain William Paulden died in the castle a month before its surrender. His brother, Captain Timothy Paulden, was killed at Wigan Lane. Thomas Paulden, another brother, suffered in the same cause, but he saved his life, and overlived the century. He was the author of a small historical tract which illustrates these depositions. It is "An Account of the taking and surrendering of Pontefract Castle, and of the surprisal of General Rainsborough in his quarters at Doncaster, Anno 1648. In a letter to a friend by Capt. Tho. Paulden. Oxford, 1747. 8vo." There was an earlier edition in 4to printed at London in 1719.

† Paulden gives an interesting account of the death of Rainsbrough. The daring assailants wished to carry him off as a prisoner that they might exchange him for Sir

heard that Lftent. Autwicke * and Marmaduke Greenfeild was there also.

John Bennington, gent., saith, that Major Marrice did give order to Captaine Alexander Ashbie,† a captaine then under him, to seize and fetch this informant goods from his chamber in Pontefract into the castle, and that he did see the said Ashbie kill a soldior for the Parliament in the street in Pontefract the same daie the castle was surprized. He saith further that one Mr. William Ramsden of Langley tould him that Michaell Blackborne, his late servant, tould him that he was one of those that runne throughe with his sword and murdered Colonell Rainsbroughe at Doncaster.

Leiftenant Thomas Farray, of Pontefract, sayth that Major Morrice issued forth warrants in his owne name as governor of Pontefract Castle for raiseing of horses, levying of money and provicions for the said castle, and for seizeing of the goods of anie townesman that was gone away with the Parliament's partie; and he heard the said Morrice say that he drew forth the forces that went against Ferrybrigges as farre as Newhall orchard himselfe, and that the said forces went against Ferribriggs by his owne appointement. He saith that the said Morrice sent for him and kept him prisoner about a fortnight, and told him that he should pay to the said Morrice 70*l.*, otherwise he would plunder all his goods and burne his howse. He saith, further, that the said Morrice did committ one John Garforth prisoner into the dungeon, and, by a councell of warre, condemned him to be hanged, for giveing intelligence to the Parliament's forces; and,

---

Marmaduke Langdale who was then in durance. He offered resistance and was killed in the affray. The Parliamentarians considered that he had been murdered.

Mr. Jackson of Doncaster is the owner of a very rare tract, the sermon that was preached at Rainsbrough's funeral. Through his kindness I am able to give a copy of the title: "The glorious day of the Saints' appearance; calling for a glorious conversation from all beleevers. Delivered in a sermon by Thomas Brooks, preacher of the gospel at Thomas Apostle's, at the interment of the corps of that renowned commander, Colonell Thomas Rainsborough, who was treacherously murdered on the Lord's Day in the morning at Doncaster, October 29, 1648, and honourably interred the 14th of November following in the chappell at Wapping, neare London. 4to. London. Printed by M. S. for Rapha Harford and Matthew Simmons, and are to be sold at the Bible in Queen's-head Alley in Pater-noster-row, and in Aldersgate streete, 1648." (Dedicated) "To the right honourable Thomas Lord Fairfax, Lord Generall of all the Parliament's Forces in England, such honour and happinesse as is promised to all that love and honour the Lord Jesus."

* Austwick, was, I believe, the person who killed Colonel Rainsbrough. He was one of the six persons excepted from the benefits of the surrender of the Castle, but he made his escape, and died in 1655.

† Ashbie was also excepted from the terms. He had carried on a treasonable correspondence with Morris before the castle was taken. He got away.

in pursuance thereof, the said Garforth was carryed to the gybbett, went upp the ladder, the rope putt about his necke by the execucioner, and there soe stood a certaine time, being mooved to make his confession, but afterwards was suffered to goe backe. He saith that when Lieftennant Generall Cromwell was to enter the towne of Pontefract, this informant did see the said Morrice draw upp his force, both horse and foot, against the said Parliament's forces, endeavoreing to resist their entry.

Marie, wife of John Tatham, of Pontefract, gentleman, saith, that in May was a twelvemoneth John Morrice did sett upp his horse at this inf^{ts} husband's house in Pontefract: that there did sometimes some souldiers come from the castle to the said Morrice and keepe him company, he then being in armes for the Parliament against the King, and was a leiutenant-collonell to Collonell Forbes,* and received pay from the Parliament accordingly, and did duty as other officers did in the leaguer before Pontefract, when the castle was held against the Parliament by Collonell John Lowther,† governor. And, att other times, one ——— Ashbie, ——— Flood, and John Smyth,‡ souldiers under Major Cotterall, who was then governor for the Parliament. And one John Battley kept him company, then an inhabitant in Pontefract, and imployed afterwards by the said Morrice after the surprizall of the castle, as an advocate for him. She further saith, that the castle was attempted to be taken by ladders about 16 dayes before that itt was taken, but by what persons she knoweth not; onely she saith that Mr. Charles Davison was att this informant's husband's house, the day before the castle was attempted soe to be taken by ladders, and that she hath heard that he was one of them that did attempt the same. She, further, sayth as she hath heard the said Major Morrice confesse, that he with Peter, his servant, an Irishman, did first enter into the castle, when itt was surprized the last summer, and that the said Peter did then shoot and wound Major Cotterall, the then governor, after that the castle was surprized. She, further, saith that the said Morrice, accompanied with Sir Hugh Cartwright, Gervas Nevill, Sir Richard Baron, and others, mett att this informant's husband's howse, and sent out warrants into the country for levying of monies, raiseing of men and arms and provisions of corn and victuall for the said castle. The said Morrice did severall times

---

* Colonel Forbes took part in the first siege of Pontefract Castle. He had one of his eyes put out by the "waff" of a cannon-ball.

† This gentleman's name was Richard and not John.

‡ These are the three who were specially excepted in the terms of the surrender, on account of their communications with the enemy.

in her presence declare that he did enter the said castle for the use of the King and the enemies against the Parliament, and that for them he did hold the same, and would doe to the uttmost of his power.

John Garforth, of Pontefract, saith, that Major Morrice did send one Richard Tailor, a soldier under him, to fetch the informant prisoner to the castle; and, when he came there, Morrice chardged him with severall false accusations, and caused him to be tried by a councell of warre, where the said Morrice, as president, gave sentence against him, and adjudged him to be hanged. And, in pursuance thereof, caused this informant to be guarded with horse and 100 muskettiers, with matches lighted, to the gallowes on Bagghill, and caused him to climbe the ladder, and putt a rope about his necke: whereupon this informant desireing the spectators to sing a psalme with him, in the time the psalme was singing, one Captaine Browne brought a reprive for eight dayes, and soe from thence they kept him in prison 7 weekes longer, and then whipped this inform^t out of towne, and charged him not to come to the towne againe upon paine of death.

Gervase Cooper, of Pontefract, draper, saith, he havinge two cowes taken from him and carryed into the castle by the sayd Marris' souldyers, and that when the Parliamentt's forces entred the towne he obtayned favour of Coll. Farefax to goe with a drumme unto the castle to procure his cowes againe. And the officers of the castle then told him thatt none but Marris could lett him have them againe; butt he, the said Marrice, toold this informantt, thatt he should not have his cowes againe if Kinge Charles should write his letter to him to deliver them: and sayd further thatt he would not leave a house standinge in Pontefract: and thereupon commanded to give fire to a morter peece, and shott a granado into the towne, and soe did twice after, whilst this informantt was in the castle: and sayd thatt he would not deliver the castle, although the King's partye in England were destroyed, he would hoold and keepe itt untill he had releefe from the Prince, for he had beene a yeare plottinge to take itt, and he was able to keepe itt three yeares.

Mary, wife of John Smyth, sayth that Morrice caused her husband, being master of the magazine under Major Cotterall, to be called forth of his bedd, and be putt a prisoner into the dungeon, where they kept him eleaven weekes. And she heard the said Morrice then say that he had beene about that plott 2 yeares; and that he hoped within a moneth to have ten castles more, and that Yorke was theire owne already. And she heard him say that there was two and twenty men* there that surprized and tooke the said castle, that should, every man, have a gold chaine with a peece of gold hung in the same, that they might be knowne from all other people in England for their service in takeing the said castle.

Alexander Stileman, gentleman, of Pontefract, saith, that after the attempt of takeing the castle by the ladder, he tooke one Mathew Adams prisoner, and brought him to Pontefract castle, who told him that Morrice was cheife in the plott for the attempt by the ladders. And he heard the said Morrice say that he had 3 times attempted the takeing of the said castle, and, if he had failed, he would have attempted itt six times more but he would have had itt. Hee saith, also, that the said Morrice did, immediately after the surprizall of the castle, commaund Gilbert Hough, Henry Sprowston, and other cannoners, to be brought into the castle, and to traverse the great gunns, and to give fire upon Captaine Browne's horse, a captaine for the Parliament, that appeared in Pontefract feild before the castle. And he heard the said Morrice say that that very day Yorke, and all, or the most, of the holds in England would be surprized. Hee saith, further, that the said Morrice gave order for the parties that went to Ollerton against Ferrybriggs, and takeing of Captaine Todd and his company att Turnebrigg, and shewed letters that Tinmouth castle † was betrayed, and other places, and caused bonefires to be made, and great gunns to be shott of for joy upon the report of takeing Newcastle, Boston, and Lincolne.

William Tatham, of Pontefract, jun., saith that, in May was a twelvemoneths, Major Morice did frequent the house of John Tatham, his father. He knoweth not by what authoritie Sir Phillip Mountaine, Kt.‡ and the rest of the officers or souldiors went from the castle to Willoughbie fight.

---

* The ordinary accounts say eight or nine. It is observable that twenty-two men went out of Pontefract to carry off Rainsbrough.

† In 1648, Colonel Lilburn, the deputy-governor of Tynemouth Castle, declared for the King. On the 11th of August Sir Arthur Haslerigg took the place by storm, and put all the garrison to the sword.

‡ The fight on Willoughby Field took place in July 1648, and was most disastrous to the Royalists. Sir Philip Monckton and some 500 others were taken prisoners. Sir Philip was a most dashing Cavalier, and went through all the dangers of the Civil War. At Marston Moor, according to the tradition in the family, he was so badly wounded that he was obliged to ride with his bridle in his teeth. He has left some remarkable memoirs of his own experiences, which have been partly printed by Mr. Hunter, in his History of South Yorkshire. It appears from them that he was mainly instrumental in admitting General Monk into York. There is a fine portrait of Sir Philip in the possession of his lineal descendant, Lord Galway.

Aug. 2, 1649. Before Sir Robert Barwicke, Kt. *Major John Cotterill** saith, that at and before the 3rd day of June, 1648, this ex^t was governor of Pontefract Castle, and garrison souldiers then belonging to the same, beinge deputed thereunto by authoritie from Major-Generall Lambert. And, by authoritie in that behalfe derived from the State, he had the charge of the said castle and garrison for the service of the Parliament and Commonwealth of England. And he saith that upon the said 3rd of June, betwixe six and seaven of the clocke in the morning, this ex^t haveing beene upon duty the night before, and haveing then newly repaired to his lodging chamber, presently there came in two men with swords and pistolls in theire hands, whome he then knew not (but afterwards heard theire names to be Paulden and Peters) who being asked by this ex^t, "Who comes there?" they answered that the castle was surprised for the King, and that this informer was in the hands of gentlemen: he might have quarter, if he pleased. But refusinge, with his weapon drawne, they fell upon him and wounded him both with sword and pistoll, and after a quarter of an houre's dispute or there abouts, growinge faint with much bleeding, was disabled to make farther opposicion; whereupon the said two men seised upon this informer, and led him into the castle yard, where he mett John Marris, comonly called Major Marris, who had formerly beene active in the Parliament service, and had assisted in the reduceing of that place to the obeidiance of the Parliament of England, when it was holden by one Lowther, formerly governor for the King. And, upon that meeting, the sayd Major Marris sayd "I am now governor of this place for the King," or words to the like effect. And the informant askinge him if he would put him into the dungion, Marris answered, with oathes and great execracions, that if both speakers of Parliament were there they should in. To which place he thereupon commanded this informant to be comitted, where this informant found then newly comitted to the same dungion about the number of thirty officers and souldiers, till that time under this deponents command. And, after he had continued in misery in the sayd place about three days and three nights, he was by order from the said Marris removed to another prison in the said castle. And the sayd Marris, after that, had the title and name of governor, and commanded the souldiers and guards in the sayd castle. And this deponent was inforced in the behalfe of the prisoners formerly under his command, as well for theire

* Major Cotterill's account of this scene differs slightly from that which is given by Captain Thomas Paulden. His resistance could not have lasted a quarter of an hour. Cotterill gives us some interesting information about Morris.

subsistance, as for theire exchange, to make his addresse to the sayd Marris, as governor; in whose power and sole command that garrison then was, from and after the time of his sayd surprisall. And the sayd Morris did constitute and appoint officers under his command for the raisinge and disciplyninge of men for defence of that castle and garrison against the authorityc of the Parliament of England. And he heard the sayd Marris say that he had beene about the surprysall of that castle any time for 2 yeares then past. And he further said, that himselfe with Col. Furbus and Col. Thomas Fairefax (who lately revolted from the Parliament and was in Scarbrough Castle) did lodge together at Knottingley in one bedd, about that time the late King came to Doncaster in a hostile manner; and that they there continued expecting command from the said King to surprise the said castle from the hands of Col. Robert Overton, then governor for the Parliament. And this informant also knoweth that there was formerly attempts made to take the castle in the night time by rearinge of ladders, which was duringe this deponent's said governement discovered and prevented. And this informer heard the sayd Marris after the surprisall aforesaid say that he was there in person when the sayd ladders were reared, and intended himselfe to be the first man that should enter, and that he then had the chiefe command of that party. And he saith, that duringe the time of his durance as prisoner in the said castle (beinge about thirteene weeks) he well knoweth that the said Marris commanded in cheife in the said castle, as governor; and did walke the rounds and commanded severall locks and barrs to be layd upon the dores where this informer was in durance. He knoweth not Blackburne by that name, but may perhaps remember both his persons and some of his actions when he seeth him.

Aug. 2, 1649. Before Sir Robert Barwicke, Kt. *John Grant, gunner,* late under the command of Major Cotterill, late governor of Pontefract Castle, saith, that he beinge the gunner of the said castle, as it was a garrison held for the Parliament, under the command of the said Major Cotterill, governor of the same. And whilst the same garrison was soe under that command, it fell out unhappily upon the third of June, 1648, that it was taken by surprisall, by Major John Marris, and others under his command, and of conspiracy with him. And, immediately upon theire entry, this deponent, and about thirtie more of the officers and souldiers of the sayd castle who continued faithfull to the Parliament, were by command of the said Marris comitted to the dungion in the said castle, beinge a darke place about forty-two steps within the earth. And, imediatly after theire comeing in,

Major Cotterill was also brought thither sore wounded in severall places of his body. And this deponent saith that the said Major John Marris was commander-in-cheife of those souldiers who were actors in the said surprisall; and that he did from thence forwards continue governor and commander-in-cheife of the said castle and garrison for the King, and held the same against the Parliament of England, until it was by force regained after a long siege. And this deponent, further, saith that he well knoweth him commonly called Major Blackburne, who was likewise an actor in the said conspiracy, and ayded to surprise the said castle, and continued there in the same under command of the said Marris; and uttered in this ex^{ts} hearing many railing words against the Parliament, and affirmed that he had gon forth upon parties and killed severall men.

Aug. 8, 1649. At York Castle: before Sir Robert Barwicke, Kt. and Tho. Dickinson, Esq. *Michael Blackburne, late of Coldhil in the parish of Almondbury*, sayth, that he was servante to Sir John Ramsden,* and waited on his chamber till the tyme of his death, and that he was not present at the surprising of the castle and garrison of Pontefract, in June was a twelmonth, by Major Marris, nor did then know him; but he came into the castle in the same month of June, and received within few days after his coming into the said garrison a commission from Sir Marmaduke Langdale as cornet of Capt. Palden's troop;† and, at that tyme when Col. Rainsbrugh was slaine at Doncaster, he went forth with the same party, but came not to Doncaster by reason that his horse tired; and he sayth that he was one amongst the rest that continued the holding of the said castle and garrison under the command of Mr. Jo. Marris; and, being questioned touching his leaving of the said castle and garrison, he sayth that he, with Col. Marris and his man, did about March last ride through the forces which had then long besieged them in the said castle, and came into Lancashire where they were apprehended.

John Marris, now prisoner in York Castle for high treason, being examined touching the surprisall of the castle and garrison of Pontefract in June last was a yeare, and whether he comanded the party who surprised and toke the said castle, he answereth that he did not surprise the said castle and garrison, for it was delivered to him, the gates being opened to him, and he

---

* Sir John Ramsden was in Pontefract Castle when it was besieged for the first time.

† The original commission to Captain William Paulden, signed by Sir Marmaduke Langdale, is now at Sledmere.

going into the same without resistance; and he was from thenceforth governor of the same, as his commission from the Prince of Wales, which he hath to shew, will expresse at large, and he did there comand in cheife the soldiers of the said garrison according to this said comission, for all the tyme he held the said castle against the forces of the Parlament.

XV. THOMAS BRIGHT. FOR HAVING AN UNLAWFUL BOOK.

Sep. 18, 1649. Before Richard Etherington, Esq. *Mathew Morley*, a trouper belonging to Collonell Robert Lilburn's regiment, saith that hee did see a booke intituled, " The Tablet or Moderacion of Charles the First and Martir," * in the hands of one Mr. Boyes; and the said Mathew Morley, upon perusall of the said booke, thought it to be very prejudiciall to the government established in England. And the said Boyes said that the booke was Thomas Bright's, of Pickring aforesaid, gentleman, and he had a frind that sent it him from beyond the sea.

XVI. MARMADUKE RICHARDSON, CLERK. FOR PRAYING FOR THE PRINCE OF WALES.

Sep. 26, 1649. Recognisances for the appearance at the assizes of Marmaduke Richardson,† of Pocklington, clerk, for praying publickly before his sermon in the parish church of Pocklington for Charles the Second, Kinge of Scotland and heire apparent to this realme.

XVII. NICHOLAS SPAVILD AND RICHARD DREW. FOR HIGHWAY ROBBERY.

Nov. 28, 1649. Before Andrew Burton, Mayor of Doncaster, &c. The Right Honn^{ble} Wm. Earle of Dunfreise‡ saith that,

---

* No early edition of this work is recorded by Watt. It was reprinted in 8vo in 1694. Another deposition describes the work as " The Tablet, &c. with an Alarum to the Subjects of England." John Musgrave, a trouper in the same regiment, supports the evidence of his comrade. Mr. Bright was bound over to keep the peace at the assizes.

† Mr. Richardson was ordered to find sureties for his good behaviour.

‡ A Scottish earl is returning from the South, and between Lincoln and Bawtry he is set upon, as he says, and robbed. He had a servant with him. It is strange that they should surrender to two assailants.

When the earl reaches Bawtry on foot there is a hue and cry after the offenders, and they are soon caught. Their story is a strange one—they say that the gentleman beinge ridinge on the high rode way betwixt Lincolne and Doncaster, he was sett uppon by Nicholas Spavild and Richard Drew, on the 26th of Nov., who tooke from him one bay mare and a black nagg with a great lether mall full of goods. Therupon hee was forced to goe to Bawtrey on foote, and there raysed hue and crye after them.

XVIII. WILLIAM MASON. FOR TREASON, &c.

Jan. 9, 1649-50. Before Isaac Newton, Esq. *William Kirkham, of Rivis*, sayth, that one Wm. Mason of Newless did relate to this informant that he brought a woman unto his brother's, Robert Mason's, bedd syde at Olde Byland, in the night time, as they were in bedd together. This informer then asked him whether or noe it was a substantiall body, and how he could see or perceave her in the darke?* Whoe answered that when it was darke to this informant it was light to him. He asked the said Mason howe he dared to doe these and other straunge matters amongst the souldyers least they should fall upon him and kill him? He answered that he had fixed them soe that they had neither power to pistoll him, stabb him, kill, or cutt him. This informant further telling the said Mason that, if he could not make good the charge which he had framed against Richard Boulbye's wyfe, he did beleeve the justices at the sessions would comitte him to the gaole or house of correccion. Whereunto he answered, if they did soe he would make some others followe him; and, when they were fast, he would goe out at his pleasure. Further, asking the said Mason whether or no there should be a King in England, he answered he would warrant there should bee a King, and that very shortely.

XIX. THOMAS WELSH. FOR SEDITIOUS WORDS.

Feb. 12, 1649-50. Before Richard Robinson, of Thickett, Esq. *John Robinson and William Iles*, souldyers under Captayn

was riding off the road over the corn: when they remonstrated with him he and his servant dismounted and walked away, leaving the horses behind them, which Spavild and Drew carried away to the pinfold. Credat Judæus!

* A deposition evidently depending upon others that are lost: it is difficult therefore to explain it. The accused person seems to have mixed politics with his diablerie, and it was for them, apparently, that he was called to account. Another witness charges him with saying at Helmsley "that hee knewe when there would be a King, and when there would be a greate fight."

Henery Ponnell, captayn in Collonell Bright's regiment,* say that, being drinking one night in theire quarters with one Thomas Welsh of North Dalton, they did heare the said Welse say these words following: That there is a King, and that England could never be governed aright without a King. That Prince Charles was crowned King of Scotland, and would shortly be amongst us. He drank an health to the sayd King and Queene's prosperity, and would have them to have pledged him with the health of Sir Marmaduke Langdale. He asked John Robinson if, when an army came against us, that he would give him quarter if he light on him, and he would doe the same by him.

XX. THOMAS ROSETER AND OTHERS. FOR PIRACY.

March 1, 1649-50. Before Jo. Overton, Esq. *Thomas Roseter, an Irishman,* saithe that, aboute sixe weekes since, he was shipped from Dunkirke in Flaunders by Lourance Dusbury, maister of this shippe now ridinge in Humber, for to goe to sea as a man of warr upon free bootie;* and that he and John Marcer, Wm. Wilson, and one Raiphe, whose sirname this ex^t knoweth not, were likewise shipped in the said shippe aboute the same time as souldiors upon free bootie; and confesseth they have Prince Charles his comission, and that they came yesterday on shoore at Easington for taking in freshe watter and gettinge victualles, haveinge been aboute sixe weekes at sea, and spent theire watter and victuall, and gott noe prize in all that. And saithe theire be only tenn other men aboarde the said shippe, and that she haithe only 2 gunnes and 12 muskittes, with pouder and amunition theireunto proportionall, sixe fyrelockes and 16 swordes and some pistolles. And, upon further examinacion, confesseth that they tooke a smale boate neare or belonginge to Lynn, loadned with oates.

At the assize begun at York on March 12, 1650 1, a Wm. Mason was indicted for uttering six pieces of bad gold coin, but was acquitted.

* Colonel Bright was a Parliamentarian, and his regiment saw much service in the Civil Wars. The offending cavalier pleaded drunkenness as his excuse, and said, probably with truth, that he remembered nothing about the alleged offence. He was ordered to find sureties for his good behaviour, and was fined 40*l*.

Sir Marmaduke Langdale's name would at this time be in the mouth of every cavalier as the most dashing and successful cavalry officer in the King's service. The sufferings and the exploits of this noble gentleman are well known. His loyalty is said to have cost him the large sum of 160,000*l*.

† A case of piracy. The adventurers had letters of marque from Prince Charles. A great deal of mischief was done on the Yorkshire coast during the Civil Wars by pirates. In 1646 the people of Scarborough complained to Sir John Lawson that they had lost as many as nine ships within eight days. After this those waters were protected by seven ships of war. At the assizes the pirates were ordered to be left in prison without bail.

William Dickinson, borne at Skarbroughe, confesseth the very same with Tho. Roserter, and, further, that the name of the capt. of the pyrates shippe is Capt. Cusye, and the name of the m^r is Lowrance Dusbury, and the name of the shipe is The Fortune. *John Marser*, was borne at Bristol, but refuseth further to be examined, savinge that he belongethe to the shipp now in Humber. *Raiphe Fletcher*, born in Bushop-warmothe, near Sunderlande, will confese nothinge.

Rositer and Fletcher say that Marser's name is Plunkett. (Yow will finde this Plunkitt a notable, cunninge, boulde rogue.)

XXI. RICHARD SMITH AND OTHERS. FOR BEING GIPSIES.

March 8, 1649-50. Before Luke Robinson, Esq. *William Allan, of Bransby, constable*, saith that divers people in the habitts of jipsey * came to Butterwicke the day before they were aprehended att Normanby, the same who are now in the Castle of Yorke. Divers of them did tell fortunes to children and to

---

* A party of poor gipsies are in trouble. We see them acting and living just as they do now, and probably no class has changed less than the gipsies. Their migratory habits and hereditary tricks and devices used to expose them to much unmerited suffering and suspicion. They generally were called Egyptians, from the country in which, it was supposed, they had their origin. Thence comes their present name. In the Register book of St. Nicholas's church, in Durham, " 1592, Aug. 8, Simson, Arrington, Fetherstone, Fenwicke, and Lanckaster, *were hanged for being Egyptians*."

The gipsies referred to in the depositions were treated in a most unjustifiable manner. The following petition declares what happened to them.

"To the right worshippfull Mr. Robinson, Esq., Justice of peace in the North Riding. The humble petition of divers distressed wandring persons, calling themselves by the name of Jepseso.

" Humbly shewith, that, whereas your worship hayth comitted us most justly, and according to our deserts, to the castle of York, where wee are; and our poore infants almost famished for want of livehood. And, much the rayther, be reason the men that by your worship's comannd brought us hither, did contrary to all equity and Christiannity, and, as we are informed, contrary to the law of this kingdom, bereft us, and tooke from us our mare, and many things of greate noate and vallew. And, withoute any neede or just cause, getting at many townes both meate and monny for theire and our use, of which your poore petitioners gott smale releife.

" In tender considderation whereof, and soe that your petitioners are most sorry for theire former leud course of life; and promisseth, by the help of Almighty God, will indeavor ourselves to direct our lives heareafter, observant to the will of God, and lawes of this land, it, therefore, would please your worship to commisserate our distressedness, and in your grave wisdom to cause the cunstable and others to restore our goods soe unjustly tacken from us. And that it would please your worship to call us to the sessions to receyve such punishment as the worshipfull bench shall think fitt, and wee shalbe bound to pray."

At the assizes all the women plead pregnancy before judgment. It was allowed in one case, that of Barbara Smith. The others were probably executed. The name of the man does not occur in the calendar.

others, and askt them money. They did some tyme speake in languages wich none who were by could understand.

Jane, wife to Thomas Savadge, of Bransby, sayth that she went to Wm. Kattill's house, where these people were, about sixe of them, and one of them, a woman, did wagge hir hand of hir, and did draw hir to a side, and told hir shee would helpe her to 60*l.*, three silver spoones and two gold rings, if she might have halfe, and one shilling, fower pence, one linning shorte and one linning pillow beare.

Richard Smith, and Barbary, whoe pretends to bee his wife, Francis Parker, Elizabeth Grey, and Elizabeth Parker.

Richard Smith doeth confesse that hee and the rest of his company weere apprehended in London as suspitious persons, for highway robbers, and were committed to Newgate and the House of Correccion, and wear in question att the sessions their, but weir, as hee pretends, ordered to bee sent to their severall dwellings or countryes, conducted by one Grey, whoe was not with them when they were apprehended. He confesses that they have beene in severall parts of this country; that they were travayling into Northumberland; that they have been in Herefordshire, Stafford, Salop, Cheshire, and Lancashire, and that they came last from the East Riding about Hesle. He denyes that any of them did professe to tell fortunes. They did likewise produce this passe, concerning which I have received since a letter from Alderman Penington, affirming itt to be forged. And likewise wee did thinke these persons were burned in the hand att theire sessions.

XXII. MARY SYKES AND ANOTHER. FOR WITCHCRAFT.

March 18, 1649-50. Before Henry Tempest, Esq. *Dorothy Rodes, of Bolling, widow,** saith, thatt, upon Sonday night was a scavennight, she and Sara Rodes, her dawghter, with a litle childe, lay all in bedd together; and, after theire first sleepe, she heareing the saide Sara quakeing and holding her hands together, she asked her what she ailed, and she answered " A, mother, Sikes wife came in att a hole att the bedd feete, and upon the bedd, and tooke me by the throate, and wold have put her fingers in

---

* Another curious story of witchcraft. I shall make no comment upon it. What a picture of credulity and folly it discloses. The depositions contain some curious local words. The poor women deny all acquaintance with the crimes imputed to them. At the assizes the bill against Susan Beaumont was ignored, and Mary Sykes was acquitted.

my mowth, and wold needes choake me." And, this informant asking her why she did not speake, she answered she cold not speake for thatt the saide Mary Sykes fumbled about her throate and tooke her left syde thatt she cold not speake. And she further saith thatt the saide Sara hath beene taken severall tymes since the saide Sonday with paines and benummednes, by six tymes of a day, in greate extremity, the use of her joynts being taken from her, her hart leapeing, the use of her tongue being taken away, and her whole body neare unto death. And those fitts continewed halfe an hower, and sometymes an hower, and when she was recovered, she continually saide thatt the saide Mary Sikes came and used her in that maner. And upon the saide Sonday the saide Sara told this informant thatt the saide Mary Sikes came unto her as she was comeing home, and tooke holde of her by the apron, and gathered itt by the bottom into her hands, and puld her soe hard by itt thatt she puld some of the gatherings out; and that she was in great feare, and wincked; and opening her eyes she saide " Mary." Butt the saide Mary Sikes wold give noe answere. And then Susan Beamont came to her. And the likenes of one Kellett wife appeared to her. Whereupon this informant told her that Kellett wife dyed about two yeares since. To which the saide Sara answered, " A, mother, but she never rests, for she appeared to me the fowlest feinde that ever I sawe, with a paire of eyes like saweers, and stood up betwixt them, and gave me a box of the eare in the gapsteade, which made the fire to flash out of my eyes."

Richard Booth, of Bolling, saith, that he saw the said Sara Rodes two severall tymes verie strangely taken, her body quakeing and dithering about halfe a quarter of an hower, her hart riseing up, and in such manner that she cold not speake but now and then a word. And the saide Mary Sikes hath divers tymes saide unto this informant, " Bless the," and " I'le crosse the," and that he hath had much loss by the death of his goods.

Henry Cordingley, of Tonge, saith, that the saide Mary Sikes hath saide unto him divers tymes, since Christenmas was twelve monthes, that he had nyne or tenn beasts and horses, but she wold make them fewer, and " Bless the," but " I'le cross the." He further saith that, some three dayes before the saide Cristenmas, he goeing to fother horses, about 12 o'clock in the night, with a candle and lanthron, his beasts standing neare his horses, he sawe the saide Mary Sikes riding upon the backe of one of his cowes. And he, endeavoring to strike att her, stumbled, and soe the saide Mary flewe out of his mistall windowe, haveing three or fower wooden stanchions, the saide cowe being then white over with an imy sweate. And he likewise saith that he had one blacke horse, worth 4*l*. 16*s*., begunn to be sicke about Tewsday was a fortnight, and continewed dithering and quakeing till Sonday following, and then dyed. And he, opening the saide horse, cold not finde an eggshell full of blood. And he is verily perswaded that the saide horse was bewitched. And he saith, allsoe, that a black meare of his hath beene sicke in like manner as the former horse was, since about Tewsday last was a fortnight, till the tyme that the saide Mary was searched by the weomen; but, since that, she hath recovered and amended, and eates hir meate verie well.

William Rodes, of Bolling, saith, that in harvest last past this informant was in the howse of William Sikes, husband to the saide Mary Sikes, and that he hearde the saide Mary say " Henry Cordingley braggs of his dawghters, what gay dawghters they are. His eldest dawghter was of her feete at once, butt, if I be owne to live, she shalbe taken off her feete and made a miracle." And than went to her parlor windowe and saide, " I'le looke if the devill be att the windowe." *Isabella Pollard, of Bierley, widow, and five other women*, say, that by vertue of a warrant from Henry Tempest, Esq., they searched the body of the saide Mary Sikes, and founde upon the side of her seate a redd lumpe about the biggnes of a nutt, being wett, and that, when they wrung it with theire fingers, moisture came out of it like lee. And they founde upon her left side neare her arme a litle lumpe like a wart, and being puld out it stretcht about halfe an inch. And they further say that they never sawe the like upon anie other weomen.

XXIII. JOSEPH CONSTANT AND OTHERS. FOR PIRACY.

Apr. 2, 1650. Scarbrough. The examinacions of Joseph Constant, captain of a vessell of warre called the St. Peter of Jersey,* &c., before Tho. Gill and Wm. Saunders, baliffes. Whoe

---

* A privateer captured off Scarbrough. Mr. Hinderwell gives an interesting account of their seizure, of which I shall avail myself. Robert Colman, master of a North Sea fishing smack, hearing of the presence of the strange ship on the coast, volunteers to Colonel Bethel, then governor of Scarbrough Castle, to capture it. The governor gives him arms and twenty-five soldiers under the command of Captain Thomas Lassells, and he had besides twenty-five seamen.

" Wee sailed forth, and that evening met with the said ship of warr, who called to us and commanded us, saying 'Strike, yee dogs, for King Charles!' and so brought their vessel aboard on us; whereupon I gave the word to the seamen then in my vessel, who immediately entered the ship of war, and, after a very hot skirmish (myselfe and three seamen being sorely wounded), we stowed the men, twenty-nine in number who were alive, besides five more slaine and drowned, tooke the vessel, and brought her

say that upon the 27th of March they came to sea from Dunkirke with 32 men or thereabouts, with commission from Charles, eldest sonne of the late Kinge of England, to apprehend and pocesse, and, in case of resistance, to sinke, fire, or otherwise destroy, all shipps and vessells, togeather with ther men, goods, ladings, and merchandize, belonginge to any places or person not in obedience to the said Charles whom they call King of England. And that, upon Monday the 1st of Aprill, towardes the evening, they espyed a vessell coming towards them, which they presantly sailed to, and laid her aboard, thinkinge to have taken her, and fireinge upon the said vessell, but they, being too stronge, tooke them and brought them into Scardbrough peare.

XXIV. JOHN PURVEYS.   A DANGEROUS PERSON.

July 17, 1650. At Rotherham. *Thomas Hartley,* of Fishlake,* saith that John Purveys, of Fishlake, was in actuall service against the Parliament, and doth continue in his malignance to this very day. That hee hath constantlie used to weare a pockitt dagger with two longe knives. That, on the 3rd of July, which was an exercise day at Fislake, he did carry privately in his pockitt the said dagger and knives to church, and said that hee did weare them for the honor of his King, and that he hoped to doe his King more service therwith then any Cropp did the Parliament with his longe sword.

XXV. ANNE CROWTHER.   FOR KILLING HER HUSBAND.

Aug. 19, 1650. Before Jo. Stanhope. *Henry Walker, of Mirfeild, clothier,*† sayth that, upon Sunday morning last but one, with one gun and other armes and provisions, and the men as prisoners, into Scarborough peares."

This deposition is signed by the captain and twenty-eight of his crew. The names show that the greater part of the men were foreigners, apparently Dutchmen.

* A Royalist who was more bold than cautious. In addition to these misdemeanors he was also charged with robbery and assault.

† A story that can scarcely be credited. A widow, three weeks after her husband's death, feels the want of another spouse—to reap her corn! An obliging friend finds one for her, and brings him on the same day, a Sunday. On the Tuesday they are married. On the Thursday she turns her husband out of bed and house. The poor wretch, who complained bitterly of the effects of a certain " clapt cake" that his wife had given him on the Tuesday, was found shivering with cold, sitting on a clog near his own door, through which he did not dare to pass. On the Friday it was broken open and he was carried in in a chair, having almost died twice whilst they were carrying him. On the Saturday he *did* die—a nice termination to the week. The woman denied the marriage!

hee, goeing to the howse of Anne Crowther, of Mirfeild, she, haveing buryed her husband about three weekes before, made a great lamentacon to him for want of some helpe to gett her corne. Whereupon he told her that hee would helpe her to a man which would helpe to gett her harvest, and told her the sayd man was a widower and that, if they pleased, they might make a marriage together. Shee asked him of what age hee was, and was so importunate with him to have a sight of the man that she procured him the same day to goe for him to Hunslett, where he dwelt, and lent him her mare, and offered to pay him for his paynes. Whereupon this informant went to Hunslett, the said day, and procured John Walker to come along with him. And John Walker and Anne Crowther meeting together the sayd Sunday att night, after some conference betwixt them, the said Anne expressed herselfe willing to marry with him, if it was that night, and carryed him along with her to her howse. And, on Munday after, they did agree to be marryed together on Tuesday, and were marryed by Mr. Robert Allanson, vicar of Mirfeild. And upon Thursday she went to the said John's bedsyde and lifted up the cloathes and desyred him to gett up, which he did. And she desyred him to goe forth of doore, and did deny to lett him come into her howse.

XXVI. THOMAS BRADLEY. FOR MANSLAUGHTER.

Oct. 18, 1650. Before Henry Tempest, Esq. *Ellen, wife of James Rodes, of West Ardesley,** saith thatt, about Midsomer last was fower yeares, Robert Allerton, her late husband, and Thomas Bradley sitt in a seate together in the church att Woodchurche. And the saide Robert, setting up his knee to write the sermon, the saide Thomas struck him with his hand severall tymes upon his right legg, which had an issue or a pipe in itt, and paused him soe vehemently that the saide Robert cryd "awe." And, by reason of the saide pawseing, the issue was stopt. And Robert said to Bradley, "thou hast given me my death."

XXVII. PETER DE BEAVOIR. A DANGEROUS PERSON.

Dec. 14, 1650. The true state or accontt of Mr. Peter de Beauvoir,† nat . . . the islande of Garnezey.

---

* A man accidentally killed by a slight blow that he received in church, whilst he was taking notes of the sermon. Bradley says that he merely pushed the leg off the other, and that no charge was made against him till he demanded 20s. of the woman for keeping an unlicensed alehouse.

† Peter de Beauvoir, a native of Jersey and a captain in the service of the Parlia-

That, the 14th day of December, 1650, as I was travellinge from the towne of Doncaster, on my march to Scottland, to repaire to Collonell Whaley's owne troope (whom by God's blessinge I did hope to have gone in), I was seiszed upon in my inne as if I had beene somme malefactor or dangerous person against this state or common whealth. That I have served this nine yeares in severall qualifications: first, at the very first beginning of these wars I have ingaged for the Parlement case with my owne horses and armes from time to time, as my little abylity did innable mee to doe; first, as a horseman-reformadoe under Collonell John Fiennes, and afterwardes was preferde to bee c^t of foote to Captn Douty, ant c^t of horse twisce under the saide Collonell Fiennes, to Captain John Hunt and Barnarde at Nazeby fight, untill wee were disbanded by order, havinge been taken before by the enemy Prince Robertt att Bristoll, and was prefferd to bee cornet to Collonell Mazzeres, under the Earle of Manchester, where at our disbandinge I rid reformadoe under Captain Fulke Grevill's troope with my man and my tow horses in Sir William Waller's army untill the said John Fiennes preferd me to be l^t of horse as abovesaide; and afterwardes have beene of my Lord Fairfax his liffe guarde, untill the disbanding thereof at London. Where, by a speciall order from Generall Fairfax, given to Doctor Stanes for my entertainemen in Collonell Whaeley's owne troope, for the space of tow years an a halfe, with my servant and tow horses and armes at my owne cost and charges, where the said Collonell did chuze mee to bee a conductor for Irelande, where I shipt neer or above heightscore souldiers as recreutes a twelve months agon at King's Roads at Bristoll. And sinsce I have ride in Captn Jinkin's troope untill I was put out of the muster rolle, in regarde I was to goe for Scottlande in the above saide Collonell Whaley's owne troope. I come from Wells to London about a moneth agone, where I come to London at the signe of the White Swan neere Holborne, where Captn Freeman did laye then, serjourninge only 8 or 9 dayes there. From whence I come with a full resoluttion to serve in Scottlande as reformadoe under my Colonel Whaley owne troope. I did mett Captn John Cresset foote company

ment is arrested at Doncaster for suspicious and extraordinary conduct, as will be seen in the charges brought against him. He seems to have been playing the part of a swaggering bully. The account that he gives of his adventurous life is interesting and was written by himself. I have seen a short petitionary letter which he addressed to the judge at York begging for a little consideration on account of his being a foreigner, and expressing his regret at what had occurred. He was indicted at the York assizes, but was discharged on finding sureties for his good behaviour. The case is a remarkable one, and the papers will be read with much interest.

belonging to Boaston garrison in the regiment of Colonell Liliarde upon their march from London towards Boaston, quartteringe with them all alonge our march as farre as it lie in my way towards Scottland, officiatinge for that present time as quarttermaester in the towne of Upton, foure milles of Stillton in Hunttingtonshire. Where I tooke my leave of him, hee being goeinge to quartter to Peterborough that night, where I did lie in the inne or alehouse in Crocksom in my roade northwardes, when I mett with Judge Tharpe's company heither to this towne of Duncaster, and did hope to have gone to Yorke still allong with him and the rest of his followers, both for my owne security and speede in my journey, having beene like to have ben set upon towards the eveninge by foure highwaymen that did endeavor to take me at advantage untill I was secured in my saide inne of Crockesam. The which things made mee be the . . . linge to goe sauve from robbery, as abovesaide, to prevent further dooings. I had forgoat to tell you that whithin fowre milles of Roiston wee did stopt and scisze 4 men, whereof 3 of them hade beene formerly cavaleers, and the other was as a servant. Wee did apprehende them, and committed 3 of them under custody in the saide towne of Roiston; and the chief of them wee sent up disarmed with Enseigne Cresset to the concell of warre at White Hall to bee adjuged as lafull prisze, and besides to know whether or no they where not in Northfolke muttiny, as I did partly discover them to be malignants newly arrived from Holland to plott mischieff, as I wrotte by Captn Cresset's ensigne to my lorde president of the concell of state from Royston; the which things I doe certifie to be the plaine truth att my perill. Peter de Beauvoir, Captn."

Articles of misdemeanors against Peter de B . . ., a Garnsey mann, whereupon, as may be concluded, he is a daingerous person and fitt to be secured.

That he tooke a jorney from London, aboute three weekes before Christide last, pretending to goe into Yorkeshire, and in his jorney his doeinges and speaches hereafter specified weere observed.

1. That he ridd armd in extraordinary manner (vizt.) with fower pistolls, a carbine, a raper and pockett dagger, and in a boufe coate. 2. That, upon discourse with Robert Sparke, he said "I tendred my service to a Parliament collonell, but he refused me because I was a Frenchman, and he is now one of the councell of state, a stately knave as all of them are." And, therewith, drawing his dagger, said these words in great passion, "I would this dagger weere in their bellies, and ere long it shalbe

in some of their bellies." 3. That upon discourse with John Rockley he said, " I have beene a sol . . . for the Parliament, but " therewith swearing a great oath " I will never serve them more." 4. That, upon discourse with Robert Sparke, he said " If I should meet with 20 or 30 men I would fire upon them all, and I care noe more for killing a man than for killing a woodcocke." 5. That he being advised by some persons of his acquaintance at Doncaster to retorne backe to London said, " I will not goe to London, for then I may venter to be hanged." 6. That he was very inquisitive in his jorney whether Judge Thorpe,[*] who was then upon the roade, was past by or not; and after he had overtaken the Judge's company, he was very inquisitive to know his jorneys and stages; and how many of the company belongd to him, and when he and the rest weere to part, and what the Judge carried in his sumpter, and whether it weere not mony. As, also, how his company was armd, and whether they would fight in case they should meete with highway robbers and cutters; and he seemed very fearefull to meete with such highway robbers and cutters, as he cald them. And, further, he said he wondred the Judge was nott sett upon by cutters, considering he had hanged so many men. 7. That he ridd thorough Brigg, Casterton, northward, about fower clocke towardes night, and came backe into the towne about eight clocke at night all in a great fright, and with his carbine and his pistolls cockt and ready to give fier, and affrighted all the people in the inne to which he came, and while he was at supper he laid his pistolls ready cockt beside his trencher; and did also their present his pistoll cockt in one hand and a naked dagger in th'other to a countryman's breast, and furiously asked him what he was, and what armes he had. 8. That upon the day when Barron Thorpe came to Doncaster, which was aboute fower clocke, the said De Bevoyr tooke occacon to stay behinde the company, and then came into the towne after them about eight clocke at night, and brought with him three or fower more persons all armd with swords and pistolls like soldiers, and wente to another inne where that company with him staid, but himselfe came to the inne where Barron Thorpe lay, pretending to belong to his company, and soe lodged their. 9. That the next morneing, being Saterday, when Barron Thorpe and his

---

[*] Did Beauvoir actually think of falling upon the Judge and his suite? Francis Thorpe, one of the Barons of the Exchequer, was frequently on duty at York.

A charge which he delivered to the grand jury at York, on March 20, 1648, was printed, in folio, by Thomas Broad, of York, in 1649.

He died and was buried at Bardsey in the West Riding, leaving behind him an unfavourable reputation.

company weere to part, and all of them to goe to their owne homes, though the day before he had charged his carbine with haileshott and killd pigeons as he roade upon the way, yett then he had charged his carbine and pistolls, some with two bulletts, some with three bulletts a peece. 10. That he said, " If I gett into Yorkeshire I will have mony enough." 11. That though he be not a soldier, but putt out of the rolle, for some misdemeanor, as may be conceived, yett he tooke upon him in his said jorny to be a quartermaster, and tooke free quarter in divers places by the way as he roade. 12. That since the said De Bevoir's comitment he hath severall tymes reviled Barron Thorpe and the maior of Doncaster, and said they weere both rogues, and if ever he gott out he would marke them for rogues, and said " I will write to Bradshawe to be freed."

XXVIII. ROBERT ASHTON. A DANGEROUS PERSON.

Dec. 25, 1650. Before Thos. Dickinson and Ralph Rymere. *John Peirse, of Bedall, Esq.* maketh oath that Robert Ashton, late of Askew, gen., comonlie called Doctor Ashton,* having a woman who charged him with bastardy, this deponent, having receaved from London an ordinance of Parliament in print against adultery, wished the said Mr. Ashton to read the same, which he did accordinglie, and withall wished him to put away the woman, in respect that he had credablie heard that he had a wife and children at Wappen neer London. The said Mr. Ashton's answer was that, before 25 June, as neer as it was, he hoped to see all the rebells that made that ordinance and act to be hanged; saying that there would be an alteracion of State, and his Majesties sonne, whose picture he kept and loved, would have his owne in despight of all rogues and rebells, and he, this deponent, would be put to his last game.

July 26, 1650. Informations against Docter Robert Ashton of Aiskew, taken before Mathew Beckwith, Esq.† That the

---

* A very singular story. Of course the articles against Dr. Ashton must be received with some caution; but how strange they are, if true ! What a union of opposites in his character ! One would like to know what became of him. Mr. Ashton was tried at the York assizes, and it was ordered that he should be kept in gaol at the pleasure of Sir Robert Barwick and Mr. Thomas Dickinson.

Mr. Peirse, a member of a family that is still resident in Bedale, was a Parliament man. I find a person called Ralph Douthwaite, of Thirsk, indicted at York for having said at Bedale on 14th June, 1652, " Mr. Pearse, the Parliament are all turned levellers, and will level every man, that the poorest soldier will bee as good as the best freeholder."

† Of Tanfield, Esq. a strong Parliamentarian and one of Oliver's captains. After

said Dr. Ashton used to reade Common Prayer, and, to the end that he might have heearers, he put upp a bell in his house, which was rung at set houres to draw his congregation togeather, which were most of them lewd people. That he pretended to have a revelacon since the late King's deceuse, to heale the evill; and soe hee solemnized the same day of the King's departure, every moneth, in a long white garment, with other ceremonies, and laid his hands upon some to heale them, saying some forme of prayers like a charme, to the delusion of the people. That hee preached divers times at the chappell of Leeming, teaching the doctrine of workes, which is meere Poperye. And there he read the Common Prayer, and since hath hired a man to reade it morneing and evening in contempt of authority. That the said Dr. Robert Ashton hath beene banished forth of Byshopbridge by Sir Arthur Hazlerigg * for theese and other disorders That he hath noe licence for practizeing of physicke, nor other degrees in the university that is knowne, and many have died very suddainly under his cure. That he is almost every day distempered with drincke, and soe very unfitt to cure the distempers of others. That he hath exprest divers base words against the present government, and those that adheares unto it, and hath scandalized many in authority most unworthily. That he doth brew and sell aile in his house without a licence, keeping a bowleing ally and butts to draw people to his house to spend their money; and besides he keepes lewd weomen in his house, and has one as his concubine; and, before his childe was borne, he said hee would give 40*l.* if Peggie would prove with childe, and what he would give att the baptiseing of it; which hee did, and played

---

the restoration he was steward to the Earl of Elgin. He built the east end of the Marmion Chantry at Tanfield, in which he lived, and put over his door in Latin
If religion flourishes I live.
M. B. 1668.
Whereupon Mr. Littleton, then rector of Tanfield, and living opposite to Mr. Beckwith, put over his door
I do not heed the man the more,
That hangs religion at his door.
* A zealous Parliamentarian, who turned the diocese of Durham upside down. I have the original manuscript of the arrangements that he made for preachers, &c. in that county. It contains much new and curious information. Sir Arthur died in the Tower before any measures had been taken against the leaders of the Cromwellian party, otherwise he would in all probability have been executed. One of the old ballads of the time thus speaks of him
What is the cause, Sir Arthur,
Your pulses go so quick ?
Tis Bishops' lands
That's in your hands
Which makes them beat so thick.

both midwife and minister, and caused the bells to be rung for joy.

Mr. Wm. Johnson, of Leeming, says that Ashton pays him 2s. a-week for the last year to say morning and evening prayers in the chappell.

XXIX. MARGARET MORTON. FOR WITCHCRAFT.

10 Jan. 1650-1. Wakefield. Before Sir John Savile, Kt. Alex. Johnson, Henry Tempest, John Stanhope, and John Hewley, Esqrs. *Joane wife of Wm. Booth, of Warmfeild,* saith that Margaret Morton,* of Kirkethorpe, came to her house, and gave her sonn (about fower yeares old) and then in good health and likeing, a peece of bread; after which time her said childe begann to bee sicke, and his body swelled very much, and his flesh did daly after much waste, till he could neither goe nor stand. This informant, mistrusting that the said Margaret Morton had bewitch her child, did send for her, who asked the child forgivenesse three times, and then this informant drew bloud of her with a pin, and imediately after the child amended. And at divers times this informant could not get butter when she chirned nor cheese when she earned.

Frances, wife of John Ward, th'elder, of Kirkethorpp, saith that she was one of the fower that searched Margaret Morton, and found upon her two black spots between her thigh and her body; they were like a wart, but it was none. And the other was black on both sides, an inch bread, and blew in the middest. And this Margaret had beene a long time suspected for a witch, and that her mother and sister, who are now both dead, were suspected to bee the like. And this ex^t had two children that dyed about two yeares agoe who were grievously perplexed with sickenes before they died; and the one of them said before it dyed, "Good mother, put out Morton," who was then in the roome.

---

* A vague and unsatisfactory case. The poor woman was tried at the assizes and was very properly acquitted. In September, 1650, a woman called Ann Hudson, of Skipsey in Holderness, was charged with witchcraft. The sick person had recovered after he had scratched her and drawn blood.

XXX. WILLIAM LAZENBY, GENT.   FOR FALSE NEWS AND
SEDITIOUS WORDS.

Jan. 22, 1650-1.   Before Richard Robinson, Esq. *James Wood, of Yorke, parchmente-maker*, sayth, that after the Lord Generall Cromwell's going into Scottland, he was at Towthrop with one William Lazenby, gent., of Haxby,* who did say, that Generall Cromwell had lost his army, and that he was taken into a castell or hold, or unto the seas. And that he hoped within a twelvemonth to see Generall Cromwell's head off, and all the heads of all the Parliament men in England that now is. And Edward Gower, George Crathorn, and Katherine his wife, and Mr. Barber, the minister, all of Towthrop, heard these words.

XXXI. GEORGE HOLROYD, CLERK.   FOR A SEDITIOUS SERMON.

Feb. 21, 1650-1.   Before D. Hotham, Jo. Peirson, and Tho. Styringe, Esqrs. *John Cuthbarte, parrishe-clarke of Foston*, sayth, that upon Thursday, being the xxxth day of Januarie, which was appoynted by an authority of Parliament as a day of thanksgiving for the good successe of our armes by sea and land, George Holroyd, minister of (Foston) did preach;† and the part of Scripture which he nominated for his text was the 14 verse of the 6 chapter of the Epistle to the Galatians, vizt., " God forbid that I should glory but in the crosse of our Lord Jesus Christ," &c. After the reading of which words the said George Holeroyd fell into a large discourse of the . . . ceding verses, expressing the joyes and rejoycing of the . . . ked; and, withall, saying that he could not very well tell whether there were more cause of humiliation then of exaltation, for that there was nowe soe much bloudshedding and cutting of the throats of our Christian brethren; which things were more cause of mourning then rejoycing. And to that purpose he did alleadge the example of David mourning

---

* A charge of using seditious language and spreading false news. The wish, in this case, was father to the thought.
  At the delivery of the gaol for the city of York in March 1657-8, William Marrison was fined 100*l*. for spreading false news.
  On Feb. 14, 1650-1, George Thorne said, at York Castle, " You see what you gett for servinge the States: as they have murdred the Kinge, soe they will likewise hang those that have done them service."

† The pulpit was at this time very much used for political purposes, but as Mr. Holroyd reflected somewhat upon the ruling powers he was called to acconnt.
  In July 1658, John Hitchmough, clerk, of Egton, in Cleveland, was charged at the York assize with uttering seditious words, but the bill was ignored.

for the death of Saule, a wicked king; and also for the death of Jonathan, Saule's sonn, for the death of Abner, who was treacherously slayne, and diverse other examples to that purpose. And, proceeding further, he sayd, that if wee looked into the miseries of these present tymes, wee should see nothing but oppression, tyranny, and butchering, and the cutting of the throats of our brethren. Yet the said George Holcroyd prayed for the good and prosperous estate of the governours, and for a peaceable conclusion betwixt the two kingdoms.

XXXII. RICHARD MONTAIGNE, GEN. AND OTHERS. FOR HIGH TREASON.

March 3, 1650-1. At New Malton, before Arthur Noel and John Worsley, Esqrs. *Chr. Holliday, of New Malton, grocer*, saith, that, about May was a twelvemonth, some foure men came about twilight, at the time of shutting up of shops, and betooke themselfes to the Cross in New Malton and had with them a wanded bottle, wherein was wyne or ther drinke, and drunk a health amongst themselfes to Charles the Second.* And, when they had done that health, one of the foure persons abovesaid, with a loud voice, proclaimed Charles the Second, King of England, Scotland, France, and Ireland. Amongst which foure persons were at that time some sword or swords drawne, and when the said proclamacion was by one of them ended, all the said foure persons came from the old cross singing, and soe went together to the taverne, where one John Williamson now dwelleth. It was said that the names of theis four men were Christopher Nendike, Capt. Denton, and Mr. Mountaine, of Westowe neere Malton. The fourth this ex[t] never heard nor can learne what his name was, it being supposed hee was a stranger. It was said, allso, that some of their horses then stood at one Robert Tyson's, and it was thought that Capt. Denton had beene in towne two or three dayes. He hath credibly heard that Capt. Denton was a pyrate at sea, and did there much hurt to the Parlaiment's freinds.

* The record of a somewhat daring adventure at Malton. A few bold Cavaliers proclaim Prince Charles King of England at the Cross. About Captain Denton more information will soon be given. He was recognised by a person who said that he had "formerly beene billited at their house, and was under Capt. Bushell in Sir Hugh Cholmley's command, when they were in the Parlaiment's service."

The person who made the proclamation was Mr. Richard Montaigne of Westow, a nephew of George Montaigne, sometime Archbishop of York. Soon after this, some persons attempted to arrest him at Kirkham, when he was in the company of Mr. Thomas Vaughan of Whitwell and others, but he made his escape. I know not what became of him. His father and his elder brother George paid 155*l.* 11*s.* as a composition for their estate, to say nothing of an annual charge upon it of 50*l.*

XXXIII. CAPTAIN DENTON. FOR PIRACY.

March 12, 1650-1. Before John Harrison and John Burton, bayliffes of Scarbrough. *Wm. Batty of Scarbrough, marriner*, sayth that betwixt Michaelmesse and Martinmesse in 1649, one John Denton,* captaine of a ketch, with one peece of ordinance, and about 30 men, did take the good ship called the Amity of Scarbrough, whereof one Robert Rogers was master, from the said Robert Rogers, betwixt Scarbrough Roade and Fyley Bay. And, after the said Denton had boarded, entered his men and taken the said ship, he did putt aboard about 7 or 8 of his men to carry the ship away, who carryed it as farre as neere to Flambrough Head, and kept the said Rogers, this inform^t and some other marriners, prisoners aboard the said ketch, until the said Rogers (being unwilling to lose his ship, being at that tyme but 2 yeare old,) did agree with Denton to pay him a certaine sum of money for to have his ship againe, which was done, and all the prisoners were sett at liberty.

Leonard Greene, of Whitby, saith, that in the yeare 1649, about Christmass, or three weeks before, being a servant in a shipp being in Tees water, and loaden with allome and butter, one Capt. John Denton, with his men, came into the said shipp, when she was on dry ground, and broke open a chest and tooke out a bagg of money, and severall suites of apparel, and tooke neare two hundred firkins of butter. Being this day with Capt. Denton in York Castle, and haveing some speach about the surprizeing of the shipp that belonged to Mr. Wiggoner and his

---

* One of the many cases of piracy that occurred about this time off Scarbrough and Whitby. The leading offender, Captain Denton, seems to have been another Paul Jones in these waters. With the story of his capture we are unacquainted, but it appears that he was taken whilst attacking a ship belonging to Mr. Wiggoner of Whitby. That this was not the only charge against him may be seen from these informations. He was evidently regarded as a prisoner of great importance. On Feb. 20, 1650-1, Bradshaw, as President of the Council of State, issued his warrant authorising Denton's detention in York castle on a charge of piracy and bearing arms against the Parliament. He was indicted at the assizes in March, and orders were given that he should be kept in prison without bail. In June he made his escape. The gaolers, Richard Lealand and Thomas Reed, had allowed him to go into the city, in the charge of a keeper, to dine with Captain William Thornton. Horses were waiting for Denton at Walmgate Bar, and he got clear away. A strict inquiry was made into the matter, and Mr. Francis Hesketh, of Heslington, was charged with assisting Denton, but he exculpated himself.

I find that on the 9th of March, 1650-1, a ship, belonging to Whitby, called the Ellis, was taken by pirates near Bridlington. Seven men were put on board, but the vessel leaking, they were obliged to put into shore and were captured. Diego Laughe was the captain of the pirate.

partners, but was hindered of his purpose by some cobble men belonging to Burlington. In revenge whearof the said Capt. Denton sayd, that if it had nott been for the company that was with him, hee would have landed his men and fired Burlington Key.

XXXIV. JOHN TAYLOR. FOR BEING A SUSPICIOUS PERSON.

March 26, 1651. Before Francis Carleill, Esq. *John Tayler*,[*] sayth, that, aboute four yeares and a halfe last past, he went to be servant to one Mr. Robert Benskyn, who, before this examinate went to serve him, had beene a Major for the late King at Basing-house. After this examinate went to serve him, the said Mr. Benskyn went to London, and this ex^t went with him. And when they came to London the said Mr. Benskyn, this ex^t, and other gentlemen gott a frigott at London, called the Wicked, carrying aboute 6 litle peice of ordinance; and from thence they, and the other gentlemen, one named Mr. Elvage, and divers others to the number of 24 persons, went to sea to Prince Rupert neare Portingall, and so were of his fleete, being in all at that tyme aboute the number of 22 ships; and also continued with the said Prince Rupert at sea, and was with him when the Malligo fleete, being in number 12 English ships, were taken by the said Prince at sea. And after that, the said Prince Rupert's fleete of shipps being scattered at sea by Generall Blague, being a commander for the Parliament of England, the ship wherein this ex^t was, and his master and divers other persons, one Capt. Bartley being then Captaine for the late King, and, since his death, for his eldest sonn, was taken before Christmas last at sea by Generall Blague's ships, and the ship wherein this ex^t went was allotted as prize to one Capt. Bradshaw, belonging to the said Generall Blague's fleete; and, after there takeing, the said Capt. Bradshaw sett this ex^t and the other persons that were in the said ship called the Wicked, upon shore at Chepstow, where they were all imprisoned untill such tyme as they were exchanged by the French who lately had fought at sea with some English ships, and tooke them and the persons in the same ships. And,

---

[*] At this unsettled time no one was allowed to travel without a pass, and all suspicious persons were arrested and obliged to give an account of themselves. The number of disbanded soldiers and sailors that were wandering up and down the country made these precautions necessary. The sailor, in the present deposition, tells a long and an interesting story of his adventures, introducing to us Prince Rupert and Blake the great sea-captain. The prisoner was sent to York Castle.

aboute 15 dayes last past, they were exchanged and sett at liberty for the English so taken. And after their release this ex^t went to Rotchdale, and so towards Newcastle-upon-Tyne, but came not to the towne, and so to Pickering and to Yeddingham, where he lay, and so to Foxheles, where he lay, and so to Agnes Burton, where he lay aboute two nights agoe att the constable's house; and from thence to Brandsburton, the 25 of March, 1651, where he was apprehended, intending to have gone to Hull, with an intent to have gone to a towne called Ashwell, in Rutlandshyre, where he was borne.

XXXV. RICHARD POLLARD, GENT., AND ANOTHER. FOR A CONSPIRACY.

June 13, 1651. Articles exhibited against Richard Pollard, of Sepulchre's, near Hedon, and against Godfrey Sommerset, of Milford. That, about the 14th or 15th of Feb., the said Richard Pollard * did repaire unto the house of Elizabeth Middleton, of Skidby, widow, late wife of Wm. Middleton, gen., deceased, hee having a wife and many children, and did make suite unto her by way of marriage. And affirmed that his wife was dead, and that hee had only two sons. And further affirmed that hee had 500*l*. by the yeare at Woodhall, neare Pomfreit. And, to perswade her thereunto, being a stranger to his estate, it was agreed that Sommersett should procure a man to represent the person of Richard Etherington, Esq., one of the justices of the peace for the East Riding, a neare kinsman unto the said Pollard, to satisfy her concerning the reality of his estate, and that hee was a widower and had noe wife. The said Pollard hath gott divers summes of moneyes of the said Mrs. Middleton upon loane, shee beleeving the premises to bee true. And, likewise, hath counterfeited and forged a deed from the said Mrs. Middleton, to passe away and sell the estate of the said Mrs. Middleton, lying neare Rippon, and sold the same.

* A charge of conspiracy and forgery. All the persons concerned occupied some position in society, and it would be curious to know what was the result. The case will remind the reader of some of the old adventures in the Fleet. Mr. Pollard was so far unsuccessful in his suit that he lost the lady, as I find her spoken of as the wife of Mr. William Oglethorpe. I know not who this gentleman was, but if he was the same person who occurs in some of the more northern informations, ten or fifteen years after this, the lady had fallen out of the frying-pan into the fire when she married him.

XXXVI. JOHN ROBINSON AND ANOTHER. FOR BEING SEMINARY PRIESTS.

June 6, 1651. Luke Robinson, Esq., certifies that the evening of the above ment^d day he aprehended two persons traveiling on the backe side of Malton, who would say nothing of themselves.* One calls himselfe John Robinson, and did produce a printed certificate signifying he had taken the engagement; the certificate was from the Com^{rs} in the plurall number, but onely signed by Sir Robert Barwicke. Hee did then owne the name mentioned in that certificate, which was Thomas Towler. The persons did acknowledge they were Roman Catholiques. The other person who calls himself John Mannering, otherwise Gravenor, did say hee was a scoole-master and did teach Mrs. Mennill's children of Kilvington. The said John Robinson saith hee was borne att Upsall.

Thomas Towler examined, 9th June, calleth himselfe now John Robinson, and saith the name hee did use yesterday was to gett the advantage of a pass. Denies to say where he was borne.†

---

* Two suspected seminary priests are arrested at Malton. There was at this time a great crusade against them and they were treated with much unmerited severity. The English mission was the destination of many of the young men in the college at Douay, and many sought their mother country merely to lay their bones in its earth. They were chased about and pounced upon by the executive as enemies to the State. It is melancholy to read the story of these bold and zealous men, availing themselves of every device to escape detection, disguising themselves, forging passes, travelling under assumed names, and undergoing every hardship for the sake of their religion. Almost every residence of an old Roman Catholic family had some hiding place for a priest, to which he could escape when the searchers were abroad. I shall revert to this subject in another place.

At the Yorkshire Assizes in March, 1651-2, Robinson was convicted of being a seminary priest, but was reprieved before judgment. I find that he was still in prison in 1660. It is probable that no proceedings were taken against his colleague.

In March 1657-8 I find that there were two other suspected seminary priests in York Castle, John Fairfax and George Anne. In April, 1660, they were still in prison, refusing to answer. Fairfax was freed by proclamation in September, 1660. His fellow-sufferer had probably died in prison.

I possess a small portrait on panel of a Yorkshire gentleman who was a missionary priest and died for his religion upon the scaffold,—Thomas Tunstall, of Scargill. It represents him with a broken rope about his neck and a knife in his bosom, an allusion to his death as a traitor. Around the picture is the following inscription, *Thomas Tunstall, pr. and suff. Mar.* 1616. *Funes ceciderunt mihi in praeclaris. Spectaculum facti sumus, &c.*—1 *Cor.* iv. 9. At the back is a little sliding panel on which is pasted an account, written in a very neat hand, of Mr. Tunstall's life and sufferings. It is taken from Mr. Knaresbrough's MSS. and is accessible elsewhere. The portrait was purchased at the dispersion of the family treasures of the Tunstalls at Wycliffe in 1812.

† It will be seen how cautiously the accused person fences with the questions that are put to him. He will bring no one into trouble. Mr. Robinson, it will be seen, shows his zeal for the Parliament in trying to connect the priest with the royal party.

Cannot answere whither hee have taken any orders from the Church of Rome. Hee mett with Mannering on Saturday last att Mr Thompson, the inkeeper, in Wetherby. Will not answere whither hee ever see him before. Acknowledgeth himselfe an Englishman and hath beene beyond the seas. The coats upon his backe came with him from beyond the seas. Hee was att Paris three yeares, and hath beene in England come Michaelmas about three yeares. Hee hath beene att Rome. Was of noe University in England. Doth not deny hee were of any University in forrayne countrys. Will not deny to have received orders from the Church of Rome. Hee saith often hee is unwilling to bring others into the bryars. Hee will not say what acquaintance hee hath in Yorkeshire. Hee did intend to goe to Pocklington last night, haveing some businesse there, but will not name with whome, because hee will wrong none. Hee landed att Dover when hee came into England. Was never in Scotland. His father's name was John Robinson, but doeth not know where he did live. Hee did see Mr Mole* in prison in Rome when he was a youth.

June 9. *Re-examined.* Asked whither he were in Yorkeshire when the Earle of Newcastle had command there, saith hee doth not know. Hee hath beene in Flanders, but not in Holland nor Spaine. Being askt whither he hath beene with him that is now called King of Scotts, saith hee was with him att Paris. Hee did not know one Coxe in Ireland, but did receive a messadge from a frend who complained that Coxe had wronged him.

John Mannering, saith that hee is some tyme called by the name of John Grosvenor, his mother being of that name. Was borne neere Stafford towne att a place called Hamton. Was bred a Roman Catholique. Served one Mr. Fowler in that county of the same proffession, and since hath lived with Mrs. Mennill of Kilvington and did teach her children. Hee mett with John Robinson att Wetherby, and stayed with him untill hee did eate meatt, and did not know of his comeing. They mett on this day sennight, and did part with him att Rippon, and mett againe upon Munday att Osmotherley. Hee doth now belong to Mr. Thomas Watterton of Walton, and doeth teach his childerne. Hee was araigned for the death of Robert Cooper the last Lammas assizes and was acquitt. Denyeth that he was in armes against the Parlament. Hee was goeing yesterday, when hee was taken att Malton, to Farburne hard by Brotherton, and saith that John

---

* The well-known Protestant martyr.

Robinson was goeing to Beverly, as hee told this ex^t, and the said Robinson did undertake to know the way.

XXXVII. THOMAS WOODROFFE. FOR SELLING UNLAWFUL BOOKS.

Aug. 13, 1651. Recognizances for the appearance at the next assizes of Thomas Woodroffe, of Leeds, bookseller, for selling of a scandalous pamphlett called *Linguæ Testium*,* which (upon his examinacion beefore the Honble Baron Thorpe) hee confesseth hee received from one Mathew Keynton, a stacyoner, liveing about Paull's churchyard in London.

XXXVIII. CHRISTOPHER WRIGHT. FOR SEDITIOUS WORDS.

Aug. 28, 1651. Before Luke Robinson, Esq. *Wm. Blanshard, of Pickering, gentleman*, saith, that he being att Thomas Norfolke's house att Whitby, one Christopher Wright came rushing in and sate downe att the table, and called for drinke; and did declare that hee was a cavaleire, and that hee was for King Charles; and that hee would fight hartily for him soe long as hee did live, though hee were hanged att the doore cheeke for itt.†

XXXIX. EDWARD CLEGG. FOR A MISDEMEANOR.

Aug. 30, 1651. Recognizances for the appearance at the assizes of Edward Clegg, one of the common sergeants at mace of

---

* One of the numerous political pamphlets of the time which the ruling powers were so anxious to suppress. I have never seen it. Baron Thorpe has been already mentioned: he was one of the tools that did so much service to the Commonwealth.

† There was a good deal of discontent in Yorkshire in the spring and summer of this year, and several insignificant risings took place. In March I find that Sutton Oglethorpe, the younger, of Escrick (Eskirk), gentleman, was convicted before the commissioners of being engaged in the late plot, and was committed to Hull. In the same month the following persons were obliged to find securities for their good behaviour on the same account: John Sisson of Hopperton, Mr. Thomas Moore of Knaresborough, Robert Powter and Lancelot Lamb of Little Ouseburn, Richard Ellis, gen., late of Plumpton, and now of Durham, Thomas Hutton of Hopperton, Richard Browne and Richard Matterson of Marton, and Mr. Richard Sissons of Allerton Mauleverer.

Thomas Mattericke, gen. was acquitted at the York assizes for saying at Connondell, on 1st June, 1651, to Francis Levy, "The King is comeing for England. I will give the a horse and armes, and prefer the to a cornet's place, for I hope to have a troope of mine owne."

Beverley, for that, after a proclamacion published by him which came from Generall Cromwell, dated 19th August, 1651, he did say "God save the King and Parliament."

XL. JOHN THOMPSON. FOR BEING A SEMINARY PRIEST.

Aug. 31, 1651. Before Luke Robinson, Esq. *John Smith, otherwise callinge himselfe John Thompson,** saith hee never went by other names than these two; saith, that hee hath no certaine abode, but where his frends doe entertaine him for the time. Being askt, amongst which frends hee doeth most reside, doeth desire to be pardoned, because hee is not willing to wrong his frends. Hee saith that hee did come from Ruston in the night; last night from Mrs. Saier's house, there haveing beene three dayes; and came from Mr. Trollop's house in the bishoprike of Durham about a fortnight agoe, and came on foote. Being askt what places hee did lodge att by the way, hee is unwilling to wrong his frends, yett confesseth hee lay att Yarme att an alehouse, and att an house beyond Blacke Hambleton, an alehouse; and that hee lay att Stangrave att an ale house. Saith hee hath beene at the house beyond Hambleton before, butt not att the other houses. Hee is by profession a schoolemaster; hath lived

---

* Another seminary priest. Bishop Chaloner, in his Memoirs of the Missionary Priests, gives the following account of him: "He was one of the secular clergy. His name was Wilks, tho' he was commonly known by the name of Tomson. He was born at Knaresbrough in Yorkshire, was taken at Malton upon a market-day, and set in the stocks to be gazed at by the people almost the whole day, till a cutler of the town making oath that he knew him to be Lord Evers his priest, he was sent to York Castle, tried and convicted, but died before execution."

Christopher Cooper, of Old Malton, deposes that before day he met Smith and one William Thompson, "goeing on the backe-side of the toune on the foote way. He said they came from Rushton. Travailed early, for they had beasts goeing before, but the beasts were not his. He then got the constable to apprehend them, and Smith confessed that he came out of the North, and confessed that he was Roman Catholique and a schoolmaster."

William Skelton, constable of Malton, says that the nightwatch of Old Malton brought the two to him as suspicious persons. "He did find popish papers about Smith, and the watchmen did bring small peices of paper which they said they did see Smith scatter."

Luke Robinson, Esq., of Thornton Risebrough, near Pickering, was an active magistrate and a very zealous Parliamentarian. He was bailiff and M. P. of Scarborough, and one of the Council of State. At the Restoration he was driven out of the House of Commons. He is thus alluded to in one of the old political ballads of that period.

> "Luke Robinson that clownado,
> Though his heart be a granado,
> Yet a high-shoe with his hand in his poke
> Is his most perfect shadow."

in diverse places, butt will not name any; saith hee is a Roman Catholique, and became one in the family of the Lady Anne Ingleby, and did live some time with old Mr. Vavasor of Heslewood five yeares, and from thence went to teaching schollars, and did teach Sir Francis Ireland his children. Being askt whether hee did never teach in any other place, hee will not answere. Being askt whether hee bee in orders from the Church of Rome or noe, hee saith hee will not say hee is or hee is not, and will not answere positively to that question. He saith hee was not beyond seas. Being askt whither a man may bee qualified for an ecclesiasticall person of that Church of Rome without hee 'goe beyond seas, hee saith hee must either goe beyond the seas or bee quallified by some person who comes from thence. Saith hee was not in prison in his life but once, being carried before Sir Robert Barwicke about two yeares agoe, who, upon examination, sett him free. Hee saith hee was then aprehended in Hemsley att one Daniell Emerson's house, and was aprehended by Major Scarffe, and was then accused for being a preist, and hee did not then deny that hee was one. Hee hath beene much att the Lord Ewres his house in the old lord's time, but not since. Hee was borne in Nitherdaile in Yorkeshire, and his father's name was William Smith. Hee did take the name of Thompson, because the times were troublesome for him. Hee came to Mrs. Sayers only to see hir.

XLI. JAMES WILLIAMS.   FOR SEDITIOUS WORDS.

Sept. 2, 1651. Before John Warde, Esq. *Thomas Hanson, of Carelton,* saith, that hee hard James Williams, of Carleton, say to a souldier in Colonell Hacker's regiment at the marching by off the army, under his excellencie the Lord Generall Cromwell, "Thou prittie face, hast thou noe better fortune then to fight against the King?" And further said, that one off these dayes they would all bee hanged, and called them trayterley rougues.

XLII. RICHARD CHAMLEY.   FOR AN ASSAULT, ETC.

Sep. 23, 1651. Before Charles Fenwicke, Esq. at Hagthorpe. *Peter Vavasor, of Spaldington, Esq.* saieth, that on Tuesday the 22d of July last, about 3 or 4 of the clock in the afternoone, there came to his house a man (unknowne to this informant) yet in gentleman's habitt, naming himself Tempest, who pretended to come as messenger from Sir Walter Vavasor to buy a cast of hawkes,* and tooke occasion of much further impertinent discourse, belching out sundry horrible oathes, and telling many great and notorious lyes, protracting tyme untill this informant was very weary both of his discourse and company; which the said Tempest (he thinketh) perceyving, and not invyted to stay, about 6 or 7 a clocke towardes night tooke horse, and, with another man who seemed to be his servant, rode away towardes Howden; and about 12 or one of the clock in that night there came to his house 7 men and horse who assaulted his house, attempting to break in by opening two slotts or boults, beating downe the window, which this informant hearing, hastily arose out of bed, not speaking to them one worde, but at an high windowe wynded an horne, which the assaylantes hearing one of them said "Sirray" if he wynded agayne he would pistoll him. Neverthelesse this informant went into another roome, and there at a window winded agayne, which being heard by the assaylants they consulted together and went from the house; but, after a little space of time, they all, together with the constable, came agayne to his house, charging the constable to comaund the dores to be opened, saying, "There is one Tempest, a rogue who hath a commission to raise forces for the King against the Parliament. Him we have sought an hundred myles, and this night he is lodged in this house; we will have him out." This informant then answered saying, "There is no such man here;" and further said, "The man naming himself Tempest went from hence about 6 or 7 a clock in the day tyme; and (saieth this informant) one of yow may be hee, for one of your voyces is very like to

---

* What a graphic picture of a startling scene! Mr. Vavasor tells his story with great simplicity, and still with considerable effect. The attack upon the house—the devices of the assailants—the winding of the horn at which no one dared to rise—are capitally described. The adventurers were more mischievous probably than malicious.

The chief culprit, Richard Chamley, *alias* Tempest, *alias* Chambers, confesses that he was at Mr. Vavasor's, and says that he met some men on the evening in question, who went to Howden. He and his servant, as he says, passed the night in a field, and crossed Booth Ferry early in the morning.

George Hagerstone, his servant, says that his master hired him at Marrick in Swaledale. He was arrested at Blyth, co. Notts., and was taken to Newark, but was released on promising to do nothing against the Commonwealth.

Elizabeth Bates, of Thorne, says that seven men like gentlemen came to her house armed with swords and pistols. One of them was Chambers, who then called himself Justice Mountaine of Lincolnshire, and another was Mr. Cressey.

The constable, Richard Westobie, says that six armed horsemen called him from his bed, and forced him to follow them in great fear. Tempest gave out "reviling speaches against Peter Vavasor, Esq. because that he sleighted and did not give him entertainement as he expected, pretending that he, the said Tempest, was *a peece of a Vavasor.*"

Tempest's." Whereat they were inraged, threatning to pistoll him at the windowe, and with greater violence still indeavoured to break in. Yet, after many attempts, and not prevayling, some of them said, "Come, let us take the gentleman's worde. Give us some beere, and we will be gone." Then this informant caused beere to be given them at a windowe, untill they all (or so many as would) had drunke. Then they desired otes for their horses, but aunswere was made that there was none otes in the house saving a small quantity for his rabbetts. So at last, desiring this informant to shake hands (who so doeing) they departed from the house, but threatned shortly to come with a stronger party, who, as he is informed, did about break of day, or before, goe over at Booth's ferry. And more also saith that the winde was that night so faire and sylent that his horne might have bene heard a mile, neverthelesse not one man durst make any helpe for want of armes to apprehend such like persons. Moreover this informant saith that, upon seryous examynacion of those passages, informacion is given by one William Smith of Burnby, sometymes quartermaster to Sir Marmaduke Langdale, that the man which to this informant named himself Tempest, his name is not so, nor Farmer, but Chambers, now or late living at Wawton, a minister's sonne, and sometymes also quartermaster to a captayne of the adverse party.

XLIII. WILLIAM BEWICK. FOR SEDITIOUS WORDS.

Oct. 2, 1651. Before Thomas Hudson, Mayor of Beverley. *Bettrice Hughes* saith, that upon the 24th of July shee heard William Bewick of Beverley, currier, say "I will drinck a health to Prince Charles, King of Scotts, and to his good successe into England, and to the confusion of all his enimies;" and thereupon drunck a silver beaker full of ale. After which the said Bewick wished Thomas Stockdale to pledge him the said health, but he refused; whereupon the said Bewick puld of the said Stockdale's hatt from his head, saying it was a health that deserved to be uncovered.

XLIV. WILLIAM CARMICHAEL AND DAVID GREY. WANDERING SOLDIERS.

Dec. 8, 1651. Before George Eure, Esq., N.R.Y. *William Carmichell and David Grey, Scotchmen,** say that they came into

---

* Two Scottish gentleman who had been in the Royal army and were making their way back to their own country. They were arrested as suspicious persons by the

England with the Scotish army, under the commaund of Charles Stuart, and that one of them, Sir William Carmighall, was servant unto one Sir Daniell Carmikell, and other, Sir David Grey, was servant unto the Earle of Lauderdale. They confess that they weare in the towne of Worcester, when the English army came down against it, but denie that they were souldiers, only attended upon the aforesaid gentlemen. They say they weare taken prisoners by the cuntry people neer Bradford, and weare committed by the maior of the said towne; and that they had libertie given them to departe from the towne by the maior of that place, about a moneth since.

XLV. HESTER FRANCE. FOR WITCHCRAFT.

Jan. 23, 1651-2. Before Henry Tempest, Esq. *Hester Spivy, of Hothersfeilde, widdow,** saith, thatt upon Thursday last she went unto the milne, and, att her comeing home att night, Elizabeth Johnson, her servant, told her thatt Hester France had beene at her howse, and, she mending the fire with the firepoite, the sayde Hester sayde, itt was a good deede to seare her lipps with itt, if she thought anie thing by itt; and soe went out of the house, but came in againe and cursed the sayde Elizabeth, and prayed to God that she shold never bake againe. And the sayde Elizabeth told her thatt she thought the sayde Hester had bewitcht her; and then this informant answered, she hoped she had a better faith then to feare either witch or devill. And, after they was gone to bedd, the sayde Hester made a greate noise in her sleepe, insomuch that she affrighted this informant; and, in the morning, she bidd her goe to some neighbors to see if her care rootes were not downe, but they were not downe. Thereupon the sayde Ellisabeth lay herself downe upon a bedd, and, this informant presently following her, she sawe that she cold not speake, and takeing her into her armes, she cold not stand, and soe she continewed speechles from six a clock untill betwixt eight or nine in the evening, saveing thatt she spoke once to her brother. Whereupon the sayde Hester France was sent for, and, she being come, the sayde Elizabeth spooke to her, and catched

---

country people near Bradford. They had escaped from the "crowning" victory at Worcester. *Floreat fidelis civitas!*

* Another case of witchcraft out of the West Riding. The girl, no doubt, was seized with catalepsy. One witness declares that Hester France had been a reputed witch for above twenty years. Another says that when he went to take her to Elizabeth Johnson's house she was very unwilling to go.

att her, and sayde "Thou art the woman that hath deard me," and soe scratched her, since which the sayde Elizabeth is somewhat better, but still continewes very ill.

John Johnson, of Hothersfeilde, the younger, saith that Robert Cliff is now very weake and sick, and hath beene sick this halfe yeare. And this morninge the sayde Robert sent unto the constable of Hothersfeilde, and desired him to send the sayde Hester France unto him; and she being come into the chamber he scratcht her very sore, and sayde, " I thinke thou art the woman that hath done me this wrong;" and then she answred and sayde that she never did hurt in her life.

XLVI. JOSEPH BANNISTER AND ANOTHER.   FOR HARBOURING A SOLDIER.*

Apr. 15, 1652. Before Henry Tempest, Esq. *Thomas Gerrard, of Hallifax*, saith, that, about a moneth after the batle att Worcester, Joseph Bannister tolld this informant that he had taken one Collonell Carr, a Scotchman, prisoner, and that he was to have 50*l.* to convey him into Northumberland to Mr. Haslerigg's at Fellton bridge, whoe maryed the sayde Collonell Carr's sister.

Elizabeth, wife of John Astin, of Hallifax, saith, thatt before, att and after the tyme that the batle was att Worcester, betweene the English and Scottish armies, she wayted upon Joseph Bannister's wife, being then in childbedd: and, upon the Friday night before the Scotts fledd by Hallifax, she went home to her owne house; and when she retourned to the said Bannister's house, she founde there a man who confessed himselfe to be a Scotchman, and called himselfe Collonell Carre, and that he was kept there and at Edward Barrowes of Scircoate for the space of a moneth.

XLVII. WILLIAM ARCHER.   FOR SEDITIOUS WORDS.

Apr. 29, 1652. At the generall sessions holden at Beverley hall garth, before Francis Thorpe, one of the Barrons of the

---

* Two Halifax men are charged with harbouring an officer of the Royal army. Colonel Carr was a Northumberland gentleman and was making his way into the North after the battle at Worcester. Bannister and Barrowes were prosecuted for entertaining him and not giving him up. Bannister has already appeared in this volume with a charge against a Mr. Clay for attempting to poison him.

publique Exchequer, Sir Wm. Strickland, Kt. and Bt., John Anlaby, Durand Hotham, Chr. Ridley, Richard Pearson, Richard Robinson, Phillipp Saltmarsh, Hugh Bethell the yonger, Francis Carliell, Thomas Stireing, Edward Wingate, Charles Fenwicke, and John Pearson, Esquires, keepers of the peace, and also justices by the keepers of the libertie of England by authoritie of Parliament.

William Archer, of Etton, yeoman, on Feb. 3, 1651-2, did speake these false and malicious and scandalous wordes, at Cherry-Burton, saying the Parliament were traitors and bloodsuckers, and that they had taken off the King's head and intended to take off his son's, but the Lord had blessed him out of their hande.*

XLVIII. WILLIAM ELRINGTON, GENT. FOR A LIBELLOUS LETTER.

July, 13, 1652. The Grand Jury presents William Elrington, late of Beverley, gent.,† for writing a challenge to Thomas Hudson, Maior of Beverley, in theis words following: "Sirrah! you have in your apprehension putt mee to disgrace; it is not your sheepskinns will repaire you. I expect satisfaccion from you this night, otherwayes I will proclaime you a coward. I scorne your basenesse, therefore I rest, my owne, not yours,—William Elrington." [*Indorsed thus:*] "To Thomas Hudson theis." And alsoe the said William Elrington did speake to the said Thomas Hudson in theis words, "Come out, and give me satisfaccion, or I wilbe revenged on thee."

---

* The country sessions, it will be seen, were, during the Commonwealth, of more consequence than they are now. The East Riding Sessions were presided over by a Baron of the Exchequer, who happened to be the Recorder of Beverley.

The offender was an unfortunate Royalist. He was not alone, however, in his wishes. In 1657, James Atkinson, of New Malton, innkeeper, was charged with saying at Kirkby Moorside, on Dec. 20, "I will drincke a health to three of the best Englishmen which are out of the nation;"—meaning the princes of the blood royal.

In 1647, Henry Revell, of Rotheram, clerk; Wm. Crofts, of Doncaster, yeoman; and Robert Browne, of Rotherham, yeoman; were charged with publishing a blasphemous and seditious libel called the Parliament's Ten Commandments. The libel consists of a most profane and wicked parody of the Lord's Prayer, the Creed, and the Ten Commandments. Revell was fined 50*l*., and the other two 100*l*. each.

† An amusing ebullition of revenge. A gentleman, who bears a Northumberland name, sends a challenge to the Mayor of Beverley, who had offended him. The result is not a combat, but a committal to the assizes. The mayor was, probably, a tanner.

XLIX. MARY FISHER.   FOR BRAWLLING IN CHURCH.

July 18, 1652. The Grand Jury presents Mary Fisher,* late of Selby, spinster, for that she on that day, being the Lord's day, did, openly in the parrish church, speake unto Richard Calvert, clerke, minister there, being in the pulpitt and preaching, these words "Come downe, come downe, thou painted beast, come downe. Thou art but an hireling, and deludest the people with thy lyes."

L. WILLIAM SYKES.   FOR A MISDEMEANOR.

Whearas it is cleare by the law of God, and the law of reason, that a tenth of oure corne and hay, in kinde, ought not to bee paid to preist or impropriator; and that hitherto wee have beene cheated by names and pretences of tithes law, and trible dammages without right or reason.†

First. Wee, whose names are hereunto subscrybed, doe, in the first place, protest against all pracktise in that kinde, past or to cume, as sinfull, ungodly, and distructive.

Secondly. And, therefore, in the second place, wee doe resolve and promiss to each other to reap and receive into our owne hands all our cropps of corne and hay, as well the tenth stacke or cocke as the other nyne, which the blessinge of God upon our labors and cost hath sent us, for the mantenance of our famylyes, and doinge other duetyes to the Common-welth and neighbourhoode that is to bee dune by us.

Thirdly. Wee will waite with patience till our representative inable us to recover reparations for those robberyes, which, under the notion of tythes, have beene drawne from us by them who are

---

* The culprit was probably a quaker, and at this time it seems to have been a part of the creed of this singular body to insult the ministers of the church in every possible way. She pleaded guilty at the assizes, and was fined the large sum of 200*l*.

At the York assizes, in August 1663, Henry Thornton, of Selby, was bound over to keep the peace for insulting Francis Sherwood, clerk, in the church, during the celebration of divine service.

† A singular case. The constable of Knottingley boldly takes upon himself to decry the payment of tithes. He writes a paper against them, putting his name to it by way of warranty. He then sent his servant with it to the common crier of the village, who proclaimed it, *ore rotundo*. The consequence was that much mischief was done. Many persons entered into an agreement to withhold their tithes from Mrs. Hamond, to whom they belonged, until she had proved her title. Others refused to pay. When the tithes had been set out by others in their fields to be carried away, Sykes had sent his cart and removed them for the use of the tenants.

as able as good Zackkeus (if as honest) to restore fowerfould, and then to learne that good lesson of the Apostle—that havinge stolne may steale noe more, but labour that they may bee helpfull.

Fourthly. Wee, as bound in duety by the bond of neighbourhoode, doe hereby bynde ourselves mutually to each other, to the utmost of our power, and as God shall inable us, to defend and save harmelesse each other from all opposers or opposisions which herein shall bee. Wittness our hands, at Knottingley, the 26th July, 1652.— *William Sykes.*

All good neighbours that getts ather hay or corne, and shall bee molested by theeves or robbers, otherwise called tithmongers, by foresinge ather stacke or cocke from of your grownde, knowe yee that, accordinge to my bounden duety, upon your notisse to mee given, I shall to the utmost of my power and place, as God shall inable mee, presarve you in both. Knottingley, the 24th July, 1652.— *William Sykes, constable.*

LI. JOHN PEACOCK, GENT. FOR SEDITIOUS WORDS.

Aug. 1, 1652. The Grand Jurors present that, on that day att Everley John Peacock, of East Ayton, gent. did drinck a health on his knees to the late King, and did say, in the hearing of many people, "I hope the sunn will once agayne shyne on mee. There are fortie thowsand cavaleirs coming into England, and upon their coming I will make some persons rue it."

LII. JANE ———. FOR ABUSING MINISTERS, ETC.

Aug. 24, 1652. Before Sir Richard Darley, Kt. *Robert Hickson, of New Malton, clarke, and preacher of the word there,* saith that one Jaine came unto the towne of New Malton about thre weekes agoe, and hath indeavoured by delusion to drawe his people away from him,* and told the people that he was a blind guid, a theife, and a robber. Upon which occasion a great number of the people are drawne from comeing to the church to heare sermons, and doe usually abuse him and call him a theife and a robber, and doe raile against the ministeriall function.

---

* A very singular case. The accused person, whose surname is unknown, must have been labouring under some extraordinary religious delusion. She seems to have been a kind of revivalist, and to have made a very great sensation at Malton, where there was at this time a more than ordinary number of weak and credulous people. She may perhaps have been a member of the Family of Love.

Uscella Stevenson, of *New Malton*, saith, that she did see the said Jaine give a younge girle a drinke out of a botle, and then immediately the girle did fall downe, and one standing by tooke her upp and held her up; and the said girle cryed "Downe with it, away with it;" and there was many in that roome and other roomes that were lyeing; and she was so frighted with the girle's falling downe so suddenly that she came away, and doth not knowe what became of the girle; and she hath heard many crye in the night time.

Anthonie Beedall, of *Hinderskelfe*, saith, that he was goeing in Gauthrope laine, where he meet with one Jaine —— on Tuesday was a fortnight (this on Sep. 3) with six others there, at a yaite in the said laine, where the said Jaine told him that he was sinnefull, and had an evill spirritt within him. He told her that he did knowe that he was sinnefull, whereupon she did bid him followe her, and she would lye his sinns before him; and soe he went alonge with her to the woolds to Litle Driffeild feilds, and there they did rest themselves, and she did there give him a drinke out of a wainded botle, which will hold about a potle of wine; and the said drinke did make him very sicke, and she told him when he was sicke that the spirritt began to worke upon him, and he was in a kind of trans for about two houres; and then the said Jaine told him that, if he would stay with her, she would show him Christ and his twelve Apostles, and, if he would fast fortie days and fortie nights, he should be as good as Christ. And he had a desire to goe home, and the said Jane bid him be sure that he came not into a boote, for if he did the boote would sinke with him, and alsoe said that he might goe thorrowe the water and not be in any danger. Soe he came away, and came over the water about Hutton-upon-Darwent; and soe comeing neare home he laide him downe on Hinderskelfe east moore, where his brother and Mr. Jackson's man found him, but he did not knowe either of them. And soe he came home, and was not right in his sences for fowre or five days after she gave him that drinke, but had a great desire to goe to her againe, but his freindes prevented him.

Thomas Dowslay, of *New Malton*, saith, that his wife doth usually resort to Roger Hebden's house, and doth not come home never a night untill twelve a clocke, and some nights not at all. And his son Thomas doth denie his true obedience unto him, and denies that he is any more to him then any other man. The said Jaine is a wandering person, and an instrument of the disturbance of the whole towne, and she is the onely instrument of draweing his wife and son from him, and she is the cause of tumults and assemblies at unseasonable times of the night; and, as it is credably reported, she hath had three bastards.

Anthonie Wright, of Westow, clarke, **and preacher of the word** *there,* saith, that upon the 8th of August last, being the Lord's Day, he was goeing into Firby feild, where he did see a great many of people assembled together, being neare thirtie there; and, as he was goeing by them, one Jaine —— fell upon him with violent tearmes, and told him that she was glad that she meet with him, and said that he was a seducer of the people, and that he was damned, and that he was a preacher for hire, and cryed out " Wo, wo!" and threatened him that he was in danger of his life.

Major Baildon, of New Malton, saith, that the said Jaine hath by delusion drawne the affeccion of his wife from him, soe as he canott keepe her at home for this Jaine, but she doth delewd and drawe her away; and he hath wanted her many days and one night, and often she hath comed into his house at unseasonable times at night home; and she saith that she ought not to owne him any more then another man. He went to Roger Hebden's house, and found the said Jaine and his wife amongst a hundred people, and he desired his wife to goe home, and she said that she would not goe, neither could she goe. And some of that partie threw him violently downe the stares, and putt him in danger of his life, and strooke him on the brest.

William Watson, of New Malton, saith, that she was an instrument of a tumult the last Lord's Day in our chappell, which had almost caused a mutinie amongst the neighbours. She is rash in condemneing many whome she never sawe before, saying they are all damned, and especially, one time, himselfe. And she uncivilly abused our minister, Mr. Hickson, and told him he was a rogue, robber, theife, deceiver, swine, drunkard, and beast.

LIII. ELIZABETH HUTTON. FOR ABUSING THE JUDGES IN COURT.

A true bill against Elizabeth Hutton,[*] spinster, for that on Sep. 9, 1652, "she did obstinately misdemeane herselfe, and uncivilly reprove the justices there assembled, and did openly say to the justices of assize upon the bench, ' Come downe, thou blynde beast.'"

---

[*] An insult to the judges upon the bench, made, probably, by a quaker. In these days the judges have more sense than to resent such outbursts of rage or insanity.

LIV. ELIZABETH LAMBE. FOR WITCHCRAFT.

March 17, 1652-3. Before Wm. Adams, Esq. *John Jonson, of Reednes,* saith that one Elizabeth Lambe,* at severall times, hath appeared unto him by night, at his bed side, and an old man in browne clothes with her, at which he was very much affrighted, but had not power to speake to her. And that after the first time she did appeare to him, his goods fell sick, and the farrier could not tell what disease they were ill of. He hath heard other of his neighbours say that they have received losse in theire goods, which they did conceive this Eliz. Lambe to be the awthor of, and that they also did beat her, and was never afterwards disquieted by her.

Thomas Rennerd, constable of Reednes, saith, that he had a child sick in 1651, and his wife said, " I feare this wife (meaninge Eliz. Lambe) hath wronged my child," and then, not long after, his wife meeting the said Eliz. at her owne doore, she did fall downe on her knees, and asked her forgivenesse, and the child did soone after recover.

Nicholas Baldwin, of Rednes, beinge sicke in bodye, saith, " This Eliz. Lamb, about the year 1648, drunde me thre younge foles ever as they were foled, by witchcraft. Sir, I did beat hir with me cain, and had it not beene for my wife, because she sat dounе of hir knesse and aske me forgivenes, I had bet her worse."

John Wreight was with one Richard Browne of Reednes in the time of his sicknes, and he said that he was cruelly handled at the heart with one Elizabeth Lambe, and that she drew his heart's blood from him, and did desire this informant to send for her to come to his house, for he desired to scratch her, saying that she had drowne blood of him, and, if he could draw blood of her, he hoped he should amend. And she, being brought by a wile, the said Browne said, " Bes, thou hast wronged me. Why dost thou soe? If thou wilt doe soe no more I will forgive thee." And she answered nothing. He then scratched her till the blood came, but within a weeke after he died; and all the time of his sicknes he complained to this informant that if he died at this time Eliz. Lambe was the causer of his death.

* A ridiculous case, and yet the guilt of the accused person would be firmly believed throughout Marshland. How sensible are the remarks of Lord Keeper Guildford: "If a judge is so clear and open as to declare against that impious vulgar opinion, that the devil himself has power to torment and kill innocent children, or that he is pleased to divert himself with the good people's cheese, butter, pigs, and geese, and the like errors of the ignorant and foolish rabble, the countrymen (the triers) cry, This judge hath no religion!"

LV. SIMON WARRINER. FOR TREASON.

May 13, 1653. Before Thomas Stockdale, Esq. *Thomas Warryner, of Knaresbrough, dyer,* sayth, that, about eight weekes since, this informer was workeinge together with his brother Symon Warryner in his father's workehouse, and his sayd brother expressed unto him that he had beene for the Kinge, and would be still for him; and told him that, when he was a souldier in Knaresbrough castle, he kild one of the Parliament's party in his father's orchards out of the castle. And this informer sayth that his brother hath made and pend a song with his owne hand about halfe a yeare since, the contents whereof beinge to this effectt; that he wisht all gallant souldiers to display their banners and sett Kinge Charles in his right againe.*

LVI. RICHARD BICKERDIKE. FOR TREASON.

July 7, 1653. Before Robert Walters, Esq. *Richard Bickerdike, of Rippon, yeoman,*† saith, that he did summon William Lumley of Carleton Miniott, George Daggett, Gregory Jackson, and John Pibus, as free holders capitall of the county, and was

---

* A man accuses his brother of treason! The siege of Knaresbrough had taken place some years before this. One would like to see a specimen of the poetical ability of the Knaresbrough muse.

† A very extraordinary case, and one which it is difficult to explain. A person from Ripon goes to London on some business of his own and falls into the hands of a fellow of the name of Elslyott, who makes him his tool. The papers to which Elslyott's name is affixed, at first sight, give one the impression that he was a madman or a fanatic, but, with all their absurdities, they are methodically drawn up, and have reference to a definite object.

When Bickerdike returns to Ripon he sets to work to find freeholders who will join with him. The depositions of three are given, Gregory Jackson, of Sandhutton, William Lumley, of Carleton Minniot, and George Daggett, of Howe. The following papers show that Bickerdike pushed his canvass for freeholders in a businesslike way.

"July 30, 1653. By vertue of a warrant directed to me Richard Bickerdike, of Rippon, agent appointed for the county of Yorkeshire, to summon threescore freeholders of the same for the suppressing of sequestracions, excise, and tythes payeing, whereof I thinke you able for the discovery, to meet me at Thomas Clarke's his house at Topcliffe, the 7th of July, there to receive further instruccions. Yours, RICH. BYKERDIKE.

"To William Lumley, of Carleton Miniott."

"Fourth of July, 1653. Whereas I am informed by Humfrey Russell, of Thornton Steward, that Mr. Humfrey Chamlen, of the same, is old, sickly, and not able to travaile to London, as a man summoned by me Richard Bickerdike, of Rippon, agent for the county of Yorkeshire, by a comission to him directed, itt is desired that he may be excused from that service. HUMFREY + RUSSELL."

It is not known what became of this case or the offender.

to summon threscore freeholders, as aforesaid. And he had his warrant and comission from one Thomas Elslyott, Esqr., armeger, or conqueror of the Long Robe. Being examined how he came acquainted with the said Elsliott, he said that, haveing occation to London aboute one Thomas Simpson's businesse, he addresed himselfe to the said Elslyott, whome he heard was readye to despatch much businesse. And the said Elslyott did dispatch his in relation to Thomas Simpson, and sent downe a commission, and wee gott itt executed. And further saith that thereuppon the said Elslyott gave him the said warrant or comission, which he once or twice refused, yett, after, accepted the same. And he conceiveth that Elslyott durst not have named the generall in his warrant, if it had not beene for the good of the contrey. And the paiper sent to William Lumley of Carleton Miniott, as a sumonse or warrant, was of this ex^{ts} owne writeinge.

Gregory Jackson, of Sandhutton, yeoman, saith, that about the 3d of July, Richard Bickerdike, of Rippon, clarke, came to this informant's house and inquired for him, whose servants answered he was gone abroad. He then sent for him and on his coming he told the deponent that he had authority to sumon him to London. Who answered he was unfitt for a London jorney. Then the said Bickerdike told him, he tooke him to be an able and fitting man to goe about such a busines as the takeing away of tythes, excise, and sequestracions. He this informant demanded where the said busines was to be gone about; the said Bickerdike answered, he was to meet him at Topcliffe upon the 7th of July last, being the faire day, at one Tho. Clarke's house, and then he should have further direccions. At which time this informant mett the said Bickerdyke, and there desired a sight of his authority, for his summons. Then the said Bickerdyke replyed that he must come on Thursday next to Rippon, and there he should see his authority. Then this informant answered he would not come there, nor follow him up and downe at his pleasure.

Jan. 9, 1651-2. These presents shall assure whome it may concerne that I, Thomas Elslyott, Esq., and member of Jesus Christ, and a free borne person of the English nation, and a free person of the same Comonwealth, and Esqr. att Arms, and Conqueror of the gentlemen of the long robe (nowe or late Sathan of this Commonwealth), by God's providence, his owne inocencye and sufferings, and by the justice of the honorable Lord Cheefe Justice Rolle, and the rest of the reverend Judges of the Upper Bench, sittinge before the Keepers of the Liberties of England, by authority of Parliament in Westminster, have, and hath, hereby constetuted and appointed Richard Bickerdicke, of Farneham, in the county of Yorkeshire, gent., to be the agent for the Commonwealth and army in the said county, by speciall direccons from the said Esqrs. superiors; the said Esq. giving unto the said Richard Bickerdike, a new sworne person unto the generall armye and Comonwealth, lawfull power to execute all such trusts for the benefitt and safetye of the said county, and generall peace and tranquilitye of this present Commonwealth and county, accordinge to those instrucions the said agent shall receive from his Exelencye's councell of warr and Esqr. att Arms, and noe other wise. And, for his wages, for his paines in the premisses, there is allowed unto him the said agent, the dayes wages of two shillings and sixpence per diem. Wittnes my hand and seale the day and yeare above written. THOMAS ELSLYOTT, Ar. Ar. Conq.

> Instruccions to be observed by Richard Bickerdike in Yorke, touchinge the causeinge of the people to joyne with the armye to take of the taxes therefore and burthens of that county.

First. You are to gett any freeholders hand to the peticion presented or to be presented to the House for that purpose, and, especially, that justice and mercy may be done freely in the Comonwealth. Then you are allwayes to have the number of 20 or 30 good able men, or their sonnes, who have with civil accomodacon of short swords and pistolls to be readie uppon a dayes warninge, when the peticon shall be delivered to the House by the generall or the armye on their behalfe, to advance itt, and that it is the full sence and desire of the county in cheife. And, together with the peticion to the Parliament house, there must be a peticion drawne in the same manner to the generall and his his great councell of warr, to be a meanes to gett your peticion read and granted in the Parliament house. And assure them that if they doe follow your councells and beare your charges, you will have nothing for your paines of them, if you misse of your markes, and untill your workes done. And aboute the latter end of Whitson weeke, as you receive instruccions from me, they must move upp to London. And this is all at present. THOMAS ELSLYOTT, Ar. Ar. Conq.

And, for further instruccions and civill distinguishment thereof, uppon subscripcion of any person who shall be convicted by the agent to be a Cavilier in hart, Presbiterian, or any who stands for tithes, his retorne shall be the parties owne subscripcion, butt with this instruccion over the same, C. for Cavalier, P. for Presbiterian, and T. for stander for tithes, to the end his Excellencye's Councell and Esqr. may the better know how the severall subscribers stands effected.—THOMAS ELSLYOTT, Ar. Ar. Conq.

The declaracion of the Esqr. att armes.

Forasmuch as the Barrons of the Exchequer, and other Judges of the Commonwealth of England, have in their predicature made a doubte whether the Parliament be desolved or not, it is declared that the Parliament is dissolved, and that all the accons of Oliver Crombwell, Esqr., Captain Gennerall of all the English forces, be just, honest, and legall, and that he ..... honest man in whatsoever he enterprized in the ..... And if any person or persons shall, by any collor or ..... whatsoever, attempt or question the authority of the Lord Generall Cromwell, or disturb the pease of this nation, the free borne persons of England, under his protection, will calle him to a severe accompt. Wittness, THOMAS ELSLYOTT, Ar. Ar. Conq. Dated the 7th of May, 1653.

To the right honorable the Generall and officers of the army sittinge att Whitthall.

The humble peticion of Richard Bickerdike, of Farnham, gentleman, agent of the county of Yorke, in his owne behalfe and the rest of the freeholders, persons of the said county. Sheweth, that whereas since his Exelencye's last declaraccions of the 22th of Aprill, and of the last of Aprill, 1653, wee, haveinge taken notice, both of the desolucion of the late Parliament, and alsoe of the greate care your honors have provided for our safety, tranquility, and good, for which wee doe retorne your honors humble thankes, approveinge all your accons, therefore wee doe hereby make bould to present our desires unto your honors in few words, that is, that your honors would take cognizance of the unsupportable taxes and excise of our country, togeither with the unnecessaryness of payment of tithes before the new representative of the well affected persons, unto your honors proceedings be called in to the supreame judicature menconed in his Excellencye's last declaracion.—THOMAS ELSLYOTT, Ar. Ar. Conq.

LVII. ROBERT WATTERS. FOR DISORDERLY BEHAVIOUR.

S. A. Robert Watters,* of Usburne, was bound to his good behaviour att the last assizes; he hath since then gone with a pole

* The families of Watter and Dickinson both arose into consideration through trade in York. In the Rebellion they took opposite sides. Hence the feud described in the deposition. Dickinson was M.P. for York during the Commonwealth, and held

axe in his hand, and beene seene neare the house of Thomas Dickinson, Esquier. That on the 6th of March, being the Lord's day, he came to the church of Kirkby Usborne, where he had not beene of eight monoths before but once, and, although his owne usuall pew doore was open and none in it, yet he, on purpose to picke a quarell, or doe some harme, as was conceived, to the said Thomas Dickinson, Esq., or some of his family, did passe by his owne pew and came to the said Mr. Dickinson's pew, and, finding the dore lockt, he did climb over the same and satt in the pew, and att Mr. Dickenson's coming thether, imediatly after, with his wife and other friends, the said Mr. Watters refused to give them place, but continued ther still, which did affright Mr. Dickinson's wife, soe as the said Mr. Dickinson was forced to call the constable and order him to sitt in the said pew with them all sarmon tyme to prevent danger. The said Robert Watters haveing beene in arms against the Parliament, and an inveterate enimy to them and all there freinds, hath demeaned himself very insolently against the said Mr. Dickinson, in so much that he did require him to find suretyes for to keepe the peace, which he not only refused, but, being upon that occasion in the presence of Mr. Dickinson, did demeane himselfe very peremtorily and uncivilly, and without takeing any notice of him as a justice of peace, did in a scornefull manner sitt downe with his hatt on.

LVIII. THOMAS CASLEY AND ANOTHER. FOR SELLING
UNLAWFUL BOOKS.

July 8, 1653. At Beverley. *Thomas Casley,* sheereman, was borne at Kendall. Sayth, hee dwellt with God, and was comanded

---

high civic honors, whilst Mr. Watter was under a cloud. The tables were turned at the Restoration.

The feud between these two gentlemen was brought before the Judges of Assize in March 1652-3. Watters was ordered to be discharged from custody; and Sir Robert Barwick, Sir Richard Darley, Robert Walters of Cundall, Esq., and Henry Bethel of Alne, Esq., were appointed arbitrators between them.

* Two Quakers are arrested at Beverley whilst attempting to disseminate their opinions. They had fastened one of their papers to the market cross, and others were found upon them. The offence might be punished under two distinct acts of Parliament. First, that against unlicensed and scandalous books, passed on Sep. 20, 1649, and that passed on August 9, 1650, against atheistical and blasphemous opinions. The printed books that were taken from the prisoners are, curiously enough, bound up with the depositions. Naylor and Farnworth were great lights among the Quakers. The pamphlets are as follows:

1. A single printed sheet, imperfect, beginning "Oh, all you hireling priests, cursed lawyers, and corrupt magistrates, take notice." Folio.

2. "A Discovery of Faith; wherein is laid down the ground of true faith, which

by God to witnesse forth the truth of God, and sayth that he fixt the printed paper upon the market's crosse in the said towne. He sayd the end was knowne to God, and divers other printed papers of the same nature founde aboute him, and allso sayd that the Bible and Scripture was not the worde of God, but a fire and a hammer.

Elizabeth Williamson, sayd, " Thou dost not know the place of my birth." She came into these partes by the will and power of God, and would give no further accounte. Shee sayth that John Harwood, by whom the printed paper is signed, shee loved him so farre as Christ was in him, and the said printed paper, with others, had to sell. And being askt the price of one of them, she answered a halfe penny. She had a husband in the flesh called John Williamson, and hee is by trade a chappman of kottans at Kendall.

LIX. ANNE GREENE. FOR WITCHCRAFT, ETC.

Feb. 16, 1653-4. Before John Assheton and Roger Coats, Esqrs. *John Tatterson, of Gargreave*, saith, that, about a forthnight after Christmas last, he was disabled in body; and one night in his father's house hee was troubled with ill spiretts, who would have advised him to worshippt the enemye. Whereof all were invisable, saveinge Ann Greene.* Butt this informant replied, " The Lord giveth, and the Lord taketh awaye, blessed bee His name." for he would give noe waye to their perswasions, though they tormented him att least foure times. Whereuppon this informant went to the said Ann, tellinge her that hee was perswaded that

---

sanctifieth and purifieth the heart, and worketh out the carnal part. Shewing the way that leadeth to Salvation." London, 1653. By Rich. Farnworth, a Quaker, with an address at the end by " James Nayler, a prisoner at Appleby in Westmorland for the truth's sake." pp. 16, 4to.

3. " A brief discovery of the kingdome of Antichrist, and the downfall of it hasteth greatly. Written by (R. F.) one the world calleth a Quaker, in March 1653." pp. 22, 4to.

4. " Moses' Message to Pharoah, or God sending to the heads of England, to undo the heavy burdens, to let the oppressed go free, to serve him in the wilderness. By Rich. Farnworth, a Quaker, whose name is written in the book of life." 4to.

All these printed papers are with the depositions.

* A reputed witch or wise woman gets into trouble. These poor creatures made this kind of life a trade, and found it to be a very remunerative one. A little knowledge of medicine, a little mysticism, and a few fortunate but accidental cures, would make a reputation, and the benighted country folks would flock to her in shoals. It was to the interest of the mediciner to keep up the delusion out of which she made her livelyhood. This old woman's medical creed was not a difficult one. It had some very ludicrous articles. The use of the hair of the sick person is derivable from classical antiquity.

she could helpe him, beeinge pained in his eare. The which disease shee told him that blacke wooll was good for itt, but he said that that was not the matter. Whereuppon she loosed the garter from her legg, and crossed his left eare 3 times therewith, and gott some heire outt of his necke, without his consent. And he askeinge her what she would doe therewith, shee tould him what matter was that to him, shee would use it att her pleasure; goe his waye home and care nott. But, goeinge home, hee was more pained then beefore, and returneinge to her he told her to looke to itt or hee would looke to her. Where uppon shee crost his eare 3 times againe, and promised hee should mend. And, accordingely, hee did, some corruptible matter runinge outt of his eare as itt did amend.

Jenett Hudson, of Gargreave, saith, that Ann Greene told her that Thomas Tatterson was overgone with ill tongues, and that hee should have one side taken from him.

Margaret Wade saith, that her doughter Elizabeth, beeinge laid uppon her bedd, fell a loughinge, and this informant runeinge to her took her upp, and she said that she saw a great bitch with a dish in her mouth, haveinge two feete, and that she sate one the bedstoope. And afterwards she said shee saw three doggs that came and scrapt aboute her bed, and said that Ann Greene was one of them, and Mary Nunweeke the other.

Ann Greene saith, that she sometimes useth a charme for cureing the heart each, and used itt twice in one night unto John Tatterson of Gargreave, by crosseinge a garter over his eare and sayeinge these words, "*Boate, a God's name,*" 9 times over. Likewise for paines in the head she requires their water and a locke of their heire, the which she boyles together, and afterwards throwes them in the fire and burnes them; and medles nott with any other diseases.

LX. JOHN PICKERING. FOR SEDITIOUS WORDS.

Aug. 4, 1654. *William Catlin, clark, minister of Crambe,* saith, that, about a month agoe, John Pickring,* of Crambe, yeoman, upon some discourse concerning tythes, in the yard of the said Pickering, burst out into these words: "Thou prayest," speaking to this informant, "in thy Babilon pulpit, against us humble saints. Dost thou think I will pay the tythes to maintaine thy pride? Thou prayest every Sonday for the upholding

---

* A fanatic who speaks his mind pretty freely to the minister of Crambe.

the beast who is falne from his first principles." And this informant asking him "What beast, John? I pray every sabath for my Lord Protector, as I have done and ever will." The said John replyed, "I, that's he, he is but an idoll. I acknowledge no outward Protector; myne is heare, heare," striking himselfe with his hand upon his heart. "Thyne is a devill; I acknowledge no outward law. This government we are under, to be ruled by a few councell men and one man, is tyrannicall. The justices you run to are tyrants. Look how it was betweene King and Parliament; so you shall se it againe; they fell from words to blowes and to blood, and so it wilbe againe."

LXI. JOHN DAY. FOR SEDITIOUS WORDS.

Aug. 19, 1654. Before Alex. Johnson, Esq. *Chr. Parkinson, of Slaidburne, the elder*, saith, that, aboute the 8th or 9th day of March last, hee was in company att Slaidburne with one John Day, of Newton, and Richard Leigh, of Birkett, which said John beinge then one of the churchwardens did demaund a church-lay of the said Leigh, whereupon he answerd that hee would pay none: but the said Day tould him that if God did blesse the Lord Protector, and the lawes of this nation did stand, hee would have itt of him: att which words the said Leigh replyed, "Is Cromwell gott to bee Lord Protector? if hee be my Lord Protector hee will sell us all, as the Scotts sould the Kinge for silver, hee haveinge beene alwayes a soldier of fortune."

LXII. ANDREW HUDDLESTON, ESQ. FOR SEDITIOUS WORDS.

A true bill against Andrew Hudleston,* of Hutton John, Esq., for saying at Hutton John, on Sept. 1, 1654, "The Parliament sitts downe on Munday next, and I thinke it is butt a course Parliament that the Lord Protector hath chosen. And if I had the keye of the Parliament house in my keeping, I would keepe both him and them till hee had cutt their throats, or they his."

* The culprit was fined 40*l.*, a sum which was afterwards reduced to 20*l.* Mr. Huddleston was one of the staunchest Royalists in the North of England. All his estates were taken from him by the Parliament, with the exception of Hutton John, in Cumberland, which was tied up by a marriage settlement, but it was sequestered until the Restoration. His son, Andrew, became a Protestant, and took a very decided part against James II. Mr. Huddleston, when he speaks of the key of the Parliament house, had in his mind a well-known historical event.

LXIII. ELIZABETH ROBERTS. FOR WITCHCRAFT.

Oct. 14, 1654. *John Greencliffe, of Beverley*, sayth, that on Saturday last, about seaven in the evening, Elizabeth Roberts* did appeare to him in her usuall wearing clothes, with a ruff about her neck, and, presently vanishing, turned herself into the similitude of a catt, which fixed close about his leg, and, after much strugling, vanished; whereupon he was much pained at his heart. Upon Wednesday there seized a catt upon his body, which did strike him on the head, upon which he fell into a swound or traunce. After he received the blow, he saw the said Elizabeth escape upon a wall in her usuall wearing apparell. Upon Thursday she appeared unto him in the likenesse of a bee, which did very much afflict him, to witt, in throwing of his body from place to place, notwithstanding there were five or six persons to hold him downe.

LXIV. ELLEN WAUDE. FOR SEDITIOUS WORDS.

Oct. 18, 1654. Before John Hewley, Esq. *Nicholas Poole of Selby*, sayeth, that Ellen Waude of Selby, widdow, about halfe a yeare since, aboute the time when the late conspiracy was had against the Lord Protector, being with this informant and his wife in his owne house, said all in the army were rogues, and she hoped to see all those rogues perish; and she further said she hoped to see my Lord Protector come to an evill end; and then presently claping her hands togeather in a rage and passion, said, "Let the rogue (the Lord Protector) looke to himselfe, for there are rodds in pickle for him."

LXV. ROBERT SAWREY, ETC. FOR STEALING A CHURCH BELL.

Jan. 14, 1654-5. Before Martin Iles, Alderman, and Francis Allanson, of Leeds. *Thomas Baxter, of Copgrave*, saith, that on or about the 24th day of December last, (beeing the Lord's Day,) hee beeing clerk of the church of Copgrave, and haveing the keyes of the church doore, missed a bell,† which he verily

---

* The woman was the wife of a joiner at Beverley, and denied any knowledge of what is charged against her.

† The bell at Copgrove church is stolen. The buyer says that he purchased the

beeleeveth at that tyme, or at some tyme the weeke beefore, was stollen out of the said church-steeple, in regard hee then found the said church doore unlocte, and the lock bended, which the Sunday beefore hee had lockt. Haveing informacon that a bell was to be sould at Leeds, and mistrusting it to be the stollen bell, he repaired thither, and, comeing to the howse of one Francis Powell there, to whom he heard the bell was sould, found there severall peeces of a bell, which hee verily beeleeveth was parte of the same bell soe stollen, in regard the smith lately beefore lyeing a band of iron upon the said bell, some parte

pieces of Robert Sawrey and Elizabeth Watson at 4*d.* per pound. Watson denies this, and says that the fragments were bought at Bolton or Tickhill Castle. Subsequently the woman confesses that the proper name of Sawrey is Barnard Bumpus, that he is her father-in-law, and that she heard him say the bell was stolen from Copgrove.

The following account of the experiences of a bell-founder at Durham will amuse some of my readers. It is taken from the unexplored mass of depositions in the chancery at Durham.

Aug. 19, 1635. Cicilie, wife of Cuthbert Cartington of Durham, gentleman, aged 36, says that she knew Humphrey Keene, a belfounder, who, about 4 yeares agoe, did cast bells att Durham, and, amongst the rest, two bells for the church of Staindropp; and, when one of those bells was in casting or runing, the sayd Humfrey, wanting mettall for the same, came to the complainant's house, which was his host house, and gott and tooke of her one brass pott, a brazen morter, two great chargers, 2 other puter dublers, 2 chamber potts, 2 quart potts, and 2 candlesticks; all which the sayd Humfrey did there estymate to cc. weight, and promised the complainant either to give her soe much mettall in liew thereof, or to pay her in money soe much as the same was. She has heard Keene say that he was to have of the defendant Toby Ewbanck 28*l.* for casting the said Staindropp bells. Keene came to remeyne att her house about the first of August, 1631, about Lammas gone 4 yeares, where he soe remeyned by the space of a yeare and halfe, or thereabouts. And he had 2 chambers, and washing and wringing for himselfe and 3 of his men; and for there dyett he did agree to give her soe much for a joint of meate, soe much for butter, and such like, which she provided and made ready for them, and hee was to pay her att the week end. Shortly after the said Keene his goeing from Durham one Tho. Sheffeild, bailiff of the Deane and Chapter of Durham, did distryne certayne bell mettall and worke geare then remayneing in a chist in the guest hall att Durham, which the said Humfrey had left behinde him, which did weigh cc and halfe a hundreth and 12 pound weight or thereabouts; and then the said mettall with the sayd worke geere was putt into the said chist agayne, and lock upp, and the key delivered to Elias Smyth, and the chist caryed into Dr. Clerke his kitchen in the colledge. The defendant Tobye Ewbancke, haveing afterwards gotten the sayd chist and mettall to Tobie Brookin's, had it caryed away to Staindropp, but she gott it stayed. Before the said Humfrey his going from Durham he did procure James Watson to write a lettre to the defendant Ewbancke, to pay him, the sayd Watson, soe much money as he was oweing him, which was about 8*l.* She did hire one to carry the sayd lettre to the sayd Tobye, who returned this answeare by the messenger by word of mouth, that he had no tyme to write, but as soone as he could gett the parishioners and chirchwardens together he would send the money. And afterwards the sayd Humfrey and Toby Ewbanck meeting on the pallace greene the sayd Humfrey was greived, as itt seamed that he could gett noe money of the sayd Toby for making his furnaces and such things for casting the sayd bells; and soe the sayd Humfrey parted from him, saying in anger in this deponent's hearing, that if he wold not lett him have money he would send theme home there bell with a silver lace about her britch.

thereof was broken of thereby, which he bringing alonge with him, and joyneing and compareing the same with the other peeces in Powell's possession, found it just to supply and fill up upp the place out of which it was broken; and, as hee verily beeleeveth, the words *Michaell th'archangell*, was engraven upon the said bell.

LXVI. KATHERINE EARLE. FOR WITCHCRAFT.

Jan. 11, 1654-5. Before John Hewley, Esq. *Henry Hatefeild, of Rhodes, par. Rodwell, gent.*, sayeth, that about August last, Katherine Earle * struck him on the neck with a docken stalke, or such like thing, and his maire upon the necke also, whereupon his maire imediately fell sicke and dyed, and he himselfe was very sore troubled and perplexed with a paine in his necke. Whereupon Ann, the daughter of the said Katharine, seing him so pained, tould him, " Doth the divell nipp the in the necke? but he will nipp the better yet." And the said Katherine hathe beene searched, and a marke founde upon her in the likenesse of a papp. And the said Katherine clapt one Mr. Franke, late of Rhodes, betwene the shoulders with her hand, and said, "You are a pretty gentleman; will you kisse mee?" Wherupon the said Mr. Franke fell sicke before he gott home, and never went out of doore after, but dyed, and complained much against the said Katherine on his death-bed.

LXVII. JOHN HUDSEY, GENT., ETC. FOR BREAKING INTO A DEER PARK.

A true bill against Thomas Johnson of Ripon, John Hudsey of Ripon, gent. Chr. Terry, barber, and Wm. Kettlewell, saddler, for having on July 5, 1654, broken the park of Sir Charles Egerton, Kt. called Markinfield Park, and chased, killed, and wounded the bucks and does.†

---

* Another case of witchcraft. The accused person was committed to the assizes by Sir John Savile. A witness says that Mr. Frank languished for three years. The woman was examined by the women of the village, and two witch-marks were found upon her—a wart behind her ear, and another upon her thigh.
What relation was Mr. Hatfield to Martha daughter of Anthony Hatfield of Laughton-en-le-Morthen who was supposed to have been bewitched? A curious little book was published about her case by her uncle, James Fisher, vicar of Sheffield. Mr. Hunter, in his History of South Yorkshire, gives an interesting account of the whole affair.

† The number of deer-parks was at this time considerable. They would afford

LXVIII. THOMAS BAYNES, GEN. FOR SCANDALOUS BEHAVIOUR.

July 17, 1654. At York assize, before Hugh Wyndham, one of the justices of assize. Thomas Baynes,* of Twisleton, gentleman, being sequestred for his delinquency and recusancy by the Comm^{rs} at York, did upon the 26th of Feb. 1652, by wryteing and words say that the said Comm^{rs} did basely and falsely and indirectly proceed against him in sequestring his estate, and that they had dealt knaveishly and rogueishly with him. That, upon the 27th of Feb. 1652, beeing the Lord's Day, hee did most falsly and unjustly read a scandallous paper in Ingleton church before the congregacion, full of malityous invectives against the said Comm^{rs}, and prohibiteing any persons, at their perills, for medleing with or giveing assistance to the agents of the said Comm^{rs} in the sequestracion of his estate. That, on the 10th of Nov^r, 1653, he did say that Alderman Geldart, the present Lord Mayor of Yorke, was the basest fellowe that ever trode upon a shooe of leather, and that hee never exchanged tenn words with a baser rogue in his life, and that the Com^{rs} for Sequestracions weere all of them caterpillers, and that there was a punishment reserved for such, and that the country all thereabouts weer satisfyed that they weere all knaves and rogues.

great temptations that were not always resisted. It must be remembered that the native deer were still very numerous in Yorkshire.

A true bill against Henry Bright of Wharlow, gen., Stephen Bright, of the same, yeo., Roger Robuck, of the same, joiner, and Cornelius Clerk, of Cathorp, co. Derby, gen., for breaking into "the forrest of Thomas Earle of Arundell, called Riveling Forrest" on 21 July, 1659, and killing a stag.

1661. George Dickinson convicted of stealinge deare out of Sheffeild Park. To be imprisoned.

1662, Apr. 8. Henry Burley for coursing, hunting, and killing of deare in Tankersley Parke.

1665, 20 July. Thomas Dodsworth of Morcarre and three others for breaking Markinfield Park and killing deer with greyhounds.

1675. John Canby, of Spofforth, John Wilson, of North Deighton, gen. and others, for killing a doe in the park at Allerton Mauleverer, the property of Sir Thomas Mauleverer.

* Mr. Baynes may well be pardoned. The word "caterpillars" was a very appropriate term to apply to the sequestrators, for they did eat up many an honest gentleman's estate. Whilst the Commissioners were at Durham they were disturbed in their work. They ran away and left their books behind them. These manuscripts, which shew their already perpetrated, as well as intended, enormities, are preserved in the fine library of the Dean and Chapter.

Mr. Geldart was a man who had made his own fortunes and had chosen the winning side.

On the 30th of March, 1650, one Richard Atkinson was charged with saying in the castle-yard at York " that all sequestrators were villaines; and, though he himself was lame, yet if hee was on horsebacke hee could beate five such Roundheads."

LXIX. CHRISTOPHER BRAMLEY.   FOR BRAWLING IN A
CHURCH.

March 28, 1655. Before Thomas Dickinson, Esq. *Josiah Hunter, minister of both Ouseburnes*, saith, that, upon the last Lord's day, being 25th of March instant, one Christopher Bramley,* of Whixley, came, as he had done severall Sundays before, to the parish church of Litle Ouseburne at the time of morning service, when he said to the informant, passing by him into the church, "Thou art going into the throne of pride;" and afterwards, being in the church he, the said Christopher Bramley, most irreverently behaved himselfe, not moving his hat all the time of the first prayer and singing of psalmes before sermon, but sat in the porch and spake to diverse as they came in, to the disturbance of them; and, after the informant had nominated his text, which was 119 Ps., 105, " Thy word is a lampe unto my feete and a light unto my path," he the said Bramley standing up said, in the hearing of the informant and one William Peele, " Where was the word? the word was not then written or but in writing;" with much more that could not be distinctly heard by reason of the noise of the people, who, being greatly disturbed as well as the informant, rose up in their seates and turnd themselves towards him who made the disturbance. Immediately the churchwarden put him the said Bramley out of the porch and lockd the doore upon him, yet he came againe and cast in a paper through a hole in the doore conteining much slanderous and reviling matter, which appears by the writing ready to be produced by the informer upon demand. The informant saith likewise that, about sixe weekes agoe, he the said Bramley came on the Lord's day in the afternoone into the parish-church of Great Ousburne in the time of sermon, when and where he did

---

* A case of brawling. The minister commits his deposition to writing and hands it in. The paper which Bramley thrust through the keyhole is also inclosed. It is a long address to the parishioners and ministers of Useburne, full of ranting and railing.

At a visitation in 1590 I find the following presentments from Little Useburne:
"They had no sermons this last yere. They have a general communion at Ester, and no oftner. Richard Scatcherd a suspectid sorcerer. A great tumult was made in ther church by Umfrey Ward, who, pretending to be parish clark, although in truth he was not, wold not be put furth by Launcelott Matterson and Richard Jackson, churchwardens."

From Aldbrough this singular presentment is made: " Henrie Robinson and Wilfrid Ingland, for behaving themselfes disorderlie in service time in piping, dauncing, and playing, Mr. Hudesley, ther vicar, being then preaching. Simon Condall plaid the foole the same time in a fowle's coat!"

We know very little indeed of the real history of the Church of England as it may be illustrated by the conduct of the country clergy and the state of their parishes.

likewise not a little disturb the informant preaching on that place of Scripture 8 Luke, 18, "Take heed how you heare," audiblye contradicting the informant with words to this purpose, "Thou hast noe such command or authoritye." After sermon alsoe he stood in a daring manner in the time of prayer and singing part of a psalme and giving the blessing, and afterwards remained most of an houre in the churchyard, labouring still to cause more disturbance, and deteining many people about him, as if it had been a place of marketting, to the great abuse of the Lord's day, &c.

LXX. CHARLES KIPLIN, CLERK. FOR TREASON.

Aug. 11, 1655. Before Edward Briggs, Esq. *Thomas Waller, of Brough*, saith, that one Charles Kilpin, of Crosbie Ravenside, clarke, hath beene an enimie against the Commonwealth ever since the beginninge of these unhappie distraccions; and he did confesse, in this informant's hearcinge, that he was a private intelligencer by the State in the yeare 1648; and, a litle before this last insurrection, this informer heard him say in February last that the Lord Protector was a traitor, for he had taken away the King's life, and hoped in a litle time that the Lord Protector and all that tooke his parte would come to a shamefull end, and that they were but rogues and theeves that tooke his parte. And the said Charles Kilpin hath passed severall times to and from the toppe of Stainemore to meet his brother Tobie Kiplin, another grand enimie against the State, about a month or three weekes before the insurrection, with a resolution, as this informant verily believes, to know when the Yorkshire and Bishopricke men would rise.

LXXI. JOHN LOFT. FOR BRAWLING IN CHURCH.

Aug. 12, 1655. On this present day, John Loft,* of Whingate Wood, came into the church of Newton Kime, in the tyme of divine service, and duringe the tyme of praier before the sermon

---

* This information is signed by the members of the congregation.

George Barker, of Tadcaster, innholder, says that on 25 July, 1654, a Sunday, Barbara Siddall interrupted Mr. Wm. Warren whilst preaching in Tadcaster church, "utteringe speeches of her owne; soe much that the said Mr. Warren was forced to forbeare preachinge, and to come out of the pulpitt; at whose comeinge forth she told him that the Bible was not the Word of God, but onely a dead letter."

preached by Mr. Thomas Clapham, minister there, stood up with his hatt on before him, and did three tymes interrupt him, sayinge the prayers of the wicked were an abomination to the Lord, and bad him cease. And, when the sermon begun, he further said he was an hyrelinge and preached for wages. He was carryed forth of the church by the constable and churchwardens there.

LXXII. WM. AND JAMES RICHARDSON. FOR SEDITIOUS WORDS.

Aug. 13, 1655. Before Edward Briggs, Esq. *Margaret Eubanke, of Stainemore, and Captain Thomas Eubanke, her husband,* say, that, on the 20th of February last, beinge with Wm. Richardson, minister of Brough, and James Richardson, his brother, they said that both her husband and she would lose both life, lands, and goods, within a little time, and all the rest of the Parliament's party that have beene against the Kinge, the lawfull heire of this kingdome, unlesse they would revolt within three moneths time. They would be laid lower then ever yet, and they deserved death, and they and such like had beene suffered too longe.

LXXIII. RICHARD BROWNE. FOR SEDITIOUS WORDS.

March 26, 1656. Before Thomas Burton and Francis Sisson, Esqrs. *John Ardsey, clerke, and Robert Miller,* say, that they heard Richard Browne,* of Cleaburne (co. Westmerland), say that the army were all plunderinge rogues and cowards, and that they had never comed to the passe they were at, but only that their army (meaninge the King's army which he was in) had some or other in it still to betray them, but he hoped to see an ill day for them all. And that he said the Lord Protector was a murtherer, and, if he and his states had their due deserts, they deserved all to be either hanged or headed, for they had both headed the Kinge, and hanged many gallant and better men than themselves, only for gettinge their estates, that they might live in pride, as now they did, and kept a company of rogues, excisemen, and, such like, to abuse the country still. And that he further sayd that if he did but know how to come privatly to the Lord Protector, and his states, that it might not be knowne, he did

---

* Browne was fined 10*l.* and was ordered to be kept in prison till the money was paid. The fine was subsequently reduced to 5*l.*

sweare, God d—— him, body and soule, if he would not cutt all their throats; and againe he wished that he had them all in an hott burninge oven, he did sweare againe, God confound him, if he would not sett up the stone and burne them all to death. All which words were spoken by the said Browne, upon the 26th day of June, 1655.

LXXIV. JENNET AND GEORGE BENTON. FOR WITCHCRAFT.

June 7, 1656. Before Jo. Warde. *Richard Jackson, of Wakefeild,* sayth, that, he beinge tennant to Mr. Stringer, of Sharlston,* for a farme called by the name of Bunny hall, nyare Wakefeild, one Jennett Benton, and George Benton, her sonn, pretended to have a high way thorough the grounds belonginge to the said farme; which one Daniell Craven, servant to the informant, and by his mayster's appoyntement, did indevor to hinder. Upon which the said George Benton did cast a stone at him, the said Craven, wherewith he cutt his overlipp, and broake two teeth out of his chaps. Soe, an action beinge brought against the said Benton for the trespass, which was submitted unto by him, and indevors used to end the difference, which was composed, and satisfaction given unto the said Craven. After which, the said Jennett Benton and her sonn did say that it should be a deare day's worke unto the said Rich. Jackson, to him or to his, before the yeare went about. Since which time his wife haith had her hearinge taken from her; a childe strangely taken with fitts in the night time; himselfe alsoe, beinge formerly of helthfull body, have beene sudenly taken without any probable reason to be given or naturall cause appearinge, beinge sometimes in such extremity that he conceived himselfe drawne in peices at the hart, backe, and shoulders. And, in the begininge of these fits, the first night, he heard a greate noyse of musicke and dancing about him. The next night, about twelve of the clocke, he was taken with another fitt, and, in the midle of it, he conceved there was a noyse like ringinge of small bells, with singinge and dancinge, and sometimes both nights a noise of deepe groninge; upon which he called of

---

* Another of these absurd cases. The accused persons deny the charge *in toto.* It is quite possible that some attempt had been made to alarm the inmates of the house, and thus to induce them to desert their quarters. The treatment of the Parliamentary Commissioners at Woodstock is a case in point.

Some time ago strange sounds were heard in a house near Newcastle, which were so peculiar and unusual that it was altogether deserted. It was found afterwards that it was built over one of the old workings of an adjacent colliery, in which some smugglers had ensconced themselves, and were working an illicit still. *Inde sonus!*

his wife and asked her if she heard it not, and soe of his man, who answered they did not. He asked them againe and againe if they heard it not; at last he, his wife, and servant, all heard it give three hevie groones ; at that instant doggs did howle and yell at the windows, as though they would have puld them in peeces. He had also a great many swine which broake thorrow two barn dores. Also the dores in the howse at that time clapt to and fro; the boxes and trunkes, as they conceived, was removed;, and severall aparitions like black doggs and catts was seene in the house. And he saith that, since the time the said Jennet and George Benton threatned him, he hath lost 18 horses and meares. And he conceives he hath had all this loss by the use and practise of some witchcraft or sorcerie by the said Gennet and George Benton.

Susanna, wife of Robert Maude, of Snow hill, saith that Jennet Benton came downe to her house to secke her son George Benton, and asked him if hee would goe home with her. He answered, "Mother, which way shall I goe? You know I can goe thorrow the stone wall if yow would have me." And further said, that either his father or the divell came to their house and tooke up the iron tongues and strooke upon the iron range. And said that the thing which soe came to their house range soe all times of the night. To which the said Gennet said, "Villaine, did it ever doe the any hurt? it will doe soe at the noone time."

Two other witnesses testify to suspicious circumstances against them; the two accused deny all.

LXXV. WILLIAM AND MARY WADE. FOR WITCHCRAFT.

July 12, 1656. Before Thomas Brathwaite, Esq. *Ann Duffeild and Mary Wilson, of Studley, spinsters,* say, that Elizabeth Mallory, daughter of the Lady Mallory, of Studley hall,* beinge

---

* A case which, from the social position of the victim, would make a great sensation in Yorkshire. The evidence is of the most contemptible description. William Wade denies the accusation against him and so does his wife. She says that the only time she gave Miss Mallory anything was three or four years ago, when Lady Mallory and her children came down to her house, and she gave them a dish of nuts. There are some ludicrous points in the narrative. Miss Mallory always knew when the fit was to be a severe one. What an idea to make a person confess a crime of which she was not guilty, and then for the sickness to depart!

The lady was a daughter of Sir John Mallory, Kt., M.P. for Ripon, a Colonel of Dragoons in the Royal Army, and a very distinguished Cavalier. She became the wife of Sir Cuthbert Heron, of Chipchase, Bt. and, at his decease, she remarried Ralph Jenison, of Elswick, Esq. I am indebted for this information to " A Genealogical and

of the age of 14 yeares or thereabouts, hath layd these twelve weekes languishinge, haveing the use of her limbs taken from her; beinge not able to rise from her bed, but as she was helpt; and in that tyme holden with strange fitts, sometimes in her armes and leggs, and moste parts of her body. Now, of late, within thre dayes, in one of her fitts she cryed out and saied, "She comes, she comes." And beinge asked who it was, she replied, "Mary, Mary." And the said Ann Duffeild nameinge diverse Maryes with their sirnames, which she had formerly knowen, unto her, she did not any way alter in her carriage till she named one Mary Waide. And, upon that, she skreaked and cryed oute, " She comes! she comes! Nowe she sitts yonder in the windowe like a catt." And once she said, " She is a tall woman att the bed's feete." And since the tyme of the nameinge of the said Mary, she hath vomited severall strange things, as blottinge paper full of pins and thred tied about, and likewise a lumpe of towe with pins and thred tied aboute it, and a peice of wooll and pins in it, and likewise two feathers and a sticke. And when she was tolde by the said Ann that she had vomited the feathers and sticke, she said she sawe them this morneinge in her hands. And beinge asked by the said Anne in whose hands; she said, " in Mary Waids:" and tolde what feathers they weere, though when she was oute of her fitts she could not tell that she was in any such fitt. And in her fitts she sayd and cryed oute that if she would confesse but in thre words that she had done her wronge, she should be well. Whereupon the said Mary was sente for and, after much intreatie, beinge perswaded to say she had done her wronge, and to aske her forgivenesse, which she did, the said Elizabeth stood upp on her feete, though imediately before her limbs were drawen upp that she could not stir, and sayd she was well, and walked upon the bed. But, presently after, the said Mary Waide denyed that she had done her wronge. Whereupon the said Elizabeth sayd, " If she denyes it, I shall be ill againe:" and presently begun with her ill fitts as formerly. And in moste of her fitts since, she sayd she should never be well till she had confessed she had done her wronge, or was carryed before a justice and punished.

Anne Duffeilde, re-examined, on July 16, says, that this day Mrs. Elizabeth Malory was in an exstreame fitt of sicknesse for the space of two howers. And this informer, with others, beeinge with her, demanded of hir what she see aboute hir in that fitt.

Biographical Memoir of the Lords of Studley," compiled by my friend Mr. Walbran, of Ripon. It was privately printed in 1840, and there was only an impression of twenty copies.

And the said Mrs. Elizabeth Mallory answered that shee see two catts, one blacke and one yellow catte. And they demaunded of hir what they weare, and she replyed "The women that sente them weare at Rippon, which yow well know." And further shee said " William " once or twice. And this informant demaunded of hir " What William?" and she replyed she knew not, but onely trusted in God; and desired them to pray with hir; which the company did. And then she named William and Mary, but when they named William Wayde she was paste holdinge, her extreamaty was such, and cryed out " William Wade thou terrifyer."

Mary Mealbancke, of Studley Magna, informeth, that, aboute the first of January laste, she beinge in the dearry or milkhouse of Studley, Mary Wayde came in to the said house: and Mrs. Elizabeth Mallory beeinge present, and haveinge a peice of breade in hir haunde, the said Mary Wayde desired her to bestow the said peice of breade upon hir. This informer replyed that breade was noe novelty in Cristmas; whereupon the said Mary answered that " your breade is novelty at any tymes;" and pressinge still upon hir to bestowe upon hir, after she haid demaunded it three tymes the said Mrs. Elizabeth Malory gave it to hir. And she thankefully received it, and tould hir that they weare very curteous gentlewomen. And beinge demaunded of this informant whether she conceived the said Mary Wayde was soe importunate for the peice of breade for wante or noe, she saith that for divers yeares bypaste she haide beene there neighbour, but she coulde not perceive but that there house was furnished with breade and good breade. She further saith that the said Mrs. Elizabeth Malory, if she had beene reedeinge upon hir booke, or upon discourse at any tyme betweene hir fitts, she woulde have leaft of, and would have given notice to the company with hir that she was to have a fitt, and would have expressed directly whether it would have beene a great fitt or an easie one, and it would have happenned accordingly. She further saith that Mrs. Elizabeth Malory affirmed that after they weare both comitted to prisson, that is to say, the said Wm. Wayde and Mary his wife, shee should have noe more sore fitts. Which, accordingly, after she was assured certaynely that they weare both in holde, she was freede from hir fitts; and hath soe contynewed for above a fortnett. And before that tyme she haid them contynewally, very many every day for the moste parte. And this informer further saith that in the exstreamety of hir fitt she cryed out, " Now she comes, Mary Wayde, Mary Wayde, Mary Wayde!"

William Wayde, of Studley, saith that this day (July 16) he was at worke, and was sent for to goe to the Ladye Mallorye aboute 12 or one of the clocke in the afternoone. And he went to the said Lady Mallorye, whoe desired him to aske hir daughter, whoe then lay sicke, forgivenesse, and to repeate some words aftir hir, or some other gentlemen which was then present, but he denied to do soe. He had noe pins in his hand. He saith that at that time that he was theire the Lady Mallorye gave order to shut two kats with a peice and he heard the peice goe of. And then the Ladye and others theire desired him to goe oute of the roome, which he did. He saith that Mrs. Elizabeth Mallorye, as he is fullye perswaded, is possesed with an evill spirit, which is the cause of hir presente mallady and sicknesse. And he is cleare of all and every accusation that now is laid against him bye the Ladye Mallorye or any other person whatsoever.

LXXVI. AGNES WILKINSON.   FOR BRAWLING IN CHURCH.

July 22, 1656. Before Roger Coats, Esq. *Thomas Danby, of Kighley, clarcke,* sayth, that yesterday, beeing the Lord's day, Agnes Wilkinson came into the church of Kighley, and at the closse of the exercisse, shee called him Antichrist, preest of Balle, flasse prophitt, with other revilleing languages.*

LXXVII. MATTHEW VASEY.   FOR HIGH TREASON.

May 30, 1657. Before Luke Robinson, Esq., N.R.Y. *Robert Anderson, gentleman,*† saith, that, about a fortnight before last

---

* The persons who disturbed the clergy at this time were, for the most part, Quakers. It was otherwise, however, in the following instances.

s. a. Paull Dawney, for disturbeing Mr. Jo. Lindley, minister of Snaith, as hee was preaching. Committed to the Sessions by Sir John Dawnay and William Adams, Esq.

A true bill against John Walker, of Mayneby, labourer, William Walker, of Kirkby Wiske, yeo., and Jane Burnett, of Newsham, for interrupting Seth Elcock, clerk, whilst he was saying prayers in the church of Kirkby Wiske, on 14 April, 18 Car. II.

26 Nov. 1663. Before Tobias Jenkins and Richard Robinson, Esqrs. Thomas Howseman, of Wheldrake, says, that yesterday John Marshal came into Wheldrake church and disturbed the preacher, saying the Lord had sent him.

† A remarkable deposition. It would be most interesting if it could be shewn that Charles II. was in Yorkshire in disguise. Vasey, perhaps, had been talking too freely. Robert Stamper, of the Marrishes, gen., deposes that Vasey told him "that hee thought hee should hee a captaine, and that hee could have men enough under him." Vasey denies having said anything of the kind to any one. At the assizes nothing was done to him, but it was left to Luke Robinson, Esq., to decide about sureties and bail. Vasey was bound over to good behaviour, himself in 40*l.*, and in two sureties of 20*l.* each. They were discharged in July, 1658.

Christenmas, he was ryding forth upon a grey gelding, and Mathew Vasey, the elder, of the Marrishes, mett this informant in the said Vasey's ground. And this informant told Vasey that he had been to shew the said horse to one Mr. Kirby. And Vasey replyed, hee was a very handsome horse, and, if he would give that horse to King Charles, it would bee five hundred pounds in his way another day. And the said Vasey did tell this informant there were three men who came from Bridlington-ward, the other day, over about that place where his, the said Vasey his dwelling is; and one of those men was thought to bee King Charles. And that the said men went to Allerston to a house there, which hee did then name; but this informant hath forgotten the name of the house; and said the said men did lye downe on a bedd there, and gott some potchett eggs, and went before day northward upon horses, each of about ten pounds price.

LXXVIII. THOMAS TAYLOR.   FOR BRAWLING IN CHURCH.

Aug. 21, 1657. Thomas Tayler,* at Appulby, did openly say to Francis Higginson, preacher there, in the publique place of meeting, "Come down, lyar, for thou speakes contrary to the doctrin of Christ, for Christ hath said, sweare not att all," whereby hee did not only molest the said Francis Higginson, but alsoe did cause greate tumult and disturbance amongst the people then and there present.

LXXIX. GEORGE HARRISON.   FOR TREASON.

Sep. 24, 1657. Before Edward Briggs, Esq., J.P. co. Westmerland. Whereas George Ottway did acciedenteley meate with one George Harieson, who by his simplisiteys did discover himselfe to be one who was imployed either for the Poppe or for Charles Stuarde, to imbroyle this nacion in bloude, and to wage warr against his Heignes the Lord Protecter. And the suteltey of the divell havinge putt the said George Harieson † into a dis-

---

* He was fined 3*l*. 6*s*. 8*d*.

† A curious case. It was not deemed a matter of much importance, as the culprit was set free by proclamation in 1658. Mr. Otway, of whom the magistrate does not speak in a complimentary manner, was a member of a good Westmerland family and makes a capital signature, whatever was the state of his mind. Mr. Briggs was the person, I believe, who plays a part in the romantic and well known story of the adventure of Robert Phillipson, Esq., better known by the name of Robin the Devil.

guise of selinge tobacco in England, with an intencion to ingage severall percons of qualiety in this quariell, the aforesaid George Ottway, being by the worlde caled a madman, but then havinge his wittes about him, did discover that the foresaid Harieson was a comon rogge, and woulde have tempted him to his owne distruction, that is to say to have .... him to have gone to Charles Sturde; sainge that he had seine the faice of Charles Sturde aboute foure weekes agoe. Uppon which the said Ottway did repley that he had foure good geldings and woulde gladle have beine with Charles Sturde. Upon which the said Harieson tould me that he woulde carie me to him within 3 weekes time. And then the said Ottwey in his Heignes the Lorde Protector's name did apprichende the said partey upon heigh treason.

Lassie Procter, of Treason feild, gen., saith, that beinge in company with George Harrison in Sedbergh, he heard him say 1. That the Lord Protector is a traitor, and all that take his part are traitors. 2. That the dregs of a Papist was to good to make Protestant off. 3. That Fox* (meaninge the grand Quaker), was one in religion with him.

Gawen Mosse, heard Harison say that he served a better maister then ever the Lord Protecter was. Further, that he came from beyond sea, and saw Charles Stuard within a month before, and, if Mr. Ottway would be pleased to goe, he would show him C. Stuard in a months time.

LXXX. CHR. FLOWER. FOR SEDITIOUS WORDS.

Apr. 26, 1658. Before Matthew Beckwith, Esq. *George Baine, of Labourne, felte maker*, saith, that he did calle Christopher Flouer, of North Couton, trator. And he did replye and said he whould furnish six cavcleares to feight against my Lord Protector,† and hee hoped to see the day to wash his hands in my Lord Protector's bloode, and that shortlye too.

---

* In Jan. 1660-1, divers persons were bound over to prosecute Thomas Wiglesworth, of Slaidburne, " touching a scandalous paper conteyning slanderous words against his Majestye, subscribed by George Fox the younger, found on and published by the said Wiglesworth. George Fox was imprisoned for a long time at Scarbrough.

† The prisoner was bound over to keep the peace. Cromwell, it will be seen, was not free from the censure of the people.

A true bill against William Leng, of Beilby, yeo., for saying at Pocklington, Feb. 2, 1649-50, " The Commons of England are fooles, and I scorne ther governement. Cromwell is the sonne of a whore."

June 9, 1654. John Field, of Thornton (in Craven), heard Lockley Allerton say " The devill confounde Cromwell and all his partakers, for he is a traitor. I drinke a health to his confusion, and you are all traytors that refuse it."

LXXXI. SIR JOHN SAVILE, KT.   FOR NOT REPAIRING THE
       CHANCEL OF WAKEFIELD CHURCH.

July 22, 1658. Sir John Savile,* of Lupset, Kt., indicted for not repairing the chancel of the church of Wakefield.

LXXXII. IZRAEL WAYD, ETC.   FOR USING A HOT PRESS.

July 25, 1659. Izrael Wayd, of Leeds, clothworker, Peter Mason, Peter Jackson, and Mathew Potter, of Leeds, clothworkers; indicted for using an hott presse.

LXXXIII. WILLIAM ELSLEY, GEN.   FOR TREASON.

The Grand Jurors present that on the 15th of October, 1659, Alexander Lambert, of Richmond, husbandman, said that hee, as he came to the assizes at Yorke, was together with one Lancelott Dent, att the house of William Elslay, gen., in Melmerby. And the said Elslay told him he had a comission from Charles Stuart to be captaine of a troope of horse in Sir George Booth † business, and proffered him a corporall place. And that

---

* He was knighted by Charles I. and was High Sheriff of Yorkshire in 1649. An interesting account of Lupset and the Saviles is to be found in a privately printed work of the late Historian of South Yorkshire, of which I possess a copy, " Antiquarian Notices of Lupset, the Heath, Sharlston, and Acton, in the County of York," 8vo. 1851. There was a little wild blood among some of the Saviles of Lupset.

† Sir George Booth, of Dunham Massey in Cheshire, headed the first movement in the North of England against the Parliament. He was a Presbyterian, and had the support or the good wishes of that party. The author of the " Iter Boreale " says, when speaking of this attempt,

"Kind Cheshire heard; and, like some son that stood
Upon the bank, strait jump'd into the flood,
Flings out his arms, and strikes some strokes to swim,
Booth ventured first, and Middleton with him;
Stout Mackworth, Egerton, and thowsands more,
Threw themselves in, and left the safer shore."

Sir George, however, was unsuccessful. He got possession of Chester, but, incautiously leaving it, was defeated by General Lambert at Winnington bridge, near Northwich, and there was an end of the whole affair.

This deposition shows that Booth had supporters out of Lancashire and Cheshire, and that the plot was more general than some have thought. The King, it will be seen, was directly connected with it, although Sir George made no allusion to him in his manifesto.

The Elsleys, mentioned in the deposition, were the ancestors of the present recorder of York. At the special assizes in Jan. 1663, Wm. Elsley, gen. was bound over to

G

one Wood was to be his lieutennant, and one William Carlile his cornett; who, together with Charles Elslay, were then present. Which Charles Elslay, though he could not stir from his owne house, would for that service assist and supply them with horses, armes, and moneys.

LXXXIV. ELIZABETH SIMPSON. FOR WITCHCRAFT.

Feb. 15, 1659-60. Before Luke Killingworth, Esq. *Michaell Mason, of Tynmouth, soldier,** saith, that, about the 20th of Jan. last, Elizabeth, wife of George Simpson, of Tynmouth, fisher, came into his house and asked a pott full of small beare from Frances Mason, daughter to this informer; and, she refusing, the said Elizabeth threatened to make her repent. He saith that upon the next day the said Frances lost the use of one of her leggs, and, within foure dayes after, the use of the other; whereupon she, becoming lame, was necessitated to keep her bed, where she lay miserably tormented, crying out that the said Elizabeth did pinch her heart and pull her in pieces; but, this informer getting blood from the said Elizabeth, she hath ever since continued quiett in her bed without any torture, but she doth not recover the use of her limmes, but pines away in a most lamentable manner.

The said Elizabeth is reported to be a charmer, and turnes the sive for money,† and hath been reputed a witch.

keep the peace, himself in 100*l*. and in two sureties—Thos. Leadom, of Lofthouse hill, yeo., and John Wandesford, of Kirklington, gen., in 50*l*. each. Was he implicated in any way in the Farneley Wood plot?

* The first case of witchcraft from Northumberland. A great raid had been made upon the reputed witches in that county some time before this, as will be seen in the preface.

† It was common enough to turn the sieve, or the riddle and sheares, for stolen property.

Dec. 13, 1598. The wife of Thomas Grace, of par. Stannington, Northumberland, was presented for turninge of the ridle for things loste and stolne.

Dec. 10, 1667. Cumberland. Before Thos. Denton, Esq. Mary, wife of Stephen Johnson, of Carleton, saith, that, as shee was comeing from Clifton, shee mett with Jo. Scott, whoe told her that his wife had cast the riddle and sheares for some cloathes of George Carre's that was stole; and one Jo. Webster, of Clifton, told them that they knew as much as he could tell them, and that it was a little bleare-eyed lasse that gott them, whoe lived neare them.

The formula used by the operator was as follows:

" By St. Peter and by St. Paul,
If —— —— has stolen ——'s ——
Turn about riddle and shears and all."

LXXXV. MARGARET DIXON.   FOR SEDITIOUS WORDS.

A true bill against Margaret Dixon,* of Newcastle, for saying, on May 13, 1660, " What! can they finde noe other man to bring in then a Scotsman? What! is there not some Englishman more fit to make a King then a Scott? There is none that loves him but drunk whores and whoremongers. I hope hee will never come into England, for that hee will sett on fire the three kingdomes as his father before him has done. God's curse light on him. I hope to see his bones hanged at a horse tayle, and the doggs runn through his puddins."

LXXXVI. JOHN BOTT, CLERK.   FOR A SEDITIOUS SERMON.

The Grand Jury find a true bill against John Botts † of Darfield, clerk, for saying in his sermon in Darfield church, on the 13th of May, 1660, " The man wee had soe long desired and expected, and that the Parliament were about to bring in, would bring in superstition and Popery, and that we must fall downe againe and worshipp stocks and images, the workes of men's hands. But, rather, let us shew ourselves men, and gird every man his sword upon his thigh, and sheath it in his neighbour's bowell, for I doe beleive too many of us have Popes in our bellies. Let us feare the King of heaven and worship Him, and bee not so desireous of an earthly King, which will tend to the imbroileing of us againe in blood."

---

* The beginning of a series of depositions, which show how unpopular Charles II. was with many of his subjects. These are the straws which tell us in which direction the wind was blowing. The whole of the Nonconformists were, sooner or later, disappointed with their new sovereign, and the winning charm of his address could not atone for the vices of the Court with persons who had been accustomed to a very different *régime*. To one royal fault there are frequent allusions:—

Sep. 15, 1665. Anthony Peele, of Ullock, co. Cumberland, says, " Hang the King. He is a knave, and a whore-maisterly rouge."

1684. Mary Watson, of par. Gisburne, says, " The devill goe with the King. He is as rank a whore-master as ever was, and as rank a rogue as ever reigned."

† This person does not appear among the vicars of Darfield, and he was probably an intruder. He pleaded the King's pardon at the assizes and the plea was allowed. The deposition shews to what length preachers would occasionally go. To " have a Pope in one's belly " passed into a proverb. It will be recollected that it was applied by a London mob to an unpopular occupant of the episcopal bench in the reign of James II. " There goes the Bishop of Chester (Cartwright) with the Pope in his belly!"

Other clergymen were also free speakers, *e.g.* Thomas Smallwood, of Batley, clerk, indicted at York, for saying in his sermon at Brears Chapel, par. Halifax, " The whore of Babilon is rising and setting up!"

LXXXVII. RICHARD ABBOT.   FOR SEDITIOUS WORDS.

A true bill against Richard Abbott, of Brighton,* for treasonable words, on May 20, 1660. Thomas Smith said, "I hope wee shall have a King." On which Abbott replied, "A King! if I had but one batt in my belly, I would give it to keep the King out, for Cromwell ruled better than ever the King will."

LXXXVIII. JOHN CAREUTH.   FOR SEDITIOUS WORDS.

May 23, 1660. *Robert Allyson, of Shields, butcher,* saith, that, about the begining of March last, John Careuth, of Tynmouth, gen., did say that the King was a son of a whore, and that the late King Charles poison'd his father, saying to this informer, "The rogue, your master, is comeing over into England, but he hath never a man that followes him that hath a principle of God in him except Sir Ralph Hopton." And he said that General Monk was a traytor, and worse than Jezabel that was eaten by doggs."†

LXXXIX. SOME PERSONS UNKNOWN.   FOR A BURGLARY.

June 6, 1660. *Jeremiah Nelson, minister of Ellesden,* saith, that on May the 7th, a litle before midnight, certain men broke into his house, and came with swords and pistolls into the said house, and shot off a pistoll, and did come into the lodging parlour, where he and his wife lyes, and did threaten him often that if he would not give them his money presently they would kill him, and one of them said often, "Kill Baal's preist," and they tooke away a purse and bag and money in it.‡

---

* This person appeared at the assizes, but nothing was done to him. In 1660, Ann wife of Andrew Key, of Tynemouth, was charged with saying "If I had the King's children I would feed them with the crumbs that fall from my table."

† Some strong speeches against persons in authority. It has been stated elsewhere that James I. was poisoned. Mr. Carruthers seems to have had little affection for the Stuarts or for the new state of things in England, and was watching with jealousy the turning tide.

Sir Ralph Hopton was one of the staunchest and most active of the Cavaliers. The old ballad says—

> "Sir Ralph and his knaves are risen from their graves,
> And cudgelled the clowns of Devon."

Alluding to his zeal for the royal cause in the West of England. The last words of Samuel Ward, the suffering and ejected Master of Sidney, were, "God bless the King and Lord Hopton."

‡ A burglary in the house of the rector of Elsdon, a village among the wilds of

XC. THOMAS LUNN.   FOR SEDITIOUS WORDS.

A true bill against Thomas Lunn,* of Bootham, labourer, for saying, on June 10, 1660, " The King shall never bee crowned, and, if hee is crowned, hee shall never live long. His father's head was taken of with an axe, but a bill shall serve to take of his."

XCI. GILBERT ROWELL, CLERK.   FOR SPEAKING AGAINST
THE PRAYER BOOK.

A true bill against Gilbert Rowell,† of Alnwick, clerk, for saying in Alnwick church, on Sep. 2, 1660, " The Common Prayer booke imposed and intruded upon the people is unlawfull

Northumberland. The rectory is an old Border peel tower, but it could not afford security to its inmates. The rector's servants gave chase to the robbers, but could not overtake them.
 I find Mr. Nelson making another deposition on May 6, 1660. He then says, " that John Shield, Quaker, did disturb him, on the 27th, in the pulpit, and on Monday last he did deny the Holy Scriptures contained in the Bible to be the word of God."
 At Durham, on Dec. 5, 1637, I find Percival Reed charged with "abuseinge Mr. Isaac Marrowe, clerke, parson of Elsden, calling him base preist, and stinking custrell, and did push the said Mr. Marrowe by the beard."
 We have a very imperfect idea of the state of the clergy, and generally of the religious feeling of the North of England in the 17th century. If we give credit to a letter written about 1750 by Charles Dodgson, another rector of Elsdon, his parish was even then in a deplorable condition.
 * The prisoner appeared at the assizes, but received no punishment.
 † Mr. Rowell was a Puritan minister who had the spiritual charge of Alnwick during the Rebellion. He had previously been an officer in the Universities of Glasgow and Aberdeen. At the Restoration, Major Orde, the churchwarden, brought to him the book of Common Prayer, desiring him to use it. His reply, made publicly from the pulpit, forms the subject of this indictment, which was pressed against him at the Newcastle assizes by Orde. The charge, which hung over him for some time, was finally given up. After Rowell was ejected from Alnwick he devoted much time to the study of physic, exercising at the same time his ministerial functions. He died at Edinburgh in the reign of William III. An account of him will be found in Palmer and Woodrow.
 Many other clergymen were in trouble at this time; e.g. :—
 Mar. 1660-1. Jeremiah Milner, of Rothwell, clerk, for not reading the Book of Common Prayer. Out on bail.
 July 29, 1661. John Noble, for the same offence. To find sureties. There is an account of this person in Mr. Robinson's History of Snaith, 127.
 A true bill against Chr. Marshall, of Horbury, clerk, for saying on the 1st of August, 1666, in the pulpit at Horbury, " Those that have taken the protestacon, and, after, come to the Common Prayer of the Church, are perjured persons before God and man."
 August 1666. An indictment against Edward Browne, of Crofton, clerk, for negligently performing the service, ignored. At this assize Brian Marsh was found guilty of assaulting John Mawman, clerk, whilst doing duty in the church, arresting and imprisoning him.

to be used, and it is not owned by God, nor hath any authority out of the word of God."

XCII. WILLIAM POOLE.   FOR SEDITIOUS WORDS.

Nov. 15, 1660. Before Sir John Kay at Woodsome. *Thomas Gibson, of Almonbury, yeoman*, saith, that on the 14th of Nov., beinge at South Crosland, William Poole,* of Barkisland, said that " the trained bands which are now rayseinge are to goe into Scotland, for Morgan and the Scotts does joyne, and these souldiers which are now disbanded does flye into Scotland and joyne with them against our Kinge, because that hee was sworne there for them, and now goes against his oath. And further sayd that the Kinge and Queene are now both come into England, and that wee should nothcinge but Popery, as formerly hath beene, and that the Queene hath broughte a Pope with her from beyond sea."

XCIII. CAPTAIN JOHN HODGSON.   FOR SEDITIOUS WORDS.

Jan. 14, 1660-1. *Daniel Lister, of Ovenden, yeoman*, sayth, that on the 10th he casually mett with John Hodgson,† of Coley Hall, late a captaine against the Kinge. And the said informer,

---

* Poole made his appearance at the next assizes, but nothing was done to him. Offences of this kind were usually passed over, the accused person finding sureties for his good behaviour.

† Captain Hodgson, of Coley Hall, in the parish of Halifax, was a well-known Republican and Independent. He fought for the Parliament by the side of Fairfax through the greater part of the civil war, and he was a person who was regarded with much respect by the members of his party. His enemies were now in power, and it is pretty certain that he was an active agent in all the Yorkshire plots after the Restoration.

Captain Hodgson, in his memoirs of his own life, which are published with those of Sir Henry Slingsby, gives a full account of the incident to which this deposition refers. He was arrested by order of Sir John Kaye and Sir John Armitage, in the night time, at Coley Hall, and was carried off to Bradford gaol. He was kept in prison without being brought before any magistrate till the next assizes. " When the assizes came, one Daniel Lyster was my prosecutor, a person that I once bound to his good behaviour, upon an information of the constable of Manningham, that this Lyster was too familiar with another man's wife, an ale-house keeper in the town, and that he spent much of his time in dishonest ale-houses and lewd company &c. And after the King was come in, he meets me, and demands the names of those that informed against him, and a copy of it; and I told him, that the business was over, and that it was not seasonable to rip into old troubles. With that he threatened me, and said, he would have them; ' The sun ' said he, ' now shines on our side of the hedge,' and so I bid him take his course. Now his information against me was, that I should say, ' There is a crown provided, but the King will never wear it;' and this was put in the indictment before the grand jury, that ' I never had been a turncoat; I never took

out of his affection to his Matie, did say, that now the sunne did shine upon the righte side of the hedge. The said John Hodgeson asked him what he ment by the sunne. He tould him, he ment our Soveraign lord the Kinge. Then the sayd Hodgson answered "Your Kinge, your Kinge ere long will have notheinge left to sett his crowne upon."

XCIV. THOMAS TAYLOR, AND OTHERS. FOR REFUSING THE OATH OF ALLEGIANCE.

March 25, 1661. Committed to gaol at the York assizes for refusing the oath of allegiance.* Tho. Taylor, Samuel Watson, Henry Jackson, John Smyth, Roger Hebden, Christofer Holyday, John Levens, George Watkinson, Peter Acklam, Isaac Linsley,

---

the oath of allegiance, nor never would do;" and these poor things were forged against me; only that I had never been a turncoat, I justified it before judge and jury. When the matter was heard against me, I had one Jeremiah Brookesbank, a neighbour, that did swear that he was in company with Lyster, and heard him say, that if ever the times changed, he would sit on Hodgson's skirts; and Lyster had overrun the court, or else had been bound to his good behaviour." Joseph Lister, the brother of Daniel, and the clerk of Sir John Armitage, tries to prove the second indictment, but Hodgson was acquitted on both: "and the foreman, one Micklethwaite, told the judge openly in the court, that if such informers or persons were suffered to go on, there would be no living for honest men." Hodgson, however, was obliged to take the oath of allegiance. For this affair he was five months in prison.

Captain Hodgson will occur again. There are some interesting notices of him in "The Life of Oliver Heywood," his pastor and neighbour. By the death of the learned editor of that work I have lost a very kind friend and Yorkshire a noble antiquary.

* Most of these people, if not all of them, were Quakers—a sect which at that time took a more prominent and obnoxious part in public affairs than it does at present. The executive was at that time very active in endeavouring to suppress their meetings, and a full account of the pains and penalties which these misguided people underwent is to be found in that very curious work " The Sufferings of the Quakers." The following extracts from the minute books, &c., will give some idea of the way in which the Quakers were persecuted.

"At the assizes at York, in July 1662, John Wilson, John Ratcliffe, and Chr. Hurdsman, of Pocklington, yeomen, Peter Pearson, of Helgrainge, yeo., Wm. Towle and Chr. Wilson, of Warter, are indicted for holding a conventicle.

"Also Edward Wilkinson and John Harper, of Leeds, labourers, Thomas Akroyd, John Levans, Thomas Thackwray, Wm. Cundall, James Burneley, Thomas Sutton, Chr. Dawson and John Holmes, of Leeds, labourers, for the like offence.

"Also Samuel Poole, of Thorne, yeo., and Baptista, his wife, Robert Eccles, Robert Stanyland, yeoman, and Anne Allenson, spinster, of Thorne, for the like.

"Also Wm. Merrison, John Bunkin, Thomas Wilson, John Melwood and Henry Doughty, of Fishlake, yeoman, for the like.

"Also Thomas and Christian Middlebrooke, Robert Burton, Thomas and Francis Burr, Godfrey Petty, Isaac Cowe, John Crabtree, John Spencer, Barth. Allinson, and John Petty, of Fishlake, yeoman, Geo. Beamont, of Sykehouse, yeo., Abraham de Cowe, Wm. Williams and Wm. Womersley, of Fishlake, yeoman, Thos. Cutt, of Thorne, yeo., for the like. Most of these persons were imprisoned for a year.

"Nov. 10, 1662. Wm. Steere and Thomas Taylor, of Thorne, gent., say that on

John Hall, Wm. Dewsbury, John Hick, Samuel Poole, Matthew Foster, John Blakeley, John Greene, Richard Blythman, Christofer Gilburne, Nicholas Pawson, Andrew Hawkes, Christopher Bramley, Wm. Lotherton, Abraham Wadsworth, John Hodgson, Wm. Siddall, Chr. Chapman.

XCV. WILLIAM LAWSON.   FOR SEDITIOUS WORDS.

A true bill against Wm. Lawson, of Leeds, labourer, for saying at Wike, on the 20th of May, 1661, " I hope the phanaticks * will disperse his Majesties trained bands like the chafe before the wind. It was justly done that the late King was beheaded."

XCVI. MARY JOHNSON AND OTHERS.   FOR WITCHCRAFT.

Aug. 8, 1661. Before John Emerson, Esq., Mayor of Newcastle. *Robert Phillip, of Newcastle, labourer,* saith, that, about fourteene dayes before Christenmas last, he fell sicke, and was sore pained at his heart, and lying awake one night about nyne or tenne of the clocke, the doores being shutt, there appeared to him one Mary, wife of Wm. Johnson, of Sandgate, labourer, one Margaret Cotherwood, with another woman; and the said Mar-

---

Nov. 9, they found divers persons in the house of Robert Burton the elder, in Thorne, under the notion of Quakers.

" March 1663. Indicted at the assizes. John Greene, the younger, of Liverseige, being indicted at Wakefeild Sessions last by the grand inquest, and contemptuously refuseing to take the oath of obedience tendered unto him, and being called in open court to plead to the said indictment, refused to doe the same, but stood mute, whereupon the sentence of *pramunire* was pronounced against him.

" Mar. 31, 1663. John Spencer, of Thorne, yeo., John Bladworth, shoemaker, Many Middlebrooke, Robert Burton, jun., yeo., Anne Rider, spinster, Eliz. Ferriby and Eliz. Allanson, of Thorne, indicted for a conventicle.

" Feb. 2, 1663-4. Anthony Knowles, of Buckden, confesses to a meeting of Quakers at his house, and to being at another at the house of George Wilson, of Cray. ' These meeteinges were to serve and seeke the Lord.'

" July 31, 1664. Anthony Hunter finds at Sunderland, par. Isell, ' assembled together in the house of one Wm. Adcocke about forty men and woemen of those called Quakers, under pretence of divine worshipp.'

" 18 July, 1669. Thomas Dowsland, of East Ayton, constable, finds a conventicle of Quakers in the house of Dorothy Coates, of East Ayton.

" June 16, 1682. Information against Mr. Samuel Poole, of Thorne, for having in his house a meeting of Quakers.

* The prisoner was bound over to keep the peace at the assizes. The disappointment which the Dissenters felt at the King's treatment of them was now being loudly expressed. Two years afterwards it broke out into open rebellion in Yorkshire. These seditious speeches were the forecast shadows of coming troubles.

Henry Welburne, of Brandesburton, labourer, was charged with saying on Feb. 16, 1660-1. " The King is a rogue, and if he does not depart the land presently hee shall die the sorest death that ever King died."

garet said to him, "Wype off that on thy forehead, for it burns me to death," (this informant having anointed his head that night with an ointment for the headache which was given him). This inform^t asking her what it was that burnt her, she answered "That ointment that is on thy brow," and puft and blew and cryed "O, burnt to the heart." Thereupon she stood a litle by, and this informer asking her if she beleeved in Jesus Christ she need not feare that ointment; and still she cryed "O, burnt to the heart; burnt to the heart." And the said Mary Johnson told him that she would be revenged of him before all men living; whereupon this informant said he trusted in Christ, He was his rock in whom he trusted. And thereupon this informer heard a voice (from whence it came he knows not) saying "Whosoever trusted in that rock Christ Jesus shall never perrish;" and the voice bid them begon, whereupon they vanished away.

XCVII. RALPH CONSTABLE, ESQ. AND OTHERS. FOR MANSLAUGHTER.

Aug. 28, 1661. *William Vernon, of London, Esq.* aged about 36, says, I saw Mr. Smith, his hand all bloodie:* askeing the said Mr. Smith who stroke him, he answered mee, "Some men in that roome," pointing at it. Whereupon I went with him to the chamber doore to demand of them in that roome whie they soe assaulted him, but, after a litle discourse, with a sword or rapier one out of the said roome runn him into the face, upon which

---

* An affray at an inn at Malton among some Yorkshire gentlemen, many of whom were soldiers. One, a Captain Smith, died of the wounds that he received. Sotheby, Constable, and Wm. Hawksworth, were tried at the assizes, and were acquitted. Constable, in his examination, is said to be of Selby, and Sotheby is described as a lieutenant-colonel, probably in some local corps.

The following cases give rather an unfavourable picture of the Yorkshire gentry:—

"July, 1659. Laurence, and John Meynell, the younger, of Thorneby, gentlemen, and Thomas Aslaby, of the same place, indicted for assaulting and beating Hugh and Robert Savile and Richard Grimston.

"Sep. 1660. Nicholas Lindley, of Aldmondbury, yeo., Mark Warren, James Hanson, of Aldmondbury, clothier, and Nicholas Fenney, of Fenney, gen., indicted for killing Edmund Lee. To appear to receive sentence when called upon.

"Aug. 3, 1663. Marmaduke Lord Langdale, Peter Pudsey, gen., and Gerard Merriman, of Holme in Spaldingmore, for an assault on Jo. Millington.

"Mar. 1666-7. W^m. Hamond, of Scarthingwell, Esq., for an assault on Thos. Robinson, of York.

"On August 18, 1668, after a dinner at Mr. James Brearey's, in York, at which Mr. John Metham, of Metham, and others, were guests, Mr. John Swann goes into the garden, and fights a duel with Mr. Richard Hodgson, and is killed.

Mar. 1669. Sir Chr. Wandesford, of Kirklington, for an assault on John Pallister. To keep the peace."

thrust the said Smith cried out "I am slayne." I beleive Mr. Smith was sober. I saw the said Smith strike with his hand Major Constable on the face before Smith received his seacond harm. I saw in the company of the said roome a drawen sword. After the said thrust, pricke, or stabb made, I went into the said roome, where Major Constable said to mee he had received much prejudice through the untrue testimony of Percyhay, and he had yet given him noe satisfaccion, which he did expect then if it could bee, or soe soone as he could. Mr Sutherby said to mee that he and others had received many abuses from most in my company, and received noe satisfaccion from them. And he further tould mee that they had beene grand traytors.

Arthur Jegon, of Lincolne Inn, gent., aged 26, saith, that hee being at the house of Lancelot Thorp, of New Malton, upon Saturday night last, with others, did there see Mr. John Smyth of Old Malton, with his hand wounded, and cut over most (if not all) his fingers. And, further saith, that the said Mr. Smyth was at the staire head neare the doore of the chamber of Mr. Constable, where there was severall swords drawne. Mr. Smyth did desire satisfaction for his wounds received; then did a certaine person in a gray coat and brownish haire, from behind Mr. Constable, with a sword or a rapier did wound the said Mr. Smyth in the face, and then Mr. Smyth fell against the wall.

Chr. Percehay, of Ryton, gent., aged 24, saith, that hee was att Lancelott Thorpe's upon Satterday last, with some other company, where Mr. Smith was cutt over the fingers. The informer heard Mr. Smith demaunding satisfacion of Mr. Constable for the wrong hee had received by himselfe or some of the company in the roome with the said Mr. Constable, whereupon one over Mr. Constable's shoulder, and out of his chamber, thrust Mr. Smith into his face with his sword, and hee fell downe and said hee was wounded.

James Strangwayes, of Pickering, gen. aged 27, sayth, that following Capt. Smith and the last in company down the staires he see Mr. Constable, with others, on the staire heades, calling some "Rouges." Mr. Smith replyed, "By whome they ment?" They answered him, by such rouges as himselfe, and thereupon drew there swordes, and wounded him on his fingers, and one of them cryed for a pistoll to pistoll him, which presently was brought, and presented it at Smith, which was prevented by the informant. Mr. Smith afterwardes returned to the stair heades, and there demanded sattisfaction on Mr. Constable. Whereupon Constable replyed he knew nott who had done him the injury, and Smith answered, for anything he knew it was himselfe, and thereupon gave Constable a blow on the face with his hand. Another standing behind Constable run at Smith with a drawne sword or raper in his hand, and wounded Smith in the face, whereupon Smith fell. Mr. Constable afterwardes reflecting upon perticular persons, Major Nary told him he did nott well to doe soe, for things were pardoned by the Act of Indemnity. Constable replyed he vallued not a fart the Act of Indemnity.

Henry Sowthebie, of the Cittie of Yorke, gent., saith, that he being att the house of Lancelott Thorpe, in Major Constable's lodgeing, John Narie, Chr. Perchey, John Smith, James Strangewaies, with others, about 8 of the clocke in the evening, did riotously attempt to enter into the lodgeing of the said Major Constable, which he perceiveing, hee, with the Major, did stand upon his guard, being altogether ignorant of what designe they had. And thereupon Major Constable haveing opened his chamber doore, did civillie demand what businesse they had there, and and wisht them to departe in civillitie, without anie further trouble; which the Major had scarce uttered, but Smith by a thrust hitt Major Constable on his left eye, in so much that blood issued out verie much by reason of the said thrust, which caused this informant to beleive that Major Constable was mortally wounded. The said Smith was drunke, and with extreame scurrilous language did abuse this informant and Major Constable. And he verilie beleives that the rest of the persons in Smith's companie were verie much intoxicated with drinke. John Narie said in a threatening manner "Sett your King asyde, wee will doe anie thing whatever with you, if you dare," and that all the parties beforenamed doe frequently meet at Narie's house and elsewhere twice everie week, upon what occasion this informant knowes not, but is most certaine that all the said persons are disaffected, and apparently by all theire accions disloyall to his Majestic's interest.

John Carre, of Skamston, husbandman, haveing occasion to be with Mr. Suddeby, whoe was his attorney-at-lawe, was present when Mr. Smith was wounded, and he belciveth that the said wound was given by Mr. Suddeby, but upon the bussell he saw Mr. Constable, Mr. Suddeby, and one Hawksworth have theire swordes drawne, and Mr. Constable and Mr. Suddeby threshing and striking with theire swordes. But Mr. Constable, after Smith was wounded, did blame Mr. Suddeby for being soe forward. And he heard Lancelot Thorp say, "O, Mr. Sudeby, fly, for you have slain a man!"

Anne, wife of Lancelot Thorpe, of New Malton, yeoman, saith, that she being in the roome with Mr. Ralph Constable, Mr. Henry

Sowtheby, Mr. Hawksworth, and John Carre, it being Mr. Constable's lodging, her husband came in with a message from Mr. Nary and Mr. Peircyhay to know whither Mr. Constable had any writt against Mr. Peircyhay or noe. Presently after his goeing out, Mr. Nary, and the rest of the gentlemen that were with him, came out of theire owne roome, and came to the chamber-doore, where these other gentlemen were, the doore being open. Thereupon Mr. Constable and the rest of the gentlemen rose up and demanded what they had to doe to come to their chamber, and after some words past amongst them they shutt their chamber doore, and some of the other gentlemen thrusting against it, Mr. Constable tooke up his pistoll, and bid them att their perill not to enter into his chamber for it was his castle, and thereupon laid downe his pistoll againe. But the other gentlemen comeing soe violently on there was swords drawne at the chamber doore, but she did not see any blowes or thrusts given, neither did she see Mr. Smyth att the doore, but after she saw him sitting on a bedside in the parlour, and his nose bled, and she gave him a napkin to wipe itt.

XCVIII. JANE WATSON. FOR WITCHCRAFT.*

Oct. 10, 1661. Before Sir John Marlay, mayor of Newcastle-on-Tyne. *Winifrid Ogle, of Winlington White-house, spinster*, saith, that, aboute three of the clocke in the afternoone yesterday, she, heareing that two of the children of Mr. Jonas Cudworth was att the house of Mr. Thomas Sherburn, watchmaker, in great paine, being bewitched, she came to see them, and she found them in great extrimity; and one of the said children and one Jane Pattison who was then there cryed out they see the witch Jane Watson, and the child said the witch brought her an apple, and was very ernest to have it, and presently after the people of the house cryed "Fire, fire!" upon which this informant see something like a flash of fire on the farr side of the roome, and she see a round thing like fire goe towards the chimney, and the said childe was severall tymes speechles, and in great torment and paine, and that halfe of the apple the child spoak of was found att the bedfoote.

---

* Another case of witchcraft from Newcastle, and a very absurd one. The mother of the children says that, in her belief, Jane Watson has thus injured her because she refused to buy oatcakes from her in consequence of her bad character. Mr. Cudworth was a woollen draper. The children blame Jane Watson and Anne Mennin. Watson asserts her innocence.

Jane Patteson, spinster, servant to Mr. John Ogle of Winlington White-house, see some children of Mr. Jonas Cudworth in great paine, and much tormented, and in extrimity, and one of the said children said, " There is the witch, there is the witch, Jane Watson." Upon which this informer said " I see the witch," she then seeing a woman in a red waist coate and greene petticoate, which woman was gon under the bed presently; upon which this informer's master, Mr. John Ogle, came with his rapier and thrust under the said bed therewith. And she further saith that some of the people in the house told her they heard something cry like a swyne upon the said thrust under the bed.

Elizabeth, wife of Thomas Richardson, of Blaydon, yeoman, aboute 8 yeares since, living in Newcastle, and being very sick, and much tormented in her body, she sent for a medicer called Jane Watson, who came to her and tooke her by the hand, but doth not now remember what she said to her, but imediately after the paine left her, and a dogg which was in the said house presently dyed.

XCIX. THOMAS HERBERT.   FOR SEDITIOUS WORDS.

March 23, 1661-2. Before Nicholas Cole, mayor of Newcastle. *Robert Wouldhave, sergeant-att-mace,* heard Thomas Herbert, weaver, say " Who would have thought that Lambert's[*] armye would have been distroyed within three yeares tyme; butt he hoped before other three yeares goe about he would see an alteration in this government. I meane the present government that now is."

[*] In 1659 General Lambert, who had during the civil war been most active against the King, did all he could to oppose the reaction. He crushed the Cheshire rising under Sir George Booth, but was unable to stop Monk. Without coming to blows, as Monk advanced, according to Captain Hodgson " Lambert and his party was mouldered away." The author of the Iter Boreale speaking of Monk observes,

> His few Scotch coal kindled with English fire
> Made Lambert's great Newcastle heaps expire.

Lambert no doubt had a wish to step into Richard Cromwell's place, and there were many who would gladly have seen him in that elevated position. The following speeches show the tendency of the popularis aura :—

" A true bill at York against Richard Smith of North Ouram for saying, on Aug. 31, 1660, at Halifax, " The King is a bastard, and the sonne of a whore. I hope to see Lord Lambert King."

A true bill against Francis Rider of Walden for saying, on Aug. 12, 1664, " Cromwell governed this land better than the Kinge. I wish that Lambert might have succeeded him, for hee would have governed it as well."

C. GEORGE TAYLOR. FOR SEDITIOUS WORDS.

A true bill against George Taylor of Kirkby Kendall, for saying, on 9th Aprill, 1662, "It was a good day when the King's head was cutt off. There hath beene noe peace like as was in Oliver* the Protector's time. It is a pitty but that all King's heads should bee cutt off."

CI. WALTER CROMPTON, GEN. FOR SEDITIOUS WORDS.

May 28, 1662. Before Tho. Crompton, Esq. *Tristram Hewbanck, of Kilham, husbandman,* sayth, that a little while before the coronation of his Matie Charles the Second, who now is Kinge, hee heard Walter Crompton,‡ of Sunderlandwick, gent., say hee hoped the Kinge would never bee crowned, for hee was a bastard. And hee hath severall times seene him clap his hand on his horse buttocks and say, "Stand up, Charles the third by the grace of God," which is an usuall expression of the said Walter Crompton's.

CII. ROBERT ROBERSON. FOR SEDITIOUS WORDS.

July 28, 1662. Before Sir Patricius Curwen, Bt., Sir Wilfrid Lawson, Kt., and John Lamplugh, Esq. *Chr. Bruntinge, of Cockermouth,* saith, that on the 17th he heard Robert Roberson, of Loweswater,‡ after some discourse of the act for hearthes and stones, say that before the said act went forward their was many in England would fight in blood to knees.

---

* Anthony Hunter, of Keswicke, said that, on 25 July, 1664, one James Wright of Darnton in the county of Durham, came to his house and begun to give ill languages, saying he valued none of the King's officers, and that Oliver Cromwell was a better man than the King. The culprit pleaded intoxication as his excuse. He was a needle-maker by trade, and sought his livelihood " by singing of songs."

† The foolish speeches of a young man of 26 or 27. The deposition was actually taken by his brother. The charge against the legitimacy of Charles I. was frequently made. The bill against Mr. Crompton was ignored at the York assizes. There is a curious account of Mr. Charles Crompton in the Lives of the Norths, ii. 232.

‡ The act taxing the hearths was one of the most unpopular measures that was ever passed in England. This is not the only instance of ill-feeling to the King at Loweswater.

"Dec. 6, 1661. Before Sir William Huddleston, Kt. Joseph Robinson, of Baryet par. Loweswater, heard Thomas Allison say that Charles the Second was a traitor and a rogue, and all those that tooke his parte; and he hoped within a short tyme they would be taken a course with."

CIII. COLUMBUS INGLEBY, GEN.   FOR MURDER.

August 4, 1662. An inquest on Brian Redman, of Ingleton. On August 2, Columbus Ingleble, of Lawkland Hall, gen., shot him with a pistol.*

CIV. CHARLES NORTH, GEN.   FOR SEDITIOUS WORDS.

Aug. 8, 1662. Before Godfrey Copley, Esq. *John Staunton, of Everton, co. Notts, gen.*, saith, that being in company on Saturday last with one Charles North,† at widow Atkins' house in Blackstone, he heard him say that he was for those men that had murthered the last King, and he would be for them as long as he had life, and that they were honest men, and that the last King did deserve the death he had.

Anthony Barton, of Blaxton, yeo., heard Mr. Charles North say that King Charles was a traitor; whereupon the said Mr. Stenton tooke the said North a boxe of the eare. And the said North said that the ould King, when he was put to death, had but his due.

CV. MICHAEL STUDHOLME, GEN.   FOR MANSLAUGHTER.

Oct. 11, 1662. *Michaell Studholme, of Wigton*, sayeth, that he, being at Carlile,‡ about 16 or 18 yeares since, accidently went

---

Pepys, in his Diary, under the 30th of June, 1662, makes the following remarks which are illustrative of the present deposition. "This I take to be as bad a juncture as ever I observed. The King and his new Queene minding their pleasures at Hampton Court. All people discontented; some that the King do not gratify them enough, and the others, fanatiques of all sorts, that the King do take away their liberty of conscience, and the height of the bishops, who I fear will ruin all again. Much clamour against the chimney-money, and the people say that they will not pay it without money."

* We have no account of this affair. Mr. Ingleby was tried and acquitted. *Verdicts*, 1657-8. Thomas Etherington, gent., dyed by the visittation of God. Wm. Brearey, gen., slaine by misfortune. 1658. Wm. Smith, of Welbury, clerk, slayne by misfortune. 1666. Ralph Babthorpe, *interfectus per infortunium*. Wm. Hotham, *felo-de-se*.

† Charles North, of Awkley, co. Notts, gen., speaks some seditious words. At the York assizes he was bound over to keep the peace, himself in the sum of 80*l*., and in two sureties of 40*l*. each, *i.e.* Francis Thornhill, of Misterton, gen., and Nicholas Hexop, clerk, of Finningley.

Mr. North's end was a tragical one. On the 28th of February, 1663-4, he was shot by Nicholas Curtis, of Doncaster, apothecary.

‡ An incident which probably occurred during the siege of Carlisle in 1644, when

to the signe of the Sune, ther being severall captaines both for King and Parliament; which said captaines had some differences at the said inn, who did part them civilly. And the said ex^t, with the said captaines for the King and Parliament, walkeing quietly in the market place, thos captaines for the King did pursue those captaines which were for King and Parliament with ther swords drawne, and calling them "Parliament rogues," and said, "Downe with this Parliament;" and soe, with that, they fell upon them with their swordes drawne, and the defence of the said deponent with the captaines for saveing their lives did defend theirselves with their sword drawne, and then rung the common bell of the said citty, and forced the said deponents with those captaines which were for King and Parliament into the guildhall; in which commotion one of either party was killed, to witt, Ensigne Hutton, who was then for King and Parliament, and Leonard Milborne, a citizen of the said citty.

CVI. HENRY THOMPSON.   FOR MURDER.

Jan. 19, 1662-3. At Rotherham, before Thomas Garnett, gent., coroner. *Anne Ashmore, of Rotherham, spinster,** sayth, that, upon the 30th of December, about eleaven of the clocke in the night, she beinge in her bed, in the almes-houses upon Rotherham bridge, did heare one Henery Thompson, laborer, and then a dweller in the said almes-houses, very vyolently fall upon, beate and strike one Margarett Hill, a poore olde widdow, with a rod or staffe for almost an hower and a halfe together, in such a vyolent manner that the said Margarett Hill cryed lamentablie out, and said he would kill her; butt still he layed the more on her, callinge her wich, and said she had bewiched his mother,

---

the city was captured by General Lesley. When peaceful times returned, Mr. Studholme found it necessary to place upon record his own account of this adventure. Possibly some false charge had been made against him and he wished to exculpate himself.

In 1663, some of the rebels concerned in the Kaber-rig plot asserted that "one Studholme" had engaged to place Carlisle garrison in their hands. Was this the person now alluded to? He was a county gentleman, and I find him more then once serving on the grand jury.

An interesting account of the siege of Carlisle, drawn up by Mr. Tullie, has been printed.

* A very cruel case. The poor old woman languished till the 18th of January, and then died from the effects of the injuries that she had received. Thompson's wife states that the old woman had charged a sister-in-law of hers with stealing apples: at this her husband was offended, and beat the old woman about the head and face for an hour and a half. I do not know what was done to Thompson.

and gave her not over untill he made (her) knell downe of her knees, and aske him forgivenes. All this while this informer durst not stir out of her bed for feare the said Thompson should beat and strike her in the like manner.

CVII. JOSHUA KIRKBY, CLERK.   FOR NONCONFORMITY.

March, 1663. Joshua Kirkby,* of Wakefeild, clerke, formerly lecterer there, haveing not subscribed the declaracion mencioned in the act of Uniformity of publicke praiers, and is not licensed to preach by the archbishopp of this province, nor hath read the thirty-nyne articles of religion mentioned in the statute of 13th of Eliz., nor read the booke of Comon Praiers, as by law is required, and dyvers tymes since his disabillity hath preached in his owne house on his usuall lecture day. Comitted by Jo. Armitage, Bart., Richard Tanckard, Knt., Thomas Stringer, Esq. Francis Whyte, Esq.

CVIII. WILLIAM CHRISTIAN, GEN.   FOR DEFRAUDING THE REVENUE.

Apr. 6, 1663. Before George Denton, Esq. *James Wood, of Rockliffe*, saith, that William Safftlay, a wayter or officer deputed by Mr. William Christian,† customer of the porte of Carlisle, and farmer of a parte of the Scotch border customes, did in the porte of Carlisle receive severall entries of wool-fells and tanned leather to be exported into Scotland. And, in particuler, in or about the midle of Jannuary 1663, did make entry of tenn packes of wooll-fells, of the goods of Richard Graham, of Harker, and Richard Fargison, of Rockliffe, in the county of Cumberland. And, about the same time, of three packes of tanned leather, of

---

* One of the ejected ministers. He went to Wakefield in 1650 as Lady Camden's lecturer. He was several times in trouble for his loyalty. On one occasion he was imprisoned for praying publicly for Charles I., and he was also punished for his share in the insurrection of Sir George Booth. The act of Uniformity silenced him, but he still preached in his own house. For this offence he was sent to York castle. One of his principal amusements in gaol was writing verses, about which a friendly pen tells us " the sense was far beyond the poetry." He died at Wakefield in the summer of 1676, and, being at that time under sentence of excommunication, was buried in his own garden.

† A charge of defrauding the revenue is brought against Mr. Christian, the customer of the port of Carlisle. The Christians, from their connection with the Isle of Man and the Derby family, are well-known both in history and romance. What was the result of the complaints now given I have been unable to discover. Mr. Christian lived, I find, until the latter part of the century. I should like to see the history of this family written at length. It would contain some very remarkable chapters.

the goods of Thomas Graham; and two packes of the same commodity, of the goods of Robert Wilson. All which said goods Mr. William Christian was knowing of, and consenting to the entries and exportation of into the kingdome of Scotland, with many other severall parcells of prohibited goods, both of wooll, tan and leather, and raw hides.

Secondly, Mr. Florence Garnet, and Mr. William Softley, officers deputed by Mr. Wm. Christian, as parte farmer of the Scotch border customes, togeither with the said Wm., did threaten not onely the collector in the porte of Carlisle for ofering to make seizure of two mares goeing for Scotland, but did say that they would have him turned out of his place, and all the rest of the wayters in the porte. The said Garnet, notwithstanding his promise and ingagement that the mares should not be exported, did privately in the night time convey them into Scotland, contrary to act of Parliament and the King's speciall warrant, commanding that that none should be exported unlesse by warrant under his hand and seale. And this by the incouragement of Mr. William Christian.

Thirdly, the officers imployed by Mr. Wm. Christian, now resideing within the porte of Carlisle, have dailey, and from time to time, advised and incouraged marchants to practice all the fraudes they could. And some of them have received monyes for the custome of cattle, and given warrants for the importation of goods out of Scotland, acknowledgeing the English custome to be paid, and assisted marchants in the private conveyance of the said goods, or advised them the way to escape the officers.

CIX. CAPTAIN MASON.   FOR HIGH TREASON.

July 27, 1663. John Turner, of Thorne, saith, that on June 26th, hee being in company of Thomas Mayson,* of Gansebrough, co. Lincolne, at Thorne, he heard him say that there would be warres shortly againe in England, and that there would be fouer

---

* This is the Captain Mason who appears in the Yorkshire Calendar in March, 1665-6, as having been committed by Sir Thomas Gower "for conspireing to raise warr against his Majestie." He was tried, together with John Browne, of Syke house, and William and Richard Wilson, of Barforth, yeomen, for high treason, and they were ordered to be kept in gaol without bail till the next assize. It was then directed that he should be admitted to bail, to make his appearance at the next gaol delivery, if two justices of peace, to be specially appointed, should think fit. No recognizances are entered into the minute book, and we may conclude therefore that the justices would not release the prisoner. This did not make much matter to him. He was being brought to York when the escort was attacked by five men at Darrington, near Pontefract, and Mason made his escape. We hear nothing of him afterwards.

for one against the cavaliers. And they being talking of the Quakers, he said that he would goe into that towne, and could have the coppy of the act before it was signed by the King, for he had as good intelligence from London as any man that lived in Lincolnshire.

CX. SARAH WALKER.   FOR SEDITIOUS WORDS.

July 28, 1663. Newcastle-on-Tyne. Before Robert Shaftoe, Esq. and Mark Milbank, Esq. *Sarah, wife of Oswald Walker, yeo.*, did say on the 13th of July these wordes (to witt): "There was never a King in England that was a chimney sweaper but this," meaning his Matie that nowe is, and that she would petition and indeavour to gett and raise an army to fight against his Matie and all his officers that came to demand any such thing as the harth money."

CXI. THOMAS LIGHTFOOT, ETC.   FOR HIGHWAY ROBBERY.

August 15, 1663. Before John Tempest, Anthony Byerley, Samuell Davison, and Stephen Thomson, Esqrs. *John Williamson, of Rawdon, clothier,** saith, that himselfe, with his servant and daughter, were travailing from his house at Rawdon on the 5th instant towards Rippon about his profession of a clothier, and that, as he was going on Killinghall moore, they were overtaken by three persons, who did assault them, clapping a pistoll to his brest, and bade him deliver his money or he should dy for it. Whearupon he was forced to submitt to them, and one of them, who, as he now understands, calls himselfe John

---

Mason was examined with reference to this charge against him, and made the following deposition: "He went to Wetherby in Yorkeshire to receave money, without any intention of goeing to the Spaw, but, being so neare the Spaw, he resolved to goe and drink some waiter. He heard of one Dr. Ritchardson, which was then at the Spaw, but denyeth that he had any conversation with him, to his knowlege."

The Spaw was Harrogate, and Dr. Richardson was one of the fomenters of the plots of 1663.

It has been seen that there was a considerable body of Quakers at Thorne. It now appears that there were among them some dangerous enemies to the state.

* A daring case of highway robbery. Thomas Lightfoot was a Quaker and lived at Richmond. He had escaped out of Durham gaol. When he was arrested a money-bag and a peculiarly marked half-crown were found upon him, to which Williamson swore. Lightfoot and Smith were convicted at the York assizes, and were executed.

Smyth, who likewise clapt the pistoll to his brest, did search his pocketts, and tooke out 14s. and one penny. Another of the said persons did thearupon cutt the wametow and tooke off the pack clouths which were upon a driven horse, and out of them took 40l. which he gave to a person who, as he understands, calls himselfe by the name of Thomas Lightfoote. The said Thomas Lightfoot did search the informant's daughter Sarah in a very rude and uncivill fashion, and did take out of her pockett a little box, whearein theare was 1s. and three pence. It was about ten of the clocke in the fore noone.

CXII. JONATHAN SHACKLETON. FOR SEDITIOUS WORDS.

Sep. 17, 1663. Before Sir John Armytage. *Tho. Shackleton, of Morton bankes, par Bingley*, sayeth, that, upon Sunday night last, he heard Jonathan Shackleton,[*] of the same place, say " Am I a phenattick? Yow shall know yet before March wind be blowne that we phenatticks will looke all those in the face which now doe oppose us, for the Kinge is a bloudy Papist, or else he would never have give consent to the putting to death of soe many honest men as he hath."

CXIII. WM. MOULTHORPE. FOR SEDITIOUS WORDS.

Oct. 17, 1663. Before Wm. Wilkinson, Esq. Mayor of Pontefract. *Nicholas Myas, of Pontefract, labourer*, sayth, that, about the 14th of September last, one Wm. Moulthrope,[†] laborer, came into his owne house at Pontefract, and told him hee had heard a pretty story that one George Marre was sworne never to bee a cavalier againe. Whereupon this informant replyed, " T'was a pitty but such rogues should be hanged that could not

---

[*] The spirit of disaffection was rapidly spreading in Yorkshire. Very soon after this it broke out in open rebellion. The accused person spoke the mind of many discontented Yorkshiremen.

A true bill against Edward Middleton, of Leeds, yeo., for saying on Oct. 20, 1663, " The Kinge and the Queene are Papish divells." The prisoner was found not guilty. The York juries seem to have been singularly lenient to all offenders of this kind. Charles II. was frequently charged with being a Roman Catholic. On Jan. 29, 1662-3. Before Mr. Richard Dawson, alderman of Richmond. Thomas Gibson of Brompton-on-Swale, gent. says that he heard Robert Blackburne, of Richmond, gent. in the house of Thomas Morley in Richmond, saye that M^{ris} Morlay the nighte before sayd that the King was a Papist.

[†] A man who knew something probably of the intended rising. He was acquitted. The speech about the evil is amusing as a piece of ingenious reasoning.

let the Kinge alone, and meddle with their owne matters." Unto which the sayd Moulthrope sayd, " What is the Kinge better than another man? for Robin Bulman, (meaninge one Robert Bulman, of Pontefract, laborer,) a seaventh sonne, can cure seaven evills, and the Kinge can but cure nine, soe that the Kinge is but two degrees better than Robin Bulman. Thou shalt see that before the moneth end as many will arise in England and Scotland as will cutt the throats of all those that were for the Kinge, and to bee sure thy throate will bee cutt for that thou hast beene soe long a cavalier, and now art in armes for the Kinge!"

CXIV. NICHOLAS BATTERSBY. FOR SORCERY.

Oct. 20, 1663. Before Cressy Burnett. *Henry Eskrigg, of the Cittie of Yorke, milloner,* saith, that Richard Readshaw, the younger, beeinge lately a prisoner in the sheriff's goale, upon suspicion of steallinge some monyes from Thomas Lord Fairefax, was declareinge to this informant how innocent hee was of the cryme imputed to him, and that hee was not guilty thereof. Whereupon this informant told him of one Nicholas Battersby,* of Bowtham, whoe had skill in the discoveringe of those persons that had stolne moneyes; and where the monyes might bee found. Soe, att the earnest desire of the said Readshawe, Battersby was sent for to the goale, and att his comeinge, beeinge acquainted with the busines, did aske the said Readshawe what tyme of the day my Lo. Fairefax monyes was gone, and when; and tooke instruccions thereof in his booke, and then departed, and the next day the said Battersby came to the sheriff's goale, and declared before this informant, and severall others, that the querent was cleare (meaninge Readshaw), and that the moneys in question was stolne by an old grey-haird man, and a young man, whoe were servants in the house, and was hid in a great sacke, which by reason of the waters none could as yett come unto; and it would

---

* A wise man is in trouble. It was certainly rather bold to come to the city gaol to exercise his art. He was bound over at the assizes to good behaviour.

The sum of 140*l.* had been stolen out of Lord Fairfax's study, at Appleton, and two men, father and son, bearing the name of Richard Readshaw, were charged with committing the offence. They were yeomen at Appleton. The case against them was merely one of suspicion, and the bill was thrown out. They were bound over, however, to keep the peace.

Joseph Wetherell, of Scarborough, labourer, was charged with having, on Oct. 11, 1678, stolen " a portmantle" containing 1,050*l.*, the property of William Lord Widdrington.

not bee discovered within 5 monthes. And the said Battersby receaved 5s. for his paines in the said business.

CXV. CAPTAIN ATKINSON AND OTHERS. FOR HIGH TREASON.

Oct. 22, 1663. Before Sir Philip Musgrave, Sir John Dalston, Richard Brathwait, Robert Hilton, and Edward Nevinson, Esqrs. *John Waterson, of Great Musgrave,* saith, that, upon Munday, the 12th,* comeinge home from Kerby Stephen, layt that night, he

---

* The account of the rising that took place in Westmerland, which is generally known by the name of the Kaber-rig plot.

The measures and conduct of Charles II. were especially distasteful to various bodies of Dissenters, especially to those which had been so active in bringing about the Restoration. His supposed leaning towards Roman Catholicism, the patronage that he gave to the Church of England, his acts against the Nonconformists, and the dissolute manners of the court, gave great offence to the Puritanical party. They remembered the strictness of the old *régime*, and contrasted it with the laxity and inequality of their present rule. A dangerous spirit soon began to spring up.

In the North of England this discontent was very strong. I have already given many of the threats and speeches of angry men which show how the tide was turning. But they did more than talk. In the autumn of 1663 a general rising in the North was concocted at Harrogate. In October the Yorkshire insurgents met at Farneley Wood, near Leeds, where they threw up some intrenchments; but being few in number, and those ill provided with arms, and badly advised and officered, they got away to their homes without shedding any blood. The original depositions, giving an account of this ill-planned affair, are not now in existence, but there are very full abstracts of them in Dr. Whitaker's Loidis and Elmet. A longer account of this rising, together with the names of those concerned in it, will be given in the preface.

Simultaneously with the attempt at Leeds there were to be others in various places, especially in the county of Durham; that also was crushed in the bud. It was called the Muggleswick Plot, and there is an account of it, with some of the depositions, in Mr. Surtees's History of Durham.

The Westmerland party, to which these depositions refer, was under the management of Captain Atkinson, an old parliamentary officer. He had gathered together and armed a few of the discontented people in the neighbourhood, and the attempt was to be made on the 13th of October. The Durham men were to have joined their brethren in Westmerland, but a change in the orders was made, and the Westcountrymen were ordered to march into the Bishoprie. Captain Atkinson marshalled his troop in the night time, and got it to a place called Birka, near Kaber. From Birka the party returned homewards. The number was so small and the enterprise so perilous that the leader deemed it more prudent to send the men to their own abodes.

So daring an attempt, in which so many were interested, could not be kept secret long. The Cavaliers, mindful of their past sufferings, were instantly on the alert, and the insurgents were detected and thrown into prison very speedily indeed. A special assize was held in the winter, and Captain Atkinson, Waller, and several others, were executed at Appleby.

The object of the insurgents was to seize the garrison towns in the North, and to arrest the chief members of the Royal party, especially that gallant gentleman Sir Philip Musgrave. They would then have endeavoured to effect an alteration in the government, setting up liberty of conscience, overthrowing the taxes, pulling down the bishops, and stopping the payment of tithes, and other obnoxious imposts. The Quakers were energetic in the scheme, and the plotters hoped to carry with them

met with a partye of horse, about the number of 30 or above. Comandinge him to stand, demanded his name, and haveinge also a horse, required him to goe along. That Capt. Atkinson was there then, and rid upon a white horse, with a case of pistolls. And, inquireinge concerning the matter, one Capt. Waller answered that Fairfax would be up in armes that night, and that they weare up in Scotland and in Cumberland, and throughout all Englande. And that there was a hatter in Ravenstondale who said he neaver took up arms in his life, yet in this designe would venture as freely as any of the old soldiers, and had kept a hors for that purpos 2 months, and had armes with him. And saith that Richard Richardson and John Waller, on Munday at night, rid for Corporall Watson, and were all to meet at Spittle that night. Askeinge whether wer armes, he was answered ther was 14 case of pistolls at Will. Goodlad's barne, and some at Capt. Atkinson's; and that they declared against bishops; and departed at Birkay, beyond Kaber-rigge, and Capt. Atkinson and Capt. Waller spoke unto them, that haveing done no harme in the country, they might returne home and not be knowne. That two men came the 12th of October, at night, out of Yorkshire, one from Holbecke, a mile from Leeds, the other from Leeds; they informed those at the meeting that they came on purpose to give them notice their frends in Yorkshire would be in armes that night. They went away towards Barnard Castle from the same place: and, the weeke before, on Chris. Dauson came out of Yorkshire upon the same account to Rich. Richardson, of Crosby Garrat. Henry Petty said to the ex[t] last night, that the same night, or the next, the prissoners should be rescued out of the gaole att Apleby.

Dec. 12, 1663. At Applebie, *Thomas Greere* confesseth, that he was at the meetinge at Kaber-rigge the 13th of October, beinge ingaged thither by Captaine Atkinson. He denyeth that he knew any more of the desygne then that they weere to follow Captaine Atkinson, who was to have ledd them that night into Bishopricke;

the whole of the old Presbyterian party. Great names were bandied about as favouring the enterpriso, as Fairfax, Wharton, Manchester, and others. It is probable that they knew nothing of the plot, for, although they could not approve of the measures that were so oppressive to their political opinions and religious creeds, they had too much good sense to involve themselves in a scheme from which no good whatever could result.

Captain Atkinson was of Winton in Westmerland. He was the commander of the garrison in Appleby Castle for the Commonwealth, and forced the townsmen, at the sword's point, to elect a Roundhead mayor. The Wallers were a most respectable family of statesmen.

The depositions will tell their own tale. It will be seen that the Westmerland insurgents were in close communication with their brethren in Yorkshire. The rising would have been a very serious one if it had been properly organized.

but upon Birkey, neare Kaber-rigge, he dismissed them without giveinge them any reasons why he did soe. He saith that he verily beleeiveth that none in this cuntrey, exceptinge Captaine Waller, Serjeant Richardson, Reignalde Fawcett, or Thomas Wharton, can give any cleare account how the desygne was laid or what they aymed at. He saith, that, 2 dayes after he was brought to Appleby, he had there some discourse with Captaine Atkinson, who then tolde him that Collonell Waters was to heade the Yorkeshire men, Generall Browne, Mason, and one Ludlow to leade the Southerne men, and one that lives neare Barnardcastle to heade the Bishopricke. He names these men to be at the meetinge upon Kaber-rigg, Captaine Atkinson, Captaine Waller, Henry Petty, Steven Wetherell, Thomas Fawcett, Yorkeshyremen, and one out of the Barrony; William Goodlad, John Waterson, John Fothergill, John Waller, Steven Bowsfeilde, Nicholas Threlkelde, John Wilkinson, John Smith. He saith that one Robert Wharton, a shoemaker in Kendall, may discover mutch, for that he harde Captaine Atkinson and Reginalde Fawcett severall tymes (of late) make mention of him, and that Thomas Wharton, of Coategill, in Orton parish, was the agent amongst them. Aboute a fortnight before the riseinge was, he had a discourse with Capt. Ro. Atkinson, who told him he had beene at the Wells, in Yorkshire, with one Richardson,* and Richardson had a declaracion drawne, and that severall gentlemen in Yorkshire were joind with Richardson in the busines; and Atkinson said he had severall agents in the county to gaine and gett men to joine with him, and that there was likly to be a risinge, and that one Walter Greathead and Mason † were all in it, and that the randavouse was to be at Northallerton, upon a Monday night the 8th of October. That the riseing was intended against the present government.

Nov. 23, 1663. Before Sir Philip Musgrave and Richard Braithwaite, Esq. *Wm. Goodlad* saith, that they had some designe upon Carlisle, and Captaine Studholme was named as the principall at their meeting at Kabur. That two men came out of Yorkshire and brought orders, both which hee doth suppose to be Quakers, and that their would some thousands of people in London joyne with them, and that in Durham and in Yorkshire weare the most considerable numbers. That hee fynds a very great discontent in the country among the commons against the

---

* A Dr. Richardson, who is several times mentioned as having been one of the inciters of this plot at Harrogate.

† This is the Captain Mason about whom some further information will soon be given.

present government, and the Quakers are ingaged in this designe. That it was discoursed to have Sir P(hilip) M(usgrave)* taken prisoner at Hartley. That they expected declaracions, but the messengers durst not bring them, nor could Capt. Atkinson have those to assist him out of the county of Durham whom he expected, but was ordered to march to them with what forces hee had. If his forces had beene considerable hee intended to have seised upon the excise money which was in the hands of the clarke of the peace at Apleby, but he doth not knowe what persons weare to bee the most eminent commanders.

Dec. 1663. Before Richard Braithwaite, of Warcop, Esq. *William Goodlad* saith, that Capt. Robert Atkinson was to be the commander of the forces he cold rayse heare, and soe was to march to Bishopricke: and had at one meeteinge neentene horse, being the 12th of October, beyond Kaber, called Birkett, wher they parted. And, as the ex^t apprehended, that the said Capt. Atkinson was informed of some disapointment of the assistance he expected, and they was therfore counselled by the said Capt. Atkinson to depart to there severall homes, in regard there was noe hurt done in the country by them, and they parted discontently, himself and one man. The ex^t receaved notice of this meeteinge not before Fryday before by Tho. Coear, of Kerby Steaven, who informed that ther was a designe in hand, and that they wer to march out of the county, and that Capt. Atkinson was to head them, and was in hope of help from Bishoprick and Yorkeshire, and to engage against his Majesty, and was told by him he was in great probability to compass their ends. Henery Petty and himself mett Capt. Atkinson comeing to Smardale Bridge, rideinge a white gray and had a case of pistolls and sword, and above ten with him, some in arms, and beleves as he heard that they were Quakers gave the notice in this country.

William Goodlad saith, that, the Thursday before the meeteinge, he mett with Henry Petty, who told him that Tho. Greare would have this informant to meete Capt. Atkinson on the Monday night followinge at Kabar; and in that night he and Petty went together armed, *videlicet*, this informant had a sword and a pistoll, and Henry Petty had a sword and a case of pistolls, and each on horse backe; and they mett Captaine Atkinson aboute 10 of the clocke in the night at Ravenstondale, nere the Scotch alehouse; that Atkinson gave the word to be " God be with us,"

---

* Sir Philip Musgrave, in whose hand this deposition is written, merely puts the initials of his own name. An autobiography of this noble gentleman was published a few years ago at Carlisle. He was as good a Christian as he was a brave soldier.

and the designe of their riseing in armes was against the present government. It was designed that Yorke and Carlile should be surpris'd, and the loyall gentlemen were to be seis'd and secur'd, and that severall partys out of Yorkeshire and Durham were to joine with those in Westmerland; and ther was a correspondency betweene the party in Yorkeshire and those in Westmerland; that two persons came to Atkinson to give him notice that that night those in Yorkeshire would be up in armes.

Dec. 17, 1663. Before Sir Philip Musgrave. *Thomas Sutton, of Graystocke*, saith, hee is well acquainted with Corporall John Watson, hee haveing scene him a corporall in Oliver's owne troope. The last tyme hee saw him was at Penrith, about 14 dayes before Lammas, and since hath not seene him: and then hee told him hee had beene in Scotland, and at Dumfrees about some bussiness, but would not tell him what. Upon further discourse, said that their should have beene a party in Scotland to have joyned with some in England, and have had a randevow att Darnton, but their designe was discovered, and some of them imprisoned. And being asked how the Scotch should have come inn, hee said they would have brooke inn with about 800 horse and joyned with the English, and that, to the beste of the ex[ts] knowledge, the tyme hee spooke of for this designe should have beene about Yorke sises, but Corporall John Watson denied to have any hand in the bussiness or knew who weare ingaged. Hee said that hee had told this to John Hall at Penrith, and hee hath not heard anything of the late plott untill it was discovered.

William Hodjon saith, that John Watterson, of Great Musgrave, came to him and tould him that he could helpe him to a souldier's place. On Munday night after the said Watterson tould him that 35 of them had beene together that night, but could not gett theire purpose about because Capt. Atkinson would not assist them, and he tould him that for all that befor Martinmas day they hope to here other news; and farther the said John said that Lord Thomas Fairfax was able to raise 3,000 men to assist them, and that he was the cheife adgeint in this designe; and the said John did report that the foot which comes from Portingall was to rise with them, being in number 5,000.

Apr. 20, 1664. Durham. Before Henry Lambton, John Tempest, Wm. Blakiston, Ralph Davison, and Cuthbert Carre, Esqrs. *John Waller,*[*] *now of Durham, late of Mallerston in*

---

[*] The witness, who was the nephew of one of the arch-rebels, had made his escape from Westmerland to Durham. In the spring of 1664 he was recognised there by Robert Hilton, Esq. of Murton, near Appleby, who swears before the Durham magis-

Westmorland, yeoman, saith, hee was acquainted with this designe of rising about 5 weekes before the meeteing at Birka neare Duckintree, not far from Kabar, which was Oct. the 12, 1663. Hee was first acquainted with it by Tho. Wright of Castlewaith in Malterstone, near Pendragon castle, a Quaker, who, meeteing with him by accident, and this ex^t telling him hee was to goe into Yorkeshire, the said Wright told him he knew his busines. Hee, denying it, told him Yes, hee was sure hee knew of a plott in agitacion, and that, before hee could returne, it would bee put into execution. After which, hee goeing his intended journey, hee called at the Well, where his unckle, Capt. Atkinson, then was, and at that tyme one Gorge Rumford was with him, who came as a messenger out of the county of Durham, and, at the first, hee, scrupleous to speake anything in the presence of this ex^t, but being assured by Capt. Atkinson that hee might relie upon his trueth and secresy, hee did then expresse himselfe at large, and told them that the county of Durham was in soe good a position that they could in a nyght's tyme raise 7 or 800 able fighting men, horse and foot, and that they could secure that county, and assist their neighbours with a considerable party, and that hee brought his assurance from John Joblin.* The next night his unckle, Capt. Atkinson, went 7 miles farther to a place within 2 miles of Bradford, where there was a meeteing of severall persons out of divers countreys, and there, as his unckle, Capt. Atkinson, told this examinate, it was resolved there should bee a riseing, which was to have beene about three weekes before the riseing which was elswhere, or they should have tymely notice accordinge. Soe it was deferred till the 12th of October last, when they did meete accordingly at Birka neare Caber, to the number of seventeen, some armed and some not. When the number appeared to bee soe inconsiderable, Capt. Atkinson told them that, since there meeteing did not answere there expectacion, hee thought it best that every man should returne to his owne home, to which some of them appeared very unwilling, protesting they would goe on, and did accordingly march to Birka, where they drew upp and then dissolved; but what was said there hee knowes not, haveing left them. Hee saith hee knowes few of the names of the persons who mett at Birka, and saith that hee beleiveth that Tho. Fothergill of

---

trates that Waller had been very actively engaged in the recent plot, and that he was indicted at the last Westmerland assizes.

* This person was actually the gaoler at Durham. He was imprisoned at York for several years.

Ravenstondale neare Newbiggon can name 8 or 9 in Orton parrish and Ravenstondale, and John Wilkinson can give an account of severall who either did, or had appointed to meete at a house on the topp of a hill neare Appleby uppon the said rebellious designe. Hee saith that hee hath heard Rumford and Capt. Atkinson declare that it was there intention that those who made noe resistance should not bee injured, but those that stood in opposicion to them should all bee putt to the sword. Hee heard Capt. Atkinson say that the Lord Wharton, Lord Fairefax, and the Earle of Manchester were acquainted with this plott, and that hee had assurance that they would joyne with them, and this hee did averr to have from persons that would not deceive him. Hee saith that Tho. Greere told him that one Studham and others in Carlisle had sent word that himselfe, with others that would joyne with him in the garrison there, would declare for them, and that the gates should be throwne open, soe that they should become master of it without bloudshed. Hee saith that there were 2 Quakers whose names hee knowes not, and pretended to be woolemen, who brought assurance from John Joblin aforesaid to Capt. Atkinson, and did likewise acquainte this ex^t that they weere able in the county of Durham, both to doe there owne busines, and assist them in Westmerland with a troop of horse, if it weere needfull, uppon intimacion to bee sent to John Joblin that they stood in need of there assistance.

May 1, 1664. Durham. Before Fr. Bowes, John Heath, and John Tempest, Esqrs. *John Waller*, being further examined, sayth, that he doth remember when he was at the Wells and Harrigate in Yorkeshire, theare were theare at that time three or fower Scottish gentlemen, with their servants, whom he conceived to be driving on the plott theare, which he doth the rather beleive because his uncle, Robert Atkinson, informed him so much, and, as he remembreth, the liveryes were yellowish with a black edging. He saith that, by the discription made of these persons by Mr. George Hume, the present gaoler of Durham, he beleiveth it was Sir Dungan Campbell and some other Scotishmen, who lay severall weekes about the Wells or Harrigate at the same time. He further sayth, that, to the best of his knowledge, and by the discription given to this ex^t of him, one John Ward was one of the partyes who came in the habit of a woolman to his uncle Robert Atkinson in Mallerstang, together with his companion, being both imployed by John Jopling, late gaoler of Durham, and some other his associates (whom he knoweth not) as they affermed; who did assure that they were all in a readiness to rise in armes; and that, if Westmerland did stand in need of assistance, John Jopling, upon notice to be given to him, would send them a party of horse. And further, that the time appointed for the rising did stand. He saith that, if he be confronted with the said John Ward, he shall be able positively to say whether he were one of the persons imployed in the message. He further sayth, that, about 3 weekes before the 12th of October last, one Robert Waller, who was this ex^{ts} uncle, and since executed at Appleby, as hee hath heard, did desire him to come into the bishoprick of Durham with a message to John Jopling, who had bin the gaoler at Durham under the late usurped powers; and, that he might have creditt with the said Jopling, the said Robert Waller gave him a word or signall, which, as he remembreth, was "God with us," and did withall assure him that upon that word or signall he should have full credence.

The effect of the message was that he the said Jopling should send them a party or troope of horse, according to a former promise that he had made them to that purpose, but this ex^t refused to take upon him that imployment. And about the same time theare came a messinger to them out of Yorkeshire signifying that the rising then designed was putt of untill the 12th of October. He further sayth that his uncle, commonly called Captaine Atkinson, tould this ex^{te} that what passed amongst them in this designe was not put into writing, and that they did manage all their intelligens by messingers, who gave account of their intentions by word of mouth; and that they did never intrust any of these things to letters. He further sayth, that the sayd Captaine Atkinson tould him that they had assurances that a considerable part of the trayned bands in the West Riding in Yorkeshire would joyne with them in their rebellious designe, and that he had this assurance from those that would not give him a wrong information, which he beleiveth were Atkinson the hosyer and others that did sitt in councell upon the late plott within two or three miles of Bradford. And having thus farr unburdned his conscience, and declared the uttmost of his knowledge, he doth earnestly profess that if he knew any thing further he would declare it, although with the certayn loss of his owne life, and ruine of his nearest relations; and if anything hearafter shall come to his memory, which at the present he can not recollect, he shall not fayle to make a just and perfect relation of it. Being asked concerning a letter now shewed unto him, he sayth that he doth acknowledge it to be his hand, but doth protest in the presence of God that it was not with an intention to send it to any man, theare being none such at Richmond, or any other place, as it is directed unto; and that he writt it meerly as scribling what came into his fancy by accident, without designe; and that it hath nothing of private meaning more than what he hath already declared. And if it shall appeare to be otherwaies he shall willingly and readily submitt himselfe to the severest punishments of the law, and expect nothing of his Majesty's mercy, in which he doth now wholy rely. He further sayth, that the person who went by the name of Docter Richardson, if he could be taken, can give the most perfect account of the whole transaction of this business; and that he hath heard his uncle Atkinson say that the said Richardson had the declaration in which were sett downe the grounds and reasons of their rising within a quarter of an hower before he was apprehended by the order of the high sheriff of Yorkeshire, and that he had layd it out of his pockett by accident within that short space before he was taken.

July 1, 1664. Before Sir Philip Musgrave, &c., at Penrith. *Joseph Adamson, jun., of Crosthwaite, co. Cumberland, yeo.*, sayth, that John Walker, of Litle Braithwaite, taylor, did, aboute the 20th of Jan. last past, at Samuel Radclife's, in Keswicke, say to this informant, that John Studdart, his maister, and hee, did fix and dresse foure case of pistols, six swords, and twentie fire lockes the Fryday next before the day of the last plott; and that night his sayd maister heareing some company about the house, caused him to looke forth of a windowe, to see what company they weare; where he saw aboute fifteen horse of the persons his master expected, three of which the sayd Walker lett in to the house of his sayd maister, of which Thomas Williamson, of Naddall, was the first, who then sayd "Now or never!" and which company the sayd John Studdartt did then furnish with armes. About a weeke after the tyme the last plott should have beene, this informant being at James Bowes' smithy in Portinshaile, one John Beebey (a servant to the sayd John Studdartt) brought thither two muskett-barrells, which hee caused the sayd smith to make into two gavelockes; and when the smith was makeing of the same, the one of them (being charged) went of, and shott a brace of bulletts.

CXVI. RALPH ROBINSON. FOR HIGH TREASON.

Oct. 23, 1663. Before Sir James Pennyman, Kt., deputy lieutenant. *Ralph Robinson, of Cockerton,** sayeth, that he with

* A deposition which throws some light upon the intended rising in the county of

divers others, both Presbiters and Anabaptists, were to rise in armes on Tuesday the 13th of this month, and to meete upon Woodam Moore, in Bishopbrigg, by 7 of the clock in the mornyng, and that one Jones was to commannd the Bishopbrigg horse, whose wife . . . . London. And he, farther, sayeth he saw the sayd Jones about 7 weekes since att Great Ackley, in Bishopbrigg, who then told him the rising was to be through England: that their pretence was to pull downe all prisons, quitt all taxes, and sett upp liberty of conscience. He further sayeth, that Theodore Parkinson was ingaged in the plott, and that when the officers tooke him att Yarme, he was comyng to him, being att Battersby, to gett him along with him to the place of meeting, and that the sayd Parkinson was to be a trooper in the busines, and that they were all to be horse and dragoones. He sayth he knew nothing of the day of rising till the sayd Parkinson sent him word from Stoxley by one Tho. Randall, a Quaker, living at Cockerton, that it was to be on the 13th. He sayth that William Carter, living at or neere Appleton, was to be a capt. of horse amongst the plotters. He sayeth that John Robinson, of Woorsall, and Wm. Massam, of Farnaby, were likewise ingaged, and that Chr. Whitton, of Little Ayton, was to be a trooper. He sayeth that one Lassells, living neere Osmotherley, was ingaged, and beleeves it is the same Capt. Lassells who lives att Mountgrace. He sayth one Major Scarth, living in Cumberland, was ingaged. The forenamed Jones gave him informacion of all the forenamed persons. He confesseth himself was to be a trooper amongst the plotters, and hath knowen of the intented rising this tenne weeks. The sayd Jones tould him there was to be a collection amongst the Presbiters and Anabaptists to pay what souldiers that (they) could rayse.

CXVII. WILLIAM ASKWITH, &C.   FOR HIGH TREASON.

Oct. 28, 1663. *William Hage, of Woodchurch, husbandman,** saith, that, on Monday the 12th of October last, he mett William Askwith, alias Sparlinge, aboute 8 of the clocke at night, nere Howley parke, and he did confesse that he and Wm. Tolson had

---

Durham, or the Bishopric, as it was very frequently called. Mr. Surtees gives an account of the Muggleswick plot, which was identical with those at Kaber and Farneley Wood. Robinson and Parkinson were kept in prison at York for many years.

* A deposition relating to the Farneley Wood plot, of which there is a full account in Dr. Whitaker's Loidis and Elmete. Sparling was a prisoner in York Castle for a long time, but escaped the gallows.

beene in the parke to search for two horses of Sir Richard Tankerd's, and that they did intend to have rise with Captaine Thomas Oates. Aboute two dayes after this informant apprehended him upon the late plott, and he told this informant that on the night after they parted he went to Morley to Oates his house, that Oates was gone to Farneley wood, and beinge too late to goe he returned home againe And one Samuell Ellis did confesse to this informant that he went to Morley to be a trumpiter to a troope of horse under Capt. Oates, and had the Lord Castleton's trumpett with him.

John Aryard saith, that he apprehended John Faweer for the late plott, and he did confesse that he was in armes in Farneley wood with Captaine Oates and others, to the number of 25 persons or thereabouts.

CXVIII. DOROTHY STRANGER. FOR WITCHCRAFT.

Nov. 10, 1663. Before Sir James Clavering, Bart., Mayor of Newcastle. *Jane, wife of Wm. Milburne, of Newcastle,** sayth, that, aboute a month agoe, shee sent her maid to one Daniell Strangers, of this towne, cooper, to gett some caskes cooped; and, when her servant came there, Dorothy, his wife, did say to her, "Whatt was the reason that your dame did not invite her to the weding supper?" And further said, that she would make her repent itt, and deare to her. This informant sayth that Fryday gone a seaven night, aboute 8 o'clock att night, she being alone and in chamber, there appeared to her something in the perfect similitude and shape of a catt. And the said catt did leape at her face, and did vocally speake with a very audible voyce, and said, that itt had gotten the life of one in this howse, and came for this informer life, and would have itt before Saturday night. To which she replyed, "I defye the, the devill and all his works." Upon which the catt did vanish. And upon Saturday last, aboute 8 of the clock in the morneing, she goeing downe to the seller for to draw a quart of beare, and opening the seller dore, which was locked, she visibly did see the said Dorothy Stranger standing in the seller, leaneing with her armes upon one of the hodgheads, and said then to this informer, "Theafe, art thow there yett? thy life I seeke, thy life I will have:" and had a small rope in her hand and did attemp to putt it over her head aboute her neck, but she

---

* The deposition of a weak deluded woman in Newcastle, who imagined that she had been bewitched. It is strange that any magistrate should write down such ridiculous evidence.

did hinder her with her hands. Further, she did take upp a quart pott, and demanded a drinke, butt she would give her none. Whereupon the said Dorothy said that she would make her rue itt. To which this informer replyed that she defyed her and all her disciples. And Stranger answered againe, "Although thow be strong in faith, Ile overcome itt att the last." Upon Sunday last aboute one of the clocke, this informer putting on her clothes in her chamber to goe to church, there did appeare to her a catt of the same shape as the former, and did leape att her throat, and said, "Theafe, I'le not overcome ye as yett." To which this informer replyed, " I hope in God nor never shall." And the said catt did bite her arme, and did hold itt very fast, and made a great impression in her arme with her teeth, and did lett her hold goe and disappeared. And yesterday, in the afternoone, aboute 2 of the clock, this informer comeing downe the stares, the said catt did violently leape aboute her neck and shoulders, and was soe ponderous that she was not able to support itt, but did bring her downe to the ground, and kept her downe for the space of a quarter of an howre. And was soe infirme and disenabled that the power of both body and tongue were taken from her. And the last night, aboute 9 of the clock, this informer being in bedd with her husband, the said Dorothy did in her perfect forme appeare to her, and tooke hold of the bed clothes and endevored to powle them of, but could not. And then and there the said Stranger tooke hold of her arme and pulled her, and would have pulld her out of bed if her husband had not held her fast, and did nip and bite her armes very sore, and tormented her body soe intollerably that she could nott rest all the night, and was like to teare her very heart in peeces, and this morneing left her. And this informer veryly beleives that the said catt which appeared to her was Dorothy Stranger, and non else. And she haveing a desire to see her did this morneing send for the said Dorothy, butt she was very loth to come, and comeing to her she gott blood of her, at the said Stranger's desire, and since hath been pritye well.

8 Aug. 1664. *Re-examined.* She sayth, that after she had gotton blood she was in very good condicon, and was not molested for a quarter of one yeare. And aboute the 16th of January, being in bedd with her husband, aboute one of the clock in the morneing, the said Dorothy Stranger, in her owne shape, appeared to this informer in the roome where she was lyeing, the dores being all lock fast, and said to her, " Jane, Jane, art thou awaken?" She replyed, " Yes." Upon which the said Stranger answered, " I am come here to aske of the forgiveness for the

wrong I have done the, and if thow will never troble me for whatt I have formerly done to the, I doe promisse never to molest or troble the as long as thow lives." Upon the speakeing of which words she did vanish away. Aboute a month before she appeared as aforesaid, this informer being sitting alone in her howse, in a roome two storey high, there did then violently come rushing in att one of the paines of the window a grey catt. And itt did transforme ittselfe into the shape of the said Dorothy Stranger, in the habitt and clothes she weares dayly, haveing an old black hatt upon her head, a greene waistcoate, and a brownish coloured petticoate. And she said, "Thou gott blood of me, but I will have blood of thee before I goe." And she did flye violentlye upon this informer, and did cutt her over the joynts of the little finger of both her hands, and did scratch her and gott blood. And havinge a black handercheife aboute her necke, she did take itt away, and never see the same since, and did then vanish away.

Eliz. Stranger, widow, sayth, that, aboute six or seaven yeares agoe, her daughter Jane, then wife to Oswald Milburne, baker and brewer, being in the Sandhill, did meete with Dorothy Stranger, who said to her, "Thou shalt never see the Sandhill againe." And comeing home imediatly she fell sick and lanwished above ½ a yeare and dyed. And in her sicknes tooke very sad and lamentable fitts, and did cry out most hydeously, saying, "Ah, that witch-theafe, my aut Dorothy, is like to pull out my heart. Doe not yow see her? Doe not yow see her, my aut Dorothy that witch?" And did to her very last howre cry out of the said Dorothy Stranger.

CXIX. WILLIAM DAY. FOR TREASON.

Nov. 21, 1663. *George Knowles, of Skipton*, sayth, that, on 29th October, comeing from Kighley in the way towards Skipton, he mett with one William Day,[*] of Skipton, sometime a souldier against his Majestie, at Steeton brow foote. And the saide Daye, laughinge and jeeringe, said that he knew well such and such men weare plotters in the late plott, but he wold be hanged before he wold discover them.

---

[*] Another witness says that Day "had formerly beene a trumpeter in the Kinge's armie, and afterwardes a trooper in Lambert's regiment, and a violent person."

CXX. HENRY HANSON. FOR HIGH TREASON.

Dec. 19, 1663. Before Cuthbert Wade, Esq. *Chr. Hodgson, of Gargrave, gentleman,** saith, that haveinge formerly lived in Broughton, where one Mr. Henry Hanson dwelleth, and beinge verie intimately acquainted with him, the said Hanson did severall times acquaint this informant that there was a greate plott or a designe on foote or in agitacion, and said that this designe was for the good of the Commonwealth, for the takeinge awaye of excise, harth-money, and other taxes. And severall times did aske this informer if he would be or weare willinge to joyne with them (sayeinge himselfe was one had promised to make one in the same designe,) to take upp armes with them; and he never mett him betweene Midsomer and Michaelmas last past, but the said Hanson did aske him if he weare resolved to goe on with him in the said designe. And the said Hanson told him that one Colonell Ludley was to heade that partie, or to be cheefe, and that one Atkinson, a stockiner, was cheefe intelligencer in these parts too and from the said Ludley, and that there was a partie in the dales to rise for the carrying on of the said plott, which Atkinson was to head, and one Iveson, his neighbor in Broughton, and formerly a servant to one quarter-maister Shrigley, wold be one, and he thought there wold be a very considerable partie in Craven willinge to joyne.

Richard Allan saith, that on the 13th of October last he inquired at Hanson's house whether he was at home or not, and his wife, cominge to the dore, said "What is your businesse with him?" This informent did answer, to knowe if they were all well, and then he demanded a delivery of what armes there were in the house. But she replyed she dirst not deliver them, and said that her husband had not beene at home of two nights before, and there were sixe score persons in number combined together, and she was affraid her husband was amongst them, and if he came home she desired that his master, Mr. Justice Drake, would use some meanes to secure him.

CXXI. JAMES PARKER. FOR SEDITIOUS WORDS.

A true bill against James Parker, of Rodwell, yeo., for saying,

---

* Another deposition relating to the Yorkshire plot. A Craven gentleman is implicated in it. He was in prison for some time, and was bound over to keep the peace.

on Nov. 18, 1663, "I served Oliver * seaven yeares as a souldier, and if any one will put up the finger on the accompt that Oliver did ingage, I will doe as much as I have done. As for the Kinge I am not beholdinge to him. I care not a fart for him."

CXXII. JEREMY BOOTH AND OTHERS. FOR TREASON.

Dec. 26, 1663. Before Walter Hawksworth, Esq. *Joshua Wilkes, of Bradford, blacksmith*, saith, that, on the 12 of October last, one Jeremy Booth, of Bradford, blacksmith, tould this ex^t that that night there would bee a riseing,† and that some persons weere to meet for that purpose in a close in Maningham called Tong lands, and that one John Lowcock, of Bradford, sadler, was to bee a leivetenant or some other officer, and that Henry Bradshaw, of Maningham, should bee a captain, and that Mr. Waterhowse, of Bradford, was to sett out a horse, and Richard Walker, of the same, was to sett out another.

Jeremy Booth, of Bradford, blacksmith, saith, that upon the 12th of October last, one John Lowcock, of Bradford aforesaid, sadler, tould this ex^t that there would bee that night a riseing in the country, and that severall persons fitted for that purpose weere to meet him in Maningham neare to Henry Bradshaw's howse there that night, and that the said Lowcock was to bee a quarter

---

* The prisoner was acquitted at the assizes. The misrule and the many vices of Charles II. made the people contrast his government very frequently with that of Cromwell. The Dissenters could not but remember the Protector, or Oliver, as he was familiarly called. It was long before this feeling was extinguished. In July, 1667, Pepys notes down in his Diary, "It is strange how everybody do now-a-days reflect upon Oliver, and commend him, what brave things he did, and made all the neighbour princes fear him; while here a prince, come in with all the love and prayers and good liking of his people, who have given greater signs of loyalty and willingness to serve him with their estates than ever was done by any people, hath lost all so soon."
On Nov. 30, 1663, John Meynel, of Thornaby, gen. deposed before Sir James Pennyman "that one John Lascells, of Little Syddell, in the parish of East Harsley, did, about March last, say that the Parliament that tooke away the King's life was legall and just, and did say to him in October last that he should see a sudden alteracion of of this present government, and that very speedily. And the wife of the said Lascells did say that the King's court was noe better than a bawdie house."
The Lascelles were engaged in the Farneley Wood plot.
Dec. 14, 1663. Arthur Shafto, of Newcastle-on-Tyne, smith, and Mungo Kell, keelman, heard, at Stella, one Edward Cuthbert say to Kell, "If thou and the King were both haugd, it would been good for the Commonweal. And he would warrant him before the best law in England."
† A deposition which shews that there were men in Bradford who were implicated in the Farneley Wood plot. That town has been already connected with it, and it is evident that the spirit of disaffection pervaded a great part of the West Riding.

master in that busines, and that the said Henry Bradshaw was to bee a captain; and that the said Lowcock had beene three nights ryding abroad about that busines, and that one William Swayne, smith, of Bradford, did lend him his mare for that service; and, further saith, that the said Lowcock further tould this ex^t that Richard Walker, of Bradford, mercer, was to sett forth a horse for that service, and that one Dawson should ryde him, and Mr. Jonas Waterhouse another, and the said William Swayne another; and saith that this ex^t askeing him, the said Lowcock, how they would doe for armes and amuniccon, hee answered they should have enough, and the said Walker would furnish them with powder. And this ex^t further saith that in the evening . . . . . one John Wilkinson, of Bradford, cloathdresser, came to this ex^t, and then tould him that hee had then beene at the howse of one Hugh Sawley, in Bradford, and that there hee had then beene with the said Henry Bradshaw, and that there was in company with him one John Kitchin, of Bradford, commonly called trooper Kitchin, and his wife, and that the said Bradshaw then offered the said Wilkinson a horse to ryde, if hee would goe to the intended riseing, and at the same tyme, likewise, another upon the same tearmes to the said Kitchen; but the said Wilkinson then tould this ex^t that the said Kitchin's wyfe replyed that her husband should not goe unles the said Bradshaw went himself, and further saith that at the tyme aforesaid the said Wilkinson further tould this ex^t that the horses which weere soe offered by Bradshaw to Wilkinson and Kitchin weere then at the said Hugh Sawley's, and that the hostler, Christopher Bawden, there should helpe them to them; and the said Wilkinson did likewise tell this ex^t that the said Bradshaw had said, that if hee had not had occacion to meet Major Gr. . . . head hee would first have secured Mr. John Weddall, Mr. Tho. Wood, and Jeremy Bower, if they had beene then at home, and then have gone along with them, meaning the said Kitchin and Wilkinson.

CXXIII. GEORGE PARKIN. FOR SEDITIOUS WORDS.

Jan. 19, 1663-4. Before Sir Francis Fane, K.B., Sir Tho. Osburne, Bt., Sir Godfrey Copley, Bt., Sir John Dawney, Kt., Sir Ralph Knight, Kt., John Wentworth, Roger Portington, Wm. Adams, Thos. Yarbrough, and Wm. Spencer, Esqrs., at the Doncaster Sessions.

William Jackson, of Attercliffe, joyner, sayth, that, the Tuesday before Whitsunday last, John Dixon was leaneing in his shopp window, and George Parkin,* of Attercliffe, a knife-maker, came, and when Dixon saw him come, hee went away, and Parkin said, "John Dixon will not stay if hee see me come." To whome the informer said, "You must bee civill, for hee is an honest poore man and the King's servant." To whom Parkin answered, "A Kinge! wee were better without a King then with one, for though wee have a Kinge, the old block remaines still; for hee first sent to see what wee would give him, then hee sent for money for our heades, and lastly, for sesements, soe hee intends to send soe long, till hee make us all beggers like to himselfe." And upon Tuesday, being the 15th of October last, hee further said that there would come a change ere long, and then hee would bannish both the informer and all his like, kebbs as they were. And, on the first of October last, hee said, "Now the trayned bands are raysed; but before the twelve month's end wee shall see Kinge Charles his head in a pooke, as his father's was."

CXXIV. JOHN LYLEY. FOR SEDITIOUS WORDS.

March 21, 1663-4. Before Walter Calverley, Esq. *Rosamond, wife of Jeremy Bower, of Bradford,† habberdasher*, says that, on the 16th of March, one John Lyley of Bradford came unto her house, and, after some discourse had with her about her husband's carrying of him to Yorke before the last goale delivery, the said Lyley questioned her what authority her husband had to carry him to Yorke. To which the said Rosamond replyed that her husband had an order to show for what he did therein. And the said Lyley said to her, "Your husband sought my life, or he would have my head upon the toll-booth of Bradford, but if his head went, more should goe with it." And he said that he had had her husband's life forty tymes offered him, and he could have hanged him when he would. And she replyed, he would not have suffered unles he went contrary to the law and government, but some had suffered unjustly, for the late King had soe suffered. Whereupon he said, "Will you say soe? (repeating the words 3 tymes). He suffered justly, and had a fair tryall, and just witnesses; but soe had not they," meaning (as the informant conceived) the persons that

* The accused was acquitted at the assizes. He had made use of violent language, but there is some sense in a portion of what he said.

† The wife of a person who seems to have played the part of a constable and an informer at Bradford, has a story to tell against a poor man who had been in trouble in 1663. She evidently tries to draw him out, and then lays an information against him. It is most unfortunate that justice should be obliged to make use of such disreputable tools.

were condemned att the last goale delivery att Yorke; whome he had formerly called upon that discourse Martyres, and said foure tymes as much blood would be required att the hands of the unrighteous. And further said, "Did not the late King and Earle of Strafford bring all this trouble upon the land? and wee were too hasty before, but within this halfe yeare they should see more then they had scene before."

CXXV. WILLIAM HURD.   FOR SEDITIOUS WORDS.

March 21, 1663-4. Before Edward Elwick, Lord Mayor of York. *Elizabeth Wall, servant to the Lord Fairfax, of Appleton,* saith, that a little before the tyme that the Duke of Buckingham came last into Yorkeshire, one Wm. Hurd came into the daryhouse at Nunappleton, and told this informant that he heard of a plott,* and that there would be some rising, or words to that effect, if they thought they might have my Lord's assistance. To which this informant made answere that she knew both my Lord and my Lady did abominate such things. And thereupon, at the same tyme, to the best of her remembrance, the said William Hurd told her that Edward Bolland was to come to my Lord Fairfax: howbeit she doth not know or beleeve that the said Edward Bolland hath beene with my Lord Fairfaxe since that tyme.

CXXVI. A LIST OF YORKSHIRE RECUSANTS.

March 25, 1664. Indicted at the Assizes for not coming to church. *Seacroft.*† Alice Mallison, sp^r, Thomas Deardon. *Seacroft.* John Ryther, sen., gen., John Ryther, jun., and Mary his wife. *Roundhay.* Wm. Huby. *Barwicke.* Sir Stephen Tempest, kt., and Anne his wife, Thomas and William Hardwick, Francis

---

* A deposition which throws some light upon Lord Fairfax's conduct during the Yorkshire rising. The insurgents, some of whom had fought with him during the wars, looked to him for countenance and aid, especially as in his religious views he had a strong leaning towards their own opinions. They were, however, disappointed. Fairfax had become disgusted with the party that he served, and he never approved of the excesses into which it ran. He was vehemently opposed to the death of the King. At his trial Lady Fairfax boldly cried out that he was too honest to be there. He permitted Monk to enter England; and now, in 1663, when it was expected that he would have supported the insurgents, his maid-servant answered very truly for him that her Lord and her Lady abominated such things.

† A summary of the lists of Nonconformists that were prepared by the village constables and forwarded to York. These lists, of which several will be given, are of great value. They are put together, it will be seen, in the most capricious manner, with no order as to districts.

Johnson, Mary Clerkeson, George Clerkeson, Wm. Huby, Wm. Smith. *Whorleton in Cleveland.* Wm. Huddleston, Eliz. wife of Richard Harker, Ellen wife of James Wetherell, Wm. Sloman, Wm. Robinson and Jane his wife, James Runinge and Susanna his wife. *Maltby.* James Lownsdale and Mary his wife, Laur. Wright and Jane his wife, Wm. Browne and Anne his wife. *Stokesley.* Sir Richard Foster, Bt., and Clare his wife, Mary Metcalfe, widow, Chr. Lowicke, Lucretia Lowicke, widow, Robert Lowicke and Mary his wife, James Kirby and Margaret his wife, Richard Wilkinson and Anne his wife, Richard Garbut and Elizabeth his wife, Stephen Wilkinson and Merial his wife, John Thomson and Katherine his wife, John Dobson and Margaret his wife. *Hilton.* Anthony Dawson, gen., Stephen and Wm. Tiplady, Michael Walker and Anne his wife, George Walker and Anne his wife, Margaret Grayson, widow, Everel Ingledew, widow, Everel Johnson, spinster, George Butler and Elizabeth his wife, Robert Bare, Thomas Marwood. *Seamer.* George Harrison and Ellen his wife, Margaret Cotham, spinster. *Busby.* John Banckes, sen., Chr. Banckes and Jane his wife, Jane Bird, spinster, John Banckes, jun., and Elizabeth his wife, John Banckes, Joan Banckes, spinster, Robert Young, Ellen Barwicke, spinster. *Kirby.* Elizabeth Jackson, spinster, Robert Simson, laborer, and Dorothy his wife, Wm. Rountree. *Hutton Rudby.* John Billerby, Oliver Nicholson and Merrill his wife, Katherine Chapman, spinster, Mary, wife of Thomas Coulson, Ann Stainthrop, widow, Margaret Stockton, spinster, Thomas Appleton, Mary Appleton, widow, Wm. Parker, Mabell wife of Wm. Sayer, Ann wife of Robert Thomson, Thomas Young and Ann his wife, John Errington and Mary his wife, Michael Errington, Jane Thomson, spinster, Ursula Slinnan, spinster, Anthony Craggs and Eliz. his wife, Thomas Hunter and Jane his wife, Susanna wife of John Sayer, Thomas Bullisie and Margaret his wife, Stephen Chapman and Frances his wife, Francis Ripley and Elizabeth his wife, Mary Burden, spinster. *Ayton Parva.* Wm. Calvert and Isabel his wife. *Holme Beacon.* Edward Clarke, Thomas Leavening and Emett his wife, Robert Smith and Margaret his wife, Richard Smith, John Alleyn and Alice his wife, Frances and Ann Fox, spinsters, Thomas Smith, Ann Marshall, spinster, Ann wife of Robert Leavening, Thomas and Stephen Horseman, Robert Nicholson. *Holme-in-Spaldingmore.* Mary Blackburne, spinster, Grace Rushton, spinster, Thomas Dolman, gen., Ellen Man, widow, Anthony Man. *Shipton.* Edward Wilberfosse and Frances his wife, James Stephenson, Frances Stephenson, widow, Ann Wood, spinster, Robert Aislaby, Robert

Appleton, George Thorley, Ann Musgrave, spinster, Barbara Aislaby, spinster, Thomas Hessey and Margaret his wife, Isabel Wood, widow, John Wood, Richard Spicer and Mary his wife, Barbara Rash, spinster. *Bubwith.* Margaret Beilby, spinster, Averil Raby, widow, Ann wife of Wm. Barton, sen., Mark Starke and Jane his wife, Mary Grisedale, widow, Thomas Barker, Peter Vavasour, John Thorpe and Eliz. his wife, Mary Steed, spinster, Eliz. wife of Ralph Smith, Margaret Hebden, spinster, Isabel wife of Rowland Gardum, George Holborne. *Melborne cum Storthwaite.* Robert Butler, Barnard Pickering and Mary his wife, Thomas Browne and Barbara his wife, Ellen Mitchinton, widow, Jane Blanshard, spinster, Margaret Webster, spinster, Thomas Blanshard, sen., Margaret wife of Robert Blanshard, Thomas Blanshard, jun. *Newsham.* David Pickering and Katharine his wife. *Aughton.* George Buttell and Mary his wife. *Skipsey.* Thos. and Wm. Rich, Jane Rich, spinster, John Becke, Mary Becke, spinster, Mary Pilkington, spinster, John Pilkington, Ann Pilkington, spinster, Thomas Thompson, Ann Stabler, spinster. *Ulrom.* Robert Lenge, John Lenge, Jane Lenge, spinster, John Ramshaw and Ann his wife, Richard Lenge, Wm. Stringer and Ann his wife, John Hudson and Ann his wife, Henry Childe, James Cooke and Margaret his wife. *Lelley.* John Eppenall and Mary his wife, Wm. Yeates and Jane his wife, John Yeates, John Sampson, Richard Appleton and Mary his wife, Ralph Balke, Eliz. Hart, spinster, Robert Gibson, Wm. Thorpe, jun., Joseph Fewson, Henry Johnson, John Thorpe, jun., Thomas Gargill and Rebecca his wife. *Ganstead.* Ann Constable, spinster, Thomas Constable, Barbara Mascon, spinster, Ann, Eliz. and Ann Burne, spinsters. *Sprotley.* Nicholas Pearson and Bridgit his wife. *South Skirley.* John Hunt and Barbara his wife, David Thewson and Anne his wife. *Waghen, alias Waune.* Robert Hardy, Thomas Clarkeson, Wm. England. *Flinton.* Marmaduke Maske and his wife, John Ellis, Robert Collison, Chr. Turner. *Elsternwicke and Danthorpe.* John Thorpe and Jane his wife, Henry Hedney and Margaret his wife, Wm. Young and Mary his wife. *West Newton, Burton, and Tanston.* George Seaton and his wife, John Hobson and his wife, Thomas Kilpin, Ann Sprotts, spinster. *Humbleton.* John Sherefon and Frances his wife, Wm. and Robert Parkin, Eliz. Hansley, spinster, Ann wife of Peter Binckes, Prudence and Margaret Wilson, spinsters. *Fitling.* Michael Morton and Katharine his wife, Henry Young. *Withernesey.* Daniel Hardy, Sarah Hardy, widow, Richard Hardy and his wife, Thomas Joy and Alice his wife, Thomas Ashborne. *Ryall and Camerton.* Thomas Calvert and his wife, Margaret Calvert, spinster, James Sumner and Frances his wife. *Puttrington.*

Eliza Toman, spinster, Thomas Standfield, Patricke Gibson and his wife, Wm. Plossum, Wm. Cocke. *Burstwicke.* Ralph Kirton and his wife, Leonard Metcalfe and his wife, Marm. Baxter and his wife, Philip Tuadon, Ann Jennison, and Ellinor Levit, spinsters, Robert Johnson and his wife. *Ottringham.* John Johnson and Mary his wife, Thomas Rosse and Jane his wife, Eliz. Tennison, spinster, Ralph Tennison, Richard Hancocke, Reuben Hancocke, Eliz. Hancocke, spinster, Robert Adam and Ann his wife, Wm. Nicholson, George Craw and Margaret his wife. *Halsam.* Wm. Owst and Secily his wife, Henry Stead and Margaret his wife, Robert Owst and Isabel his wife, Anthony Audas, Ursula Audas, spinster, Robert Owst and Anne his wife, Robert Owst and Mary his wife, Francis Thornely, John Dinnis and Alice his wife, Eliz. Norton, spinster. *Holleym.* Gabriel Tomlinson, Margaret and Isabella Tomlinson, spinsters, Wm. Witwan, Eliz. Kitching, spinster, Robert Wood and Ann his wife, James Walker and his wife, Peter Johnson and his wife. *Boulton Bart.* Isabel wife of Richard Blanshard, Mary Hargill, widow. *Wilberfosse.* Joan wife of Robert Wright, Mary and Dorothy Wright, spinsters. *Newton.* Mary wife of Richard Bovill. *Barneby.* Frances wife of George Tenney, John Wilson and Eliz. his wife, George Dewsbury and Anne his wife. *Austbers (sic).* Robert Dolman and his wife, Ellen Oglethorpe, spinster, John Dolman and Ann his wife, Mary Langley spinster. *Wressell.* Eliz. Brunton and Mary Thistlewood, spinsters. *Goodmadam.* James Noble. *Cottingwith.* Mary Milner, spinster. *Gristropp.* John Vavasour and Julian his wife, Wm. Young and his wife, Isabel Story, spinster, John Story. *Ilton cum Pottoe.* Robert, Thomas, and John Ward, Ann and Elizabeth Ward, spinsters, Richard King and Elizabeth his wife, Richard Handley. *Swinton cum Warthermuske.* Anthony Adamson, Henry Adamson and Eliz. his wife, George Jackson and Frances his wife, Symon Pickersgill and Mary his wife, Wm. Smith and Alice his wife, John Smith and Alice his wife, Ann Thwaites, spinster. *Massam.* Jane Bridgewater, widow. *Ellington.* Wm. Thwaite, Wm. Body, spinster. *Ellingstring.* Jane Smorthwaite, spinster. *Fearby.* Edward Ryley and Isabel his wife, John Ryley. *Healey cum Sutton.* Anthony Wade and Jane his wife, Francis Wade. *Burton super Ure.* Roger Beckwith, Esq., Isabel Beckwith, spinster. *Beedall.* Marmaduke Grannge, Richard Pearson and his wife, Ralph Grannge and his wife, Mathew Ingleton and his wife, Wm. Lodge and his wife, Sara Smeaton, spinster, Chr. Lodge and his wife, Thomas Lodge, Bridget Stanley, spinster, George Petch and his wife, Eliz. Wilson, spinster, George Pearson and his wife. *Welmarch.* Robert Lumley and Alice his wife. *Thorneton Watlas.* Ann Williamson, spinster. *Rookewith cum Therne and Clifton.* John Wray and Eliz. his wife. *Catfosse.* Richard Woodell. *Upton, Dringoe, and Brough..* Thomas Nayler and Ann his wife. *Beeforth.* Leonard Browne, Jane Browne, George Ditch and Margaret his wife, Peter Seller and his wife, Thomas Sellar. *Hornesey cum Burton.* Alice Acklam, spinster, Jane Thorpe, spinster, John Centleman, Prescilla Newsam, spinster, Oliver Richadge and Margaret his wife, Wm. Lister and his wife, Robert Lamplough and Jane his wife, Ann wife of Thomas Acklam. *Arnold, Ruston, and North Skirley.* Thomas Thorpe and Dorothy his wife, George Gibson and Mary his wife. *Brandsburton.* Nicholas Watkin and Alice his wife, Katharine wife of John Fenby. *Hatfeild.* Hugh Bagley and Mercy his wife. *Bewhall super Nunkeeling.* John Raley and Ann his wife, Wm. Mitchell and Alice his wife, Joseph Mitchell, Margaret Mitchell, spinster, Ursula wife of Thomas Graunge, George Acklam, sen., and Eliz. his wife, George Acklam, jun., and Margaret his wife, Sarah Acklam, spinster, Peter Fusley and his wife, Secily Weeke, widow, John Walker and Dorothy his wife, Matthew Pearson, Ann Peirson, spinster. *North Froddingham,* Ralph Slater and Mary his wife, Wm. Jarrat, John Sugden. *Colden.* Edward Collinson, Wm. Royce, Robert Burill. *Siglesthorne.* Margaret Blashell, spinster. *Barmiston.* John Watson and Anne his wife, Matthew Watson, John Winter, Dorothy Gibson, spinster. *Withernwicke.* Mary Jackson, spinster. *Hempholme, Hayholme, and Halletrome.* Francis Fisher and his wife, John Fisher. *Seaton.* George Smith, John Menpast, Anne Welborne, spinster, Mary Gartham, spinster.

CXXVII. THOMAS ROWNTHWAITE. FOR SACRILEGE.

A true bill against Thomas Rownthwaite, of Studley Roger, labourer, for that he on 23 April, 1664, " capellam * apud Studley Roger fregit," and carried from it two waine loades of stones, and one waine loade of timber, ad valorem 40s.

---

* One of the many chapels in the neighbourhood of Fountains Abbey. All traces of it are now gone, and the very site is unknown. There were two other indictments preferred against Rownthwaite: viz., for breaking into the close of Wm. Ullithorne, and assaulting him. He was bound over to keep the peace.

In 1666 Wm. Walsh of Altofts and eleven others were charged with breaking into the chapel at Shadwell, and were bound over to keep the peace.

CXXVIII. ROBERT THORNBURROW.   FOR SEDITIOUS WORDS.

June 6, 1664. Before Edw. Nevinson, Esq. *John Hewatson*, saith, that Robert Thornburrow, of Woodend, and he, beinge at some variance, about two days before last Christmas, the said Robert did say, " Thou thinks because thou art a soldjer noe body will meddle with the, but thou and all thy brave captaines will be forc'd to take a hold tree or it be long."*

CXXIX. WM. DALSTON, ESQ.   FOR SEDITIOUS WORDS.

July 1, 1664. Before Sir Philip Musgrave, &c. *Chr. Irton, of Threlkeld, gen.*, says, that Wm. Dalston,† of Thwaite, Esq., did say, that those persons that sufferd at Appleby, at the last goale delivery, were stoote men and innocent men.

CXXX. JANE SIMPSON AND ANOTHER.   FOR WITCHCRAFT.

July 20, 1664. Before Sir James Clavering, Bart., Mayor of Newcastle. *Anthony Hearon,‡ baker and brewer*, sayth, that aboute

---

* A Cumberland information. The prisoner evidently was wishful that the plot should be revived, and is bold enough to say so to a soldier.

Richard Marsingill of Stacksby, mariner, was indicted for saying, on Jan. 14, 1667-8, " If our Kinge had beene right hee would not have imployed such rogues to have beene souldiers. The land is badly ruled, and the King may come to make the same end his father made."

† Mr. Dalston, a gentleman of antient family, is referring to Captain Atkinson, and his party of plotters, who were executed at Appleby. He denies using the words. There are, however, six witnesses against him. One of them charges Mr. Dalston with having said, " The men that sufferd at Appleby were proper and able men, and dyed sacklesse." Another heard him say, " That he would spend his blood in that same cause wich they died in."

A true bill was found at Carlisle against John Sixton, of Bowness, clerk, for saying in his sermon in Bowness church, on July 1, 1664, " Charles Stewart the Second is a tyrant, and brought in an army to destroy this nation."

‡ A case of witchcraft from Newcastle. The sick person draws blood from the suspected witch and recovers. The poor woman asserts that she is innocent. A month after this the following depositions were taken. " Aug. 18, 1664. Before Sir James Clavering, Bt., Mayor of Newcastle, Wm. Thompson, of Newcastle, yeo., sayth that his daughter Alice, of the age of 17, hath beene for six weeks last by past most strangfully and wonderfully handled, insoemuch that she does continually cry out of one Katherine Currey, alias Potts, that wrongs her, saying, " Doe you not see her? doe you not see her, where the witch theafe stands ?" And she doth continually cry out that she pulls her heart; she pricks her heart, and is in the roome to carry her away. By reason whereof she is in great danger of her life.

" Ellinor Thompson, sayth, that, by the space of these seaven yeares bypast, she hath

five weeks agoe, one Jane Simpson, huckster, haveing chirryes to sell, Dorothy, wife to this informer, bought of her a pound, and payd her 8*d*. And, reproveing her for takeing more of her then she did of others per 2*d*. in the pound, the said Jane gave her very scurrellous and threating words. And within a fewe dayes after, the saide Dorothy tooke sicknes and hath beene most strangly and wonderfully handled, and in bedd had most sad and lamentable fitts, to the admiration and astonishment of all spectators, being sometymes rageing madd, other tymes laughing and singing, other tymes dispareing and disconsolate, other tymes very solitary and mute. And, on Saturday last, aboute three of the clock in the morneing, she tooke a most sadd fitt, crying outt to this informer, who was in bedd with her, that one Isabell Atcheson and Jane Simpson did torment her, and were aboute the bedd to carry her away. And he had much to doe to hold and keap her in bedd. And she did cry, " Doe yow not see them? Looke where they both stand." And the said Dorothy putting by the curten, he did clearly see Isable Atcheson standing att the bedd side, in her owne shape, clothed with a green waiscoate. And he calling upon the Lord to be present with him, the said Isabell did vanish.

CXXXI. LIONEL COPLEY, ESQ. FOR A MISDEMEANOR.

A true bill against Lionel Copley, Esq.,* for having at Rotherham, on the 25th of Sept. 1664, beaten Richard Firth, put a bridle into his mouth, got on his back, and ridden him about for half an houre, kicking him to make him move.

beene trobled by one Katherine Currey, widdow, severall tymes appearing in the night to her. And the weeke before Fasterne-evening gone a twelve month she came to this informer in the markett and layd her hands upon this informer's shoulder, and sayd, " My peck of meale sett thy kill on fire." And, within two dayes after, the kill was on fire, to her great losse and damage."

* A most extraordinary charge, so strange, indeed, that it can scarcely be credited. I know nothing further of the case; but the culprit, if really he was guilty, must have been deranged. He was a gentleman of high family in the county, and his son Lionel became Governor of Hull and afterwards of Maryland.

It is evident that they were some peculiarities about Mr. Copley, and that he was not on the best of terms with his neighbours. In August 1666, Samuel and Ruth Wood were convicted of a conspiracy to defraud Lionel Copley, Esq. They were fined 13*s*. 4*d*. each, and were to be placed in the pillory at Rotheram on two several market days. In March, 1667, I find that Francis Mountney, of Rotherham, gent., was convicted of inciting the Woods to make their charge against Copley. It would be interesting to know more of this affair.

CXXXII. THOMAS SIMPSON. FOR SACRILEGE.

A true bill against Thomas Simpson,* of York, labourer, for breaking into Whitby Church, on 23 Nov. 1664, and carrying off a surplice, a hood, a silke carpet, and two pulpit clothes.

CXXXIII. ANTHONY GARFORTH, GEN. FOR SEDITIOUS WORDS.

Jan. 31, 1664-5. *John Hoyle, of Kighley,* saith, before Sir John Armitage, that, a month or five weekes before the discovery of the late plott, he heard Mr. Anthony Garforth,† of Steeton, say, "I desire you to lend mee ten pounds." And this inf^t tould him hee had it not. Then Mr. Garforth saide, if hee had it not, hee would have it some where, for hee would have tenne or twenty pounds lyeinge by him, for there will bee such a stirr as never was yett, for the Kinge hath declared himselfe to be a Romane Catholicke, and went to masse with the Queene, and saide that hee had the declaracon in his pocket. He would have declared the above unto Mr. Justice Waide, but that hee was interrupted by Leivetenant-Collonell Malham.

---

* In the Calendar in March 1664-5. Simpson is thus described, "Thomas Simpson, a desperate person, confiderate with Wood and Leightfoote, which was executed Lent Assizes last, denieing his name and calling himselfe John Readhead. Charged alsoe with robbinge of churches, and the felonious takeinge of two mares, haveinge a surplice, a minister's hood, and other church ornaments taken with him, and likewise confessing to have broken the goal att Owsebridge in York, and violently endeavored to make an escape after his apprehention." He was executed.

At Pontefract Sessions, 23 April, 1661, Richard Mathewman, of Wombwell, yeoman, was charged with having, on 15th Jan., 1642-3, broken into Emley church and stolen a silver bowl, val. 10*l.*, two communyon table cloathes, and several bonds, bookes, and other wryteings, to the value of 70*l.* Not guilty.

Jan. 1665-6. John Spight, charged with stealing lead from Brinkburn church.

A true bill against Michael Dent, of Richmond, jun., for that he, on July 22, 1693, broke into the church of Kirkby Ravensworth, and took away three silver chalices, a silver plate, a linen table cloth, and 2*s.*

In 1778 or 1779, in the valley of Turvin, in the parish of Halifax, a robber's cave was discovered among the rocks, in which, among many other things, were two surplices belonging to the church of Rochdale, and the scarlet hood of a doctor of divinity. The inmate of the cave opposed the entrance of the searcher, pistol in hand, but he was arrested and transported for life.

† A Yorkshire gentleman of family is charged with being concerned in the plot of 1663, and his hands, in all probability, were not clean. A witness says that Mr. Garforth declared " that this government would alter, and very shortly, for their docinges were naught, and could never stand," and that after the plot was discovered he absented himself for five weeks. Mr. Garforth was fined 20*l.* and was bound over to keep the peace, himself in the sum of 200*l.*, and in two sureties of 100*l.* each, viz., William Garforth, of Garforth, gen., and Edmund Garforth, of Gargrave, clerk.

CXXXIV. MRS. PEPPER. FOR USING CHARMS, ETC.

Feb. 3, 1664-5, Newcastle-on-Tyne, before Sir Francis Liddle, Kt., mayor. *Margaret, wife of Robert Pyle, pittman,** sayth, that, aboute halfe a yeare agoe, her husband, being not well, sent his water to Mrs. Pepper, a midwife, and one that uses to cast water. And the same day Mrs. Pepper came to see him, and did give him a little water in a bottle to tast, which he took and tasted, and forbad him to drink much of itt, but reserve itt to take when he tooke his fitts: and desired him to goe to the dore, which he did at her request. And, imediately after, Mrs. Pepper and Tomisin Young did bring him with his leggs traileing upon the ground into his howse. And he was in the fitt by the space of one houre and a halfe and was most strangely handled. And the said Mrs. Pepper did take water and throwed itt upon his face, and touke this informer's child, and another sucking child, and laid them to his mouth. And, shee demanding the reason why she did soe, she replyed, that the breath of the children would suck the evill spirritt out of him, for he was possessed with an evill spirritt; and she said she would prove itt either before mayor or ministers that he was bewitched.

Elizabeth, wife of Richard Rutherford, taylor, sayth, that she found Robert Pyle in a very sad condicion, lookeing with a distracted looke, every part of his body shaking and tremblinge, being deprived of the use of his body and seneeces. Where there was then there one Mrs. Pepper, a midwife, and she did see her call for a bottle of holy water, and tooke the same, and sprinkled itt upon a redd hott spott which was upon the back of his right hand; and did take a silver crucifix out of her breast, and laid itt upon the said spott. And did then say that shee knewe by the said spott what his disease was, and did take the said crucifix and putt itt in his mouth.

---

* A very singular case. The accused person seems to have been a Roman Catholic, and made use of her religion to supply her deficiency in medical knowledge.

It is curious to find children laid to the mouth of the afflicted person to charm away his disease. Other things were applied for the same purpose, as will be seen from the following presentment from a parish in Northumberland.

"July 23, 1604. Office against Katharine Thompson and Anne Nevelson, pretended to be common charmers of sick folkes and their goodes, and that they use to bring white ducks or drakes, and to sett the bill thereof to the mouth of the sick person, and mumble upp their charmes in such strange manner as is damnible and horrible."

CXXXV. JOHN BURROWES.   FOR MURDER.

Feb. 9, 1664-5. At Hatfield house, in Ecclesfield. Before Thomas Garnett, gent. *John Mathewman, of Sheffield, sheather*, saith that, upon Wednesday the 8th instant, about eleaven of the clocke in the forenoone, he was travelling on the high way nere a place called Langley, and then and there came a woman out of a house cryinge out, and said that there was a madman * killinge of her husband, and did entreat this informer to help her husband. Then he went to gett some more ayde, and came speedilie backe againe, and then did see one John Burrowes hewinge and hackinge att the throat of one John Jones, the said woman's husband, with one iron wood bill in his hands, and had given the said Jones many greivous severall wounds upon the head, face, and throate, and elsewhere; and then the said Jones lay dead and mortally wounded, and never moved hand nor foott, to this informer's knowledge. And the said Burrowes did threaten this informer and the said woman to doe the like by them if they would nott lett him alone, or come nere him.

John Burrowes, late of Rotheram, apothecary, saith, he had slaine a monster with one watch bill or broome hooke; and did confesse that he begun the fray aboute the takeinge of certaine pieces of wood out of one close nere to the cottage of the said John Jones, which this examinat did justifie to be his owne. He doth nott deny that after he had given the said Jones some wounds upon the head with the said watch-bill, or broome-hooke, he did cutt or hacke his throate with the same to make him lye still.

CXXXVI. JOHN NICHOLSON AND OTHERS.   DANGEROUS PERSONS.

Feb. 21, 1664-5. At Beverley. Before Sir Robert Hildyard, Kt., &c. &c. *Henry Lalley,† of Hollim, clarke*, saith that, in or about

---

* A poor maniac commits a frightful murder. There was no such thing as an asylum in those days, and dreadful catastrophes occasionally resulted from the freedom that insane persons were permitted to enjoy. Burrowes was acquitted at the assizes, and was set free!

† Mr. Lalley had been at Hollym for some time. In September, 1649, I find that he was in trouble " for intruding himselfe into the personage and rectory house of Hollam, being a notorious delinquent." At the Restoration he was secure, but he found himself in a nest of Quakers. In the following depositions there is an amusing account of his troubles. He says that Peter Johnson is unmarried and has children

the beginning of Desember 1664, he heard John Nichelson, of Risam, say, that if God put the sword into his hand he must strike. He saith that severall bookes of the Quackers which tended to the advance of their owne wayes of worshipp have beene sent to him, and that Hope Kitching, of Holme, tould him that he saw a booke concerning the sufferings of the Quackers and the deliverance of seaven of them sent to be banisht in the shipp called the Anne of London, which shipp had beene at sea three moneths and bett back by stresse of weather. About Desember last John Nichelson, in the parish of Hollen, said to him, that the Quackers had shipps of their owne bought with their moneyes that they imployed for intelligence beyond the seas.

John Thompson, of Hollim, yeaman, saith, that, about Michaellmas 1663, discourseing with Peter Johnson, of Hollim, conserning tithes, the said Peter tooke this deponent, gripte him and shakte him, and tould him tythes should quicly be put downe, and if the Lord would put the sword into their hand wee should see they would fight the Lord's battle. And, on Sunday after Lamis day 1663, the said Peter said to Mr. Henry Lathley, minister of Hollim, as he was goeing to Killnsey to preach, " Hary, art thou goeing to tell lyes as thou hast done in Hollim; repent, repent, thy callamityes draws neare," which he often repeated.

CXXXVII. MATTHEW DALE AND OTHERS.   FOR AN ASSAULT.

May 4, 1665. Before Sir Henry Cholmeley, Kt. *Thomas Slinger, vicar of Helmsley*, saith, that being, on the 29 Aprill, about to enterr the corps of John Bolby, I was openly assalted by a party of Quakers, which booth* tore the surplisse and book

unbaptized, and that he, John Nicholson and his family, Ralph Barber and his wife, Robert Wood and his wife, John and Francis Wetwan, Thomas Eshton and Richard Harde did not come to Hollym Church on Jan. 30, in accordance with the King's proclamation. Nicholson and Johnson were bound over to keep the peace, &c.

Timothy Rhodes, of Hornsey, clerk, deposes that on the 10th of February he saw about 100 people go into the house of Peter Acklom, of Hornsey, and stay there two honrs and a half, and that Acklom has had meetings in his house since he was released from his imprisonment in Hull.

It will be seen that there was a large body of Quakers in Holderness—now there are hardly any of that creed in that district. In Poulson's History of Holderness there is an engraving of an old meeting house of the Quakers at Owstwick.

* A set of these turbulent men attack and maltreat the vicar of Helmsley whilst he was burying a parishioner. The early history of the Quakers has still to be written. There were swarms of them in the North of England in the seventeenth century. The following letter from a Yorkshire magistrate is interesting:—

K

of Common Prayer: viz. Matthew Dale of Helmesley, Thomas Yowart of Antofts, W. Fryar of Bilsdale, John Day of Ampleford, Wm. Rowland of the Oldstead.

CXXXVIII. HENRY ASHTON.   FOR SEDITIOUS WORDS.

May 19, 1665. Before Sir Ralph Delaval. *Ann Allison, of North Sheilds,* saith, that Henry Ashton upon the 27th of Dec. being triming here father Robert Allison, and specking of his being a good marksman, sayd that, if he had not shot well, he could never have killed twenty-five cavaliers in a day, and he thought it as pleasant to hime as killing of bukes or doces. Where upon her mother saying shee would warrant he would doe the like to the King if he hade hym, he answered he would doe anything for a livelyhood; all was fish that came to the nett.

CXXXIX. WILLIAM UBANKE.   FOR CUTTING AND WOUNDING.

May 9, 1665. *Edward Nettleton, constable of Hunsworth,* saith, that John and Wm. Bankes, children of Paull Bankes (they being both wounded*), came to his house, and did tell him that their father, and Judith their mother, and Hannah Bankes their sister, were dangerously wounded by bayliffes. Whereupon

"Sweet cosen,—I thanke you for your affectionat expressions towards me in your letter, and the care you seem to have of me by sending me the opinion of other men that I may therto frame my owne. I have seen a pamphlet called a Declaration of the Quakers, which methinkes hath more of simplicity, and lesse of rancor, than this paper which you now sent me. To speake truth, they both of them strive against a known law, and the magistrate hath it not in his power which of the lawes he will put in execution, and which of them he will forbear; and, for this paper now sent, it seemes to be of another and a higher strain against rulers than the former. If men of the same perswasion did write them both, then the Quakers have by this late writing growen higher in their invectives against magistracy. But I am apt to think that this writing comes from another party, who have made bolls, and put them into the hands of Quakers to shoot them; and then, cosen, who are the fooles? Or, if it come originally from the Quakers, they then, I say, (are) worse men and subjects than they were before. Good cosen, let you and me study to be quiet, and to do our owne busines, to live peaceably, and not to push incentives to warre, and let the legislative power make lawes . . . . All my family salute you, and I in particular remaine, cosen, your very affectionate kinseman to serve you, RIC. ROBINSON.

"Thickett, 11th June, '70. These for Mrs. Skipwith at Skipwith."

* A most murderous assault by some bailiffs at Horton near Bradford. They had broken into the house and attacked the inmates. Paul Bankes had a most dangerous wound in the throat, which was given him by Ubanke. Ubanke denies injuring any one, but his companions throw all the blame upon him. Richard Coore, of Tong, clerk, a clerical physician, deposes to the nature of the wounds. Ubanke was fined 5*l*.

he went downe to the house and found there Wm. Ubanke, Joseph Priestley, Robert Hirst, and David Millington, and thereupon arrested them, the said Paull Bankes being soe wounded that he conceives him in danger of death, and likewise Judith his wife, who being with child, is likewise dangerously wounded, and Hannah Bankes hath a cutt in her forehead, and William Bankes is soe dangerously wounded that he is greatly endangered of his life, being about the age of tenn or eleven yeares.

CXL. JEREMY SMITHSON, ESQ. FOR LIBELLOUS WORDS.

A true bill against Jeremy Smithson,* of Stanig (Stanwick), Esq., for saying, on June 24, 1665, to Sir Joseph Cradock, "Thou art a base fellow. You thinke yourself impowered by being in the comission of peace. I am in the comission, and care not a fart for the commission or you."

CXLI. ANNE LINSCALE. FOR CHILD MURDER.

July 10, 1665. Before Edward Trotter, Esq. *Henry Sole* saith, that Sissilye Linscale † toold him that, the same day that her cousin Ann Linscale was delivered of a childe, that she came to her father's house aboute noone, and she, the said Sissilye, had beene chirning, and had made a cake for her owne dinner, and would have given her cosen Ann some with her, but she refused, and went away as though she had not beene well. And the said day, about cowe-time, the said Sissilye was goeing to fetch home a cowe from a place called Hoggard garth; and,

---

* Jeremy, afterwards Sir Jerome Smithson, of Stanwick, is in trouble. He loses his temper with a very active magistrate, Sir Joseph Cradock, and vents his displeasure in terms that the other would not be disposed to overlook. The Smithsons had only recently become the owners of Stanwick, and their position among the leading gentry of the Riding was at present a doubtful one. Mr. Smithson in this instance wished to lead Sir J. Cradock into a duel, and he was bound over in consequence to keep the peace.

Mr. Smithson was in other troubles besides this. In July, 1668, John Wake of Stanwix was indicted at York for tempting one Chr. Francklin to leave Mr. Smithson's service and to carry off his clothes. Thomas Swinburne, of Barmton, co. Durham, was also indicted for speaking slanderingly of Smithson in reference to the aforesaid case, and for assaulting Francklin.

† A startling case which had been hushed up for some time. The informer tells her tale, as she says, because Agar had abused her master. Her evidence therefore must be received with suspicion, although it is clearly given. All the women were tried at the assizes, but they were acquitted, and were freed by proclamation.

passing by her aunt's house, the mother of the said Ann, she
heard the said Ann cry out very greviously, upon which she
went in to se what was the matter; and, as soone as she came in,
her ant, Jane Linscale, sent her to Elizabeth Agarr to desire her
to come to her daughter Ann, for she was very sicke, and desired
to speake with her. She, goeing, and not finding her at home,
came back againe and told them that she was not in the house; and
so goeing to Hoggard-garth for her cowe, as she either went or
came back she mett the said Elizabeth Agarr, and toold her
that she had beene at her house lookeing for her, for her cosen
Ann was very sick and desired to speake with her, who went
hastily away from her towardes her owne house. And she
went on and did fetch her cowe; and, as she came back with her,
she turned her downe the streete, and went herself againe to her
ant house to see how her cosen Ann did, and when she came at
the fore dore it was shutt, so goeing on to the other dore, thurst-
ing it from her, it opened, and she went in; and at her comeing
in they did looke straingely upon her, and did shut the dore and
keept her in; and the said Elizabeth Agarr had a bottle and a
paper in her hand, and she tooke something forth of the paper,
but she knew not what it was, and rowled it betweene her hands,
and gave it to the said Ann, and bid her swallow it downe. That
being done, she gave her the bottle, and she dranke of it.
Whereupon presently after she brought a childe from her; and,
when she had it, she whispered with Em. Linscale, the sister of
the said Ann, but she knew not what she said. This being done
her ant Jane came to her and said, " Good Sisse, do not speake
of this, for, if thou doest, we are all undone." Also the said
Elizabeth Agarr came to her, and tooke her to the table side,
and smote very earnestly with one of her hands upon the table,
and vowed that, if ever she heard any worde that she should
speake of it, she would be the death of her. Then the said
Elizabeth Agarr said to the said Em, " Go and doe as I bidd
the." Whereupon she tooke the childe, and wrapt it in a ragg,
and then they opened the dores and let her out, and the said Em
and her sister Pegg brought forth the child and put it in a hole,
and she, the said Sisse, did stand and looke at them when they
did it. Also the said Henry saith that he did aske her what was
the reason that she did not reveale it noe sooner, and she said
that she had manie times beene troubled aboute it, yet durst not
speake of it for feare of getting some ill by them. And further
the said Henry saith, that three daies after the said Sisse had discovered it, that the said Jane and Em came before the house
where the said Sisse was, and did revile her with very bad words,

and did say there was two dores, and, "If we had the out at either of them, we would pull thy throate out." Whereupon she said, "Master, did not I tell you that, if ever I did speake of it, I was sure to have a mischiefe by them?" Upon which she, the said Sisse, did start up and looked out at the windowe and said, "Em, is not this true that I have said? Did not I se the and thy sister Pegg burie the childe hard by where thou standest? I pray God I may never se such a sight againe." Whereupon they went away and gave not a word more.

CXLII. A LIST OF RECUSANTS

July 17, 1665. For being absent from church for a month.
Dent. Alexander Heblethwaite, Thomas Wilkinson, Chr. Wood. *Sedberge.* John Blakelin, Richard Robinson, Thomas Holme, Edward Atkinson, John Croft, John Langton, Richard Atkinson, Francis Blakelin, Edward Trotter, John Dawson, Henry Dennison, Thomas Branthwaite, John Holme, Edward Branthwaite, Richard Speight, Wm. Farrer, James Shaw. *Awstwicke.* Margaret Franckland, Margaret Johnson, spinster, Nicholas Moore, John Moore and Ann his wife, Edward and Giles Moore, Margaret Cowper and Isabella Chapman, spinsters, Thomas Chapman, Lawrence Peacocke. *Clapham.* Thomas Robinson, Alice Atkinson, spinster. *Thorneton.* John Topham and Mary his wife, Thomas Addison and Rebecca his wife, Jeffrey Wildeman and Anne his wife. *Ingleton.* Clement Stephenson. *Horton.* Matthew Wildeman, Richard Benson, John Bentham, John Moore, Richard Guy, George Bland, Wm. Redman, Wm. Kendall, Thomas Gibson, Thomas Banckes, John Wearing, Easter Tenant, spinster, James Tenant, Eliz. Tenant, spinster, John Bents. *Birdsall.* Layton Firbancke and Frances his wife. *Acklam cum Leavening.* John Day, Robert Bowser, Thomas Holmes, Mary Jackson, spinster. *Kirby Grindelythe.* Wm. Sheppardson. *Duggleby.* Robert Tyndall. *Arkesey.* Samuel Barley, Robert Scott, Eliz. Bradford, widow. *Hooton Pannell.* Alice Shore, spinster. *Watton.* Wm. Dawson and Jane his wife. *Southburne.* Thomas Nicholson and Mary his wife. *Skerne.* James Canaby, Isabel Langdale, spinster, Wm. Jarrett, and Margaret his wife.

CXLIII. WILLIAM KNAPTON.   FOR SEDITIOUS WORDS.

The Grand Jury find a true bill against Wm. Knapton,* of Barwick in Elmet, for saying, on the 4th of August, 1665, to Martin Prince, "How now, thou rebell? What art thou better beinge a soldier for the Kinge? For where is your Kinge now, that grand Papish? Hee flyeth from the plague, but it will follow him, I'le warrant."

CXLIV. JOHN MUSGRAVE, GEN.   FOR SEDITIOUS WORDS.

A true bill against John Musgrave,† of London, Gen. for saying at Rothwell, on Aug. 20, 1665, "Now is the time, if we will stirre, for the Annabaptists ‡ and Quakers are not afraid of the plague."

CXLV. CHR. MAUD.   FOR SEDITIOUS WORDS.

Chr. Maud, of Ellerton, milner, indicted for saying, on the 28th of November, 1665, "There will bee blood spilt before all the assessments § be payd. He thought in regard the assess-

---

* The plague was now raging, and that awful visitation was laid at the King's door. The vice of the Court, and the general profligacy of the nation, in the opinion of many, had been the cause of it. Knapton was bound over to keep the peace, himself in the sum of 100*l.*, and in two sureties of 50*l.* each.

The Grand Jury find a true bill against Wm. Thomson of Collingham for saying on the first of August, 1665, "The King is the onely causer of the plague and pestilence, and hath provoked God to send this judgment upon us by taxing and assessing the poor. If this Kinge had been hanged when the other was beheaded wee should have had none of these taxes; but I think wee must all rise." Not guilty.

† The prisoner, who lived in Cripplegate, was acquitted and was discharged on his recognisances. It will be seen that even in that time of danger and dismay there were some turbulent spirits who thought there was a chance of making a change in the government.

A charge of another kind was, I have found, made against the King with reference to the Anabaptists.

Jeremiah Denby, of Steaton, was indicted at York for saying at Kildwick, on 26 July, 1684, to Richard Pollerd, clerk, "The King himself is a great favourer of the Anabaptists, and those are the best Cristians that come least to church, for all I know."

‡ The culprit was allowed to escape without any punishment whatever.

§ The many taxes imposed by Charles II. were excessively distasteful to the people, especially as the money raised by them was practically wasted.

Oct. 21, 1664. At Rocke before John Salkeld and Jo. Clarke, Esqs. Thomas Busby, of Alnwicke, saith, that, on the 12th of August, being walking in the company of Henry Elder of Alnwicke, and saying, "What can become of all the money that was collected in the cuntrey?" the said Henry replied, "What should become

ments were soe great now, that people had the best time in respect that they had sowen downe their seed; that it was their best course to releive themselves from the great burden of assessments that lay soe heavy upon them, to take clubs and pitchforkes, and such weapons as they could gett, and goe to the Kinge."

CXLVI. NONCONFORMIST MINISTERS, AND THE DECLARATION.

March 7, 1665-6. Northumberland. We, John Pringle of Newcastle, clerke, John Weld of Lamesley in the county of Durham, John Thompson of Peglesworth in the county of Northumberland, Thomas Willson of Lamesley in the county of Durham, Thomas Truercn of Harla Hill in the county of Northumberland, and Robert Pleasance of Newcastle aforesaid, clerkes,* doe sweare that it is not lawfull, upon any pretence whatsoever, to take up armes against the King; and that we doe abhorre that trayterous position of takeing armes by his authority against his person, or against those that are commissionated by him in pursueance of such commissions; and that we will not at any time endeavour any alteration of government, either in Church or

of it? There was non to destroy it but a company of ranting fellows; and, for his Majesty, hee had taken up the bones of an honester man then himselfe, and, in his thoughts, there would be noe quietenes till hee went the way his father went."

Chr. Peares, of Thornaby, gen., was indicted at York for saying, on March 31, 1679, " I heare there is a new assessement comeing forth, which is strange, for I beleive there is noe act of Parliament for itt, and this assessement hath been demanded in the Bishoppricke of Durham, but they denyed to pay itt."

* A declaration which some of the ejected ministers in the North were required to make. It is signed by eight of those devoted men.

John Pringle was ejected from Eglingham, and came to Newcastle, where he spent his time in preaching for Mr. Gilpin, ahd practising physic. He was in gaol for his religious opinions, and died in Newcastle about 1690.

John Weld is not mentioned by the historians of the Nonconformists. He was a kinsman probably of Thomas Weld, the silenced rector of Gateshead.

John Thompson was ejected from the rich rectory of Bothal. He was in prison for his opinions, and the confinement generated an illness that carried him off.

Thomas Wilson was ejected from Lamesley. He held a meeting in his house for two years with the assistance of Mr. Robert Lever.

Thomas Trewren lost the vicarage of Ovingham. He went to Harrow in Middlesex, where he had a congregation. He died in 1676.

Robert Pleasance was ejected from the rectory of Boldon, co. Durham. He was connected with the parish of St. Mary-in-the-South Bailey, Durham, and I have a good deal of information about him. I possess a beautifully written MS. containing the sermons that he preached at Boldon in 1658-9.

Ralph Wicliffe was the son of Wm. Wycliffe, of Offerton, a cadet of the great Yorkshire family of that name. He preached in Durham and Northumberland, and died in 1683.

It must be observed that there were many other ejected ministers in the neighbourhood of Newcastle whose names are not appended to this declaration.

State.—Jo. Pringle, John Weld, John Thompson, Tho. Wilson, John Davies, Tho. Trewren, Rob. Pleasaunce, Ralph Wickliffe.

CXLVII. A LIST OF YORKSHIRE RECUSANTS.

March, 1665-6. *Kirkby Hill.** John Harrison, Peter Harrison and Margaret his wife, Wm. and George Pinckney, Ellen Anderson, spinster. *Barford.* Michaell Pudsey and Mary his wife, Thomas Dodsworth and Katharine his wife, John Berry and Elizabeth his wife. *Forcett.* Thomas Leath and Eliz. his wife, Job Shutt and Mary his wife, Henry Barwicke and Anne his wife, Mary Frinny, Hellen Firth and Jane Porcivell, spinsters, Wm. Pearson and Bridget his wife, George Berry and Mary his wife, Faith Cornforth and Margaret Gibson, spinsters. *Caldwell.* Frances wife of James Gregory, Alice Gregory, widow, Alice Gregory, spinster, Wm. Stockdale and Anne his wife, Ellenor Stockdale, widow. *Carleton.* John Catterick, Esq., and Margaret his wife, John Catterick, gen., Isabel, Mary and Margaret Catterick, spinsters, Isabel Catterick, widow, Robert Walker and Anne his wife, James Walker and Margery his wife, Matthew Walker, Ellioner Walker, spinster, Henry Lawson and Frances his wife, Robert Mansfeild and Frances his wife, Isabel wife of Wm. Mansfield, Barth. Robinson and Mary his wife. *Melsonby.* Robert Pearson and Isabel his wife, Thomas Pearson, John Thompson and Alice his wife, Nicholas Stubbs and Margaret his wife, Mary Watson, Anne Clerke and Eliz. Blacket, spinsters. *Dalton cum Gailes.* Roger Mennell and Mary his wife, Chr. Wade and Isabel his wife, Robert Ackman and Eliz. his wife, Francis Skaife and Isabel his wife, Jane Mennell, spinster, George Watson and Ellen his wife, Trinian Anderson and Eliz. his wife, James Kilburne and Eliz. his wife. *Eppleby.* Robert Ovington and Anne his wife, Margaret Preston, spinster, James Moore, Anna Moore. *Laytons Ambo.* Marmaduke Wilson and Katharine his wife, Francis Wiseman and Margaret his wife, Robert Peirson and Ellen his wife, Robert Leatch and Jane his wife, Anne wife of James Stubbs, Anthony Pearson and Jane his wife, Anthony Foster and Jane his wife, James Hutchinson and Mary his wife, Robert Cutter and Elizabeth his wife, Henry Killinghall

---

* Another, and a more extended, list of recusants. The greater part, if not the whole, of them were Roman Catholics. The names that are given are but a small section of that great religious party in the county of York. Out of the whole number five or six of the leading gentry made their appearance at the assizes.

and Anne his wife, Katharine wife of Robert Dunn, Francis Dunn. *Gilling.* Brian Corby and Mary his wife, Eliz. wife of John Wallis. *Ravensworth.* Robert Richardson and Bridget his wife, George Smith and Frances his wife, Margaret wife of Wm. Gibson, Cecily Atkinson, spinster, Anne wife of Clement Browne, Micha Norton and Eliz. his wife, Anne wife of Cuthbert Cowling, Nicholas Allen, gen., Anthony Allen, gen., and Anne his wife, George Allen and Eliz. his wife. *Aldbrough.* George Mennell, gen., and Ellen his wife, Anthony Metcalfe, gen., and Frances his wife, John Roome and Anne his wife, Richard Piburne and Mary his wife, Stephen Dalton and Ellenor his wife, Robert Walker, Edward Birkebecke, Bridget Birkebecke, spinster, George Walbancke and Anne his wife, Frances Ridd, widow, John Graine and Mary his wife, John Sigsworth and Grace his wife. *Easby.* Anne Colson, widow, Francis Tunstall, gen., and Anne his wife, John Hugginson, Mary Hugginson, Lawrence Lowesh, Mark Appleby, Eliz. Wray, spinster, Dorothy Summerside, Dorothy Barker, spinster. *Hutton.* Wm. Tunstall, Esq., Eliz. Ubancke, spinster, John Hort and Mary his wife, Anne wife of Francis Thomson. *Cliffe.* George Witham, Esq., and Grace his wife.

——— *Heworth.* Edward Thwinge and his wife, Wm. Thwing and his wife, John Hargrave and his wife. *Hinderskelfe.* Ann Kendall, widow, Ralph Kendall and Mary his wife. *Farlington.* Francis Blakeston, Charles Dixon and Anne his wife, Alice Dixon, spinster. *Bransby.* Edward Cornforth, Katharine Rawdon, spinster, Ann Shirwan and Isabel Jackson, spinsters. *Skewsby.* Allen Aiscough, Esq., and Anne his wife, Francis Aiscough, John Dresser, Eliz. Stibin, Anne wife of Edward Halliday, George Cooper and Mary his wife, George and Valentine Turner, Robert Harry, Joan wife of Wm. Harrison, Mary Wier, spinster, Chr. Wilson and Anne his wife, Phillis Hornesey, widow. *Sheriffehutton.* John Jackson and Isabel his wife. *Bulmer.* Michael and George Nicholson, John Hicke and Anne his wife. *Welburne.* John Tiplady and Alice his wife. *Whenby.* Alice Barton, spinster, Wm. Walworth, sen. and jun., Matthew Stonecliffe, Eliz. Ellis, Ursula Rivis and Mary Wood, spinsters, Wm. Dresser, Francis Bossell, Grace and Isabel Hall, spinsters.

Hallifax. Nathaniel Crowther, John Hooker, Thomas Holmes. *Haworth.* Chr. and Jonas Smith, Wm. Clayton, jun., John Clayton, jun., Wm. Clayton, Joseph Smith, John Pighills. *Idle.* Francis Drake and Frances his wife, Alice Crowther, George Booth and Isabel his wife, George Booth. *Bradford.* Mary

Squire, spinster, Richard Jowett, Anne Crowther. *Warley.*
Henry and Timothy Wadsworth. *Ovenden.* Richard Longbotham, Robert Wright. *Skircoate.* Abraham Hodgson. *South-
owram.* Grace and Mary Hemingway, spinsters. *Stansfeild-
cum-Langfeild.* John Feilding, sen. and jun., Mary Feilding,
spinster. *Rishworth.* Mary Earnshaw. *Rastricke.* John Eccles,
Richard Hanson. *Wadsworth.* Edward Turner. *Pudsey.* Wm.
Crabtree. *Erringdon.* James Barrett. *Wyke.* Mary Bentley
and Mary Greenwood, spinsters. *Thorneton.* Edward Hulley.
Calverley. Thomas Dodgson, Hugh Lickbarrow. *Gomersall.*
Marmaduke Cowling. *Heckmondwicke.* Michael Mitchell. *Hep-
tonstall.* John Crabtree. *Allerton cum Wilsden.* George Faber.
Heaton cum Clayton. John Bradley, Wm. Kellett. *Clackheaton.*
James Grave. *Okenshaw.* Wm. Pearson. *Barnoldswicke.* Richard
Bootham and Alice his wife, Richard Bootham, jun., Henry
Bowtham, Mary wife of Henry Hartley. *Newsholme.* Chr. Batty,
Mary Tatham, spinster. *Bradford.* Isabel wife of Brian Parker,
Henry Bayly. *Slaidburne.* Thomas Wigglesworth, Robert Proc-
ter, Ellinor Cutler, spinster. *Newton.* Dorothy Hodgskinson,
spinster, Robert Walbancke and Ellianor his wife, Thomas Stack-
house, Wm. Birkett, Jonathan Scott, Jane Walne, sen. and jun.,
Isabella Knowe, spinster, Thomas Knowe, Jane Knowe, spinster,
Henry Baitson. *Birkett.* Jane wife of Richard Leigh. *Knowle-
stones.* Thomas Turner and Agnes his wife. *Stainforth.* Samuel
Watson, Richard Wharfe, Thomas Rudd.

Hunton. Jane Wylde, spr., Elianor wife of John Theakeston,
Jane Wilde, spinster, Chr. Askwith and his wife, Chr. Dent and
his wife, Cuthbert Banckes and his wife, Chr. Hawkins and his
wife. *Horneby.* George Pearson and Margaret his wife, Jane
Peirson, spinster, Eliz. wife of John Reed. *Osmotherley.* John
Johnson, Gregory Kendraw. *Thornton in le Beanes.* Anne wife
of Wm. Burton. *High Worsall.* Robert Berry, John Rocke.
Brompton. Thomas Wheldin and Frances his wife, Thomas
Smith, Margaret Hutchinson, spinster. *West Rounton.* Nicholas
and Henry Robinson, Wm. Robinson, Eliz. wife of Edward
Grimes, gen.

Bolton hill. Anthony Myers, Richard Smith. *Skipton.* John
Hawkeshead and Eliz. his wife. *Hebden.* Robert Rathmell and
Agnes his wife. *Broughton.* Thomas Tempest, gen., and Eliz. his
wife, John Yorke, gen., and Eliz. his wife, Richard Tempest, gen.,
and Eliz. his wife, George Fell and Elianor his wife, Richard Firth,
Jane wife of Thomas Tempest, George Butler, James Wolsing-
den and Elizabeth his wife, Stephen Wolsingden, Thomas Heaker,
John Tempest. *Hewby.* Edward Jennings, Richard Rossell,

— Woodward and Jane his wife, Richard Maisterman and Eliz. his wife, Anne Carleton, spinster, John Tayler and Mary his wife, Syth Maisterman, widow, Andrew Vaux and Jane his wife, Walter Merry and Hester his wife, John Dinnis. *Myton.* Wm. Walker, Richard Scott, Thomas Loncaster. *Linton cum Youlton.* Thomas Appleby, Esq., and Eliz. his wife, Henry Hunt. *Newton.* Roger Baker, Wm. Masterman. *Stillington.* Richard Smith and Anne his wife.

———— Thomas Baites and Jane his wife, George Headlam and Jane his wife, John Foster and Jane his wife, John Hewitson and Anne his wife, Philip Hildreth and Jane his wife, Wm. Hildreth and Anne his wife, Thomas Wilson and Jane his wife, Eliz. Wilson, spinster, Jane Pinckney, spinster, John Cuthbertson, Eliz. Cuthbertson, spinster, Jane Smith, spinster, Isabel Hall, widow, Margaret Westwood, spinster. *Great Smeaton.* Richard Smith and Anne his wife. *Cleasby.* Anthony Singleton, Eliz. Singleton, spinster, Ralph Todd and Anne his wife. *Brompton-super-Swale.* John Pearson and Mary his wife. *Warlaby.* John Coggs and Anne his wife. *Stappleton.* Lawrence Heddon.

Sheffeild. Francis Ratcliffe and his wife, Edward Murphy and his wife, — Champnoone, widow, Mary Sergison, widow. *Hansworth.* George Greates and Joan his wife. *Cantley.* Mary wife of Henry Smith. *Hutton Roberts.* Eliz. wife of Edward Pearson.

Halsham. Robert Owst and Ann his wife, Henry Sled, Robert Owst, jun., and Mary his wife, Ursula Awdas, widow, Anthony Awdas, Thomas Moody and Ursula his wife.

Alwoodley. Jane Smith, widow. *Yeadon.* Robert Marshall, John Burrow, Anne Laycocke, Margaret Walker and Mary Pollard, spinsters. *Rawden.* Wm. Butterfeild and his wife, Eliz. Wilson, spinster. *Harwood.* Peter Wright, John Jessop, — Nicholson, labourer.

Cridlingstubbs. Wm. Briggs and Mary his wife. *Smeaton parva.* Philip Heptenstall and Anne his wife, Joan Heptenstall.

Hooke. Thomas Empson and Isabel his wife. *Gowle.* Anthony Empson and Dorothy his wife. *Armine.* Francis Binckes, gen., and Eliz. his wife, George Harrison. *Whitgnift.* Mary wife of Thomas Sellier. *Swinfleet.* Mary Pennithorne, widow, Eliz. Raper, widow, Mary wife of Thomas Spincke. *Usfleet.* Francis Penington and Anne his wife.

Boulton. Isabel Blanshard and Mary Hargill, spinsters. *Barnby-super-Moram.* Frances wife of George Tenney. *Newton-super-Derwent.* Mary wife of Richard Bovill. *Barwicke-in-Elmett.*

Sir Thomas Gascoigne, Kt., Sir Stephen Tempest, Kt., and Anne his wife, — Errington, gen., and his wife, Francis Johnson and his wife, Wm. Brame, Wm. Smith and his wife, Andrew Slater, Mary Shippen, Robert Franckland and his wife, Wm. Vevers, Richard Prince, Robert Oddy, Isabel Deardon, spinster. *Kippax.* Wm. Graycocke and Frances his wife, Peter Graycocke, Richard Graycocke and Eliz. his wife. *East Keswicke.* George Hopwood, Francis Easterby, Thomas Hopwood, Anne Sutton, spinster. *Seacroft.* Thomas Deardon. *Scarcroft.* John Ryther, Esq.

Thornton in Pickering. Thomas Dutton, Robert Rogerson and Katharine his wife. *Pickering.* Ellianor wife of Thomas Dickinson, Stephen Reddy, Wm. Coullam, Robert Coullam, Robert Kinge, James Jackson, Isabella Robinson, John Pates, Eliz. Norcliffe, spinster, Ann Pennocke, spinster, Richard Dobson, John Browne, Richard Barnard, Thomas Collin, Richard Foster, Wm. Pilmer, Anne Sharples, spinster.

Aislaby. Roger and Thomas Chapman, Mary and Isabella Chapman, spinsters. *Pateley briggs.* George Barwicke, blacksmith, Eliz. Lowcocke, spinster.

Hacknes. Thomas Moore, gen., James Boyes and Isabel his wife. *Harwood dale.* Gideon Clapham, Richard Dobson, Matthew Poskitt and Anne his wife, Wm. Addison and Mary his wife, James Reachee, Eliz. Reachee, spinster, Wm. Coverdale. *Smeaton.* John Coward, Ellis Blackburne, widow. *Filingdales.* James Poskit, Stephen Dickinson, Anne Dickinson, spinster. *Whitton hill.* Wm. Norrison and Joseph Thornehill.

CXLVIII. MATTHEW HARWOOD. FOR HIGHWAY ROBBERY.

April 24, 1666. *Peter Gervise, of Hutton, laborer,** saith, that on Sunday morning last, between eleven and twelve o'clocke, as hee was going to give his master's horse some oates through a wood, that Mathew Harwood was in the wood, and bid him stand, and then he asked him " For what?" and Harwood told him he wanted money. He tould him he had none for him, and said hee might seeke itt somewhere else. And replied he would make him seeke his life, and then Peter Gervice run away, and Mathew Harwood run after him, overtook him, and, with a stroke

---

* A case of highway robbery with violence. The attempt was made in the broad daylight. The culprit denies his guilt. He was sentenced to death at the assizes, but was reprieved.

with a stick, knocked him downe to the grownd. And then gott upon him and demanded his purse, and said that if hee would not give itt him hee would rip him up, and let him see his hart; and soe opened his buttons, and gave him some rippills with his knife on his brest, and tooke his purse out of his pockett, and tooke 6s. out of itt, being all he had; and he tooke a handchercher out of his pockett.

CXLIX. WM. KNAPTON AND ANOTHER. FOR SEDITIOUS WORDS.

Whitehall, Apr. 30, 1666. Before Sir John Armytage and Walter Hauksworth, Esq. *Peter Holmes, of Leeds,** *bailiff within the wapentak of Scarwick*,† informeth that William Knapton of Barwick, farmer, did at Leeds, on the 17th instant, say that he hoped to see his Majesty destroyed before the moneth of May were finally ended.

And that Joseph Welch, clothmaker, being at Kirstall, on Thursday, the 19th, said that the plot was basely carried at Farneley wood, and that he would fight bloud up to the knees rather then the next plot should be so carried; and that it would not be long before he hoped to see a fight.

CL. EDWARD RUDDOCKE. FOR MURDER.

May 2, 1666. Before Wm. Gray, gent., coroner. *Thomas Bell, of Birdsall, blacksmith*,‡ saith, that the last day of Aprill last, about aleaven a clocke in the night of the same day, he did repaire, together with severall young men and boyes of the towne of Birdsall, unto a woodclose, or wood, belonging to Eddlethorpe grainge, being about the number of fourteene. He and William Knaggs, soe soone as they were within the wood, went a part from the rest of the companyall, their intencon then being to chuse and gett a young ash tree for a May poll to carry to the

---

* Some regrets are expressed at the failure of the Farneley Wood plot. One of the speakers, Wm. Knapton, had been in trouble before.

† *i. e.* Scyrack, or Shire oak.

‡ The record of a night adventure in the East Riding. On the night before the first of May some of the villagers at Birdsal go into Eddlethorpe woods in quest of a young tree to serve as a Maypole. They are caught in the woods by a person of the name of Ruddock, who shoots one of the poor fellows, and kills him on the spot. The culprit pleads an alibi, and says that he was at home all night. He was acquitted at the assizes, it being probably thought that the evidence was insufficient.

town of Birdsall. But immediately after this deponent and the said William Knaggs was parted a little distance from the other part of their partners, they heard some speake, but did not well understand what they said; and, imediately after, was a gun discharged, and the said William Knaggs, being then close by this examinate, gave a skrike, and turned round, and fell downe dead: whoe, as this deponent conceives, received the shott from the same gun, but being something darke this deponent could not discover whoe shott of the same gunne. And, imediatley after the gunne was discharged, one Mr. Edward Ruddocke and another person, unknowne to this examinate, came up to this deponent, saying, "Ho rogues! Ho rogues! Have we mett with you. Ile make rogues on you. It's more fitt you were in your bedds then here at this tyme of night," or words to that purpose. And the said Mr. Edward Ruddocke hadd in his hand one gun, and the other man that came with him an iron forke. And this deponent, being lifting up his partner, the said Mr. Ruddocke asked if there were any life in him; to which this ex^t replyed none to his thinking; and then he bid this deponent take him on his backe, and carry him home. He then asked this ex^t where the rest of his partners were, who told him he thought they were downe in the wood. And Mr. Ruddocke then told him he hoped to meet with some of the rest of them; and then goeing a little distance, as this ex^t conceives, the said Mr. Ruddocke did charge the gunne againe. The other man, which he knewe not, asked this ex^t what he called the man which was killed. He answered Wm. Knaggs: to which the strainger replyed he was sory for that, he had rather it had been any else. Then Mr. Ruddocke told this deponent that he would make him an example for all the rest, and then went both away.

CLI. SAMUEL WORTLEY, GEN. FOR MURDER.

May 3, 1666. Barnsley. Before Thomas Garnett and Charles Jackson, gent. coroners. *Richard Wainewright, of Cawthorne,*[*] *bayliffe*, sayth, that, the first day of May, he beinge a bayliffe and assistant to Thomas Wildsmith, a bayliffe, went, with him, Wm. Skelton, and another man to assist them, to Wm. Hinch-

---

[*] A murder at Barnsley, in which a bailiff is the victim. The culprit was an attorney in that place. He was captured and tried at York, but, strange to say, he was acquitted. The widow of the slain person begged that he might be punished. Her husband had left a large family, encumbered by debt, behind him.

clyffe's howse in Barnesley, to arreast Samuell Wortley and the sayd Hinchclyffe, upon a writt at the suite of the Queene Mother for 300*l*. And at theire entrance into the howse they called for a quart of ale, and desired to speake with Wm. Hinchclyffe; whereupon Edward Hinchclyffe, his brother, desired Wm. Hinchclyffe to come to speake with Thomas Wildsmith; and when he came Thomas Wildsmith drunke to him, and when the sayd Wm. had drunke, Thomas Wildsmyth rose up, and told him hee arrested him. Which when he had done, Wm. and Edward Hinchclyffe desired Wildsmith to goe into the parlor with them, and he did so. And Edward Hinchclyffe, Wm. Hinchclyffe, and Eliz. his wife, sayd to this informer, which was in the howse, " If yow will be content, wee will give you 500*l*. bond, or what yow please." Then Wm. Hinchclyffe's wife went into the chamber to Samuell Wortley; whereupon Samuell Wortley came downe with a drawne sword or rapier under his coate, and went into the parlor, and Wm. Hinchclyffe's wife suddenly shut the doore after him. And, presently after, Edward Hinchclyffe went into the parlor, and shut the doore after him alsoe. Then Wildsmith asked Samuel Wortley how hee did, and sayd to him, " Sir, I arrest yow at the suite of the Queen Mother." Then Wortley said, " I will run thee through, thou shalt arrest none of mee." And when this informer heard those words hee went to the parlor doore, and would have gone into the parlor, but Edward Hinchclyffe kept the doore fast, soe that he could not goe in. Then this informer looked through a hole in the doore, and saw Wortley make two passes at the said Wildsmith with his rapier, the one of them he put by, and turned himselfe to the doore, and would very gladly have gone forth. And this informer then did see Edward Hinchlyffe stop him, and would not let him depart till he was wounded, soe that, at the second passe, Wortley run him through his body. And then the doore was opened, and they thrust Wildsmith out of the roome and barrd the doore after him. And Wildsmith cryed out to this informer, and said, " Ah, Dicke, I am slayne." And this informer heard the words that past betweene Samuell Wortley, Wm. Hinchclyffe, and Wildsmith, but Wildsmith gave neither Hinchclyffe nor Wortley a foule word.

Buckley Wilsford, of Barnesley, gent., sayth, that, the first of May, he hearinge that one Thomas Wildsmyth, bayliffe, was allmost slayne, went to se him, then found him under the hands of a chirurghion then dresseinge of his wounds. And the said Wildsmyth severall tymes tould this informer that Samuell Wortley gave him the said wound, and with a sword or rapier strucke quite through his bodie against the doore.

Richard Smith, of Barnesley, clerke, sayth, that upon Wednesday, the 2d of May, about two of the clocke in the morneinge, he was att Old Barnesley, att the house of Wm. Rooke, where he now liveth, and then and there came a man ridinge into the fouldstead, and tould this informer he was desyred by Mr. Buckley Wilford and Thomas Wildsmith to goe to Barnesley, to the house of Richard Lambert, to pray with and for the said Wildsmith, who then lay languishing upon some wounde he had gott the day before, as he tould this informer. Then this informer asked Wildsmith who gave him the said wounds, and he answered "Samuel Wortley, ah, fye on him!" Then this informer desyred him to make his peace with God, and tould him he could nott live; and then Wildsmith answered, "Noe, Noe, hee was a dead man, if he had a thousand lives (he said) they was all gone."

William Houldgat, of Barnesley, laborer, was charged by James Bird, one of the constables of Barnesley, to goe and help to apprehend Samuell Wortley. And he did his best endeavoure, and rune after the said Wortley, and did see him rune away, and was very neere him, and did se him gett of horse backe, and soe the said Wortley ride quite away out of his sight, soe that he never did see him since that time.

CLII. WILLIAM HUNSLOE. FOR SEDITIOUS WORDS.

July 21, 1666. Before William Gee, Esq. *Arthur Alford,* saith, that William Hunsloe,[*] of Walkington, upon the 20th of this instant, with others, being speaking about the late battell betwixt his Majesties fleete and the Dutch navy, did say that the Dutch had got the better and were landed upon the coast at Bridlington, and that hee would lead them on. What was the King? Hee was but a chimney-sweeper, and hee would justifie it.

---

[*] Hunsloe was tried at the assizes, and was ordered to be put in the pillory at York, Beverley, and Bridlington, on three several market days, with a paper affixed to his head declaring his offence. The naval war with the Dutch was being fought with varying success. The English had sometimes much the worst of it, and any allusion to their disasters would be sure to be resented.

CLIII. STEPHEN BULKELEY.   FOR PUBLISHING CONTRARY
TO THE STATUTE.

At the York City Assize, August, 1666. Stephen Bulkeley * was indicted "*pro imprimando libellos, Anglice Ballads, et non apponendo manum suam, contra statutum.*"

CLIV. GEORGE ATKINSON.   FOR SEDITIOUS WORDS.

Aug. 2, 1666. Before Sir Joseph Cradock and James Metcalfe, Esq. *Edmond Harcour, alias Metcalfe, of Muker*, sath, that, within these two yeares last past, one George Atkinson,† now of Muker, did severall tymes say that the surplice was the hower's smock, and that the King had broken his oath which he made to the Scotts by seting up this government, and if there were any riseing people would be flocking to them.

CLV. JOHN FAWSIT.   A DANGEROUS PERSON.

Sept. 11, 1666. Before Sir Joseph Cradock and James Metcalfe, Esq. *Margaret, wife of Enock Hodgson, of Richmond, taylor*, sayth, that a strainger (who is now in hold and calls himselfe by the name of John Fawsit) came yesterday, about fower a clocke in the afternoone, into her husband's house, and begged money of her, and said hee was newly come from the fleete. Whereupon shee asked him what victory wee had got.

---

* This indictment was ignored by the grand jury. The accused person had printed and published a volume of ballads anonymously. No such book is now known to be in existence, and it is probable, therefore, that it was suppressed.

Stephen Bulkeley was a well-known printer in the North. I have a book which he printed at York in 1642. In 1649 his press was busy in Newcastle, and shortly after this he was in Gateshead; but soon after the Restoration he removed to Newcastle. After this he took up his quarters in York, and there he produced many of those curious little books which are now so difficult to obtain.

† The accused person was the reader at Muker chapel and brings a countercharge against Metcalfe. He says that "Mettcalfe called him Baall's preist and asked him how he durst take upon him to be reader att Muker without the consent of all the neighbors." He denies saying anything about the surplice and the King. The grand jury threw out the bill.

A bill ignored against Frances, wife of Ralph Wythes, gen. On 12 Sept., 1666, John Waddington, of Burton Leonard, yeoman, said to her, "Thou art a rogue and a rascall. Now that Oliver is dead, wee dare speake to you. Now we have a King, God blesse him." She replied, "Thou dost not knowe how long, knave!"

To which hee replyed, wee had gotten none since the former. And, further, askeing him what newes from London, hee said there was fowerscore parrishes burnt. And being asked whether Whitehall were safe or not, hee said it was burnt, and that hee saw the King and the Queene . . . . . which was theire habittation at that time. And this informant said, "God knowes this hath beene a sore plott." Hee said, Yes. Hee had a letter from his brother out of France three months agoe, by which hee (knew) of it. And that Captaine Mayson of Yorke and young Rymer were the cheife agents to carry on that plott * for this country and for Yorke. And this informant bewailing of the citty of London's losse, hee said, they would not leave the face of a divill in it, before they had done with it.

Michaell Jackson, of Richmond, labourer, heard the above, and alsoe that the said strainger said that hee could lay a ball and goe an hundred miles before it should take fire.†

CLVI. WILLIAM GILL, CLERK. FOR SEDITIOUS WORDS.

Sept. 18, 1666. Before Sir John Armitage, Bt. *Thomas Senior, of Hopton, gen.*, saith, that upon Sundaye, the 9th of Sept., Doctor William Gill,‡ sometymes called Doctor Bridges, sometymes called Doctor Douglas, did in a sermon by him preached in the churche att Mirfeild, speakinge of the sinns of the people of England, and particulerly of the royall familie, did ex-

---

* A most curious and remarkable deposition. Many people believed that the Roman Catholics were the authors of the great fire of London, but the charge appears to be a groundless one. It was boldly made on the Monument, and Pope is alluding to this accusation when he says of that ugly pillar,

—— London's column, pointing at the skies,
Like a tall bully, rears its head and lies.

Little credit can be placed upon the statements of the accused person that are recorded in this deposition. He was bound over at the assizes to keep the peace.

Captain Mason, a month or two before this, had been arrested, with several others, for some offence against the state. As they were being brought to York Castle, by order of Lord Arlington, the escort was attacked by five men at the little village of Darrington, near Pontefract. The result was that Mason made his escape. (Thoresby's Diary, i. 261.) "Young Rymer" was probably the same person who was concerned in the Farneley Wood plot, and the kinsman, if not father, of the well-known author of the Fœdera.

† Fire-balls, which are said to have been used in London.

‡ The name of this person does not appear among the vicars of Mirfield, and he was probably an impostor. He was convicted at the next assizes and fined 13s. 4d., in addition to which, he was to stand in the pillory in the market-places of Leeds, Wakefield, Halifax, and Bradford.

presse and deliver these followinge words (to wit) that nothinge but reproache, shame, and confusion of face belonged to the royall famillie for their sinns and wickednesse.

Thomas Mann, of Mirfeild, heard in December last one Doctor Gill preach a sermon in Mirfeild church and deliver theise wordes, "The King and Queene are both idolaters, and soe are all the royall family. It is I that have said it."

Mary, wife of Thomas Foe, of Tote hill, clothier, on Tuesday the 5th of Sept., heard Mr. Gills (a wanderinge preacher) say theise wordes, " I have bene the Kinge's chaplin, but I never made it knowne before, and I have it in my power to burne Fekisby,* and, if I save it, it is for the old Mrs. Thornhill's sake, for shee is a good woman:" and then saide to this informant, " Lett theise wordes dye at thy foot, lett them goe no further, I say, for, if thou do, I shall heare of them againe."

CLVII. WM. KIRKE. FOR SEDITIOUS WORDS.

Nov. 10, 1666. Before Wm. Wickham, Esq. *Thomas Holt, of Hallyfax, gent.*, saith, that drinkeing a cupp of ale at Egton † with Wm. Kirke of Esdale side, the said Kirke said to the landlord of the house, being one of my soldiers, " Their major is growne so high that he saith never a papist shall weare a sword, not soe much as a stick in his hand. I say never a cavalier shall weare a sword. Within a few daies thou shalt not se a King in England."

CLVIII. JAMES, GEORGE, AND JOHN ALDERSON. FOR MURDER.‡

Before Sir Joseph Cradock and James Metcalfe, Esq. Dec. 11, 1666. *James Hutchinson, of Hartly, in Westmerland, minor*,

---

* Fixby, in the parish of Halifax, the old seat of the Thornhills.

† There were a great many Roman Catholics in the neighbourhood of Whitby, especially at Egton.

‡ A most extraordinary story of a murder said to have been committed among the moors between Askrigg and Westmerland.

That there had been a murder is probable enough. Chr. Alderson, of Askrigg, deposes that a person of the name of John Smith, who used to buy stockings at Askrigg, slept at his father's house in Swaledale on the 23d of March two years ago, and that he went towards Kirkby Stephen next day, and that he had heard it said that the man had never been seen again. A woman called Helen Alderson, of West Stonesdale, says, that, on the day on which " the plotters were executed at Appleby," she came from Mallerstang to her master's house at West Stonesdale; and, at a place called

sayth, that, in spring was two yeares, hee went from his owne howse with one Thomas Whitcheele, his neighbour, to seeke for two young horses upon the moore; and, being parted, he heard a voice cry out " Murder!" and did verily beleive hee heard the noise of a blow given, and two other men's voices; and after a litle while after he saw a horse with a rideing sadle on his backe coming towards him,* and a man following him on foote; whom hee asked if hee saw not two staggs, and hee said " Noe." Then this informant said unto him, " You have sure beene fighting, for you are all bloody," though hee saw no blood on him; and then that man replied " Noe." This informant then asked him who was with him; hee said it was his father and a neighbour who did followe a poore man who had lodged at his father's, and had stolne something there, and soe went away. And this informant went unto a place called Hollow Mill, and looked downe the gill and saw two men standing together with their backs towards him, and something lyeing on the ground . . . . if it were cloathes; and then hee went a litle further and . . . . . said Whitheele and told him what he had hard and seen. Then . . . . to see what would become of the men that were . . . .

Hawkinge Bower, near Hollow-mill-crosse, she saw a man restinge himselfe against a hray *with a kind of packe on his backe.*

Whiteheele or Whitehead, Hutchinson's companion, says that be saw nothing on the moors, and that they never found any bones at all! He deposes that, on the first occasion, Hutchinson told him of the cry that he had heard and of the men that he had seen. The Aldersons deny any connection with the affair. The informant's tale is partially confirmed, and it is a most marvellous one. The interest of it is heightened by the spiritual appearance mentioned at the end. Hutchinson was probably concerned in the murder himself, if he was not the sole perpetrator of it. He tells a somewhat incoherent story; but what a picture it gives us of the terrors of a guilty conscience!

I have found a certificate on behalf of the Aldersons to the following effect: " Whereas one James Hutchinson, of Hartley in Westmerland, who maliciously has gone about by his informacion to take away the lives, good name, fame, and reputacions of James Alderson, of Thwaite in Swaledale, and George and John his sonns, wee certifie that they have alwayes beene reputed and well knowne to be of good name, &c., not at all in any wise attainteud, nor supposed to be of any leude or vicious behaviour, but honnest in all their dealeings with all men, fathfull subjects to his Majestye and his late Majesty of blessed memory, and lovers of all his Majesties liege people. And wee are fully perswaded that the informacion of the said Hutchinson and his complices is false, and by the instigation of that wicked one the enimie of mankind." Feb. 26, 1666.

Appended to it are the signatures of 106 persons, including George and Francis Atkinson, ministers, Edmund Milner, and James Fryer, bailiff of the manor of Helagh. To shew how the dales were divided among clans I may say that the petition is signed by 33 Aldersons, 18 Milners, 11 Harkers, and 7 Metcalfes.

The bill against the Aldersons was ignored by the York Grand Jury.

* One Elizabeth Harrison of Nateby deposes before Sir Philip Musgrave that " she did see a man following a horse that had got from him. There was a yellow sadle cloth under his sadle; the horse couler gray. She did nott know the man, nor how long it is since shee saw him."

and by and by they came towards this informer and Whitcheele, and then this informer did perceive they were bearing something betweene them, and told the said Whitcheele therof, whereupon they went towards them, but they tooke horse and went away. Yet afterwards this informant and Whitcheele met a footman who came up the way that the 2 horsmen went down, and asked him if hee knew the 2 horsmen, and hee said " Noe," soe they returnd home. And at the latter end of summer they went unto the moore to seeke their staggs againe; and, coming nere to the place where they saw the two men bearing something, they began to looke aboute, and, in a waterhole, to their thinking, they saw the ribs of a man sticking in the bray, which, when they had moved with a staffe, fell into the water and swome, and then this informant did conceive their was the corpse and head of a man with haire on it. And this informant further saith that, about this time twelve month, one George Alderson, of Spennhouse in Swaildaile, meeting with this informant at Kirby Stephen, asked him if hee did not use sometimes to bee upon the moores, and this informant said " Yes;" then the said George Alderson said hee was the footman that belonged to the two horsmen that you saw in the gill, whom you asked if I knew them. And this informant then asked him who they were, and hee said his father and his brother John. And then this informant said " Was that your brother? Where got hee his horse againe?" and hee said, " At a house hard about the towne head," and, being asked what occasioned his coming thither that day, hee said his father and his brother were gone out before after a poore fellow that was lodged there, and had stolne something, and hee followed them for feare they should get some harme, but, before hee came to them, the deed was done. Hee said alsoe that his father was a very wicked man,* and did not repent him of anything hee had done; to which this informant replied, " Tell him from mee he shall heare from mee if I bee troubled in conscience or any other way." And this informer further sayth that, about Candlemas after, as hee stood at his owne doore about daygate, with his wife and ... Hartly aforesaid not being farr off, there came a strange lookeing man with a sad coloured coat, and a poake tied about his shoulder, and a staffe in his hand, and this informant bad him good even, and put of his hat, but the man said nothing at all, nor moved his hat. Whereupon this informant's wife † said she wondered

---

* The Aldersons deny all this, especially George. Isabel Hutchinson, the informant's wife, swears that he used the words in question about the wickedness of his father.

† The woman's deposition will illustrate this passage, " Shee was standing within

what kinde of man that was, to whom this informer said, "Sure he is a Quaker." Then the straing person said, "The Quakers' religion is better then yours, for yours is a murthering religion." Then this informant replied, "I defie thee and all the world for any such things;" and then hee said, "Hee that hath concealed murther is as bad as a murtherer." And this informant further sayth that, hee being in bedd one night this last summer, hee heard a voice, which he knew not, say unto him, "Speake, for I am sure thou art not asleepe." Then this informant said, "I command thee in the name of the Father, Sonn, and Holy Ghost to tell mee what thou art; and, if thou bee sent by God to declare what thou hast to say," and it denied that it was sent by God, or to tell what it was.

CLIX. LUKE WETHERHEAD, ETC. TREASURE TROVE.*

Feb. 28, 1666-7. Before John Clarke, Esq. *Mary Davison, of Alnewicke*, sayth, that the 1st of Feb. she liveing with Mr. Thomas Medcalf in Alnewicke, one Luke Wetherhead comminge home to the said house from plough was exceeding merry. She asking him the reason of his mirth, he answered her, that in the five acres where he had that daye ploughed he had found a pott full of silver, and much gold in the midle of it, and that it was all chested about, and that he would fetch it home at night. And at supper he told her that he and Robert Sanderson had beene fetching home the gold and silver, and that he had lifted

the doore when *this supposed man* came by there doore, whom shee did see, but tooke noe notice what kynde of person hee was, nor did she heare him say anything to hir husband; but she heard hir husband say, "I defie thee and all the broad world in that kynde." The tyme, to the best of hir remembrance, was betwixt Christmas and Candlemas last. One night, being in bed with her husband, she did wake out of sleepe and thought shee heard her husband talke, and asked him if he did speeke, and hee answered he spooke to noe body, but he never told hir anything that he was frighted untill lately that it was comonly discoursed off."

* A curious story of a case of treasure-trove in Northumberland. The discoveries of money and plate in that county have been numerous. Roman remains of great value have been found from the very earliest times, nay, in the first rituals of the Northern church there are special prayers for the consecration of vessels that were found in heathen places. The Corbridge lanx, now in the possession of the Duke of Northumberland, is very well known.

During the wars with Scotland a good deal of English treasure was lost on the Borders. I remember ten years ago at Carlisle examining a hoard containing several thousands of the silver pennies o. the Edwards. They had been brought to an ironmonger by two labourers who had found them near the Roman Wall. One had got his hat full of coins, and the other two stocking-feet crammed with them. They were being sold at the uniform price of 6d. a piece, and I became the purchaser of some fine specimens.

it up upon Robert Saunderson's backe, and that hee did not think he could have carried soe greate a weight of silver and gold in a great pott. And moreover one Jane Bell brought home a greate deale of it in a poke under her arme. She asked him when he would part it, he answered, here is soe dunes much of it that he could not gett time to partt it untill some hollydaye or some afternoone. The next daye being Candlemas daye, the said Mr. Medcalf being to hyre Robert Saunderson, the said Luke told him, "What neede hadst thou be hyred haveing soe much money? Thow mayst have bought land of thine owne and stockd it. For my part I shall garr two oxen and two horses mainetaine me like a man all my life time." He asked her how bigg a 5s. peece of gold was. She answered as bigg as three pence. He answered, then the gold that we have found are 20s. peeces, for they were as bigg as 12d. and that they had enough of them. And he told her that the pott was as bigg as the large brass pott she was scowringe.

CLX. WM. OGLETHORPE, GEN. ETC. FOR A MISDEMEANOR.*

March 13, 1666-7. Before Sir George Fletcher and Thomas Denton, Esq. *Thomas Pattinson*, saith, that when he should have come to give in evidence at the last gaole delivery held at Carlile, against Thomas Law, James Bridon, and John Bell,† whoe were at the breakeing of the house of Christ. Wannoppe of

---

* A case which gives a vivid picture of the state of society in Cumberland—and what a picture it is—outrages of the most dreadful kind—gentlemen by birth assisting the villains, and magistrates of the county defeating the ends of justice, and drinking with them in the common public houses. The account of the robbery is most graphic.

† At the gaol delivery at Carlisle, in December, 1666, John Bell was sentenced to death for this burglary, Law was acquitted, and Briden died before the assize began. Edward Birney was out on bail, and, as there is no mark against his name, it seems probable that he did not surrender. Pattinson and Law were bound over to keep the peace, and to appear at the next assize. Pattinson lived at Crosby; Law, Bell, Birney, and Noble, were "Bewcastlers," and lived in the most disreputable village in the North of England. Bell was probably some kinsman to the worthy who was commemorated by the following inscription in the churchyard of Farlam near Bewcastle:

> John Bell, broken brow,
> Ligs und'er this stean :
> Four of mine own sons
> Laid it on my weam.
> I was a man of my meate,
> Master of my wife ;
> I lived on my own land
> Without mickle strife.

the Holm . . ., this informant was threatened by Mr. William Oglethorpe,* that if he did give in evidence against Law, hee would bringe in James Briden, whoe was then at liberty, to come in, and sweare away his life. And that if there were not another man in England to come to doe the said Pattinson a mischeife, he, the said Mr. Oglethorpe, would either doe him a mischeife as to his person or estate himselfe. And Christ. Wannope hath confest that Mr. Oglethorpe would have given him 5*l.* not to have prosecuted Bell. The said Mr. Oglethorpe gave many harsh and terrible threatening words against the informant, which made him not soe cleare in his evidence against Law as he would have beene; which caused this informant to make his complaintt to Mr. Denton,† in hopes that course might have been taken with the said Oglethorpe, that soe he might have given in more clearer evidence. But the said Oglethorpe recciving noe rebuke, made this informant more slow in his evidence, as also because Henry Dacree, Esq., did wish him not to give in evidence against Law, for that the Earle of Carlile was out of the county, and that his Lordshipp had noe spleane to him,‡ which did more win upon the informant. He further saith, that about a weeke before the said house was broken, the said Law, Bridon, Bell, together with Edward Birney, Mungoe Noble,§ and one George Routledge,‖ went almost to the house of the said Christ. Wannope, to have broken the same; but they, hearing people abroad that night,

* Mr. William Oglethorpe was a thief himself, as well as a companion and encourager of thieves. He was tried at Carlisle, in August, 1667, for cattle stealing, and, pleading guilty, his case was referred to the Earl of Carlisle. There must have been something very attractive and romantic to a person like Oglethorpe in living the life of an outlaw and receiving the rude homage of the freebooters around him. I find that, in 1667, Richard Lascelles, of Gawthorpe, co. York, Gen., was in Newcastle gaol for frequenting the society of thieves. In the same year James Irwen, Esq., was charged at Carlisle with being a person of evil name and reputation, and Lord Carlisle was desired to settle what was to be done with him.

† Thomas Denton, Esq. was one the most active of the Cumberland magistrates. He wrote a peculiarly neat hand, and it is quite a treat to find a deposition which he took down. Mr. Denton, Sir Wm. Dalston, Bt., and Sir George Fletcher, Bart., were the royal commissioners who condemned Bell at Carlisle.

‡ This will give the reader an unpleasant insight into the state of Cumberland. The Earl of Carlisle, like Belted Will, was lord-paramount in the county. He had but recently returned from his expedition into Russia, of which an amusing account was published in 1669. There is much about him in that choice and splendid book, "The Memorials of the Howard Family," which was privately printed by the late Mr. Howard of Corby. I possess both these works.

§ Of this arch-thief some more information will soon be given.

‖ The Routledges lived in that den of wickedness, Bewcastle. They were also called Kirkbeck. There was no one in this county at that time who did not possess an alias.

returned againe in very great wrath and fury; the said Noble declareing that he had put the inside of his coate (out) on purpose to goe downe the chimney. And that he had three dayes veiwed the house where they might best (enter), and he found noe place soe convenient as the chimney. He, further, saith, that aboute a weeke after the attempt, the same persons came againe, except Noble and Routledge, accedentally meeting with Squire Dacree, as he was comeing to Harper-hill, all the said partyes fell into drinke with the said Mr. Dacrees, at Jenkin Armstrong's, at Greenes burne, and soe stayed till the busieness of the house-breakeing was over, at which James Bridon and Tho. Law was very angry. And Bridon declareing to this informant upon the saying he was afraide that Noble would discover them, said, "what, man!" that the said Noble could not deny his helpeing him to drive the seaven beasts which they stole out of Long Martin, from one Atkinson, about Brough faire last, with many other slouths and roberryes that the said Noble was in with the said Bridon, and therefore he durst not make any discoverye to the Squire for his life. Alsoe this informant further saith that he heard the said Bridon declare the said night that they broke the house of Wannope, that he had a mare of Mr. William Oglethorpe's, which he lent him when he and Noble went to stealc the seaven beasts of ..... Raylton's, of Newbiggin, and soe brought them unto Bewcastle; and he told this informant that Bridon, Oglethorpe, and Noble did devide the said goods amongest them. And about Michaelmas last Thomas Lawe told him that Mr. Oglethorpe would joyne with them in the breakeing of Wannope's house, and that of one Robert Blacklocke, of Rickerby, which they resolved to have gone to have broken if Bell had not bled soe ill in loseing two of his teeth. And he told him that William Oglethorpe had beene at severall such like busienesses before, for that there was a house broken about Kirk Oswald, and in makeing their attempt, one of the company had a stone throwne at him by one of the house as he was goeing upp the ladder, which feld him to the ground. Upon which they left the house and tooke the corps, and carried them to Bewcastle, and there buried him. And soe the said partyes smothered it the dead man's freinds, and said he had beene sicke a weeke before.

CLXI. ELIZABETH DUFFIELD.   FOR A MISDEMEANOR.

July, 1667. Elizabetha Duffeild, de Cawood, vidua, pro dispergendo diversa plasimata peste infecta * infra villam de Cawood.

CLXII. EMMY GASKIN.   FOR WITCHCRAFT.

July 4, 1667. Newcastle-upon-Tyne. Before John Emerson, mayor. *Margaret, wife of Thomas Sherburne, watchmaker*, saith, that, on Munday last, one Emmy Gaskin, of Sandgate, came to this informer's doore, and one Elizabeth Gibson her servant came to the doore, and the said Emmy asked something for God's sake; the said Elizabeth told her she had nothing for her, for she had gott too much ill by her allreadye. And this informer, lookeing out of the windoe, asked this said Gaskin what she did there, and bid her begone, for she had nothing for her. She replyed againe, if she had nothing for her, she said God give her lucke on it; and the said Emmy said to the maide, that she hoped either she would breake her necke or hang herselfe before night. And the said maide hath never been well since, for the night after she tooke her fitt which she had done many tymes before, and lay that she could not speake for about half an houre, and when she was in that condicion there begun a thing to cry like a henn among the people's feet, and assone as it begun to cry, the said Elizabeth did begin to smile and laugh, and then the thing that cryed like a henn did, as they thought, flawter with the wings against the bords of the floor, and when it left off the said Elizabeth came out of her fitt, and asked what that was that cryed, as she thought, like a henn, for she heard it, and saw the women that came to ask something for God's sake goe out at the doore, and is still worse and worse.

CLXIII. ARCHIBALD LITTLE AND ANOTHER.   FOR CATTLE STEALING.

Aug. 16, 1667. At Newcastle, before Charles Earle of Car-

---

* A very singular indictment. A woman exposes in the little village of Cawood some clothes, which, as it was supposed, were infected with the plague. The villagers are up in arms, and she is sent to the assizes. The plague paid many visits to York and its neighbourhood during this century, and did much mischief. The country people, as it will be seen, took the utmost precautions against its spreading. The disease was very fatal in the diocese of Durham at this time. Among the Mickleton MSS. in Bishop Cosin's library at Durham are many papers relating to its progress.

lisle. *Ann Armestrange* * deposeth, that, about a weeke or forthnight before Martinmas, Arch. Litle brought a blunt taled nag out of Cumberland, which he delivered to one Robert Moore, son of Geo. Moore, of Long Witton. That tyme More helped Little to a booty to carry backe. They first attempted to steale a white maire with a fole about Wooler, but were chased from her. The next night Little and Moore stole 2 horses, one from Barber of Long Witton, a maire coloured dun, another from Greene Leyton, a bl. dun nag. They carryed these to Darder, where they were kept by Robert Henderson, nephew to Robert Snawden, and by Sim. Elliott alias Cully, whoe likewise had a booty of five beastes and one maire. The next night Little and Moore stole five great beastes from Long Witton, and brought them to Dardar, where they had left the horses. They had their meat at Ann Henderson, of Rimpside, durcing this tyme. The next night being Saturday, Arch. Little, Sim. Cully, and the informant went away with the beastes and horses, and by the way neare Wascow Sheild they tooke away with them those beastes belonging to William Clea. Then they drive the beastes to Tho. Scott's,† of Dodbogg, where Scott would not let them come into the house because there was a fox-thatcher there, but carryed them to a sheyld hard by his house, where he made them a fire and got them meate. After 2 howers stay they went out a mile further to Jo. Rackas sheild, where they part two beasts amongest Mr. Charleton's ‡ of the Boure, and stayed there all day. Geo. Telfare came thither at that tyme, and proffered to send them meat from his sheild, but they did not accept it. Then next night, being Sunday, they drive their beastes to Mongo Noble's,§ save two that tyred, which

---

* The confession of a woman who had been a companion of thieves. She reveals the exploits of a marauding party, and her story possesses all the interest of a romance. This deposition must be read with No. CLX., as the one illustrates the other. I know not what becaune of the woman, who had been arrested on a charge of larceny, but Archibald Little, alias Scald-Arch, was tried at the Cumberland Assizes in March, 1666-7, and was sentenced to death, but was subsequently reprieved.

† Thomas Scott was acquitted at the Northumberland assizes in April, 1667.

‡ This person seems to have had a very bad character. I have seen him mentioned in several instances as either thieving himself or assisting thieves.

§ This Mungo Noble inherited all the thieving propensities of the famous Hobbie Noble, and was one of the greatest rogues on the Borders. He was a native of Bewcastle, and was very frequently in trouble, but generally contrived to make his escape. In 1663 he was charged with buying sheep and lambs knowing them to be stolen. In April, 1665, he was tried at the gaol delivery at Hexham, but was acquitted. In 1668 he was out on bail for divers felonies in Cumberland. The following extract refers to him:—

"When his Lordship held the assizes at Newcastle, there was one Mungo Noble (supposed a great thief) brought to trial before his lordship, upon four several indictments; and his lordship was so much a South-country judge, as not to think any of

weare left at Dodbogg, and belonged to Sim. Cully's share. Mongo Noble was from home, and his wife was fearfull to receive them, James Briden being newly taken: yett shee, after a little, tooke them into the house and gave them meat, and putt Little and Cully into a barne where Mongo his man lay called Wm. Nixon. The next morneing, being Munday, Cully sent this informant backe to Dodbocke to carry a bay horse, which was stole out of Yorkeshire, to Rimpside, which she did, and came backe to them to Mongo Noble's upon Wednesday following, where Cully still was, and told this informant that Little was gone to William Oglethorpe. The informant went then to Jo. Martine's of Rideings, where shee stole some cloathes, which she brought first to her uncle Jo. Armestrang's, and, after, her uncle went with her to Mongo Noble's, where Cully was afraid and threatened her because he thought shee had betrayed them to her uncle. She got the cloathes from Martine's before shee went with the gray horse to Rimpside. While shee was at Mongo Noble's there (came) a little man with a red face bl. haire wellkled. The people called him Sir. Shee conceived it was William Oglethorpe. He was about buying the dun maire and a cow that was stole or estrayed from them, offering eight shillings to Little whether shee was found or not, but the cow being found againe, Little would not take soe little. She further deposeth that Tho. Moralee * came to her last night and advised her to keepe her tongue, and hee and his freinds would warrant her. Shee further saith that the cloathes that she stole from Barwicke shee brought to Edward Charleton, of Newton, who advised her to put on man's cloathes, which shee did, and left both her cloathes and other things that shee gott their with him; which cloathes she could never get againe. There was of the Barwicke goods a bl. gowne, two ould peices of gold, three gold ringes, a silver bodkin, a greene petticoat with silver lace, hoods and scarfes, and severall other thinges. She afterwards by Robert Snawden's advise went to Edward Charleton to demand her cloathes. He told her he

---

them well proved. One was for stealing a horse of a person unknown, and the evidence amounted to no more than that a horse was seen feeding upon a heath near his shiel (which is a cottage made in open places of turf and flag) and none could tell who was the owner of it. In short, the man escaped, much to the regret of divers gentlemen, who thought he deserved to be hanged ; and that was enough. While the judge, at the trial, discoursed of the evidence and its defects, a Scotch gentleman upon the bench, who was a Border commissioner, made a long neck towards the judge and said, ' My laird,' said he, ' send him to huzz, and yees neer see him mere.' " (Life of Lord Keeper Guildford, i. 286.)

* This person, and one of the name of Gerard Morale, were indicted at the Northumberland assizes in March, 1665-6, and were bound over to keep the peace.

would give her none, but threatened her to deliver them to a justice of peace, if shee demanded any. Shee further saith that the cloathes for which she is now prosecuted she had them from Eliz. Gibson, daughter of Anthony Gibson. Shee further deposeth that Robert Snawden brought out of the west country a gray horse, for which he exchanged a broune one of his owne that was got in Yorkshire when he went thither with Edward Conyers. This gray horse is still in the possession of Jo. Hall, of Rodbury. Elinor Jorden, of Biskerton, is a receptor of ill company. About the latter end of harvest last, Robert Snawden had two bl. steers which came out of the west countrey, but knowes not whose goodes they were, nor from whom he had them. Sim. Cully and Arch. Little stole the beasts from Clenell, which were all gott againe but foure, which they blamed Oglethorpe for imbesleing. They were first carryed to Mongo Noble's; this Little and Cully told this informant.

CLXIV. JOHN PLATTS, ETC. FOR HIGH TREASON.

Oct. 6, 1667, *Samuell Swayne, of Sowerby*, saith, he was an apprentice with one John Platts, of Stanering End, above Sowerby, and about one month or five weekes before the discovery of the late plott,* the saide John Platts desired him to ryd a meare for the said John, under Capt. Hodgson, of Coley Hall, against his Matie that now is, which meare was well kept and very privately for the space of one quarter of the yeare or thereabouts for that purpose; and the saide John told him that he should have a case of pistolls and bullitts, and a sword, which he then had, and if that were not good enough he would buy him a better and provide him with what other armor that was fitting. After the saide plott was discovered Capt. Hodgson was taken prisoner and sent to Yorke; the saide John Platts hereinge thereof saide to this informant that if he had bene there when he was taken he would have lost his life before that Capt. Hodgson should have beene taken. And the saide John Platts did incurrage him to goe, and tould him that he might gett one hundreth pounds in the yeare by that business, if God blessed them that the plott

---

* The Sowerby plot, as it is called, was in the summer of 1661. There is little known about it. There is something concerning it in the Memoirs of Captain Hodgson, 1733-4. That gentleman had some share in it and was arrested. His ill fortune, we see, won him some sympathy, as he was greatly esteemed in the parish of Halifax. This was the first movement made in Yorkshire by the discontented Independents, but nothing came of it.

went forward, and that he would have had him ridd his meare, before one Josias Stansfeilde and others, which said Josias answered and saide, that he should have discovered it within foure and twenty houres, for now (said he) it is too late. And when this informant denied to ride the saide meare the saide John did sore beate him, and caused him to leave that part of the country.

CLXV. JOHN LEE.   FOR SEDITIOUS WORDS.

March 31, 1668. Before Sir Robert Shafto, at Newcastle. *Robert Fryzer, Serjeant-att-Mace*, saith, that, on the 15th of Oct., being att Wm. Mason's house in the Bigg markett, in company with Capt. Richard Mason, and some other gentlemen of this towne, and John Lee,* yeoman, and the company discoursing of his late Maties unjust and unlawfull sufferings, the said Lee (though not att all spoke to) said that he had often spoke to his Matie, and that the towne of Newcastle could not afford soe ill-favored a face as he had; upon which he being desired to hold his peace or begon, he replied, "What better is the present King, for there hath been no grace in the land since he came to it."†

William Hall, saith that, being then present, John Lee spoke that there were none that bare office in the excise but rogues, and what he did say to the rogue Mason, the exciseman, (meaneing the said Captaine Mason) he would prove and vindicate it; and what was Henry Brabant‡ (meaneing the present right wor^pll maior) but an exciseman? and none but broken rogues had such places.

* A person who speaks very freely against Royalty and the excise. Whatever faults Charles I. had, he certainly had no " ill-favoured face." That monarch was in Newcastle in 1639 and 1646. In the latter year he spent about nine months in the town, being at that time a prisoner. There are several anecdotes connected with his residence, which will be found in the local histories. I will give another, referring to an incident that occurred in the neighbourhood of Auckland. The King, it is well known, had an excessive dislike to smoking. The soldiers who were guarding the King were making use of their pipes without any regard to royalty, when a Mrs. Wren, of Binchester, went up to them and broke them in their mouths. " Lady," said the King, " I thank you. You have done more than I durst have done."

† John Mayling was charged with saying at Newcastle, on March 10, 1667-8, " God d—— his Majestie, what was hee more then another man that soe many men had suffered death for him? It were a good deed if all England would rise upp against him, and make quite of him, and then they would be quiett." He was acquitted, as also was Lee.

‡ In June, 1660, Mr. Brabant was made collector of the Customs, Subsidies, &c. at Newcastle. He was afterwards knighted, and in Feb. 1672 the reversion of his office was given to his son Henry.

CLXVI. WILLIAM SKELTON, GEN., AND OTHERS. FOR MURDER.

Apr. 28, 1668. Before Thomas Denton, Esq. *Dorothy Skelton, widdow, relict of Lancelott Skelton, late of High-house, co. Cumberland, gentleman, deceased,** saith that, aboute the last Twelftide, her said husband happened to have a defluction of rheum, and a distemper in his teeth, which impostumated, and, for want of skilfull chirurgions, put him into great paine and extremety of illnesse. About which time one Wm. Skelton of Penreth, gentleman, one of the brothers of the said Lancelott (who was at that time owing unto the said Lancelott the sume of 160*l*.) did, with many fair perswasions and flatteries, prevaile with the said Lancelott to come to Penreth to the house of the said Wm., and that Joyce, wife of the said Wm., did both write and speake unto the said Lancelott to come to her uncle, Thomas Gasgarthe, clerke of the parish of Penreth, and she was confident, next under God, he would cure him. Whereupon the said Lancelot was perswaded, contrary to this informant's minde, to go to his said brother's house in Penreth. And when they had him there, the three did make him believe that his distemper was the French-pox; as they both afterwards confessed they did to this informant, for which they gave him an oyntment, which they applyed to his backe; which Gasgarth confessed to this deponent would have killed him, if he had given him soe much more of that oyntment as the breadth of his finger. Afterward, aboute the beginning of March last, she, fearing that they had some designe upon her said husband, and that, partly by designe, and partly by want of judgment, they might endanger his life, did bring one Dr. Warton, an eminent physitian in Lancashire, to see him, and to know of him what was her said husband's distemper, who, haveing seen him, told her that he that had him in hand was an asse and a knave to take a man under cure, and not to know the nature of his disease. And he further said that his disease was the scurvy onely and noe other disease: and he gave this informant directions what he should take for the cure of it. But before the druggs could be procured, and the physick administered, they had drawn in his body soe weake with their tampering that his body was not fitt to receive it. And of that weaknesse he dyed suddenly after. And she further saith that they the said William, Joyce, and Skelton, did dureing the time of his illnesse,

---

* A Cumberland gentleman falls into the hands of quacks, and dies in consequence of their treatment. The case, however, was never brought before a court.

by all possible meanes endeavour to alienate the affection of the said Lancelot from her. And when she brought the said Dr. Warton to see him, they made him beleive that she brought him to destroy him. And, in the time of his illnesse they got the said Lancelott to signe a release of the said debt of 160*l.*, if it soe happend that he should die of that sicknesse. And the said Gasgarth, about a week before the death of the said Lancelot, did confesse that he was mistaken in his disease. And she further saith that he did never professe physick, nor chyrurgery, but hath ever been and yet is a parish clarke. And she doth verily beleive that by their unlawfull tamperings and clandestine practices the said Lancellott came by his death.

CLXVII. JOHN MELMERBY. FOR SACRILEGE.

June 19, 1668. Before Sir Conyers Darcy. *Ellin Wasse, of Ellerton,* saith, that John Melmerby came to her house, and confessed that on a night of publick ringing (which she beleeves was the 5th of November) he did lye concealed in a stall in Catherick church,* untill all the people were gone out, and then he tooke from thence the tippett, surplesse, and plate. And laughing merrily he sayd that Mr. Anthony was not able to gett another

---

* Sacrilege at Catterick. The case was a trumpery one, and Melmerby was acquitted at York. Mrs. Wasse's testimony was not believed. It was shown that she was influenced by her husband, who had made his escape from York Castle and wished to injure Melmerby. It appears that Melmerby, hearing of the robbery, got a search-warrant from Major Smithson, and went with it to the constable at Catterick, who was angry at him for interfering. By the advice of the vicar and Mr. Crofts of Appleton, Melmerby was arrested and carried to Richmond before Sir Joseph Cradock.

In the indictment the articles stolen are described as, a tippet, a surplice, a silver bowl, a woollen table cloth, a linen table cloth, a pulpit cloth, a hearse cloth, a napkin, and a basin.

I could say much about Charles Anthony, the vicar. The following entry which he made in his parish register bears directly upon this deposition and shews how he replaced what had been carried away.

"Deo Optimo, Maximo, calicem argenteum Carolus Anthonius, ecclesiæ de Catherick vicarius, dedicavit 25to die Decembris, anno Christi 1681.

" Oratio ejusdem ad calicis dedicationem.

" Omnipotens, Sempiterne Deus, Qui liberaliter omnibus tribuis, humillime confiteor nihil me de me habere, præter quod de Tua benignitate accepi. In testimonium largitatis Tuæ, et gratitudinis meæ, de Tuis retribui; et Majestati Tuæ hunc calicem dedico et consecro, non inanis gloriæ avidus, nec terrenæ remunerationis cupidus, sed devotissimo corde motus et humillimo animo promptus. Obsecro, ut hanc liberam meam oblationem benigne accipias, gratiose per manus meas sanctifices, et potenti Tua manu conserves et custodies, in usum perpetuum hujus ecclesiæ de Catherick, *ab omni furto et periculo:* Per Jesum Christum, Unicum Dominum, Unicum Redemptorem, et Unicum Salvatorem nostrum.

Gloria in excelsis Deo Patri, et Jesu Christo, Filio Ejus Unigenito, et Spiritui

tippett.* And he confessed that he did hide the said goods in a hole behind the doore within his house, and covered the same with a board and other trash which he threw upon it. And he sayd also that he went to a justice of peace for a warrant to search for the sayd goods, for feare people should thinke that he had stolne them himselfe.

CLXVIII. JOHN BOWMAN'S DEPOSITION.

June 26, 1668. Before Francis Barker, Esq. *John Bowman, of Greenhill, co. Darby, taylor,*† saith, that, upon the Tuesday before Assention Day last, hee was comeing home from Sheffield market on the footway towards Highley; and about the mid-way there was one John Brumhead overtooke him, and they past along untill they came against the cutlers bridge. And when they came at the said bridge they had some discourse concerneing an apparition that had beene seene theere, as it was reported, in the shape and corporall forme of a man that they called Earle George.‡

Sancto, ex utroque procedenti. Sicut in principio fuit, nunc est, et in sempiternum erit, per secula seculorum. Amen.
Dedicavit item lintea pro altari, et pulvinar pro suggesto."
Some other depositions about Melmerby will be given afterwards.
* This reminds us of the old song :
  "Without any surplice, or tippett behind,
  "The priest shall say service."

† An extraordinary story ; and it is difficult to see why the man should make a deposition in this matter before a magistrate.

‡ Earl George must be George Earl of Shrewsbury who died in 1590. He was a distinguished and prudent statesman and a person of the highest rank and consequence. The brachet or hound, which he led, makes us acquainted with his favourite amusement. In the tomb of the great Earl of Westmorland in Staindrop Church, there was found, a few years ago, the skull of a greyhound.
Capgrave gives us a picturesque story when he tells us how in 1343 the restless spirit of Bishop Burghersh, of Lincoln, " appered onto on of his swyeres, with a bow, arrowes, and horne, in a schort grene cote," and desired that reparation should be made for a misdemeanour that he had committed.
The story of Bishop Bek, of Durham, and Hugh the black huntsman of Galtres, will not be forgotten, " how the busshop chasid the wild hart in Galtres forest, and sodainly ther met with him Hugh de Pontchardin that was afore deid, on a wythe horse; and the said Hugh loked earnestly on the busshop and the busshop said unto him, " Hughe, what makethe thee here." And he spake never word, but lifte up his cloke, and then he shewed Sir Anton his ribbes set with bones and nothing more ; and none other of the varlets saw him, but the busshop only. And the said Hugh went his way, and Sir Anton toke corage, and cheered the dogges, and shortly after he was made Patriarque of Hierusalem, and he saw nothing no more. And this Hugh is him that the silly people in Galtres doe call Le Gros Veneur, and he was seen twice efter that by simple folk, afore yat the forest was felled in the tyme of Henry, father of Henry yat now ys."
It is unnecessary to allude to the ballad of the wild huntsman.

And as they were speakeinge of itt, of a sudden there visibly appeared unto them a man lyke unto a prince with a greene doublet and ruff, and holdinge a brachete in his hande. Whereupon this examinate was sorelye affrighted and fell into a swound or trannce, and contynued in the same, as hee conceiveth, for the space of aboute halfe an houre. And when he awakend he saw a man passinge with two loadend horses, and he went with him towardes Highley.

CLXIX. PATRICIUS CURWEN, GEN. FOR MURDER.

Aug. 8, 1668. Before Thomas Denton and John Aglionby, Esqrs. *Patritius Curwen,** gentleman*, saith, that he being in company with Mr. William Howard and Mr. Henry Howard, and Mr. Grimston last night, there happened to be a difference between Mr. Wm. Howard and Mr. Curwen aboute the drinking of (a) glasse of wine, whereupon Mr. Henry Howard, upon some language passing between Mr. Wm. Howard and Mr. Curwen, tooke Mr. Curwen by the eares, and threatened to kick him out of the roome: and Mr. Grimston fell upon the said Mr. Curwen with his fists to beat him, till Mr. Broadwood, m^r of the house, tooke Mr. Curwen out of the roome and carryed him to a bed, where he lay for some time in his cloathes, and arose againe and went out into the towne to buy a sworde of Leiutenant Neale's in the presence of Mr. Basill Feilding, for which sword he had long before been treating to buy. And upon his returne he went into the chamber to challenge Mr. Henry Howard to fight upon the Sands adjoyning to the towne. The said Mr. Howard with Mr.

---

* A duel arises out of some angry words that were spoken at a party of Cumberland gentlemen in the house of Mr. John Broadwood of Carlisle. Mr. Stephen Grimston says that the cause of the affray was the hasty temper of Mr. Curwen, who "spoke contemptibly of all the family of Howards." We might think that Pope had seen this deposition.

After they were separated, they go to rest.

The two Howards occupy one bed. In the morning Curwen comes into the room to demand satisfaction, and, after another message, the meeting on the Sands is arranged—the fons et origo mali.

Mr. Curwen was a member of a junior branch of the house of Workington. That great property came into the possession of his family on the decease of his namesake Sir Patricius Curwen. The two Howards were sons of Sir Francis Howard of Corby, although they are omitted in the elaborate pedigree of that family which was compiled by the late Mr. Henry Howard.

On the 8th of August, Wm. Tallentyre, of Carlisle, certifies that Mr. Curwen is very seriously wounded, and that it is doubtful whether he will recover or not. He recovered, and, after a short sojourn in Carlisle gaol, was discharged, with his fellow-prisoner, Meales.

Robert Strickland did meet the said Mr. Curwen with Sergeant Meales, and there the said Mr. Curwen engaged in duell with Mr. Henry Howard, and after he had wounded him twice desired him to give over, but Mr. Howard refuseing he killed him by running him through the body; and upon the said place also the said Mr. Strickland and Sergeant Meales engaged in fight as seconds.

CLXX. ELIZABETH TEASDALE. FOR MURDER.

Sept. 17, 1668. At Rokeby, before Wm. Robinson, Esq. *Margett Atkinson, of Eppleby Low-feild,** sayth, that her husband, John Atkinson, about 14 dayes since, hired a servant cauled Elizabeth Teasdale untill Martinmas, who, the same day she was hired, did speake in this informer's hearing some words, as if she knew something of the barborus murder that was lately committed att Thorpe upon Phillis Gilpin and her maid, saying that she heard say that there was 2 that murdered the said Phillis Gillpin, and that they chased the maid about the house, and proded her from under the bed and borde with a spitt whilest one kept the dore; faltering in her relation, saying sonetimes it was a boy, other sometimes a girle, never shewing anny thing of regrette for so horrid a fact, but laughing at those who seamed to be troubled at it, seeming to lessen it, saying she was but a gogle-eyd quean; and, during her aboad with the said John Atkinson, which was but five dayes, her discourse was frequently of this murder; and, being pressed to declare how she came to know these things, she did, much against the mind, and without the privity or knowledge of this informer and her husband, she did desert their service.

---

* A murder is committed in the quiet little village of Thorp, near Greta-bridge. A servant girl in the neighbourhood lets fall some mysterious words which seem to imply that she knew something of the horrid deed. When some stir is made she runs away from her place, and gets away into Westmerland. When she is found she denies having ever spoken the words assigned to her.

A person called Henry Carter, of Piercebridge, deposes that the woman told him that when the murder took place she was at Crosby Ravensworth, whereas she was really in the house of Chr. Thwaytes at Greta-bridge. He says also that Thos. Tolson, who lodged with Mrs. Dethick, not 30 yards from the place where the murder was committed, "had his dyett with the wooman until the murder done, and that blood was found in the house of M[rs] Dithick, and afterwards blood was found upon the horse's maine under the place where Tolson lay."

I cannot find that anything was done in this matter.

CLXXI. WM. INMAN AND TWO OTHERS. FOR MURDER.

Oct. 17, 1668. *George Batty, of St. Martin's-in-the-Feilds, taylor*, saith, that Richard Batty,* his father, was keeper of Newby parke, belonging to Sir Metcalfe Robison, and that he was walkinge out from his lodge to the castle on the 11th of June, 1660, between the houres of 10 and 11 at night, when he was mett by Wm. Inman, Chr. Fish, and Marmaduke Horseman, who had a leash of greyhounds, and came to the said parke to steale deere. Whilst the said Richard Batty did resist them he was knocked down by Inman, and he heard one of them say, "Hange him, and throw him into the pond."

CLXXII. STEPHEN ELLIS, GEN. FOR SLANDEROUS WORDS.

A true bill against Stephen Ellis, of Hipperholme, gen., for that he, on the 10th of May, 1669, said to Michael Armitage, son of Sir John Armitage,† then high sheriff of Yorkshire,

---

* An affray in the park at Newby. Three noted poachers from Ripon had slipped their dogs at the herd of deer, when the keeper came up and shot one of the dogs. Upon this he was assaulted by the three, and was severely wounded by Inman. He lived for 24 hours. His gun and the dog that he had shot were thrown into the pond.

Sir Metcalfe Robinson, who was in London, offered a reward of 10*l.* for the capture of each murderer. It was regularly announced in the market towns, and an unsuccessful hue and cry was made after the offenders.

The murderers had fled the country. Eight years afterwards two of them seem to have been arrested in London, having been challenged by the old keeper's son.

Chr. Fish confesses that he is a native of Andfield. He knows nothing of the murder or of the men since he left Ripon. He was once accused by Sir William Ingleby of stealing a deer. Has been at sea for more than six years, and came home twelve months since in the Rupert. Before that, he was in the Fountaine, commanded by Captain Leggat. Lodges in the Angell in Well Alley in Wapping. Has a wife and three children at Ripon, but has not heard of them since he left.

Marmaduke Horseman confesses that he was in the park with the other two, and that Inman struck the blow. They did not think that any harm had been done. He fled to Ireland, and has just come to England.

The three were indicted at the Yorkshire assizes in Sept. 1660, and, on the 30th of March, 15 Car. II. they were outlawed. Fish and Horseman were sentenced to death at the next assize after the taking of these depositions, and were executed.

† Sir John Armitage of Kirklees, another Sir John Fielding in the West Riding of Yorkshire. He was a great enemy to Nonconformists of every description, and was most active in suppressing conventicles. In this year he was High Sheriff of Yorkshire, and captain of the trained bands. He married a daughter of Thomas Thornhill, Esq., of Fixby, by whom he had eight sons, all of whom were childless. He fell from his horse as he was returning home from a drinking party at Nunbrook in April, 1677, and broke his neck. Oliver Heywood describes the scene, and evidently looked upon it as a judgment for Sir John's harshness to Dissenters.

"Sirrah! goe to Hallifax. And come, I am as good a man as thy father, but that thy father has some more meanes. And that which hee has hee gott by his poore tennants by racking theim. I gott nott myne by coseming and cheating."

CLXXIII. WM. WARREN.   FOR A CONSPIRACY.

June 27, 1669. Before Ralph Hebburne and Wm. Warren, Esqrs. *Adam Bell, marchant and burgess of Edenbrough*, saith, that, about the beginning of November last past, William Warren, late of Wooler, being then in Edenbrough, came to him, and would have perswaded him to (have) gone along with him to have taken away the moneyes of James Walker of Hamblton, being then in Scotland with an intention to buy beasts (being a drover); and, finding the informant alltogether averse to his desiers, he further moved him to goe with him into Northumberland, and lye in waite on Rimside Moore for William Warren, Esq. or John Clerke, gent., who were to pass that way, with a considerable summ of moneyes belonging to the right hon[ble] William Lord Grey, Barron of Werke, to Newcastle-upon Tyne, with intention to have murthered them, telling the informant, and shewing him a dagger, with an ivory haft, that he intended to ride up with the aforesaid William Warren and John Clerke, or either of them, with which dagger he would stabb one of them, and give a signe by a himm or cough to the rest of his partners to doe the like to those that were in the company; and, haveing done that, to take away the money and horses belonging to the officers of the said Lord Grey, and to pistoll the horses of the said William Warren and partners, and to have then fled for either Ireland or Holland; and he told him that he thought that Conyers would goe along with them, and that Thomas Bayley, then liveing in Scotland, would be one of his assistants.

Sir John was buried in Hardger Church, with a most gorgeous ceremonial, Samuel Drake, vicar of Pontefract, preaching the funeral sermon. He was also Sir John's chaplain whilst he was high sheriff, and printed the discourse which he delivered in York—I have a copy of it. The title runs as follows : " Totum Hominis, or the Decalogue in three words: viz., Justice, Mercy, and Humility. Being a Sermon upon Micah 6th, vers. 8th. Preached in the Cathedral of St. Peter's, York, upon Monday the 15th day of March, 1668-9, before the Right Honourable Baron Turner and Baron Rainsford, the Right Worshipful Sir Jo. Armitage, Bart., being then high sheriff of Yorkshire. By Samuel Drake, D.D. Vicar of Pontefract, and sometime Fellow of St. John's Coll. Camb. London, 1670." 4to. pp. 27. Dedicated to the Lady Margaret Armitage, of whom the writer says, " Residing at London, you have the glory of art and nature in your eye; but the ornament of a meek and quiet spirit in God's sight is of greater price."

Ellis pleaded guilty at the assizes, and was bound over to keep the peace.

CLXXIV. A LIST OF YORKSHIRE RECUSANTS.

July 6, 1669. *Drighlinton.* Robert Hollins.* *Barkisland.* John Fletcher. *Erringden.* James Barrett. *Rishworth.* Henry Dyson and Mary his wife, Mary Earnshaw. *Wadsworth.* Edmond Turner. *Pudsey.* Thomas Rainde. *Midgeley.* Abraham Helliwell. *Wareley.* John and Michael Bentley. *Greatland.* Timothy Hoyle, Martha Crosley, spinster. *Langfield.* John Whally. *Harshead.* Sarah Denholme, spinster, Wm. Denholme, Mary Denholme, spinster, Henry Reyner. *Cleckheaton.* Wm. Pearson, James Greave. *Fixby.* Mary Appleyard, spinster. *Idle.* George Booth and Eliz. his wife, Ephraim Sandall and his wife, Alice Woother, spinster, Francis Drake and his wife. *Hallifax.* Thomas Holmes, Wm. Rigby, Mary Rigby, spinster. *Calverley.* Hugh Jackson. *Stainland.* Eliz. Helliwell, spinster, John Wormall, John Copley. *North Byreley.* John Verity. *Heckmondwicke.* John Mallinson. *Northowram.* Thomas Pollard. *Tonge.* Grace Kitchin, spinster. *Horton.* Thomas Clough, John Peghells. *Thornton.* Edward Halley. *Heaton cum Clayton.* James Bradley, —— Jowett, widow. *Hoyland.* John Firth. *Bradford.* James Marshall, James Bond, Moses Sykes, Matthew Wright, Wm. Dawson and Mary his wife. *Wilsden.* Jonas Bothomley, Jonas Willman. *Hipperholme.* John Hodgson. *Haworth.* Chr. Jonas, and Joseph Smith, Wm. Clayton, jun. John Pighells, John Tayler, Jonas Turner, Nathan Heaton.

Hepworth par. Crofton. Ralph Champney, John Walker, Eliz. Champney, spinster, Joseph Warde, Margaret Bealley, spinster. *Warmfeild cum Heath.* Eliz. Barker, widow, Alice Cautheran, widow. *Shitlington.* Eliz. Clegge, spinster. *Ossett.* Widow Passeley, Thomas Passeley, Eliz. and Grace Passeley, spinsters. *Horbury.* John Issott, sen. and jun., Sarah Issott, spinster, Jephat Issott, Margaret Healde, spinster.

Pattrington. Patrick Gibson and Eliz. his wife, Geo. Simpson and his wife, Francis Thornley, Eliz. Tornholne, widow. *Burstwicke.* Leonard Metcalfe and his wife, Ralph Kyrton and Katherine his wife, Philip Headon and Anne his wife, George Cronfurth and Mary his wife, Mark Baxter and Mary his wife. *Halsam.* Robert Owst and Anne his wife, Henry Sled, Anthony Audas, Isabel Owst, spinster, Francis Thornley, John Dynnis and Alice his wife, Eliz. Norton, widow. *Watton.* Mary Suddaby, spinster,

---

* Another list of persons who had been absent from church for a month or upwards. It will be found that most of them were Roman Catholics.

Richard Purslove and Sarah his wife. *Driffield.* Silvester Simpson, James Blackburne, Thos. Pearson, Robert Etherington. *Naborn.* Wm. Palmes, gen., and Mary his wife, Wm. Boyes, Mary Todd, spinster, Richard Leng, milner, and Mary his wife, Thomas Ryeley and Ellen his wife, Henry Granger, George Browne, Joan wife of George Foster, Mary Bovill, spinster. *Dunnington.* Robert Hargrave and Jane his wife, Richard Marshall, John Harrison, Michael Tayler. *South Duffeild.* Thomas Bollen. *Bradfeild.* Wm. Downer, Henry Charlesworth, John Woodhouse, Ralph Saunderson, Hellen Simster, spinster, John Saunderson and his wife, Richard Bovill, John Brittlebancke, Thomas Revill, Sarah Webster, spinster, —— Greaves, widow.

Clapham. Chr. Squire and Eliz. his wife, Chr. Foster. *Sedbergh.* Francis Blenckarne, Wm. Ferry, Edward Trott, John Grysdale, Francis Blackling, Richard Speight, John Blackling, John Holme. *Hutton Pannell.* Margaret Purdue, spinster, Dorothy Fletcher, spinster, John Borges and Alice his wife. *Ingleton.* Thomas Baines and Isabel his wife, Geoffrey Leake, Thomas Leake and Eliz. his wife, Anthony Leake and Agnes his wife, Faith Calvert, spinster, Richard Beesley, and Agnes his wife, John Tayler and Eliz. his wife, Clement Stevenson. *Horton.* Matthew Wyldeman and Mary his wife, John Moore, John Bentham. *Bentham.* Wm. Ellershow, Wm. Gibson, James Parker, George Bland, James Balderston, Wm. Redmaine. *Wintersett.* Wm. Champney, sen. and jun., gen., Anne and Eliz. Champney, spinsters, Edmond Schoro, Thomas Schoroe, Mary Schoroe, spinster, John Brownnilay, Matthew Baminont, Dorothy Baminont, spinster. *Brearley.* George Holgate and Anne his wife, Robert Holgate, Anne and Mary Holgate, spinsters. *Havercroft.* John Clarkeson, Frances and Katharine Clarkeson, spinsters. *Cudworth.* Richard Whittie, Alice Stamadin, spinster. *Castleford.* Frances Rasin, widow, Wm. Beckwith, gen. *Kirke Smeaton.* George Holgate, gen. *Houghton.* John Huntres and Mary his wife, Wm. Bilcliffe and Mary his wife, Richard Bilcliffe and Mary his wife, Anne wife of Thomas Hill. *Featherston.* George Hippon, gen., John Hippon, Anne Corkar, Alice Hippon, and Bridget Scholey, spinsters, Oliver Freeman and Dina his wife, John Darley and Mary his wife. *Campsall.* Francis Middleton, gen., Thomas Watterton, Robert Abbey, Thomas Cooke. *Preston.* Philip Hamerton, Esq. John Hamerton, Esq., Philip Hamerton, jun. gen. and his wife, Francis Womesley, Anne and Eliz. Womesley, Isabel Wylding and Alice Walbancke, spinsters. *Newsholme.* Chr. Batty, Mary Tatham. *Waddington cum Bradforth.* John Boardman, Margaret wife of John Mentis, Isabel Parker, spinster. *Rimington.*

Thomas Driver. *Mitton cum Bashall.* Thomas Singleton. *Barnsley.* Thomas Dearlove, gen. and Anne his wife. *Stratforth.* Thomas Bulmer, Thomas Milborne, Thomas Snaith. *Bowes.* Henry Wenington and Alice his wife, James Raine, yeoman, and Jane his wife, Mary Richardson, spinster, Hannah Richardson. *Marwicke.* Ralph Dent and Isabel his wife, Robert Dent and Anne his wife, Ursula Croft, spinster, Robert Maultus and Mary his wife, Wm. Dent, Charles Wyllis, Wm. Orton and Isabel his wife, John Key and Isabel his wife. *Muker.* Edward and Joseph Milner, Wm. Garth, Symon Milner, John Harker, James Milner. *Reath.* John, George, and Wm. Kearton. *Seargill.* Christian Barnes, Eliz. wife of John Whittell. *Barningham.* Anthony Metcalfe and Eliz. his wife, Anne Apleby, spinster, Margaret wife of George Barsley. *Hinderthwaite.* Eliz. Allenson, spinster. *Marske.* Frances Hutton, widow. *Arkengarthdale.* John Barningham and Hannah his wife, Brian Peacocke and Anne his wife, James Peacocke and Anne his wife, Chr. Barringham and Anne his wife, John Hird and Margaret his wife, Ralph Peacocke, John Colling, Richard Hird, John Cowlin, James Crathorne, Vincent Peacocke and Eliz. his wife, John Raw. *Lartington.* Francis Wrightson, Robert Parkin and Anne his wife, Chr. Goodson, George Rayne, Charles Kay and Ellinor his wife, Chr. Heslop and Dorothy his wife, John Wrightson, Robert Bolron, Michaell Wrightson, Chr. Key, Ralph Key. *Cotherston.* John Walker, John Longerwood, John Bowson, Henry Bowson, Margaret Bowson, spinster, George Wilson, Jane Wilson, spinster, Andrew and George Appleby, Matthew Hutchinson.

Ganstead. Thomas Constable, gen., Anne Constable, spinster, Magdalen wife of George Hodgshon, Anne wife of Marmaduke Catterill, Francis Cowlman. *Sprotlay.* Nicholas Pearson and Bridget his wife, Richard Sharpe and Mary his wife, James Bainton and Jane his wife, John Pearson, Dorothy Bainton, spinster, Wm. Young and Mary his wife, Edward and Thomas Young, Margaret Young, Margaret Gedney, Ellen and Margaret Gedney, spinsters. *Flinton.* John Ellis, John Isaack, Joseph Thomson. *Swine.* Thomas Dalton, gen., Thomas Nodar, Ellen wife of John Linsley, Anne Dixon and Prudence Wilson, spinsters, Wm. Hay, Thomas Pinder, Jennet Lidfurth, spinster, Margaret Tislay, Anne wife of Marmaduke Catterill, George Hodshon. *Danthorpe.* John Thorpe and Jane his wife. *Humbleton.* John Shearson and Frances his wife, Anne wife of Peter Binckes. *Garton cum Grimston.* Robert Acklam, Ellen Acklam, widow, John Estropp and Ellen his wife. *Lelly.* Anne Moody, spinster. *Bilton.* Francis Burton, Henry Wells, Robert Hull and Eliz. his wife. *Fittling.*

Michael Morton and Katherine his wife. *Rouse.* Ralph Westerdale and Constance his wife, Wm. Mercer and his wife, Matthew Moore, Thomas Tindall, John Spencer, Francis Smith, —— Billaney, widow, Jane Harland, spinster, Wm. Morrill, Ruth Harland, spinster.
Killinghall. John Wardman, Alice and Eliz. Wardman, John Handlesworth. *Stainley cum Caton.* Henry Swaile and his wife, Michael Mawde and his wife. *Knaresbrough.* Thomas Jefferson and Anne his wife, Mary wife of John Cundle, Katherine Wheelas. *Burrowbridge.* James Homerton and his wife, Francis Calvert and his wife, —— Smithson, —— Loupe, —— Thorpe, gen. and his wife, —— wife of Francis Wilkinson. *Farnham.* —— Wincopp, gen., Barbarah Bickerdyke, widow, Ellen Wincopp, Eliz. and Jane Lascells, spinsters. *Beckwith.* Margaret Thomson, Edward Thomson and his wife, Ralph Reynolds. *Harrigate.* John Fawcett and his wife, Wm. Dobson, Robert Yong and his wife, Thomas Squire and his wife, Thomas Grimston and his wife. *Skriven.* Francis Hill. *Steanbecke downe.* George Smith, Thomas Spence and Cecily his wife, Joan Butler, Richard Gill, Richard Raynard and Joan his wife, Helen Raynard, Francis Gill, Francis Shaw and Anne his wife, Anne Thackwray, Robert, Wm., and Anne Grange, Mary Bell, Francis Baine. ——, George Norman, Jane Norman, Debora Baker. *Larton.* John Baxter and Eliz. his wife. *Rocliffe.* Isabel Warde, Marmaduke Grange, Anne Yonge, Eliz. Fawcett, John Yong, Wm. Treese and Jane his wife, Judith Treese, John Yong and Mary his wife. *Steanbecke.* John Tulley and Eliz. his wife, Thomas Beckwith, gen., Julian Beckwith, Margaret Bayne. *Scotton.* George Watkinson and Anne his wife, Thomas Watkinson, Sarah Burrow, spinster, Peter Blakey and Eliz. his wife. *Azerley.* Alice Duffeild, Charles Duffeild, Chr. Netherwood, Henry Duffeild and Margaret his wife, Katherine Rounthwaite, widow, George Rounthwaite, Chr. Coates and Eliz. his wife. *Burton Leonard.* Francis Duffeild and Jane his wife, Ninian Morris. *Healey cum Sutton.* Anthony Wade and Jane his wife, Dorothy Jackson, widow. *Fearby.* John Ryeley, Isabel and Mary Ryeley, Eliz. Bowes. *Ellington.* Thomas Hayton, —— Blackburne, widow. *Illon cum Pott.* Robert Warde, John Warde, Anne and Jane Warde, spinsters, Humphrey Baine and Susanna his wife, Richard King and Dorothy his wife, Richard Hanley. *Burton super Yore.* Marmaduke Beckwith and Eliz. his wife, Wm. Beckwith. *Rookwith, Thurne, and Clifton.* John Wray and Eliz. his wife, Eliz Wray, spinster. *Bedall.* Anthony Metcalfe, gen. and his wife, Timothy

Waine, Ralph Grange and Susan his wife, Chr. Lodge and Dorothy his wife, Anthony Lodge, Frances Petch, spinster, Thomas Lodge, Jane Petch, spinster, Matthew Engleton and Ellen his wife, Eliz. Wilson, widow, George Pearson and Margaret his wife, Wm. Lodge and Hannah his wife, Anne Dodsworth, widow. *Thornton.* Anne Williamson. *Tunstall.* Thomas Bainbrige and Ellen his wife. *Morton-flatt.* Robert Bulmer. *Pattericke cum Brumpton.* Thomas Whitton and Katherine his wife, Alice Clerke, spinster. *Burgh.* Sir John Lawson, kt. and bt., Wm. Edisforth and his wife, Richard Haw and Anne his wife, ——— Wickett, widow, Wm. Snell and his wife. *Coulburne.* James Fawcett, Eliz. Fawcett, spinster, James Hard and Anne his wife, Margaret Hard and Jane Spence, Wm. Bulmer and Anne his wife, Francis Corby, Thomas Corby and Grace his wife, John Fawcitt.

Burley. John Lowby. *Menston.* Miles Franckland and Agnes his wife. *Alwoodleyes.* Jane wife of Wm. Smith. *Baildon.* John Fowler. *Poole.* John Sparrow. *Otley.* Anthony West and Mary his wife. *Farmanby.* Daniel Hayes and Eliz. his wife. *Thornton.* Robert Rogerson and Katharine his wife, Thomas Dutton.

Pickering. Stephen Keddey and Katherine his wife, Dorothy Bell, spinster, John Keddy, Roger Chapman, Thomas Chapman, Richard Chapman, Mary Chapman and Alice Coultman, spinsters, Ellinor wife of Thomas Derixon, Eliz. wife of Francis Ellerton, Wm. Coulam, Robert King and Frances his wife, James Jackson and Anne his wife, John Jackson, Isabel Robinson, Eliz. Newtrice, widow, Anne Pennocke, widow, Richard Dobson and Mary his wife, John Cowlam and Anne his wife, Jane Campion, Thomas Collin and Margery his wife, Richard Barnard and Anne his wife, Nicholas Pilmoore and his wife, Robert Halliday and his wife, Anne Dring, widow.

Kirby Hill. John Harrison, Peter Harrison and Margery his wife, Jane Pinking, spinster, George Pinking and Jane his wife, *Laton.* Marmaduke Wilson and Katherine his wife, John Wiseman and Margaret his wife, Anne Stubbs, spinster, Robert Leath, Anthony Pearson and Jane his wife, James Hutchinson and Mary his wife, Anthony Foster and Jane his wife, Dorothy Wilkin. *Forcett.* Robert Shutt and Mary his wife, Anne Borrick, Mary Tindall, Mary Fenne. *Laton.* Eliz. Wilkinson, widow, Wm. Pearson and Bridget his wife, Mary Berry, Faith Cornfurth, John Berry and Eliz. his wife, Thomas Leatch and his wife, Robert Richardson and Bridget his wife, John Hurstt and Mary his wife, Mary Neesham, Anne Thomson, Mary Johnson, widow,

John Harrison and Anne his wife. *Barford.* Michael Pudsey, gen. and Jane his wife, Galfrid Appleby and Mary his wife, Richard Clifton and his wife, John Berry and his wife, Thomas Dodsworth and Katherine his wife, Eliz. Parkin. *Ovington.* Francis Tunstall, gen. and Anne his wife, Marmaduke Appleby, Eliz. Hodgshon, Mary Todd, Rowland Lowish and Jane his wife, Eliz. Wray, Dorothy Somersides, Mary Hodgshon, John Hodgshon and Seth his wife, Dorothy Parker. *Newsham.* Wm. Smithson, John Smithson and Julian his wife, George Smith and Ellinor his wife, Anne Johnson, Robert Smithson and Grace his wife, Grace wife of James Frest, Ellen wife of Thomas Brignall. *Gilling.* Bryan Corby and Mary his wife, Francis Simpson and Frances his wife, Eliz. wife of John Wallis, Eliz. Thomson, Philip Smailes and Isabel his wife, Mary Smailes, Richard Butterfeild and Grace his wife, Alice Butterfeild. *Dalton.* Roger Mennell, Esq. and Mary his wife, Chr. Wade and Isabel his wife, Robert Ayleman and Eliz. his wife, Francis Scaife and Isabel his wife, Wm. Menell and Eliz. his wife, Eliz. Messenger. *Caldwell.* Wm. Stocktell and Anne his wife, Ellinor Stocktell, Frances wife of James Gregory, Eliz. Gregory, widow, Alice Gregory, spinster. *Melsonby.* John Boolmer and Jane his wife, Robert Pearson and Isabel his wife, Thomas Pearson, Nicholas Stubbs and Margaret his wife, John Thomson and Eliz. his wife, Mary wife of Richard Watson, Anne Clerke, widow. *Sutton super Derwent.* John Yorke, Peter Laycocke. *Thornton.* Edward Gower, Hester and John Frame, John Day, taylor, Symon Scroope, Esq. and Mary his wife, Bridget Scroope, James Thornton, Tristram Driffeild, Anthony Appleby, Symon Staveley, Mary Singleton, Katherine Bickerdike, John Petch, Henry Atkinson and Anne his wife, Thomas Chambers, Chr. Dent and Philippa his wife, Ralph Morland and Barbara his wife, John Skelton and Frances his wife, George Carter and Dorothy his wife, Diana Atkinson. *Bellerby.* John Wetherill and Mary his wife, Ralph Aulle and his wife. *Coverham cum Oglethorpe.* John Smithson, Anthony Bradrake, Wm. Coates and his wife. *Hunton.* Ellen Theakston, Jane Wylde, Chr. Askew and his wife, John Dent and his wife, Cuthbert Bankes and his wife, Chr. Hawkins, Eliz. Theakston. *Holme.* Wm. Franckland, gen. and Eliz. his wife, James Alcocke and Anne his wife.

CLXXV. THOMAS FISHER. FOR MURDER.

July 24, 1669. *William Warde, of Beverley, ale-house-keeper*, saith, that Thomas Fisher,* labourer, and others, being att his house and discoursing concerning the murther of Elizabeth Wright, and that the said Fisher was suspected to have murthered her, and likewise that itt was beleived hee would be forcd to touch her body; the said Fisher said, if hee were forcd to goe to touch her body hee would have other two or three persons to doe the like.

CLXXVI. RICHARD GILPIN, CLERK, AND OTHERS. FOR HOLDING A CONVENTICLE.

Aug. 4, 1669. Before Ralph Jenison, Mayor of Newcastle, *Cuthbert Nicholson, cordyner*,† saith, that upon Sunday last, about

---

* A murder at Beverley. The victim was a woman who had been Fisher's paramour. Many suspicious circumstances were brought forward against him—he had been seen with the woman—he had been heard to threaten her—it was evidently to his interest to get her out of the way. He was convicted and executed at York.

The custom of obliging the supposed murderer to touch the body is alluded to. It was commonly believed that blood would flow from the corpse when this was done, and this was considered to be a proof of guilt. Several remarkable instances of this have been printed and commented upon, but people quite forget that this flow of blood is easily to be accounted for by natural causes. Webster, in his Discovery of Supposed Witchcraft, alludes to this subject, and overthrows the popular superstition.

† A deposition which throws a good deal of light upon the early history of the Nonconformists in Newcastle. They were a very numerous and influential body. I have found but few indictments against these people at York, and it is probable enough that many of them were tried at the sessions. The following deposition relates to an arrest of another party of Dissenters in Newcastle in another place, and at a little earlier period.

"July 22, 1669. Before Ralph Jenison, Mayor of Newcastle-on-Tyne. Cuthbert Nicholson, cordwainer, saith, that, upon Sunday last, there was assembled at the house of Wm. Dewrant's, in Pilgraham streete, a great multitude of people, consisting to the number of 150 persons or there aboutes, under the pretence of religious worship and service, for he heard them sing psalmes. And, after singing was done, he did see and heare the said Wm. Dewrant pray amongst the said people. And Robert Fryzer, one of the cerjeants-att-mace, being with the churchwardens of the same parish, did in the name of Mr. Mayor discharge them there unlawfull assembly, and, upon that, they dispersed themselves. Amongst whom was Geo. Thursby, draper, and his wife, John Tompson, draper, Lyonell Blagdon, merchant, Wm. Dent, merchant, Suzann Bonner, widdow, Charles Newton, gentleman, Thomas Smith, barber-chyrurgion, etc. etc."

"Mr. Durant, brother to John Durant, of Canterbury. He married the sister of Sir James Clavering, Bart." (MS. Memoir of Alderman Barnes.) He died in 1681, and his tombstone which was found under a staircase in one of Sir Walter Blackett's stables in Pilgrim Street, is preserved in the chapel of the Unitarians, who claim him as the founder of their congregation, originally Trinitarians. The only ground of such

five or six of the clock in the morneing, he did see a great nomber of people goe inn to the howse of Mr. Richard Gilpyn, minister, in the White Freers,* and, afterward, he went to parson Joⁿ Shaw,† and acquainted him with the premisses. Whereupon the said Mr. Shaw, togeither with the churchwardens, constables, and serjeants-att-mace, by the comaund of Mr. Maior, did repaire to the said Richard Gilpin's howse. And when they came there all the dores were shutt and made fast. And after the dores were broken open he did see these severall persons come out, viz. Robert Johnson, merchant, Dr. Tunstall,‡ Wm. Cutter, James Hargraves, merchant, Wm. Hutchinson, Geo. Headlyn, fitter, Charles Newton, gent., Humphrey Gill, gent., Jno. Bittleston, tanner, Matthew Soulsbey, roper, Michaell Jobling, pullymaker, Robert Finley, chapman, and diverse other persons to the nomber of fortie.

The information of Cuthbert Nicholas, cordwainer, against the persons hereunder named for being att meetings and convinticles:

an opinion seems to be the probability that on Durant's death the congregation of Gilpin, their undoubted pastor, received the deceased's friends into their flock. Durant had formerly officiated in All Saints Church. W.H.D.L.

* It is remarkable that, in 1728, Mr. Gilpin's congregation purchased property in the White Friars, and erected the Hanover Street chapel. They had previously assembled outside the Close Gate. The deposition points to an earlier locality before their worship was tolerated.

" Mr. Richard Gilpin claimed to be of Bernard Gilpin's line, and had his scutcheon pinned at his coffin." (Memoir of Barnes.) Something about his family may be seen in Nicolson and Burn's History of Cumberland, under Scaleby, and of himself in Calamy. He was ancestor of Wm. Gilpin, the author of many delightful works on picturesque beauty. After he had surrendered the rectory of Greystock he practised medicine at Newcastle. " Doctor Gilpin, having outlived all the ministers of his own age and time, many his superiors and most of them his equals, became the leading man of these Northern parts, and was by some styled the worst of the best, and the best of the worst sort of ministers." (Memoir of Barnes.) He died in 1700. W. H. D. L. There is a quarto sermon of Gilpin's in print, which he published when he was at Greystock.

† John Shaw was lecturer at St. John's and rector of Whalton. He was the author of two controversial works which were published at the expense of the corporation of Newcastle, *i. e.* Origo Protestantium, or an answer to a Popish Manuscript, 4to. 1677, and, No Reformation of the Established Reformation, 1685.

‡ Dr. George Tunstall, a Yorkshire gentlewoman by birth, was town's physician at Newcastle. Dr. Tunstall was bold enough to rush into the Scarborough Spaw controversy, and to break a lance with the belligerent Dr. Witty. He began the onset with " Scarbrough Spaw spagyrically anatomized. By Geo. Tonstall, doctor of physick. London. 1670." This provoked a rejoinder from Witty, to which Tunstall replied with " A New Year's Gift for Dr. Witty ; or the Dissector Anatomized. London. 1672." Witty called his antagonist a mountebank, and the compliment was fully returned. The whole controversy was a most amusing one.

Mr. Richard Gilping, Mr. William Deurant, Mr. John Pringle,* Mr. Henry Lever,† preachers.‡

Mr. Geo. Dawson and Katherine his wife, Mr. Geo. Thursby § and his wife, Mr. Lyonall Blaigdon and wife, Mr. Wm. Hutchinson and wife, Mr. Wm. Johnson, Mr. John Thompson and wife, Mr. James Hartgrave, Mr. Samuell Powell, Mr. Thomas Powell, Mr. Peter Sanderson, Edward Kirton and wife, Wm. Cutter and wife, Mr. Robert Johnson, Mr. Richard Baker and wife, Mr. Thomas Blair, George Hedlam, Robert Cay, Rich. Jones, Mr. Geo. Bednall, James Jackson, Wm. Wilkinson, sadler, Matthew Soulsby, Thomas Dawson, Robert Wilkinson, Mary Bainbrigg, widdow, John Greene, William Sherwood, John Emerson, potter, David Sherwood, John Ward, Mr. Tho. Ledger, and wife, Michaell Jopling, George Waugh, schoolemaister, John Bittleston, John Shacklock, Richard Righ, Rich Readhead, Mrs. Thompson, John Pigg, Humphrey Gill, Mr. John Carr, Titus Pithey, Widdow Jefferson, Christo. Gibson, John Hornesby.

CLXXVII. EDWARD CANBY AND OTHERS.   FOR A RIOT.

Jan. 25, 1669-70. Before Godfrey Copley, Esq. *Henry Riley, servant to Nathaniel Redding of Santoft, in the county of Lincoln, Esq.,*|| saith, that, on Friday last being the 21st, about ten a'clock

---

* "Dr. Pringle, another physician and pastor for some time of a congregation there, who married a choice good woman, with whom he got a very great fortune." (Memoir of Barnes.) He died in or before 1693.

† Ejected from St. John's, Newcastle; buried at All Saints in 1673.

‡ In 1663 Bishop Cosin wrote to the Mayor of Newcastle, telling him to look sharply after "the caterpillars," naming as the ringleaders "William Durant, Henry Leaver, Richard Gilpin, and John Pringle." (Bourne's Newcastle.)

§ Brother of Ralph Thoresby, the antiquary. It is singular that Mr. Ambrose Barnes's name does not occur in this list.

|| An account of one of the many scenes of violence that were witnessed on Hatfield chase during the drainage of the levels. I have already stated how unpopular that scheme was, and to what insults and perils the foreign settlers were exposed.

In 1655 Nathaniel Reading was sent from London to collect the rents which had been granted to the Duchess of Buckingham, and to keep down the opponents of the Dutch drainers. He was a man of immense energy and daring, but in Yorkshire he met with difficulties that would have overwhelmed any ordinary person. He fought, as he says, as many as thirty-one pitched battles, some of his men being killed, and many maimed or wounded. I have already given a deposition which describes an attack that was made on the house of Mr. Van Valkenburgh. The following notices relate to the same subject.

"Nov. 3, 1649. Richard Lee, of Beusley, co. Hants, &c. indicted for entering the house of Sir Gabriel Vernat, at Hatfield, called Nortoft, and detaining it.

"1657. Indictment against Mark Van Volkenburgh, of Hatfield, Esq., Walter

in the morning, he saw Mr. Edward Canby, Richard Starkey, Cornelius Prole, Humphrey Tonge, John More, Mark Matthews, Richard Carlisle, Abraham Bar..., Francis Wood, Richard Read, Benjamin Guy, and Jacob Lecon..., of the parish of Hatfield, and other persons, to the number of fifty, as he believes, armed with swords, pistolls, gunns, and other armes, come to Santoft aforesaid, where the said persons did assault, shoot, and wound the said Mr. Redding, without any provocation on his part, or any servant of his, for that the said Mr. Redding, in the hearing of this informant, had severall times commanded his servants that that they should not resist or provoke any of the said persons. And the said persons did violently assault, beat, and wound Robert Wiburn, in so much that he lost much blood, which this informant seeing, and being afraid of himself, he ran away. He further saith that his said master sending the last night Thomas Coupland to Roger Portington,* of Barnby Dun, Esq., who was

Wray, Esq., George Gibbon, gen., George Wood, gen., and many others, of the same place, for taking two mares from James Pinckson at Hatfield.

" March 1657-8. Indictment against Nathaniel Reading, of Hatfield, Esq., Jacob de Can, gen., and others, for a riot.

" Sept. 1660. John Popplewell, of Belton, co. Lincoln, labourer, and 23 others, indicted for killing John Pattricke.

" March, 1660-1. A bill against Nath¹. Reading and three others for stealing a horse from Daniel Duverley, ignored.

" March, 1660-1. Mark Van Volkenburgh and 28 others indicted for taking three horses from Robert Maignon, James Poulson, and Andrew Waterloe.

" July, 1661. Richard Maw and 28 others, to keep the peace, for a riot at Thorne.

" March 16, 1671-2. Before Sir Henry Thompson, Lord Mayor of York, Nathaniel Reading, of London, Esq., sayth that, upon the 21th of Jan. 1669, Humfrey Tonge, of Hatfield, laborer, came to his house, and there, without any provocaccion given to him, did shoot this informant into the leggs (haveing before threatned to come to his house and put a brace of bulletts in his belly), and did break open his stable dore and steale one or two bridles, and he stroke one Robert Wayborne, servant to this informer, on the head and felld him to the ground.

" March 11, 1672-3. Nathaniel Reading, and others, indicted for a riot, and for driving away the cattle of Robert Martison, Richard Read, Francis Rooke.

" 5 Feb. 1680-1. Nath. Reading, Esq., says, that, having on 27 Jan., in virtue of an order of the House of Lords, made a distress of several horses belonging to Henry Moore and brought them to Santoft, the said Henry, and others with him, came and used violent language and threatened to shoot him, of which he is much afraid.

A long and most interesting account of Reading is to be found in the History of South Yorkshire. In early life he had thrown up his law books and wandered to Naples, where he allied himself to Massaniello, and only won his life by the eloquence with which he begged for mercy. In 1679 he was counsel to the Roman Catholic lords, and was charged with tampering with the witnesses on the other side. For this he was put in the pillory, fined 1,000*l.*, and imprisoned for a year. After this he returned to Lincolnshire and was subjected to the same persecutions with which he had formerly been annoyed. In 1696 his house was barricaded and set on fire, and the inmates made their escape with very great difficulty. He died about 1712, broken down with poverty and age.

* The Portingtons of Barnby Dun were favourers of the insurgents.

the next justice of peace, with a letter that he would please to come to suppress the rioters, the said Coupland returned this day from Mr. Portington wounded in four severall places of his head, and so beaten of his armes and bodie as he was not able to come to make his own complaint, and he told this informant that the said Humphrey Tonge .... to Mr. John Bradburne had done it, and did pursue him a mile and a half from the high way before he overtook him; and further saith he heard some of the said persons say, they neither cared for the Duke, nor for those commissioned by him, for as they light on them they would knock them in the head.

CLXXVIII. JOHN BROWNE. FOR SEDITIOUS WORDS.

Feb. 3, 1669-70. Before Godfrey Copley, Esq. *John Walker, of Sikehouse, yeoman*, sayeth, that, at this informant's owne house in Sykehouse, John Browne,[*] reading his Ma^{ts} speech to both houses of Parliament, dated the 18th of Januarie, 1666, wherein his Matie sayeth that "the nation had never lesse cause to complaine of greivances, or the least injustice or oppression, then in these seaven yeares it hath pleased God to restore me to you," that, upon readinge those wordes the said Browne did say the King was the veriest rogue that ever reigned; and, as for the the Stewards, one of them formerly runne away into another land, and gott to be steward to some great man there, and soe changed theire name to bee Stewart.

CLXXIX. ANNE WILKINSON. FOR WITCHCRAFT.

Apr. 1, 1670. Before Fr. Driffield, Esq. *Anne Mattson* saith, that yesterday, Mary Earnley, daughter of Mr. John Earnley, of Alne, fell into a very sicke fitt,[†] in which shee continued a longe time, sometimes cryinge out that Wilkinson wyfe prickt her with pins, clappinge her hands upon her thighs, intimatinge, as this informant thinketh, that shee pricked her thighes. And other times shee cryed out, "That is shee," and said Wilkinson's

---

[*] An old soldier who had been in some trouble for clipping money. He made use of some other words not complimentary to Royalty. He was acquitted at the assizes, and was bound over in his recognizances to keep the peace. Sir Philip Monckton, then High Sheriff of Yorkshire, was one of his bondsmen. The accused person had probably been a soldier under him.

[†] An old woman is charged with witchcraft, but was acquitted at the assizes.

wyfe run a spitt into her. Whereupon Mr. Earnley sent for Anne Wilkinson, widdow; and, when as the said Wilkinson came into the parlour where the said Mary Earnley lay, the said Mary Earnley shooted out, and cried, " Burne her, burne her, shee tormented two of my sisters." Shee saith further that two sisters of the said Mary Earnleye's dyed since Candlemasse last, and one of them upon the 19th of March last dyed, and, a little before her death, there was taken out her mouth a blacke ribbond with a crooked pinne at the end of it.

George Wrightson, of Alne, saith, that yesterday Mary dau. of John Earnley, gent. fell into a violent and sicke fitt, and continued therein one houre and more, all that time crying out in a most sad and lamentable manner that Anne Wilkinson was cruelly prickinge and tormentinge her with pins, as the said Anne was sittinge by her owne fire upon a little chaire; and presently Mrs. Earnley sent this informant to the said Anne Wilkinson's house, whoe brought word shee was then sittinge by the fire upon a little chaire when he suddenly came into her house.

Anne Wilkinson, of Alne, widdow, saith that shee never did Mr. Earnley, nor any that belonged him, any harme, nor would shee doe; and, as for the bewitchinge of any of his children, shee is sackless.

Margarett, wife of Richard Wilson, sayth, that, in her former husband John Akers' lifetime, she once lost out of her purse 50s. all but three halfe pence; and, shortly after, there hapned to be a great wind, and, after the wind was downe, she, this ex^t, mett with Anne Wilkinson, who fell into a great rage, bitterly cursing this ex^t, and telling her that she had bene att a wise man, and had raisd this wind which had put out her eyes, and that she was stout now she had gott her money againe, and fell to cursing her againe, wishing she might never thrive, which cursing of the said Anne did soe trouble this ex^t that she fell a weeping, and, coming home, told her mother what had hapned, and her mother bad her put her trust in God, and she hoped she could doe her noe harme. And the next day she churned but could gitt noe butter; and, presently after, this ex^t fell sicke, and soe continued for neere upon two yeeres, till a Scotch physitian came to Tollerton, to whom this ex^t went, and the phisityane told her that she had harme done her. And she further sayth that her then said husband, John Acres, fell shortly after ill, and dy'd of a lingring disease, but, till then, he was very strong and healthfull.

CLXXX. ADAM BLAND, ESQ. FOR MANSLAUGHTER.

Apr. 4, 1670. Before Sandford Nevill and Francis White, Esqrs. *Adam Bland, Esq.*,* sayth, that, on Munday the 28th of March, hee and one Mr. Conway and Mr. Gargrave were together at Methley, and Mr. James Strangewayes, and one Mr. Willughby, came rideing by, where, seeing this ex^t in the yeard of one Burton, the sayd Mr. Strangewayes lighted and saluted this ex^t in a freindly maner, but, after a little pause, Mr. Strangewayes taxed the ex^t with some words that he should speake of the sayd Mr. Strangewayes, which this ex^t (in justice to himselfe) utterly denyed; wherupon Mr. Strangewayes seamed to bee very well satisfyed; and thereuppon they went into the house of the sayd Burton; and, about eleaven of the clocke at night, the ex^t went with Mr. Conway into a chamber of the sayd house, to see him in bed, leaveing Mr. Strangewayes and Mr. Willoughby below in the roome where they had beene drinkeing; and, when this ex^t came downe, Mr. Willoughby was gone out and Mr. Strangewayes left alone; where this ex^t sat him downe by him in a freindly maner, and Mr. Strangewayes started upp uppon a sudden, and drew his sword, and swore, G—— d—— him, hee would kill the ex^t if hee would not fight him, and with that made a passe at this ex^t, which hee avoyded by leaping backe till he came with his backe against a livery cupboard beeing against the wall at the farthest side of the roome, and then the sayd Mr. Strangewayes made a second passe which the ex^t put by, and got a prick in the knee with Mr. Strangewaye's sword, and then the sayd Mr. Strangewayes made a third violent passe at the ex^t, which this ex^t put by with his left hand; and haveing his sword (for his defence) poynted against Mr. Strangewayes' hee runn himselfe uppon it, by which this ex^t conceives hee received his wound.

* Another of the quarrels that were so frequent among the country gentlemen. It took place, as usual, at an inn, and one of the combatants, Mr. James Strangeways, died on the spot. A few years before this he had witnessed a similar scene at Pickering, of which I have given an account, but it had given him no warning. Robert Nun, of Methley, gen., Edward Ashton, gen., Richard Willoughby, gen., and others, were of the party, but their evidence was of little use, as they were not present at the affray.

Mr. Bland was the second son of Sir Thomas Bland of Kippax. He pledges himself at the assizes to procure the King's pardon, and is required to do so, himself in the sum of 100*l.* and in two sureties of 50*l.* each, i.e. Edward Copley, of Batley, Esq. and Lionel Copley, Esq. jun., of Wadworth.

CLXXXI. A LIST OF YORKSHIRE RECUSANTS.

July 8, 1670. *Azerley.** Chr. Coates and his wife, Charles Duffill, Alice Duffill, Henry Duffill and his wife. *Minskip.* Michael Wright and Ursula his wife, Mary, Peter, and Richard Earle, Anne Gray, and Barbara Simpson. *Burton Leonard.* Francis Driffield and Jane his wife, Ninian Morris. *Grewillthorpe.* James Metcalfe, Margaret and Jane Walker, Mary Atkinson. *Killinghall.* Jennett Holdsworth, Alice, Eliz., and John Wardeman. *Steanbeck.* Margaret Baine, widow, Jane, and Thomas Beckwith, John Tullie and Eliz. his wife, Eliz. wife of Richard Baine. *Klint.* John Kendall, John Milner, Wm. Shan and his wife, Wm. Thomson, John Thomson and his wife, Robert Bucke and his wife, Peter Shann and his wife, Thomasin Askwith, Robert Joy and his wife, Jane Thomson, Wm. Wheelas and his wife, Francis Fish and his wife, Thomas Hardcastle, sen. and jun., Chr. Mautus, sen. and jun., Margaret Watson, Mary Hebden, Jane Steele, Anne Hopperton, John Mautus, Anne Gratewood, Katherin Smith. *Larcon.* Charles Baxter and his wife. *Kirby Malzard.* John Fish and Mary his wife, Katherine Brafill. *Aldfeild cum Studly.* Wm., Beatrix, Philip, and Simon Maultus. *Harrigate.* John Fawcitt and his wife, Thomas Squire and his wife, Robert Yong and Anne his wife, Thomas Grimston and Eliz. his wife, Wm. Dobson, Mary Hogg. *Bewerley.* Wm. King and his wife. *Arkendale.* Wm. Knaresborough, gen., and his wife, Chr. Smith and his wife, John Jesse and Margaret his wife, Mary Pullen, widow, Ellen wife of John North. *Scotton.* John Watkinson and Anne his wife, Thomas Watkinson, Peter and Sarah Blakey. *Fountaines earth.* George Swainson and Eliz. his wife, Katherine Craven, Magdalen Bayne, Margaret Rayner, Dorothy Scott, Margaret Horner, John Bridge. *Knaresborough.* Thomas Jefferson and Anne his wife, Richard Casse, George Casse and his wife, Boswell Middleton and his wife, Marmaduke Inman and his wife, Daniel Dodgshon. *Waitwith.* Matthew Burnitt and his wife, James Wheelehouse and Mary his wife, Thomas Harrison and Grace his wife, John Kendall and his wife, John Askwith and his wife, Francis Bucke and his wife, Francis Wheelehouse and his wife. *Pannell.* Edward Thomson and his wife, Ralph Reynald, Margaret Thomson, spinster. *Staveley.* George Norman, Jane Norman, spinster,

---

* A long list of Recusants. They are charged with being absent from church for a month. I cannot find that any punishment was inflicted on them.

Eborah Bacon, Robert Fosewicke, Eliz. Fosewicke. *Rocliffe.* Isabel Warde, spinster, Anne and John Yong, Eliz. Fawcitt, spinster, Judith Treese, Wm. Treese and his wife, John Yong, sen., and his wife, Richard Robinson. *Burrowbridge.* Francis Calvert and Anne his wife, James, John, and Wm. Calvert, Eliz., Anne, and Dorothy Calvert, spinsters, Eliz. Barker, spinster, John Lindley, James Hamerton and Mary his wife, Francis Thorpe and Jane his wife, Anne Loope and Mary Wilkinson, spinsters. *Stranbeckdowne.* Wm. Ward, sen., Frances wife of Wm. Baine, Mary Bell, Michael Pigott, Jane Spence, widow, Mary Thackwray, Anne, Robert, and Wm. Grange, Francis Gill, Anne Thackwray, widow, Margaret Lancaster, widow, Francis Shaw and Anne his wife, Alice and Richard Gill, Robert Browne, Anne Suttell, spinster, Ralph Suttell and Anne his wife, Thomas Spence, George and Wm. Smith.

South Owram. —— Ealey, widow. *Skircoate.* Edward Usherwood, Joseph Ushard. *Bowling.* Chrysis Wamesley, spinster. *Horton.* Mary wife of Thomas Clough. *Calverley.* Hugh Jackson. *East Witton.* Francis Eventine, Dorothy Gill, Anthony Appleby and Jane his wife, Dorothy Appleby, Chr. Petch, Wm. Wolmesley and his wife, —— Wolmesley, Wm. Withrington, John Cowell, Ellen and Mary Watson, Francis Halliwell, John Shaw and Magdalen his wife, John Bartlett and his wife. *Thornton Steward.* Simon Scroope, Esq., and Mary his wife, Bridget Scroope, James Thornton, Tristram Duffeild, Simon Staveley, Henry Atkinson and Anne his wife, John Atkinson, Dinah Atkinson, Thomas Chambers, Chr. Dent and Philippa his wife, Ralph Morland and Barbarah his wife, John Skelton and Frances his wife, George Carter and Dorothy his wife, *Gumpton.* John Simpson and Jane his wife, Mary Close, John Keirton and Eliz. his wife, Anne wife of Marmaduke Maultus. *Finghall.* Chr. Cundall and Mary his wife, Jane wife of Henry Clarkeson. *Burton.* Eliz. Hutchinson, widow, Eliz. Hutchinson, jun., Anne wife of John Milnes, Alice Dawson, widow, John Robinson and his wife, John Petch, sen. and jun., and their wives, Eliz. wife of George Lelley, Eliz. and John Horseman, Castinia Barker, widow. *Coniescoate.* John Wedrell and his wife, Mary Wedrell, Ralph Ansley and his wife, Dorothy Peacocke, Chr. Collinson. *Hunton.* Chr. Aisker, Cuthbert Bankes and Cecily his wife, Matthew Husband and Jane his wife, John Dent and Mary his wife, John and Katharine Fenwicke, Anne wife of Elias Dodsworth, Chr. Hawkins, Anne Barker, widow, Eliz. wife of Edward Theakston, Ellen, wife of John Theakston, Chr. Stanley. *Arrathorne.* Christina wife of Marmaduke Richardson. *Laborne.*

George Waite and Mary his wife, James Allen and Anne his wife, John Allen and Eliz. his wife, Robert Reynoldson and Eliz. his wife, Dorothy wife of James Wray, Magdalen Garison, spinster, Margaret and Eliz. Baine, Katharine Vittie, Anne Russell, Mary Hobson, widow, Ellen wife of George Allen, James Buck. *Wensley.* Eliz. Atkinson, Henry Robinson and Katherine his wife, Anthony and Dorothy Robinson, John Willis and Ellen his wife, Anne Braithricke, Anne Fishwicke, Margaret Chesney. *Downeholme.* Wm. Franckland and Eliz. his wife, James Alcocke and Anne his wife, Lucy wife of Robert Wiggin. *Harnby.* Francis Morland. *Ellerton.* Nicholas Adcock, Eliz. Morley. *Spenithorne.* Simon Jefferson and Jane his wife, Margaret Scurray, widow, Margery wife of Ralph Chayter, Brian Sclater and Eliz. his wife, Anne Thomson, widow, Jane Ingram, widow, Dorothy Gill, widow, John Wray. *Coverham cum Oglethorpe.* Margery Croft, Anne Hemesworth, John Smithson, Anthony Bradricke, Wm. Cowest and his wife.

Danthorpe, John Thorpe and Jane his wife.

Aldbrough. George Mennell and Olive his wife, Anthony Metcalfe, gen., and Frances his wife, Edward Birckbeck, gen., Jane and Bridget Birckbeck, John Roome and Anne his wife, Eliz. Roome, spinster, Stephan Dalton and Ellen his wife, Francis Dalton, James, Anthony and John Scorrey, Matthew Todd and Eliz. his wife, Marmaduke Spence and Eliz. his wife, Mary Browne, Anne and Mary Bussley, Eliz. Roberts, Jane Stockton, James Scamer, Francis Rudd, John Rudd, Robert Walker, sen. and jun., Margaret Walker, spinster, Thomas Walker and Eliz. his wife, Mary Burden and Bridget Stubbs, spinsters, John Sidgeworth and Grace his wife, Chr. Bucke and Dorothy his wife, George and Anne Welbancke, Ellen Pyburne, spinster, Mary Pyburne, sen. and jun., Margaret Pyburne, Richard Todd and Isabel his wife, Henry Hudson and Mary his wife. *Drighlington.* George Rigg, John Hardy. *Pudsey.* Wm. Pudsey. *Eccleshill.* George Smith. *Cleckheaton.* Richard Scholefeild. *Boulton.* Mary Jewitt. *Rishworth.* John Bothomley. *Leversedye.* Martha Horsefeild. *Allerton.* Jonas Bothomley and his wife. *Wadworth.* Edmund Turner *Heworth.* Chr. Smith, Jonas and Joseph Smith, John Pighells, John Tayler, Jonas Turnor. *Clifton.* Sarah Denholme. *Ovenden.* Thomas Law. *Idle.* Alice Crowther, Sampson Bawmforth. *Hipperholme.* Thomas Taylor, Mary Pellington. *Tonge.* Wm. Goodall. *North Byerley.* Jane Wharter. *Thornton.* Anne Todd. *Rastricke.* Thomas Firth, sen. *Hecknondyke.* Thomas Mercer. *Heaton.* James Bradley. *Warley.* Michael and John Bentley. *Barkisland.* Thomas Teale, Jeremiah Lang. *Shelfe.*

Wm. Jackson. *Midgeley.* Samuel and John Turner, Henry Bolles. *Ealand.* Martha Crosland, spinster, Timothy Hoyle. *Stainland.* John Copley.
West Tanfeild. Sir Wm. Tanfeild, kt., and dame Eliz. his wife, Eliz. Plaine, Richard Tayler, Wm. Currier. *Middleton Quarnehow.* —— Vadcoe. *Pickall.* Mary Lumley, widow. *Hallikeld.* Edward Blackburne, Wm. Blackburne, Thomas Foster.
Elsternwicke. Wm. Yong and Mary his wife, Edward, William and Thomas Yong, Margaret, Ellen and Margaret Gedney. *Fitlinge.* Michael Norton and Margaret his wife. *Bilton.* Francis Burton, Henry Wells, Robert Hall. *Sprotley.* Nicholas Pearson and Bridget his wife, Richard Sharpe and Mary his wife, John Pearson and Rebecca his wife, Jane Baynton. *Witton.* Henry Brigham, Dorothy, Richard and Mary Brigham, George Farthing and Mary his wife. *Humbleton.* John Stearson and Frances his wife, Anne wife of Peter Binckes. *Lelley.* Anne Mody.
Ellington. Thomas Hayton and Hannah his wife, —— Blackburne, Anne and Matthew Scott. *Firby.* John and Sibil Ryley, Eliz. Bowes. *Swinton.* Henry Adamson and Eliz. his wife, Anthony and Margaret Adamson, George Jackson and Frances his wife, George Jackson and Ellen his wife, John Smith, Thomas Smith and Sarah his wife, Wm. Smith and Alice his wife. *Masham.* Robert Lodge and Hester his wife, Jane Bridgwater, widow, Thomas Bridgwater. *Ilton cum Pott.* Humphrey Bane and Susanna his wife, Richard Kinge and Eliz. his wife, Robert, John and Thomas Warde, Richard Jackson. *Burrell cum Coolinge.* Mary wife of Wm. Ecopp. *Bedall.* Ralph Grainge and Susan his wife, Anthony Metcalfe, gen., and Eliz. his wife, Timothy Wayne, Wm. Lodge and Anne his wife, Mary Binckes, Sarah Smeaton, Miles and Thomas Lodge, Chr. Lodge and Dorothy his wife, Bridgett Stainley, Eliz. Wilson, Matthew Ingleton and Ellen his wife, John Ingleton, Anthony Lodge, George Pearson and Margaret his wife, Margery Tennant, Anne Dodsworth, Ann Bell. *Rookwith and Thurne.* John Wray and Eliz. his wife, Eliz. Wray. *Tunstall.* Thomas Bainbrige and Ellinor his wife. *Snape cum Thorpe.* Ralph Erington and his wife, Wm. May, Mary Rylead. *Screwton.* Robert Bulmer and Anne his wife, Robert Bulmer, Bartholomew Bulmer, Eliz. Pallister. *Brough.* Sir John Lawson, kt., Anne Odesforth, widow, Richard Hall and Anne his wife, Isabel wife of Wm. Sewell, Mary Wickett. *Cathericke.* Marmaduke Thwaites and Eliz. his wife, Robert Jaques, Mary Wastell, Eliz. Metcalfe, Wm. Loftous and Anne his wife, John Loftous. *Cowburne.* James Fawcitt, John Fawcitt and Alice his wife, Eliz. Fawcit, Thomas Cooby and

Grace his wife, Frances Cowby, Jane Spence, Edward Rudd and Isabel his wife, John Marley and Mary his wife, John Wood and Eliz. his wife, Thomas Langchester and Eliz. his wife, Matthew and John Todd, Thomas Faweitt, Jane Pearson, Anne Walker, Mary Foster, John Manfeild, John Goldsbrough, —— Simpson. *Ovington.* Anne Tunstall, Mark Appleby, John Huggison and Sith his wife, Lawrence Lowesh and Jane his wife, Mary Huggison, widow. *Standwicke.* Edward Birkbeck, Thomas Girlington, John Dobson and Anne his wife, Matthew Walker and his wife, Mary Walker, widow, Robert Walker, Robert Manfeild and his wife, John Manfeild. *Dalton.* Roger Menell and Mary his wife, Mary Messenger, Chr. Waide, Thomas Foster, Robert Akeman, Wm. Mennell and Eliz. his wife, Trinian Anderson and Eliz. his wife, Eliz. Messenger, Gabriel Appleby, James Kilborne and Eliz. his wife. *Laton.* Marmaduke Wilson and Katherine his wife, James Hutchinson and Mary his wife, Anthony Hesle and Jane his wife, Robert Leach, Anne Stubbes. *Gilling.* Brian Cooby and Mary his wife, Francis Sampson and Frances his wife, Eliz. Wallis, Philip Swailes and Isabel his wife, Richard Butterfeild and Grace his wife. *Newsam.* Wm. Smithson, John Smithson and Julian his wife, George Smith and Ellinor his wife, Ellinor Warde, Anthony Shutt and Katharine his wife, Grace Prest, Ralph Shaw and Mary his wife, Robert Smithson and Grace his wife, Ellinor Brignall. *Caudwill.* James Gregory, —— Gregory, widow, Hellen and Wm. Stockton, Frances and Grace Berry. *Ravensworth.* Nicholas Allen, Anthony Allen and Anne his wife, John Allen, George Allen and Eliz. his wife, Mark Allen and Anne his wife, Nicholas Cargraive and Ellen his wife, Anthony Coates and Mary his wife, Jane wife of John Hall, Margaret Anderson, John Walker, Simon Bradley, Francis Catton and Mary his wife, Michael and Eliz. Norton. *Newsam.* Cuthbert Cowling and Anne his wife, Michael Wiseman, Margaret wife of Edward Cowling, Cecily Atkinson, Margaret wife of Wm. Gibson, Anne wife of Clement Rowne, Dorothy wife of John Colling, Robert Cutter and Eliz. his wife. *Skeeby.* Valentine Allen. *Howton.* Robert Richardson and Bridget his wife, John Hart and Mary his wife, Mary Nesom, Mary Johnson, John Harrison and Anne his wife, Eliz. Ellis, spinster, Jane wife of Robert Sheilds. *Forcett.* Robert Shutt and Mary his wife, Thomas Leach, John Berry and Eliz. his wife, Wm. Pearson and his wife, Eliz. Wilkinson, widow, Marmaduke Cornforth and Faith his wife. *Barford.* Michael Pudsey and Mary his wife, John Berry and Eliz. his wife, Matthew and Wm. Berry, Eliz. Parkins, Isabel Wetherill, widow, Gabriel Appleby, Richard

Clifton and Anne his wife. *Appleby (Eppleby).* Mary Shutt. widow, Mary Atkinson, widow, Anne wife of Richard Shutt, *Melsonby.* Robert Pearson and Isabel his wife, Wm. Lightfoot and Eliz. his wife, Wm. Massam and Anne his wife. *Burford.* John Turnor and Mirrill his wife, John Thomson and Alice his wife, Mary Watson, Winifred Fetham, Anne Dickinson, Anne Clearke, Robert Ritchinson. *Kirby Hill.* John Harrison, Peter Harrison and Margaret his wife, Eliz. Harrison, spinster, Joan Pinckney, George Pinckney and Jane his wife.

Remington. Thomas Driver. *Newsholme.* Chr. Batty, Mary Tatham, widow. *Malham.* John Beckwith. *Boulton juxta Bolland.* Thomas Fletcher, Isabel Wilding, widow, Alice Walbancke, —— Womesley, widow. *Mitton.* Brian Singleton and his wife. *Waddington in Bradford.* Margaret wife of John Meautys, John Boardman and Isabel his wife, Brian Parker, Henry Bayley and Isabel his wife, James Harrison and Margaret his wife, George Crumbleholme and his wife, Cecily wife of Wm. Walker. *Barnoldswicke.* Richard Boothman and Alice his wife, Richard filius ejus et Henricus frater ejus. *Bowland.* James, John, and Thomas Driver, Edward Heskitt, and his wife, Margaret and Eliz. Turner, Eliz. Hewson. *Walton cum Bretton.* Anne Watterton, Eliz. Browne, filia ejus. *Bolland.* Lawrence Copeland and his wife, Robert Seele and Frances his wife, Mary Broadhead, —— Watterton, Matthew Mooke. *Ossett.* Alice Passhley, widow, Thomas and Mary Passhley. *Wakefeild.* Edward Nettleton. *Sugdell.* Charles, Ellinor, and Anne Thimleby, —— Nettleton, widow, Robert Hemesworth, Wm. Gooderidge, Jane and Mary Pease, Margaret Orre.

CLXXXII. THOMAS CARR, GEN., AND OTHERS.   FOR ARSON.

A true bill against Thomas, James, and John Carr, of Ford, gentlemen, Matthew Carr, alias Pearson, of Ford, gen., Jane Fenwick, spinster, Jane and Margaret Carr, of Ford, spinsters, and others, for that they on Jan. 17, 1671, set fire to the house of Susan Carr, widow, of Bromerigg.*

* We know nothing more of this case. It originated no doubt in some family feuds, for which the county of Northumberland has been unhappily remarkable.

CLXXXIII. MR. HODGSON. FOR AN ASSAULT.

Jan. 24, 1670-1. Before Thomas Bawtry, Lord mayor of York. *Jonathan Welburne, of Yorke, merchant,** saith, that, on Thursday last, two doggs feighting in Micklegate, Mr. Hodgson, one of my Lord Freschevile's troope, came out of Mr. Hillary's house and drew his rapier and struck at a brewer's servant, whoe owned one of the doggs, and cutt him cross over his cheeke. Whereupon Mr. Perott, one of the sheriffs, did goe to him and desired him to putt upp his sword, telling him it was not fitt to draw in the streete upon a naked man. To which Mr. Hodgson answered that, if he (meaning the sheriff) should lift upp his staff against him, he would run him through; and, as the sheriff was goeing away, he called him "Pale-faced rascall," and said he would marke him against another tyme. And the sheriff told Mr. Hodgson, he should know he bore as much rule in the citty as he did, and should know it shortly.

CLXXXIV. MARGARET PINCHBECK AND HER DAUGHTER. FOR MURDER.

Oct. 29, 1671. Before Wm. Gray, gen., coroner.† *Elizabeth Pinchbecke, daughter of John Pinchbecke, deceased*, saith, that, about 8 or 9 a'clocke in the evening on Fryday last, this informate's father and mother being falln out before their goeing to bed, after some ill words there was some strokes betwixt them, and her father tooke the sticke from her mother, and severall strokes was given. But this informate being in bed is uncertain who gave the more strokes, but she perceived her mother to bring an ax from under the cupbord, where it usually lay, and carryed itt to the bedside, and went into bed to her father, and seamed to lye very quietly, until this informate thought they had beene both asleepe; but, about 3 or 4 a'clocke in the next morneing, as she beleives, she heard her mother rise out of bedd and take the axe. This informate being amaised does not remember whether she had a candle or noe; but this informate heard a

---

* An affray in the streets of York in which the sheriff is insulted. The indignant official brings the offender before the lord-mayor, and he is bound over at the assizes to keep the peace.

† The history of a frightful crime—a woman murders her husband in cold blood! Her punishment was a fearful one—she was burnt alive, and her daughter was acquitted. The story is told with painful minuteness.

great stroke given, which she beleives was upon her father's head by her mother with the ax. And, upon the first stroke, her father gave a great skrike, and after that this informate heard a stroke or two more, but her father crye no more; but her mother caused her to gett up and putt on her close. And this informant's mother then tooke her father on her backe with one of his armes above her shoulder, and the other of his armes under her other arme, and commanded this informant to carrey his feet, which she did as well as she could, but she was scarce able to beare them, but was forced severall tymes to lett them fall. They carryed him downe the hill by John Smith's doore stead, and turned againe on the right hand towards the mill, on along by the doores till they came att Morgan's doore, which is a deepe part of the becke, and this informate is certaine that they putt him into the becke at Morgan's doore, where Alice Morgan dyed;* and, after this informat and her mother came in, her mother charged her that she should never tell to anyone that she killed her father, for, if she ever spoke of itt to any one, she would kill her; and that her mother warmed water, and with itt washed the bench by the bedside which was all bloody, and allsoe washed severall other bloody places within the house.

William Salton, of Pickering, was present on Saturday morning last about 7 a'clocke at the becke side neare Pickering upper mill, where was found lying the dead corps of John Pinchbecke in the water with two daingerous wounds upon his head, one upon his forehead, by which the scalpe broke, and a great cutt overthwart his head, both which wounds this informat beleives has beene done with such an instrument as an ax. And afterwards this informat, goeing towards the testator's house, found an ax nigh the doorestead very bloody, and found blood on the long settle and seat by the bedd side, and upon the bedd and chest, and in severall other places of the wall and other parts of the house. And this informate, being this day charged by the constable to attend Margarett the testator's wife to secure her, hath heard her severall tymes this day deny that she knew anything of her husband's death; but since she has confessed to this deponent and John Hewlin that she did take the ax and knocked him in the harnes her owne selfe, and that she carryed him downe and threw him in the becke, and that he swattled after he came in the becke. And further, in these words, she tugged him with the might she had.

Elizabeth, wife of Richard Wilson, saith, that she examined

---

* She had probably been drowned in the beck at this place.

the girle, Pinchbeck's daughter, if she knew whoe killed her father, who answered that her father and she heard a knocking on the top of the house, and he went out and shee see him noe more. Margrett, the testator's wife, sitting in the house, was exclaimeing against her husband, and said, "Ah, Pinchbecke, thou has sought to breake my hart, but I live still, and hast thou putt thyselfe away."

Margrett, the testator's wife, sayth that she did take the ax, and knocked her husband's harnes out, for he had done her a great injury and did deserve it.

CLXXXV. ANDREW CARR, GEN.   FOR MANSLAUGHTER.

Apr. 20, 1672. Before Robert Widdrington, coroner. *Richard Hendersone,* sayth, that, in or about the 22d or 23d of Feb. last, being at Chillingham in the company of Mr. Gilbart Swineho and James Swinho,* Mr. Andrew Carr and severall others, he heard

---

* A duel between two Northumbrian gentlemen which had a fatal issue. Mr. Swinhoe was killed. A witness says that he heard him say that he was not hurt till Robert Gray, of Turvelawes, came with his sword drawn and bade him point his sword: in the meantime Carr gave him his wound. He says, also, that Mr. Swinhowe resided at Chatton.

My father knew nothing of this rencontre when he drew up his pedigree of Swinhoe, of Goswick, for his History of North Durham. He would have read this deposition with much interest. The brother of the gentleman who was killed, and who had somewhat to do with the origin of the quarrel, Mr. Gilbert Swinhoe, was, I believe, a person of some little literary distinction. There is lying before me a play of which he is supposed to have been the author. As there is, in all probability, no other copy of it in the North of England, the reader will thank me for a farther account of it. The title runs as follows, "The tragedy of the unhappy fair Irene. By Gilbert Swinhoe, Esq. London, printed by J. Streater, for W. Place, at Grays-Inn gate, next Holborn, M.DC.LVIII." 4to. pp. 30.—The play, which is a very respectable composition, is prefaced by three copies of verses. One is by F.S., and is addressed "To the most ingenious author, his much honoured countreyman;" another by Eldred Revett, is inscribed "To the hopefull youth of his much honoured kinsman, Gilbert Swinhoe, Esq." The other is by his brother James, who was killed; I give it in extenso.

TO HIS DEAR BROTHER THE AUTHOR.

I gratulate, Sir, that we see so soon,
While we but for a morning look'd, your noon.
We (could not yet believe that right-way;
And see! Thou do'st awake into full day.
Nor have I ought to vouch thy beams) begun,
But gnats have leave to play within the sun:
And though thy worth not needs that we stand by,
We may, however, with our votes comply,
And speak what all must do: that thou hast writ
Scenes that have in them, spirit, judgment, wit;

some crossing words betwixt Mr. Gilbart Swinhoe and Mr. Carr, and afterwards he saw Mr. Gilbartt give Mr. Carr a blow, being highly provocked to it. And all the tyme they stayd togeather that night very hye and provoking words betwixt James Swinhoe and Carr. They being parted that night, and Mr. Gilbert and James goeing to another house, being on Mathasis, and there went to bed togeather. And upon there goeing into bed Ensigne Horne's man brought a payper to the sayd Gilbart Swinhoe, whoe oppend the same and red on lyne of it, and sayd "This is a challang." The next morning, little after son rys, suspecting sume

> Who from thy pen shall reade Irene's fate
> Will think her now not so unfortunate,
> Let others to their merit speak thee high,
> I but a tribute bring of piety.
>
> J.A. SWINHOE.

The verse is uncouth but characteristic of the period and the district. In the 17th century Northumberland produced very few authors. The gentry were too busy with their flocks and herds and their petty feuds to attend to literature. The following notices will illustrate this deposition and show the state of society among the upper classes in Northumberland.

"1661. Musgrave Ridley, of Witchells par. Haltwhistle, gen., Wm. Ridley of the same parish, yeoman, and Hugh Ridley, of Hutton Bushell, gent., are bound in their recognizances to appear at the next York assizes for killing Francis Robinson, of Hackness, gent." Musgrave Ridley lost his estate for his loyalty during the civil wars, and it was in reference to him that the late Mr. Surtees wrote the following lines —

> When fell the Ridley's martial line,
>   Lord William's antient towers,
> Fair Ridley on the silver Tyne,
>   And sweet Thorngrafton's bowers;
> All felt the plunderer's cruel hand,
> When legal rapine through the land
>   Stalk'd forth with giant stride;
> When loyalty, successless, bled,
> And truth and honour vainly sped
>   Against misfortune's tide.

"In July, 1665, Mr. Wm. Selby, of Pawston, kills Simon Stobart by thrusting his rapier through a door. He was burned in the hand.

"1665, 20 Sep. Sir Thomas Carnaby is killed in an affray with Richard Harland in his house in Blake Street, York."

"March 8, 1679-80. At Craister, Ellioner Gilchrist, saith, that upon Thursday last, betwixt 3 and 4 a'cloke afternoone, she being in Esq. Craister's garden, and there she hoard a noyse. Therupon she went to the top of the garden wall to se what made the noyse. There she saw Mr. Edward Forster lyinge, and she also saw on Mr. Tho. Craister walking from him, and she see two swords drawen lying besides Mr. Ed. Forster's drawen. Then she called unto Mr. Craister, saying, 'What have yow donn to Mr. Forster?' but she heard no answere."

"Feb., 1683-4. Edward Ogle, of Ogle, yeo., charged with knocking Michael Hall off his horse, whereby his leg was broken and he died."

"June 1, 1686. Mr. John Thirlwall, of Newbiggin, is shot with a pistol in Hexham lane, near Gaoler's style, by Mr. Richard Hayles, with whom he was fighting. Mr. Thirlwall was greatly to blame.

mischeif, the ex^t came up to Anthony Dunstoll's garden, where he found the sayd J. Swinho and A. Carr with drawen swords fyghting, and the informer seazed upon Mr. Carr and so parted them without any harm done, and came into Dunston's house and drunk togeather about an houre. Then the sayd Carr went out of Dunston's house, and so parted. And about 3 or 4 of the clock in the afternoon of the same day, being in Anthony Dunstol's stable, heard a woeman cry out that there was two fyghting in garden. Soe the informer run in to the sayd garden and did fynd James Swinho and Mr. Carr's swords drawen and Robert Gray with them, and, the sayd James Swinhoe being wounded in the arme, did help to bring him in to the sayd Dunstall's, and he bled to death of that wound.

CLXXXVI. JOHN BOOTH, CLERK. FOR CLIPPING MONEY.

May 8, 1672. Before Sir Henry Goodrick and Sir Richard Hutton.* *Mrs. Anne Smithson, of Stainley,* sayth, that, near Lent in the year 1670-1, she being at Bothwell Castle, was informed by Ann Martin, servant to Mr. John Booth, parson of Bothwell Castle, that the said Mr. Booth was a clipper of coyn. She further sayth that shee was an eye witness of it, as also Roger Ambrey, who had part of the clippings. She saw through the crannys of boards and observed a furnace about a yard high with

* A most remarkable case. The rector of Bothal, near Morpeth, is charged with clipping, and he had evidently been guilty of other offences. Many witnesses support the charge of clipping. Ralph Daglish says that he built a fire-hearth for the rector in a corner near a window in a room over the gateway in Bothall Castle. Booth had borrowed a pair of bellows from the village smith, and a person comes forward who heard the smith say " he wondred what the parson did with his bellowes, for they have a better blast then they had before." Ramsey, a Newcastle goldsmith, deposes that he bought of Booth "about 900 ounces of rund silver or bullion at twice," thus shewing the large scale on which the operations had been carried on.
When everything was revealed, Booth at once fled, and, not content with that, he seems to have done his best to keep the witnesses against him out of the way. The absence of Henry Thompson is mentioned in the deposition. He had been got away into Yorkshire, but after some time he wrote to Sir Henry Goodricke, professing his readiness to swear against Booth. He makes some revelations against him. " Now, by reason of my tender yeares, he perswaded me to goe out of the country till his troubles were over, for he told me that there was none knew of his actings save myself, and a made in the house. But for hir he would give hir a dose. Which young made was taken away with on Douty, a highwayman, by Booth's order, and brought to Knasebrough, where she dyed very strangely and suddenly."
Booth was not content with this. On March 15, 1672-3, one of the days of assize, Mrs. Smithson deposed before the Judge, that Booth, with one Marm. Scott, his attorney, had offered her 12*l.* if she would sign a paper stating that James Bell, of Bothal, had induced her to give false evidence. She took the money, but kept the paper and brought it to the judge!

panns and sheers fastned in a table. He had an assistant called Henry Thompson, now sayd to be at Tangier, although beleeved to be near Islip, in Darbyshire. Upon his defrauding my Lord Newcastle and flight upon it, the said Booth sent to his wife to be sure to pull down the furnace and to throw the iron pinns over the leads.

Chr. Smithson, of Staveley, gen., sayth, that Mr. Booth did clip the King's coyne for lucre sake, and sold it to one Ramsgill, of Newcastle, a goldsmith, and one Andrew Bell told him that he did carry a cloth bag from Bothell to Newcastle of Mr. Booth's, with great lumps of silver melted in it which thumpt him upon back like boolder stones.

CLXXXVII. WM. FAWCETT AND OTHERS. FOR SACRILEGE.

Jan. 8, 1672-3. Before Sir Henry Thompson, Lord Mayor of York. *John Harrison, an officer of the Cathedrall Church of Chester*,[*] saith, that, on the 15th of December last, the Cathedrall Church of Chester was robd of two silver candlestickes richly guilt and imbossed, and one large silver charger guilt, and that a silver head guilt with a face upon it, now shewed him, is parte of one of the said candlestickes, and that he knoweth it as well as any friende's face hee ever was acquainted with; and that he likewise saith that a peece of silver plate guilt now shewed to him he veryly beleeves is parte of the said charger.

[*] A case of sacrilege. Chester Cathedral had been plundered, and the thieves are captured in York. At Christmas, 1672, three men, called Wm. Fawcett, Tristram Barwick, alias Ralph Thomson, and James Noble, were arrested in York. Their language had caused them to be suspected. When they were searched, picklocks, files, and pistols were found in their possession. Thompson had five rings, one with the King's picture, another with a cornelian stone. A servant of Sir Christopher Wandesford says, that in Ireland, in Sept. last, Sir Christopher was robbed of 307*l*. and a gold ring, which he believes to be that with the cornelian stone. The retainer had his suspicions that the men were highwaymen, and, by a most lucky chance, he had got them arrested. They had a horse with them, which they say was lent to them at Greta Bridge. It had been stolen, however, from Sir Jerome Smithson's, at Stanwick. The men confess that they had been in Chester and Ireland, but deny the charges against them. It is proved that Thomson offered for sale the silver, cut in pieces, at the shop of Henry Mangey, goldsmith, in York, telling him that his grandmother had been a Papist, and that the plate had been used upon an altar. The evidence of the verger is strong. Barwick died in York Castle, and I do not know what became of the other two.

CLXXXVIII. ANNE BAITES AND OTHERS.   FOR WITCHCRAFT.

Apr. 2, 1673. Before Humphrey Mitford, Esq. *Ann Armstrong, of Birchen-nooke, spinster,** saith, that Ann, wife of Thomas Baites, of Morpeth, tanner, hath beene severall times in the company of the rest of the witches, both att Barwick, Barrasford, and at Ridingbridg-end, and once att the house of Mr. Francis Pye, in Morpeth, in the seller there. The said Ann Baites hath severall times danced with the divell att the places aforesaid, calling him, sometimes, her protector, and, other sometimes, her blessed saviour. She hath seen the said Ann Baites severall times att the places aforesaid rideing upon wooden dishes and egg-shells, both in the rideinge house and in the close adjoyninge. She further saith that the said Ann hath been severall times in the shape of a catt and a hare, and in the shape of a greyhound and a bee, letting the divell see how many shapes she could turn herself into.

Apr. 4. Before Sir Richard Stote. The same witness saith, that since she gave information against severall persons who ridd her to severall places where they had conversation with the divell, she hath beene severall times lately ridden by Anne Driden and Anne Forster, and was last night ridden by them to the rideing house in the close on the common, where the said Anne Forster, Anne Driden, Lucy Thompson, John Crawforth, Wm. Wright, Elizabeth Pickering, Anne Usher, Michaell Aynesley, and Margaret his wife, and one Margarett, whose surname she knowes not, but she said to the protector she came from Corbridge, and thre more, whose names she knowes not, were all present with their protector: and had all sorts of meates and drinke, they named siltt, upon the table by pulling a rope, and they tooke the bridle of this informant, and made her singe to them whilst they danced; and all of them who had donne harme gave an account thereof to their protector, who made most of them that did most harme, and beate those who had donne no harme. And Mary Hunter

---

* One of the most extraordinary cases of witchcraft that has ever been printed. I know of nothing that surpasses it in interest, save the great Lancashire case, which has been re-published by the Chetham Society, and illustrated with an admirable preface by its learned President, Mr. Crossley.

We are here introduced to a witch-finder, who plays the part of Matthew Hopkins, and tells us her experiences, which are of the most peculiar description. The reader must test her depositions with his own critical acumen. He must draw his own conclusions as to the accuracy of a tale that would run like wildfire through Durham and Northumberland. I know nothing of the result of the affair. I need not say that all the accused persons deny their guilt.

said she had killed George Taylor's filly, and had power over his mare, and that she had power of the farre hinder leg of John Marche.

Feb. 5, 1672-3. Newcastle-on-Tyne, before Ralph Jenison. *Anne Armstrong, of Birks-nooke*, saith, that, being servant to one Mable Fouler, of Burtree house, in August last, her dame sent her to seeke eggs of one Anne Forster, of Stocksfield; but as they could not agree for the price, the said Anne desired her to sitt downe and looke her head, which, accordingly, she did. And then the said Anne lookt this informant's head. And, when they had done, she went home. And, about three dayes after, seekeing the cowes in the pasture, a little after day-breake, she mett, as she thought, an old man with ragg'd cloaths, who askt this informant where she was on the Friday last. She tould him she was seekeing eggs at Stocksfield. So he tould her that the same woman that lookt her head should be the first that made a horse of her spirit, and who should be the next that would ride her; and into what shape and liknesses she should be changed, if she would turne to there God. And withall tould this informer how they would use all meanes they could to allure her: first, by there tricks, by rideing in the house in empty wood dishes that had never beene wett, and also in egg shells; and how to obtaine whatever they desired by swinging in a rope; and with severall dishes of meate and drinke. But, if she eate not of their meate, they could not harme her. And, at last, tould her how it should be divulgd by eateing a piece of cheese, which should be laid by her when she laie downe in a field with her apron cast over her head, and so left her. But after he was gone she fell suddainely downe dead and continued dead till towards six that morneing. And, when she arose, went home, but kept all these things secrett. And since that time, for the most parte every day, and sometimes two or three times in the day, she has taken of these fitts, and continued as dead often from evening till cockcrow. And whilst she was lying in that condition, which happend one night a little before Christmas, about the change of the moone, this informant see the said Anne Forster come with a bridle, and bridled her and ridd upon her crosse-leggd, till they came to (the) rest of her companions at Rideing millne bridg-end, where they usually mett. And when she light of her back, pulld the bridle of this informer's head, now in the likenesse of a horse; but, when the bridle was taken of, she stood up in her owne shape, and then she see the said Anne Forster, Anne Dryden, of Prudhoe, and Luce Thompson, of Mickley, and tenne more unknowne to her, and a long black man rideing on a bay galloway, as she thought, which they calld there protector. And when they had hankt theire horses, they stood all upon a bare spott of ground, and bid this informer sing whilst they danced in severall shapes; first, of a haire, then in their owne, and then in a catt, sometimes in a mouse, and in severall other shapes. And when they had done, bridled this informer, and the rest of the horses, and rid home with their protector first. And for six or seaven nights together they did the same. And the last night this informer was with them they mett all at a house called the Rideinge house, where she saw Forster, Drydon, and Thompson, and the rest, and theire protector, which they call'd their god, sitting at the head of the table in a gold chaire, as she thought; and a rope hanging over the roome, which every one touch'd three several times, and what ever was desired was sett upon the table, of several kindes of meate and drinke; and when they had eaten, she that was last drew the table and kept the reversions. This was their custome which they usually did. But when this informer used meanes to avoyd theire company they came in theire owne shapes, and threatned her, if she would not turne to theire god, the last shift should be the worst. And from that time they have not troubled her. But further saith that, on St. John day last, being in the field, seeking sheep, she sitt downe, being weary, and cast her apron over her head. And when she gott upp she found a piece cheese lying at her head, which she tooke up and brought home, and did eate of it, and since that time hath disclosed all which she formerly kept secrett.

Apr. 9, 1673. At the Sessions at Morpeth before Sir Thomas Horsley and Sir Richard Stote, knights, James Howard, Humphrey Mitford, Ralph Jenison, and John Salkeld, Esqrs.

Ann Armstrong, of Birks-nuke, spinster, saith, that the information she hath already given is truth. She now further saith that Lucy Thompson of Mickley, widdow, upon Thursday in the evening, being the 3rd of Aprill, att the house of John Newton off the Riding, swinging upon a rope which went crosse the balkes, she, the said Lucy, wished that a boyl'd capon with silver scrues might come down to her and the rest, which were five coveys consisting of thirteen person in every covey; and that the said Lucy did swing thrice, and then the said capon with silver scrues did, as she thinketh, come downe, which capon the said Lucy sett before the rest off the company, whereof the divell, which they called their protector, and sometimes their blessed saviour, was their cheif, sitting in a chair like unto bright gold. And the said Lucy further did swing, and demanded the plumbroth which the capon was boyled in, and thereupon it did immediately come down in a dish, and likewise a botle of wine which came down upon the first swing.

She further saith that Ann, the wife of Richard Forster off Stocksfeild, did swing upon the rope, and, upon the first swing, she gott a cheese, and upon the second she gott a beakment of wheat flower, and upon the third swing she gott about halfe a quarter of butter to knead the said flower withall, they haveing noe power to gett water.

She further saith Ann Drydon, of Pruddow, widdow, did swing thrice; and, att the first swing, she gott a pound of curraines to putt in the flower for bread; and, att the second swing, she gott a quarter of mutton to sett before their protector; and, at the third swing, she got a bottle of sacke.

She further saith that Margrett the wife of Michaell Aynsley of Riding did swing, and she gott a flackett of ale containing, as she thought, about three quarts, a kening of wheat flower for pyes, and a peice of beife.

She further saith that every person had their swings in the said rope, and did gett severall dishes of provision upon their severall swings according as they did desire, which this informant cannot repeat or remember, there beinge soe many persons and such variety of meat; and those that came last att the said meeting did carry away the remainder of the meat.

And she further saith that she particularly knew at the said meeting one Michael Aynsly of the Rideing, Mary Hunter of Birkenside, widdow, Dorothy Green of Edmondsbyers in the county of Durham, widdow, Anne Usher of Fairlymay, widdow, Eliz. Pickering of Whittingeslaw, widdow, Jane wife of Wm. Makepeace of New Ridley, yeo., Anthony Hunter of Birkenside, yeo., John Whitfeild of Edmondbyers, Anne Whitfeild of the same, spinster, Chr. Dixon of Muglesworth park and Alice his wife, Catherine Ellott of Ebchester, Elsabeth Atchinson of Ebchester widdow, and Issabell Andrew of Crooked-oake widdow, with many others both in Morpeth and other places, whose faces this informer knowes, but cannot tell their names. All which persons had their severall meetings at diverse other places at other times: viz. upon Collupp Munday last, being the tenth of February, the said persons met at Allensford, where this informant was ridden upon by an inchanted bridle by Michael Aynsly and Margaret his wife. Which inchanted bridle, when they tooke it off from her head, she stood upp in her owne proper person, and see all the said persons beforemencioned danceing, some in the likenesse of haires, some in the likenesse of catts, others in likenesse of bees, and some in their owne likenesse, and made this informant sing till they danced, and every thirteen of them had a divell with them in sundry shapes. And at the said meeting their particular divell tooke them that did most evill, and danced with them first, and called every of them to an account, and those that did most evill he maid most of.

And this informant saith that she can very well remember the particular confessions that the severall persons hereunder named made to the divell then and there, as well as other times: and first

Lucy Thompson of Mickly confessed to the divell that she had wronged Edward Lumly, of Mickly, goods by witcheing them; and in particular one horse by pineing to death, and one ox which suddainly dyed in the draught, and the divell incouraged her for it.

Ann Drydon of Pruddoe confessed to the divill that, on the Thursday night after Fasten's even last, when they were drinking wine in Franck Pye's celler in Morpeth, that shee witched suddenly to death her neighbor's horse in Pruddoe.

Anne wife of Richard Forster of Stocksfield confessed that she bewitched Robert Newton's horses of Stocksfeild, and that there was one of them that had but one shew on, which she took and presented with the foot and all to the divell at next meeting. And she further confessed to her protector that she had power of a childe of the said Robert Newton's called Issabell, ever since she was four yeare olde, and she is now about eight yeares old, and she is now pined to nothing, and continues soe.

Moreover Michaell Ainsly and Anne Drydon confessed to the divill that they had power of Mr. Thomas Errington's horse, of Rideing mill, and they ridd behinde his man upon the said horse from Newcastle like two bees, and the horse, immediately after he came home, dyed; and this was but about a moneth since.

The said Anne Forster, Michaell Ainsly, and Lucy Thompson confessed to the divell, and the said Michaell told the divell that he called 3 severall times at Mr. Errington's kitchen dore, and made a noise like an host of men. And that night, the divell asking them how they sped, they answered, nothing, for they had not got power of the miller, but they got the shirt of his bak, as he was lyeing betwixt women, and laid it under his head, and stroke him dead another time, in revenge he was an instrument to save Raiph Elrington's draught from goeing downe the water and drowneing, as they intended to have done. And that they confessed to the divell that they made all the geer goe of the mill, and that they intended to have made the stones all grinde till they had flowne all in peeces.

Mary Hunter confessed to the divill that she had wronged George Tayler of Edgebrigg's goods, and told her protector that she had gotten the power of a fole of his soe that it pined away to death. And she had gott power of the dam of the said fole, and that they had an intention, the last Thursday at night, to have taken away the power of the limbs of the said mare. About Michaelmas last she did come to one John Marsh, of Edgebrigg, when he and his wife was rideing from Bywell, and flew sometimes under his mare's belly and sometimes before its breast, in the likenesse of a swallow, untill she got the power of it, and it dyed within a week after. And she and Dorothy Green confessed to the divill that they got power of the said John Marshe's oxe's far hinder legg. And this is all within the space of a year halfe or thereabouts.

Ann Usher, of Fairly May, confessed to the divell that by his help she was a medciner, and that she had within a litle space done 100l. hurt to one George Stobbart, of New Ridly, in his goods. And that she and Jane Makepeace, of New Ridly, had trailed a horse of the said Geo. downe a great scarr, and that they have now power of a quye of the said Geo., which now pines away.

Elizabeth Pickering, of Whittingstall, widdow, confessed, that she had power of a neighbor's beasts of her owne in Whittingstall, and that she had killed a child of the said neighbors.

And this informer saith that all the said persons were frequently at the meetings and rideings with the divill, and craved his assistance, and consulted with him about all the aforesaid accions.

She further saith, that Jane Hopper of the Hill confessed to the divill that she had power over Wm. Swinburne, of Newfeild, for near the space of two yeares last past, by which he is sore pined, and she hopes to have his life. And Anthony Hunter, of Birkenside, confessed he had power over Anne, wife of Thomas Richardson, of Crooked oak; that he tooke away the power of her limbs, and askt the divill's assistance to take away her life. And Jane Makepeace was at all the meetings among the witches, and helped to destroy the goods of George Stobbart.

And this informer deposeth that Ann Drydon had a lease for fifty yeares of the divill, whereof ten ar expired. Ann Forster had a lease of her life for 47 yeares, whereof seaven are yet to come. Lucy Thompson had a lease of two and forty, whereof two are yet to come, and, her lease being near out, they would have perswaded this informer to have taken a lease of three score yeares or upwards, and that she should never want gold or mony, or, if she had but one cow, they should let her know a way to get as much milk as them that had tenn.

And further this informer cannot as yet well remember.

Apr. 21, 1673. The said witness, Anne Armstrong, deposes further, before Ralph Jenison, Esq.

On Monday last, at night, she, being in her father's house, see one Jane Baites, of Corbridge, come in the forme of a gray catt with a bridle hanging on her foote, and breath'd upon her and struck her dead, and bridled her, and rid upon her in the name of the devill, southward, but the name of the place she does not now remember. And after the said Jane allighted and pulld the bridle of her head, and she and the rest had drawne their compasse nigh to a bridg end, and the devil placed a stone in the middle of the compasse; they sett themselves downe, and bending towards the stone, repeated the Lord's prayer backwards. And, when they had done, the devill, in the forme of a little black man and black cloaths, calld of one Isabell Thompson, of Slealy, widdow, by name, and required of her what service she had done him. She replyd she had gott power of the body of one Margarett Teasdale. And after he had danced with her he dismissed her, and call'd of one Thomasine, wife of Edward Watson, of Slealy, who confessed to the devill that she had likwise power of the body of the said Margaret Teasdle, and would keepe power of her till she gott her life.

At severall of their meetings she has seene Michaell Aynsley and Margaret his wife, now prisoners in his Maties goale, and Jane Baites, of Corbridge, ride upon one James Anderson, of Corbridge, chapman, to their meetings, and hankt him to a stobb, whilst they were at their sports; and, when they had done, ridd upon him homeward.

May 12. She further saith, that, on the second day of May laste, at nighte, the witches carried her to Berwicke bridge end, where she see a greate number of them: and amongste the reste she see one Anne Parteis, of Hollisfeild, and heard her declare to the devill that she did enter into the house of one John Maughan, of the pareshe of Haydon, and found his wife's rocke lyinge upon the table. And she tooke up the rocke to spinne of it, and by spincinge of the rocke she had gotten the power of the said Anne that she should never spinne more, and would still torment her till she had her life.

May 14. She being brought into Allandaile by the parishiners, for the discovery of witches, Isabell Johnson, being under suspition, was brought before her; and shee breathing uppon the said Anne, immediately the said Anne did fall downe in a sound and laid three quarters of an houre: and after her recovery she said, if there were any witches in England, Isabell Johnson was one.

At Morpeth Sessions, as aforesaid. *Robert Johnson, of Rydeing Mill,* saith, that, about the latter end of August last, late at night, lyeing in his bed at Rydeing Mill, betwixt two of his fellow-servants, he herd a man, as he thought, call at the dore, and ask whoe was within. Upon which this informant rose, and went, and layd his head against the chamber window to know whoe it was that called, and he heard a great noise of horse feet, as though it had been an army of men. Whereupon he called, but none would answer. Soe he returned to his bed, and the next morneing, riseing out of his bed, he wanted his shirt, which seeking after he accused his two fellow-servants, which were amazed at the thing and denyed that ever they knew of it, which this informant further searching after, found it lapt upp under his pillow at his bed head. He further saith, that Mr. Errington's draught, and Ra. Elrington's, being away at Stiford, leading tyth corne there, and being late in comeing home, this informer could not rest satisfyed, but went to seek the draughts, and to know what was become of them: and met them comeing out of Stiford towne end, and came homeward with them, till they came to the water. And Mr. Errington's draught being got through, he herd the people with the other draught cry that they were goeing downe the water. And then he got on to a horse, and rode downe after them some 3 score yards or thereabouts, where he came to them just at the entring into a great deep pool, where, if he had not made great help, they might have been lost, both men and beasts. And getting them turned and brought upp to the other draught, they came all home together; and this informant, haveing loosed the beasts out of his maister's draught and goeing to bed, was that night suddainly strucken dead in the kitchen to the sight of his fellow-servant. He further saith that, about some sixteen dayes before Christmas last, he could not by any meanes he could use gett the mill sett, and, about the hinder end of Christmas hollidayes, being sheeling some oats, about two hours before the sunn-setting, all the geer, vizt. hopper and hoops, and all other things but the stones, flew downe and were casten of, and he himselfe almost killed with them, they comeing against him with such force and violence.

He further saith that, about a moneth since, one Wm. Olliver, his fellow-servant, went to Newcastle in the morneing, and rode upon a gray gelding of his maister's, which, to all their sights, was as well and as good like as any horse could bee. And his fellow-servant sayed that he came as well home and rode as heartily as any horse could doe. And after he is come home this informant went to the dore, and tooke the horse by the bridle, and led him into the stable where he usually stood. And there haveing him in his hand by the bridle reen, and haveing not gott him fastened nor out of his hand, till suddainly the horse rushed downe, he being not hott at all with rideing: and soe continued a good while, sometimes lookeing very cheerily about him, and other sometimes striveing, as it were, for life and death, soe that this informer was forced to goe to bed and leave him, and in the morneing when he came to the stable again he found him lyeing dead, and takeing him out of the stable they rippt him upp to see what might be the cause, and could finde nothing but that the horse was all right enough in his body.

John March, of Edgebrigg, yeoman, saith, that, about a month since, he went to a place called Birkside nook, and there Ann Armstrong heareing him named began to speak to him, and askt him if he had not an ox that had the power of one of his limbs taken from him. And he telling her he had, and enquireing how she came to know, she told him that she heard Mary Hunter of Birkside, and another, at a meeting amongst diverse witches, confesse to the divell that they had taken the power of that beast; and she not knowing her name, Sir James Clavering and Sir Richard Stote thought proper to carry her to Edenbyers, and there to cause the woman to come to her ther, to the intent she might challenge her. And she challenged one Dorothy Green, a widdow, and said she was the person that joyned with Mary Hunter in the bewitcheing the said ox. And the ox now continues lame, and has noe use of his farr hinder legg, but pines away, and likely to dye. He saith that Ann Armstrong told him that the said persons confessed before the devill that they bewitched a gray mare of his; and he saith that about a fortnight before Michaelmas last, he and his wife were rideing home from Bywell on a Sunday at night upon the same mare, about sun-sett; and there came a swallow, which above forty times and more flew through under the mare's belly, and crossed her way before her brest. And this informant strook at it with his rod above twenty times, and could by noe meanes hinder it, untill of its owne accion it went away. And the mare went very well home, and within four dayes dyed: and, before she dead, was two dayes soe mad that she was past holding, and was strucke blinde for four and twenty houres before she dead.

He further saith, that the said Mary Hunter came downe to his house on Munday last, where he had Ann Armstrong; and she askt her what she had to say to her. And she told her that she was a witch, and that she had seen her at the devill's meetinges. The other askt her where, and she answered, "In this same house, last night, being Sunday, amongst all the companye." And the said informer saith, that that very night when she said they mett, he was soe sore affrighted that he was in a manner dead; and afterward comeing to himselfe againe he herd a great thundring, and saw a great lighteninge in the house, and to the number of twenty creatures in the resemblances of catts, and other shapes, lyeing on the floores and creeping upon the walls. And immediately after I herd the girll singing to them. And his servants, being in bed with the young woman, awakened, and came downe out of the roome where the girll lay, and said, "Alas! the witches were gone with the girll." And he went upp and found her body lyeing in the bed, as she were dead, neither breath nor life being to be discerned in her: and continued soe for the most part of an hour, till he fetched in two or three neighbors to see her in that condition. And presently after they came in she began to stir and open her eyes, and loked on them for about an hour before she spake anything. And when she spoke she said that all the companyes were there, and were endeavouringe to get her away, but were prevented. And further he saith, the said Ann Armstrong enquired of the said Mary Hunter for her sonn Anton, and there being one of her sonns called Cuthbert, wee told her that he was the man she askt for, which she denyed, and said that it was not the man, for she knew him very well, and had seen him severall tymes at their meetings; and desired her to send him downe, and a lass that she, the said Mary, severall times ride upon and singe unto them, and she would resolve her whether it were they or not. Thereupon Anton afterwards came downe, and questioned her what she had to say to him. She said she would lett him know at the sessions, hearing he was to be there: and because he had threatened her, she would say noe more, but told this informer, after he was gone, that Anton had confessed before the devill he had taken the power of Anne wife of Tho. Richardson of Crooked oak's limbs from her, and had likewise bewitched severall cattell to death. And further saith, that he knowes that the said Ann Richardson is in a very bad condicion, being sometimes able to goe, and other times that she cannot goe without help. He never see the said Ann in his life before, neither, to his knowledge, was she ever where he was, nor never saw none of his beasts, but told him all this when he went to see her.

Geo. Tayler, of Edgebridge, yeoman, saith, that, coming to Birkside nook to speak with one Ann Armestrong, whoe had oftentimes formerly desired to have seen him, and, she being asleep upon a bed, her sister awakened her and raised her, and being asked if she knew him, or could name him, she answered that if he were the man that had a fole lately dead, and if he lived at Edgebrigg, his name was Geo. Tayler. Upon his demanding on her how she came to know it, she told him that she herd Mary Hunter of Birkenside, widdow, confesse itt before the divell at meetinge they had that she had gotten the power and the life of his fole. The said fole began not be well about Michaelmas last, and dyed about a moneth since, and it had noe naturall disease to his knowledge, but often swelled in severall parts of the body of it; and its head and lipps would have been sore swelld, and letten him have endeavoured never soe often to blood it, thinking thereby to prevent its death, he could never get any in noe part of the body of it. And, when it was dead, he opened it to see if there were any blood or not, and he saith that he thinks, very, a quart pott would have holden all that it had and more, and that litle that it had was all drawne about the heart thereof.

He saith that Ann Armestrong told him that she heard when the said Mary Hunter and Dorothy Green, of Edmondbyers, confesse to the devill that they had the power of his oxen and kyne, horses and mares, and that now, at this present, he has a grey mare, the dam of the said fole, pineing away, and in the same condition that the fole was in. And he thinks that all his goods doe not thrive nor are like his neighbours goods, notwithstanding he feeds them as well as he can, but are like anatomyes.

Apr. 21, 1673. *Marke Humble, of Slealy, tayler*, saith, that he, betwixt 7 and 8 yeares agoe, walking towards the high end of Slealy, mett one Isabell Thompson walking downward. And when she was gone past him, she being formerly suspected of witchcraft, he lookt back over his shoulder, and did see the said Isable hould up her hands towards his back. And when he came home, he grew very sick, and tould the people in the house that he was afraid Isabell Thompson had done him wrong. And for some 3 or 4 yeares continued very ill by fitts in a most violent manner, to the sight and admiration of all neighbours. And, whilst he continued in this distemper, the said Isabell came to his house, and said it was reported she had bewitchd him. She tould him if it were so, it would soone be knowne. And further saith that his mother Margaret Humble then lyeing not well, Isabell Thompson tooke some of her haire to medicine her.

CLXXXIX. MARGARET MILBURNE. FOR WITCHCRAFT.

May 17, 1673. Before Sir Thomas Horsley, Knight. *Dorothy Himers, of Morpeth*,* saith, that, about three years agoe, she being washing at the water side, one Margaret Milbourne helping her to wash, Margaret Milbourne, the said Margaret's mother-in-law, came to this informer wher she was washing with the other, haveing her sonne's child in her armes, and was angry with her daughter-in-law for comeing to wash, and troubleing her to keepe her child; and said she was an ill housewife that cannot be worth a groat in her owne house. Upon which this informer said, she might worke her owne worke at home when she could not addle a groat abroad. Upon which the said Margaret said she was old, and was not able to keepe the child. Upon which this informer said ther was a tough sinew in an old wife's hough. Upon which the said Margaret told her she would never be soe old with as much honesty. This informer, further, saith, that since that time she hathe been in a languishing condition, and hath not had her health, as formerly, nor able for any servile worke. She further saith that, on 25th day of Aprill last, in the night time, she being very sick, lieing in her bed, did apprehend she see a light about her bed like starrs. And then she did apprehend that she did see the said Margaret Milbourne, widdow, standing on an oate scepp att her bed feet, thinkeing she was pulling her heart with something like a threed. Upon which this informer cald on her master's daughter that lay by her, who cald of other people out of the roome below. Who comeing up found this informer in a swound, who continued not able to speake for three or foure howers. She verily believes that Margaret Milbourne is the cause of her grievances; and she doth often take very sick fitts, and in her fitts apprehends she sees the said Margaret.

Isabell Fletcher, of Morpeth, saith, that, on the 12th of May, she was watching clothes with some others upon a piece of ground called the Stanners, neare Morpeth, in the night time. And goeing from the rest of the company to fetch a cloake, which she had left a distance of, see a white thing comeing through the water, like a woman, and she stood still till it came to her. And then it appeared to be a woman, who spoke to this informer, and asked her how she did. This informer asked her againe, "Who is this that knoweth me, and asketh how I doe?" The woman

---

* This is almost the last case of reputed witchcraft that I find in Northumberland. The accused person asserts her innocence.

then answered, "Doe you not know me?" This informer then apprehended her to be one Margaret Milbourne late of Bedlington, whome she was very well acquainted with, she being servant lately to Wm. Milbourne, her sonne, liveing in Morpeth. Then she said to this informer, "Wilt thou goe see thy dame?" Upon which she replied she would neither goe see master nor dame at that time a night. Upon which she said, that if she would not goe with her, it would be worse for her or ought be long: and soe turnd her back and went away. Upon which this informer came towards her company and sate downe; and, presently after, lookeing back she thought she did see her come towards her againe: upon which she fell into a swoune. And then her company comeing to her, they held her up, and, when she came out of the swound, she continued in a distracted condition all the night, soe that the company could scarce hold her. And this informer formerly heard her reputed for a witch. And she saith that the day following, in the afternoone, being dressing a roome, she apprehended the said Margaret put her head in at the window. Upon which she fell into her distracted condition againe and continued soe five or six houers, insomuch that she was holden by severall people.

CXC. CALVERT SMITHSON, GEN. FOR SEDITIOUS WORDS.

Jan. 6, 1673-4. Calvert Smythson,* of Kipling, gen., said at Beedall, "The Parliament is prorogued till October next. I have forty men ready to rise att the holding upp of my finger, and when I come on the feild I will give noe quarter. I hope to see five hundred men killed in halfe a yeares tyme betwixt Allerton and Kipling."

---

* A turbulent member of the North Riding family of Smithson. For these incautious words he was indicted, and was fined 10*l*.

He was again in trouble in 1678, the year of the plot. He was probably a Roman Catholic. He was charged by John Foster, of Great Fencote, with saying at Bedale on the 5th of Nov. 1678, "I and my company will destroy the King." The evidence against him was but weak, and he denied the charge altogether. A man of the name of Leonard Butterfeild who was present on the occasion said that no such words were used, but that Smithson said "that all Bedill men was roges and knaves, and this informant the worst of them all."

In 1670 Mr. Smithson charged Leonard Hartley, of Brettonby, with assaulting him, but the indictment was ignored.

CXCI. PETER BANKS. FOR BEING AN IMPOSTOR.

Jan. 19, 1673-4. Before Robert Roddam, Mayor of Newcastle. *Jane, wife of Cuthbert Burrell, shipwright,* deposeth that Peter Banks is a most strange seducer * and inticer of the King's subjects and people, and deludes them in a wonderfull manner, perswadeing and makeing them beleive that he cann lett leases to people for tearme of yeares and life. Whereupon diverse seamen repair to him and putt trust in his conjurations, and pay him 20s. a peice for such leases. And, about a yeare and an halfe since, the said Banks came to this informer's husband, he useing to goe to sea, and stopped one of these leases into his hands. Which when this informer discovered, she was mighty angry, and much greived. And haveing read the same the contents were these, " I charge you and all of you, in the high sword name, to assist and blesse Cuth. Burrell belonging to——(*such a ship*) from all rocks and sands, storms and tempests thereunto belonging, for this yeare." After which the informer did forthwith burne the same in the fire; for which the said Banks threatned he would plague the informer that she should never be worth a groat. And since that time she and her family have been mightily perplexed, and in great straits and necessities, though she trusts in God, and is not affraid of the devill, yet the said Banks by his strange stratagems afrights her. The said Peter Banks hath often confessed to her and others that he used inchantments, conjuracions, and magick arts; and, in perticuler, in conjureing evill and malitious spiritts; and, espetially, about a young woman that lived in Gateshead, whose name she knows not, who came to him when the informer was present, and discovered about her being molested with a spirit and the like. Whereupon he looked in his books, and writt something out of the same into a paper, and delivered it to that young woman. And told her that when the spirit appeared lett her open that paper, and she would be noe more molested. And afterwards, as Banks confessed, the same woman came back again, and gave him thanks and payment. And he told this informant, for he made his cracks and boasts of it, that he medecined and conjured an evill spirit that Thomas Newton's daughter was troubled with, and in the night time he burnt peices

---

* A wise-man is in trouble. The depositions are amusing and will recall to the minds of my readers many stories that they have heard themselves. This race of impostors is not yet extinct, and as long as there are weak and credulous people in the world the trade will be found to be a lucrative one.

of paper in the fire written on for that end, and a certaine number
in the night, at a certaine time, and used words that he had
mastered the spirit. He likewise said that he could compell
people that had ill husbands to be good to their wifes. And he
did nominate one Jane Crossby, to whom he had letten a lease for
that end, and had gott 10s. and two new shirts for his pains; and
that the same lease endured for a yeare, and, durcing that time,
her husband was loveing and kind; but the yeare expireing, and
she not renewing her lease, her said husband was ill and untoward
againe. And he also declared that he could take away a man's
life a yeare before his appointed time, or make him live a yeare
longer.

Ellinor Pattison, alias Phillipps, deposeth, that, contention
having arisen between her and one Peter Banks, she often in the
night time was terrified and affrighted with visions and appari-
tions; and in such manner as she thought the said Banks was
standing up in flames of fire, and could never be att rest and
quietnesse till she made agreement with him. But, before the
agreement, he repaired to her, and told her he knew she was
wronged and bewitched and he could cure her. Therefore by his
perswasions she permitted him to cutt a litle haire out of the back
side of her neck in order to medecine and cure her. After which
he putt the haire into a paper, and, haveing sealed it upp, gave it
againe to the informer, and bidd her burne it. After which she
amended and grew better.

CXCII. ROBERT RAWNSLEY AND ANOTHER. FOR MURDER.

March 19, 1673-4. Before John Hargreaves, coroner. *Jonathan Drake* sayeth, that, about Mayday last, Sara his wife, now
deceased,* told him that one Robert Rawnsley and Nathan Holdsworth came to his house, and made a distresse upon an attach-
ment, as they said, and tooke a caddow from her. And the said
Rawnsley tooke her in his armes and threw her downe, and
kneeled upon her, and stopt her winde by graspinge her by the
throate with his hands till shee was blacke in the face, and he
trod upon her and strucke her with his feete, and bett the skinne
of her knees and legges in severall places. And the said Rawnsley

---

* A cruel assault at Horton, near Bradford, which was fatal to the poor woman,
who languished for some time and then died. The cowardly assailants pretended to be
bailiffs. Some parts of the story remind us of the famous exploit of Wild Darell at
Littlecote Hall.

struck this informant down twice, and threw one of his children on the fyer.

CXCIII. A LIST OF NORTHUMBRIAN RECUSANTS.

June 20, 1674. Wm. Hall, of Durtrees, yeoman,* Matthew ......, of Wooler, Wm. Hickson, of Otterburn, Wm. Browne, of Elsdon, and his wife, John Hall, of Townhead, and Isabell his wife, George Aydon, of Hexham, and his wife, Anne Gibson, of Coftly, John Gatenbee, of ...., yeoman, Francis and Luke Gatenbee, Mary Gatenby, of Walsend panns, spinster, Zachariah Tysycke, of Howdon panns, ... Horsley, of Long Horsley, Anne and Margaret Wilson, of the same, John Foster, sen. and jun., of Lee Ryden, Thomas Smart and his wife, and George Tayler, of the same place, Wm. Ord, sen. of Grange, gen. and Eliz. his wife, Wm. Ord, jun., and Jane Fletcher, of the same, spinster, Thomas Selby, of Swarland, gen., Anne Embleton, of Felton, widow, Katherine wife of Thomas Nicholson, and .... Calverlaw, spinster, of the same place, ... Orkenhead, yeo., Joseph Greaves, sen., George Joblin and his wife, Bartholomew Wintrup, yeoman, all of Felton, Robert Todd, of Brinkburne, and Margaret his wife, Anne Rennison, of Netherhaye, Edward Struther, of Alnwick, gen., and Mary his wife, Anne wife of Henry Finney, Eliz. and Frances Brandlinge, Wm. Gare, jun. and his wife, Robert Anderson, Mary Sanderson, widow, Robert Stephenson, Jane Watson, widow, Elizabeth Hunter, and Jane wife of John Scott, all of Alnwick, Wm. Robson, of Heale, yeo., and his wife, Rowland and Lewes Robson, yeomen, Galfrid Robson, labourer, Isabel Greene, John and Wm. Hunter, yeomen, all of Healle, John Potts, of .... haugh, yeo., Robert and Roger Potts, Edward Hunter and Deborah Potts, of the same place, Francis Withrington, of ——, gen., and his wife, Peter Snawdon, of the same, yeoman, Grace Snawden, of Bickerton, spinster, Wm. Solsby, of Whitton, ... Wilson, of .... peth highware, yeo., and Faith his wife, John and Eliz. Watson, Mary Cotes, Bartholomew Gibson and Barbara his wife, John Thompson, Thomas Jennison, and Thomas Shipley, of the same place, Eliz. Joplinge, of Newton hall, spinster, Cuthbert Softley, and Edward Robson, of Horsley, yeomen, Wm. and Anthony Tayler, and Thomas Newton, of Bromeley, yeomen, Eliz. Rowell, of Raichell foot, spinster, John

---

* The names have been carelessly transcribed by the clerk. It will be observed that this is a very imperfect list. It seems to have been customary to send up a list, when it was called for, almost entirely different from its predecessor.

Nicholas, Edward and George Rowell, of the same place, Wm. Snowball, of Hindley sheale, Gawin Castinton, of Broughs house, yeoman, Margaret Collingwood, Ralph Davison, Barbara Smyth, and Wm. Watson, of Lanton, Thomas Wilson, and Thomas Trumble of West Newton, Thomas Emerson and George Pringle, gen., of Kelham. Robert Enkrein, of Thornington, Nicholas Pearson of Downham, Anne wife of Oswald Creswell, gen., and Eliz. Fenwick, of Lesbury, Peter Wilson and Thomas Atkinson and his wife, of Belford, Thomas Foster and the wife of Archibald Johnson, of Edderston, George F..... am, of Bradford, the wife of John Harrison, and the wife of Marmaduke Mattison, of Spinnelston, Wm. Hall, of Dortres, Anne Hall of Birkhill, Mark Hedley, of Stobes, Matthew Anderson of Berchow cragg, Thomas Charter, Margaret Tarlett, Edward Stansey and Anne his wife, and Thomas Tendall, of Chatton, Robert Forten, of Humbleton, John Thomson and Eleanor his wife, Wm. Gray and Christiana his wife, Philip Tayler and Elizabeth his wife, Thomas Smyth and Margaret his wife, Edward Thomson, sen. and Elleanor his wife, Edward Thomson, jun. and Eliz. his wife, and Wm. Smith, of Heslerigg, Henry Hain and Catharine his wife, Katherine Anderson, George Main and his wife, of Lyham, Anne Millison, Edward Grey, Oswald and John Garrand, George Pattison, Ralph Carre, Eliz. Thomson, Anne Strawhin, Eliz. Anderson, Jane Waite, Anne Trumbell, Elleanor Thomson, Dorothy Alder, and Jane Hardy, of Wooler, John Cunningham and Eliz. his wife, James Strother and John Carse, of Lowesk, Thomas Selby and Eliz. his wife, Mary Bambarrow and Wm. Mackrelle, of Barmoor, Ralph Clavering, of Calliley, Esq. and his wife, George Collingwood, of Eslington, Esq., Robert Beednall, of Lemmonton, gen., Roger Huntridge, gen., and Robert Trumble, yeo. and his wife, of Abberwick, Ralph Weddall, of Bolton, yeoman, Henry Ogle, of Harup, gen., Robert Milne, of Edlington, yeo., Robert Smers, of Broom parke, yeoman, Richard and Cuthbert White, of ——, yeoman, Michael Winigates and Isabel his wife, of Stanton, Francis Ratcliffe and Joan his wife, of Witton shells, Thomas Browne and Isabel his wife, of Hungry side, Walter Watson, Anne Gare, widow, Patience Gare, spinster, Dennis and Wm. Smyth, James Pixerem, George Bawcham, Wm. Fletcher, Chr. Snawden, and George Turner, of ——, Robert Fenwicke, gen. and his wife, and Ralph Carnaby, of Lanches.

CXCIV. ANDREW RUTHERFORD. FOR MURDER.

July 16, 1674. Before Tho. Davison, Mayor of Newcastle. Sir *William Douglas, of Cavers, in Scotland*, saith, that on or about the 10th instant, about one or two o'clock in the morneing, there was a murther comitted in and upon the body of James Douglas,* his brother german, and he hath in suspition one Andrew Rotherford, of Townhead, who, as he informed, is now fled to this towne.

CXCV. SUSAN HINCHCLIFFE AND ANOTHER. FOR WITCHCRAFT.

Aug. 26, 1674. Before Darcy Wentworth, Esq., at Woolley. *Mary Moor, of Clayton, spinster,*† saith, that, on the 14th day of

---

* James Douglas, of Camerton, the brother of Sir Wm. Douglas, of Cavers, who had in his veins the best blood in Scotland, is killed on the Borders. Sir William, after the Scottish fashion, pursues the murderer, one Andrew Rotherford, of Townhead, in Jedburgh, as far as Newcastle. Had he caught the fugitive there, he would probably have taken the law into his own hands, but being baffled in the chase he has recourse to the mayor. One Andrew Rutherford, a Newcastle gentleman, who, judging from the identity of names, must have been a kinsman of the murderer, was summoned to give evidence. He said that, on the Tuesday before, he saw the murderer in the Shieldfield, and he told him "that he had done a mischeife, and sighed." The witness, who seems to have heard of the crime, then charged him with killing Douglas, and he confessed it, and told him that he was on his way either to Hull or Hartlepool, probably to escape beyond sea. The witness saw his namesake as late as yesterday afternoon at an alehouse in Pipergate.

† Another of these strange cases which occurred in the West Riding of Yorkshire. The evidence is plainly that of a malicious and ignorant person, and one would scarcely believe it possible that any magistrate could sit down to write such nonsense from the lips of any one. The idea of any person carrying home with him from a distance in his mouth nine pieces of bread and nine of butter! Appended to the deposition is a petition, signed by more than fifty persons, addressed to the magistrates for the West Riding. Many respectable names appear on it. It states that the accuser is only a girl of sixteen, and then it goes on, as follows:

"Some of us have well knowne the said Susanna and Anne, by the space of twenty years and upwards; others of us fifteene years and upwards; others of us tenne years and upwards. And have by the said space observed and knowne the life and conversation of the said Susanna to be not only very sober, orderly, and unblameable in every respect; but also of good example, and very helpfull and usefull in the neighborhood, according to her poore ability. That shee was a constant frequenter of publicke ordinances while she was able, and to the best of our understanding made conscience of her wayes in more than common sort. That we never heard, or had the least ground to suspect her, or her said daughter, to be in any sort guilty of so foule a crime, but do fully believe that the said information against them both is a most gross and groundless (if not malitious) prosecution. And this we humblie certifie, as our very true apprehensions, as in the sight and presence of Him, who will judge the secrets of all hearts. And as touching the said girle who now informs, some of us could say too

August, shee heard Susann, the wife of Joseph Hinchliffe, and Ann, the wife of Thomas Shillitoe, both of Denbigh, discourseing thus together. The said Susan said to Ann, "If thou canst but gett young Thomas Haigh to buy thee threepennyworth of indicoe, and look him in the face when hee gives it thee, and touch his locks, wee shall have power enough to take life." And shee alsoe sayd, "Nanny, wilt thou not goe to day and make hay att Thomas Haigh's?" to which the said Ann answered "Yes." Then sayd Susan, "If thou canst but bring nyne bitts of bread away, and nyne bitts of butter in thy mouth, wee shall have power enough to take the life of their goods. They need not be in such pomp, for we will nether leave him cowe nor horse at house." The said Ann askt Susan, "Mother, did you doe Dame Haigh any hurte?" The said Susan answered, "I, that did I, for after I toucht the cadgeings of her skirts, shee stept not many steps after. I shortned her walk." And this informant saith that, at another time before, shee heard the said Susan say to the said Ann, "I think I must give this Thomas Bramhall over, for they tye soe much whighen about him, I cannot come to my purpose, else I could have worn him away once in two yeares." Then said the said Ann to the said Susan, her mother, "Would I was as free as I was within this two yeares." The said Susan replyed, "Thou art too farr worne." Then the said Susan sayd to her daughter, "Nanny, did thou not hear that Timothy Haigh had like to have been drowned i'th water-hall dyke?" To which shee answered shee did not hear. Then the sayd Susan sayd, "I lead him up and down the moor, with an intention hee should either have broak his neck or have drownd himselfe: but at last his horse threw him, and hee then went over the bridge, and I had a foot in. How hee gott over the bridge I cannot tell, except the Lord lead him by the hand. I had him not at that time. But the next time, lett the horse and him look both to themselves." The said Ann askt the said Susan, her mother, if ever shee had done John Moor any hurt. To which she answered "Yes." And sayd, "I tooke the life of two swine,

---

much concerning her, of a quite different nature, but that we judge recrimination to be but an indirect way of clearing the innocent."

On the assize records there is nothing to tell us how the case terminated. The deposition itself is torn in two, which seems to shew that the matter came to nothing. A note in Mr. Hunter's Life of Oliver Heywood fills up the blank, and gives a very melancholy termination to the affair. It appears that Hinchcliffe and his wife were bound over to answer the charge at the next assizes. It preyed upon his mind so much that on Thursday morning, Feb. 4, 1675-6, he hanged himself in a wood near his house, and was not found till the Sunday. In the mean time his wife died, praying on her deathbed for her accusers.

and did hurt to a childe." And shee heard the said Susan say to the said Ann, that if her father had but toucht Martha Haigh, before shee had spoken to him, they could have had power enough to taken away her life. To which Susan replyed, "There is noe tyme bye-past." The informant, further, saith, that, aboute the midle of July last past, goeing to borrow a line wheele, she heard Ann Shillito say to Susan Hinchlife, "I saw my father play such a trick last night as I never saw in my life." Susan asked her what yt was. She said, "He asked for butter, and there came butter on to his knee in a wooden sawser." Susan said that "That was but a little. Has thou lived in this house soe long and never saw none of thy father's trick. Dost not thou know that thy father went to John Walker's to steime a pare of shooes, and he would not let him have them without he had money in his hand, but he never made pare after. Likewise he went to George Coppley's to steime a wastcoate cloth, and he would not let him have it without he had silver in hand; and, because he would not let him have it, he never made peice att affter but two. If any body would not let them have what they wanted, they would take life of any body." She heard Susan Hinchlife say to Ann Shillito that Joseph Hinchlife was as ill as they, but would not be scene in it. He bare it farr off. Ann Shillito further saith that if they weere knowne they might be hanged. But Susan Hinchlife replied noe hempe would hang them. But Ann Shillito said, they might be burnt then. Susan said, nay, they would never tell untill they died. She further saith that Ann Shillito said, "Ile warrant ye thou shall but say little when thou comes before the bench."

Timothy Hayne, of Denby, saith, that he was present when Mary Moore did vomitt a peice of bended wyer and a peice of paper with two crooked pinns in it, and hath att severall other tymes scene her vomitt crooked pinns.

CXCVI. JONATHAN JENNINGS, ESQ. FOR MANSLAUGHTER.

Jan. 11, 1674-5. Before Jo. Yeates and Philip Waide, coroners. *John Hargraves, of the Citty of Yorke*,* sayth, that, on the

---

* A duel that created a greater sensation in Yorkshire than any other affray in the seventeenth century. Some family differences seem to have originated it. Mr. Aislaby, the *novus homo* of the Aislabies, had married the second of the daughters and coheirs of Sir John Mallory of Studley Royal, and Mr. Jonathan Jennings was affianced to the elder sister. Tradition says that Mr. Jennings and Miss Aislaby had been at a party at Buckingham House on Bishophill, and when the gentleman escorted the lady

10th of Jan., imediatly after dinner, Mr. George Aislaby, this ex^ts maister, sent this ex^t with a lettre directed to Mr. Jonathan Jennings, and ordered him to deliver it to Mr. Jennings' owne hand, but Mr. Jennings then beeinge att dinner, hee left the same with

home to Mr. Aislaby's house they could not get in. When the inmates were aroused, Mr. Jennings, in answer to Aislaby's question, told him that the heiress of Studley Royal was waiting outside, and that it was a strange thing that a daughter of Sir John Mallory should be kept waiting at George Aislaby's door. *Hinc illæ lachrymæ!* Another account ascribes the quarrel to a wish to sacrifice the honor of Miss Mallory to the too notorious Duke of Buckingham. The lady, it is to be remarked, died unmarried.

A duel took place next morning, a Sunday, and, as the story goes, the signal for the meeting was the ringing of the minster prayer bell. It ended, as it is well known, in the death of Aislaby. In the Life of Oliver Heywood there is an account of the affray which is too important to be omitted here.

" Mr. George Aislaby, the register of the spiritual court at York, did challenge Mr. Jonathan Jennings to a single duel, by whom he was slain, on Jan. 10, 1675, being Lord's day. The occasion was this: the Duke of Buckingham, living at his own house in York, hath several masks, plays, interludes, dancings, at which, a day or two before, was, among the rest, Sir John Mallory's daughter, living with Mr. Aislaby, whose wife was her own sister. They stayed at the masking very late at night. Mr. Aislaby and his family went to bed, left a man up to wait for his sister's coming home and open the gates. The man went to the Duke's house to meet them, but missed them, for Mr. Jon. Jennings (Sir Edward Jennings' brother, of Ripon,) had taken her into his coach. They, coming to the gates in the man's absence, knocked, but got not admitted, whereupon Mr. Jennings takes her to his brother-in-law's, Dr. Watkinson's, house, where he lodged. The day after Mr. Aislaby and Mr. Jennings met together; had some words about it; were sharp. Mr. Jennings told him it was hard Sir John Mallory's daughter must wait at George Aislaby's gates and not be admitted. It ran so high, that Mr. Jennings told him he was the scum of the country. This stuck upon Mr. Aislaby's big spirit. Thereupon, after he had been to church in the forenoon, on Sabbath day noon, Jan. 10, 1675, he sent a challenge to Mr. Jennings, charged the servant to deliver it to his own hands, but he, being at dinner, could not but give it to one of the servants. He inquired what answer he brought, who telling him 'none,' sent him again to him, commanding him to bring a positive answer. Having delivered the note, Mr. Jennings said, 'Go, tell your master I will wait upon him presently.' The place was called Pen-roes without Boulen-bar. The sign was, the tolling of the bell to church. Mr. Jennings took a boy with him, as though he would walk, who directed him to that place or near it, and sent him back, none suspecting the business. Mr. Aislaby kissed his wife when he went out. She said, ' Love, will you not go to church?' 'Yes,' said he, 'but not to the church you go to;' so went out. They met; Mr. Aislaby was come first; they fell to it with their swords; Mr. Jennings run him up the right arm; his body was untouched; so many veins being cut he bled excessively. Mr. Jennings led him by the arm, then left him; went and told his servants to go and fetch their master; who made ready his coach; got him into it. The last words he was heard speak were, ' I had him once in my power,' so died. By that time he was got home, his wife, being Sir John Mallory's daughter, came to the coach, being big with the twelfth child, fell down in a swound. He was searched by surgeons, who had no hurt upon his body, but arms. Mr. Jennings was at Dr. Watkinson's; when he heard it, was ready to tear the flesh off himself; when recovering, he got the Duke's coach, and went out of town; is gone straight to London, post, to beg his pardon. Mr. Jennings took two men; went to the high sheriff; they were bound with him in 500*l.* a piece for his appearance at the assizes, and got his pardon from the King, and walked up and down York streets with confidence."

the maidservant of the house to deliver to him; which answer hee
retorned to Mr. Aislaby, his maister, when hee retorned back.
Whereupon the said Mr. Aislaby sent this ex^t back againe to enquire of the said maid servant whether shee had delivered the
lettre to Mr. Jennings' hand or noe, but the answer was made to
him by severall of the servants, " the lettre was delivered to Mr.
Jennings' owne hand," and soe brought his maister back that
answer, who was then out of Monckbarr expectinge an answer,
which when this ex^t brought to him, hee bid him goe hence.
And this ex^t, further, saith that, about two of the clocke, (which
was within an houre after the delivery of the said lettre,) the said
Mr. Jennings came to this ex^t and askt him if Mr. Aislabie, his
maister, was with him, who told him that hee was gone out: and
then the said Mr. Jennings askt him the way to a close, but remembers not the name of it; whereupon the said Mr. Jennings
went directly downe a certaine lane leadinge to certaine closes
called Penley Crofts, and, shortly after, suspectinge some mischeife
might ensue, hee, this ex^t, together with one John Metcalfe, went
towards Penley Crofts aforesaid, where att a distance hee thought
hee heard the clashinge of swords, and, shortly after, (goeinge
forward to see the event) hee found Mr. Jennings leadinge the
said Mr. Aislabie, who had received a wound and was bleedinge
and almost spent for want of breath. And this ex^t further saith
that, when the said John Metcalfe beckned of this ex^t to come to
his maister, Mr. Aislabie, then the said Mr. Jennings left the said
Mr. Aislabie.

John Metcalfe, of the Citty of Yorke, sayth, that, on the 10th of
Jan., after two of the clocke in the afternoon, hee this ex^t, with
one John Hargraves, of what hee had observed, they then began
to suspect some mischeife might happen betwixt Mr. George
Aislabie their maister, and one Mr. Jonathan Jennings: whereupon, imediatley, this ex^t, together with the said John Hargraves,
went towardes Penley Crofts, beinge a certaine peece of ground
nigh the city of Yorke, where hee saw the said Mr. Aislabie and
Mr. Jennings with their swordes drawne and glitteringe before
hee came to them, none beinge with them but themselves. But
when hee came to them hee found the said Mr. Aislabie wounded
and ready to swound, and the said Mr. Jennings leadinge of him
(the said Mr. Jennings haveinge ther a long small rapier by his
side), and this ex^t told the said Mr. Jennings hee had done a sad
dayes worke; who replyed little or nothinge, but then left this
ex^t with the said Mr. Aislabie, beinge not able to goe any further,
haveinge lost so much blood and wantinge breath. And this ex^t
further saith that the said Mr. Jennings face was all bloody, sup-

poseinge that hee had besmeered his face over with blood that hee might not be knowne.

James Collins, of the Citty of Yorke, gentleman, sayth that, on the 10th of Jan., about five a clocke in the afternoone of the same day, one Mr. Jonathan Jennings came to this ex^{ts} house, who was then wounded in his right hand, and told him that Mr. Aislabie had given him the said wound. And this ex^t further saith that Mr. Jennings told him that hee had received a lettre from Mr. Aislabie, the said day, the contents whereof, to the best of this ex^{ts} remembrance, are as followeth. "Sir, I desire you to meete mee in Penley Crofts, where wee may discourse somethinge concerninge the honor of the Mallory family." And this ex^t further saith that Mr. Jennings told him that they had beene discourseinge of it a whole weeke. And, further, the said Mr. Jennings told this ex^t that when they met, Mr. Jennings askt Mr. Aislabie what should bee the meaninge of this, to which Mr. Aislabie answered that it was not a tyme to use words: and soe Mr. Aislabie drew upon him; and, further, the said Mr. Jennings told him that Mr. Aislabie satt himselfe upon the ground, and then Mr. Jennings askt him if hee had gott a wound; and Mr. Aislabie told him hee had got on in the arme, and desired him to leave him. To whom Mr. Jennings replyed hee hoped hee was not hurt, and that hee would not leave him.

Jan. 19, 1674-5. Before Richard Metcalfe, Lord Mayor. *Jonathan Jennings, Esq.*,* sayth, that he and Mr. George Ayslabye were for a longe tyme very kind and intimate freinds, and, on Sunday the xth of January, Mr. Aislaby sent writeinge to this ex^t concerneinge some decre which this ex^t was to help him and Wm. Palmes Esq. unto, and intimateinge his owne desire to speake with this ex^t; whereupon he went to his house, and when he heard that he was walked forth he found the place and came to him with intent freindly to discourse. The said Mr. Ayslaby drew out his sword, refuseinge to intertayne any discourse, but furiously run upon him with his sword, soe that this ex^t, being surprised, retyred and went backe untill he had like to have falne into a ditch. And, beinge in great perill, he did draw a short walkinge sword, wch he usually wore, and indeavoured to defend himselfe therwith, yet the said Mr. Ayslaby wounded this ex^t in his right hand, and soe being disabled, closeinge, both fell to the ground, but how Mr. Ayslaby could gett any wound he knoweth not, unlesse by runninge himselfe upon this ex^{ts} sword.

* Mr. Jennings, at the time of the duel, was staying at the house of Mr. Chancellor Watkinson, but after the fatal issue of the affray he absconded, and did not appear before the magistrates, as it will be seen, for several days.

CXCVII. ABRAHAM IBBITSON. FOR HORSE STEALING.

26 Jan. 1674-5. *Abraham Ibbitson, of Leedes, cordwyner,*[*] being charged with the felonious takeing away of twoe geldings, one chesnutt colour, another coloured gray, of the goods and chattells of Wm. Hutchinson, Esq., and, alsoe, with a gelding or galloway of the goods and chattells of Joseph Ibbitson, gen., saith, that, about twoe yeares agoe, hee became acquainted with one Thomas Bancroft (formerly servant or apprentice unto Joseph Turner, of Leedes, sheere grinder). And that, about the latter end of November last, this ex^t mett with the said Bancroft in the highway from Yorke towards Leedes: and, walking thither togeather, the said Bancroft declared and sayd unto him, "If thou wilt goe along with me, thou neede not to want money," and then and there shew'd him a handfull of money. And, att some short tyme after, this ex^t, haveing occasion to Yorke, mett with the said Bancroft againe, who persuaded him to turne back againe to Leedes, att whose instance hee did. And the same night the said Bancroft went into the grounds of the sayd Mr. Hutchinson, and then and there did take away the sayd chesnutt geldeings. And he tooke away the horse or galloway of the said Mr. Ibbitson's. After which takeing the sayd Bancroft appointed him to stay for him about Mooretowne, untill he came unto him there; which accordeingly this ex^t did that night, and they both ridd to Beedall, and there this ex^t sold Mr. Ibbetson's geldeing for 6s. 8d. And, after such sale, the sayd Bancroft ridd away with the chesnutt geldeing, and ledd the gray gelding in his hand, and ordered this ex^t to meete him att Richmond. To which towne this ex^t went, and not meeting with him there, he put himselfe into service to a cordwyner, and stayd there from Munday to Fryday then after. And not findeing the said Bancroft to come there hee retorned the direct way to Leedes. And intendeing afterwards for Yorke (with a designe to take shippeing for Virgenia) this ex^t mett againe this said Bancroft on Bramham moore, where Bancroft did much persuade this ex^t to turne highwayman with him, and told him that hee had sold the galloway, and kept the geldeing in a woode neare Bramham moore. And after this discourse they went togeather unto a certaine alehouse in the Streete houses, in the way betwixt Tadcaster and Yorke, where there was a bush as a signe, and there they drunke togeather, and hee left Bancroft att that house.

---

[*] The confession of a horse-stealer. In the 17th century horse-stealing was a very common offence in the North of England.

CXCVIII. DANIEL AWTY.   FOR CLIPPING MONEY.

Apr. 28, 1675. Before Edward Copley, Esq. *Wm. Fryer, of Leeds*, saith, that Daniell Auty,* of Dewsbury, often tolde this informant that he colde clip as well as any man, and that, aboute a weeke since, he shewed this informant aboute fowerteene ounces of bullion, which he confest he had clipt, and he exchanged part of itt with this informant for 2 silver spoones; which bullion this informant delevered to Mr. Peables last Thursday, and, haveinge received a gratuity of Mr. Peables, for his discovery, of eight halfe crownes, he carried the same to the said Auty, whoe clipt seven of them, and delivered them clipt into this informant's handes.

Jaine Fryer, of Leeds, sawe aboute 14 ounces of bullain in the hands of Daniell Auty, part whereof he exchanged with Wm. Fryer, her husband, for two silver spoones; and the same day the said Wm. brought to Auty 8 halfe crownes, seaven of which the said Auty clipt that night, for she hearde the knopinge of them, being in the next roome.

Wm. Batley, of Leeds, June 2, 1675, saith, that Daniell Autye, late of Dewsbury, did come to his house, and desired him to procure of Mr. Beacham or any other 100*l*., or what other sum he could best procure for two or thre days, and he would allow this inform^t reasonable profitt for the loane thereof, for the said Autye told him he could clipp about 3*s*. of every pound, and doe it as well as any man in England could doe it, and further he told him that it was noe treason to talke of it.

Mr. Wm. Frier, of Leeds, 11 June, 1675, saith, that he beinge

---

* Daniel Awty was one of the most notorious thieves and clippers in England. He was a native of Dewsbury, at that time one of the most disreputable villages in Yorkshire. The whole of his kith and kin seem to have been adepts in dishonest practices. Awty was frequently in gaol for clipping money, but, by marvellous good fortune, he escaped scathless. His name will occur more than once in this volume, especially in connection with the robbery of the communion plate at York Minster. The practice of deteriorating and clipping money was carried on to a most appalling extent. There was hardly a single silversmith who had not trafficked in such iniquitous bargains and devices, and it was occasionally necessary to make a very severe example of buyers as well as sellers. On one occasion a wealthy goldsmith, Arthur Mangey, the father of Thomas Mangey, a well known divine, was executed for this offence.

Awty's life was passed in wickedness and crime, and ended in bloodshed. In 1702 he was living at a farmhouse between Ripon and Thirsk, which he had fitted up as a place for coining. A son-in-law, called Busby, resided with him. A quarrel arose between the two about their illegal trade, and in the end Awty was murdered by his son-in-law. Busby was convicted, and was hung in chains near Sandhutton, and the gibbet was long known by the name of Busby-stoop. Thoresby saw the murderer hanging in chains in 1702, and speaks of Awty as having been a Leeds clothier.

one at Wm. Shepley's house in Dewsbery, in the beginning of May last, Alice Awty, wife of Edward Awty, of Dewsbery moore side, came to him, as he was sitting, and desired to speake with him privately, and she told him that she heard that he had delivered to Mr. Peoples a peice of bullion which he had received from her sonn Daniell Awty, and desired him, for the Lord's sake, that hee would keepe theire counsell, for if hee should att any time be discovered they was undone for ever, and in case he kept theire counsell, if att any time he brought a stolne horse or any thing else they would safely secure itt;* and further said that there was nothing that her sonn Daniell did but she knew of it as to that bussiness.

June 16, 1675. Before Edw. Copley, Esq. *Mr. Wm. Frier, of Leeds,* saith, that, being in the company of Richard Oldroyd,† of Water yate, in Dewsbery, he told this informant that if he would att any time procure him moneys he would clipp it upon reasonable tearms. And, further, said that there was a neighbour, one Daniell Awty, could doe itt better then himselfe, and that he had sold severall peices of bullion to the goldsmith of Leeds, which was betwixt Daniell Awty and himselfe. He had fourty pounds in the hands of Mr. Peoples, of Dewsbery, clerk of the peace, which was granted him att Knaseborough sessions for his good service formerly done for the country, which said summe Richard Oldroyd told him, if he would intrust him with it, he would clipp it upon reasonable tearms, and that two shillings in the pound he could easily take of. And the aforesaid Rich. Oldroyd invited him to come to Dewsbery, for he had a chamber that was very convenient for discovering the Ratchdale ‡ clothiers in Lancashire, which trade from thence to Wakefeild weekely, for the taking of theire moneys from them as they returned from theire markett, and that what prises he gott from them he would be very civill in his requitall.

* 28 June, 1675, Wm. Batley, of Leeds, cloth dresser, confesses that Mercy Hutchinson, Awty's sister, had given him money to bribe Freare, of Leeds, and that both had been ready to take it, and that Freare would not give evidence. Awty was then in York Castle.

† A person of the same name, who bore the unenviable *soubriquet* of "The Devil of Dewsbury," was executed at York, in 1664, for his share in the Farneley wood plot. This person was probably his son.

‡ The Lancashire clothiers carried their wares to Leeds and the West Riding towns across the hills on pack-horses.

CXCIX. ROBERT THOMPSON. FOR MURDER.

May 6, 1675. Before Hen. Atkinson, Esq. *Alice, wife of Christopher Outhwaite, of Sawley, mason*,* saith that, her husband keeping an ale house in Sawley, a man aged twixt 40 and 50 yeares, and a young man aged about 17, upon Munday was fortnight, about three of the clocke in the afternoone, came into the house to drinke ale, and, the young man being sickly, the elder man desired her to warme a flaggon of ale for ye young man, and did shew himselfe very tender and carefull over the young man, and stayed about three houres, and would have stayed all night, but this informant refused to lodge them, she dislikeing them by reason of their often whispering. And the man, now present att the time of her informacion takeing, who now saith his name is Robert Thomson, is, as she verily beleiveth, the same elder man. And, dureing their stay, they were talking of their journey, which they said was to Skipton in Craven; and, as she remembers, th'elder call'd the young man Jacke, and paid for him, and told the young man he might call him master.

Jane, wife of John Tayler, of Buerley, smelter, saith that, on Tuesday was fortnight, two men came to her husband's house, he keeping an ale house, th'elder aged twixt 40 and 50 yeares, the younger about 17, and sickly; and they there drunke two flaggons of ale, and one pennyworth burnt for the young man, and they said they were to goe to Skipton; and, about two of the clocke, went away, th'elder paying sixepence; and gave 6 boddells to the younger, which he also paid. And she saith a man was found dead about a quarter of a mile from her husband's house, about twelve score out of the road to Skipton, upon Tuesday was sennight; whom she did see, lying in a hollow place twixt two little hills, his face and head so bruised that this informant could make noe discovery of the young man by his countenance; but, by his hatt and apparell, she saith she verily beleiveth it was the young man that was at her husband's house with the man now present, who saith his name is Robert Thomson, whom this informant did this day challenge in the markett in Ripon, and charged him with the premisses, but he denyed all.

---

* A murder at Bewerley near Ripon. From the evidence it seems probable that the culprit had some very strong reason for getting the young lad out of the way. Thompson lived at Sutton Howgrave, and, in his defence, asserted that on the day and night in question he was staying with his brother-in-law, John Metcalfe, at Thoralby, and that he knew nothing of the affair. Metcalfe, however, denies that he was at his house, and three witnesses speak to the fact of their seeing Thompson at or near Bewerley on the day of the murder. Thompson was probably executed.

Richard Sill, of Bainbrigg, in Wensidaile, sayeth, he knows Robert Thompson very well, who is now suspected for the murderinge of his sonne John Sill, and belcives the same to be true, for that his sonne had given out in speeches that Robert Thompson had promissed him 5*l*. if he would not appeare against him att Richmond sessions, which he agreed to, but belcives Robert did not yett pay it him, though he came severall tymes to demaund it. And this deponent, further, sayth that upon the 14th instant he viewed the cloathes of the murdered personn, and upon the 15th viewed the body of the murdered personn, and findes it to be his sonne.

CC. JOHN MELMERBY. FOR A ROBBERY.

May 11, 1675. Before Ro. Hutton, Esq. *John Barnit* saith, that John Melmerby,* of Brunton, neare Richmond, sold to Urseley, wife of Edward Wharton, of Harrigate, a piece of rowd ticking, some white ticking and also one rowle of ribin and one bunch of black thrid, all which was stolen out of a shoop att Newbaud, also a silver peper box, a silver mustard box, and a silver salt with a coote of armes cut on them which was thre combs,† and also a duzan of wood combs, all taken out of the pack of John Chambers, a Richmond carrier, at Burrowbridg. And the said John Barnit and Melmorby likewise sold to the said Urslay a silver taster, a silver tankard, which they with others tooke out of ye study of Doctor Samways,‡ of Beadall; and they also sold two lased hankirchers and seaventy yeards of Indian sersnit for 25*l*., which was taken out of ye said Chambers' packs.

1675, July 21. Before Sir Joseph Cradock. *Anne Wilkinson, of Hartforth, spinster*, saith, that, about St. Thomas' day was a twelfthmonth, this ex^t was spining woolen at the howse of John Wharton, att Catterick bridg-end, and she saw John Melmerby, with three other of his comrades, bring into the house of the said John Wharton two silver bowles, nine silver spoons, three silver tumblers, who sold the same to John Wharton and Elizabeth

---
* A notorious burglar and highway robber, who, after several escapes, was sent beyond the seas. I have already printed a deposition in which he is charged with having robbed Catterick Church. I now give two more charges against him.

† The three combs were the arms of the family of Tunstall of Wycliffe. The *novus homo* of the house, according to tradition, was barber to William the Conqueror, and his descendants were not ashamed to shew the allusion to the office of their ancestor on their shield.

‡ Dr. Samways was a person of high preferment, as well as of literary distinction. But more of him elsewhere.

his daughter. Which was the plate of Captain Robinson's, of Kirby Hill, as the said Melmerby then said, and, that the said Melmerby with his companions did light a candle in the house of the said Captain Robinson and cut a pye in the same house before they came out, as the said John Melmerby said.

CCI. THOMAS WILY.   AN IMPOSTOR.

Jan. 11, 1675-6. These are to certifie whome it may concerne, that I, Robert Ashburne, of Yorke, booke-seller,* travelling from Whitgift to Yorke, in my way at a place commonly called Hayle Mill, neare Holden, found a man, whitch I suppose to be a tinker, in a ditch, and a woman pulling him out; which woman exprest these wordes, that it was a good deed to suffer the man to drownd himselfe, for he had like to have killed her yesterday, and that he had killed a man at the other end of the towne, and willfull murther would out.

CCII. JOHN NEVINSON AND OTHERS.   FOR HIGHWAY ROBBERY.

March 3, 1675-6. Before Sir Henry Thompson, Kt. and Richard Robinson, Esq. *Peter Skipwith*,† aged about 14, saith, that

---

* An impostor who was probably playing a trick to attract the sympathy and loose the purse strings of some wayfarer. The following note, relating to the case, is in the handwriting of Mr. Robinson of Thicket. " Upon this writing of Ashburne's, this tinker was brought before me by the constable of Howden, and, upon examination, I found him to have been long an incorrigible rogue; so that, partly for his roguish kind of life, and partly upon this charge, I committed him to the gaole. This tinker calles himselfe Thomas Wily, and sayes he dwelles at Barnsley. Ric. Robinson."

† A deposition referring to John Nevinson, the famous highwayman, who is commemorated in an old ballad, of which two stanzas may be taken as a sample :—

" Did you ever hear tell of that hero,
 Bold Nevison that was his name?
He rode about like a bold hero,
 And with that he gained great fame.

" He maintained himself like a gentleman,
 Besides he was good to the poor ;
He rode about like a bold hero,
 And he gain'd himself favour therefore."

Nevinson may be appropriately called the Claude Duval of the North. The story of his ride from London to York is too well-known to be repeated, and even Lord Macaulay introduces him into his history of England. The depositions now given are imperfect, so that we cannot well tell what the crime was for which Nevinson was condemned in 1675-6. He was, however, reprieved, together with a woman of the name of Jane Nelson, in the expectation that he would discover his accomplices. The hope

the letter now shewed unto him, beginning "Intillmen," for Gentlemen, and underwritten, "Old Bomcocke," was of his writing; and that his mother told him what he should write; and beleeves that his father, George Skipwith, first told his mother what should be written. And that his father and one Mr. Tankered had wont to sport with one another about balmcockes, and, therefore, the said Tankered called his father Bomcock, and his mother wisht him to subscribe the letter Old Bomcock. And, as to the figures underneath the letter, viz. ii. 10 10, he saith that the latter should have been put out, and that the two former figures of ii. and 10 were intended for the one and twentieth day of February.

George Skipwith, of Howden, saith, that the letter above-mentioned by Peter Skipwith, was written by his sonn at his appointment; and that the meaning of that letter written to Mr. Brace or Bracey was, that the abovenamed Tankered and Brace, or Bracy, would perform theire promise made to him, which was to pay to his wife 19s. 2d., which they owed to her. And that he caused the letter to be signed Old Bomcock. And further saith that the reason of those words in the letter, viz: "It is very hard if nothing redound to me out of such a summe as between fower and five hundred pounds, and that I do expect every day to be carried to prison, or else my house to be broken up by execution, and my wife and children thrown into the street," was, because Brace, or Bracy, and Tankered had promised to lend him . . . . . pounds, and that they would pay his debts, and that if he would keepe their counsell he should never want. And sayes he knowes no persons likely to be highwaymen save Tankered and Brace or Bracey: and that Tankered's aboad is for the most part at

seems to have been a vain one, and the pardoned culprit was draughted into a regiment destined for Tangier. He soon deserted from it, and we shall meet with him again.

It seems to have been a custom among the highwaymen to have receiving houses in different parts of the country. This put them at the mercy of the receivers, and they were obliged to conciliate them by gifts.

A life of Nevinson has been published, which is excessively rare.

There are several scarce pamphlets describing robberies and other crimes that took place about this time in Yorkshire, in some of which, perhaps, Nevinson played his part.

"Bloody news from Yorkshire: or the great robbery committed by twenty highwaymen upon fifteen butchers, as they were riding to Northallerton fair." 4to. London. 1674.

"A true relation of the proceedings at York assizes, with an account of the condemnation of the young man who murdered another man's wife near Leeds." 4to. London. 1677.

"A full and true relation of a most barbarous and cruel robbery and murder committed by six men and one woman, near Wakefield, in Yorkshire." 4to. London. 1677.

Mr. Wright's, in Lincolnshire, at some town nigh unto Gainsborough. And that he and Brace, or Bracy, do often frequent Wentbridge, at Robert Blowes his house there; and they oftentimes lodge at Tuxford, at Mr. Rodes his house there; and that they are men who live by robbing; but knowes no particular man they did rob, onely Tankered told him about halfe a yeere since that they had taken about 100*l*. or 150*l*. from Botterill, a barley-buyer, at or about Brigham-baulke-end. And the said Tankered, at Mrs. Freer's house in Howden, asked if he knew of any man that had 100*l*. or 200*l*. to get, for they lived by their witts and wanted at that time. And the said Tankered, further, urged him to have informed them of some of his neighbors that had money, or, however, to keepe theire counsell, which he promised to do. He beleeves that Tankered's right name may be Thomas Pearson, and saith that Blowes at Wentbridge, and Rodes at Tuxford, can inform their names and places of aboad. And this ex[t] being asked where he was when absent from Howden severall dayes about the time of the robbery committed in the West Riding, he saith that he was at Hillam for the most part of those dayes, but first went to Wentbridge to seeke out Tankered and Brace, or Bracy, but could not finde them. And saith that he knows Brace, or Bracy, and Tankered to be companions, and thinks that Brace, or Bracy, his true name to be John Nevison; and that somtime heertofore he lived at Agnes Burton, and hath an uncle lives therabouts, and that this Nevison is now married and lives beyond Pontefract. And he saith that Tankered bid him come to him at Blowes' house in Wentbridge, and he would lend him some money, and accordingly he went the last summer to him, but Tankered pretended he then wanted money, and so got none of him. He further saith that Mistresse Blowes, at Wentbridge, told him that they, meaning Brace and Tankered, had got a good summe of money. And this was after the robery committed in the West Riding. And she further told him that the country laughed at the excisemen, saying they had robbed themselves, but she beleeved they were robbed by Tankered and Brace, or Bracy, and their companions, for that Tankered, since the robbery, had paid them off their reckonings, and Tankered and Brace had either of them bought horses of thirty pounds a peece: and, besides these horses, Tankered had bought an horse of 30*l*. price upon the Woldes. Lastly, he saith that Edmund Brace, or Bracy, is a companion of Tankered, alias Pearson, and of John Brace, or Bracy, alias Nevison, and lives at Ragnall, four miles from Tuxford, and he thinkes that he also goes by the name of Nevison.

CCIII. JOHN ACKLAM. A ROMAN CATHOLIC PRIEST.

March 16, 1675-6. Before Sir Richard Osbaldeston, Kt. *Charles Chauncy, of Burlington, gent.,** saith that, upon the first of this instant, he went by the comand of his captaine, Andrewe Hayes, to search the house of John Constable, Esq., being a Papist, for horses.... And upon his search he seisd two gueldings ... mare, and two fowleing pieces. And in his search .... one who was sett in a roome ne .... to another roome, where there was a table spread with a linnen cloath: and at one end a surplice, and at another end a vestment, which he believ'd belong'd to a Popish preist. And this informant returnd with Mr. Constable to his cap ... at Burlington, who then .... that he had seized the said person. Whereupon this informant took horse immediately and went to Mr. Constable's house againe, and there found and seized the said person, who then called himselfe John Acklam, with the surplice and vestments, and carryed them all to his captaine at Burlington. And then he searched the said party who called himselfe Acklam (and found) a ring of brasse, with tenne small notches and a large one; a tinne box, wherein was severall wafers or parts of wafers with impressions upon them, with two written letters, and some notes about paying of mild moneyes for guineyes, with some other papers. But afterwards he was told that the said party who called himselfe Acklam was one John May, and was looked upon to be a Popish priest.

CCIV. THOMAS HEBER, GEN., AND OTHERS. FOR A BURGLARY.

March 30, 1676. Before Walter Hauksworth, Esq. *Alexander*

---

* The penal statutes against the Roman Catholics were at this time very vigorously enforced. The houses of the gentry were being constantly searched for horses and arms; the oath of allegiance was frequently put to them; and they were subjected, generally, to much harsh treatment. We cannot understand, in these days, the fever of anxiety which was excited by the real or pretended plots that were then being brought to light.

The officer's evidence is confirmed by a serjeant of the name of James Lawson. The prisoner, who signs his deposition with the name of John May, says that he has been called so for 30 years. He denies that he is a priest. He says that he was born at a single house called Ash on Blakesmoor. He confesses that the box and its contents are his own property, and says that the vestments and other things belong to Mr. Constable, and that "most of the Popish gentlemen have such."

Squire, of Ilkley, deposeth,* that, upon Fryday, in the night of the 17th day of March, about one of the clocke, his dwelling-house was broken open, and that thre persons entred his said house, one of which persons came to him with an ax, threatning to murder him, and gave him many sore blows. And this informant got hold of the head or web of the ax, and said " I fear God and not man," and strugled with him, and got hold of one of his hands, and held it to save himselfe from being murthered, and felt it was a very soft hand. He was a tall man. And another of the said persons went to his daughter, Elizabeth Beecroft, being in bed in a roome near adjoyning, and would have smothered her in the bed cloths. And one of the said persons, being a tall man, broke open a cupboard and a deske and tooke from thence above 2*l*. 10*s*. and a little peice of beefe. And on their goeing away they left behind them one iron gavelocke, one staff, and a wood wedge. There were other persons att the doore whom he heard whistle when they went away. And, the said persons being gone, he went to one Jane Beanlands, who that night lodged in his barne adjoyning to his house, and asked her if she heard nothing; to which she replied that about one of the clocke that night she heard Mr. Thomas Heber, of Hollinghall, and Wm. Hudson, of Ilkley, shoemaker, their voyces near the doore, and presently heard a great rushing or noise att the doore, as if it were in breaking open. And this informant saith that afterward the above mentioned staffe was knowne to belong to the said Thomas Heber, who did afterward challeng the same to be his. And the said Thomas Heber was within his house when the burglary was committed, and he did well perceive him by the light of the moone depart out of his house.

Elizabeth Beecroft saith, that Mr. Thomas Heber came to her father's house, the Thursday next after the said burglary committed, and told her that he knew the persons had robbed her father, and likewise told her how they broke the cupboard-doore with a gavelocke att two knocks, and the deske with a wedge; and likewise said they would never have robbed the house had they knowne there had beene no more money in it then was found.

* A deposition which connects a Craven gentleman with a very serious offence. The Hebers of Holling-hall were a younger branch of the family at Marton. I do not know what was the result of the case, but it is probable enough that, in spite of the suspicious circumstances against him, Mr. Heber was acquitted. The Yorkshire juries were singularly lenient to the county gentlemen. It was easy enough to put their lives in jeopardy by false testimony.

Mr. Heber acknowledged that the staff found in the house was his own, but denied any knowledge of the burglary. The gavelock was sworn to by its owner, having been lent by him to a man of the name of Bibby. Beecroft swore to Pollard on account of a peculiar stutter in his voice.

Elizabeth Longfellow, of Ilkley, saith that she went into the house of Josias Laycocke, of Ilkley, alehouse-keeper, and one Walter Pollard of Ilkley, being one suspected for the breakeing of Alexander Squire's house, was drinking in company. The said Pollard asked her how she did, and further said, " I am now makeing Bess Squire halfe crownes fly." (She being then called by the name of Squire, since married to one Richard Beecroft.)

CCV. JOHN KAY, CLERK, AND OTHERS. FOR PRACTISING PHYSIC WITHOUT A LICENCE.

A true bill against John Kay, of Leeds, clerk, for practising medicine* without a license on May 1, 1676. Also, against

---

* A special licence was required to enable any one " to practise medicine," but the study of it has at all times been a favourite pursuit among the clergy, and for a very good reason. A line in the epitaph of John Favour, vicar of Halifax, who died in 1623, thus summarily gives the three accomplishments in which he was a match for any one in his extensive parish :

> Theologus, Medicusque obiit, Jurisque peritus.

Among the Puritan ministers a knowledge of medicine was very common, and, after the black Bartholomew Act, many of them threw up their gowns and adopted that profession. Some of the gentlemen mentioned in the bill were not Puritans. Mr. Kay, of Leeds, was a great friend of Ralph Thoresby, the antiquary, who frequently mentions him in his Diary.

About Matthew Robinson, the vicar of Burneston, and his acquaintance with medicine, there is a long account in the life of that gentleman which has been published by Mr. Mayor of Cambridge. In the following extract it will be seen that Mr. Robinson removed at least one cause of complaint which properly-appointed physicians had against him.

" Many well knew that he was brought up a physician, and therefore consulted him in their distempers and infirmities. Amongst many gentlemen thus applying to him, was Sir Joseph Cradock, the commissary of the Archdeaconry of Richmond, who often consulted him for himself and family with great success; but, finding him shy and nice in writing bills or anything that looked like a professed physician, he sent to him under the seal of the office a licence to practice physic, that he might not have any excuses longer, and this proved to him a great unhappiness. For he was sent for by some dukes and peers, with many baronets, knights, and great men, upon that account; some of whom (as being at too great a distance,) he absolutely refused ; others he was induced to gratify, that of friends he might not make them enemies. Insomuch that in short time he had but little time left him to his own studies, being three or four days per week, and often more, carried unwillingly abroad to visit patients ; and, when he was at home, his house was much visited by friends of the best quality.

" In his medicinal practice he had prodigious success, especially in the checking and curing of consumptions, being well instructed from his own hectical constitution, as well as from books. And in that he had a peculiar method of his own, known then to few or none, but such as after took it up from him. No man had a steadier judgement of pulses and patients, for he could see danger at a great distance, and rarely missed in his prognostications ; and, therefore, in all such cases he pressed the counsels of abler physicians. And though he refused to undertake the cases of many patients, seeing them desperate, he never denied any to join in counsel with the most learned

Richard Humber, of Midlam, gen.; Matthew Robinson, of Burniston, clerk; Thomas Bonnell, of Hunsingore, clerk; and John Coar, of Tong, clerk; for the same offence.

CCVI. SAMUEL BANCKES. FOR BEING A ROMISH PRIEST.

Aug. 14, 1676. Before Yorke Horner, Lord Mayor of York. *Thomas Thomas, of Yorke, gen.*, sayth, that, within twelve dayes past, he see Samuell Banckes,* of this Citty, writeinge-master, act in the office of a Roman preist within his owne house, and that he see him say masse in his owne person, haveinge upon him the robes of a preist at that tyme before an alter, and that he see the wyne in the Sacrament in his hand, severall people to the number of about seaventeene beinge then present.

CCVII. JOHN BARNET. FOR HIGHWAY ROBBERY.

Sep. 13, 1676. Before Sir Joseph Cradock, Kt. *James Darnell, of Brompton-super-Swayle*,† saith, that comeing with two horse load of cheeses, which he had bought att Manchester, on Thursday, the 7th instant, he went homeward, when it was darke; and as he came to the turne of the laine that goeth to Killerby causey, 2 men rideing very fast overtook him, and stroke att him, as fast as they could, one after another. And this informant defending himself by lifting his armes above his head, his armes were thereby exceedingly bruised, as appeared att the time of this informacion given, they being both black and blew. At last he

---

physicians of the land; often reporting those odd cases of patients even to the college of physicians by a polite Latin pen, whereof he was a great master, as well as of the Latin tongue."

But I must stop. I may give here, appropriately enough, what a Doncaster physician says about himself:—

"Feb. 17, 1651-2. Mr. Wm. Gray, of Doncaster, sayth that he is noe phisition quallifyed according to the lawes of the land, but is a chirurgeon and hath served his father, and hath beene bred in the art of surgery under his father, and that he giveth phisick to divers that doe desire him, and that he thinkes itt lawfull for him soe to doe, butt that he doth not assume to himselfe the name of a doctor of phisick, though some people doe give him that title."

* Another proof of the active measures that were being now taken against the Roman Catholics. The accused person denies the charge.

† A case of highway robbery. A man called John Barnet, who had just been released from York Castle, where he had been burned in the hand, was charged with the offence. The prosecutor swears to some money that was found in Barnet's possession, also to some cheese, and to the bridle of the robber's horse. Barnet, who lived at Newsham, was in all probability convicted.

fell of his horse, and then they, or one of them, burst open his drawers, and putt their, or one of their, hands into his private pocket, which was within his breeches, and took out thereof above 40s., a carvatt, a handcherchief, the key of his chist and some papers, and left this informant for dead: who laid soe till the next morning he found they had cutt the wanty that tyed his pack fast to his panyers, which he found was fallen downe, and most of his cheeses throwne abroad, of which he wanted two or three, and perceived a great quantity of blood that had come from the wounds in his head.

CCVIII. JOHN WALTON AND OTHERS. FOR SPEAKING AGAINST THE CHURCH OF ENGLAND.

Feb. 9, 1676-7. Before Sir Philip Musgrave, Bt. *Thomas Walton, of Aldstone moore, gent.*,* saith, that, being in the company of Lionell Walton, of the Bridge end, his son John Walton, etc., and discoursing about a minister, Mr. Burnard, who related to this informer some discourse that past betwixt himselfe and one John Walton of Gateshead concerning the Church of England, which Church Mr. Burnand held to be a true church, the said John Walton denied it. The company now present said they thought that John Walton was in the right. They did also endeavour to prove by arguments that the Church of England was a false Church; namely, 'The Kinge is a foresworne man, then how could he establish a true church: that the Church of England is eronious, and therefore could not be a true church: and that a corrupt tree cannot bring forth good fruite, the Church of England is universily corrupt, therefore it cannot be a true church. They did also affirme that the Church of England was goeing on the broad way to destruction. They alsoe said that if the Church of England went to heaven, hell would be very empty. They alsoe affirmed and tooke in hand to prove that those that used the Comon Prayer would be dammed. They endeavoured to prove it out of some text in the Collossians, chap. 2^d, 21 and 22 ver.

CCIX. A LIST OF ROMAN CATHOLIC RECUSANTS.

Northumberland, 1677. Wm. Ridley, of Crawhall, Esq., and

---

* A severe attack upon the Church of England. Some objection, however, may be taken to the logic!

Truth his wife, Arnold Burdett, of Williamontswick, gent., and Katharine his wife, Ralph Ridley, of Waltowne, gen., Robert Errington, de eadem, gen., Thomas Armestrong, of Bradley, yeoman, and Margaret his wife, Wm. Smyth, of Housesteads, yeoman, and Mary his wife, Andrew Jopling, of Newlands, yeo., and Mary his wife, John Gill, de eadem, yeo., and Elizabeth his wife, Richard and Thomas Gibson, of Corbridge, yeo., Cuthbert Hudspeth, de eadem, yeo., Elizabeth Algood, de eadem, spinster, Katherine Sympson and Isabella, wife of Henry Forster, de eadem, Thomas Riddell, of Fenham, Esq., Edward Widdrington, of Felton, Esq., and Dorothy his wife, Robert Brandling, of Alnwicke abbey, Esq., John Smythworth, alias Smurfitt, of Alnwick, gen., Edward Strother, of Alnwicke, gen., Mary wife of James Rutherford, de eadem, yeo., Anne wife of Henry Farey, de eadem, Robert Anderson, de eadem, yeoman, John Sanderson, de Parke, yeo., Wm. Ord, of Grange, gen., Elizabeth Ord, of Grange, widow, Henry Widrington, of Ritton, gen., Henry Thornton, of Witton Sheilds, gen., Wm. Thornton, of Netherwitton, gen., Cuthbert Fenwicke, of South Midleton, gen., Elizabeth Atkinson, de eadem, Bartholomew Wintrees, of Gallowhill, yeoman, Sir John Swinburne, of Capheaton, Bart., John Fenwicke, of Denham, gen., —— Withrington, of Westharle, spinster, Dame Cristiana Widrington, of Cartington, widow, Dame Mary Charleton, de eadem, widow, Francis Widdrington, of Heapall, gen., Wm. Hall, of Kestron, gen., Grace Snawden, of Bickarton, —— Greene, of Healle, widow, Wm. Robson, de eadem, Roland Robson, de eadem, yeoman, Bernard Romney, of Rothberry, yeo., Richard Wilson, de eadem, yeo., Alex. Watson, de eadem, yeo., Matthew Robson, of Thropton, yeo., Thomas Selby, of Bittleston, Esq., Charles Selby, of Farnham, yeoman, Thomas Clennall, of Clennall, Esq, Mary Hall, de eadem, spinster, Robert Browne, of Allanton, yeo., Lancelot Ord, of Wetwood, gen., Catherine Anderson, de eadem, Matthew Coxon, of Woolaw, yeo., Wm. Hall, of Durtrees, yeo., Margaret Collingwood, of Lanton, Robert Gray, of Berchall, gen., William Errington, of Beaufront, Esq., John Thirlewall, of Newbiggin, Esq., Wm. Welken, of par. Hexham, yeo., Nicholas Welken, de eadem, —— Carnaby, of Nabbock, widow, Benony Carre, of Hexham, yeo., Philip & Thomas Jefferson, de eadem, yeo., Mary wife of Robert Hutchinson, yeo., Wm. Hutchinson, yeo., Thomas Kirsopp, yeo., Mathew Younger, yeo., Richard Gibson, sadler, John Cooke, yeo., George Gibson, yeo., Jane Dickinson, widow, John Armestrong, yeo., Margaret Dickinson, widow, Barbara Stewart, widow, Ann Blenkinsopp, spinster, Bridget wife of John Fenwicke, yeo., Laurence Cooke, yeo., George Nixon, yeo., Thomas Noble, yeo., Richard Lambert, yeo., John Heron, yeo., all of Hexham, Bartram Oddy, of the Hermitage, yeo., John Bartram, sen. and jun., of Hexhamshyre, yeo., Wm. Thornton, of Witton, gen., Wm. Errington, of Wallicke grainge, gen., Mark Grey, of Heslysyde, gen., Thomas Mountney, of Stonecroft, gen., Thomas Morraley, of Morraley, gen., Sir Francis Ratcliffe, of Develstone, Bart., and Catharine his wife, Allan Swinburne, of Nafferton, gen., John Halsell, of Ovingham, gen., James Fenwicke, of Spittall, par. Ovingham, gen., George Collingwood, of Eslington, Esq., Ralph Clavering, of Callolee, Esq., Thomas Riddell, of Unthanke, gen., Wm. Fenwicke, of Bywell, Esq., Robert Fenwicke, de eadem, gen., Katherine Fenwicke, de eadem, spinster, Lancelot Newton, de Stocksfeild hall, gen., William Lord Widrington, of Widrington, and Bridget Lady Widrington, Ambrose Fenwicke, of Matfin, gen., Gerrard Fenwicke, de eadem, gen., Henry Grey, of Betchfeild, gen., Wm. Widrington, of Bootland, gen.

CCX. THOMAS HARLAND AND OTHERS. FOR A RIOT AND CONSPIRACY.

Jan. 3, 1677-8. Before Thomas Hesletyne, Esq. *Dorothy Bilton, of Huby, widow,** saith, that, about February last, John Maisterman, of Huby, came to this informant, and desired her and Wm. Sergeant to burne Mr. Sampson's gate of his close called Booncroft, and did offer to give each of them 12*d*. a peice for soe doeing, but they did refuse to doe it. And Thomas Harland, and Anne his wife, did severall tymes, about two yeares since, importune this informant and John Myers to disguise themselves; and, to that end, did proffer to furnish this informant with a perriwigg, and the said John Myers with a visard mask, and they to lay in waite att a place called Slecarre gate, neare Huby; and there to knock downe the said Mr. Sampson from his horse as hee came from Yorke.

John Myers, of Huby, yeoman, saith, that, in March was a twelve moneth, hee by the direccion of Thomas Harland, of Huby, and with the knowledge of John Maisterman, did carry about

---

* A case of conspiracy and arson that presents some singular features. A person of the name of Harland, living in Huby, wishes to annoy and get rid of his neighbour, a Mr. Sampson, and, on that account, he troubles him as much as he can. He burns down one of his gates, and tries to induce the villagers to do him further injury, promising to stand between them and harm. It is amusing to find an old woman saying that he wished to put a wig upon her, and to convert her into a highway robber.

nyne or ten kidds of whinns, and lay them to a gate of John Sampson, Esq., and, about twelve or one of the clocke in the night tyme, did carry fyre in an earthen pott, and placed it among the whinns, whereby the said gate was burnt down. And, about a moneth after the burning the said gate, the aforesaid Thomas Harland did advise and direct this informant to prepare a squybb, and to throw the same in att the window of the lodgeing room of the said John Sampson in the night tyme, when the said Mr. Sampson was asleep in bedd; and, alsoe, to sett fyre on about threescore kidds of whinns then lying nigh to a spring of wood of the said Mr. Sampson's in Huby, that it might bee burnt. And then the said Harland told this informant that thereby the said Mr. Sampson would bee soe affrighted that hee would leave the towne, and then the inheritance wilbe our owne.

CCXI. WILLIAM CRESSWELL, GENT., AND OTHERS. WRECKERS.

July 30, 1678. At Elswick, before Ralph Jenison, Esq. *William Berry and Thomas Bowman*,* say, that, on Satturday, the 10th of November last past, betwixt two and three of the clocke in the morning, the good shipp or barke, called the Margarett of Leath, whereof John Finley was then maister, came on shoare at Seaton seas, at the port of Blyth's nuke. And they being in dainger to be lost, and the shipp in dainger to be suncke or broke, the passengers being afraid of ther lives, being a dossin or sixteene in number, would not stay aboard the said shipp, but were sett ashoare. And before the shipp's company could returne againe to there shipp, one William Creswell of Creswell, gent., and John Boult and William Curry, booth of Bedlinton, came aboard the said shipp, and brooke open the doores and hatches, and went downe into the hould; and did likewise breake open severall trunkes and boxes, and tooke away severall goods, which these deponents doe conceive to be worth at least 200*l.*

CCXII. DANIEL O'FERRELL. A SUSPICIOUS PERSON.

Dec. 2, 1678. Before Bradwardine Tindall, of Brotherton, Esq. *John Megan, of Brotherton*, saith, that Daniell O'Farrell, ales

---

* A ship goes ashore near Blyth Nook, on the Northumbrian coast, and the wreckers make it their prey. Among them was Mr. Cresswell of Cresswell. The crew, it will be observed, had deserted the vessel. The coast of that county is a very dangerous one, and mishaps very frequently occur there.

Moore, came into his house, the 24th of November, beinge the Lord's day, and called for a flaggon of ayle. The said John Megan beinge then reading in a sermon booke, he interrupted him, and said he would give him a flaggon of ayle if he would sing him a Scotch songe; and rather then he should want a song he would give him a shilling. But Megan denying to sing, he asked him "what newes?" Megan said, he must know that of him, because he supposed he was lately come from London. He then said that the Kinge had throwne up his crowne to the Parliament, and they to chuse who should weare it. How doe you like that? And said there would be a change, and that you will see shortly. And made insulting jeasts and severall other jeastures.

Daniell o' Farrell, alias Moore, saith, that hee came into England halfe a yeare agone. In which time hee hath been in London, for the most, and served one Mr. John Fitzgerrard, a resident with the Venitian Ambassador. Hee received a little paper, now showne to him, in which is mencioned "Mr. Harecourt ten masses, &c.," from Mr. Fitzgerrard aforesaid. Hee was borne in Ireland, but bred up in Germany. Hee came into this countrey to teach French and Italian and Dutch languages, and hee was travelling for that purpose, and for noe other intent.

CCXIII. NICHOLAS POSTGATE. FOR BEING A SEMINARY PRIEST.

Dec. 9, 1678. At Brompton, before Sir Wm. Cayley and Wm. Cayley, Esq. jun. *John Reeves, his Majestie's surveyor, or gauger, for the towne of Whitby*, saith, that upon the 7th instant, he was informed that Matthew Lith,† of Sleights, being at a

---

* A suspicious person is arrested. This was an evil time for the Roman Catholics, and every strange looking person was stopped. O'Ferrall was in York Castle in July 1679. Mr. Harcourt was one of the victims in the Plot.

† An aged Roman Catholic priest is arrested near Whitby. He was condemned to death at the York assizes, and was actually hanged, drawn, and quartered.

There has at all times, since the Reformation, been a strong body of Roman Catholics near Whitby and Egton. Mr. Postgate is said to have worked among them for more than fifty years.

A witness of the name of Wm. Cockerill deposed that he heard Lith say, "Wee should have a sorrowfull Christmas, a bloody Fastnes, and a joyfull Easter." Henry Cockerill said he went with Reeves, and that Lith tried " to hide Postgate by standing before him untill the said Reeves did pull him away." Both say that Postgate was a reputed priest. Two women of Whitby, who had become Protestants, depose that they heard Postgate say mass, at John Hodgson's, at Biggin-house, near Ugthorpe, at Thomas Pattinson's, at Ugthorpe, and at Timothy Lyth's, near Grosmont Bridge.

wedding, should speake these words, "You talk of Papists and Protestants, but, when the roast is ready, I 'know who shall have the first cutt." Upon notice whereof, this informer thought himselfe obliged to search the said Matthew's house, which accordingly he did upon the 8th instant, supposeing that some armes or ammunicion might be found there, the said Matthew and his family being all Papists. And he saith that though he was interrupted by the said Matthew, he did finde a supposed Popish preist there (called Postgate), and, alsoe, Popish bookes, relicks, wafers, and severall other things, all which the said Postgate owned to be his. The said Postgate said that he was called Watson, but afterwards being called by others by the name of Postgate, he owned that to be his right name.

Nicholas Postgate, about the age of fourscore years, saith that, about 40 yeares since, he lived at Saxton with the Lady Hungate, untill she dyed. And, since, he hath lived with the old Lady Dunbar, but how long it is since he knoweth not. Of late he hath had noe certaine residence, but hath travailed about among his friends. Being demanded whether he be a Popish priest or noe, he saith, "Let them prove it," and would give noe other direct answer. Being demanded how he came by, and what use he made of the bookes, wafers, and other things which were found with him, and which hee owned, he saith that some of them were given him by Mr. Goodricke, a Roman Catholicke, and other

The following account of Postgate's death is taken from Chaloner's Memoirs of the Missionary Priests.

"The day allotted for his triumphant exit was the 7th of August, 1679; on which day, in the morning, amongst other visitors, went to see him Mrs. Fairfax, wife to Mr. Charles Fairfax of York, and Mrs. Meynel of Kilvington. These ladies having done their devotions, went together to his room, to take their last leave of him, and to crave his blessing. The confessor, seeing them in great concern, whereas he was chearful, came up to them, and laying his right hand upon the one and his left upon the other, they being both at that time big with child, he spoke these words to them: *Be of good heart, children, you shall both be delivered of sons, and they will be both saved.* Immediately after he was laid upon a sledge, and drawn through the streets to the place of execution, where he suffered with great constancy. The two ladies were soon after brought to bed of sons, who were both baptized, and both died in their infancy.

"He was executed according to sentence; his quartered body was given to his friends and interr'd. One of his hands is preserved in Douay College. The following inscription was put upon a copper plate, and thrown into his coffin:

"'Here lies that reverend and pious divine, Dr. Nicholas Postgate, who was educated in the English college at Doway. And after he had laboured fifty years (to the admirable benefit and conversion of hundreds of souls) was at last advanced to a glorious crown of martyrdom at the city of York, on the 7th of August, 1679, having been priest 51 years, aged 82.'

"The unhappy Reeves who, apprehended him, never had the 20*l.* reward which he looked for; but, after having suffered for some time an extreme torture in body and mind, was found drowned in a small brook."

some by one Mr. Jowsie,* a supposed Romish priest, both which are dead; and that hee made use of them by disposeing them to severall persons who desired them for helping their infirmities. Being demanded why he named himself, att the first, Watson, he saith that he hath sometimes been soe called, his grandmother on his father-side being soe called, and he being like that kindred.

CCXIV. JOHN CORNWALLIS, ETC.   SUSPICIOUS PERSONS.

Dec. 17, 1678. Before John Assheton and Henry Marsden, Esqrs. *Capt. Thomas Hebar* sayth, that, beeing att Skipton, in the house of Robert Michell, upon the 13th instant, a gentleman comeing thorow the roome wheare I, with some company,† was

---

* On Dec. 9, 1678, Andrew Jowsey, of Egton, was charged before Edward Trotter and Constable Bradshaw, Esqrs., with being a priest. He denies the fact. He will not take the oaths of allegiance and supremacy now offered to him. Matthew Morgan, of Egton, deposes to having heard Jowsey say that he was a priest, and that he had come from Ireland. Jowsey was acquitted.

† Some depositions of great interest and value. The real or pretended plots that were now being discovered, all of which were said to be originated by the Roman Catholics, filled the whole country with alarm. The most vigorous measures were taken by the executive, and a most virulent persecution commenced, which was fostered with the utmost energies of a few interested and pestilential informers. It is now pretty well ascertained that many of the accusations that were brought against Roman Catholics were base forgeries. There were many Roman Catholics, doubtless, who looked upon this period as a great crisis in the history of their religion, and who were fully prepared to undergo any penalty or peril to maintain it; but, with the exception perhaps of a few cases, it was reserved for others to give the false colouring to their sympathies and words and to array them in the garb of treason. It is pitiable to think that in the North, as well as in the South, there were wicked and untruthful men who sought to make capital out of the religious opinions of others which common Christian charity should have taught them to respect, and to build up their own fortunes upon the ruins of many loyal and noble houses.

In these depositions we have a graphic account of the arrest of two ladies and a gentleman, all of whom were Roman Catholics. The gentleman was seized at a little inn at Skipton, in Craven. Some light is thrown upon the adventures of the party by the account of the trial of Sir Thomas Gascoigne.

It seems to have been the desire of the Northern Roman Catholics to establish a Nunnery in Yorkshire, for the propagation of their religion. The place, in the first instance, marked out for it was Heworth, near York, the residence of a very ancient Roman Catholic family of the name of Thweng. Broughton Hall, in Craven, the residence of Lady Tempest, was also spoken of. The place, however, that was ultimately selected was Dolbank, in the neighbourhood of Ripley, and there a nunnery seems to have been actually established, and endowed with 90l. per annum by Sir Thomas Gascoigne.

A Mrs. Lascells was appointed lady abbess, and several other ladies are mentioned as becoming nuns, among whom were the two who were captured with the principal subject of the following depositions. Cornwallis himself, as we are told in the trial of Sir Thomas Gascoigne, was to be the father-confessor of the nuns. He also bore the name of Pracid, and several letters written by him under that name were produced at the trial of Gascoigne. What shifts the Roman Catholic priests were put to! They

sitting, I inquired of my landlord, Michell, who the gentleman was. Hee tould mee he knew nott, but hee would fetch him doune into my roome againe, if I pleased. I desired him to doe soe; and accordingly hee did. And the gentleman beeing set doune by mee, I asked him which way he travilled. Hee tould mee, to Broughton hall, and intended theire to inhabit. And hee likewise tould mee hee intended to follow his calling theire of pollishing glasses for prospectives and spectackles and mycroscops. I asked him wheare hee was borne, what was his name, and where hee had lived. To the first, hee answered hee was borne at Yorke, and that his name was John Cornewalls, and that hee had lived att London, butt came doune to York about six months since, and from Yorke hee was then travilling to Broughton hall, the joynter house of the Lady Tempest. Wheareupon hee offered to take his leave, butt I tould him I had something more to say, and then asked him what religion hee was of. Hee tould mee, perhaps hee was a seeker; which indirect answer gave mee occation to send for the captain of the gard. And by his assistance and the constabl's, we sought a trunk of the said Cornewallis, out of which were taken 5 letters, one in English, and 4 composed of Lattin, Greeke, and Hebern. Which letters, with the prissoner, wee sent by the constable of Skipton to John Assheton and Henery Marsden, Esqrs., two of his Magesty's justices of peace. And upon his examination, theire was 5 letters produced, which I verily beeleive was the same which I see taken out of the trunk att Skipton; and the prisoner owned as much beefore the above named justices.

John Cornwallis, saith, that hee was borne in the city of Yorke, as he hath heard and verily believes, and was removed to Beverley about the third or fourth yeare of his age. And that he went to schoole in Holdernes, and did, about the age of 17, goe to London, and stayed there with some freinds, Roman Catholiques, about three yeares. And then he went to Paris, where he stayed about foure or five yeares, where he made perspective and other sort of glasses. And then he went from thence into Italay, to Florrence, and Siena, and from thence to Roome, where he stayed about three yeares and a halfe. And then he came back to Marcellis, where he stayd about halfe a yeare; and from thence to Paris,

---

became masters in the art of deception. They were obliged to be prepared for every emergency. They had an answer ready for every possible question. And thus they kept flitting up and down the country in strange dresses, and under feigned names, halting here and there at some chosen place, and leaving it before it was known that they had arrived. There was a great deal of romance in the life that they were obliged to lead.

where he stayed about seaven or eight yeares, upon the same imploy of glasse makeing. He afterwards reterned back into England, about foure yeares since, and came to London, where he did reside till about May last, and did there continue his art about glasses, and did goe to severall Catholique houses and others where he did vend the same, by which he did support himselfe. And hee sayes he cannot declare any of the places of his residence in London, but the last place was nere Chareing Crosse, but remembers not the name of the house or the owner. And as to the five letters now showne unto him, they were in his custody, and hee received them at Catholique houses, but he is ignorant of the contents of every of them. And alsoe sayth hee hath not, nor had, any other letters, papers, or any other truncks, bookes, or goods at Skipton, or elsewhere, save what have beene now showne and produced, saveing his gowne, a paire of shooes and a cane.

The same witness, re-examined, sayth himselfe to be 41, or thereabouts. Hee was borne in Yorke, as hee hath heard say, and never knew his father; yett was brought up by frends at a schoole in Holdernesse, and cannott name them whoe they was that gave him his education; but sayth hee went to London younge, and there, of his owne industery, learned the art of makeing prospective glasses, spectacles, and looking glasses, here and there amonght workmen in London, and never was bound to the said calling. Hee confesses hee understands a little Lattin, not much, and resided in London from the time that hee was 18 or 19. Hee sayth himselfe to bee a Roman Catholicke, and, as he hopes to bee saved, he denyes to bee in any orders of priesthood or Jesuit; and likwise sayth it is not requisitt for him to say what Catholicks hee knows in London, or required of a magistrate to aske him such questions. That weare to discover and bring an odyum of such that hee knowes nothing but well by. His residence was in diverse places in London, and his last residence at London was neare Cheareing crosse. It is more then God Almighty requires to devulge the place of his last lodgings in London. But and syth hee came to Yorke from London in May last for his health, where his aboad hath beene since; and came downe in the company of Mr. Jo. Stapleton of Warter, Mr. Hitch of Leathey, and Mr. Shaw a marchant in York, in a coatch. Denyeth his sister Cissyly Cornewallis did come downe with him. Since his coming to Yorke his lodging hath beene at halfe a doz. inns in Yorke; and his last place of his inns was at Mr. Wharton's, gardiner, howse in the Fryars' garden, neare Tanner row, a Protestant. Hee came to Skipton because he desired to suggerne at Broughton in the joynter house of the Lady Tempest.* Hee was recommended thither, although hee had noe letter to any for it, by her Ladyshipp, daughter to Sir Tho. Gascoigne of Barnbowe, at whose howse hee hath beene twice since hee came to Yorke, and knowes Sir Thomas and his sonne and the Lady Tempest his daughter. The last-named it was that offerd this kindnesse to the ex^t to give him entertainement at her house, the hall in Broughton in Craven, whither this ex^t was goeing, and a sister and a cozen with him, namly his cozen Christina Anderton, of what place hee will not discover, for feare of doeing mischeiffe, as hee sayth hee is in conscience bound to conceale, and is an utter stranger to all hir relations in England. He sayth that the five letters now shewed unto him whereunto the name of Jo. Assheton and Hen. Marsden, Esqrs. is indorsed, weare in his trunke at Skipton; but hee thinks that hee is not obliged to tell from whome he had them, and reffuseth to declare further to that poynt.†

Cæcilia Cornewallis, spinster, sayth shee was borne in London, and was the daughter of one Francis Cornewallis, Esq. a Suffolke gentleman, and her mother's name was Katherine Arrundell of the family of the Lord Arrundell of Warder, before shee maried her sayd father.‡ Her father dyed eleaven yeares agoe, about June last. She sayth that, since the now Dutchesse of Yorke came into England, her mother hath beene a retainer to her, and is yet, for any thing shee knowes to the contrary, in the quality of one of the women of her bed-chamber. She declares shee is about twenty-two yeares of age, and hath lived with her mother in London all her time, till about three monthes last past. Att which tyme shee received letters from one Mr. John Cornewallis and Mrs. Christiana Anderton, her relacions, liveing then in the city of Yorke, to desire her company to abide and reside with them there for some tyme. Upon which shee did then remove from London to Yorke, and did continue there ever since; and upon Wednesday last came from thence with the sayd Cornewallis and Anderton in the company of one Mathew Wharton, with

---

* Broughton Hall, the ancient residence of the Tempests, was spoken of as the Nunnery. Lady Tempest was the daughter of Sir Thomas Gascoigne, and the widow of Sir Stephen Tempest. She was in all the troubles that came upon her father, and was tried at York for her life, but was acquitted. Before she was sent to York she was for some time a prisoner in the " Gatehouse." I have not found any account whatever of her trial.

† The witness and the two ladies were for some time in York Castle as suspicious persons. They refused to take the oaths of allegiance.

‡ The evidence of these two ladies must be read with great caution. In the Calendar they were charged with having given a false account of themselves, and there seems to be little doubt that this was actually the case.

whom they all last lodged at Yorke, and one John Wharton, his brother, to Skipton, with intencion to reside at Broughton Hall in Craven, a house of the Lady Tempest, daughter to Sir Thomas Gascoigne of Barnbow, by agreement and appointment of the said Lady Tempest. She confesseth that shee hath beene acquainted with her cosen Anderton about nyne yeares, and with her cosen Cornewallis about three yeares, and sometymes he used to pay some visits to her and her mother. And acknowledges that her mother, herselfe, her cosens Cornewallis and Anderton are and have beene Popish recusants, but knowes not her sayd cosen Cornewallis is or ever was in holy orders in the church of Roome. She doth acknowledge that her mother is sister to the now Lord Arrundell of Warder, but knowes nothing of the plott.

Cicily Cornwallis sayth, shee was borne in Leicestershire at Ashby, and that her father and mother were Popish recusants, and that she is of that perswacion. Shee hath lived most at Nottingham, Ashby, and Wollerhampton with an aunt, whose name was Butler, but her husband's Christian name shee remembers not, though he was her owne uncle by the mother side. For six monethes last past she hath lived in Yorke with one Mr. Wharton, a gardiner, in the Shambles, and came thither in a hackney coach. Before her comeing to Yorke shee lived with the same aunt and uncle in the square in Southampton buildings, who were lodgers in one Mr. Conquest's house, within 2 or 3 dores of one Mr. Whitnell's house nere King's Street, for one yeare last past. She came to Yorke with her brother Cornewallis with a designe to inhabit at Broughton, in the house of one Dame Lady Tempest. Shee hath seene her brother in London often, but never knew his place of residence there or els where; but beleeves hee is a Popish recusant, and that he hath beene beyond the seas.

Christiana Anderton, spinster, who was yesterday examined by the name of Christian Cornwallis, (Dec. 14), sayth, that shee was borne in Leicestershire at a towne called Ashby, and that her father name was Henry Anderton, a younger brother, a gentleman of smale estayt, and that her mother's name was Butler, of the best of that family in Leicestershire; but cannot declare her mother's father's christian name. Shee went over into France when shee was about nyne yeares of age, and resided in a nunnery at Paris called Val-de-Grace till about seaven yeares since. Then shee retorned into England, and hath beene in London and Leicestershire most part since. Shee inhabited in London for a yeare last before June last, and about that time she came downe to Yorke with a designe to goe to Broughton. And not long before her comeing shee had some discourse with Lady Tempest, and made some agreement with her to reside in the said house, her brother, Mr. Thomas Gaiscoigne, then being with her in London. Shee knowes nothing of a Popish plot, or designe of Popish recusants against his Majestie, the religion establisht, or government. Shee hath beene in company with Mr. Coleman,* but never knew any thinge of his designes, or did discourse with him five words.

CCXV. MR. JOHN VAVASOUR.   FOR SEDITIOUS WORDS.

May 19, 1679. Before Richard Shaw, Lord Mayor of York. *Mr. Ambrosse Girdler* sayth, that, about three weekes agoe, beinge in company with one Mr. John Vavasour † in a publique house, the said Vavasour said publiquely that the company there was not to beleive their was a plott (meaneinge as this informer beleives the Papist plott that now is) except the Kinge should say it. And Jonathan Hobson beinge then present, told the said Vavasour that he chanlenged the justice of our kingdome; to which the said Vavasour answered and said, "Goe and call in thy neighbours, and take what advantage thou can;" and the said Vavasour is a Popish recusant.

CCXVI. ELIZABETH ABBOTT.   A DANGEROUS PERSON.

May 21, 1679. Newcastle-on-Tyne. Before Ralph Jenison, Esq. *Gilbert Errington, of Pontisland, gen.*, deposeth that one Elizabeth Abbott, spinster,‡ the 20th May, told him that she was

---

* Edward Coleman, a very well known person, was executed for high treason in 1678. He was a person of great influence among the Roman Catholics.

† The Vavasors were strong Roman Catholics, and more than one of them was in trouble at this eventful period. The disinclination of the King to believe in the existence of a plot was, it will be seen, generally known.

‡ The accused was acquitted. She said she was a Roman Catholic, and went to Mr. Riddell's house in hope of finding a priest to comfort her, as she was troubled in conscience; and, thinking that they slighted her, she thought of this revenge. Mary Armstrong was charged with firing a house in North Shields on August 10, 1667, and threatening to burn the whole town. There was no prosecution against her. These silly women had their heads filled with the stories that were then afloat about the fire at London, and other intended conflagrations.

Newcastle had a very narrow escape about 1684. An apprentice going up with a candle into a loft which contained many barrells of gunpowder and much combustible material, thoughtlessly stuck the candle into a barrell, of which the head had been knocked off, to serve for a candlestick. He saw the danger and fled. "A labourer

resolved to goe to Fenham, hearing Mr. Ridle was att home, and that if he denyed hir request, as his lady had formerly done, she would doe the strangest act that ever was done, for she would sett the towne of Newcastle on fire; and that she had viewed the place where she resolved to doe it, for she would gett pitch and tarr, and sett fire in the Maior's shopp, or in some other shopp where there was lint and tow, and would stand by it that she might be taken, and would own herselfe to have done it, and would sweare before any authority that Mr. Riddle and his lady, and Mrs. Errington, of Denton, and some others, were the cause thereof.

Thomas Peirson, gent., saw Mr. Errington and Eliz. Abbot discourseing together, and Mr. Errington told him that the said Eliz. had said to him that she would fire Newcastle. This deponent said " God forbidd," but she said she would doe it. Then this informer told hir that he thought she was possessed with the devill, and Mr. Errington said he thought she was possessed with an evill spirritt.

CCXVII. ANTHONY CROFT. FOR SEDITIOUS WORDS.

A true bill against Anthony Croft,[*] of York Castle, for saying on May 28, 1679, " The Parliament will downe with the Lords and Bisshopps, and will doe with this King as they did with the last; and then wee shall be men."

CCXVIII. WM. TROTTER. FOR SPREADING FALSE NEWS.

June 5, 1679. Before Mat. Jeffreyson, Mayor of Newcastle. *Elizabeth, wife of James Craister, yeo.*, saith, that hir husband and Mrs. Eliz. Hodshon, wife of Mr. Albert Hodshon, discourseing about the oath of allegiance,[†] and the King's authoritye, and

---

ran into the loft, and joining both his hands together, drew the candle softly up between his middlemost fingers, so that if any snuff had dropped, it must have fallen into the hollow of the man's hand."

[*] A Quaker. He was tried at the assizes and was acquitted. He evidently approved of the sentiment of the old ballad:
> Lawn sleeves and rochets shall go down,
> And hey then up go we!

[†] At Newcastle, in March 1682-3, Albert Hodgson, Lancelot Errington, Robert Lawson, John Pepper, Thomas Robinson and Cuthbert Henderson, were committed to gaol for refusing the oaths of allegiance.

In July 1683, the following persons, natives of Northumberland, were in gaol for the same reason. Thomas Riddle, John and Ralph Clavering, Thomas Clennell, Wm.

that of the Pope's in England, one Wm. Trotter, a skipper, comeing into the company, said he heard say there was noe King in England, and the apprentices * of London had declared there was noe King in England.

CCXIX. WM. MANDEVILLE, GEN.   FOR SEDITIOUS WORDS.

A true bill against Wm. Mandeville,† of Rotheram, gentleman, for saying at Rotheram, on June 17, 1679, in reference to the rebellion in Scotland, " If there bee forty thousand men upp in Scotland they will beat all England. Though the Duke of Monmouth bee gone downe to suppresse them, its thought hee is gone to take their and the Kirke's part. I dare not whistle treason, but I know what I thinke. I hope to see the Church downe and the preists buryed in their surplices; for I know noe good they do, but are a great charge to the parish in washing them."

Collingwood, John Fenwicke, Henry and Wm. Thornton, Thomas Riddell, Edward Strother, Francis and Wm. Widdrington, Thomas and John Fenwicke, Luke Avery, Wm. Aynsley, John Browne, Cuthbert Blacklocke, Nicholas Browne, Edward Byars, Thomas Beadnell, James Browne, Nicholas Bell, Mark Blakelocke, Andrew Currey, Robert Collingwood, Robert Clarke, Ralph Carnaby, George Chater, Thomas Davison, Richard Dobson, Wm. Errington, Luke, Henry, John and James Gardner, Thomas Gibson, Andrew Hunter, Chr. and John Hall, John Heron, Wm. Hunter, Wm. and Lancelot Hall, Robert Jefferson, John and Robert Moody, James Morrison, Henry Nevill, Andrew Pringle, Chr. Perry, John and Nich. Rowell, Wm. and Geoffrey Robson, George Ridley, George Rotherford, Wm. Rowell, Robert Snawdon, Thomas Swan, John Swinhoe, Roger Snawdon, Richard and George Smirke, George Todd and Richard Wardell.

Mr. Albert Hodgson was again in trouble in 1684.

"Nov. 22, 1684. Anthony Spencely, of Newcastle, skinner and glover, deposes that on the 20th, being in company with Albert Hodgshon, a Romaine Catholique, and some discourse happening about Mr. Alderman Davison, the said Albart Hodgshon did much abuse him, and said G—d—him, he is a whigg, and all that will take his part are whiggs, and did with much invitracye and malice asperce and abuse Mr. Davison ; and, one Richard Fleck offering to reprove him, he threw a cupp of drinke att him, and threatned to beate any that would oppose itt, and said that none of the Aldermen were worth anything except Mr. Brabant, and did much extoll and cry upp his religion, being a Papist, and that few else were loyall."

* The power of the London apprentices was considerable, but it had little effect beyond the walls of the city itself. The times were dangerous, otherwise an idle speech of this nature would not have been attended to.

At the York assizes in July, 1679, Michael Pudsey was indicted for saying, " If wee kill the Kinge, or any other person, or do any sinn, if wee have a pardon from the Pope, all our sinns are forgiven, and soe, he said, he verely beleived." The culprit was sent to Durham, as, at that time, he resided in that county. Some illustrious blood was flowing in his veins.

† A Rotheram gentleman speaks his mind pretty freely, and is subjected to a fine. The murder of Archbishop Sharpe had recently occurred, and the Covenanters had broken out into open rebellion. The Duke of Monmouth had been sent down to chastise them, and he did so with a very gentle hand at Bothwell Bridge. Many comments were made upon his leniency to the vanquished Covenanters.

CCXX. JOHN ANDREWES.   FOR BEING A SEMINARY PRIEST.

July 8, 1679. Before Richard Shaw, Lord Mayor of York. *Robert Bolron,** *of Shippon hall, par.* Barwick-in-Elmet, saith, that, aboute twelve monthes agoe, he see one who goes by the name of Andrewes,† exercise the office of a Romish preist at Romanby, neare Northallerton, att one Mrs. Metcalfe's house, and he see him in his robes and administer the Sacrament to aboute ten persons, among whom was Adrian Metcalfe and others. And he never see the said Andrewes since, untill the last night that search

---

* A notorious personage—the Titus Oates of the North of England, of whom it will be necessary to give a somewhat lengthy account. It is principally derived from a pamphlet intituled,
 "An abstract of the accusation of Robert Bolron and Lawrence Maybury, servants, against their late master, Sir Thomas Gascoigne, kt. and bart. of Barnbow in Yorkshire, for High Treason : with his trial and acquittal, Feb. 11, 1680. 'Fit error novissimus pejor priore.' Printed for C. R. 1680."
 Robert Bolron was a native of Newcastle-on-Tyne, and in early life was bound apprentice to a jeweller in London in Pye Corner, where the famous fire was stopped. After remaining there a year he ran away and enlisted as a soldier, and soon found himself in Tynemouth Castle. From thence he was sent aboard the Rainbow frigate to fight against the Dutch. From this service he deserted, and thrust himself upon Sir Thomas Gascoigne of Barnbow, having a friend of the name of Richard Pepper among the retainers of that house. From Barnbow he went to Newcastle; and, at Pepper's recommendation, Sir Thomas made him the inspector of one of his coalmines near Newcastle. In this position he was guilty of gross peculation, which his master very generously overlooked, although he removed him from his place. Bolron was still kindly treated by Sir Thomas till it was necessary to eject him, and then in base revenge he brought that accusation of treason against his benefactor which will shortly be mentioned. The result happily ended in an acquittal.
 Bolron was now fairly embarked in the wretched profession that he had adopted. To strengthen himself he takes into his confidence a fellow of the name of Maybury, or Mowbray, and the two begin to carry on their iniquitous trade. Mr. Ingleby, Lady Tempest, Sir Miles Stapleton, and other persons of high position and character, were falsely charged by them; but in one instance only, that of Mr. Thweng, did they succeed in securing a conviction. The Northern juries, always loth to condemn for political offences, refused to believe them. The informers were openly charged with lying; and, happily for themselves, they seem to have been allowed to slink away into that obscurity from which they ought never to have emerged. In August, 1681, there was a rumour, as Narcissus Luttrell tells us, that Bolron had changed sides, and was resolved to accuse Oates.

Clodius accusat mæchos, Catalina Cethegum?

There was much reckless audacity about the man. He spoke boldly before the judges; but, had their minds not been blinded by party feeling and prejudice, they must have detected many inconsistencies in his statements. He brought forward his mother and his wife to assist him with their evidence. For some time he had actually a general search warrant from the Privy Council, and he was a person of importance; but no one knows what became of him, and no one will care to enquire.

† A person of the name of Andrews, a suspected priest, is arrested in York. He was in prison for several years. Mrs. Lascells, at whose house he was found, was, I believe, the Abbess of the Nunnery at Dolbank.

was made for one Mr. Thwinge,* a Romish priest, who was found in that search in the house of one Mrs. Lascells in Yorke, a Roman Catholicke, as alsoe the said Andrewes, whom this deponent seeinge chalenged for a Popish preist.

John Andrewes confesseth that he was borne in Monmouthshire, near Abergavenny, and that about seaven yeares agoe he went to Calice in France to learne the language there, where he stayd about halfe a year: from thence he went to St. Omer's, where he stayd only one night, from thence to Birge and Newport; and from thence to Bruges, where he stayed about a quarter and a halfe of year, haveing an aunt there; from thence to Newport and Ipres and Lyle, and from thence to Doway, where he stayd about twelve monthes; from thence to Arras, Amyens and Paris; and from Callice to England, where he hath been about two yeares. He saw one who goes by the name of Robert Bolron, about October last, at one Mrs. Metcalfe's house in Rummonby. The occation of his comeinge to this place was upon the account of his health. He hath not taken priestly orders accordinge to the Romish usuage, and, as to his weareinge preistly robes, or administeringe the sacrament, he sayth that hath not beene proved upon him.

CCXXI. JOHN LEAMON.   FOR SEDITIOUS WORDS.

July 19, 1679.   Before Matt. Jeffreyson, Mayor of Newcastle. *Simon Robson, cordwainer,* deposeth, that, yesterday in the afternoon about five a'clock, being in company at the house of Mr. John Squires, with Dr. Young, Mr. Robert Fenwick, John Wilson, John Leamon, and others, and discourseing about the late rebellion in Scotland occasioned by the Whiggs, &c., and the

---

* A son of George Thweng, of Heworth, near York, Esq., and the victim of Bolron's devices   He was the nephew of Sir Thomas Gascoigne, and was indicted at York, together with Mary wife of Thomas Pressick, for high treason. On Feb. 20, 1679-80, Richard Pepper, Bolron's old friend, was sent to Newgate for endeavouring to corrupt the King's witnesses against Thweng and Pressick, who were then in that gaol. (Luttrell's Diary, i. 36.)   Bolron thus got rid of a dangerous person. In March following the trial began at York, but the accused objected to so many jurors that it was obliged to be deferred. (Ibid. 38.)   In July they were again indicted, and Thweng was found guilty and was sentenced to death. (Ibid. p. 51.)   Thoresby was present, and says that he was condemned " for saying at a consult at Sir Tho. Gascoyne's at Barnbow, that, if they lost this opportunity of killing the King, they could never expect such another." (Diary, i. 51.)   A full account of the case is given in the State Trials, from which it will be seen that Mr. Thweng was condemned by the evidence of Bolron and his comrade. He was respited on the 4th of August, but on the 15th of Oct. there came down an order from the Privy Council that the law should take its course. He was accordingly executed on Oct. 23, and his mutilated remains were interred in St. Mary's, Castlegate. (Drake, 286, &c.)   Cf. Challoner's Memoirs of the Missionary Priests, 449.

conduct of his Highnesse the Duke of Monmouth there, the said John Leamon did declare that the Duke's soldiers killed those innocent people in cold blood;* and the reason why the Duke did not eat att Newcastle was his often being drunk in Scotland.

CCXXII. ROBERT DOLMAN, AND OTHERS.   FOR HIGH TREASON.

Oct. 27, 1679. Before Richard Shaw, Lord Mayor of York. *Robert Bolron* † sayth that, in the yeares 1676, 1677, 1678, he was steward to Sir Thomas Gascoigne,‡ of Barnbow in Yorkeshire, of his coale mynes, dureinge which tyme he severall tymes heard severall consultations for killinge the Kinge, and promoteinge the Roman Catholicke religion, and establishinge a nunnery at Dolbancke near Ripley. At some of which consultations the persons hereafter named were present (vizt.) Sir Thomas Gascoigne aforesaid, Thomas Gascoigne, Esq.,§ John Middleton, of

---

* Some strictures upon the Duke of Monmouth's conduct in Scotland may be read in No. CCXVIII. He certainly did not lay himself open to the charge of cruelty, as he was most merciful to the Covenanters.

† Robert Dolman, Esq., a Roman Catholic gentleman of ancient descent, is accused by Bolron of treason. He was bound over to appear at the assizes, himself in 400*l*. and in two sureties of 200*l*. each. He was probably acquitted, as the evidence against him was of the most flimsy description.

‡ Sir Thomas Gascoigne, of Barnbow, the head of a distinguished Yorkshire family, was accused of treason by an old retainer of his of the name of Bolron. I have already given some account of this fellow to show by what base motives he was actuated. The charge against Sir Thomas was that he encouraged and contributed to a subscription for setting up the Roman Catholic religion, that he established and endowed a nunnery at Dolbank near Ripley, and that meetings of Roman Catholics were held at his house, at which the propriety of killing the King was gravely discussed and sanctioned, Bolron himself having been desired to carry it into effect.

Several pamphlets were published in connection with this alleged plot, one of which has been already mentioned. The first was by Bolron himself.

" The Papist's bloody oath of Secrecy, and Litany of Intercession for England: with the Manner of taking the oath upon their entering into any grand conspiracy against Protestants. As it was taken in the chapel belonging to Barnbow-hall, the residence of Sir Thomas Gascoigne, from William Rushton, a Popish priest." 1680.

" The Deposition and further discovery of the late horrid plot, by one Mr. C——, late servant to Sir T—— G——, in Yorkshire. London." s. a.

In Jan. 1679-80. Bolron, and his fellow informer, Mowbray, who were about to bear evidence against Sir Thomas Gascoigne, had a pardon granted to them for their own share in the plot. Sir Thomas was placed at the bar of the King's Bench on the 24th of Jan., but, owing to a difficulty in making up a jury, the trial did not begin till Feb. the 11th. It was a cruel sight to see a gentleman of 85 tried for his life on the evidence of an ungrateful servant. There was little alleged against him except by Bolron and Mowbray, and several witnesses were brought forward by the prisoner who threw the greatest discredit upon their assertions and motives. The Yorkshire jury acquitted their fellow countryman, who ought never to have been subjected to such unworthy treatment.

§ The eldest son of Sir Thomas Gascoigne. He was accused by Bolron; but it was

Stockhill hall, Esq. with severall other persons, Popish recusants. And he further deposeth, that, in the year 1677, he saw a list in the chamber of Sir Thomas Gascoigne, the title of which list was, " A list of the Actors and Contributors designed in the promoteinge of the Roman Catholicke religion, and for establishinge a Nunery." Amongst severall names in the said list this informant saw the name of Esq. Dolman of Yorke, which list he hath heard severall Papists say was the list of those that had ingaged themselves in the designe of killinge the Kinge. And he further sayth that he also see in the said list severall contributions given by severall persons of quality of the Romish religion for carryinge on the said plott, but doth not remember the particular contribution or sume of mony given by the said Esq. Dolman; but sayth that the said Sir Thomas Gascoigne, with others then in his company, did severall tymes mention the name of Esqr. Dolman, liveinge in Peasholme Greene in Yorke, but his Christian name he doth not of his owne knowledge remember, but hath in his letters by the particular order of Sir Thomas Gascoigne, Thomas Gascoigne, Esq., and Lady Tempest, been desired to recomend them kindly unto Mr. Dolman and Esqr. Dolman, which letters were directed to Wm. Horncastle, servant to old Mr. Dolman: and hath likewise received severall recomendations backe againe to Sir Thomas Gascoigne, Esqr. Gascoigne, and Lady Tempest, before mentioned. And this informant further deposeth that at the same tyme he see the said list he also heard the said Sir Thomas Gascoigne, Thomas Gascoigne, Esq., Lady Tempest, Sir Walter Vavasour,* deceased, Sir Francis Hungate,† John Middleton, of Stockhill hall, with severall others, then and there present, say unanimously, and resolve the killinge of the Kinge, and establishinge the Roman Catholicke religion in England. And he then heard Sir Myles Stapylton, of Carlton, kt.,‡ utter these words, that he would give two hundred pounds towards carrying on the plott, meancing the plott aforesaid about killinge the Kinge; and that if the Duke of York did not

found out that, at the time when he was charged with hatching treason in England, Mr. Gascoigne was actually abroad, having obtained the King's leave to travel! Bolron afterwards modified his evidence so as to include him in the plot, and Mr. Gascoigne was tried at York in March, 1681-2, together with Mr. (Stephen) Tempest and Mr. York. Bolron and Mowbray gave evidence against them, but they were all acquitted. (Luttrel, i. 173.)

Mr. Middleton, a young gentleman of very high family, went into France with Mr. Gascoigne. Nothing seems to have been done to him.

* Of Haslewood; a gentleman who had fought and suffered greatly for Charles I. Dr. Peter Vavasor was his brother.

† Of Saxton; a baronet connected with some of the best families in England.

‡ Some notice of Sir Miles Stapleton will be given afterwards.

please them they would serve him as they did intend to serve his brother. And he see in the said list the name of Doctor Peter Vavasour, and he heard some Papists say that he was gone to London with an intent to get an order from his Matie and Privy Councell to goe beyond sea, for fear he should be discovered to be concerned in the plott.

Lawrence Mowbray * saith, that aboute Michaelmasse 1676, there was an assembly of severall preists or Jesuitts att the house of Sir Thomas Gascoigne, att Barnbow, and that the said assembly did then generally conclude and agree that the Kinge was to be killed, for that he was a heretique, and excommunicated by the Pope, and that itt was nott onely lawfull butt meritorious to kill the said Kinge, or any other heretique, and that they likewise said that all or most of the Catholicks in England were ingaged in the same designe. After which discourse one William Riston,† preist to Sir Thomas Gascoigne, produced a list of names, which he did declare were ingaged in and contributors to the said designe. Amongst which names he mentioned Mr. Dolman and Dr. Peter Vavasour ‡ of this city.

CCXXIII. FRANCIS COLLINGWOOD. FOR BEING A SEMINARY PRIEST.

Oct. 27, 1679. Before Richard Shaw, Lord Mayor of York. *Robert Bolron, gentleman,*§ saith, that last night beinge upon a

---

* Lawrence Maybury, or Mowbray, the accomplice of Bolron, was originally a footman in the service of Sir Thomas Gascoigne. Having stolen some money and jewels belonging to Lady Tempest, he was turned out of his place, and after wasting his ill-gotten gains in dissolute living, he was prevailed upon by Bolron to join him in his design. I have before me a folio pamphlet containing much information about Mowbray and his proceedings. It is entitled:

"The narrative of Lawrence Mowbray, of Leeds, in the county of York, gent., concerning the bloody Popish conspiracy against the life of his sacred Majesty, the government, and the Protestant religion, &c. &c. London. 1680."

Mowbray was henceforward identified with the fortunes of Bolron, and seems to have sunk with him into insignificance when no one believed what they said.

† This person is frequently mentioned in the account of the trial of Sir Thos. Gascoigne. According to Bolron he was deeply implicated in the plot.

‡ The fifth and youngest son of Sir Thomas Vavasor of Haslewood, and the brother of Sir Walter Vavasor, who has been already mentioned. He was bound over to appear at the assizes, himself in 400*l.* and two sureties in 200*l.* each.

§ The accused person asserts his innocence. He says that he was servant to Mr. Philip Constable, of Everingham. He was bound over to appear at the assizes, himself in 200*l.*, and in two sureties of 100*l.* each.

At this time there were several persons in York Castle charged with similar offences about whom there are no depositions in existence. "John and Robert Berry accused of a treasonable and dangerous conspiracy. Francis Ascough, gent., and Thomas

search with his assistants for priests and Jesuitts, he found in the house of the Lady Widdrington a man in bedd, who calls himselfe Francis Collingwood, and that in the trunck of the said Collingwood this informant found a pewther box used by Popish priests for holy unction, and, likewise, that he found in his pocketts a paper, with characters on itt, entitled "Edward Coleman's Characters," a booke concerninge babtisme of infants, used onely by Popish priests, and a blew ribbon with a crucifix on it called a stolle, used by Popish priests upon christininge of childer.

CCXXIV. THOMAS RIDDELL, ESQ.   FOR HIGH TREASON.

Nov. 14, 1679. Before Sir Rich. Stote, Bt., Robert Jenyson and Richard Neile, Esqrs. *Robert Bolron, of Newcastle-upon-Tyne,* myllyner*, saith, that at Barmbow hall, in the county of Yorke, in the yeare 1677, he see one — Killingbeck,† a Romish priest, say mass in Barmbow chappell, haveing on the vestments used by the Romish priests when at any time mass is said. This informant, further, sayes that, in the said yeare, he did see the said — Killingbeck at a generall consultation held in Barmbow hall, where it was concluded the murthering of the King, and of all Protestants that would not immediately turne Roman Catholicks. This informant, further, sayes that the said — Killingbecke did promiss in the name of his master, Thomas Riddall, of Fenham, Esqr., that he should contribute liberally for the carrying on the said designe, and that his master had given him such instructions before he came from home. This informant further

---

Coates, for the same. Francis Osbaldeston, Anthony Langworth, Wm. Allanson, and Simon Nicholson, upon suspicion of being Popish priests." All these persons had refused to take the oath of allegiance, and were detained in prison in consequence.

* The informer is busy at his native place, Newcastle on-Tyne. He tries to make victims of two of the greatest gentlemen in Northumberland, but without success, although he would be sure to cause them much annoyance and vexation.

Mr. Riddell was the son of a well-known cavalier, Sir Thomas Riddell of Fenham. The services of the father ought to have been a sufficient guarantee for the loyalty of the son. Sir Thomas was governor of Tynemouth Castle, and the colonel of a regiment of foot for Charles I. He was so conspicuous a person that a price of 1,000*l*. was put on his head. He escaped to Antwerp in a Berwick fishing smack, and died there, a ruined exile, in 1652.

Sir Thomas Haggerston, of Haggerston, in Islandshire, was Governor of Berwick. His father, the first baronet, had been colonel of a regiment of horse and foot under the Earl of Newcastle, and his brother John Haggerston was killed at Ormskirk, *ex parte Regis*, in 1644.

† Robert Killingbeck was mentioned more than once by the witnesses at Sir Thos. Gascoigne's trial.

says that he see a list, intituled " A list of the Actors and Contributors ingadged in the designe of promoting the Roman Catholicke religion, and establishing a Nunery, &c.," which list he hath heard severall Papists say was the list of those that had ingadged themselves in the designe of killing the King; amongst which names he see the particuler names of Thomas Riddall, of Fenham, Esqr., Sir Tho. Haggerston, of Haggerston, Barrt., as also the contribucions given by them for the carrying on the said designe, but does not remember how much it was they or either of them did give for the carrying on of the said designe. And this informant further sayes, that he did heare them conclude and agree immediately to establish a nunery at Dolbanck, near Ripley, in hopes that there designe of killing the King should take effect, which nunery was accordingly established about Michelmas 77. And this informant further sayes, that he suspects there may be found in the house or custody of the said Thomas Riddall, of Fenham, Esq., severall papers or writeings relateing to the horrid plot against the life of his sacred Majesty and government, as also that there does ly lurking in the said house the said Killingbeck, or some other Romish priest.

CCXXV. WILLIAM BATTLY. FOR PERJURY.

July 9, 1680. An indictment against William Battly,* of Leeds, yeoman, for charging Lawrence Mowbray and Robert Bolron with giving false evidence, in the following note. "After that Sir Thomas Gascon was impeached by Bouldrun, I was in company with Bouldrun at one widdow Latham's house in Leeds, and being in discours with him about our cockes, and telling of our former acquaintance, wee fell into discours about Sir Thom. Gascon. He desired me for to goe to borrow him an Almanacke, either new or old; to which I did borow him four, but none of them would serve him. What is the matter, said I, Mr. Bouldrun, that you ar soe scrupulus for Almanackes? to which he replyed that Lawrance Moubury and he was contriving to bring Sir Miles Staplton and the Lady Tempest to be gilty of the plot with Sir Thomas Gascon. And if we can but hit our tyme we shall doe their jobs, for now I am resolved to be revenged on Sir Thomas and his relations for the abuse he puts upon me, for he sues me

* Battley was one of the persons who gave evidence at Sir Thomas Gascoigne's trial, and endeavoured to impugn the evidence of Bolron. Bolron charged him with perjury. I know not what became of the matter, but it must be remarked that Battley was by no means a solitary witness against the informers.

and seekes my destruction, or els I would never have troubled him nor none that belongs to him."

CCXXVI. ELIZABETH FENWICK.   FOR WITCHCRAFT.

Dec. 11, 1680. Before (Sir) Thos. Loraine. Wheareas information uppon oath is made before me by Nicolas Rames, that one Elizabeth Fenwicke, of Longwitton,* did threathen the sayde Nicolas Raymes what he had done she, the saide Elizabeth Fenwicke would make him repent it; and she, the sayde Elizabeth Fenwicke, being a woman of bad fame for withcraff severall yeares hearetofore, he the saide Nicolas Rames doth affirme and complaine that his wife, lyeing under a sad and lamentable torment of sickeness, doth daylye complaine that she the sayde Elizabeth Fenwicke doth continuallye torment her, and is disabell to her in her saide perplexatye; and, withall, in her due senses doth acknowledge she rydes on her, and endeavours to pull her on to the flower; and a blacke man, thinkeing the deavil, and the said Elizabeth Fenwicke dane togeather. And the sayde Nicolas Rames did goe and desired her to come to his wife: wheareuppon she came, and cominge to the said Nicolas Rames his wife, she tolde her she must have blood for bewitching of her; and the saide Elizabeth answesheard again that if her blood would doe her any good she might have had it long since, and the saide Elizabeth would ha cutt her finger, and the sayde Anne Rames answeared againe, " I will have it uppon the brow wheare other people give it uppon witches;" and the sayde Elizabeth answeareth againe that if her chyldren should get notice of the saide blooding they would goe madde. And againe, by the consent of the saide Elizabeth, she bid her draw blood uppon her brow. Her condition be exceading weake by all probabalye of witchcraft in this woman. The sayde Elizabeth called the said Nicolas ... her fre consent to assist his wife; and the saide Nicolas runne in a grat ... thre severall tymes before she would bleade, and she, the sayde Elizabeth, desired him nott to discloase it, and he declared that if no further prejudice was to him or his wife he would not prosecute her.

* The last case of reputed witchcraft that has occurred to me. The poor woman was acquitted.

CCXXVII. RALPH MADDISON * AND OTHERS. FOR ARSON, ETC.

May 30, 1681. Before Utrick Whitfield, Esq., and Francis Addison, Esq. *John Ellrington, and Margaret his wife*, saye, that Ralph Maddison, Joseph Maddison, Thos. Pattyson, of Unthanke, and Robert Thompson, of ..... this informer's house at Acton, and did carry away four oxen, six cowes, ... young beasts and five score tenn of weathers, yewes and hoggs. Ralph Maddison did confess to this informer that in March 1678 that he burnt Jo. Rawe's houses at Benfullside, and Nuns-house stable, with match, gunpowder, and tow.

William Egelston, of Rukton, saith that Isaac Warde, of Cronkley, spoke these words in the hearing of this informer, " There was a sakles man goeing to jaole," meaning Ralph Maddison, and further saidd, that they who burned Espersheilds was in a quandary wheither to burne Espersheilds or Cronkley.

CCXXVIII. MARY COATES. FOR HIGH TREASON.

A true bill against Mary Coates of Morpeth, June 10, 1681, for sending her son John to school at St. Omer's.†

---

* A singular deposition. There was evidently a very violent feud between Maddison and his son-in-law, who seems to have been a weak foolish person. If, however, a little of what is said against Maddison be true he must have been a consummate villain.

Mr. Elrington sends a petition to the Judges from which I made a few extracts.

" A petition to the Justices of Assize at Newcastle from John Elrington, of Unthanke, Esq.

That he being a gentleman of a good extraction, and endued with an estate of nigh 300*l*. a yeare, hath had the bad fortune to match himselfe to the daughter of one Ralph Maddison ; who being a person of very bad life and conversation hath perswaded him to convey his estate to the said Maddison, and his heires. That he is now but tenant for life, and by his ill ways did get the said petitioner to sell 40*l*. or 50*l*. a yeare of his estate for the saveing of his life at the last assizes ; and, this yeare, falling into the same danger againe, hath endeavoured, by the meanes of Captaine Fetherstone and Mr. Thomas Hunter, to raise him more money. Not getting it he threatens violence. He hath debauched the petitioner's wife, his own daughter. He threatens to kill him, and hath stolen away the deeds and writings of the petitioner's estate. He begs for protection against Maddison and his son Joseph."

What was done on this petition we know not, but Maddison was ordered to be burned in the hand at the assizes. His son Joseph was acquitted. He was connected with a family of some importance in the western part of the county of Durham. The last of the Maddisons died at Paris in the beginning of this century, deeply regretted by his native dalesmen and the whole county, not without some suspicion of his having been poisoned.

" Far off on the banks of the Seine,
" Thy darling, thy Maddison dies."

† Bills are also found at the same time against Ralph Clavering of Callaly, Esq.,

CCXXIX. ARCHIBALD EARL OF EGLINTON. FOR MURDER.

Jan. 21, 1680-1. Before Ralph Hassell, Mayor and Coroner of Doncaster. *Jasper Blythman, Esq., of Newlathes,* saith, that, upon Tuesday the 18th, hee was in company with Lord Egglington,* Mr. Thomas Maddox, and Mr. Tho. Derby, att the signe of the Angell in Doncaster. My Lord bid Mr. Maddox fetch upp disc and a box, which hee did, and soe they two fell to a play called hazard, and in a very little time Mr. Maddox wone all the moneys that my Lord Egglington had in his pockett (as hee said), and then my Lord plaid upon the tick, and had lost 50s. to him; but the disc came into my Lord's hands, and he wan the 50s. back, and 20s. more, which he demanded Maddox to pay him, which he refused, saying his Lordshipp ought him 3l. which hee won of him in the cockpitt, and —— him why should hee pay when my Lord would not pay him. My Lord replyed hee lyed, and —— him hee would have it, and soe laid his hand upon the moneys that was upon the table; and the said Maddox paid him. Upon which my Lord told him hee was a —— dog, and did arise from his seate and phillipped him over the noase. Then they plaid againe, and my Lord went on the tick againe, and lost about the former summe to Maddox; but when the disc came into his hand wan it againe, and about 10s. more, which hee demanded of him, but Maddox made the same answere, or to the effect, as before. Upon that my Lord arose

---

for sending his son John to the same place; against Edward Widdrington, of Felton, Esq., Henry Thornton of Witton Sheeles, gen., and Wm. Thornton of Netherwitton, gen. for sending to the same college Nicholas Thornton, Esq., and Henry Thornton, gen., and against Thomas Riddell, Esq., of Fenham, for sending his son Mark to be educated abroad.

* The record of a fatal affray in the Angel inn at Doncaster, between the Earl of Eglinton and a Mr. Maddox.

Archibald, eighth Earl of Eglinton, was at this time residing at Bretton, in right of a Yorkshire lady whom he had married, the widow of Sir Thomas Wentworth.

These depositions disclose a very discreditable scene at Doncaster in which a man was killed by the Earl at the gaming table. The drawer at the inn deposes that the affray took place on the Tuesday night between 12 and 2 o'clock; and Roger Perkins, the apothecary, says that Mr. Maddox had two mortal wounds, one in the left side, and the other in the thigh. He was buried at Doncaster on the 21st of January.

Wm. Squire, of Doncaster, gen., deposes that Lord Eglinton sent for him. When he came there were with him Blythman and Derby. "His Lordshipp said hee was glad to see him, and presented him with a glasse of white wine; and, seing he did not drinke it of forthwith, his Lordshipp heaved up his caine, and said hee would Maddox him." This occurred on the day of the affray.

Lord Eglinton was found guilty at York, and was sentenced to death, but he was reprieved till the King's pleasure was known, and he was subsequently set free. His grandson in after years was shot in a contest with a poaching exciseman.

from his seate and tooke the box in his hand and said, "—— you, I will have the moneys I have won," and offred to strike him but did not. Whereupon Maddox laughed and said, "Your Lordshipp may make me do anythinge," and soe paid, and then fell to play againe. After this manner for severall times were they quarrelling; att the last my Lord wan 20s. of him, and demanded it, but hee refused to pay, replyeing as before that my Lord ought him moneys. Soe Maddox paused upon it; and, being muche in drinke, hee did forgett himselfe. For which my Lord asked him a second time. Hee told my Lord that by —— hee had paid it. "Sounds," saith my Lord, "you are a dog; you paid me none; and I will bee judged by these two gentlemen in the roome whether have you paid me or noe, and —— you I will have it." And soe risse from his seate and tooke the box in his hand. But this informant thought it would not have come to blows tooke the lesse notice. My Lord made a blow at him, and Maddox standing up to defende himselfe, my Lord drew his sowrd and made passes att him. But this informant doth verily beleive that Maddox was sett att the time of the first passe makeing. And then this informant stept in and laid hold on my Lord and putt him from Mr. Maddox, who followed my Lord and gott hold of my Lord's wigg. And in that bussell he supposes he gott his wound in the thigh. Then this informant drove them into a corner of the roome that hee might have the better advantage to part him and Maddox, whoe pulling at my Lord's perriwigg, my Lord said, "—— you, I will kill you," and shortned his sword, and he thought he was about to stabb him, and this informant cried out, "For Christ's sake, my Lord, bee quiett, there is too much harme done allready." And soe this informant struck upp the point of the sword, and then tooke hold of the hilt, and told my lord that hee would have him putt it upp, and caused him to putt it upp. My Lord said, "Bear witnesse hee runne upon my sword." And this informant told my Lord that his Lordshipp made severall passes att him, and was afraid hee had wounded him. Maddox replyed, "The Scotch dog has wounded me," and "None but a pittifull Scotch Lord would have done it," and then gave him very badd words. After that my Lord offred to strike att him, but this informant kept him of. And Maddox continueing ill language, my Lord was provoked and made towards him, but, in putting of my Lord from him he fell betwixt Edward, the drawer att the Angell, and this informant, and this informant went about to helpe my Lord upp, and begged his pardon, and told him that hee did not intend to throwe him downe. And in the fall my Lord's hatt and wigg fell on the ground, soe this informant takeing them upp, in the mean time my Lord gave him a violent blow over the head with his cane, which made Maddox crye, " Oh!" Then this informant laid hold on my Lord and desired him to goe out of the roome, and went downe staires with him into the yard.

CCXXX. WILLIAM WIDDOWS.   FOR A MISDEMEANOR.

Oct. 10, 1681. Before Thomas Hesletine, Esq. *William Widdows, of Yorke,** mercer*, being examined concerning the printing of the tryall of Sir Miles Stapleton, confesseth that at the last assizes held at the castle of Yorke, he was present at the tryall of the said Sir Miles Stapleton, and did take and write the same tryall in short hand. And, after the end of the said assizes, he did transcribe the same faire over, and send that copy to one Mr. Thomas Simmons, a bookeseller in Ludgate Street, in London: and he has received above fourty bookes from the said Mr. Simmons, which he believes were printed by that copy.

CCXXXI. RALPH GARDINER.   FOR AN ASSAULT.

" May it please your Lordshipps. One Mr. Ralph Gardiner,† who is now in his Majestie's present servis in the hors guard, and

---

* A York tradesman is charged with publishing an account of the trial of Sir Miles Stapleton, not having obtained permission to do so from the court. It was, probably, suppressed, and I have never heard of the existence of a copy. An official account of the case is printed among the State Trials.

Sir Miles Stapleton, of Carlton, was charged by the informer, Bolron, with being concerned in the plot of Sir Thomas Gascoigne. In June 1680, he was sent down from London to be tried at York (Luttrel, i. 48.) He was brought to the bar in the following month, but he challenged so many of the jurors that the trial was deferred. It came off in July 1681, and there were three witnesses against him, Bolron, Mowbray, and John Smith, of Walworth, co. Durham, otherwise called " Narrative Smith," from the pamphlet which he published. Sir Miles defended himself energetically, and brought many persons to throw discredit upon the evidence of the informers, and the jury immediately acquitted him. He was mainly indebted for his escape to the evidence in his behalf of his friends and neighbours, Sir Thomas Yarburgh and his lady.

Sir Miles Stapleton was a gentleman of great honour, position, and ability. The antiquary Thoresby speaks favourably of the courteous reception that he gave him.

† This is the gentleman who made an attack upon the corporation of Newcastle, in a scarce and curious little book, which was published in 4to. in 1655, and dedicated to the Protector. It is intituled, " England's grievance discovered in relation to the coal trade." The late Mr. Thos. Bell, of Newcastle, had in his library another of Gardiner's works in MS.

These works, which were of the most controversial character, made the writer very unpopular in Newcastle, especially with the Mayor and Aldermen, whom he especially

bound to appeare to an indictment of trespasse and assault, pretended to be done by him in the Citty of Yorke, these are humbly to request your Lordshipps will be pleased to respite the recognizances of the said Mr. Gardiner until the next assizes, by reason he is ordred to waite upon the King in a party to Newmarkett, in order to keep guard during his Majestie's stay there.

"Your Lordship's most humble servant, DAVENPORT LUCY."

"*March the 4th*, 1681-2.

"*In dorso.* To the honorable the Judges of the assizes for the Citty and County of Yorke."

CCXXXII. MR. WM. BROWNRIGG.   FOR LIBELLOUS WORDS.

May 1, 1682. Before the Justices at Knaresbro'. *Mr. William Lingard, of Scotton, saith,* that hee, accidentally meeting with Mr. Wm. Brownrigg,* and Mr. Catterall, in Scotton, was requested by them to goe to an alehouse in Scotton to drink a cup of ale with them, which he was willing too. That the said Catterall goeing from their company, the said Brownrigg began to relate what greivances he had suffred by Sir Jonathan Jennings and Sir Richard Graham, two justices of the peace, and fell into revileing tearmes against them, and declared they were both rogues, and that they had done him injustice, and caused him to be wrongfully imprisoned against law, and said he was now resolved to put them in print for rogues, and make it appear to the world what kind of men they were, or words to this purpose. And this deponant saith that he wished the said Brownrigg to forbear such revileing expressions; but he replyed he cared nott who heard him, for hee was resolved to question greater persons

attacked. Mr. Alderman Barnes, who was certainly a religious-minded person, says of the author in a satisfied tone, "but he got his reward, being afterwards at York hanged for coining." This, as will be seen from this letter, was altogether incorrect. Mr. Gardiner had been committing an assault in York, of which there is no account preserved, but it is evident that it was not of a serious or heinous character.

It has not yet been ascertained what became of Gardiner when he left the North. It now appears that he entered the army, and was in the royal horse guard.

* A gentleman is charged with abusing two magistrates and a judge. He, evidently, was a person fond of litigation, and had lost his suit.

He was again in trouble in June 1683. He had refused to drink the King's health, and had said "Hang the King, he is good for nothing else." After this he seems to have fled the country, and another person, it will be seen, gets into trouble on his account.

"July 1683. Harrogate. Mr. Jefferson asking what had become of Mr. Brownerigg, and said that he had heard that he was fled for speaking treason,—Geo. Cass, said, not for speakeing treason, but reason."

then they were, and did then instanc Judg Dolbin,* and did also affirme the said Judg Dolbin was a rogue, and had done him injustice two severall times. And further said he had a paper in his pockett ready drawne, which he intended for the press, which would sett forth what rogues these three were, and did thereupon produce the same, which was very close writt, but he would not suffer this deponant to read the same.

CCXXXIII. CHARLES BROWNING.   FOR BURGLARY.

May 13, 1682. Before James Clayton, Esq. *Charles Browninge*,† saith, that, upon Wensday last, hee came from Newcastle towards New Bolton, in Yorkeshire, and, the 12 day of this instant May, hee came to New Bolton, about 2 of the clocke in the night, and, knowing my Lord Wiltshire's closet where he used sometimes to lay some gold, hee fetched a lader forth of the gardins, and brought the same lader, and sett it up to the closet window, and then went up it, and broake a pane out of the casement and opened it, and soe entred into the said closett; and from thence hee tooke a cabinett in which hee thought there might be gold or some other treasure, and carried the cabinet away, but beinge closely pursued hee was forced to throw the said cabinet away.

CCXXXIV. RALPH HOLROYD, ETC.   FOR MURDER.

July 26, 1682. Before Wm. Pickering and Jos. Bawmer. *Hester Webster*,‡ being aged 24 years or upwards, sayes, that

* Mr. Justice Dolben was one of the Judges that tried the Roman Catholic gentlemen for their supposed share in the plot. Some of the observations that he made were by no means seemly or decorous.

† The confession of a burglar.

‡ One of the most appalling tragedies in this century, and one that made a very great sensation in Yorkshire. Mr. Leonard Scurr was a native of Pontefract, and was educated at Sidney College, Cambridge. During the Commonwealth he officiated at the chapel of Beeston, near Leeds, and Calamy says that he, " though a good preacher, was a man of a bad character and a scandal to his profession."

At the Restoration, he threw off his gown, and, having some means of his own, undertook the management of a coalmine and lived in a lonely house in Beeston Park. The family consisted only of Mr. Scurr, his aged mother, and a maid servant. He cared not for the solitary situation, as he was a vigorous and a daring man.

At the end of January 1679-80 the house was attacked by some of his own workmen, possibly to gratify their revenge, but, more probably, in the hope of securing some plunder. Then the frightful scene was enacted which is described in this deposition. The struggle was a terrific one, and the half-naked man fought with the boldness of despair

being in the house of one Isaac Clark, upon the Comb, in Dublin, in the chamber over the house, in company at dinner with one Phœbe, once servant to Mr. Scurre, and who is now in Ireland, and one Elizabeth Clark who lives beyond London at present, these 3 persons being together, there came in Ralph Howroyde and his wife into the roome, and the aforesaid Phœbe askd if her Mr. Scurre was alive; to which Ralph Howroyde replyed, he was barbarously murthered, and sayd that Littlewood was felling a tree with Scurre the day before, and he sayd they came home (but named no persons), and the beasts were put out of the cow house, and the doors all made fast, and that there was a trapp-doore out of the house into the cow-house which was also made fast, and they went to the old woman in bed, (still naming no persons,) and the old woman sayd 3 times "Lord have mercy upon me, what would you do with mee?" Upon that Mr. Scurre, hearing, came down in his shirt with a rapier drawn in his hand

and nearly overpowered his assailants. They had him, however, in a trap, and the end was that he and his mother and servant were murdered under circumstances of the greatest barbarity. The house was set fire to and the ruffians made their escape.

It was not known for a long time that a murder had been committed, although there were many suspicions.

On the 24th of January Thoresby rode from Leeds to Beeston, "to see the most dreadful spectacle that was ever beheld in these parts. Mr. Scurr, his mother, and a maid servant, every one burnt to death, last Thursday, at night between eleven and one o'clock, but whether accidentally, or designedly by the malice of some, (whom perhaps he was in suit with,) is yet uncertain. The old gentlewoman was most burnt; her face, legs, and feet quite consumed to ashes, the trunk of her body much burnt, her heart hanging as a coal out of the midst of it. Part of his face and arms, with the whole body, unburnt, but as black as the coals, his hands and feet quite consumed. Very little of the maid was to be found, only I saw her head; a most piteous sight! Some observe all their skulls are broken, as it were, in the same place, which causes some to suspect it is wilfully done; but if so, the Lord will reveal it, so that, in all probability, those inhuman murderers may have their deserts in this life."

An account of this fearful tragedy was printed, and it was soon discovered that a murder had been committed. The motive for the crime is not so easily explained. Some thought that it was done in the desire of plunder, as Mr. Scurr was known to be thinking of a journey to London in connection with his affairs. Dr. Whitaker, however, remarks that it was suspected that the murderers had been instigated by some person of property at Beeston, who got possession of a part of Scurr's estate, and had some papers belonging to him. In the minute books of the assizes I find some entries that throw some light on this mysterious assertion. In July, 1665, Richard Sykes, of Hunslet, gen., Robert Batt, of Farneley, gen., and others, were charged with riotously entering upon a certain tenement belonging to Leonard Scurr, and were bound over to keep the peace. Thirteen months after this the same parties appear at the assizes with charges and countercharges of riot and assault.

Mr. Scurr wrote "Some brief Instructions for Churchwardens and others to observe in all Episcopal and Archidiaconal Visitations," which he published without his name. The paper was written against Ecclesiastical discipline and authority. I find that in July, 1664, Thomas Burwell, doctor of laws, was charged at the York assizes with illegally citing and excommunicating Leonard Scurr. This case had, probably, some connection with the printed paper.

and he wounded them all, and he (that is Howroyd) thought two
of them would dye upon their wounds: and Mr. Scurre thinking
to escape (after he had wounded them) at the trapp-door there,
he could not get out, and there they knockd him in the head with
an axe. Then they brought him down and threw him upon his
mother in her bed. And there was a pretty young woman, she
beggd her life of them, and told them she would be rackd in
peeces before she would tell of them, if they would spare her life.
The men did grant her her life, but there was a woman she would
not grant her her life, but choppt of her head betwixt the parlour
doore and the house door. And they, thinking to make people
beleive that it was done by accident, sett the house on fire. And,
further, this Ralph Howroyde sayd that Thomas Webster went to
the coale pitt in the morning, and he wondred his maister Scurre
did not come. He lookt over towards the house and they all
came to it, and Thomas Webster would have taken Mr. Scurr's
body out with a spitt, and they would not suffer him. Ralph
Howroyde's wife was by and present all along, and seemingly
talked to the same purpose. And this deponent and others with
her asking if any of the murderers were taken, hee, that is Howroyde, sayd, Littlewood was suspected, and named Katherine
Winne, the midwife, and another man or two he named, which
were under suspicion, whome this deponent doth not now remember. This was within 2 dayes that Howroyde and his wife
were come over for Ireland.*

* The sequel of the story must be told. Holroyd and his wife go to Ireland, and
there, by a most providential circumstance, they meet a woman, unknown to them, who
had once been in Mr. Scurr's service. They talk of the murder, without much reserve.
The girl sees upon Holroyd's wife a scarlet petticoat and a gown which she remembers
to have seen Mrs. Scurr wearing. She informs against them, and when the two are
separately examined before the magistrate they contradict each other. Other evidence
was gathered together, and Littlewood as well as Holroyd were sentenced to death at the
York assizes in 1682. Littlewood was reprieved in hopes of some farther revelations
from him which were never made, but Holroyd was hung, afterwards in chains, on
Holbeck Moor, in the presence of 30,000 spectators. He halted, on his way through
Leeds, at the vicarage, and had some talk with Mr. Milner, but it did him no good.
Thoresby, speaking of the 14th of August, 1682, says, " Most of the day taken up with
visitants, to see Holroyd pass by to his execution, for the horrid murder of Mr. Scurr,
his mother, and a maid-servant. After, rode to the Moor, where were many thousand
spectators ; but, alas! frustrated exceedingly in their expectations, he dying in the
most resolute manner that ever eye beheld, wishing (upon the top of the ladder) he
might never come where God had anything to do if he was guilty, and so threw himself off in an anger as it were, without any recommendation of himself to God that any
could observe, which struck tears into my eyes, and terror to my heart, for his poor
soul, earnestly imploring, while I saw any signs of life, that God would give him re-
pentance for his crying sins, and be better to him than his desires."

CCXXXV. JOHN REED AND ANOTHER.   FOR BURGLARY.

July 14, 1683. Before Peter Hudson, Mayor of Doncaster, and Thomas Lee. *Mary, wife of John Oddy, of Rossington bridge end*, saith, that the taller man, who calls himselfe by the name of John Reed,* came to her house yesterday about noone (this deponent and her husband keeping a publique house att Rossington bridge), and pretended to stay for some company to call of him there; but, noe body calling of him, this deponent used arguaments for him to bee gone, saying they had noe lodging for him. Hee still alledged that the said company would come, and that hee must have lodging there, for that they would call either that night or next morninge. This deponent was over perswaded to lett him have lodging. And in the night, about one or two a clocke, the lesser man, who calls himselfe by the name of John Squire, came to the house, and called and knocked att the dores and asked for a pott of ale. She refuseing to open the dores, hee threatened to breake the windows, and asked if they had noe lodgers in the house. She told him "Noe." He replyed they had one, a young man, and then called, "Jack!" Upon which the lodger rose and spoake to him out of the window, and the lesser man asked him if hee would goe with him, and hee answered "Yes." After much noise and stirr this deponent was forced to open the chamber dore, where the lodger laid, and hee came down and opened the outward dore to the other, whoe then came into the house togeather, and called for ale and tobacco. When they had drunke the ale, the taller man locked the dore, and the lesser man seized upon a boy, called Francis Chambers, apprentice to this deponent's husband, who filled them ale, and told him G—d —— him, if hee did not tell him where the money lay hee would run him through, as the boy informed this deponent. And the boy escapeing from him, they both came into the roome where this deponent and her husband lay, the lesser man haveing his sword drawn, and severall times threatened this deponent and her husband to kill them, unless they would tell them where their money was. Whereupon this informant told them that they had noe money in the house. Hee told them that they had, and swore, and offered his sword att them, and said hee would run them through. Shee told them that, if they would save their lives, they should have all they had. Whereupon this deponent

---

* A burglary with violence at Rossington. The scene is very minutely described. A little lad makes his escape and alarms the villagers, who capture the thieves. The two men were condemned to death, but were reprieved.

gave them their keys, but they, alledging they could not open the locks, forced her to rise and open the locks and deliver them their money, which was about 12s. They swore that there was more money in the house, and that they had lately sold land, and received for itt fifty pounds, which they would have, or else swore they would kill them, and searched all the house and chests for itt. And when they could not find itt, they retorned and made a thrust att this deponent's husband, and pricked him in the side; which hee, endeavouringe to putt by, cutt his hand upon the sword. Whereupon this deponent catched hold of the raper, and, to prevent mischife, bent itt. Then they went out of the house, and locked the dore after them, and, shortly after, came back againe, and searched the house againe, and forced this deponent to give them all the money shee had in her pockett, which was about 3s. in a little wood box. Dureing all this, Francis Chambers, the prentice, hadd gott out of the chamber window and raised the constable and some of the inhabitants att Rossington, who pursued them and tooke them.

CCXXXVI. STEPHEN THOMPSON, GENT., ETC. FOR TREASON.

July 16, 1683. Before Timothy Foord and Nicholas Saunders, bayliffes of Scarborough. *Peter Posgate, of Scarbrough, mr. and marriner,*[*] sayth, that, uppon the 27th day of June, about the houres of nine o'clocke, this deponent's mother informed him that Mr. Stephen Thompson, of Scarbrough, had sent his made twice to her to speake with this deponent. Whereupon he went immediately to Mr. Thompson's house, where he found him and his wife and Mr. Cornelius Moone. Then Mr. Thompson desired this deponent to give two gentlemen passage for Holland, and to be kind and civill to them, and they would content him for their passage. And the said Mr. Thompson desired this deponent to order the cobble that attended his ship to come privately on the backe of the castle, to take them in, and pretended to this deponent, that they

---

[*] Two Scarborough gentlemen, Mr. Thompson and Mr. Cornelius Moone, are accused of furthering the escape beyond the seas of two dangerous and suspicious persons. Mr. Thompson, in his defence, asserts, that one of the two was a kinsman of his, Richard Nelthorp, the other a Leeds merchant of the name of Layne. They told him that they were obliged to flee for debt, and he assisted them to escape, not being aware at the time that there was a proclamation for the capture of Nelthorp or any one else. The strangers had been at Whitby, Cloughton, and in the neighbourhood, for some days.

There is a certificate appended to the depositions excepting Postgate from blame, as he had been imposed upon by Thompson. It is signed by L. Williamson, Denis Grenville, Nic. Conyers, Thomas Legard, Anth. Salvin, Isaac Basire and Noel Boteler.

were persons that were in debt and forced to abscond for the same, and afraid to come to a publique place where boates usually goe from, by reason they were afraid to meet with my Lord Marquesses of Winchester * servants, because they were indebted to my Lord. Whereupon this deponent ordered the cobble to goe accordingly and take them in. And this deponent went and cald of the said passengers about twelve a'clocke of the same day, at Mr. Thompson's house, and went aboard with them in the said cobble. He further sayth, that he delivered them safely ashore at Rotterdam, and they gave him five pounds for there passage, which hee thought was too much (having not usually such pay) and proffered them three pounds againe, but they would not receive it, but thought it well bestowed for there safe passage. And the day after they were arrived, comming from the church, a Bristoe merchant living at Roterdam challenged one of them, which was the taller man, and lyke hard something short, and called him by the name of Mr. Ward, pretending that they were schoole-fellowes together at Bristoe, and that he was bred as an attorney. He sayth that at that tyme he heard nothing of any plot, or that any proclamation was issued out from his Matie for the apprehending of any persons.

CCXXXVII. MR. JAMES CALVERT. FOR TREASON.

July 19, 1683. Before Sir John Legard, Bt., Wm. Osbaldeston, Esq., and Sir Richard Osbaldeston, Kt. *Mr. James Calvert, of Boynton,*† *Nonconformist,* saith, that upon Thursday, being the

---

* Sir John Reresby, in his Memoirs, gives an amusing account of this nobleman. He paid him a visit. "He had four coaches and a hundred horses in his retinue, and staid ten days at a house he borrowed in our parts. His custom was to dine at six or seven in the evening, and his meal always lasted till six or seven the next morning; during which he sometimes drank; sometimes he listened to music; sometimes he fell into discourse; sometimes he took tobacco; and sometimes he ate his victuals; while the company had free choice to sit or rise, to go or come, to sleep or not. The dishes and bottles were all the time before them on the table; and when it was morning, he would hunt or hawk, if the weather was fair; if not, he would dance, go to bed at eleven, and repose himself till the evening. Notwithstanding this irregularity, he was a man of great sense, and though, as I just now said, some took him to be mad, it is certain his meaning was to keep himself out of the way of more serious censure in these ticklish days, and preserve his estate, which he took great care of." I have heard a somewhat similar story of him when Duke of Bolton. He feigned insanity for a time, for political reasons, and used to hunt by torchlight among the woods and cliffs that are near Marske, in Swaledale.

† The well-known and very learned Nonconformist minister, James Calvert, is in trouble. He had been unwittingly committing treason, by aiding the sailing of two gentlemen from England. They were suspicious persons, and there was a royal procla-

28th of June, there came to the house of Sir Thomas Strickland, Barr¹, at Boynton, one Sir John Cockroom, (a Scotchman, who married the said Sir Thomas Strickland's sister,) and his sonn, and another gentleman, who, as the servants said, his name was Duglas, and two young men, servants to the said Sir John. The said Sir John declard he had a desire to goe by sea into Holland; and to that end inployed one Mr. Rickeby to provide a shipp for them; but the informant apprehending the said Sir John desired to be gon asoon as he could, voluntarily went to Bridlington key, to Mr. Rickeby, to know whether a vessell was provided or noe. But he could not be resolved that a vessell was hired for them, so he returned to Boynton, and told Sir John that Mr. Rickeby was looking after a shipp for him. The next morning, being Friday, about six a'clock, he in the company of the said Sir John and his sonn, the said Duglas (he being a middle sized man for stature, inclining to be corpulent, sharpe visage and short black curld hair,) and one Duke Raine, gardiner to Sir Thomas Strickland, went to the sea side near Barmston dock, where they stayd about halfe an houre; and in that time, upon some signes being made by the said Sir John and others, by waving of there hatts, there came from a shipp riding near the shore a boate, which carryed from on shore to the said vessell the said sir John, his sonn, and the gentleman named Duglas. He saith that Sir John ordered that his servants should stay at Boynton untill he returned, or that they heard further from him. A letter was brought to him, being directed for him, which was from Sir John's sonn, the contents of which was to returne thankes to all at Boynton, and especially to Mr. William Strickland and his selfe, and nothing else. He allso saith, that at Sir Johne's first coming to Boynton, he desired that the busines might be kept private, and that no noise might be made of itt.

CCXXXVIII. JOHN NEVINSON, ETC. FOR HIGHWAY ROBBERY.

Jan. 3. s. a. Before Sir John Reresby, Bt. *Elizabeth Burton* *

mation to the effect that men of that description were to be arrested, and were not to be allowed to leave the country.

The strange gentlemen had been visiting at some of the first houses in the East Riding. John Thompson, Sir John Cockroom's groom, says that they spent one night at Sir Barrington Bourchier's, at Beningbrough. From thence they went to Mr. St. Quintin's, at Scampston, and then to Boynton.

Mr. Calvert was at this time chaplain to the family of Strickland. He was brought there by Sir William Strickland, and remained at Boynton preaching and educating Sir William's son, till the death of the baronet and his lady.

* A most interesting deposition, which throws great light upon the proceedings of

saith, that shee, beinge discontented with her freinds, went to service in Newarke, where shee fell accquainted with Edmond Bracy, of the county of Nottingham, John Nevison, of the county of Yorke, Thomas Wilbore, of the county of Nottingham, Thomas Tankard, of the county of Lincolne, John Bromett, W^m. or Robert Everson, of noe certaine abode, but commonly at the Talbott in Newarke, all high-waymen, whoe tabled this informant at a house in Newarke, and maintained her with apparrell, and all other necessaryes, for two yeares, and as much as since May last. That the said Bracy, &c., have committed severall robberyes within the time before mentioned; and hired a roome by the yeare at the Talbott, in Newarke, where they comonly mett, after any robbery donne, and devided the spoyle; to which place they did usually send for this ex^t, and did give her some part of what they gott. The robberyes which this ex^t did heare them confess they had comitted weare as followe:

1. One betweene Grantham and Stamford, donne by three of them (viz.) Nevison, Everson, and Bromett, where they tooke about 300l. from a shop-keeper; of which this ex^t had as much as paid for a quarter's table.

2. One neare to Maultby in Yorkeshire, donne by three, Nevison, Bracy, and Tankerd, where they tooke about 200l. from one Malim of Rotheram, when he was goinge towards Gainsbrough mart was a twelve month; whereof they gave this ex^t 2l.

3. That of Lyncolneshire, where they tooke a greate booty, but which of them committed the same shee knoweth not.

4. One in Yorkeshire, committed by Nevison, Bracy, Tankerd, and Wilbore, where they tooke above 300l., of which this ex^t had 9s. to buy her a white petticoate.

5. One betweene Gainsbrough and Newarke, committed by Nevison, Everson, and Tankerd, where they tooke about 200l.

Nevinson, the famous highwayman. A woman, who had been an accomplice, is charged with stealing clothes at Mansfield. She expected that her old companions would be able to set her free, but, as they failed her, she makes a clean breast, and discloses all the robberies that they had committed.

The exploits of Nevinson have been made famous by popular tradition and the ballad literature of the country. The chroniclers of his deeds have told us of his daring and his charities, for he gave away to the poor much of the money that he took away from the rich. We do not hear of his taking a lady out of her coach to dance a minuet with him, but he was renowned for his courtesy, and, like the famous Duval,

"Taught the wild Arabs on the road
To act in a more gentle mode."

Nevinson had a long career of success, but it terminated at last. In 1676 he was tried and condemned for a robbery at York, but was reprieved. He returned to his old courses, and was arrested in March 1683-4 in a public-house near Sandal, for a trifling robbery. He was sent to York, and was executed in May.

from a Londoner, that had beene at the last mart; as alsoe one caudle cup of silver and a tankerd and two silver bodkins. All which she found in the portmanture, and is now, or was lately, in their roome at the Talbot, marked with the letter T, except the two bodkins, which they gave her, one of which shee lost, the other shee yet hath. As alsoe 25s. to (buy) her a serge petticoate, and a paire of bodyes.

6. One betweene Longe Billington and Gunnerby, on Whitsun-Monday last, comitted by Bromett and Bracy, where they tooke about 30l. from a drovier, supposed to bee a Yorkeshireman. Of this they gave this ex^t soe much as paid for a quarter's table, and bought the wastecoate on her back.

7. One neare Edlington in Yorkeshire, comitted by Nevison and Bracy, between Martinmas and Christenmas last, where they got about 50l.

8. One neare Stilton, in Huntingtonshire, about May was a twelvemonth, committed by Tankerd and Bromett, where he tooke but 5l., of which they only gave this ex^t a new halfe crowne.

9. That neare Rotheram, from a butcher on Rotheram faire day was twelve months, comitted by Bracy and Nevison, where they tooke 30l., and gave to this ex^t 16s., wherewith shee bought foure els of holland.

10. One neare Roistone, betweene Mayday and Lammas last, comitted by all the sixe, where they tooke 250l., of which this ex^t had two peeces of goold, as much silver as paid for halfe a yeares table, and 6s. 8d. more, to buy her some shifts.

Shee further saith that shee thinkes the master of the Talbot is privy to their carriages, for that shee hath often scene them whisper togather; as alsoe one William Anwood, the ostler there, shee haveinge often seene the said partyes give him good summs of money, and order him to keepe their horses close, and never to water them but in the night time. Shee further saith, that they doe keepe another woman at Lyncolne in Castlegate, at the house betweene the signes of the Swan and the Crowne. One Hugh Peter lives at one end of the house, shee at the other. Shee hath beene mantained by them foure yeares, and hath had a childe to Bracy, which is deade. Shee further saith that shee came from Newark to see some freinds about Sheffeild, but was diverted to Rotheram by reason of hideinge herselfe after the cloaths taken at Mansfeild. And that the two men that came to her at Rotheram the Monday before Christmas day last was Bracy and Tankerd. They came to see her, and to charge her to keepe counsell, and gave her two peeces of goold.

March 26, 1684. *Peter Shippen* saith, that he was at the foot-race at Chappell-town-moor, the 23 of August last past. That, the night before, he laid at the hous of Mrs. Rushton in Barnbo, and went to the race the morning after about nine of the clock with Nicholas Shippen and others. That he continued ther till about four a'clock in the afternoon, and then returned to the company of Mr. Hall of Swillinton, the saxton of that place. He stayed and drunke with him at the hous of one Grant, in Whitechurch, till about 7 of the clock, and then went to Barnbo. The next morning getting up early he went to Shippen to the house of the said Nicholas Shippen very early, and desired him to lend him some mony to carry him to London, for that he designed for that place, but had lost all his own the day before at the foot-race. He could only furnish him with 10s., which obliged him to goe to Garford, halfe a mile distance from thence, to one Tho. Hunt, of whom he further did borrow 20s. From thence he went to the house of Hall, the saxton of Swillinton, with whom he stayed from eight in the morning till two in the afternoon. From thence he went to Pewill Hill, near Barnsley. From thence he went for Oxford, wher he stayed five days with a sister that was married, and soe came to London, wher he hath continued ever since with his master, Mr. Thomas Gascoin. He saith that he knoweth Mr. Nevison, that he did frequent him sometimes, but it was to gett some mony of him that he owed him, but not uppon any other account. He hath seen Will. Knight, but not since Mielemas 1682, and that he went under the reputation of Nevison's man, but that he knoweth not wher he is.

CCXXXIX. MR. ANDREW TAYLOR, ETC. FOR HOLDING A CONVENTICLE.

June 22, 1684. Before Robert Waller, Lord-mayor of York. *Francis Thomlinson, grocer,** *Wm. Lister and Henry Sparlinge*,

---

* An interesting account of the seizure of a Presbyterian congregation in York. There was a large number of Nonconformists at that time in the city. The chapel in St. Saviourgate was not yet built, and their meetings for religious exercises were held in private houses. There was frequently an assembly, according to Oliver Heywood, at the house of Mr. Andrew Taylor in Micklegate. On this occasion the meeting was held at the house of Mrs. Rokeby. She was either the mother or the wife of Thomas Rokeby, Esq., (afterwards a judge,) at that time the great legal adviser of the Nonconformists in the North of England. In his private note-book he speaks of his having had a share of imprisonment. Possibly he had got into trouble for affording shelter to some of the persecuted ministers of his party.

Mr. Ward and Mr. Taylor were fined 50l. each, and were committed to Ousebridge gaol. Oliver Heywood saw Mr. Ward there in the course of the following year.

say, that, this day, beinge inform'd of a tumultuous meeteinge at one Mrs. Rooksbye's house without Micklegate barr, they, together with Ald^n Constable, went there about 8 or 9 of the clocke this morneinge, and demanded entrance, but were denyed. Whereupon by order of the said Ald^n Constable they were admitted, and they found there the followinge persons, to witt, Mr. Andrew Taylor, Ralph Ward, a pretended minister, John Gowland, of Knapton, Wm. Banckes, Thomas Raine and his wife, Jane Dodsworth, Richard Fisher, Abraham Smyth, Wm. Garforth, James Beverley, Wm. Gowland and Eliz. his wife, Richard Overend, of Foulforth, Henry Whales and Joshuah Habber, John Ridsdale, of Naburne, Charles Waterhouse, Hannah Thompson, John Carter, Anne Walker, Ald^n Dawson's wife, Mercy Puckeringe, Abigall Taylor, Judith Robinson, Knightley Hickson, of Leeds, Katherine Hobson, Francis Ward and Mary Ward, Mathew Birkett, Obedd. Lupton, Robert Slayter, Martin Hotham, Wm. Halleday, of Huntinton, Thomas Blackett, and divers others unknowne to these deponents; some of whom they found in lofts above the garretts, and Mr. Ward and Mr. Taylor in a closett lockt up; and the rest in severall other roomes.

There is a long account of Ralph Ward in Calamy, to whose pages my readers must be referred. The same author speaks of Mr. Taylor as " that public-spirited merchant, who opened his door for private meetings in the straitest times." Martin Hotham was a merchant in the city. His son afterwards officiated at the chapel in St. Saviourgate.
I find several indictments preferred for holding conventicles.
" May 24, 1674. Against John Thoresby, gent., Susanna Idle, Brian Dixon and his wife, Hannah Scatcherd, the wife of Joseph Ibbetson, the wife of — Bickerdike, gen., Jeremiah Thoresby, &c., for being at a conventicle at Leeds in a house called Sibills.
" June 7, 1674. A conventicle at the house of Robert Armitage, clerk, in Holbeck.
" Jan. 17, 1677-8. Against John Loxley, Samuel Thornes and Richard Dawson, for holding conventicles at Wakefield."
The Nonconformists were, I believe, generally indicted at the sessions.
The following deposition reveals the delinquencies of a Cumberland magistrate who fell into the hands of Chief Justice Jeffreys.
"Aug. 6, 1684. Before Lord Cheifo Justice Jefferies. *James Appleby, gent.*, sayes that Henry Foster, of Stonegartbside, in the county of Cumberland, Esq., one of his Maties Justices of the peace for the said county, and, alsoe, the said Henry Foster's wife, declared before this informant and others that they did keepe a conventicle in their house, and would contynue the same. And this informant; in Dec. 1682, gave in an informacon against severall dissenters to the said Henry Foster, and prayed proceedings thereon, but he never prosecuted such dissenters, although often requested. Hee was credibly informed by severall of the servants of the said Mr. Foster that hee nor his lady never takes the sacrament or goes to the parish church, nor does baptize their children according to the liturgy of the Church of England, but hath them baptized in his owne house by some fannaticall feild preacher in Scotland."

CCXL. THOMAS ASWALL.   FOR BURGLARY.

July 19, 1684. Before Sir Richard Neile. *Robert Porter, a prisoner in Morpeth goale,** saith that Thomas Aswall, one of the smiths belonging to the garrison of Tinmouth, in which garrison this informant was a souldier, haveing by this informant bene seene and observed 6 or 7 severall tymes to come out of the gun-roome belonging to the said garrison, and perticularly one morne-ing about 5 or 6 a'clock, this informant in the darke went in at the same doore he came out of, then open, which he tooke to be the gun-roome, and there groping about he found a barrell in which there was about 5 or 6 cartaridges of powder, which he tooke away, and which was that powder that was fyred in the smith's shop at Sheilds, which powder this informant had not taken, nor ever found the way into the gun-roome, but he have-ing received severall parcells of powder from the said Aswall to sell, which he sold, and he then, with the (said) Thomas divided the money, being 5 or 6 pounds of powder each tyme for five tymes at the least, which he sold to Isaac Hunter, of Shields, who willingly bought it. But he beleiveth he knew noething how he came by it. This informant was first sent to sell powder to Hun-ter by Aswall, and by watching him where he gott the powder he found the way into the gun-roome, where he beleiveth the said Asswall had often bene, his shop haveinge not longe before this informant tooke the said powder bene blowne up, which was arched over with the stone. All which he hopeth the officers of Tinmouth well remember, and that there was iron instruments for opening locks taken belonging to Aswall, which he first denyed and then owned. And this informant sayth that about seaven weeks since there was brought to him in the goale 10s. by one Thomas Jackson of North Sheilds, who said he brought it from Thomas Aswall to give this informant, and told him the said Thomas bid him keepe his owne councell, and noe harm would come either to this informant or the said Aswall, for it would onely be a little imprisonment, and at Lammas he would be cleere.

---

* A soldier belonging to the garrison of Tynemouth, who had got into trouble, ac-cuses a comrade of stealing powder out of the gun-room. The character of Porter had been a very indifferent one. He had been charged with horse-stealing, and breaking into two shops. It is quite possible that his story is a made-up one.

CCXLI. WILLIAM BECKWITH.   FOR SEDITIOUS WORDS.

Aug. 19, 1684. Before Wm. Christian, Esq. *John Kerren, of Whitehaven, gen.*,* saith, that, being in company of Roger Hendley, of Workington, gen., in the house of Thomas Jackson, in Whitehaven, one Wm. Beckwith, (an officer of the customes in this port,) said, " that, if ever a Parliament did sitt in England, the Duke of York would appeare more guilty than the Duke of Monmouth in any of his actions." And, on the 9th of April, being on board the ship Pearl of Whitehaven, he caused severall of the seamen to drink the Duke of Monmouth's health, and afterwards swearing by — he hoped to see him (meaning the Duke of Monmouth) farr above the Duke of York, and that he would fight for him as long as hee had blood. And " When a Parliament sitts, then wee shall see how York will appear, and the greatest friends he hath," and, " The Parliament will lopp off his head."

CCXLII. EDMUND APPELBY.   FOR SEDITIOUS WORDS.

Nov. 20, 1684. Before Wm. Bridgeman, Esq. Memorandum, that, one day about the latter end of winter or beginning of the spring 1677-8, Edmund Appelby † was drinking pretty briskly in the house of William Orfeur, and was using severall diswasive arguments, most of them consisting of ambiguous terms, viz., from Wm. Orfeur, his keeping or managing any farm, or any other of

---

* The first of a series of depositions relating to the Monmouth controversy and the intrigues of the Protestant and Roman Catholic parties in favour of their respective champions. It will be seen how popular the ill-fated Monmouth was in the North of England.

Mr. Beckwith speaks his mind very freely. Henry Nicholson, the constable of Whitehaven, says that he went to apprehend him, and found him in the house of Henry Brunton, mariner, who locked the door and refused to let him in. Brunton and a man called Levett Thompson detained the constable till Beckwith made his escape. The officer followed him to the house of Henry Tubman, who refused to allow him to arrest the fugitive, but put him off by promising to bail his guest if he was left alone till the morrow. With Tubman's aid Beckwith got away, it was supposed, to Ireland.

† A very singular deposition. It is written in the neatest and most precise hand, and is signed by Mr. Orfeur. The scribe was probably a neighbouring schoolmaster who wrote down the story at the Squire's dictation. The peculiar, and occasionally grandiloquent, style of the deposition is amusing.

The Orfeurs were a very ancient family. The gentleman who is now mentioned seems to have been a person of singular habits. Mr. Appelby denies the truth of the story.

that perswasion, as a reputed Papist, &c. And, att severall times before, in Edmund Appelby his own house, had made use of strong sophisticall arguments to the disparagement of monarchichall government of England. As alsoe by justifying the death of the late King, Charles the First, to have been deserving, as a combiner with and intentionary introducer of Popery. And that his murdering his subjects in Ireland deserved as many deaths to him as he had haires of his head, if possibly he could have had so many lives to have lost, being worse then the massacry of France. As also that this Charles the Second was going the same rode, and had made further progress in the same, and such like matters, and consequently better deserved to undergoe the same punishment then his father. And that to his knowledge he would as sure gett itt, as he had done that was gone, before the expiracion of Wm. Orfeur his four years lease, which was then within less then 13 or 14 months or thereabouts. And, therefore, "I advise you," said Appelby to Orfeur, "to look to yourself, for as soon as God sends us the King's business done, there will not one Papist be permitted to be within the compass of the sea." And withall he threatned that he should not speak of it, for being none but their two selves, if he would be so ingratefull for his kindness to discover him, he would both deny it and sue him for a slander. But so it was that Wm. Orfeur his servant heard the same and more than he could remember, which of late she voluntarily discovered to him: and signified the same by the specificall token that above or a litle after that juncture of time a violent wind blew over her litle child, then about four years old, with such force against a great stone, that it had almost bled to death And in that passion for the child she cursed all traytors, either by word or deed, or any that bare with them.

And the said Edmund Appelby further intimated to Wm. Orfeur that if it was his fortune to have the same power in the Commonwealth of England, as formerly he had in Oliver's time, as he then said he had often formerly told Wm. Orfeur in Mr. Menel's case of Kilvington, when he was a superintendant to the sequestrators of the delinquents' estates, which indeed he did at severall times before notifie to the said Wm. Orfeur, that then he would have a dispensation for the litle man, meaning Wm. Orfeur, for his banishment (but not from Rome, he said by way of derision, &c.) if he would be kind to him in surrendering of a lease which he then had.

Memorandum, that James Appelby, about 15 or 16 months after, in the year 1679, when Wm. Orfeur and his servants demanded a gun from him which he kept and detained without leave, his answer was, that he had authority to keep a gun, but the Papists had none, neither for gun or other weapons. But then a litle time after it happened that one of the said servants asked him againe for the gune, and by what authority he detained it, whose answer was, by vertue of the law and severall acts of Parliament which was in force against Papists bearing or wearing of arms. And the said Wm. Orfeur being nigh to the said servant, (though not in James Appelby his view,) prompted him to ask whether he had the King's commission to put such laws in execucion against the Papists or no. His answer was, "The King! no! he had better warrant then either King or Papist. He had the fundamentall laws of the kingdom for his warrant, and hop'd in few days now that the Commonwealth of England should be once up againe, and should gett their hearts all well cas'd of this King and the Papists, as formerly they had done of his father and them in those days." The servant replyed she hoped for better things, and James Appelby his rejoinder to that was, "That it was but bare hopes, for the law hath as good right to try a King as a subject, as experience the fair tryall of the last King Charles the First. And the same law hath the same power over this Charles the Second; which if he see not before he be a yeare elder, I'll be content to hang for him, therefore never feed yourselves fatt with vaine hopes of a boasting sound and ring, a King! a King! No. Let him be sure that his treacherous wayes and his red letter men's (meaning the King and Papist's) will not many years after seventy-eight be engraven upon his neck with letters of blood, as sure as his father's was in forty-eight; he need expect no other."

Dorothy Stephenson, being servant to Mr. Wm. Orfeur of Allergarth, about eight years ago, heard him say to Mr. Edmond Appleby, "Before the Papists be wronged I will goe to the King." Upon which Mr. Appleby replyed, "For ought I knowe the King is but a rogue and beares with Papists;" and Mr. Orfeur said, "That is more then you can prove." She further sayth that she hath scene Mr. Edmond Appleby both clip and coyne silver at Asherton, she being then his servant, about twenty yeares agoe.

CCXLIII. PETER RAYNING. FOR SEDITIOUS WORDS.

Feb. 19. 1684-5. Before Sir Richard Neile. *Mary Darley, of North Sheilds, widdow,** sayeth, that shee, coming in company in a wherry from Newcastle to Sheilds, with Peter Rayning, of North Sheilds, who hath lived there severall years as a Scotch chapman, some discourse being betwixt the master and Peter Rayning that our gracious King, Charles the Second, being dead, under whome there had been peaceable tymes, and, by there discourse, fearcing that under our new King, James the Second, that there would be troubles, this informant, being laid downe in the wherry, it being night tyme, rose up and said, " Here hath bene hard tymes already for a poore widdow to make shift with a charge of children, pray God send us peace and quietnes." The said Peter Rayning said in answere, " Wee had better have a redd warr then a peace, unles it be to the honor of God." The said Peter is a dissenter from the Church of England, and is an inhabitant in the house of George Wilson, who is the like, and hath been questioned for the same, as shee hath heard; and shee sayeth that, the 15th instant, shee goeing into the house of Patrick Atking, of North Sheilds, a Scotchman and a cobler, to light a candle, Margarett Atking his wife said, " Neighbour, did not you heare the post of last night?" " Yes, I heard and saw it, but what is the newes, neighbour?" Whereupon shee answered and said, " Very badd newes, for our new King James is dead,† and they say they have surfeited him, and he hath bene thrice lett blood since his brother died." To which this informer said, " God forbid," and then this informer in an amasement went to Mr. James Hebden's house, the deputie-water-

---

* A Scottish pedlar at North Shields is in trouble. We should call him, in these days, a red-republican. Mrs. Darley seems to have been a very mischievous person. The scarcity of newspapers at that time made the dissemination of false news a very venial offence.

† The following deposition illustrates this, and shows the strong Protestant feeling that prevailed at that time in Newcastle. " Feb. 11, 1684-5. Before Wm. Aubone, Mayor of Newcastle. Henry Alder, merchant, servant to Ralph Elstob, merchant, deposeth that, this afternoone, one Ann Baxter told this deponent she see Jonathan Carr, merchant, servant to George Huntley, merchant, receive a letter from the post-boy, and open the same; and asking him what news, he said ' Bad news, the King is ill of the same distemper his late Matie dyed off.' And further sayth, that afterwards he was in company with the said Jonathan Carr, and Samuell Hancock, another of the servants of the said George Huntley, and this deponent asked Carr about the letter and words, to which, after a little pause, he answered, ' I wish it may be soe ;' upon which Hancock reproved him, bidding him have a care what he said ; to which he againe replied, ' It were better for the nation if it were soe.' "

bayliffe and land-bayliffe, and told him and his wife with sorrow what shee had heard, and asked him whether it was true. The said Hebden's answere was, "I heare noe such newes, and God forbid it should be true, and I advice you to speake noe more of it;" and this informant sayeth shee never spoake more of it till she was sent for to give information, and since she was sent for, Abigall Turner hath abuesed this informant and her children, and sayth shee is fitt to be whipped through the towne for informing against her neighbours, and shee sayth that Isabell Trumble alsoe hath abuesed her about the same matter, and badd her goe and forsweare herselfe as she had done.

CCXLIV. A LIST OF ROMAN CATHOLICS IN PRISON AT YORK.

March 10, 1684-5.

A true list of the prisoners in Ouse bridge, who were inhabitants in the Citty of York, and at a session their were comitted to a præmunire * by the Mayor, Aldermen, Sheriff, and Recorder of the said Citty of Yorke. Certified by Jo. Constable and Jo. Wood.

The hon^{ble} Mary Fairfax,† wife to the hon^{ble} John Fairfax,

---

* Two very interesting lists. In the latter part of the reign of Charles II. the Statute of Præmunire was put in force, and many Roman Catholics, who refused to take the Oath of Allegiance, were thrown into prison, and subjected to other inconveniences. These severe measures were rendered necessary by the discovery of the plots.

In July, 1680, I find that the following persons were in confinement in York Castle for refusing the oaths :
John and Robert Berry, Francis Aiscough, Thomas Coates, John Atkinson, Francis Osbaldeston, Anthony Langworth, John Cornwallis, alias Prassett, William Allanson, Simon Nicholson, Sir John Lawson, Bt. George Meynill, Esq. Francis Tunstall, Esq. Anthony Metcalf, gen. Edward Birbecke, gen. Anchetel Bulmer, gen. George Allen, Robert Wilson, gen. Wm. Hildreth, gen. John Dawson, Mary Waite, widow, John Lambert, gen. Roger Meynill, Esq. Peter Midleton, Esq. James Thornton, gen. Katherine Witham, widow, Richard Snow, Philip Constable, Esq. Francis Mollineux, Mary Hogg, Mary Moore, Eliz. wife of Thomas Clarke.

When James II. came to the throne the tables were turned, and there was every desire to help those who were still in gaol on account of their religion. Orders were, in all probability, sent from the King to the country prisons directing lists of the sufferers to be made out, and every circumstance to be mentioned which was in the favour of the prisoners. These two lists seem fully to warrant what I say, and they were most probably drawn up for the King's perusal. Every thing that the sufferers had done for Charles I. and II. is carefully specified. We may be very sure that they would be released from gaol, but the confinement had done its work with many of them. Some, no doubt, had taken the oaths and had been released after a short imprisonment ; others would procure the King's pardon.

† The wife of John Fairfax, Esq., a younger son of Thomas Viscount Fairfax, by a daughter of Sir Philip Howard, of Naworth. Her father, Colonel Hungate, was

daughter to Collonell Francis Hungate, colonell of horse, who was in the service of his late Majesty of happy memory; his estate sequestred from his wife and children, by which this prisoner is a great sufferer.

The worshipful Magdalen Metham,* wife to George Metham of Metham, Esq., whose father George Metham, Esq. was wounded, taken prisoner at Willoughby fight; whose grandfather, Sir Jordan Metham, was a great agent at the setting up of the King's standert in Yorkshire; whose wife and children were sequestred; whose uncle, Sir Thomas Metham, was slain at Hessay moor: by which this prisoner and her husband are great sufferers.

The honour'd Catherine Lassells, widdow to Edward Lassells, a leiftenant in his late Majesty's service, whose father George Thwing, Esq., rais'd a troop of horse; whose brother, Alphonso Thweng,† levied a company of foot for his late Majesty's service; for which their estates were sequestred, and this prisoner at ten years old was imprisoned by Young Hotham, for being the daughter and sister of such royallists; and has suffred other wayes.

The hon^d George Thwaites,‡ (and Mary his wife), lieftenant of a company of foot in his late Majesty's service; taken prisoner, sequestred untill his late Majesty's happy return; by which these prisoners were great sufferers.

The much esteem'd John Andrews,§ gent., of a loyall family in Wales, his nearest relations having bin great sufferers for his late Majesty's service; who coming to the spaws for his health, was seiz'd upon as a stranger, and clapt into præmunire, by which this prisoner has much suffer'd.

We, whose names are heere subscrib'd, do know and ar well satisfied that the within-named prisoners have bin and are loyall and peacefull subjects to his late and present Majesty, and, in

---

killed fighting for Charles I. at Chester. What an outrage to decency and Christian charity it was, to speak mildly, to confine ladies in a prison which, when the Ouse was high, was partially under water!

* Any one might be proud of such a pedigree of loyal ancestors. The Methams of Metham were one of the most illustrious families in Yorkshire. Sir Thomas Metham fell at Marston Moor, with many of the Northern gentlemen. Jordan, the eldest son of Sir Jordan Metham, was killed at the siege of Pontefract Castle.

† The Thwengs, of Heworth, near York, were an ancient Roman Catholic family. It must not be forgotten that this lady's brother, Thomas Thweng, a priest, was executed for high treason at York in 1681. She was a niece, also, of Sir Thomas Gascoine, of Barnbow.

‡ Of Marston, near York, and a member of a family that had been seated there for a very long time.

§ The account of the arrest of this person has been already printed. Nothing whatever is said of his being a Roman Catholic priest.

themselves, parents and familys, have bin great sufferers for their loyalty. Which we, being desired to certifie to whom it may concern, in love to their persons and pitty to their sufferings, have subscribed our names.

A list of the prisoners in præmunire in the castle of York, comitted to that prison from severall Sessions held in that County. Certified by Sir Tho. Mauleverer and Sir Thomas Rudston.

Francis Aiscough,* Esq., who was lieftenant of a troop of horse rais'd by his brother James Aiscough. The said Francis was wounded, imprison'd, sequestred for his loyalty and service to his late Majesty.

Ancketillus Bulmer,† the son of Anthony Bulmer, lieutenant-colonell in his late Majesty's service; the which has sufferd much.

Robert Wilson, gent.
William Hildred, gent.
Robert Berry, gentleman,
Anthony Medcaff, gent.
Edward Burbeck, gent.

All souldiers sequestred, and sufferers for their loyalty and service to his late Majestie.‡

Thomas Cotes, servant to the old Lord Falconberg.

Francis Molineux, servant to the worshipful family of the Constables of Everingham, loyall subjects and sufferers.

Francis Osbaldeston,§ son of Sir Francis Osbaldeston, a loyall person, who with imprisonment lyes bed-ridden in the prison neare upon these two years, being 80 years old.

Anthony Langworth, gent.; whose father was turn'd out of his estate; whose uncle, Sir John Langworth, colonell under his late Majesty, and his present Majesty's father, and his uncle Sir Francis Prujean, was knighted by his late Majesty. This prisoner is loyall, and a great sufferer in himselfe and relations.

Simon Nicholson, gent., an Irishman and a stranger, who tra-

* A son of Alan Ayscough, Esq. of Skewsby, and brother of James Ayscough, of Middleton-one-row. Mr. Ayscough had been in prison for five or six years. He has been already mentioned.

† Grandson of Sir Bertram Bulmer, of Tursdale, co. Durham, and one of the last representatives of a great and most illustrious house. He died in 1718, aged 84. Sir Bertram ruined the family estates, and raised and led a troop to the Low Country Wars. In 1726 a person of the name of Bertram Bulmer " kept the cock-pit and bowling green in Gray's Inn, and was in possession of an ancient emblazoned pedigree of Bulmer extending beyond the Conquest !"

‡ North Riding gentlemen, several of whom had been in gaol for a very long time.

§ This gentleman, and Langworth and Nicholson, had been in prison for some years. They were reputed priests. Mr. Osbaldeston is mentioned in the State Trials, in connection with Bolron, the informer, who made a ludicrous mistake with reference to him.

velling through the county was apprehended, and clapt in præmunire; his selfe loyall, and his family, and great sufferers.

John Lambert, shopkeeper, a loyall subject and sufferer.

George Allen, } all common souldiers in his late Majesty's and
Richard Snow, } present Majesty's father's service; sequestred,
John Dawson, } and now maintain'd in prison by common alms.

Women prisoners.

The worshipful Mary and Margarett More,* living in this county upon a farm of their mother's, were committ to præmunire (the said Margarett dyed in prison), the daughters of Thomas More, Esq., the grandchildren of Chrizaker More, who was the grandchild of Sir Thomas More, quondam Lord Chancelour of England. The prisoner, in herselfe and family, loyall, and a great sufferer.

Mrs. Mary Wayt,† widdow to George Wayt, gent., whose brother was mortally wounded at Hessay Moor, and dyed presently after his wound; whose said husband George Wayt was lieftennant to Major Markham of a troop of horse; she being of a loyall family of the Lanetons, in Lancashire, whose estate was sould from them for their loyalty; her estate sequestred, by which she is a great sufferer.

Mrs. Mary Hoog, the daughter of Lieftenant Hoog, the grandchild of Captaine William Hoog, in the Lord of Newcastle's army, who for their loyalty and service were plunder'd and sequesterd; by which this prisoner is a great sufferer.

Catharine Wilson, whose husband was a souldier under his present Majesty's father; who for his loyalty and service was plunder'd and sequestred; by which his widdow, the prisoner, is reduced to such poverty, that she is maintain'd in prison by common alms.

John Cornwally,‡ alias Brand, in whose behalfe the Duke of Newbourg writt two letters to his late Majesty, and Monsieur de Thun, the Emperor's embassador, interceded for his liberty as an alien and stranger.

Elizabeth Clark, once a servant to the family of Constables.

* A most valuable notice of the descendants of the famous Sir Thomas More. Mr. Hunter would have read it with great interest. It corrects an error in his pedigree of More, and throws some light upon the history of that ill-used and unfortunate family. Cresacre More, it must be observed, was the great-grandson of the Chancellor. How sad that any of his descendants should be permitted to die in a gaol!

† A daughter of Abraham Langton, of the Lowe, in Lancashire, and widow of George Wayte, of Layburn, Esq.

‡ This is the person who was arrested in 1678. He was supposed to be a Roman Catholic priest, and to be implicated more or less in the plots of the time. An account of him has been already given.

CCXLV. SIR WM. SCOTT, ETC. FOR TREASON.

May 22, 1685. Before Timothy Davison, Esq. *Frederick Challenar*, one of the waters and searchers of the Customes house at *Newcastle*, saith, that, in the month of February, he being aboard of the shipp or pinck called the Content of Newcastle,* whereof John Ward was and is now maister, then under sale, makeing for sea, outward bound for Holland or some part beyond the seas; and, demanding of the said John Ward whether he had any passengers aboard of his said vessle, he replyed he had none. Whereupon this informer makeing deligent search he found a certaine gentleman hidd and concealed in a cabbyn in the round house of the said shipp; and, after examinacion and inquiry made, findeing the said gentleman to be a suspected and dangerous person, he carryed him ashoare, and comitted him into the custody of Capt. Villiers into Tynmouth castle, and he examining the matter whether there were any goods or things appertaineing to the said gentleman on board of his vessle, he denyed that he had any, and said that one James Clay, waterman, who brought him aboard of the said vessell, told him that he was an inhabitant in Newcastle, and soe went directly to sea with his said shipp; and that the said gentleman did appeare and prove to be and goe under the name of Sir Wm. Scott; and, as this informer is told, that there was a trunck and a box belonging to the said Sir Wm. Scott, seized upon beyond seas on board of the said shipp.

CCXLVI. JOHN CUNNINGHAM. FOR SEDITIOUS WORDS.

June 13, 1685. Before Wm Aubone, Mayor of Newcastle. *James Mow, tailor*,† sayth, that, haveing occasion to goe to drinke a glasse of ale, he went into the house of one Michaell Clerke, tailor; and falling into the company of one John Cunningham, had some discourse about the news. The said Cunningham fell out in speeches and said that, if Argile ‡ had got nere Clide (he

---

* A gentleman is found concealed on board a Newcastle vessel by a Custom house officer. He is arrested as a suspicious character.

† A party of tailors in Newcastle begin to discuss politics: one of them speaks so strongly that his freedom of speech cost him 5l. at the assizes.

At no town perhaps in England was the dislike to James II. more strongly manifested than at Newcastle. It was at this time that the unhappy Monmouth was in England on his illfated expedition, and the hearts of the people were with him. The depositions that I give will show how strong that feeling was.

‡ The Earl of Argyle made an attempt in Scotland about the same time that Mon-

the said Cunningham knew the countrey soe well,) that Argile had then conquered Scotland; and, in a short time, England would be nothing to him. And he begunn a health to the Duke of Monmouth, which this deponent refused to drinke, and thereupon the said Cunningham broke out in idle speeches, and said there was noe King in England, for Monmouth was the anointed; and, before another yeare goe about, you will heare another story.

Richard Stephenson, tailor, saith, that he heard Cunningham say "the Duke of Monmouth's gone, and that the King's forces were not soe strong as Monmouth's. Richard, have a care; hereafter will pay for all." And allsoe said, sometime before that, " Sir John Fenwicke * is come to the towne, but I doubt its to take upp forces for Monmouth, and not for the King;" and said, " O, have they taken Monmouth's life, he is an anointed prince, and they are rebellious for soe doeing."

CCXLVII. RICHARD HUNTER. FOR AN ASSAULT.

June 25, 1685. Before Wm. Aubone, Mayor of Newcastle. *George Thompson* saith, that, upon Tuesday the 16th day of June, one Richard Hunter † came to the sentre, and would have

---

mouth's insurrection began in England. Both, it is well known, were unsuccessful. The following depositions refer to the Scottish affair.

"June 15, 1685. Before Wm. Aubone, Mayor of Newcastle, and Henry Brabant. John Otway, merchant, deposeth, that this day, being at Mr. George Story the barber's shopp, one John Clerke and this deponent discourseing about Argile's being in armes, the said Clerke said that none could blame Argile for looking for his owne againe, he being banished three years; and said, ' Give him his owne againe and he would be quiett;' and added, ' Mr. Story, you would take itt ill if any should robb you of the house you live in.''

"June 10, 1685. John Hodge of Newcastle, discourseing with George Marshall, a prisoner in his Maties gaol, about the news in Scotland, he said he hoped very shortly to have a comission from Earlston (being one of the fugitives or rebells there), and to be in office under him."

* Sir John Fenwick of Wallington. He certainly would not have supported Monmouth, as the witness observes. In 1696 he was mixed up in a conspiracy against William III. for which he lost his life. His character and family made him very popular in the North; and there was an old song of which the burthen was,

"Sir John Fenwick's the flower amang them."

† The town of Newcastle was at this time very strictly guarded. Its dislike to James II. would be well known, and every precaution would be taken to suppress the rebellious spirit of the inhabitants. A bold fellow, it will be seen, makes an assault upon a sentry.

The following persons were committed to gaol at the same assizes by Lord Chief Justice Jeffreys for an assembly to subvert the Government, and for subscribing a treasonable paper of association and secrecy, Thomas Thompson, John Foster alias

passed into the guard or sentry that was standing at Sandgate gate; but, one of them opposeing and hindring him, the said Richard Hunter tripped upp one of the sentries, and tooke his fauchett from him; upon which, this deponent, being a corporall of the said company, seeing such abuse done to the sentre by the said Hunter, tooke a pike and stopped him, desireing him to restore the fauchett againe, and to goe home and be quiett; but the said Hunter, being resolute, cutt the pike which was in this deponent's hand in two peices, and aimed at this deponent's neck with the said fauchett; and, missing his aime, cutt this deponent's thumb of by the lower joynt.

CCXLVIII. WM. HINDMERSH, GEN. FOR LIBELLOUS WORDS.

A true bill against Wm. Hindmersh, of Newcastle, gen. for saying, on July 13, 1685, " I heare sixteene or seaventeen thousand were to contribute . . . . hundred thousand pounds towards Monmouth's designe, and that the present Mayor, Mr. Alderman Davison, Mr. Morton,* and Mr. Councellor Blakiston, were suspected to be contributors, and would be one hundred pounds a peice."†

CCXLIX. JOHN SAYLES. FOR TREASON.

May 29, 1685. Before Sir Richard Neile. *Robert Bell, of Pont-island, walker,*‡ saith, that, on the 23d of May, being at

Forster, John Ornsby, Michael Dent, Thomas Rushton . . . . Joseph Porter, Thomas Bilton, Thomas Verner, Ely Bilton, Joseph Dixon, Matthew White, Benjamin . . . son, March . . . Wm. Robson, John Kay, Leonard Johnson, George Airey, John Cooke, Joseph Sharpe, and James . . .

* " A true bill against Richard Willans of Newcastle, hatter, for saying, on Feb. 20, 1681, that George Morton, Esq. did harbor and entertaine Mr. Welsh, the Scotch minister, a preacher, in his house, when he was mayor, some dayes and nights."

† The accused says that he was at North Shields, and heard the contribution mentioned, but without any names. Party spirit was at this time running very high.

"July 12, 1685. Before John Thomson, lord mayor of York. Captaine George Butler of Yorke sayth, that Mr. Henry Sparlinge told him that he was a Monmouth teare-rogue, and that he had raysed men and sent them away privately by his two serjants for Monmouth's service. And very great provoakeinge language he gave this deponent; and sayd the Lord Mayor of Yorke was a sonne of a whore, and a rogue, and soe were the rest of the aldermen ungone to Hull for goeinge thither, and that he could hange this deponent when he would."

‡ An amusing and curious deposition. There were certainly strange stories about the death of Charles II.; and Monmouth, in his proclamation, did not hesitate to charge his uncle with his death, but there seems to be no possible foundation for the slander. The memory of James II. has faults enough to bear without the crime of murder.

Newcastle, one John Sayles, a Scotchman, told him, " I will tell you a peice of newes that I heare, that King Charles the Second doeth appeare to his brother King James the Second, and soe troubles and disturbs him that he is very sadly troubled and disturbed and almost distracted and not himselfe." And he said further, that the ghost of King Charles; when he appeared to his brother, held a bottle of coffee to the said King James his face or nose, and said, " This is such coffee as you gave me when I was alive."

CCL. JOHN HOWDEN.   FOR SEDITIOUS WORDS.

July 13, 1685. Before Sir Wm. Lowther. *Wm. Robinson, of Saxton, husbandman,** sayeth, that, as he was goeing to worke with John Howden, betwixt the crosseing of the streets and Scardingwell gate, upon a discourse of drinking the King's health at the bonefire over night, the deponent said to Howden, " Did you drinke the King's health, for you weare an Oliver souldier?" He replied, " I served Oliver no longer then he lived; they say in our towne that the Duke of Monmouth is taken, and they say they'l hang him, but I say by the lawes of armes they cannot hang him." The deponent replied that if they could not hang him by the lawes of armes they might behead him by the lawes of the land. But the said Howden answered they would not, and said, " If thy father had left thee an estate, and thy unckle should seek to wrong thee of it, thou would fight for it, wouldst thou not?" to which he replied " No, it may be not." One Richard Parke, being by, said, " Yes, or else thou would sue for it;" and Howden concluded with these words, " It is a pittie that the Duke should loose his right."†

CCLI. FRANCIS THOMPSON.   FOR SEDITIOUS WORDS.

July 22, 1685. Before John Atkinson, Esq., Mayor of Ap-

---

* Two days after this, on the 15th of July, Monmouth lost his head.

† It will be seen that the feeling in favour of Monmouth ran over all the North of England. I give three cases in point.

" July 19, 1683. At Wakefield, Richard Barker begunne the Duke of Monmouth's health, and said hee was the King's own sonne, and that hee hoped to see a change before twelve monthes should come about."

" 13 Feb. 1684-5. Margaret Johnson, of York, says that Andrew Younge comeinge to her house as a beggar told her that the Scotch were all in armes, and that the Duke of Monmouth was cominge over the sea."

" Feb. 28, 1685. John Ingham, of Luddenden, blacksmith, says at Hallifax, ' Wee have a King but he is uncrown'd, for the crowne belongs to the Duke of Monmouth.'"

pleby. *John Poulter, elder and younger,** say, that they came to Sandford and enquired for the constable there. Whereupon they were directed to one Francis Thompson, and, shewinge him theire pass, did desire some releife of him, to helpe them in theire journey to Whitehaven. Upon which he asked them if theire pass was in the Queene's name. They said it was in the King's Majestie's name. He then said he did beleive theire was noe Kinge in England. The said Poulter askinge his reason why he should soe say, he answered the Kinge was dead. Thereupon Poulter told him he harde of noe such thinge all the way he came. Whereupon Tompson asked him, whether he did beleive that James Duke of Yorke was heire to the crowne. Upon that Poulter replyed he did beleive soe. And Tompson then replyed that did not hee. Was the Duke of Monmouth a bastard? To which the said Poulter replyed he was neither bolster nor pilloe to the King's concernements.

CCLII. THOMAS MOFFETT. FOR SEDITIOUS WORDS.

July 23, 1685. Before Sir Richard Neile. *William Alder, of Clifton Loneinge, in the parish of Stannington, yeoman*, saith that, on the 6th, in the rode betwixt Glanton and Wooler, he mett Thomas Moffett,† of Fawdon, who asked him " What news?" " I heard noe news," said this informant, " but that there is some shipps taken with great store of arms and moneys belonginge to him that they call'd the late Duke of Monmouth." In answer the said Moffett said, " Out, that's nothinge." " But," says this informant," theres many of opinion he cannot (meaninge the Duke of Monmouth) subsist longe." " Whough," says Moffett, " he has more men then the Kinge of England has." " Ei, faith, has he?" said Thomas Dodds. And Moffett said, " Else how came the Duke of Albemarle and the Duke of Sumerset to be killed?"

---

* A parish constable in Westmerland speaks treason. He seems to have been in complete ignorance of the political news of the day. Some time would elapse before the tidings of the death of Charles II. and the accession of James II. penetrated into the wilds of Westmerland. I have heard a strange story connected with the county of Durham. In the beginning of the reign of George III. Mr. Ambler was holding a court at Stanhope or Wolsingham. In the course of the proceedings some document was read in which the name of the reigning sovereign was mentioned. Upon that an old woman lifted up her hands in astonishment, and cried out, " Lord bless us, is Queen Anne deed?"

† A man spreads false news and speaks treason. Nothing had happened to Albemarle or Somerset, and Monmouth had been executed on the 15th.

meaninge by the forces of the late Duke of Monmouth. Whereupon this informant answered, "There is many such idle people as you both are in this countrey, and if I knewe where there were authority I would leave my journey and cause you to be apprehended to give account where you had this news, for I beleive you are some confederates, or holds intelligence with some confederates, of that partye."

CCLIII. JOHN HEY AND MARY LEE. FOR SEDITIOUS WORDS.

August 25, 1685. Before George Thornhill, Esq. *William Dex, of Heckmondwike, slater,** saith, that, on the 24th of July last, goeinge into a privat house in Hull, and meeteing there with one John Hey, of Heckmondwike, butcher, and Mary wife of Tobie Lee, of the same towne, and they beinge his acquentance, he tould them that he had listed himselfe a soulger under Captain Collingwood, but they wood not beleive him untill he had made severall prodestations to confirme the same. They replied and bad the devil goe with him, and said that before they wood goe to be a soulger under the Kinge they wood run their knifes to his hart if they could gett an oportonaty. And, further, replied that they wood both be soulgers under the Duke of Monmouth, and gett him what strength they could. And the said Mary Lee tould him she wood disguise herselfe in man's apparill, and that the aforesaid Hey and she wood lye together, for she could travell seaven yeares before she was knowne.

CCLIV. A RIOT IN YORK MINSTER.†

Jan. 30, 1685-6. Before the Dean of York. *Bartholomew Collier, one of the Sergeants of Sir John Reresby's company of*

---

* Monmouth is again the subject of the deposition. The accused persons fled the country.

† An account of a most scandalous and disgraceful scene in York Minster at the funeral of the Lady Strafford. She died on the 27th of December, to the great grief of her illustrious husband. She was a daughter of the loyal Earl of Derby, and a lady of exalted character as well as birth.

As a compliment, and as a matter of precaution, a company of Sir John Reresby's grenadiers, at that time quartered in York, was directed to accompany the funeral procession. The soldiers met the hearse at the wind-mills beyond Micklegate bar. When they got to the Minster, at the choir door, "they stood on either side of the corps, to let the same be carryed quietly in, and to hinder the rabble from stealing the escutcheons off from the pall and herse, and to let the clergy and gentry that attended

Granadiers, saith, that having received orders from Mr. George Butler, lievetenant to Sir John Reresby, (who told this informant that he had received a lettre from Sir John to the purpose hereafter mencioned,) to go along with the said company of granadiers to attend the corps of the late Countesse of Strafford, that was then coming downe to be buryed in York Minster, and to see that no violence or rudenesse should be then offered, did, accordingly, upon Wensday the 13th, command the said company, and did attend the herse, where the corps of the said Countesse was, from Micklegate bar, and guard it into the Minster-yard. And as soone as the said herse came to the west end of the Minster, and the corps were taken downe, there was a great rabble or rout of ordinary people, that pressed very rudely upon this informant and his souldiers, and would needs take the escutcheons from the herse by force. Which he and his company did endeavour to hinder them from doing; whereupon severall of the said rabble struck at the said souldiers with great sticks or staves. And he and the said company did guard the said corps within the Minster till they came at the quire doore, where they made a stand, and let the corps be carryed in. And the said rabble did then presse and croud very rudely to come in, and follow the said corps, which he and his company, endeavouring to hinder them from doing with as much civility as they well could, a great many persons of the said rabble struck at this informant and his souldiers, and knockt some of them downe, and among the rest this informant himself was knockt downe twice at the doore of the quire. Whereupon he was forced to draw off his souldiers to a more open place in the Minster, to hinder them from being further abused. And the said rabble pursued them still and used great violence to them, and struck at them with sticks, and made great shouts and noyse, and some of them cryed out, " Let's kill the dogs, we are ten to one," and repeated this severall times. And this informant had much a doe to prevent great mischeif,

the corps to go quietly in." The depositions describe the scene that ensued. The "old countess dowager" could scarcely get into the church. The mob called the soldiers the " black-guard "; they struggled and fought in a disgraceful manner.

There is some conflicting evidence, as several persons justify the proceedings of the mob. It is to be remarked, also, that this is not the first occasion on which this regiment came into collision with the populace. The soldiers made a great riot at Doncaster in 1684, in which the mayor and the justices of the peace were roughly handled. There is an account of this affair in Mr. Hunter's South Yorkshire.

On Shrove Tuesday, 1672-3, there was "a great company of people in the Minster yard, about 5 in the evening, and many puld up the pales before the Deanry and Dr. Lake's house."

There was a riot, or something like it, about the same time, when the Chapter tried to prevent people from walking in the nave of the Minster in service time.

but, as soone as he could conveniently, he drew his men out of the church in to the Minster yard; where the said rabble still pursued them, shouting and throwing sticks, stones, and dirt at them as they went, and did seize on severall muskets, and broke them; so that this informant, seeing there was no way to pacify the tumult without doing some mischeif to them, was forced to draw off his men into the citty, and leave the crowd.

Richard Hewitt, gentleman, saith, that haveing a curiosity to see the solemnitys of the funerall performed, hee attended the corps to the Cathedrall. Which was guarded thither with a company of granadeers, marching in two fyles, on either side the hearse, to keepe of a crowd of rabble that followed them, from disordering the hearse, and crowding the attendants. The soldiers soe guarded the corps to the Cathedrall, and soe upp the body of the Church unto the great doer, which enters into the quier; where they stood and made a guard, untill the corps was carryed into the quier, and the attendants weere gone in. The crowd of comon people which weere gott into the Church would have pressed in after; which the soldiers would have hindred, but they indeavouring to force their passage by crowding, the souldiers would have prevented them. And one of the soldiers with an halbert crosse-in-hands, (and as this informant beleives) to keepe them out of the quier, pushed att some of the formost of the rabble, which was returned by blowes upon the soldiers, and returned by the soldiers upon the rabble. The crowd pressing close upon the soldiers they begunn to defend themselves with their fusees club'd; in which recounter severall of the rabble were knocked downe, and severall of their fusees broken. This informant seeing this, and beleiveing that in all likelyhood, if some care weere not taken to suppresse the ryot, and secure his Majestie's peace, some persons night be killed, went betweene the rabble and the soldiers, and did use arguments to perswade them to desist, saying to them the horridnesse of the crime. Whereupon they drew a little back from the soldiers, and then the informant turned to the soldiers and advised them to march forth of the Church, which they seemed ready and willing to doe. But as they weere goeing away, the rabble pursued them and shouted att them, and, as this informant was told, and veryly beleives, threw staves at them to incense them, whereupon the serjants who headed the company gave out the command to face about, and to stand to their armes, which was readily donn by the soldiers, who marched upp towards the crowd, their fusees presented with their byonets in the mussles. And soe standing att bay, one att another, some of the fyle leaders thinking (as this informant beleeves) to terrifye them into quietnesse, threatned to fyre at them, and some of them did fyre; but, noe harme being donn, they being onely (as this inform^t beleeves) charged with powder, it made the rabble more insolent; and then some gentlemen drawing neare this informant desired their assistance to hinder such riotous proceedings, who advised them to desist, and the soldiers to march forth of the Church, which they did accordingly, the rabble pursuing them with shouts and cryes. When the soldiers weere gonn forth of the Church, as sonne as this informant could gett through the crowd that followed them, hee went to call the constable for the said liberty, who imediately came with this informant; and this informant advised him to command the King's peace, and to command him, or what persons else he thought convenient, to assist him to quell the ryot, and to secure what persons he found guilty; but, upon the appearance of the constable, the rabble dispersed. He is credably informed the escutcheons of the deceased Countesse that were placed round the quire weere all torne downe before the service was donn; and, when the corps was brought to the place of interrment, whilst the Deane was in performing the service, this informant see severall persons teare downe the escutchions that weere placed over the place of interment.

CCLV. DANIEL AWTY. FOR SACRILEGE.

Feb. 11, 1685-6. Before Toby Conyers, D.D. and Dr. Wickham, Dean of York. *Joseph Lockwood, of Kirkheaton,** *clothyer*, saith, that one Mercy Hutchinson, widow, sister to Daniell

---

* An interesting deposition. The splendid communion plate used in York Minster was stolen in 1677, and, after a lapse of some years, these informations were laid. Mr. Lockwood had, I believe, been gaoler of York Castle. Awty and his sister were in prison for some time on this charge, but it could not be brought home to them. Awty himself denies all knowledge of the offence, but confesses that, on the day of the robbery, he was at service in the body of the choir towards the altar.

An account has been already given of the loss of the Chester plate. About this time Westminster Abbey suffered a similar privation.

The following information relates to Awty, who has been mentioned several times already:

"Aug. 1, 1685. Benedict Horsley, of Yorke, painter-stainer, sayth that he was one of the city grand jury that did throw out a bill of indictment brought by Daniel Awty of York, whitesmith. The said Awty meeting him said, 'Thou art a pittifull fellow. There is thirteene or fourteene of you—I would sell you all to the devill for two pence a peice,' meaneing the grand jury."

This Mr. Horsley is believed to have been a very near kinsman of the author of the Britannia Romana.

Awty, alias Otty, of the city of York, did severall times at Dewisbury, about two or three yeares ago, as allso severall times in York within the space of six monthes last past, tell this deponent that her said brother got the plate which was stolne out of York Minster some yeares ago, and that itt was conveyed to the house of Alice Awty, widow, in Dewisbury, who is mother to the said Daniell. And the said Mercy Hutchinson did att the said house shew this deponent a course canvase bagg, and told him that the said Minster plate was brought thither in that bagg. And he has sometimes urged the said Mercy to discover what she knew of this matter to a magistrate: at which times she has usually replyed, " What! would you have mee hang my owne brother?" And he saith that, a litle before the said plate was stolne, the said Daniell Awty told this deponent that he and some who were prisoners in York Castle had been discoursing about the Minster plate, and what a rare booty itt would bee, if it could bee gott; and talked as if hee would have had this deponent concerned with him in getting and helping to convey and conceal the same, and said that he this deponent's living near might bee helpfull to them in their designe. Att that time this deponent was servant to the Lady Beaumont in Lord Irwin's house.

James Dinsdall, in the Minster Yard, saith, that, about two or three moneths ago, one Mercy Hutchinson came to live in the house where one Mrs. Morley lives, in the Bederne, where he hath severall times seen her; and, since Martinmas last, he hath severall times heard the said Mercy owne that she had the Minster plate, which was stolen from thence some yeares agoe, in her armes at her mother's house at Dewisbury, when and where her brother Daniell Autie was present. She further said that the said plate, or a great part of it, was there melted downe, and that part of the table upon which it was melted was burnt in the melting of it. And hee also heard her at somtimes, speaking of the said plate, say that she would make the Minster bells ring, and that, if she pleased, she could hang a hundred of them. And he hath heard her say that her brother would have given her money to be gone out of the citty of York to Dewisbury because she made such talk and discourse of him. He hath also heard the said Mary call one Elizabeth Richardson, who lives in Swinegate, and is commonly reported to have been naught with the said Autie, " clipping whore," and tell her that it was the Minster plate that made her to flourish.

CCLVI. ALEXANDER CRANSTON.   FOR SEDITIOUS WORDS.

Oct. 29, 1686. *Thomas Condon, gent.*, was, together with one Timothy Tayler and Madam Clement, on the 28th instant, in the house of Robert Walker, in Staynton dale, in the way for Scarbrough, where he mett with a man who called himselfe Alexander Cranston, who, upon discourse, sayd that the Duke of Munmoth was alive,* and that he could goe to him before night, and that one Collonell White † was beheaded in his stead; and the sayd Cranston sayd he hopd that Monnmoth would weare the crowne of England on his head in two yeares time.

CCLVII. STEPHEN DUFFEILD.   FOR SEDITIOUS WORDS.

Jan. 31, 1686-7. Before Sir Jonathan Jenings, Kt. *John Peatch, of Ripon, boddy-maker,* saith, that, yesterday morning, being Sunday, and in the time of divine service, this informant being churchwarden, together with William Walker and James Suttrice, alias Clarkeson, his fellow churchwardens, entring into the house of James Foxton, to see what order was therein kept, one Stephen Duffeild, of Ripon, came in, and, entring into discourse with them, told them that the Queene told the King that she could not conceive unlesse she dranke Charles Monmouth's blood; upon which the King told her that he would send for him and that he should be lett blood, that she might drinke it: upon which she replyed, that unlesse she might drinke his heart's blood it would doe her noe good.

---

* A rumour was spread abroad that Monmouth was alive. The same story has been circulated, at different times, about many persons of distinction. The love of the people for their favourite Monmouth was very great."

" 6 July, 1685. Robert Sutton heard George Levitt, of York, say at Hull, that it was talked frequently in London that the late Duke of Monmouth was within three or four dayes march of London, and that parte of the artillery was taken from the King's forces."

" Dec. 17, 1685. Mr. Richard Marsden, rector of Slaidborne, deposes that yesterday, at Slaidborne, Ralph Dobson gave out that there was a rebellion, and should be a rebellion, and whether the Duke of Monmouth was in England or not in England at the springe this informant's coat should be turned."

" 5 June, 1687. At York. The King's health being drunk, one Peter Barker did refuse to drink the same, and sayd that he would drink Munmoth's, for he was alive."

† Colonel White was a well known personage.

CCLVIII. PETER HUTCHINSON.   FOR SEDITIOUS WORDS.

May 3, 1687. Before Sir Wm. Bowes, Kt., Fr. Tonstall, and George Meynel, Esqrs. *Ralph Walker, of Whashton, yeoman,*[*] saith that, on the 25th of April, he met with one Peter Hutchinson, blacksmith, at the house of Francis Allen, in Kirkby Ravensworth, alehouse-keeper, where, having drank together, the said Hutchinson began a health to the Duke of Monmouth, wch this informant refusing to pledge, and reprehending him for begining it, the said Hutchinson did affirm the said Duke to be alive as certainly as he himself was, and added that he had sown oats which were now growing for Monmouth's horses to eat. Thereupon this informant told him that he would make informacion of his discourse before George Meynel, Esq.; whereupon the said Hutchinson said that neither he, the said George Meynel, nor any of those Popish dogs, the new justices of peace, had any power to hurt him. And the said Hutchinson, on the same day, in the house of one Anne Wiseman, said, with severall oaths, " Hang these Popish dogs, wil we have any of these Popish dogs to be our King ?"

CCLIX. MICHAEL THEAKSTON.   FOR AN ASSAULT, ETC.

June 15, 1688. Ripon. Before Wm. Chambers, Mayor, and Sir Jonathan Jennings, Kt. *George Murgetroyd, of Ripon,*[†] sayth that, last night about tenne of the clocke, a fire being kindled neare Mr. William Heslinton's house in or neare the old markett place, this informer went to see what was the meaneing of it, and there found the fire was built of strawe and dry small sticks, soe that, as the wind stood, severall (thatched) houses were in danger of being burnt, the same fire being built in as dangerous a place for doeing a mischeife as is in the towne of Ripon. One James Turpin, who was then upon the watch, came up to the place where the fire was, and being also apprehensive of the danger, endeavoured to putt out the fire with his watchbill, whereupon one Michael Theakestone tooke hold of the watchbill and would have taken the same from the said James Turpin if he could. About halfe an houre after, he and George Pinckney were together

---

[*] Another deposition about Monmouth. The King had been putting many of the Roman Catholic gentlemen on the list of justices of the peace. Two of the magistrates before whom Hutchinson was brought were Roman Catholics.

[†] An amusing deposition, which gives quite a little picture of the town of Ripon.

when Mr. Mayor's serjeant went to discharge the said Mich. Theakstone from makeing a bonefire in that place: the said Theakstone then answered the serj^t, that he would make a bonefire upon his owne frontstead let Mr. Mayor doe what he would, and other words, in contempt of Mr. Mayor. After the serj^t was gone, this informant told the said Michael, that he wondred why he should make a fire in that place, and of such combustable matter, that might have done more harme then his estate was able to repaire. He answerd that it was time enough to complaine when harme was done, and in a ridiculing way said of Mr. Mayor, that he was a very loyall Mayor, and it was a loyall corporation, and the King should know it, and Mr. Mayor was as honest a man as ever broke a house, and he cared not for him. Adding these further words, viz., " Wee'l be with you," to which this informant answered, 'twas not question but their mind and their hearts were willing enough, but they wanted strength; and the said Michael replyed, there was strength enough over the water, or words to that effect.

Elizabeth Parving, of Rippon, widdow, went to desire them to putt out the fire, and when she spoke to the said Michael Theakestone, he strucke her over the head twice with a pair of bellowes, told her that she was a witch, and her picture was burnt att London, and he would burne her, and said if he had her son he would make gunpowder of him.

CCLX. EDMOND JOHNSON. A ROMAN CATHOLIC PRIEST.

Dec. 19, 1688. Before Thomas Denton, Esq., Cumberland, *Edmond Johnson*,* *late of Dundalke, in the county of Louth*, saith, that he was borne at Killen, neare Dundalk, and was educated att Reins in Champaigne in France, in the colledge of St. Patrick,

---

* A Romish priest is arrested in Cumberland, and is compelled to give the history of his life. I find that he was in prison in August, 1690, and, probably, he continued in durance much longer. The times were fraught with danger, and every Roman Catholic would be looked upon with suspicion.

In the month of August, 1690, I find the following persons detained in gaol in Cumberland as dangerous and disaffected people. Bryan Mackguier, Matthew Carroll, Edward Plunkett, Phillip Really, Charles Mackdonell, John Davis, John Mackguillim, and Richard Fryan. Wm. Legg, Esq., was also there, having been committed, on suspicion of treason, on August 1, 1689 ; John Standley, an Irishman, was likewise in prison, it being supposed that he was a disaffected person.

There was a true bill found against Thomas Williamson, of Egremont, gen., for inciting sedition at Egremont on June 1, 3 James II.

In 1679 Wm. Huddleston, Chr. Jefferson, and Catherine Blenkinsop, were committed to Appleby gaol for refusing the oath of allegiance. Huddleston took it in the following year.

for three years; afterwards went to Brussels in Flanders, learning devinity with some seculars, where he remain'd about a yeare; then he traveld through Sweden, Denmark, and Norway; from whence he came and arrived att Sheilds, in Northumberland, the 7th instant, and came from thence to Newcastle, and to Mr. Swinburn's of Naferton; from thence to Corby, from whence he came yesterday morning. That he tooke orders of a secular preist from Oliver Plunkett,* titular bishopp of Armaugh, att Arpatrick, fourteen years since, and is now going towards Whithaven in order to goe to his native cuntry.

CCLXI. CUTHBERT GASCARTH, ETC. FOR A BURGLARY.

Dec. 20, 1688. Before Andrew Hudleston, Esq. *Will. Holmes* saith, that, on Sunday night last, the house on the Iland, belonging to the Lord Darwentwater, was broken,† and that, att the instance of one Mary Ratcliff, he was prevailed with to goe about to discover who it was that had done the same. And, goeing towards St. Herbert's Ile, he did discover Cuthbert Gasketh and Ralph Heaton endeavouring to make their escape in a boat from thence, and he did see them throw out of the boat a great number of botles, two runletts with some ale in them, and a chist with some pappers in it, and they were apprehended.

CCLXII. ABRAHAM COSIN. FOR MURDER.

March 11, 1689. Before John Hargreaves, Coroner, at Huddersfield. *Easter Parker, of Dewisbury,*‡ saith that, on Munday

---

* Oliver Plunket, a victim to the persecuting spirit of the times, was executed at Tyburn in July, 1681.

† A burglary at the ancient seat of the Ratcliffes on the Isle. It had been held for the King, during the Civil Wars, by Colonel Philipson, who from his well known and daring exploits earned for himself the soubriquet of Robin the Devil.
  The robbers steal away on the lake, and drop with their prey
  > Down by St. Herbert's consecrated grove.

A chase ensues, and the burglars are seized, having first thrown their plunder into the lake. What a striking and exciting scene it must have been! The men were tried at Carlisle, and escaped with a term of imprisonment.

Gascarth's end was a melancholy one. He was found entangled in a fishing net in Derwentwater, and there were many suspicions of foul play, but nothing was ever proved. A witness came forward at the inquest, and said that she had seen Gascarth pass her window some time after he must have been drowned in the lake! Here is something for those who seek after the supernatural!

‡ A very cruel case. A poor boy comes to Dewsbury very ill. He is kindly treated by some of the villagers, and the constable hires a man to take him on horseback to his

the 28th of February last, James Stancliffe, a boye of about 14 yeares of age, came to this deponent's house in Dewisbury, about daye-gate, and came to the fyer, and desired lodginge, and so shee made him some warme meate, and ordered him to be lodged in the barne, and that he might have strawe enough; and he tolde her, when shee went to him after to see how he was, that he was warme; and hee alsoe told her that he was sicke sometimes, and desired he might be helpt home, for he was not able of himselfe to goe home, his leggs wold not carry him. And, in the next morninge, shee gave him warme meate againe, and shee acquainted the constable and others of the towne how it was with the boye, and the boye lodged the next night at Roger Holgate's in Dewisbury, and she sent him some warme meate; and the constable did order her to sett him a pennyworth of ale by him where he was to lye, that he might drinke it in case he was drye in the night. And the next morninge the constable ordered her to make James some warme meate, and shee did so, and gave it him, and he did eate parte of it, and the residue, beinge the thinne of it, was kept warme for him to drinke on when he went away, and he was not waked withall, that shee knowes of. She heard that the constable did give order to Abraham Cosin to carry the said James to Mirfeild, where he was borne, and she sawe him set on horsebacke, and ropes was tyed to the sadle for him to stay himselff by. And the morninge he went away he desired her to give him a litle cheese and breade to take with him, and she did so.

Jane Holgate, of Dewisbury, sayth, that, on Tuesday the 26th of February, a litle before night, James Stancliff came to her house, and sate him downe, and fell asleepe, and slept about halff an hower; and, a litle after, he went out of doore and the constable and others sought him, and he was found amongst some strawe in Michael Parker fold, and then he went into Parker's house, as she has heard, and then he came to her house. And, presently after, Parker's wife brought him some warme ale, meate, and, after, the constable came and desired her husband to let James staye there all night, and hee wold content them, and they let him lye by the fier-side in an old coverlet, and a quishinge under his heade. And, after they were gone to bed, Michaell Parker wife

home, which was in the parish of Huddersfield. The boy is so unwell that he is actually tied to the saddle. Instead of being sheltered on the road, he is sent on from constable to constable in the most heartless way. The driver of the horse seems to have been a most unfeeling wretch, and the sufferings of the poor child were very great. The tale is a most affecting one.

Cosin lays the blame on the constables, who refused to receive the child. He says that the day was very cold, and that there were many hail-showers. As soon as the boy was taken from the horse he died instantly.

sent a pennyworth of ale for him, and it was brought about nine a'clock. And about twelve a'clocke James wakned, and went forth of the house himselff, and came in againe, and layd him downe. And, after, he made a noyce as though he wold vomit, and she bid her husband rise and turne him to the other side, and he did so, and mended the fyer, and layde more coales on, and James said, "Now it is almost daye." And at daye he rose up, and sat by the fyer, and the constable askt him what he wold have, and he said he wold have some warme ale; and they brought him about a pinte of ale made warme, and James dranke it of; and then the constable asked him how he wold ride, and he said either in a hackney sadle or a pack-sadle. And so Abraham Cosin came into her house and askt James if he might be his man that daye, and James turned his head towards him and smiled. And Easter Parker brought him a white cap, and put it on his head, and gave him some bread and cheese, and then he went out of dore. And shee and her husband askt James severall times in the night time how he did, and hee alwayes said he was not sicke, but he was weake. The constable gave them two pence for his lodginge, and for fier and waytinge on him.

Joseph Allison, of Mirfeild, sayth, that Abraham Cosin came to him, and he had a boye tyed on horsebacke, with a coard about his midle, and tyed in a packe sadle. He was then set astryde. It was about tenn a'clocke afore noone, and it was pretty good weather. The boye spoke pretty hartily, but Cosin sayde they had waked with him all the last night, and he had brought him by vertue of a paper signed by the minister and constable of Dewisbury. This deponent told him he was unwillinge to receive him; and he told him, if he would not receive him, he wold set him downe at his dore, this deponent being constable. He then desired Cosin to goe with the boye to the next constable, and he refused to goe without wage. And this deponent give him 4*d.*, and a pennyworth of ale, and he said he would have another pott when he came backe.

Grace Jepson, of Kirk-heaton, saith, that Abraham Cosin brought a boye on horsebacke to her house, her husband beinge constable, and the boye was then very sicke, and tyed in a packsadle, with a coard, and nothinge but a straw wispe under him, and had very bad cloathes; and she askt the childe why he had no better cloathes, but he cold not speake then, but beinge taken off the horse and warmed, he cold then speake at sometimes, and but seldome, beinge very weake. And this deponent burned him some drinke, but he was not able to drinke it, but desired some small drinke, and drank some of that. And this deponent tolde Cosin that her husband was not at home, and she had nobody to send with the boye to the constable of Dalton, beinge the next constable; and he said he wold carrye him for paye, and demanded a shilling for goinge thither, it beinge but twoe myles. And at last shee agreed to give him nine pence, and some meate, drinke, and tobacco; and then he tooke the boye, and tyed him on the horse backe againe with a coard, he not beinge able to sitt on by himselff. And Cosin went into the house to light his tobacco, and the boye called on him, and said, " Let us goe," and so they went towards Dalton.

Joseph Dyson, of Dalton, yeoman, sayth, that, on Wednesday the 27th, betwixt one and two a'clocke after noone, there came to his house, he beinge constable of Dalton, a man and a boye with him tyed on horse-backe with ropes; and the boye was then so badd, that he did not heare him speake whilest hee was there. And the man said the constable of Mirfield and Kirk-heaton had hyred him, and, if he pleased to hyer him, hee wold carry him to Huddersfield, beinge the next constablery, and demanded 12*d*. for it, beinge but a myle. And this deponent gave him six pence, and, the boye mutteringe some thinge, the man that brought him sayde, " Hold thy tongue, for thou shalt not be taken of, for thow has wanted for nothinge, and it is but a myle thou hast to goe." And the man desired a botle of strawe to lye betwixt the boye and the fore-parte of the sadle to leane on. And he gave it him, and layde it in the sadle himselff, and so they went awaye.

Joshua Eastwood, of Dalton, clothier, sayth, that, on Wednesday last, he sawe a man drivinge a horse with a childe tyed on in a packsadle, and the constable and hee discoursed together, but he heard not what they said; but when he came nere them, hee heard the man say, " If yow and I can agree, yow shall not be troubled with the childe, I'le cary him to the constable of Huddersfeild myselff." And he heard him aske a shillinge of the constable, but they agreed for sixpence. The childe was very sicke and lookt as he wold dye, and the childe desired to be taken off, and the man said, " I had him but off very lately, and he was much made on, and shold have no more till he came at the constable of Huddersfeild." And then he turned the horse downe the folde, and the childe's heade hung downe, first one waye and then another, and wold have falne off, but he was tyed on with coardes. And the man tooke holde on him, and bid him sitt up for he cold ryde well enough, and gave him hard wordes, and told him he shold but goe to Huddersfeild one litle myle, and might goe up by the church-yard-side, and might see the place where he might be buryed. He saw them goe a litle way towards Huddersfeild, and the horse was a bad one and went ill, and he desired the man to get up behinde the boye and holde him on. He heard the man say that the boye had beene aboute a weeke in Dewisbury, and had outrun his master, and was falne sicke there, and said he knew he was very weake, for hee had beene waked twoe nights then last past.

Richard Thewlis, of Huddersfeild, sayth, that Abraham Cosin did bringe a boye on horse-backe to his house, beinge constable of Huddersfeild. Hee was in a packe sadle, and was tyed on with coardes, and was so weake with sicknes that hee cold not hold up his heade, but it hunge below the sadle crutch on the farr side, and some parte of his face did, by the movinge of the horse, knocke against the sadle crutch. And soone after he got James into his dwelling house he dyed.

Marye Shawe, of Huddersfield, sawe a man leadinge a horse at Huddersfeild towne end, and there was a boye on his backe, and, because shee saw his heade hange downe very lowe, she went nere and tooke hold of the boye's hand, and said to the man, "I think this childe is deade;" and he said to her, "Hold of him, and let him alone, for I have but to goe to the constable with him."

CCLXIII. RICHARD DICKINS. FOR SEDITIOUS WORDS.

March 20, 1689. Before Thomas Kitchingham, Mayor, and Wm. Massie, Esq., of Leeds. *James Sinemond, of Leeds, barber*, saith, that, on Sunday night, Mr. Richard Dickins, of Leeds,* attorney-att-law, told him that if Tyrconnell did arive in England with thirty thousand men, he would himselfe add one more to the number. And he said that he had lately beene in the company of himselfe and six more persons, drinking; one of which began a health to the confusion of King William, and he, the said Mr. Dickins, and the rest of the company, did pledge the aforesaid health.

---

* A Leeds lawyer gets into trouble. Tyrconnell was one of the staunchest supporters of James II.

"Dec. 11, 1690. Francis Calvert, of Boroughbridge, gen., sayd, 'I do not vallue King William's authority, nor will I submit to his government.'

"April 9, 1691. George Beckwith, of Potternewton, said that he loved King James, and would be for him, and that he hated King William.

"July 20, 1691. Mr. Peter Peeile, of Ullocke, merchant, being at Cockermouth, John Fallowfeild, mercer, said that King William was a rogue, and he hoped to see his head upon Cripplegate the next time he went to London."

CCLXIV. SARAH CLERK AND OTHERS. FOR MURDER.

April 10, 1689. Before Francis Whyte. *John Walker, of Carnonley, clothworker,** saith, that hee was att the house of Awrelius Clerk, of Batley, yeoman, on Friday the 25th of March, att night, with one Josias Swallow, of Heckmondwike, dyer; and Sarah, wife of the said Awrelius Clerk, did att that time make a contract with them, and proferd to givem (give them) 20s. if they would murther her husband. And they undertooke to performe the same, which they did, comeing into the house that same night in att a back doore, where they mett the said Clerk in an entry, and Swallow struck twice att him with a club, and knockt him downe, and killed him. And the said Sarah ordered them to bury him in the midden, which they did, with all his clothes on. And a while after the body was taken thereout, and conveyed he knows not whither; but this deponent believeth that this was done by Swallow and Sarah Clerk.

Edward Brooke, of Bradford, saith, that, having discourse with Sarah Clarke upon Tuesday the 9th where her husband was, she said that Josias Swallow and one John Walker knockt him in the head, and buried him in the muck-midding till Sunday morneing after; and that morneing the said Swallow tooke him out of the midding, and carryed his body on horseback before him, and threw him into the deep pitt att Carlinghow shayes, and there this informant might finde him.

CCLXV. GEORGE DENTON, ESQ., AND OTHERS. FOR HIGH TREASON.

May 9, 1689. Before Thomas Denton, Esq. *Thomas Pingney, of Brumfeild-raw, co. Cumberland, mason*, saith, that, upon Thursday the 18th of Aprill last, George Denton,† late of Cardew,

---

" April 20, 1692. Benjamin Hudson, of Bridlington, said, ' Here's a good health to King James, and here's a good health to the Prince of Wales.' "

* The record of a frightful crime. A woman deliberately hires two men to murder her husband, and all the persons implicated acknowledge their guilt, apparently without the slightest compunction.

† Some account of the movements of the Jacobites in Cumberland. A rising was evidently intended, but it was nipped in the bud. The information contained in these depositions is entirely new. There was a strong spirit of disaffection in the North long before the rising of 1715. Sir Richard Graham, Viscount Preston, was tried for high treason in 1691, and some years afterwards Sir John Fenwick died upon the scaffold. Their names, it will be observed, are mentioned in these depositions.

Esq. desired this informant to go along with him into Northumberland, and had borrowed a horse for him, but desired him to go to Mr. Joseph Read's in Carlisle for 3*l*., and to meet him at the dubb at Warwick-briggs, whether this informant came before Mr. Denton came thither. Soe this informant went to meet him as farr as Carleton-thwaite, where he met the said Mr. Denton and Mr Graham of Newbiggin, with Thomas Bowman, who had Mr. Denton's sword under his coat. So this informant and Tom Bowman went on with the said Mr. Denton to the dubb, where Mr. Denton put on his sword when it was night, and desired a guide. So young Wm. Nicholson of Newby did guide him to Robert Graham's of the Bush, beyond Longtown; and Robert Graham guided him the next day to Haggtown to his brother George Graham's, where they mett with four gentlemen, who treated him there, and allmost fuddled him. Then Robert Graham carried him from thence to Mowesknoue, where he should have stayd, but there had been so many gentlemen before that time that there was no provision left for horse nor man. So they went on to Allison's bank; and the next morning Mr. Denton came back with this informant to Robert Graham's, where above a dozen gentlemen were to dine that day. And he desired one of those gentlemen to lend this informant his horse to guide him over Esk, for they had all large trooping horses, with pistalls and all accoutrements for warr, and were at least 60 in number, as Mr. Denton desired the informant to tell William Lowther. So this informant came to Carlisle to Mr. Reed for 10*l*., which if he sent him, he would trouble him no more. So Mr. Reed sent him about 6*l*. in dollers, which this informant carried him the Thursday following to Allison's bank. And Mr. Denton sent this informant back for 5*l*. more, but Mr. Reed said he would see him the Munday following, and would not then furnish him with any more money, though he had a trunk full of linen in pawn. And the said Mr. Denton desired this informant to bring him his pistolls from Dalston hall (where they yet are), but he refused. He saith that one Anth. Haldin, who rode in the late King's guards, had a case of pistolls, holsters and breastgirth at Dalston hall, and a sword at Elizabeth Riddal's. And Mr. Denton maintained the said Haldin, and left half a crown for him at Durdar when he went into Scotland. And Haldin had gone to him into Scotland on Munday last if Mr. Denton had not been taken the day before. Haldin came divers times to this informant to desire him to show him the way to Mr. Denton at Allison's bank, who harbours about John Sowerbie's in Brownelston, and sometimes at Tho. Blaylock, butcher in

Botcherd-gate. And Mr. Denton did desire this informant to speak to William Lowther to come to him, but he would not.

Anthony Alldin, late of Swallow-street in St. James's parish, London, saith, that he was born at Hingham in Norfolk, and had dwelt in London about twelve years, part of which time he was a servant, and afterwards an alehouse-keeper, till within this three years, that he was listed in the Duke of Albemarl's troop of granadeers in the King's guards. At which time he was then a Protestant, and was brought over to the Roman Catholick religion about two years since by some preists with whom he had been acquainted in France. And he was turned out of service when the late King James discerted the government, for being a Roman Catholique, and was since then in London, untill the later end of March, when he came by sea to Newcastle, and so to Carlisle, upon that Saturday when the Lord Preston gave an alarum to this garrison. Since then he hath been in Dalston parish, where he saw George Denton, Esq. with whom he was acquainted in London, and hath been divers times in his company at Dalston-hall, where Mr. Denton payd his reckonings; but he never gave him any money, save that he left half a crown to be drunk at Thomas Bowman's at Durdar. And after the said George Denton was gone into Scotland, this ex^t did enquire of Thomas Pingney, his guide, where he was, and would have been glad to see him, and said, if the said Thomas went back to the said George, that he would have gone along with him, to see him and to drink with him. But denies that he was to be listed as a soldier for the late King, or that the said George Denton did invite him into the Border.

He, further, saith, that he hearing in London that the late King James was in Ireland, and was comeing into Scotland, so he thought to come into this country, and brought his pistolls down, and thought to get a horse and saddle here, and so to enter into that service again.* And Thomas Pinkney told him that

---

* A passage which recalls the beautiful old Jacobite ballad:

"It was all for my rightful King
   I left my native strand,
It was all for my rightful King
   I e'er saw Irish land.

The trooper turn'd him round about
   Upon the Irish shore,
He gave his bridle reins a shake,
   Said 'Adieu for evermore,
               My love!
And adieu for evermore!'"

Mr. Georg Denton and they upon the Borders would speak with him. He answer'd that he would go, but would not stay.

Feb. 23, 1690-1. Before Thomas Denton, Esq. *John Storie, of Bewcastle, gentleman*, saith that he knows nothing of any intended conspiracy upon the Borders of England and Scotland the last summer, nor at any time before or since, by any person or persons, to levy warre against King William and Queen Mary or the Government established, but onely what the generall report of the countrey was, that divers gentlemen of the Borders were mett together near Cissenbury-craggs, to the number of sixty. And sometimes it was said they were an hundred persons; but, upon enquiry made of the inhabitants nearest adjacent to that place, he could not finde that there was any truth in those reports. And he saith that he never saw the Lord Preston but twice, when he was last in Cumberland, the last summer was a 12 month, for when he then came, he mett him near the abbey-miln at Lanercost with Sir John Fenwick. And his Lordshipp desired this informant to guide him to Kirkandrews, which he did, and stayd there all night. And he went to waite upon his Lordshipp there a little before he went into Yorkshire, but he never heard his Lordshipp speak one sylable of any treasonable matters. And he hath not received a letter from his said Lordshipp this three years, nor from his brother Collonell James Graham; nor hath he corresponded with his said brother this seaven years.

CCLXVI. AN UNKNOWN PERSON. FOR MURDER.

May 11, 1689. Before Thomas Allgood, Esq., one of the Coroners for Northumberland. At an inquest sitten att Gunnerton, upon view of the body of Wm. Brearcliffe alias Braidclyffe, late of Farrburne in the parish of Brotherton in the county of Yorke, gen., who was yesterday found upon Gunnerton-fell.

Edward Shaftoe, of Gunnerton, gen., saith that hee goeing out into Gunnerton moores a gunning,* very early yesterday morning, upon the breake of day, at a place called Stone-gapps in Gunnerton moores, hee see two gray maires, both sadled and bridled, and the one of their bridles tyed to the other's sturrup-iron. And, seeing none near the said maires, hee brought them to the common

---

* An account of a very mysterious murder among the Northumbrian moors. The description possesses all the interest of a romance. It does not appear that the murderer was ever discovered. The evidence of Mr. Shafto was confirmed by two others of the same name, William and Arthur Shafto, of Gunnerton, gentlemen.

pinfold of Gunnerton, and putt them therein. After which hee called of his brother, William Shaftoe, and told him they would goe and see if they could see the owners of the said maires. And, rideing on the said moore to a place called Whitley Knoake, being further on the moore and higher then ordinary, they hollowed there to know if any would answere them. And, goeing northward on the said hill, they heard a voice of a man crying out " Help, for Christ Jesus' sake !" and wished hee had but a man to speake to him before he dyed. Whereupon this informant and his brother goes northward to a burne side, and hee spoake over the burne and asked him what the matter was, and what hee wanted. Who replyed hee wanted nothing but a man to speake to him before hee dyed, for he was a dyeing man. And this informer askeing him how, or by whome, he said there was a rogue had shott and murdered him. This informant asked him if he knew him that did soe; and he said, Yes, he knew him well enough. And askeing him what they called him, he answered " Roger." This informant asked him if he knew his surname; he said noe, he did not, but one Mr. Errington, of the Linnells, knew him well enough, and could give a better account of him than hee, hee being once the said Mr. Errington's servant. And this informant and his brother rode through the burne, and went to the place where he was lyeing waltering in his owne blood. This informant said, " Sir, what's the matter with you?" and he said he was shott and murdered by a rogue. This informant asked him if the rogue had gott any money from him, and he said he had gott two guinnies, one silver watch, one crowne peice of silver, three or four shillings, his crivitt and sleeves. This informant askeing him if he had not a hatt, hee said, noe, he had not a hatt, but he had a velvett capp, which the rogue was gone with. This informant asked him if he had noe spurrs, and he said, " Oh dear, is he gone with my spurrs too?" And findeing a part of a pistoll stock, this informant said, " Sir, here's a peice of a pistoll stocke:" and he, " Oh dear, hee had two pistolls." And this informant, searching among the hather, found the stock and lock of the other pistoll, and asked him how the rogue came by the pistolls; who replyed, " Mr. Errington lent him them before they came away." And this informant asked how he came to be soe farr out of the way, and he said they were goeing up to the high-lands to see the rogue's mother. And the maires were both his owne, and he lent the rogue one to ride one, and now hee's gone with them both. The rogue pretended himselfe to be sleepy and weary, and had a desire that they should light and rest themselves a litle, and when they came and lay downe, the deceased lyeing on his belly with his head upon his arme, never feareing anything, the said Roger shott him in at his back betwixt his shoulders. And after he had shott him he fell upon, beating and cutting of his head in severall places with the pistolls. And he prayed him for Christ Jesus sake not to beat or cutt his head with the pistolls, and he would quitt him all that he had in the world freely, but the rogue said he would not; of which shott and wounds the said deceased dyed.

CCLXVII. EDWARD CHARLTON, ESQ. FOR TREASON.

"Mr. Hodgson,*—My brother Jake is not yet comed home, but this week we exspect him. As sonne as he comse I will sind mony for the hatte. As for news, we heare that six thusand

---

* Mr. Charlton, of Hesleyside, in Northumberland, the head of an ancient Border family, is charged with spreading false news. A letter had been intercepted, which he was supposed to have written. He was arrested in virtue of the following order from Lord Shrewsbury:—

"Whitehall, 22 June, '89.

"Sir,—I send you here inclosed a letter writt, as is said, by one Mr. Charleton, at whose house in Northumberland several disaffected persons are observed to meet. The person to whom it is writt is already committed by my Lord Lumley upon another account. You are to apply to the next justice of peace for his assistance in examining the said Charleton, when he is apprehended, concerning the contents of this letter, and I doubt not but there will be sufficient reason to secure him likewise; at least, to bind him over to answer this false and seditious news at the next sessions. You will send me a copy of his examinations.—I am, Sir, your faithfull humble servant,

SHREWSBURY.

"Coll. Fitzwilliam (Heyford), or Commander-in-chief at Newcastle."

Mr. Hodgson and Mr. Charlton were Roman Catholics and Jacobites. Some account of Mr. Hodgson has been already given.

Political and religious feeling ran very high in Northumberland during the reigns of James II. and William and Mary. In 1687 seven Roman Catholic gentlemen were placed upon the commission of peace, *i. e.*, Sir Nicholas Sherburn, Edward Charlton, Ralph Clavering, John Errington, Thomas Riddell, Charles Selby, and James Wallis, Esqrs., and in 1688, Sir Wm. Creagh, another Roman Catholic, was made Mayor of Newcastle, by royal mandate. At this time the insignia of the city, "the cap, the the mace, and the sword, were one day carried to the church, another day to the Roman Catholic chapel, and on the third to the dissenting meeting-house."

In November, 1688, Newcastle welcomed Lord Lumley with open arms, and declared for the Prince of Orange. The splendid equestrian statue of James II. was torn from its pedestal and was thrown into the Tyne. I have seen a deposition about this affair at York, but it was too much mutilated to be deciphered. The Roman Catholic gentry were now under a cloud. They were subjected to domiciliary visits, and treated with a severity that would, no doubt, induce many of them to enter into the Jacobite plots of the period.

Mr. Charlton's offence was spreading false and dangerous news, which the ruling powers were always anxious to suppress.

In 1685, Wm. Drake, Esq., of Barnoldswick, co. York, a justice of the peace, was

of K. J. forsis sartainly landed at Kintir in the Hiylands. They prist all bots and visills in K. J. name to goe back for Ierland for more forsis, and they are gon, and the rist following fast. Allso there master, whoe sartanly lands in Skotland. The K. standerd will be set up be the end of May. Fortty thusand Frinch landed in Ierland. All this from a good hand, so it is sartanlye credetted by all, which is all I can tell you in this, other ways wod say more. You wod dissire to here the new landed forsis is with Clavours and Makdonills and Makeleanes, who joyns together; and we hear that K. J. has made the lord of Macklane Earl of Argille. This is all I have time to say. We exspet souldgers heare this night or to morrow, for we hear they have bine in most plasis, and has got severall horsis out of Quokit, and five horsis from Mr. Howard.* Y^r sar^{tt} ——

"Pray sind me too botells of your vere bist Rinnis, and two botells of whit wine, the bist you have. The clarred was so bad as we weare forst to sind for better, but I emadgen you had noo better. Lit the Rinnis and whit wine be the bist you have. Sind me 3 bottells of your bist mum to be had.

In dorso.—" *For Mr. Allbertt Hodyshon, in Newcashill.*"

July 1, 1689. Before Sir Robert Fenwick, of Bywell, Kt. *Edward Charlton*,† *of Hesslyside, Esq.*, saith, that the letter shewn to him is not of this ex^{ts} hand, nor did he know anything of the writeing thereof, or who writ the same. He did not, nor doth keepe any person or persons aboute his house, or in his family, that gave or gives any disturbance to the present government, to his knowledge.

CCLXVIII. ROBERT JEFFERSON. FOR SEDITIOUS WORDS.

July 5, 1689. Before Sir Robert Fenwick, Kt. *Wm. Ashburne, of Hexham, gentleman,* saith, that he heard one Robert

charged with this offence. He was, however, in so infirm a state of health, that no notice was taken of his words.

"An indictment against Leonard Ash, of Knaresbro', clerk, for saying, on the 16th of August, 1695, at Boro'bridge, 'The towne of Namur is retaken by the French, and forty thousand French fell upon our foot and cut off a great many of them, but some of our horse broak through them and scampered away.'"

* Probably Charles Howard, of Overacres, in Redesdale.

† A nephew of Sir Edward Charlton, of Hesleyside, Bt. who raised a troop of horse for Charles I., and whose estates were sequestered by the Parliament. He married, in 1680, Margaret, daughter of Sir Francis Salkeld, of Whitehall, in Cumberland. Mr. Charlton died in 1710, aged 50. His widow survived him, and died at York in 1729. E. C.

Jefferson, of Hexham, say that there was a great rogury done in Whitehall to King James. And being askt who had done it or what it was, he said that the Prince of Orange took downe all his rich hangings, both their and in other places, and had carryed them to some place to be transported into Holland, which was robbery. And that he had robd Whitehall of King James' plait, and had smelted itt, and some of itt had coyned into money, and the rest he made into piggs like lead and sent itt into Holland, and he hoped that he would follow it himselfe or long.

CCLXIX. MR. RICHARD JACKSON. FOR SEDITIOUS WORDS.

Aug. 4, 1689. Before Richard Patrickson, Esq. *Mr. John Stevens, quarter-master in L^t. Coll. Leryson's troope of dragoons in the Queen's regiment*, saith that, on Friday, being in company with Mr. Richard Jackson, schoolemaster of St. Beese,* the said Mr. Jackson did suddenly rise upp from his seate, and askte him who he was for. He replyed he was for King William; but Mr. Jackson said he was for King James. And being askte by this ex^t if he knew what he said, Mr. Jackson answered he did, and clapeing his hand on the table said he woo'd stand by it soe longe as he had a drope of blood in his body. And he further said itt was noe treason to drinke King James' health.

CCLXX. TEDY MURFEW. FOR SEDITIOUS WORDS.

Oct. 25, 1689. *John Wiggins, of Bramham,*† being at John

---

* The master of the endowed school at St. Bees avows himself a Jacobite in the presence of some soldiers, who make him their prisoner.

† An Irish soldier is committed to York Castle for speaking treason. On Feb. 26, 1689-90, an Irishman of the name of Brian O'Brian, was examined before Sir William Lowther, being charged with treason. A scrap of paper was found upon him containing the addresses of eleven Roman Catholics, among whom were the names of Mr. Gascoigne, of Parlington, and Mr. Scrope, of Danby. There is given with the deposition a printed proclamation, which was in the possession of the prisoner, "From his most sacred majesty, King James the Second, to all his most loving subjects in the Kingdom of England," dated from Dublin Castle, May 8, 1689. The man was, in all probability, engaged in some Jacobite plot. He gives the following account of himself.

"Bryan O'Bryan sayeth that he hath been employed in worke in the county of York for a whole yeare past, and that he was goeing to Esq. Rookeby's to Morton, or Mr. Watterton, or to Sir Henry Slingsby's to Red house, there to be employed att one of those places; and the late King's declaration being found about him, he sayeth he had it from one Elizabeth Maskey, a servant to Mr. Watterton of Wallton, who, he says, was reading of it."

Smith's, heard two persons very abusive, and said that they would serve King James: upon which they were conveyed before Sir Thomas Armitage to his house at Biggin, and one of them, who calls himselfe Tedy Murfew, did assawlt and beat the deponent upon his breast with his staff, and said that he would fight for King James as long as he lived.

Tedy Murfew, of Crumlin, near Dublin, soldier,—had been a soldier under the late King James here in England, and arrived in this kingdom Oct. the 5th, 1688, and that he had been a begger up and down the contrey ever since the late King went away, but if he had his liberty he would live upon his calling, fencing and dancing. He was drunk, and could not tell what he said and did. He is a Roman Catholic.

CCLXXI. THE LAIRD OF STABLETON. FOR SEDITIOUS WORDS.

Dec. 26, 1689. Before James Nicholson, Esq., Maior of Carlisle. *Mrs. Jane Wallas* saith, that, on Tuesday last, three persons (whose names this informer does not well know, but one of them is the Laird of Stableton and one other, his brother, the Laird of Stanke), were drinking at her house, and desired this informer to sit downe and drinke with them; and the person who had a laced coat, and who is called Laird of Stableton, began the King's health. This informer said she would pledge King William's health; the said Laird of Stableton asked who she meant of, whether or noe it was not the Prince of Orange, and whether he was brought in by God or the people? and further said he knewe no King but King James. This informer replyed she hop'd King William would be shortly in Scotland, and then they would all owne him. Upon which Laird Stableton answered, that if King William went into Scotland he should find hot comeing thither.

CCLXXII. ROBERT GRAHAM. FOR HIGH TREASON.

May 10, 1690. Before Thomas Denton and John Briscoe, Esqrs. *Thomas Lund, a private soldier in Capt. Wolf's company in Carlisle garrison*, saith that, upon Tuesday last, and at severall times before, one Robert Graham, of Gariston,[*] gentleman, did

---

[*] A Cumberland gentleman is charged with treason. He has been already mentioned in No. cclxiv., and it is evident that he was a strong Jacobite. It would be curious to know something more about Thomas Lund. Was he at all related to the

tell this informant that King William was an outcomelin rebell, and had banished the right King from his crown and dignitie; and he hoped to see King James sett in his throne before Martinmas day next: and he told me that we were all rebells both to the King and his government. And the said Graham would gladly have perswaded this informant to desert his colours, and to go along with him to Brecon hill, or to Dilston, to the Earl of Derwentwater's,* if he had a minde, that he might thence get safe into Lancashire (being this informant's countrey); and that he would take five Grahams to himselfe, who would beat all the souldiers in Rowcliffe and Gargoe into the citty's gates at Carlisle; and that fifteen thousand men were comeing out of the Scotch Hylands towards Sterling, and that they would beat us into the hole like rogues as we were. And further saith that upon notice of a party going out of Carlisle, one John Goodfellow† of Rowcliffe got upon a black mare and rode to Robert Graham's house to Garistown and bid him begone, for there was mischeife against him; whereupon he fled to the moor, where he was taken, haveing, before the party came, conveyd away his armes, vizt., 4 swords and 2 guns.

Robert Graham, of Garistown, saith, that he was a trooper in Scotland under Captain Clavers, late Lord Dundee, about seaven yeares since. He knows one Thomas Lund, who was quartered at his brothers, and the said Lund came thither on Tuesday night much concern'd in drink, and began to abuse the house, till this ex^t rebuked him for it; whereupon the said Lund did threaten to pull out a pistall and to shoot this ex^t. Denies that they had any discourse concerning King William or King James.

man who took so prominent a position in the well-known Lancashire plot? The Grahams, during this century, were the most turbulent family in Cumberland.

* It is most interesting to see how the Jacobites in the North were beginning, even now, to regard the head of the house of Radcliffe as their leader. Five and twenty years after this the son of the nobleman who is here mentioned lost his life and his estates, and, in the words of the touching ballad, bade

> " Farewell to pleasant Dilston Hall,
>   My father's ancient seat!
> A stranger now must call thee his,
>   Which gars my heart to greet!"

The memory of this high-spirited and ill-fated nobleman is still cherished in the North with affectionate regret. Every relic of the rising and its leader has been most carefully treasured up. I have had in my hands one of the white cockades that was mounted in the insurrection.

† Goodfellow denies giving any information, and says that he went to Mr. Graham's house at Garistown " to desire liberty to grave stacks in his ground."

GLOSSARY.

ANCIENT-BEARER, 1. The bearer of a flag, or ensign. "Saul and his *ancients*." "Phillop Grondye the *anncient*."—*Eccl. Proc.* 222.

BATT, 84. ? a gut. A bate in Craven is a fibre of wood.

BEATMENT, 194. A measure containing about a quarter of a peck. Common in the North.

BEDSTOOPE, 65. One of the principal timbers in a bed that runs into the posts or stocks. The thin laths or spars that run across the bed from one stoop to another were called bedstaves.—*Eccl. Proc. Durham*, 1630.

BILL, 85, 128. A halbert-shaped piece of iron with a hook at the end, used by hedgers and countrypeople. Called a *broome-hooke*, 128, and a *watch-bill*, 128, 284. In the latter case it is the ordinary pike or halbert used by the officer of the Corporation of Ripon.

BOATE, boote. A-S. help, aid.

"What is good for a *bootlesse* bene?" She answered, "Endless sorrow."

BODDELLS, 217. A small brass coin worth about the 3rd of a half-penny. They have the Scottish thistle on them, and were very common in the North in the 17th century.

BOTLE, 289. A small bundle or wisp. "To seek a needle in a *bottle* of hay."

BRABLER, 10. A quarreller.—*Cf. Eccl. Proc. Dunelm.*, 259.

"In private *brabble* did we apprehend him."
    (Twelfth Night, Act v. Sc. 1.)

BRACHET, 161, 162. A little dog used for scenting and hunting—perhaps a terrier or spaniel. It calls to mind the little brachet of La Beale Isoud that recognised Sir Tristram in his madness.—*Cf. Morte d'Arthur*, 1, 343.

BUNCH, 10. To beat. A word still common in the North.

CADDOW, 205. A woollen covering or blanket.

CADGEINGS, 209. The edges.—*Cf. Wright.*

CAST, 127. To examine.

CHEEKE, 46. The posts of a door, the side posts.

CHURCH-LAY, 66. A church rate or cess. Common in the North. Office against Humphrey Dalton, "He denyeth to pay 2d. for his *churche-lay*."—*Ealand*, 1586.

COLLER, 3. Choler, anger.

CORONETT, 16. A cornet.

CRACKS, 204. Boasting or bragging.

"Æthiops of their sweet complexion *crack*."—(Love's Labour Lost, Act iv. Sc. 3.)

CROPP, 31. A Roundhead.

"Kentish Sir Byng stood for his King, Bidding the *crop-headed* Parliament swing."

CROSSING, 188. Angry or contradictious.

CUSTRELL, 85 n. A beggar, a pitiful wretch.

"He's a coward and a *coystril* that will not drink to my neice."
    (Twelfth Night, Act i. Sc. 3.)

CUTTERS, 35. Highwaymen, or robbers.

DAYGATE, 287. Sunset. "About *daygate* he found the barn-doore open."—*Durham Chancery Papers*, 1675.

DEAD, 192. In a fit or swoon.

DEARD, 52. Frightened or injured.

DISENABLED, 113. Disabled.

DISTEMPERED, 37. Distracted or disordered. "*Distempered* with drinck." —*Court Papers, Durham*, 1607.

"It is but as a body yet *distemper'd*." (Hen. IV., Act iii. Sc. 1.)

DITHERING, 29. Shaking, trembling. In 1678 Thoresby was sick of the ague "not only with the *dithering*, but a violent pain in the back of my head."—*Diary*, i. 23.

DOCKEN, 69. The dock.

DUBB, 292. A reach, or piece of still water in a river. A pond. In 1624 Isabel Walker called Ralph Blakeston "Popish rogue and Popish rascall, and said the devill and he danced in a *dubb* together."—*Eccl. Proc. Durham*.

DUNES, 151. ?

EARNED, 9 n, 38. To curdle.

"Since naething awa, as we can learn, The kirns to kirn, and milk to *earn*."

FANONES, 4. ?

FASTENES, 230. Shrove-tide.—*Cf. Eccl. Proc. Durham*, 69. 87, 308.

FAUCHETT, 275. A sword, or faulchion.

FIRE-POITE, 51. A poker.—*Craven Glossary*.

FLACKETT, 194. A flask, or wood-bottle.

FLAWTER, 154. To flap. In the North, *flacker*, hodie.

FORESWORNE, 226, 269. Perjured. A true bill against Wm. Whaley of Appleby, for saying on Jan. 10, 28 Car. II., to Robert Westmerland, "Thou art a *forsworne* fellow, and I will prove it."—*York Castle Papers*.

"Your oath once broke, you force not to *forswear*." (Love's Labour Lost, Act V. Sc. 2.)

FOX-THATCHER, 155. ? an earth-stopper.

FRONTSTEAD, 285. The front of a house.

GAPSTEAD, 29. A gap, or hole in a hedge.

GARR, 151. To make.

"A stranger now must call thee his, Which *garrs* my heart to greet."

GAVELOCKES, 110, 223. Crowbars. A common word in the North.

GILL, 148, 9. A small wooded glen, generally with a stream running through it.

GRANADO, 19, 47, n. A grenade. —*Wright*.

GRAVE, 300, n. To cut or dig.

GRIPTE, 129. Grasped, seized hold of. A common word.

HANKT, 193, 197. Hooked or fastened. Still in use, "*hanking* fish."

HARNES, 186, 7. The brains.

HEADED, 73. Beheaded.

HOUGH, 202. A heel or foot.

ILL, 8. Bad, evil. "She had many *ill* fitts.—*Eccl. Proc. Durham*, 1616.

IMY, 30. White, recking. Ime in the North is hoar frost.

KEBDS. Rogues, villains.—*Wright*.

KENING, 194. Half a bushel.

KETCH, 41. A keel or barge.—*Cf. Gloss. to York Fabric rolls*.

KIDDS, 229. Faggots.

LEE, 30. Urine.—*Wright*.

LOOKT, 192, 209. Knotted or tied. This was thought to be the work of witches or fairies, and the knot placed the victim in their power. Of these elf-locks, *cf. Rokeby*, canto iv, *the Scottish ballad of the Witch Mother*—

O wha has loos'd the nine witch-knots, That was amang that lady's locks." —and *Romeo and Juliet*.

LYKE, 258. Seemingly, to all appearance.

MALL, 25. Mail. A trunk or portmanteau.

MART, 260, 1. Market. "He gave them one ox to make a *mart* upon."—*Eccl. Proc. Durham*, 1572.

MEDICER, 93, 196 A mediciner, or quack doctor.

MIDDEN, 291. A dunghill. Very common.

MISTALL, 29. A cowhouse or byar. At Cumberworth, in 1671, "a lath sett on fire and burned downe to the ground, with the *mistulls* and other outhouscinge adjoyninge."—*York Castle Papers*.

MUM, 297. A kind of liquor.

NAKED, 185. Unarmed.

NAUGHT, 126 n, 282. Generally lascivious or lewd.

OR, 298. Before. "And the lions brake all their bones in pieces *or* ever they came to the bottom of the den."

OUTCOMELIN, 300. A stranger. In 1621 a person calls the vicar of Heddon "an *outcome* lad."—*Eccl. Proc. Durham.*

OVERGONE, 65. Hurt or injured.

PAUSE, 32. To strike or beat. παιω.
PEECE, 49 n. A piece with. Akin to.
PILLOWBEARE, 28. A pillow-case.
PINCK, 273. A small vessel with a narrow straight stern.—*Wright.*
PIPE, 32. An issue or abscess.
PRODED, 163. Punched or poked. A common word.

QUEAN, 163. A young girl; occasionally used in a bad sense. A Scottish word.

RECEPTOR, 157. A receiver, "a *recettor* of theives."—*Eccl. Proc. Durham,* 1575.
REFORMADO, 33 (*Span.*) An officer, who, for some disgrace, was deprived of his command, but retained his rank.—*Wright.*
REPPILLS, 141. Scratches or slits.
ROCK, 197. A distaff.
ROWD, 218. Worked in rows.
RUND, 189 n. Clipped or rounded.

SACKLESS, 124 n, 248. Innocent.
SHEYLL, 155, 156 n. A rude hovel for fishermen or shepherds,—*unde North and South Shields.*

SILLT, 191. The food used by witches, dwarfs, fairies, &c.
SKREAKED, 76, 142. Shrieked or screamed.
SLOTTS, 49. The sliding bolts or bars that run across a door from wall to wall.
SLOUTHS, 153. Sleuths, or the pursuit of robbers; generally made with dogs that were called sleuth-hounds.
SMOTHERED, 153. Concealed from.
SPRING, 229. A young wood or plantation.
STAGGS, 148-9. Young horses.
STEIME, 210. To order or buy.
STOWLED, 6. Cut off, or perhaps drilled through.
SWATTLE, 186. To splash or rise in the water. Ducks are said to *swattle* when they are drinking.

TABLED, 260-1. To have one's table or board.

WAGGE, 28. Beckon.
WAKED, 288-90. To watch or sit up all night with. Generally with a sick person or a corpse.

"The watchman *waketh* but in vain."

WALKER, 275. A fuller.
WAME-TOW, 100, 226. A girth. The belly-band of a horse.
WANDED, 40, 56. Covered with wickerwork, like a flask.
WELLKED, 156. Spotted or marked.
WHIGHEN, 209. The mountain ash. The rowan-tree, which witches hated.
WOOL-FELLS, 97. Sheepskins.

YAITE, 56. A gate.

INDEX OF NAMES.

N. B. *The letter* n *after the Number of the page refers to the Note.*

A.

Abbey, Robert, 167
Abbott, Eliz., 237, 237 *n*., 238; Richard, 84
Acaster, Thos., 16
Acklam, Alice, 123; Ellen, 168; George, 123; Eliz., wife of, 123; George, jun. 123; Margt., wife of, 123; John, 222; Peter, 87; Robt., 168; Sarah, 123; Thos., Anne wife of, 123
Acklom, Peter, 129 *n*
Ackman, Robt., 136; Eliz., wife of, 123
Acres, Akers, John, 177
Adam, Robt., 122; Anne, wife of, 122
Adams, Mathew, 20; Wm. esq., 58, 78 *n*., 117
Adamson, Anthony, 122, 182; Henry, 122, 182; Eliz., wife of, 122, 182; Joseph, 110; Margt., 182
Adcock, Nicholas, 181
Adcocke, Wm., 88 *n*
Addison, Francis, 248; Thos., 133; Rebecca, wife of, 133; Wm., 140; Mary, wife of, 140
Agarr, Eliz., 131 *n*., 132
Aglionby, John, esq., 162
Ainsly, Aynsley, Aynsly, Michael, 191, 194, 197; Margt., wife of, 191, 194, 197
Airey, George, 275 *n*
Aisker, Chr., 180
Aislaby, Barbara, 121; Aislabye, Mr. Geo., 210 *n*., 211, 211 *n*., 212, 213; Miss, 210 *n*.; Robt., 120
Akeman, Robt., 183
Akroyd, Thos., 87 *n*
Albemarle, Duke of. 277, 277 *n*., 293
Alcocke, James, 171, 181; Anne, wife of, 171, 181
Alder, Dorothy, 207; Henry, 268 *n*.; Wm., 277
Alderson, Chr. 147 *n*.; Helen, 147 *n*.; George, 147, 149, 149 *n*.; James, 147; John, 147, 148 *n*., 149

Alford, Arthur, 144
Algood, Eliz., 227
Allan, Rich., 115; William, 27
Allanson, Eliz., 88 *n*.; Francis, esq., 67; Robt., clerk, 32; Wm. 245 *n*., 269 *n*.;
Alldin, Haldin, Anthony, 292, 293
Allen, Anthony, 137, 183; Anne, wife of, 137, 183; Francis, 284; George, 183, 269 *n*., 272; Eliz., wife of, 137, 183; Ellen, wife of, 181; James, 181; Anne, wife of, 181; John of Ravensworth, 183; Eliz., wife of, 181; Mark, 183; Anne, wife of, 183; Nicholas, 137, 183; Valentine, 183
Allenson, Anne, 87 *n*.; Eliz., 168; Sir Wm., 1
Allerton, Lockley, 30 *n*.; Rob., 32
Alleyn, John, 120; Alice, wife of, 120
Allgood, Mr. Thos., 294
Allinson, Barth., 87 *n*
Allison, Joseph, 288; Thos., 94 *n*
Allyson, Rob., 84
Ambler, Mr., 227 *n*
Ambrey, Roger, 189
Anderson, Catharine, 227; Eliz., 207; Ellen, 136; James, 197; Kath., 207; Margaret, 183; Matthew, 207; Rob., 206, 227; Trinian, 136, 183; Eliz., wife of, 136, 183
Anderton, Christiana, 235, 236; Henry, 236
Andrew, Isabel, 194
Andrewes, John, 240, 240 *n*., 241, 270
Anlaby, John, esq., 53
Ansley, Ralph, 180
Anthony, Chas., Vicar of Catterick, 160, 160 *n*
Anwood, Will., 261
Apleby, Appleby, Anne, 168; Andrew, 168; Anthony, 171, 180; Jane, wife of, 180; Edmund, 265, 266, 267; Dorothy, 180; Gabriel, 183; Galfrid, 171; Mary, wife of, 171; George, 168; Jas., esq. 263 *n*., 267; Mark, 137, 183; Marmaduke, 171; Thos., 139; Eliz., wife of, 139

x

INDEX OF NAMES.

Appleton, Nicholas, 121; Mary, wife of, 121; Rob. 121; Thos, 120; Mary, wife of, 120
Appleyard, Mary, 166
Archer, Will., 52, 53
Ardsey, John, 73
Argyle, Argile, Earl of, 273, 273 n., 274, 274 n.; 297
Arlington, Lord, 146 n
Armitage, Sir John, 86 n., 87, 97, 100, 126, 141, 146, 164, 164 n., 165 n; Lady Margaret, 165 n.; Mich., esq., 164; Rob., 263 n.; Sir Thos., 299; Wm., esq., 12
Armstrong, Armestrong, Armestrange, Anne, 155, 191, 192, 193, 197, 199, 200, 201; Jenkin, 153; Jo., 156, 227; Mary, 237 n.; Thos. 227; Margaret, wife of, 227
Arrington, 27 n
Arrundell, Kath., 235; Lord, 233, 236
Ash, Leonard, 297 n
Ashborne, Thos., 121
Ashburne, Rob., 219, 219 n.; Wm. esq., 297
Ashby, Ashbie, Capt. Alex.; 17, 17 n.; Major, 14 n., 15, 18
Ashmore, Anne, 96
Ashton, Edward, 178 n.; Dr. Robt., 33, 36, 36 n., 37, 38
Assheton, John, esq., 64, 232, 233, 235.
Askew, Chr. and wife, 171
Askwith, Chr. and wife, 138; John, and wife, 179; Thomasin, 179; Will., 111
Aslaby, Thos., 89 n
Aston, John, Eliz., wife of, 52
Asswall, Aswall, Thos, 264, 265
Atcheson, Isab., 125
Atking, Peter, 268; Margaret, wife of, 268
Atkins, widow, 95
Atkinson, ———, 115, 153
Atkinson, Alice, 133; Cecily, 137, 183; Diana, 171; Dinah, 180; Eliz., 181, 227; Edward, 133; Francis, 148 n.; Geo., 145, 148. n; Henry, esq., 217; Henry, 171, 180; Anne, wife of, 171, 180; James, 53 n.; John, esq., mayor of Appleby, 276; John, 180, 269 n.; John (of Eppleby), 163; Margt., wife of, 163; Mary, 179, 184; Rich., 70 n., 133; Capt. Rob., 102, 102 n., 103, 103 n., 104, 105, 107, 108, 109, 110, 124 n.; Thos. and wife, 207
Aubone, Wm., 268 n., 273, 274, 274 n
Audas, Awdas, Anthony, 122, 139, 166; Ursula, 122, 139

Aulle, Ralph, and wife, 171
Aune, Geo., 44 n
Autey, Autie, Awty, Otty, Daniel, 215, 215 n., 216, 281, 281 n., 282; Alice, wife of Edward, 216, 282
Autwicke, Austwick, Lieut., 14 n., 17, 17 n
Avery, Luke, 239 n
Avyard, John, 112
Awderson, Robt., 78
Aydon, Geo., and wife, 206
Aylemian, Robt., 171; Eliz., wife of, 171
Aynsley, Wm., 239 n
Ayscough, Aiscough, Alan, 137, 271 n.; Anne, wife of, 137; Francis, esq., 137, 244, 269 n., 271; Mr. James, 271, 271 n

B

Babthorpe, Robt., 95 n
Bacon, Eborah, 180.
Bagley, Hugh, 123; Mercy, wife of, 123
Baildon, Major, 57
Bainbrige, Bainbrigg, Bainbridge, Mary, 174; Thomas, 170, 182; Ellinor, wife of, 170, 182
Baine, Eliz., 181; Francis, 169; George, 80; Humphrey, 169, 182; Susanna, wife of, 169, 182; Margt., 179, 181; Richard, Eliz., wife of, 179; Wm., Frances, wife of, 180
Baines, Thos., 167; Isabel, wife of, 167
Bainton, Dorothy, 168; James, 168; Jane, wife of, 168
Baites, Jane, 197; Thos., Ann, wife of, 191; Thos., 139; Jane, wife of, 139
Baitson, Henry, 138
Baker, Debora, 169; Rich. and wife, 174; Roger, 139
Balderston, James, 167
Baldwin, Nicholas, 58
Balke, Ralph, 121
Bamborrow, Mary, 207
Baminont, Dorothy, 167; Matt., 167
Banckes, Chr., 120; Jane, wife of, 120; Joan, 120; John, 120; junr., 120; Eliz. wife of, 120; Sam., 225; Thos. 133; Wm., 263
Bancroft, Thos., 214
Bankes, Banckes, Cuthbert, 138, 171, 180; Cecily, wife of, 138, 171, 180; Hannah, 130, 131; John, 130, 131; Judith, 130, 131; Paull, 130, 130 n., 131; Wm., 130, 131
Banks, Peter, 204, 205
Bannister, Joseph, 11, 52, 52 n

INDEX OF NAMES.

Barbar, Ralph, and wife, 129 n
Barber, Mr., 39; of Long Witton, 155
Bare, Robt., 120
Barker, Anne, 180; Castinia, 180; Dorothy, 137; Eliz., 166, 180; Francis, esq., 161; George, 72 n.; Peter, 283 n.; Richard, 276 n.; Thos., 121
Barley, Sam., 133
Barnard, Richard, 170; Anne, wife of, 170; of Thornton in Pickering, 140
Barnarde, ——, 33
Barnes, Alderman, 172 n., 252 n.; Ambrose, 174 n.; Christian, 168
Barnet, John, 218, 225, 225 n
Barningham, John, 168; Hannah, wife of, 168
Baron, Sir Richard, 18
Barrett, James, 138, 166
Barringham, Chr. 168; Anne, wife of, 168
Barrowes, Edw., 52, 52 n
Barsley, George, Margt. wife of, 168
Bartlett, John, and wife, 180
Bartley, Capt., 40
Barton, Alice, 137; Anthony, 95; Wm. Anne, wife of, 121
Bartram, John, senr., 228; junr, 228
Barwick, Barwicke, Ellen, 120; George, 140; Henry, 136; Anne, wife of, 136; Sir Robert, kt., 11, 21, 22, 23, 36n., 44, 48, 63 n.; Tristram, 190 n
Basire, Isaac, 257 n
Bates, Eliz., 49 n
Batley, Batly, Battley, Wm., 215, 216 n, 246, 246 n
Batt, Robt. esq., 254 n
Battersby, Nich., 101, 102
Battley, John, 18
Batty, Chr., 138, 167, 184; Geo., 164; Rich., 164; Wm., 41
Bawcham, Geo., 207
Bawden, Chr., 117
Bawmer, Jos., esq. 253
Bawmforth, Sampson, 181
Baxter, Anne, 268 n.; Charles, and wife, 179; John, 169; Eliz., 169; Mark, 166; Mary, wife of, 166
Baxter, Marmaduke, and wife, 166; Thos., 67
Bayley, Henry, 138, 184; Isabel, wife of, 184; Thos., 165
Bayne, Magdalen, 179; Margt., 169
Baynes, Thos., 70, 70 n
Baynton, Jane, 182
Beacham, Mr., 215
Beadnell, Beadnal, Bednall, Geo., 174; Rob., esq., 207; Thos., 239
Bealley, Margt., 166

Beamont, Beaumont, Geo., 87 n.; Lady, 282; Susan, 28 n., 29
Beanlands, Jane, 223
Beauvoir, Beauvoir, Bevoyr, Capt. Peter de, 32, 32 n., 34, 35, 35 n, 36
Becke, John, 121; Mary, 121
Beckwith, Geo., 290 n.; Isabella, 122; Jane, 179; John, 184; Julian, 169; Marmaduke, 169; Eliz., wife of, 169; Math., esq., 36, 37 n., 80; Roger, esq. 122; Thos., esq., 169, 179; Wm., 167, 169, 265, 265 n
Beeby, John, 110
Beecroft, Eliz., 223, 223 n.; Rich., 224
Beedal, Anthonie, 56
Beesley, Rich., 167; Agnes, wife of, 167
Beevers, Thos., 6
Beilby, Margt., 121
Bek, Bp. of Durham, 161 n
Bell, Adam, 165; Andrew, 190; Ann, 182; Dorothy, 170; Jane, 151; James, 189 n.; John, 151, 151 n., 152, 152 n., 153; Mary, 169, 180; Nicholas, 239n.; Robt., 275; Thos., 141, 151 n
Bennington, John, 17
Benson, Rich., 133
Benskyn, Mr. Rob., 42
Bentham, John, 133, 167
Bentley, John, 166, 181; Mary, 138; Michael, 166, 181
Benton, Jennet, 74, 75; Geo., 74, 75
Bents, John, 133
Berry, Frances, 183; Geo., 136; Mary, wife of, 136; Grace, 183; John, esq., 244 n., 269 n.; of Barford, 136, 171, 183; Eliz., wife of, 136, 171, 183; John of Forcett, 183; Eliz., wife of, 183; John, of Laton, 170; Eliz., wife of, 170; Mary, 170; Mathew, 183; Robt., esq., 138, 244 n., 269 n., 271; Wm., 183, 229
Bethel, Bethell, Col., 30 n.; Henry, 63 n.; Hugh, esq., 53
Beverley, Jas., 263; Mayor of, 50, 53 n.; Recorder of, 53 n
Bewick, Will., 50
Bibby, —— 223 n
Bickerdyke, Barbara, 169; Kath., 171, Richard, 59, 59 n., 60, 61, 62
Bilcliffe, Rich., 167; Mary, wife of, 167; Wm., 167; Mary, wife of, 167
Billany, widow, 169
Billerby, John, 120
Bilton, Ely, 275 n.; Dorothy, 228; Thos., 275 n
Binckes, Francis, esq., 139; Eliz., wife of, 139; Mary, 182; Peter, Anne, wife of, 121, 168, 182

x 2

308   INDEX OF NAMES.

Bird, Jane, 120; James, 144
Birkbeck, Birkebecke, Bridget, 137, 181; Edward, 137, 181, 183, 269 n.; Jane, 181
Birkett, Math., 263; Wm., 138
Bittleston, John, 173, 174
Blackburne, Edward, 182; Ellis, 140; James, 167; Major, 23; Mary, 120; Michaell, 13, 14 n., 16, 17, 22, 23; Rob., 100 n.; Widow, 169; Wm. 182
Blackett, Eliz., 136; Thos., 263; Sir Walter, 172 n
Blackling, Francis, 167; John, 167
Blacklocke, Blakelocke, Cuthbert, 239 n.; Mark, 239 n.; Rob., 153
Bladworth, John, 88 n
Blagdon, Blaigdon, Lyonell, and wife, 172 n., 174
Blair, Thomas, 174
Blake, Blaque, Gen., 42, 42 n
Blakeley, John, 88
Blakelin, John, 133; Francis, 133
Blakey, Peter, 169, 179; Eliz., wife of, 169; Sarah, 179
Blakiston, Mr. Councellor, 275; Francis, 137; Wm., esq., 106
Bland, Adam, 178, 178 n.; Geo., 133, 167; Sir Thos., 178 n
Blanshard, Jane, 121; Rich., Isab. wife of, 122, 139; Rob., Margt. wife of, 121; Thos., 121; Thos. junr., 121; Wm., 46
Blashell, Margt., 123
Blaylock, Thos., 292
Blenckarne, Francis, 167
Blenkinsopp, Ann, 227; Catherine, 285 n
Blowes, Mistresse, 221; Rob., 221
Blythman, Blytheman, Jasper, esq., 249, 249 n.; Richard, 88
Boardman, John, 167, 184; Isab., wife of, 184
Body, Wm., 122
Bolby, John, 129
Bolland, Ed., 119
Bollen, Thos., 167
Bolles, Hy., 182
Bolron, Bouldron, Rob., 168, 240, 240 n., 241, 241 n., 242, 242 n., 243 n., 244, 244 n., 245, 246, 246 n., 251 n., 271 n
Bolt, Boult, John, 83, 229
Bolton, Duke of, 258 n
Bond, James, 166
Bonnell, Thos., clerk, 225
Bonner, Suzann, 172 n
Bonnyvant, Major, 16
Boolmer, John, 171; Jane, wife of, 171
Booth, Geo., 137, 166; Eliz., wife of, 166

Booth, Geo., 137; Isab., wife of, 137; George, Sir, 81, 81 n., 93 n., 97 n.; John, clerk, 189, 189 n., 190; Jeremy, 116; Rich., 29; Wm., Joan wife of, 38
Boothman, Bootham, Bowtham, Henry, 138, 184; Richard, 138, 184; Alice, wife of, 138, 184; Rich., junr., 138, 184
Borges, John, 167; Alice, wife of, 167
Borrick, Anne, 170
Bossell, Francis, 137
Boteler, Noel, 257 n
Bothomley, John, 181; Jonas, and wife, 166, 181
Boulbye, Rich., 25
Boulton, Barth., 122
Bourchier, Sir Barrington, 259 n
Bovill, Rich., 167; Mary, wife of, 122, 139; Mary, 167
Bower, Jeremy, 117, 118; Rosamond, wife of, 118
Bowes, Eliz., 169, 182; Francis, esq., 108; James, 110; Sir Wm., 284
Bowman, John, 161; Thos., 229, 292, 293
Bowser, Rob., 133
Bowsfeild, Steven, 104
Bowson, John, 168; Henry, 168; Margaret, 168
Boyes, Mr., 24; Jas., 140; Isab., wife of, 140; Wm., 167
Brabant, Henry, 158, 158 n., 239 n.; Henry, junr., 158 n
Brace, Bracey, Bracy, Edmund, 220, 221, 260, 261; John, 220, 221
Bradburne, John, 176
Bradford, Eliz., 133
Bradley, James, 166, 181; John, 138; Mr., 1, 1 n., 2 n.; Savile, 2 n.; Simon, 183; Thos., 32, 32 n
Bradrake, Bradricke, Anthony, 171, 181
Bradshaw, Capt., 42; Constable, esq., 232 n.; Henry, 116, 117; —— President of Council, 36, 41 n
Braithricke, Anne, 181
Braithwaite, Brathwaite, Rich., esq., 102, 104; Thos., esq., 75
Brame, Wm., 140
Bramhall, Thos., 209
Bramley, Chr., 71, 71 n., 88
Brandling, Eliz., 206; Frances, 206; Robt., esq., 227
Branthwaite, Edw., 133; Thos. 133
Brasill, Katherine, 179
Brearcliffe or Braidcliffe, Wm., esq., 294
Brearey, James, 89 n; Wm., 95 n
Briden, Bridon, James, 151, 151 n., 152, 153, 156

INDEX OF NAMES. 309

Bridge, John, 179
Bridgeman, Wm., 265, 265 n
Bridges, Dr., 146
Bridgewater, Jane, 122, 182; Thos., 182
Briggs, Edw., esq., 72, 73, 79, 79 n.; John, 1; Dan., 7; Mary, 8; Wm., 139; Mary, wife of, 139
Brigham, Dorothy, 182; Henry, 182; Mary, 182; Richard, 182
Bright, Brights, Col., 26, 26 n.; Henry, 70 n.; Stephen, 70 n.; Thos., 24, 24 n
Brignall, Ellinor, 183; Thos., 171; Ellen, wife of. 171
Briscoe, John, esq., 299
Brittane, John, 1
Brittlebancke, John, 167
Broad, Thos., 35 n
Broadhead, Mary, 184
Broadwood, Mr. John, 162, 162 n
Brooke, Edw., 291; Rich., 14 n
Brookin, Toby, 68 n
Brooks, Thos., 17 n
Brooksbank, Jeremiah, 87 n
Bromitt, John, 260, 261
Browne, Capt., 19, 20; Clement, Anne, wife of, 137; Edw., 85 n.; Eliz., 184; Gen., 104; George, 167; Jane, 123; Jas., 239 n; John, 98 n., 140, 176, 239 n.; Leonard, 123; Mary, 181; Nich., 239 n.; Rich., 46 n., 58, 73, 73 n., 74; Robt., 180, 227; Thos., 121; Barbara, wife of, 121; Thos., 207; Isabel, wife of, 207; Wm., 120, 206; Anne, wife of, 120, 206
— Browning, Chas., 253
Brownnilay, John, 167
Brownrigg, Mr. Wm., 252
Brumhead, John, 161
Bruntinge, Chr., 94
Brunton, Eliz., 122; Hen., 265 n
Bucke, Chr., 181; Dorothy, wife of, 181; Francis, and wife, 179; James, 181; Robt. and wife, 179
Buckingham, Duchess of, 174 n.; Duke of, 119, 175, 211 n
Bulkeley, Stephen, 145, 145 n
Bullisie, Thos., 120; Margt., 120
Bullocke, Marmaduke, 4
Bulman, Robt., 101
Bulmer, Anchetel, Ancketillus, esq., 269 n., 271; Anthony, 271; Bartholomew, 182; Bertram, Sir, 271 n.; Bertram, 271 n.; Robt., 182; Anne, wife of, 182; Robt., 170, 182; Thos., 168; Wm., 170; Anne, wife of, 170
Bumpus, Barnard, 68 n

Bunkin, John, 87 n
Burbeck, Edw., esq., 271
Burden, Mary, 120, 181
Burdett, Arnold, esq., 227; Katherine, wife of, 227
Burghersh, Bp., 161 n
Burill, Burrell, Cuthbert, Jane, wife of, 204; Robert, 123
Burley, Hen., 70 n
Burnand, Burnard, Mr., 226
Burne, Anne, 121; Eliz., 121
Burne, Hist. of Cumberland, 173 n., 174 n
Burneley, Jas., 87 n
Burnett, Cressy, esq., 101; Jane, 78 n
Burnitt, Matt., and wife, 179
Burr, Francis, 87 n.; Thos., 87 n
Burrow, John, 139; Sarah, 169
Burrowes, Burrose, Rich., 5, 6; John, 128, 128 n
Burton, ——, 178; Andrew, 24; Eliz., 259; Francis, 168, 182; John, esq., 41; Robt., 87 n, 81, 88 n.; Thos., esq., 73; Wm., Anne, wife of, 138
Burwell, Thos., D.C.L, 254 n
Busby, ——, 215 n.; Thos., 134 n
Bushell, Capt., 40 n
Bussley, Anne, 181; Mary, 181
Butler, ——, 236; George, 120, 138, 275 n., 279; Eliz., wife of, 120; Joan, 169; Mrs., 236; Robt., 121
Buttell, Geo., 121; Mary, wife of, 121
Butterfield, Alice, 171; Leonard, 203 n.; Rich., 171, 183; Grace, wife of, 171, 183; Wm., 139
Byars, Edw., 239 n
Byerley, Anthony, esq., 99

C.

Calamy, ——, 173 n., 253 n., 263 n
Calverlaw, ——, 206
Calverley, Walter, esq., 118
Calvert, Anne, 180; Dorothy, 180; Eliz., 180; Faith, 167; Francis, 169, 180, 290 n.; Anne, wife of, 169, 180; James, 180, 258, 258 n., 259 n.; John, 180; Margaret, 121; Rich., 54; Thos. and wife, 121; Wm., 120, 180; Isabel, wife of, 120
Camden, Lady, 97 n
Campbell, Sir Dungan, 108; Mrs., 1 n
Campion, Jane, 170
Can, Jacob de, 175 n
Canaby, Jas., 133
Canby, Edward, 174, 175; John, 70 n
Canterbury, Dean of, 4 n

310   INDEX OF NAMES.

Cargrave, Nicholas, 183 ; Ellen, wife of, 183
Carleill, Carliell, Francis, esq., 42, 53
Carleton, Anne, 139
Carlile, Carlisle, Earl of, 152, 152 n., Richard, 175; Will., 82
Carmichael, Sir Wm., 50, 51
Carnaby, Ralph, 207, 239 n. ; Sir Thos. 188 n. ; Widow, 227
Carr, Carre, Andrew, 187, 188, 189 ; Benomy, 227 ; Col., 52 ; Cuth., esq., 106 ; Geo., 82 n. ; Jane, 184 ; James, 91, 92, 174, 184 ; Jonathan, 268 n. ; Margt., 184 ; Math., 184 ; Ralph, 207 ; Susan, 184
Carroll, Matth., 285 n
Carruthers, Careuth, Mr. John, 84
Carse, John, 207
Carter, Geo., 171, 180 ; Dorothy, wife of, 171, 180 ; Henry, 163 n. ; John, 263 ; Wm., 111
Cartington, Cuthbt., Cecilie, wife of, 68 n
Cartwright, Bp. of Chester, 83 n.; Sir Hugh, 18
Casley, Thos., 63
Cass, Casse, Geo., and wife, 179, 252 n. ; Rich., 179
Castinton, Gawin, 207
Castleton, Lord, 112
Catherine, Queen, 46, 95 n., 100 n., 126, 147
Catlin, Wm., 65
Catterall, Mr., 252 ; Marmaduke, Anne, wife of, 168
Catterick, Isabel, 136 ; widow, 136 ; John, 136; Margaret, wife of, 136 ; John, 136 ; Margaret, 136 ; Mary, 136
Catton, Francis, 183 ; Mary, wife of, 183
Cautheran, Alice, 166
Cay, Robt., 174
Cayley, Sir Wm., 230 ; Wm., junr., 230
Centleman, John, 123
Challenar, Fred., esq., 273
Challoner, Chaloner, 47 n., 231 n., 241 n
Chambers, Francis, 256, 257 ; John, 218 ; Rich., 49 n., 50 ; Thos., 171, 180 ; Wm., 284, 285
Chamlen, Humfrey, 59 n
Chamley, Rich., 48, 49 n
Champney, Anne, 167 ; Eliz., 166, 167 ; Ralph, 166 ; Wm., 167 ; Wm., jun., 167
Champnoone, ——, 139

Chapman, Chr., 88 ; Isabella, 133, 140 ; Kath., 120 ; Mary, 140, 170 ; Rich., 140, 170 ; Roger, 140, 170 ; Stephen, 120 ; Frances, wife of, 120 ; Thos., 133, 140, 170
Charles I., 1 n., 3, 4, 5, 6, 9, 15 n., 16, 18, 19, 20 n., 21, 22, 24, 37, 39 n., 42, 53, 55, 66, 72, 73, 81 n., 84, 84 n., 88, 94, 94 n., 95, 96, 97 n., 116 n., 118, 119, 119 n., 148 n., 158, 158 n., 243 n., 245 n., 266, 267, 269 n., 270 n., 297 n
Charles II., *passim*
Charles, Prince, 14 n., 15, 19, 26, 26 n., 50
Charlesworth, Henry, 167
Charlton, Charleton, Edward, esq., 155, 156, 296, 296 n., 297, 297 n. ; Sir Edw., 297 n. ; Dame Mary, 227
Charter, Thos., 207
Chater, Geo., 239 n
Chauncey, Chas., esq., 222
Chaytor, Ralph, 181 ; Margt., wife of, 181
Chesney, Margt., 181
Childe, Henry, 121
Cholmeley, Cholmley, Sir Henry, 129 ; Sir Hugh, 40 n
Christian, Wm., esq., 97, 97 n., 98, 265
Clapham, Gideon, 140 ; Mr. Thos., 73
Clarke, Clearke, Clerke, Anne, 136, 171, 180 ; Alice, 170 ; Aurelius, 291 ; Sarah, wife of, 291 ; Cornelius, 70 n., Dr., 68 n. ; Edw., 120 ; Eliz., 254, 272 ; Isaac, 254 ; John, esq., 14 n., 134 n., 150, 165, 274 n.; Michael, 273 ; Rob., 239 n. ; Sarah, 291 ; Thos., 59 n., 60, 269 n. ; Eliz., wife of, 269 n
Clarkeson, Clerkeson, Frances, 167 ; Geo., 120 ; Henry, Jane wife of, 180 ; John, 167 ; Kath., 167 ; Mary, 120 ; Thos., 121
Clavering, Sir Jas., 112, 124, 124 n., 172 n., 199 ; John, 249 n. ; Ralph, esq., and wife, 207, 228, 238 n., 248, 296 n
Clavers, Clavour, Capt., 297, 300
Clay, Geo., 11, 12, 12 n.; Jas., 273 ; Mr., 52 n.; Rob., Dr., 11 n
Clayton, Jas., esq., 253 ; John, 137 ; Wm., 137 ; Wm., jun., 137, 166
Clea, Wm., 155
Clegg, Clegge, Ed., 46 ; Eliz., 166
Clement, Madam, 283 ; Rich., 16
Clennell, Thos., esq., 227, 238 n
Cliff, Rob., 52

INDEX OF NAMES. 311

Clifton, Rich., 171, 184; Anne, wife of, 171, 184
Close, Mary, 180
Clough, Thos., 166, 180; Mary, wife of, 180
Coar, Coear, John, 225; Thos., 105
Coates, Cotes, Anthony, 183; Mary, wife of, 183; Chr., 169, 179; Eliz., wife of, 169, 179; Dorothy, 88 n., John, 248; Mary, 206, 248; Roger, esq., 64, 78, 245 n., 269, 271; Wm., and wife, 171
Cockcroft, Henry, 6, 7
Cocke, Wm., 122
Cockerill, Henry, 230 n.; Wm., 230 n
Cockroom, Sir John, 259, 259 n
Coggs, John, 139; Anne, wife of, 139
Cole, Nich., 93
Coleman, Colman, Edw., 237, 237 n., 245; Rob., 30 n
Collier, Barth., 278
Collin, Thos., 140, 170; Margery, wife of, 170
Colling, John, 168; Dorothy, wife of, 183
Collingwood, Capt., 270; Francis, 244, 245; Geo., esq., 207, 228; Margt., 207, 228; Robt., 239 n.; Wm. 239 n
Collins, Jas. 213
Collinson, Chr., 180; Edw., 123
Collison, Rob., 121
Colson, Ann, 137
Condall, Simon, 71 n
Condon, Thos., esq., 283
Conquest, Mr., 236
Constable, Mr. Alderman, 263; Ann, 121, 168; family of, 272; John, esq., 222, 222 n.; Geo.; Philip, esq. 244 n, 269 n.; Major Ralph, 89, 89 n., 90, 91, 92; Thos. 121, 168
Constant, Joseph, 30
Conway, Mrs., 178
Conyers, Edw., 157, 165; Nich., 257 n.; Dr. Toby, 281
Cooby, Corby, Brian, 137, 171, 183; Mary, wife of, 137, 171, 183; Francis, 170; Thos., 170, 182; Grace, wife of, 170, 182
Cooke, Jas., 121; Margt., wife of, 121; John, 227, 275 n.; Herbert, 10; Laurence, 227; Thos. 167
Cooper, Geo., 137; Mary, wife of, 137; Gervase, 19; Rob. 45
Coore, Rich., 130 n
Copeland, Lawrence, and wife, 184
Copeley, Copley, Coppley, Edw., 178 n., 215, 216; Geo., 210; Godfrey, 95, 174, 176; Sir Godfrey, 117; John, 166, 182; Lionel, esq., 125, 125 n.; Lionel, jun. 178 n
Cordingley, Henry, 29, 30
Corkar, Anne, 167
Cornforth, Ed., 137; Faith, 136, 170; Marmaduke, 183; Faith, wife of, 183
Cornewallis, Cornwally, Cecilia, 234, 235, 236; Christiana, 236; Francis, esq., 235; John, alias Pracid, 232, 232 n., 233, 235, 269 n., 272
Cosin, Abraham, 286, 287, 287 n., 288, 289, 290; Bishop, 154 n., 174 n
Cotham, Margaret, 120
Cotherwood, Mary, 88
Cotterrall, Cotteril, Major J., 14 n., 18, 19, 21, 21 n., 22, 23
Coulam, Coullam, Wm., 140, 170; Rob. 140
Coulson, Thos., 120; Mary, wife of, 120
Coultman, Alice, 170
Coupland, Thos., 175, 176
Coverdale, Wm., 140
Coward, John, 140
Cowby, Frances, 182
Cowe, Abraham de, 87 n.; Isaac, 87 n
Cowell, John, 180
Cowlam, John, 170; Anne, wife of, 170
Cowlin, John, 168
Cowling, Cuthb., 137, 183; Anne, wife of, 137, 183; Edward, Anne, wife of, 183; Marmaduke, 138
Cowest, Wm., and wife, 181
Cowlman, Francis, 168
Cowper, John, 13; Margt. 133
Coxe, ——, 45
Coxon, Matth., 227
Crabtree, John, 87 n., 138; Wm. 138
Cradock, Sir Joseph, 10 n., 131, 131 n., 145, 147, 160 n., 218, 224 n., 225
Craggs, Anth., 120; Eliz. wife of, 120
Craister, Jas., Eliz. wife of, 238; Mr. 288 n.
Cranston, Alex., 283
Crathorne, Geo., 39; Kath. wife of, 39; Jas., 168
Craven, Dan., 74; Kath., 179
Crawforth, John, 191
Creagh, Sir Wm., 296 n
Cresset, Capt. John, 33, 34
Cressey, Mr., 49 n
Creswell, Oswald, esq., 207; Anne, wife of, 207; Wm., esq., 229, 229 n
Croft, Crofts, Anthony, 238; John, 133; Margery, 181; Mr., 160 n.; Ursula, 168

Crompton, Thos., esq., 94 ; Walter, 94, 94 n
Cromwell, Oliver, Lord Protector, 14 n., 16, 18, 36 n., 39, 47, 48, 62, 66, 67, 72, 73, 79, 80, 80 n., 84, 93 n., 94, 94 n., 106, 116, 116 n., 145 n., 251 n., 266, 276; Rich. 93 n
Cronfurth, George, 166 ; Mary, wife of, 166
Crosland, Martha, 182
Crosley, Crossley, Eliz., 6, 7, 8; Jane, 205 ; Martha, 166 ; Mr., 191 n.; Sarah, 7
Crow, Geo., 122 ; Margt., wife of, 122
Crowther, Alice, 138, 181 ; Anne, 31, 32, 138; Nathaniel, 137
Crumbleholme, Geo., and wife, 184
Cudworth, Mr. Jonas, 92, 92 n., 93
Cully, Simon, 155. 156, 157
Cundall, Cundle, Chr. 180; Mary, wife of, 180 ; John, 169 ; Mary, wife of, 169 ; Wm., 87 n
Cunningham, John, 207, 273, 274 ; Eliz., wife of, 207
Currier, Wm., 182
Currey, Curry, Andrew, 239 n.; Kath., 124 n., 125 n.; Wm., 229
Curtis, Mich., 95 n
Cusye, Capt., 27
Cuthbarte, Cuthbert, Edw., 116 n.; John, 39
Cuthbertson, Eliz., 139 ; John, 139
Cutler, Elinor, 138
Cutt, Thos., 87 n
Cutter, Robt., 136, 183 ; Eliz., wife of, 136, 183; Wm., and wife, 173, 174
Curwen, Mr. Patricius, 162, 162 n., 163 ; Sir Pat., 94, 162 n

D

Dacree, Hy., esq., 53, 122
Daggett, Geo., 59, 59 n
Daglish, Ralph, 189
Dale, Matt., 129, 130
Dalston, Sir John, 102 ; Wm., esq., 124, 124 n.; Sir Wm. 152 n
Dalton, Francis, 181 ; Stephen, 137, 181; Ellen, wife of, 137, 181 ; Thos., esq., 164
Danby, Thos., 78
Darcy, Sir Conyers, 160 ; James, esq., 10 n
Darell, ——, of Littlecote Hall, 205 n
Darley, John, 167 ; Mary, wife of, 167 ; Mary, 268, 268 n.; Sir Richard, 55, 63 n

Darnebrough, Sampson, 14 n
Darnell, Jas., 225
Davies, John, 136
Davis, John, 285 n
Davison, Mr. Alderman, 239 n., 275 ; Mr. Charles, 18 ; Mary, 150 ; Ralph, 106, 207 ; Saml. 99; Timothy, 273 ; Thos., esq., 208, 239 n
Dawnay, Dawney, Sir John, 78 n., 117 ; Paull, 78 n
Dawson, ——, 117 ; Alderman, and wife, 263 ; Alice, 180; Anthony, 120 ; Chr. 87 n., 103 ; George, 174 ; Kath., wife of John, 133, 269 n., 272 ; Rich., 100 n., 263 n.; Thos., 174 ; Wm. 133, Jane, wife of, 133 ; Wm., 166 ; Mary, wife of, 166
Day, John, 66, 130, 133, 171 ; Wm. 114, 114 n
Deardon, Isabel, 140 ; Thos. 119, 140
Dearlove, Thos., esq., 168 ; Anne, wife of, 168 ; Wm., 5 n
Denby, Jeremiah, 134 n
Denholme, Mary, 166 ; Sarah, 166, 181 ; Wm., 166
Denmark, Anne of, 4 n
Dennison, Henry, 133
Dent, Chr., 138, 171, 180 ; Philippa, wife of, 171, 180 ; John, 171, 180 ; Mary, wife of, 171, 180 ; Lancelot, 81 ; Michael, 126 n., 275 n.; Ralph, 168 ; Isabel, wife of, 168 ; Robt. 168 ; Anne, wife of, 168 ; Wm. 168, 172 n
Denton, Capt., 40, 40 n., 41, 41 n., 42 ; George, esq., 97, 292, 293, 294 ; Mr. 152 n.; Thos., esq., 82 n., 152, 152 n., 159, 162, 285, 294, 299
Derby, Earl of, 278 n. ; Family of, 97 n.; Mr. Thos. 249, 249 n
Derison, Thos., Ellinor, wife of, 170
Derwentwater, Earl of, 286, 300
Dethick, Dithick, Mrs., 163 n
Dewsbury, Geo., 122 ; Anne, wife of, 122 ; Wm., 88
Dex, Wm., 278
Dickins. Rich., 290
Dickinson, Anne, 140, 184 ; Geo. 70 n. ; Jane, 227 ; Margt. 227 ; Stephen, 140 ; Thos., Ellianor, wife of, 140 ; Thos., esq., 9, 23, 36, 36 n., 62 n., 63, 71 ; Wm., 27
Dickson, George, 3
Dinnis, Dynnis, John, 122, 139, 166 ; Alice, wife of, 122, 166
Dinsdall, James, 282
Ditch, Geo., 123 ; Margt., wife of, 123
Dixon, Anne, 168; Alice, 137 ; Brian, and wife, 263 n.; Chas. 137 ; Anne,

INDEX OF NAMES. 313

wife of, 137 ; Chr. 194 ; Alice, wife of, 194 ; John, 117, 118 ; Joseph, 275 n.; Margt. 83
Dobson, John, 183 ; Anne, wife of, 183 ; John, 120; Margt., wife of, 120; Ralph, 283 n.; Richard, 140, 170, 239 n.; Mary, wife of, 170 ; Wm. 169, 179
Dodds, Thos., 277
Dodgson, Dodgshon, Charles, 85 n ; Daniel, 179 ; Thos., 138
Dodsworth, Anne, 170, 182; Elias, Anne, wife of, 180 ; Jane, 263 ; Thos., 70 n., 136, 171 ; Kath., wife of, 136, 171
Dolben, Dolbin, Mr. Justice, 253, 253 n
Dolman, ——, esq., 243, 244; John, 122; Anne, wife of, 122 ; Robt., esq., 122, 242, 242 n., 243, and wife, 122 ; Thos. 120
Doncaster, Mayor of, 36
Doughty, Henry, 87 n
Douglas, Dr., 146; James, 208, 208 n.; Sir Wm. 208, 208 n
Douthwaite, Ralph, 36 n
Douty, ——, 189 n.; Capt. 33
Downer, Wm. 167
Dowsland, Thos., 88 n
Dowslay, Thos., 56, 88 n.; junr., 56
Drake, ——, 241 n.; family of, 15 n.; Francis, 137, 166 ; Frances, wife of, 137, 166 ; Jonathan, 205 ; Sarah, wife of, 205 ; Mr. Justice, 115 ; Nathan, 13 n.; Saml., 65 n.; Wm., esq., 296 n
Dresser, John, 137 ; Wm., 137
Drew, Richard, 24, 24 n., 25
Driffield, Francis, 176, 179 ; Jane, wife of, 179 ; Tristram, 171
Dring, Anne, 170
Driver, James, 184; John, 184 ; Thos., 184
Droninge, Mrs., 12
Dryden, Drydon, Driden, Anne, 191, 192, 193, 194, 195
Duffield, Alice, 169; Ann, 75, 76 ; Charles, 169; Eliz., 154; Francis, 169; Jane, wife of, 169; Henry, 169; Margt., wife of, 169; Stephen, 283 ; Tristram, 180
Duffill, Alice, 179 ; Charles, 179 ; Hen., and wife, 179
Duglas, ——, 259
Dunbarr, Lady, 231
Dundee, Lord, 300
Dunfriese, Earle of, 24
Dunn, Francis, 137 ; Robt., 137 ; Kath., wife of, 137
Dunstall, Dunstoll, Anthony, 189

Dunwell, Richard, 9, 10, 10 n
Durant, Deurant, Dewrant, John, 171 n., Wm., 172 n., 173 n., 174, 174 n
Durham, Dean and Chapter of, 68 n
Durtrees, Matt., 206
Dusbury, Lawrence, 26, 27
Dutton, Thos., 140, 170
Duval, Claude, 219 n., 260 n
Duverley, Daniel, 175 n
Dyson, Henry, 166 ; Mary, wife of, 166.; Joseph, 289

E.

Eatey, ——, widow, 180
Earle, Charles, 154 ; Katherine, 69; Mary, 179 ; Peter, 179 ; Richard, 179 ; Thos., 70 n
Earlston, 274 n
Earnley, Earneley, Mr. John, 176, 177 ; Mary, 176, 177 ; Mrs., 177
Earnshaw, Mary, 138, 166
Easterby, Francis, 140
Eastwood, Joshua, 289
Eccles, John, 138 ; Robt., 87 n
Ecopp, Wm., Mary, wife of, 182
Edisforth, Wm., and wife, 170
Egerton, ——, 81 n.; Sir Charles, 69
Egleston, Wm., 248
Eglinton, Egglington, Archibald Earl of, 249, 249 n., 250, 251
Elcock, Seth, 78 n
Elder, Henry, 134 n
Elgin, Earl of, 37 n
Elizabeth, Queen, 97
Ellershow, Wm., 167
Ellerton, Francis, Eliz., wife of, 178
Elliot, Sim., 155
Ellis, Eliz., 137, 183 ; John, 6 n., 121, 168 ; Rich., 46 n., Sam., 112 ; Stephen, 164, 165 n
Ellot, Cath., 194
Ellrington, Elrington, John, 248, 248 n.; Margaret, wife of, 248 ; Ralph, 195, 198 ; Wm., 53
Elslay, Elsley, Chas., 82 ; Wm., 81, 81 n
Elslyott, Elyslyott, Thos., 59 n., 60, 61, 62
Elvage, Mr., 42
Elwick, Ed., esq., 119
Embleton, Anne, 206
Emerson, Danl., 48 ; John, 88, 154, 174 ; Thos., 207
Empson, Anth., 139 ; Dorothy, wife of, 139 ; Thos., 139 ; Isab., wife of, 139
Enkrein, Rob., 207

314   INDEX OF NAMES.

England, Wm., 121
Engleton, Matt., 170; Ellen, wife of, 170
Eppenall, John, 121; Mary, wife of, 121
Errinton, Errington, Gilbert, and wife, 237, 238; John, 120, 296 n.; Mary, wife of, 120; Launcelot, 238 n.; Luke, 239 n.; Michael, 120; Mr., 140, 198, 295; Ralph, and wife, 182; Rob., 227; Wm., 227, 228
Eshton, Thos., 129 n
Eskrigg, Henry, 101
Estropp, John, 168; Ellen, wife of, 168
Etherington, Rich., esq., 24, 43; Rob., 167; Thos., 95 n
Eton, Provost of, 5 n
Eure, Geo., esq., 14 n., 50
Eventine, Francis, 180
Evers, Ewers, Lord, 47 n, 48
Everson, Rob., 260; Wm., 260
Ewbanck, Ewbanke, Eubancke, Hewbanck, Ubanke, Eliz., 137; Margt., 73; Thos., Capt., 73; Toby, 68 n.; Tristram, 94; Wm., 130, 130 n., 131
Exchequer, Barons of, 62

F.

Faber, Geo., 138
Fairfax, Fairefax, Farefax, Chas., esq., and wife, 6, 231 n.; Geo., 44 n., Honble. John, 269, 269 n.; Honble. Mary, wife of, 269; Lady, 119, 119 n., Lord General, 9, 11, 11 n., 17 n., 19, 22, 33, 86 n., 101, 101 n., 103, 103 n., 106, 108, 119, 119 n., 269 n
Falconberg, Lord, 271
Fallowfield, John, 290 n
Fane, Sir Francis, 117
Farcy, Hen., Anne, wife of, 227
Fargison, Rich., 97
Farmer, ——, 50
Farnworth, Rich., 64 n
Farray, Lieut., Thos., 17
Farrer, Wm., 133
Farthing, Geo., 182; Mary, wife of, 182
Favour, John, 224 n.; Vicar, 7 n
Fawcer, John, 112
Fawcet, Fawcett, Fawcitt, Fawsit, Eliz., 169, 170, 180, 182; James, 170, 182; John, 145, 169, 170, 179, 182; Alice, wife of, 182; Reginalde, 184; Thos., 104, 183; Wm., 190, 190 n
Fearne, Mary, 170

Fell, Geo., 138; Eleanor, wife of, 138
Fenby, John, 123; Alice, wife of, 123
Fenney, Rich., 89 n
Fenwicke, Ambrose, esq., 27 n., 228; Chas., 43, 53; Cuthbert, esq., 227; Eliz., 207, 247; Gerrard, 228; Jas., esq., 228; Jane, 184; John, 227; John, esq., 180, 227, 239 n.; Bridget, wife of, 227; Sir John, 274, 274 n., 291 n., 294 n., 294; Katherine, 180, 228; Robert, and wife, 207, 228, 241; Sir Robert, 297; Thomas, 239 n.; Wm. 28
Ferrell, Dan. O', 229, 230, 230 n
Ferriby, Eliz., 88 n
Ferry, Wm., 167
Fetham, Winifred, 184
Fetherstone, ——, 27 n.; Capt., 248 n
Fewson, Jos., 121
Field, Feild, Ed., 13; John, 80 n
Fielding, Feilding, Mr. Basill, 162; John, 138; John, jun., 138; Sir John, 164 n.; Mary, 138
Fiennes, Col. John, 33
Finley, John, 229; Robt., 173
Finney, Hen., 206; Anne, wife of, 206
Firbancke, Layton, 133; Frances, wife of, 133
Firth, John, 166; Hellen, 136; Rich., 138, 125; Thos., 181
Fish, Chr., 164, 164 n.; Francis, and wife, 179; John, 179; Mary, wife of, 179
Fisher, Francis, and wife, 123; Jas., 69 n.; John, 123; Mary, 54; Rich. 263; Thos., 172, 172 n
Fishwicke, Anne, 181
Fitzgerrard, Mr. John, 230
Fitzwilliam, Col., 296 n
Fleck, Rich., 239 n
Fletcher, Dorothy, 167; Sir Geo., 151; 152 n., Isabell, 202; Jane, 206; John, 166; Ralph, 27; Thos., 184; Wm, 207
Flood, Floyd, Sergt., 14 n.; 18
Flower, Flouer, Chr., 80
Foord, Timothy, 257
Forbes, Furbus, Col., 18, 18 n., 22
Forster, Foster, Anne, 191, 192, 193; Anth., 136, 170; Jane, wife of, 136, 170; Chr., 167; Mr. Ed., 188 n.; Geo., Joan, wife of, 167; Hen., 227, 263 n.; Isabella, wife of, 227, 263 n., John, 139, 203 n., 206, 274 n., 275 n.; Jane, wife of, 139; John, jun., 206; Mary, 183; Math. 88; Rich., 140; Ann, wife of, 194, 195, 196; Sir

INDEX OF NAMES. 315

Rich., 120; Clare, wife of, 120; Thos., 182, 183, 207; Wm., 13
Fosewicke, Eliz., 180; Rob., 180
Forten, Rob., 207
Fothergill, John, 104; Thos., 107
Fouler, Fowler, John, 170; Mable, 192; Mr., 45
Fox, Ann, 120; Frances, 120; Geo., 80, 80 n.; Thos., Mary, wife of, 147
Foxton, Jas., 283
France, Hester, 51, 51 n., 171; John, 171
Franck, Frank, Math., 13; Mr., 69, 69 n
Franckland, Margt., 133; Miles, 170; Agnes, wife of, 170; Robt., and wife, 140; Wm., esq., 171, 181; Eliz., wife of, 171, 181
Francklin, Chr., 131 n
Freazer, Walter, 15 n
Freeman, Capt., 33; Oliver, 167; Dina, wife of, 167
Freer, Mrs., 221
Freschevile, Lord, 185
Frest, James, 171; Grace, wife of, 171
Frinny, Mary, 136
Fryan, Rich., 285 n
Fryar, Edm., 148 n.; Wm., 136
Fryer, Freare, Frier, Wm., 215, 216, 216 n.; Jane, wife of, 215, 216, 216 n
Fryzer, Rob., 158, 172 n
Fusley, Peter, and wife, 123

G.

Galway, Lord, 20 n
Garbut, Rich., 120; Eliza, wife of, 120
Gardiner, Gardner, Henry, 239 n.; Jas., 239 n.; John, 239 n.; Luke, 239 n.; Ralph, 251, 251 n., 252, 252 n.; Rowland, 121; Isabella, wife of, 121
Gare, Anne, 207; Patience, 207; Wm., junr., and wife, 206
Garforth, Anth., esq., 126, 126 n.; Edmund, 126, 126 n.; John, 17, 18, 19; Wm., 126, 126 n., 263
Gargill, Thos., 121; Rebecca, wife of, 121
Gargrave, Mr., 178
Garison, Magdalen, 181
Garnett, Mr. Florence, 98; Thos., 96, 128, 142
Garrand, John, 207; Oswald, 207
Garth, Wm., 168
Gartham, Mary, 123
Garthwaite, Garthwayt, John, 10, 10 n

Gascarth, Gasketh, Gasgarthe, Cuthbert, 286, 286 n.; Thos., 159, 160
Gascoigne, Gascoin, Gascon, Mr. Thos., 237, 242, 242 n., 243, 243 n., 262, 298 n.; Sir Thos., 140, 232 n., 235, 235 n., 236, 240, 242, 242 n., 243, 244, 244 n., 245 n., 246, 246 n., 251 n., 270 n
Gaskin, Emmy, 154
Gatenbee, Gatenby, Francis, 206; Luke, 206; Mary, 206
Gedney, Ellen, 168, 182; Margt., 168, 182
Gee, Will., 144
Geldart, Mr., Lord Mayor of York, 70, 70 n
George III., 277 n
Germany, Emperor of, 272
Gerrard, Thos., 52
Gervise, Pet., 140
Gibbon, Geo., 175 n
Gibson, Anne, 206; Anthony, 157; Bartholomew, 206; Barbara, wife of, 206; Chr., 174; Dorothy, 123; Eliz., 154, 157; Geo., 123, 227; Mary, wife of, 123; Margt., 186; Patrick, 122, 166; Eliz., wife of, 122, 166; Rich., 227; Thos., 86, 100 n., 133, 227, 239 n.; Rob., 121; Wm., 137, 167, 183; Margt., wife of, 137, 183
Giffard, Mr. Francis, 4 n., 5
Gilburn, Chr., 88
Gilchrist, Ellioner, 188 n
Gill, Alice, 180; Dorothy, 180, 181; Francis, 169, 180; Humphrey, 173, 174; John, 227; Eliz., wife of, 227; Rich., 169, 180; Thos., 30; Will., 146, 146 n., 147
Gills, Mr., 147
Gilpin, Gillpin, Gilping, Gilpyn, Bernard, 9 n., 173 n.; Mr., 153 n.; Phillis, 163; Rich., clerk, 172, 173, 173 n., 174, 174 n.; Wm., 173 n
Girdler, Mr. Ambrosse, 237
Girlington, Thos., 183
Goldsborough, John, 183
Goodall, Wm., 181
Gooderidge, Wm., 184
Goodfellow, John, 300, 300 n
Goodlad, Wm., 103, 104
Goodricke, Sir John, 4; Mr., 231; Sir Hen., 189, 189 n
Goodson, Chr., 168
Goreing, Gowring, Lord, 11, 11 n
Gower, Ed., 39, 171; Sir Thos., 98 n
Gowland, John, 263; Wm., 263; Eliz. wife of, 263
Grace, Thos., 82 n

INDEX OF NAMES.

Grainge, Grange, Graunge, Anne, 169, 180; Marmaduke, 122, 169; Ralph, 122, 170, 182; Susan, wife of, 122, 170, 182; Rob., 169, 180; Thos., Ursula, wife of, 123; Wm., 169, 180
Graham, Graime, family of, 300 n.; Geo., 292; Col. Jas, 294; John, 137; Mary, wife of, 137; Mr., 292; Rich., 97; Sir Richard, 252, 291 n.; Rob., 98, 292, 299, 300, 300 n.; Thos., 292
Granger, Hen., 167
Grant, John, 22, 262
Gratewood, Anne, 179
Grave, Jas., 138
Gray, Anne, 179; Rob., 187 n., 189, 227; Wm., 141, 185, 207; Christiana, wife of, 207; Mr. Wm., of Doncaster, 225 n
Graycocke, Peter, 140; Rich., 140; Eliz., wife of, 140; Wm., 140; Frances, wife of, 140
Grayson, Mary, 120
Greates, Geo., 139; Joan, wife of, 139
Greathed, Walter, 104
Greave, James, 166
Greaves, Joseph, 206; Widow, 167
Green, Dorothy, 194, 196, 199, 201
Greencliffe, John, 67
Greene, Anne, 64, 65; John, 88, 88 n., 174; Isabel, 206; Leonard, 41; Widow, 227
Greenfeild, Marmaduke, 17
Greenwood, Mary, 138
Greere, Thos., 103, 105, 108
Gregory, Alice, 136, 171; Eliz., 171; James, Frances, wife of, 136, 171; James, 183; Widow, 171
Grenville, Denis, 257 n
Grey, ——, 28; Sir David, 50, 51; Edw., 207; Eliz., 28; Henry, esq., 228; Mark, esq., 228.; Rich., 133; Wm. Lord, 165
Greville, Capt. Fulke, 33
Grimes, Edw., Eliz. wife of, 138
Grimston, Rich., 89 n.; Mr. Stephen, 162, 162 n.; Thos., 179; Eliz. wife of, 169, 179
Grisedale, Mary, 121
Grosvenor, Gravenor, John, 44, 45
Grysdale, John, 167
Guildford, Lord Keeper, 58 n., 155 n., 156 n
Guy, Benjamin, 175

H

Habber, Joshuah, 263
Hage, Wm., 111
Hagerston, George, 49 n
Haggerston, Sir Thos., 245 n., 246
Haigh, Hague, Dame, 209; Martha, 210; Timothy, 210; Thos. 209
Hain, Henry, 207; Cath., wife of, 207
Hall, Anne, 207; Christ., 239 n; Grace, 137; Isabel, 137, 139; John, 88, 106, 157, 239 n.; John, Isabell, wife of, 206; John, Mary, wife of, 183; Lancelot, 239 n; Mary, 227; Mich., 183 n.; Mr., 262; Rich., 182; Anne, wife of, 182; Robt., 182; Wm., 158, 206, 207, 227, 239 n
Halleday, Wm., 263
Halley, Edw., 166
Halliday, Edw., Anne, wife of, 137; Robt., and wife, 170
Halliwell, Francis, 180
Halsell, John, esq., 228
Hamerton, James, 180; Mary, wife of, 180; John, 167; Philip, 167; Philip, junr., wife of, 167
Hamond, Mrs., 54 n.; Wm., 89 n
Hancock, Saml., 268 n
Hancocke, Eliz., 122.; Reuben, 122; Rich., 122
Handley, Rich., 122
Handlesworth, John, 169
Hanley, Rich., 169
Hansley, Eliz., 121
Hanson, James, 89 n.; Henry, 115; Rich., 138; Thos., 48
Harcour, Edmond, 145
Harcourt, Mr., 230, 230 n
Hard, James, 170; Anne, wife of, 170; Margaret, 170
Hardcastle, Thos., 179; Thos., junr., 179
Harde, Rich., 129 n
Hardwick, Thos., 119; Wm., 119
Hardy, Danl., 121; Jane, 207; John, 181; Rich., and wife, 121; Robt. 121; Sarah, 121
Harford, Rapha, 17 n
Hargill, Mary, 122, 139
Hargrave, Eliz., 13; John, and wife, 137; Robt., 167; Jane, wife of, 167
Hargraves, James, 173; John, 210, 212
Hargreaves, John, esq., 205, 286
Harker, ——, 148 n.; Col. 48; John, 168; Rich., Eliz., wife of, 120
Harland, Jane, 169; Rich., 188 n; Ruth, 169; Thos. 228, 228 n., 229; Anne, wife of, 228, 228 n., 229
Harper, John, 87 n.; Wm. 153
Harrison, Harieson, Eliz., 148 n., 184; Geo., 79, 80, 120, 139; Eliz., wife

INDEX OF NAMES. 317

of, 120; James, 184; Margt., wife
of, 184; John, 136, 167, 170, 171,
183, 184, 190, 207; Anne, wife of,
171, 183, 207; Peter, 136, 173,
184; Margt., wife of, 136, 170, 184;
John, esq., 41; Thos., 179; Grace,
wife of, 179; Wm., Joan, wife of,
137
Harry, Robt., 137
Hart, Eliz., 121; John, 103; Mary, wife
of, 103
Hartgrave, James, 174
Hartley, Henry, Mary, wife of, 138;
Leonard, 203n.; Thos. 31
Hartly, ——, 149
Harwood, John, 64; Matt., 140
Hasclerig, Haslerigg, Hazlerigg, Sir Arthur, 11 n., 20 n, 37, 37 n., 52
Hassell, Ralph, 249
Hatefeild, Hatfield, Anthony, 69 n.;
Henry, 69; Martha, 69 n
Haw, Rich., 170; Anne, wife of, 170
Hawkes, And., 88
Hawkins, Chr., 138, 171, 180; wife of,
138
Hawkeshead, John, 138; Eliz., wife of,
138
Hawksworth, Hauksworth, Walter, esq.,
116, 141, 222
Hay, Laurence, 7; Wm., 168
Hayes, Andrewe, 222; Danl., 170; Eliz.,
wife of, 170
Hayles, Mr. Rich., 188 n
Hayton, Thos., 169, 182; Hannah, wife
of, 182
Headon, Philip, 166; Anne, wife of,
166
Headlam, Geo., 139; Jane, wife of, 139
Headlyn, Geo. 173
Heaker, Thos., 138
Healde, Margt., 166
Hearon, Anthony, 124, 125; Dorothy,
wife of, 125
Heath, John, esq., 108
Heaton, Nathan, 166; Ralph, 286
Hebar, Capt. Thos., 232
Hebburne, Ralph, esq., 165
Hebden, Mr. James, 268, 269; Margt.,
121, 179; Roger, 56, 57, 87
Heber, family of, 233 n.; Mr. Thos.,
222, 223
Heblethwaite, Alex., 133
Heddon, Lancelot, 139
Hedlam, Geo., 174
Hedley, Mark, 207
Hedney, Henry, 121; Margt., wife of,
121
Helliwell, Abraham, 166; Eliz., 166

Hemesworth, Anne, 181; Robt., 184
Hemingway, Grace, 138; Mary, 138
Henderson, Hendersone, Ann, 155;
Cuthbert, 238 n.; Rich., 187; Robt.,
155
Hendley, Robt., 10 n.; Roger, esq., 265
Henrietta-Maria, Queen, 6, 6 n., 12,
143
Heptenstall, Joan, 139; Phillip, 139;
Anne, wife of, 139
Herbert, Thos., 93
Heron, Sir Cuthbert, 75 n.; John 228,
239 n
Hesketh, Heskitt, Edw., and wife, 184;
Mr. Francis, 41 n
Hesle, Anthony, 183; Jane, wife of,
183
Hesletine, Hesletyne, Thos., esq., 228,
251
Heslinton, Mr. Wm., 284
Heslop, Chr., 168; Dorothy, wife of,
168
Hessey, Thos., 121; Margaret, wife of,
121
Hewan, John, 14 n
Hewatson, John, 124
Hewbanck, Tristram, 94
Hewitson, John, 139; Anne, wife of,
139
Hewitt, Rich., 280
Hewley, John, esq., 6, 38, 67, 69
Hewlin, John, 186
Hewson, Eliz., 184
Hexop, Nich., 95 n
Hey, John, 278
Heywood, Oliver, 87 n., 164 n., 209,
211 n., 262 n
Hick, John, 88
Hicke, John, 137; Anne, wife of, 137
Hickson, Knightley, 263; Mr. 57; Robt.,
55; Wm. 206
Higginson, Francis, 79
Hildred, Wm., 271
Hildreth, Philip, 139; Jane, wife of, 139;
Wm., junr., 139; Anne, wife of, 139;
Wm., esq., 269 n
Hildyard, Sir Robt., 128
Hill, Francis, 169; Margt., 96; Thos.,
Anne, wife of, 167
Hillary, Mr., 186
Hilton, Robt., esq., 102, 106
Himers, Dorothy, 202
Hinchcliffe, Hinchlife, Edw., 143; Joseph, 209, 210; Susanna, wife of,
208, 208 n., 209 n., 210; Wm., 143;
Eliz., wife of, 142, 143
Hinderwell, Mr., 30 n
Hindmersh, Wm., gen., 275

Hippon, Alice, 167; George, 167; John, 167
Hird, John, 168; Margt., wife of, 168; Rich., 168
Hirst, Robt., 131
Hitch, Mr., 234
Hitchmough, John, 39 n
Hobson, John, and wife, 121; Jonathan, 237; Kath., 263; Mary, 181
Hodge, John, 274n
Hodgskinson, Dorothy, 138
Hodgson, Hodgshon, Hodshon, Abraham, 138; Albert, Mr., 238, 238 n., 239 n., 297; Eliz., wife of, 238; Alderman, 3; Chr., 115; Eliz. 171; Enoch, Margt., wife of, 145; Geo., 168; Magdalen, wife of, 168; Capt. John, 86, 86 n., 87, 87 n., 93 n., 157, 157 n.; John, 88, 166, 230 n.; John, Seth, wife of, 171; Mary, 171; Mr., 185, 296, 296 n.; Mr. Rich., 89 n
Hodjon, Will., 106
Hogg, Mary, 179, 269 n
Holborne, Geo., 121
Holdsworth, Jennett, 179; Nathan, 205
Holgate, Anne, 167; Geo., 167; Anne, wife of, 167; Jane, 287; Mary, 167; Robt., 167; Roger, 287
Holliday, Holyday, Chr., 40, 87
Hollings, Roger, 5
Hollins, Robt., 166
Holme, John, 133, 167; Thos., 133
Holmes, John, 87 n.; Peter, 141; Thos., 133, 137, 166; Wm., 286
Holroyd, Holeroyde, Howroyde, George, 39, 39 n., 40; Ralph, and wife, 253, 254, 255, 255 n
Holt, Thos., 147
Homerton, James, and his wife, 169
Homesby, John, 174
Hoog, Lieut. ——, 272; Mrs. Mary, 272; Capt., Wm., 272
Hooker, John, 137
Hopkins, Matt., 191 n
Hopper, Jane, 196
Hopperton, Anne, 179
Hopton, Sir Ralph, 84, 84 n
Hopwood, George, 140; Thomas, 140
Horncastle, Wm., 243
Horne, Ensign, 188
Horner, Margt., 179; Yorke, 225
Hornesey, Phillis, 137
Horsefcild, Martha, 181
Horseman, Eliz., 180; John, 180; Marmaduke, 164, 164 n., Steph., 120; Thos., 120
Horsley, ——, 206; Benedict, 281 n.; Sir Thos., 193, 202

Hort, John, 137; Mary, wife of, 137
Hotham, Durand, esq., 39, 53; —— jun., 270; Martin, 263, 263 n.; Wm., 95 n
Hough, Gilbert, 20
Houldgat, Wm., 144
Howard, Mr. Chas., 297, 297 n.; Sir Francis, 162 n.; Hen., 162, 162 n.; Jas., 193; Mr., 152 n.; Sir Philip, 269 n.; Wm., 162, 162 n
Howden, John, 276
Howseman, Thos., 78 n
Hoyle, John, 126; Timothy, 166, 182
Huty, Wm., 119, 120
Huddleston, Hudles, Hudleson, Andrew, 66, 66 n., 286; Wm., 94 n., 120, 285 n
Hudesley, Mr., 71 n
Hudsey, John, 69
Hudson, Anne, 38 n.; Benj., 291 n.; Hen., 181; Mary, wife of, 181; Jennett, 65; John, 121; Anne, wife of, 121; Peter, 256; Thos., 50, 53; Wm., 223
Hudspeth, Cuthbert, 227
Huggison, John, 183; Sith, wife of, 183; Mary, 183
Hugginson, John, 137; Mary, 137
Hughes, Bettrice, 169
Hull, Robt., 168; Eliz., wife of, 168
Hulley, Edw., 138
Humble, Margt., 201; Marke, 201
Humber, Rich., esq., 225
Hume, Geo., 108
Hungate, Col. Francis, 269, 270; Sir Francis, 243; Lady, 231
Hunt, Capt. John, 33; John, 121; Barbara, wife of, 121; Henry, 139; Thos., 262
Hunter, Andrew, 239 n.; Anthony, 88 n., 94 n., 194, 196, 199, 200, 201; Cuthbert, 199, 201; Edward, 206; Eliz., 206; Isaac, 264; John, 206; Josiah, 71; Mary, 191, 194, 196; Mr., (historian), 12 n., 20 n., 69 n., 209 n., 272 n., 279 n.; Rich. 274, 275; Thos., 120; Jane, wife of, 120; Mr. Thos., 248 n.; Wm., 206, 239 n
Huntley, George, 268 n
Huntrees, John, 167; Mary, wife of, 167
Huntridge, Roger, esq., 207
Hunsloe, Wm., 144, 144 n
Hurd, Edw., 119
Hurdsman, Chr, 87 n
Hurstt, John, 170; Mary, wife of, 170

INDEX OF NAMES.

Husband, Matt., 180; Jane, wife of, 180
Hutchinson, Eliz., 180; Eliz. jun., 180; Isabel, 149 n.; James, 136, 147, 148 n., 170, 183; Mary, wife of, 136, 170, 183; Matt., 168; Mercy, 216 n., 281, 282; Peter, 284, 284 n.; Robt., Mary, wife of, 227; Wm., 173, 174, 214, 227, and wife, 174
Hutton, Eliz., 57; Ensigne, 96; Francis, 168; Margt., 138; Sir Rich., 189; Robt., esq., 218; Thos., 46 n
Hyde, Anne, Duchess of York, 277 n

I.

Ibbetson, Joseph, and wife, 263 n
Ibbitson, Abraham, 214; Joseph, esq., 214
Iles, Martin, Alderman, 67; Wm., 25
Ingham, ———, 9; John, 276 n
Ingland, Wilfrid, 71 n
Ingleby, Inglebie, Lady Anne, 48; Columbus, 95, 95 n.; Mr., 240 n.; Sir Wm., 164 n
Ingledew, Everard, 120
Ingleton, John, 182; Matt., 122, 182; Ellen, wife of, 122, 182
Ingram, Jane, 181
Inman, Marmaduke, and wife, 179; Wm., 164, 164 n
Ireland, Sir Francis, 48
Irton, Chr., 124
Irwen, Jas., esq., 152 n
Irwin, Lord, 282
Isaack, John, 168
Issot, Jephat, 166; John, 166; John, junr., 166; Sarah, 166
Iveson, ———, 115

J.

Jackson, Chas., 142; Dorothy, 169; Eliz., 120; Geo., 182; Ellen, wife of, 182; Geo., 122, 182; Frances, wife of, 122, 182; Gregory, 59, 59 n., 60; Henry, 87; Hugh, 166, 180; Isabella, 137; James, 140, 174; James, 170; Anne, wife of, 170; John, 170; John, 137; Isab., wife of, 137; Mary, 123, 133; Michaell, 146; Mr., 17 n., 56; Peter, 81; Rich., 71 n., 74, 182; Mr. Rich., 298; Thos., 264, 265; Wm., 117, 182
James I., 84 n., 271
James II., 66 n., 83 n., 203 n., 211 n., 226, 239 n., 266, 267, 268, 268 n., 269 n., 270, 271, 272, 273 n., 274, 274 n., 275 n., 276, 276 n., 277, 277 n., 278, 280, 281, 283 n., 284, 284 n., 285 n., 290, 291 n., 292, 293, 293 n., 296 n., 297, 298, 298 n., 299, 300
Jaques, Robt., 182
Jarratt, Jerrett, Wm., 123, 133; Margt., wife of, 133
Jefferson, Chr., 285 n.; Mr. 252 n.; Mrs., 174; Philip, 227; Robt., 239 n., 297, 298; Simon, 181; Jane, wife of, 181; Thos., 169, 179; Anne, wife of, 169, 179
Jeffreys, Lord Chief Justice, 263 n., 274 n.
Jeffreyson, Matt., 238, 241
Jegon, Arthur, 90
Jenison, Jennison, Jenyson, Anne, 122; Ralph, esq., 75 n., 172, 173, 229, 237; Robt., 245; Thos., 206
Jenkins, Capt., 33; Tobias, esq., 78 n
Jennings, Edw., 138; Sir Edw., 211 n.; Jonathan, 210, 210 n., 211, 211 n., 212, 213, 213 n.; Sir Jonathan, 252, 283, 284
Jepson, Grace, 288
Jewitt, Mary, 181
Jesse, John, 179; Margt. wife of, 179
Jessop, John, 139
Joblin, Jobling, Geo., and wife, 206; John, 107, 107 n., 108, 109; Michaell, 173
Johnson, Jonson, Alex., esq., 38, 66; Anne, 171; Arch., and wife, 207; Edm., 285; Eliz., 51, 51 n., 52; Everard, 120; Francis, 119; Francis and wife, 140; Henry, 121; Isabel, 197; John, 52, 58, 138; John, 122; Mary, wife of, 122; Leonard, 275 n.; Margt., 276 n.; Mary, 88, 89, 133, 170, 183; Peter, and wife, 122, 128 n., 129; Robt., 9, 9 n., 122, 173, 174, 198; and wife, 122; Stephen, Mary wife of, 82 n.; Thos., 69; Wm., 14 n., 38, 88, 174
Jonas, Chr., 166
Jones, ———, 111; John, 128; Rich., 174
Jopling, Joplinge, And., Mary wife of, 227; Eliz., 206; Michaell, 174
Jopson, Thos., 167
Jorden, Elinor, 157
Jowett, ———, 166; Rich., 138
Jowsey, Jowsie, And., 232, 232 n
Joy, Robt. and wife, 179; Thos., 121; Alice, wife of, 121

K.

Kattill, Wm., 28
Kay, Chas., 168; Ellinor, wife of, 168; John, clerk, 224, 224 n., 275 n.; Sir J., 86, 86 n
Kearton, Keirton, Geo., 168; John, 168, 180; Eliz. wife of. 180; Wm., 168
Keddey, Keddy, John, 170; Stephen, 170; Kath. wife of, 170
Keene Humphrey, 28 n
Kell, Mungo, 116 n
Kellett, Wm., 138
Kendall, Ann, 137; John, and wife, 179; Ralph, 137; Mary, wife of, 137; Wm., 133
Kendraw, Gregory, 138
Kerren, John, 265
Kettlewell, Wm., 69
Key, Andrew, Ann, wife of, 84 n ; Chr., 168; John, 168; Isab. wife of, 168; Ralph, 168
Keynton, Matt., 46
Kilborne, Kilburne, Henry, Anne, wife of, 10 n.; Jas., 136, 183; Eliz., wife of, 136, 183
Killingbeck, Rob., 245, 245 n
Killinghall, Henry, 137; Anne, wife of, 137
Killingworth, Luke, esq., 82
Kilpin, Kiplin, Chas., 72; Thos., 121; Tobie, 72
King, Rich., 169; Dorothy, wife of, 169; Rich., 122, 182; Eliz., wife of, 122, 182; Rob., 140, 170; Frances, wife of, 170; Wm., and wife, 179
Kirk, Wm., 147
Kirkbeck, family of, 152 n
Kirby, Jas., 120; Margt., wife of, 120; Mr., 79
Kirkby, Joshua, 97
Kirkham, Wm., 25
Kirton, Kyrton, Edward, and wife, 174; Ralph, 166; Kath., wife of, 166
Kirsopp, Thos., 227
Kitchin, Kitching, Kitchinge, Eliz., 122; Grace, 166; Hope, 129; John, and wife, 117; Mary, 7
Kitchingham, Thos., 290
Knaggs, Wm., 141, 142
Knapton, Wm., 134, 134 n., 141, 141 n
Knaresbrough, Mr., 44 n., 59, 59 n.; Wm., and wife, 179
Knight, Sir Ralph, 117; Wm. 262
Knowe, Isab., 138; Jane, 138; Thos., 138
Knowles, Anthony, 88 n.; Geo., 114

L

Ladler, John, 10 n
Lake, Dr., 279
Lalley, Hen., 128, 128 n
Lamb, Lambe, Eliz., 58; Lancelot, 46 n
Lambert, Alex., 81; Gen., 12, 12 n., 14 n., 81 n., 93 n., 114; John, 269 n., 272; Rich., 144, 228
Lamhton, Hen., esq., 106
Lamplough, Lamplugh, John, esq., 94; Robt., 123; Jane, wife of, 123
Lancaster, Margt., 180; Thos., 139
Lancton, family of, 272
Lang, Jeremiah, 181
Langchester, Thos., 183; Eliz., wife of, 183
Langdale, Isab., 133; Sir Marm., 14 n.; 17 n., 23, 23 n., 26 n., 50, 89 n
Langley, Mary, 122
Langton, Sir Abraham, 272 n.; John, 133
Langworth, Anthony, esq., 245 n., 269 n., 271, 271 n.; Sir John, 271
Lascelles, Lascells, Lassells, Cath., 270; Capt., 111; Edw., 270; Eliz., 169; Jane, 169; John, 116 n.; Mrs., 232 n., 240 n., 241; Rich., 15 n.; Capt. Thos., 30 n
Latham, ——, widow, 246
Lathley, Hen., 129
Lauderdale, Earl of, 51
Laughe, Diego, 41 n
Law, Lawe, Thos., 151, 151 n., 152, 153, 181
Lawson, Hen., 136; Frances, wife of, 136; James, 222 n.; Sir John, 26 n., 170, 182. 269 n.; Robt., 238 n.; Sir Wilfrid, 94; Wm., 88
Laycocke, Anne, 139; Josias, 224; Peter, 171
Layne, ——, 257 n
Lazenby, Wm., 39
Leach, Leatch, Robt., 136, 183; Jane, wife of, 136; Thos., 170, 183, and wife, 170
Leadom, Thos., 82 n
Leake, Anth., 167; Agnes, wife of, 167; Geoffry, 167; Thos., 167; Eliz., wife of, 167
Lealand, Rich., 41 n
Leamon, John, 241, 242
Leath, Robt., 170; Thos., 136; Eliz., wife of, 136
Leavening, Robt., 120; Anne, wife of, 120; Thos., 120; Emett, wife of, 120

INDEX OF NAMES.

Lecon, Jacob, 175
Ledger, Thos., and wife, 174
Lee, Edmund, 89 n.; Sir John, 158, 158 n.; Mary, 27; Rich., 174 n.; Thos., 256; Tobie, Mary, wife of, 278
Legard, Sir John, 258; Thos., 257 n
Legg, Wm, esq., 285
Leggatt, Capt., 164 n
Leigh, Richard, 66, 138; Jane, wife of, 138
Leightfoote, ——, 126 n
Lelley, Geo., Eliz., wife of, 180
Leng, Jane, 121; John, 121; Rich., 121, 167; Mary, wife of, 167; Robt., 121; Wm., 80 n
Lesley, Lashlaye, Gen., 1 n., 4 n., 96 n
Levans, Levens, John, 87, 87 n.
Lever, Leaver, Hen., 174, 174 n.; Mr. Robert, 135 n
Levitt, Levit, Ellinor, 122; Geo., 283 n
Levyson, Lt. Col., 298
Levy, Francis, 46 n
Lewby, John, 170
Lickbarrow, Hugh, 138
Liddle, Sir Francis, 127
Lidfurth, Jennet, 168
Lightfoot, Thos., 99, 99 n., 100; Wm., 184; Eliz., wife of, 184
Lilburn, Col. Robt., 20 n., 24
Lile, Rich., 16
Lindley, John, 78 n., 180; Mich., 89 n
Lingard, Mr. Wm., 252
Linscale, Anne, 131, 132; Em, 132, 133; Jane, 132; Margt., 132, 133; Sissilie, 131, 132
Linsley, Isaac, 87; John, Ellen wife of, 168
Lister, Lyster, Dan., 86, 86 n., 87 n.; Joseph, 87 n., Wm., and wife, 123, 262
Lith, Matt., 230, 230 n., 231
Little, Litle, Archibald, 154, 155, 155 n., 156, 157
Littleton, Mr., 37 n
Littlewood, ——, 254, 255, 255 n
Lockwood, Jos., 281
Lodge, Anthony, 170, 182; Chr., 122, 170, 182; Dorothy, wife of, 122, 170, 182; Miles, 182; Robt., 182; Hester, wife of, 182; Thos., 122, 170, 182; Wm., 122, 172, 182; Anne, wife of, 170, 182
Loft, John, 72
Lofthouse, Wm., 82
Loftous, John, 182; Wm., 182; Anne, wife of, 182
Long, Martin, 153
Longbotham, Rich., 138
Longerwood, John, 168
Longfellow, Eliz., 224

Loope, Anne, 180
Loraine, Sir Thos., 247
Losh, James. 6
Lotherton, Wm., 88
Loupe, ——, 169
Lowcock, Lowcocke, Eliz., 140; John, 116, 117
Lowesh, Lowish, Lawrence, 137, 183; Jane, wife of, 183; Rowland, 171; Jane, wife of, 171
Lowicke, Chr., 120; Lucretia, 120; Robt., 120; Mary, wife of, 120
Lownsdale, Jas., 120; Mary, wife of, 120
Lowther, Col. John, 18, 21; Rich., 18 n.; Wm., 292, 293; Sir Wm., 276, 298 n
Loxley, John. 263 n
Lucy, Davenport, 252
Ludley, Col., 115
Ludlow, ——, 104
Lumley, Lumly, Edw., 195; Lord, 296 n.; Mary, 182; Robt., 123; Alice, wife of, 123; Wm., 59, 59 n., 60
Lund, Thos., 299, 299 n., 300
Lunn, Thos., 85
Lupton, Obedd., 263
Luttrell, Narcissus, Diary of, 240 n., 241 n., 243 n., 251
Lyley, John, 118
Lyth, Tim., 230 n

M.

Macaulay, Lord, 219 n
Mackdonnell, Makdonill, Chas., 285 n., 297
Macguellim, John, 285 n
Mackrille, Wm., 207
Maclane, Macleane, Lord of, 297
Macquier, Bryan, 285 n
Maddison, Joseph, 248, 248 n.; Ralph, 248, 249 n
Maddox, Mr. Thos., 249, 249 n., 250, 251
Maignon, Rob., 175 n
Main, Geo., and wife, 207
Makepeace, Wm., Jane, wife of, 194, 196
Malham, Licut.-Col., 126
Malim, ——, 260
Mallinson, John, 166
Mallison, Alice. 119
Mallory, Malory, Malorye, Eliz., 75, 75 n., 76, 77, 78; Sir John, 75 n.; 210 n., 211 n.; Lady, 75, 75 n., 78.; Miss, 211 n., 213
Man, Mann, Anthony, 120; Ellin, 120; Thos., 147
Manchester, Earl of, 33, 103 n., 108

INDEX OF NAMES.

Mandeville, Wm., 239
Manfeild, John, 183 ; Robert, and wife, 183
Mangey, Arthur, 215 n. ; Henry, 190n.; Thos., 215 n
Mannering, John, 44, 45
Mansfeild, Rob., 136 ; Frances, wife of, 136 ; Wm., 136; Isab., wife of, 136
Marcer, Marser, John, 26, 27
March, Marshe, John, 192, 196, 199
Markham, Major, 272
Marlay, Sir John, 92 ; John, 183 ; Mary, wife of, 183
Marlison, Rob., 175 n
Marre, Geo., 100
Marrowe, Mr. Isaac, 85 n
Marsden, Henry, 232, 233, 235 ; Mr. Rich., 283 n
Marsh, Brian, 85 n
Marshall, Ann, 120 ; Chr., 85 n.; Geo., 274 n.; James, 166; John, 78 n.; Rich., 167; Rob., 139
Marsingill, Rich., 124 n
Martin, Anne, 189 ; John, 156
Marwood, Thos., 120
Mary of Modena. Queen, 277, 283
Mary, Queen, 294, 296 n
Mascow, Barbara, 121
Maske, Marm., and wife, 121
Maskey, Eliz., 298 n
Mason, Mayson, Frances, 82; Michael, 82; Peter, 81; Capt. Rich., 146, 146 n., 158; Rob., 25; Capt. Thos., 98, 98 n., 99 n., 104, 104 n.; Wm., 26 n., 158
Massam, Wm., 111, 184; Anne, wife of, 184
Massaniello, 175 n
Massie, Wm., esq., 290
Masterman, Maisterman, John, 228; Rich., 139; Eliz., wife of, 139; Syth, 139; Wm., 139
Mathewman, John, 128; Rich., 126 n
Mattericke, Thos., 46 n
Matterson, Launcelott, 71 n.; Rich., 46 n
Matteson, Marmaduke, and wife, 207
Matthews, Mark, 175
Mattson, Anne, 176
Maude, Mawde, Chr., 134; Michael, and wife, 169; Rob., Susanna, wife of, 75
Maughan, John, 197
Mauleverer, Malliverer, Mr. Thos., 1, 1 n.; Sir Thos., 70 n., 271
Maultus, Beatrix, 179 ; Marmaduke, Anne, wife of, 180; Philip, 179; Rob., 168; Mary, wife of, 168; Simon, 179; Wm., 179
Mautus, Chr., 179; Chr., junr., 179; John, 179

Maw, Rich., 175 n
Mawman, 85 n
May, John, 222, 222 n.; Wm., 182
Maybury, or Mowbray, Laurence, 242 n., 243 n., 244, 244 n., 246, 246 n
Mayling, John, 158 n
Mayor, Mr., 224 n
Mazzeres, Col., 33
Mealbancke, Mary, 77
Meale, Sergt., 162 n., 163
Meautys, John, Margt., wife of, 184
Medd, Abraham, 9
Megan, John, 229, 230
Melmerby, Melmorby, John, 160, 160 n., 161, 218, 219
Melwood, John, 87 n
Menfast, John, 123
Mennin, Ann, 92 n
Mentis, John, Margaret, wife of, 167
Mercer, Thos., 181; Wm., and wife, 169
Merriman, Gerrard, 89 n
Merrison, Wm., 87 n
Merry, Walter, 139; Hester, wife of, 139
Messenger, Eliz., 171, 183; Mary 183
Metcalf, Medcalf, Adrian, 240; Anthony, esqr., 269 n., 271 ; and wife, 169; Anthony, and Eliz , wife of, 168, 182; Anthony, and Frances his wife, 137, 181; Edmond, 145, 145 n.; James, 145, 147, 179 ; John, 212, 217, 217 n., Leonard, and wife, 122, 166, 148 n.; Mary, 16, 120; Mrs., 240, 241; Rich., 213; Thos., 150, 151
Metham, Geo., esqr., 270, 270 n.; Magdalen, wife of, 270, 270 n.; Mr. John, 89 n.; Sir Jordan, 270, 270 n.; Sir Thos., 270, 270 n
Meynel, Meynill, Menel, Mennell, Geo., esqr., 269 n., 284; Geo., and Ellen his wife, 137; Geo., and Olive his wife, 181; Jane, 136; John, 116 n.; Lawrence, 89 n.; Mr., 266 ; Mrs., 44, 45, 231 n.; Roger, 136, 171, 183, 269 n.; Mary, wife of, 136, 171, 183 ; Thos., 89 n.; Wm., 171, 183 ; Eliz., wife of, 171, 183
Michell, Rich., 232 ; Rob., 233
Micklethwaite, ——, 87 n
Mickleton, ——, MSS. of, 11 n., 154 n
Middlebrocke, Christian, 87 n.; Mary, 88 n.; Thos.,87 n
Middleton, Midleton, Bosvell, and wife, 179 ; Edw., 100 n., Eliz., 43 ; Francis, 167 ; John, esq., 242, 243, 243 n.; Peter, esq., 269 n.; Wm., 43
Midgley, Mary, 7, 8, 9, 9 n.; Samuel, 7
Milbank, Mark, esq., 99
Milborne, Milburne, Leonard, 96; Margt.

INDEX OF NAMES. 323

202, 203; Margt, junr., 202, 203;
Oswald, 114; Thos., 168; Wm., 203;
Wm., and Jane, wife of, 112, 113
Miller, Rob., 73
Millington, David, 131; John, 89 *n*
Millison, Anne, 207
Milne, Rob., 207
Milner, Edw., 168; Edmund, 148 *n*.;
Jas., 168; Jeremiah, 85 *n*.; John,
179; Joseph, 168; Mary, 122; Mr.,
255 *n*.; Symon, 168
Milnes, John, Anne, wife of, 180
Mitchell, Joseph. 123; Margt., 123;
Michael, 138; Wm., 123; Alice, wife
of, 123
Mitchinton, Ellen, 121
Mitford, Humphrey, 191, 193
Mody, Anne, 182
Moffett, Thos., 277
Mole, Mr., 45
Molineux, Francis, 269 *n*., 271
Monckton, Mountain, Sir Philip, 20,176*n*
Monk, General, 20 *n*., 84, 93, 119 *n*
Monmouth, Munmouth, Duke of, 239
239 *n*., 242, 243, 265, 265 *n*., 273 *n*.,
274, 274 *n*., 275, 275 *n*., 276, 276 *n*.,
277, 277 *n*., 278, 278 *n*., 283, 283 *n*.,
284, 284 *n*
Montaigne, Mountaigne, Mountaine, Geo.,
Archbp. York, 40 *n*.; Geo., 40 *n*.;
Rich., 40, 40 *n*.; Justice, 49 *n*
Moody, Anne, 168; John, 239 *n*.; Rob.,
239 *n*.; Thos., 139; Ursula, wife of, 139
Mooke, Math., 184
Moone, Mr. Cornelius, 257, 257 *n*
Moore, Anna, 136; Edw., 133; Geo.,
155; Giles, 133; Hy., 175; Jas., 136;
John, 133, 167; Anne, wife of, 133;
John, and Mary, his wife, 209, 210;
Mary, 208, 269 *n*.; Matt., 169;
Nicholas, 133; Rob., 155; Thos.
46 *n*., 140
Morale, Moralee, Gerard, 156 *n*.; Thos.,
156
More, Chrizake, Cresacre, 272, 272 *n*.;
John, 175; Marg., 272; Mary, 272;
Thos., esq., 272; Sir Thos., 272, 272 *n*
Morgan, 186; Alice, 186; Matt.. 232 *n*
Morland, Francis, 181; Ralph, 171, 180;
Barbara, wife, 171, 180
Morley, Morlay, Eliz., 181; Matt., 24;
Mrs., 100 *n*., 282; Thos., 100 *n*
Morraley, Thos., esq., 228
Morrill, Wm., 169
Morris, Marrice, Marris, Morrice, Castilian, 15 *n*.; Col. John, 13, 13 *n*.,
14 *n*, 15, 15 *n*., 16, 17, 17 *n*., 19, 20,
21, 22, 23; Ninian, 169, 179

Morrison, Marrison, James, 239 *n*.;
Willm., 39 *n*
Morton, Geo., esq., 275 *n*.; Margt., 38;
Mich., 121, 169; Kath., wife of, 121,
169
Mosse, Gawen, 80
Moulthorpe, Wm., 100, 101
Mountney, Francis, 125 *n*.; Thos., esq.,
228
Mow, James, 273
Mowbray, Moubray, Maybury, 251 *n*.;
Lawrence, 242 *n*., 243 *n*., 244, 244 *n*.,
246, 246 *n*.—*See* Maybury.
Murfew, Tedy, 298, 299
Murgetroyd, Geo., 284
Murphy, Edw., and wife, 139
Musgrave, Anne, 121; John, 24 *n*.,
134 *n*.; Sir Phil., 102, 102 *n*., 104,
105, 105 *n*., 106, 110, 124, 148 *n*.,
226
Myers, Anth., 138; John, 228; Nich.,
100

N

Narie, Nary, Major, 91, 92
Nayler, Naylor, Jas., 63 *n*., 64 *n*.; Thos.,
123; Anne, wife of, 123
Neale, Lieut., 162
Neesham, Mary, 170
Neile, Rich., esq., 245; Sir Rich., 264,
268, 275, 277
Nelson, Jane, 219 *n*.; Jeremiah, 84, 85
Nelthorpe, Rich., 257 *n*
Nendike, Chr., 40
Nesom, Mary, 183
Netherwood, Chr. 169
Nettleton, Edw., 130, 184;——, widow,
184
Nevelson, Anne, 127 *n*
Nevill, Gervas, 18; Henry, 239; Sandford, esq., 178
Nevinson, Nevison, Ed., esq., 102, 124;
John, 219, 219 *n*., 220 *n*., 221, 259,
260, 260 *n*., 261, 262
Newbourg, Duke of, 272
Newcastle, Earl of, 11, 11 *n*., 45, 190,
245 *n*., 272
Newsam, Priscilla, 123
Newton, Chas., 172, 173; Isaac, esq.,
25; Isab., 195; John, 193; Lancelot,
228; Rob., 195; Thos., 5, 6, 204, 206
Newtrice, Eliz., 170
Nicholas, Cuthbert, 173; John, 207
Nicholson, Cuthbert, 172; Geo., 137;
Henry, 265 *n*.; Jas., 299; Michael,
137; Oliver, 120; Merrill, wife of,

120; Rob., 120; Sara, 245 n.;
Simon, 269 n., 271, 271 n.; Thos.
and Kath., his wife, 206; Thos. and
Mary his wife, 133; Wm., 122, 192
Nixon, Geo., 227; Wm., 156
Noble, Hobbie, 155 n., 156; Jas., 122,
190 n.; John, 85 n.; Mungo, 152,
153, 155, 155 n., 157, 181 n.; Thos.
228
Noder, Thos., 168
Noel, Arthur, esq., 40
Norcliffe, Eliz., 140
Norfolke, Thos., 46
Norman, Jane, 169, 179; Geo., 169,
179
Norrison, Wm., 140
North, Chas., 95; John, Mary, wife of,
179
Northumberland, Duke of, 150 n
Norton, Eliz., 122, 166, 183; Michael,
137, 183; Eliz., wife of, 137, 183;
Mich., 182; Margt., wife of, 182
Nun, Robt., 178 n
Nunwicke, Mary, 65

O

Oates, Titus, 240 n.; Capt. Thos., 112
O'Brian, O'Bryan, Brian, 298 n
Oddy, Bartram, 228; John, 256; Mary,
wife of, 256; Robt., 140
Odesforth, Anne, 182
Ogle, Edw., 148 n.; Henry, esq., 207;
John; Winifred, 92
Oglethorpe, Ellen, 122; Sutton, 46 n.;
Wm., esq., 43 n., 151, 152, 152 n.,
153, 156, 157
Oldridge, Wm., 14 n
Oldroyd, Rich., 216
Olliver, Wm., 198
Orange, Prince of, 296 n., 298, 299
Ord, Orde, Lancelot, esq, 227; Major,
85 n.; Wm., 206, 227; Eliz., wife of
206, 227; Wm., jun., 206
Orfeur, Wm., 265, 266, 267
Orkenhead, 206
Ornsby, John, 275 n
Orre, Margt., 184
Orrick, ——, 3
Orton, Wm., and Isabel his wife, 168
Osbaldeston, Francis, esq., 245 n., 269 n.,
271, 271 n.; Sir Francis, 271; Sir
Rich., 222, 258; Wm., esq., 258
Osburne, Sir Thos., 117
Otty, alias Awty, see Awty
Otway, Ottway, Otwey, Geo., 79, 80;
John, 274; Mr., 79 n

Outhwaite, Chr., 217; Alice, wife, 217
Overend, Rich., 263
Overton, John, esq., 26; Robt., 22
Ovington, Rob., 136; Anne, wife of,
136
Owst, Isab., 166; Robt., and Anne his
wife, 122, 139, 166; Robt., and
Isabel his wife, 122; Robt., jun., and
Mary his wife, 122, 139; Wm., and
Sccily his wife, 122

P

Pallister, Eliz., 182; John, 89 n
Palmes, Wm., 167, 213; Mary, wife of,
167
Parke, Rich., 276
Parker, Brian, 138, 184; Isab, wife of,
138; Dorothy, 171; Easter, 286,
288; Eliz, 28; Francis, 28; Isabel,
167; James, 115, 167; Michael, and
wife, 287; Rob., 168; Anne, wife of,
168; Wm., 120
Parkin, Eliz., 5, 171; Geo. 117, 118;
Rob., 121; Wm., 121
Parkins, Eliz.; 183
Parkinson, Chr., 66; Theodore, 111,
111 n
Parteis, Anne, 197
Parving, Eliz., 285
Passeley, Eliz., 166; Grace, 166; Thos.,
166; widow, 166
Passhley, Alice, 184; Mary, 184;
Thos., 184
Pates, John, 140
Patrickson, Rich., 298
Patteson, Pattison, Pattyson, Ellinor,
205; Geo., 207; Jane, 92, 93;
Thos., 248
Pattinson, Thos., 151, 151 n., 152, 230 n
Pattricke, John, 175 n
Paulden, Palden, Capt. Timothy, 16 n.;
Capt. Thos., 16 n., 21, 21 n.; Capt.
Wm., 16, 16 n., 23, 23 n
Pawson, Nicholas, 88
Payler, Edw., esq., 3
Peables, Peoples, Mr. 215, 216
Peacocke, Brian, 168; Anne, wife of,
168; Dorothy, 180; James, 168;
Anne, wife of, 168; John, 55; Lan-
celot, 133; Ralph, 168; Vincent,
168; Eliz., wife of, 168
Peares, Chr., 135 n
Pearson, Peirson, Ann, 123; Anthony,
and Jane his wife, 136, 170; Edw.,
and Eliz., his wife, 139; Geo., and
Margt. his wife, 122, 138, 170, 182;

Jane, 138, 183; John, 39; 53, 168; John, and Mary his wife, 139; John, and Rebecca his wife, 182; Matthew, 123; Nicholas, 121, 168, 182, 207; Bridget, wife of, 121. 168, 182; Peter, 87 n.; Rich., and wife, 53, 122; Robt., and Ellen his wife, 136; Robt., and Isab., his wife, 136, 171, 184; Thos., 136, 167, 171, 221, 238; Wm., 136, 138, 166, 170, 183; Bridget, wife of, 136, 170, 183
Pease, Jane, 184; Mary, 184
Peatch, John, 283
Peele, Anthony, 83 n.; Henry, 14 n.; Peter, 290 n.; Wm., 71
Peircyhay, Perchy, Percyhay, Chr., 90, 91, 92
Peirse, John, 36, 36 n
Pellington, Mary, 181
Penington, Alderman, 28; Francis, 139; Anne, wife of, 139
Pennithorne, Mary, 139
Pennocke, Ann, 140, 170
Pennyman, Sir James, 110, 116 n
Penrose, John, 4; Rich., 4
Pepper, Mrs., 127; Rich., 240 n., 241 n
Pepys, Diary of, 95 n., 116 n
Perkins, Roger, 249 n
Perott, Mr., 185
Perry, Chr., 239 n
Petch, Chr., 180; Frances, 170; Geo., and wife, 122; Jane, 170; John, 171; and wife, 180; John, jun., and wife, 180
Peter, Hugh, 261
Peters, ——, 21
Petty, Godfrey, 87 n.; Henry, 103, 104, 105; John, 87 n.
Philipson, Phillipson, Col., 286 n.; Robt., esq., 79 n.
Phillip, Robt., 88
Phillipps, Ellinor, 205
Pibus, John, 59
Pickering, Pickring, Barnard, 121; Mary, wife of, 121; David, 121; Kath., wife of, 121; Eliz., 191, 194, 196; John, 65, 66; Mercy, 263; Wm., 253
Pickersgill, Symon, 122; Mary, wife of, 122
Pigg, John, 174
Pighells, Pegheils, Pighills, John, 137, 166, 181
Pigott, Michael, 180
Pilkington, Ann, 121; John, 121; Mary, 121
Pilmer, Wm., 140
Pilmoore, Nicholas, and his wife, 170

Pinchbeck, Eliz., 185, 186, 187; John, 185, 186, 187
Pinckney, Pingney, Pinkney, Geo., and Jane his wife, 136, 184, 284; Jane, 139; Joan, 184; Thos., 291, 293; Wm., 136
Pinckson, Jas., 175 n
Pinder, Thos, 168
Pinking, Geo., 170; Jane, his wife, 170; Jane, 170
Pithey, Titus, 174
Pixerem, Jas., 207
Place, Wm., 187 n
Plaine, Eliz., 182
Platts, John, 157, 158
Pleasance, Robt., 135, 135 n., 136
Plossom, Wm., 122
Plunkett, ——, 27; Edw., 285 n.; Oliv., 286, 286 n
Pollard, Pollerd, Isabella, 30; Mary, 139; Rich., 43, 43 n., 131 n.; Thos., 166; Walter, 223, 224 n
Ponnell, Henry, Capt., 26
Pontchardin, Hugh de, 161 n
Poole, Rich., 67; Sam., 87 n., 88, 88 n.; Baptista, wife of, 87 n.; Wm., 86, 86 n
Pope, Alex., 146 n., 162 n
Popplewell, John, 175 n
Porcivell, Jane, 136
Porter, Joseph, 275 n.; Robt., 264, 264 n
Portington, Roger, 117, 175, 175 n., 176
Posgate, Postgate. Nich., Dr., 230, 230 n., 231, 231 n., 232; Peter, 257, 257 n
Poskit, Poskitt, James, 140; Matt., 140; Anne, wife of, 140
Potter, Math., 81
Potts, Deborah, 206; John, 206; Kath., 124 n.; Robt., 206; Roger, 206
Poulson, Hist, 129 n.; James, 175 n
Poulter, John, 277
Powell, Francis, 68, 69; Sam., 174; Thos., 174
Powter, Robt., 46 n
Pressick, Thos., Mary, wife of, 241 n
Prest, Grace, 183
Preston, Lord, 291 n., 293, 294; Margt., 136
Priestley, Jos., 131
Prince, Martin, 134; Rich., 140
Pringle, And., 239 n.; Geo., esq., 207; John, 135, 135 n., 136, 174, 174 n
Procter, Lassie, 80; Robt., 138
Prole, Cornelius, 175
Prujean, Sir Francis, 271
Pudsey, Michael, 136, 171, 183, 239 n.; Jane, wife of, 171; Mary, wife of, 136, 183; Peter, 89 n.; Wm., 181
Pullen, Mary, 179

INDEX OF NAMES.

Puleston, Judge, 14 n
Purdue, Margt., 167
Purslove, Rich., 197; Sarah, wife of, 167
Purveys. John, 31
Puryer, Geo., 3
Pyburne, Piburne, Ellen, 181; Mary, 181; Mary, jun., 181; Margt., 181; Rich., 137; Mary, wife of, 137
Pye, Francis, 191, 195
Pyle, Robt., 127; Margt., wife of, 127

Q.

Quentin, Mr. St., 259 n.; Sir Wm. 14 n

R

Raby, Averil, 121
Rackas, Jo., 155
Raine, Rainde, James, 168; Jane, wife of, 168; Marmaduke, 259; Thos., 166; Thos., and wife, 263
Rainsbrough, Rainsbrugh, Col., 14 n., 15 n., 16, 17, 17 n., 20 n., 23
Rainsford. Baron, 165 n
Raley, John, 123; Ann, wife of, 123
Rames, Nich., 247; Anne, wife of, 247
Ramsden, Sir John, 23, 23 n.; Mr. Wm., 17
Ramsey, ——, 189 n
Ramsgill, ——, 190
Ramshaw, John, and Ann his wife, 121
Randall, Thos., 111
Raper, Eliz., 139
Rash, Barbara, 121
Rasin, Frances, 169
Ratcliffe, Radclife, Radclyffe, family of, 300 n.; Francis, and wife, 139; Fran., 207; Joan, wife of, 207; Sir Francis, 228; Cath., wife of, 228; Mary, 286; John, 87 n.; Sam., 110
Rathmell, Robt., 138; Agnes, wife of, 138
Raw, Rawe, Jo., 168, 248
Rawdon, Kath., 137
Rawnsley, Robt., 205
Raylton, ——, 153
Raynard, Helen, 169; Rich., 169; Joan, wife of, 169
Rayner, Margt., 179
Rayning, Peter, 268
Reachee, Eliz., 140; James, 140
Read, Reed, Sir Joseph, 292; Rich., 175, 175 n
Readhead, John, 126 n.; Rich., 174
Readshawe, Rich., 101, 101 n
Really, Phillip, 285 n
Redding, Reading, Nathaniel, 174, 174 n., 175, 175 n

Reddy, Stephen, 140
Redmaine, Wm., 167
Redman, Brian, 94 n.; Wm., 133
Reed, John, 256; Eliz., wife of, 138; Mr., 292; Percival, 85 n.; Thos., 41 n
Reeves, John, 230, 231 n
Rennerd, Thos., 58
Rennison, Anne, 206
Reresby, Rearsbie, Reasbie, John, 1, 1 n.; Sir John, 258 n,, 259, 278, 278 n., 279
Revett, Eldred, 187 n
Revill, Henry, 53 n.; Thos., 167
Reynald, Ralph, 179
Reyner, Hen., 166
Reynolds, Ralph, 169; Thos., 14 n
Reynoldson, Robt., 181; Eliz., wife of,181
Rhodes, Timothy, 129 n
Rich, Jane, 121; Thos., 121; Will., 121
Richadge, Oliver, 123; Margt., wife of, 123
Richardson, Dr., 99 n., 104, 104 n., 110; Eliz., 282; Hannah, 168; James, 73; Marmaduke, 24, 24 n., 26; Christina, wife of, 180; Mary, 168; Rich., 103, 104; Robt., 137, 170, 183; Bridget, 137, 170, 183; Thos., Anne, wife of, 196, 200; Thos., Eliz., wife of, 93
Rickeby, Mr., 259
Ridd, Francis, 137
Riddell, Riddal, Ridle, Eliz., 292; Mark, 249 n.; Mr., and wife, 237 n., 238.; Thos., 227, 228, 238 n., 239 n., 245, 245 n., 246, 249 n., 296 n.; Sir Thos., 245 n
Rider, Anne, 88 n.; Francis, 93 n
Ridley, Chr., 53; Geo., 239 n.; Hugh, 188 n.; Musgrave, 188 n.; Ralph, 227; Wm., 188 n., 226; Truth, wife of, 226
Ridsdale, John, 263
Rigby, Mary, 166; Wm. 166
Rigg, Geo, 181; Righ, Rich., 174
Riley, Hen., 174
Ripley, Fran., 120; Eliz., wife of, 120
Riston, Wm., 244
Ritchinson, Robt., 184
Rivis, Ursula, 137
Roberson, Roht. 94
Roberts, Eliz., 67, 181
Robinson, Robison, Anthony, 181; Sir Arthur, 4; Barth., 136; Mary, wife of, 136; Capt., 219; Dorothy, 181; Francis, 188 n.; Henry, 71 n., 138, 181; Kath., wife of, 181; Isabel, 9 n., 140, 170; John, 25, 26, 44, 44 n., 45, 46, 111; John and wife, 180; Joseph, 94 n.; Judith, 263; Luke, 9, 27, 27 n., 44, 44 n. 46, 47, 47 n., 78, 78 n.; Matt., 224 n.,

INDEX OF NAMES.

225; Sir Metcalfe, 164, 164 n.; Mr., 85 n., 219 n.; Nich., 138; Ralph, 110, 111 n.; Rich., 25, 39, 53, 78 n., 130 n., 133, 180, 219, 219 n.; Thos., 89 n., 133, 238 n.; Wm., 14 n., 120, 138, 163, 276; Jane, wife of, 120
Robson, Edw., 206; Galfrid, 206; Geoffrey, 239 n.; Lewes, 207; Matth., 227; Rowland, 206, 227; Simon, 241; Wm., and wife, 206, 227; 239 n., 275 n
Robuck, Roger, 70 n
Rocke, John, 138
Rockley, John, 34
Roddam, Rob., esq., 204
Rodes, Dorothy, 28; James, Ellen wife of, 32.; Mr. —— 221; Sara, 28, 29; Wm., 30
Rogers, Robt., 41
Rogerson, Robt., 140, 170; Kath., wife of, 140, 170
Rokeby, Rookeby, Mr., 298 n; Mrs., 262 n.; Thos., 262 n
Rolle, Lord Chief Justice, 60
Romney, Bernard, 227
Rooke, Franc., 175 n., Wm., 144
Rookesby, Rooksbye, J., 14 n; Mrs., 263
Roome, Eliz., 181; John, 137, 181; Anne, wife of, 137, 181
Roseter, Roserter, Thos., 26, 27
Rosse, Thos., 122; Jane, wife of, 122
Rotherford, Geo., 239 n.; Rich., Eliz., wife of, 127
Rounthwaite, Rownthwaite, Geo., 169; Kath., 169; Thos., 123, 123 n
Rountree, Wm., 120
Routledge, Geo., 152, 152 n., 153
Rowell, Edw., 207; Eliz., 206; Geo., 207; Gilbert, 85, 85 n.; John, 239 n.; Rich., 239 n.; Wm., 239 n
Rowland, Wm., 130
Rowne, Clement, Anne, wife of, 183
Royce, Wm., 123
Rudd, Edw., 183.; Isab., wife of, 183; Francis, 181; John, 181; Thos., 138
Ruddocke, Edw., 141, 141 n., 142
Rudstow, Sir Thos., 271
Rumford, Geo., 107, 108
Runinge, Jas., 120; Susanna, wife of, 120
Rupert, Robertt, Prince, 33, 42, 42 n
Rushton, Grace, 120; Mrs. 262.; Thos., 275 n., Wm., 242 n
Russell, Anne, 181; Humfrey, 59 n
Rutherford, Rotherford, Andrew, 208, 208 n.; James, Mary, wife of, 227
Ryeley, Ryley, Anthony, and Isabel his wife, 122; Isab., 169; John, 122, 169, 182; Mary, 169; Sibil, 182; Thos., 167; Ellen, wife of, 167
Rylead, Mary, 182
Rymer, ——, 146, 146 n.; Ralph, 36
Ryther, John, 119, 140; John, jun., 119; Mary, wife of, 119

S

Saffltlay, Softlay, Wm., 97, 98
Salkeld, Sir Francis, 297 n.; John, 134 n., 193; Margt., 297 n
Saltmarsh, Philip, 53
Salton, Wm., 186
Salvin, Anth., 257 n
Sampson, Francis, 183; Frances, wife of, 183; John, 121, 228, 228 n., 229
Samways, Dr., 218, 218 n
Sandall, Ephraim, and wife, 166
Sanderson, Saunderson, John and wife, 167, 227; Mary, 206; Ralph, 167; Peter, 174; Rob., 150, 151
Saunders, Nich., 257; Wm., 30
Savadge, Thos., Jane, wife of, 28
Savile, Hugh, 89 n.; family of, 81 n.; John, esq., 5; Sir John, 2 n., 5 n., 38, 69 n., 81; Rob., 89 n
Sawley, Hugh, 117
Sawrey, Rob., 67, 68 n
Sayer, Saiers, John, 120; Susan, wife of, 120; Mrs., 47, 48; Wm., 120; Mabell, wife of, 120
Sayles, John, 275, 276
Scaife, Skaife, Francis, 136, 171; Isab., wife of, 136, 171
Scarffe, Major, 48
Scarth, Major, 111
Scatcherd, Hannah, 263 n.; Rich., 71 n
Scholefeild, Rich., 181
Schoro, Schoroe, Edmund, 167; Mary, 167; Thos., 167
Scluter, Brian, 181; Eliz., wife of, 181
Scorrey, Anth., 181; Jas., 181; John, 181
Scott, Anne, 182; Dorothy; 179; John, 82 n., 206; Jane, wife, 206; Jonathan, 138; Marm., 189 n.; Matt., 182; Rich., 139; Rob., 133; Thos., 155, 155 n.; Sir Wm., 273
Scrope, Scroope, Bridget, 171, 180; Mr., 298; Simon, esq., 171, 180; Mary, wife of, 171, 180
Scurr, Scurre, John, 13; Leonard, 253 n., 254, 254 n., 255, 255 n
Scurray, Margt., 181
Seaton, Geo., and wife, 121

Seamer, Jas., 181
Seele, Rob., 184 ; Frances, wife of, 184
Selby, Chas., 227, 296 n.; Thos., 206, 207, 227 ; Eliz., wife of, 207 ; Wm., 188 n
Seller, Peter, and wife, 123 ; Thos., 123
Sellier, Thos., Mary wife of, 139
Senior, Thos., 146
Sergeant, Wm., 228
Sergison, Mary, 139
Sewell, Wm., Isab., wife of, 182
Shackleton, John, 7 ; Jonathan, 100
Shacklock, John, 174
Shafto, Shaftoe, Arthur, 116 n., 294 n.; Edw., esq., 294, 294 n.; Rob., 99; Sir Rob., 158 ; Wm., 294 n., 295
Shan, Shann, Peter, and wife, 179 ; Wm. and wife, 179
Sharpe, Archbp., 239 n.; Joseph, 275 n.; Rich., 168, 182; Mary, 168, 182
Sharples, Ann, 140
Shaw, Francis, 169, 180; Anne, wife of, 169, 180 ; Jas., 133; John, 173, 173 n., 180 ; Magdalen, wife of, 180 ; Mary, 290 ; Mr., 234 ; Ralph, and Mary his wife, 183 ; Rich., 237, 240, 242, 244
Shearson, John, 168 ; Frances, wife of, 168
Sheffeild, Thos., 68 n
Sherburn, Sir Nich., 296 n.; Thos., 92, 154 ; Margt., wife of, 154
Sherefon, John, 121 ; Frances, wife of, 121
Sherwood, David, 174 ; Francis, 54 n.; Wm., 174
Shield, Shields, John, 85 n.; Robt., Jane, wife of, 183
Shilleto, Thos., Anne, wife of, 209, 210
Shipley, Thos., 206
Shippen, Mary, 140 ; Nicholas, 262; Peter, 262
Shipperdson, Wm., 133
Shirwan, Ann, 137
Shore, Alice, 133
Shrewsbury, George, Earl of, 161, 161 n., 296 n
Shrigley, ——, 115
Shutt, Anthony, 183 ; Kath., wife of, 183 ; Job, 136 ; Mary, wife of, 136 ; Mary, 184 ; Rich., Ann, wife of, 184 ; Rob., 170, 183 ; Mary, wife of, 170, 183
Siddall, Barbara, 72 n.; Wm., 88
Sigsworth, Sidgeworth, John, 137, 181; Grace, wife of, 137, 181
Sikes, Wm., 30
Sill, John, 218 ; Rich., 218

Simmons, Matth., 17 n.; Mr. Thos., 251
Simpson, Simson, Barbara, 179 ; Eliz., 82 ; Francis, 171 ; Frances, 171 ; Geo., and wife, 82, 166 ; ——, 27 n., 183 ; John, 180 ; Jane, 124, 125, 180 ; Rob., 120 ; Doroth., 120 ; Silvester, 167 ; Thos., 60, 126, 126 n
Simster, Hellen, 167
Sinemond, Jas., 290
Singleton, Anthony, 139 ; Brian, and wife, 184 ; Eliz., 139 ; Mary, 171 ; Thos., 168
Sisson, Sissons, John, 46 n.; Francis, 73 ; Rich., 46 n
Sixton, John, 124 n
Skelton, Dorothy, 159 ; John, 171, 180; Frances, wife of, 171 ; Lancelott, 159, 160 ; Wm., 47 n., 142, 159; Joyce, wife of, 159
Skipwith, Geo., 220 ; Mrs., 130 n.; Peter, 219, 220
Slater, Slayter, Andrew, 140 ; Ralph, 123 ; Mary, wife of, 123 ; Rob., 263
Sled, Henry, 139, 166
Slinger, Thos., 129
Slingsby, Sir Henry, 11 n., 86 n., 298 n
Slinnan, Ursula, 120
Sloman, Wm., 120
Smailes, Mary, 171 ; Philip, 171 ; Isabel, wife of, 171
Smallwood, Thos., 83 n
Smart, Thos., and wife, 206
Smeaton, Sara, 122, 182
Smers, Rob., 207
Smirke, Geo., 239 n.; Rich., 239 n
Smith, Smyth, Abraham, 263 ; Barbara, 27 n., 28, 207 ; Chr., 137, 179, 181 ; Dennis, 207 ; Elias, 68 n.; Francis, 169 ; Geo., 123, 137, 169, 171, 180, 181, 183 ; Ellenor, wife of, 171, 183 ; Frances, wife of Geo., 181 ; Henry, Mary, wife of, 139 ; Jane, 139 ; John, 14 n., 18, 19, 47, 87, 89, 89 n., 90, 91, 99 n., 100, 104, 147 n., 182, 186, 251 n., 299 ; John, and Mary, his wife, 19; 137, 181 ; Joseph, 137, 166, 181 ; Kath., 179 ; Ralph, Eliz., wife of, 121 ; Rich., 27, 28, 93 n., 120, 138, 139, 144 ; Anne, wife of, 139 ; Rob., 120, Margt., 120 ; Thos., 84, 120, 138, 172 n., 182 ; Thos., and Margt., his wife, 207 ; Thos., and Sarah, his wife, 182 ; Wm., 48, 50, 95 n., 120, 140, 180, 207 ; Wm., and Alice his wife, 122, 182 ; Wm., and

INDEX OF NAMES. 329

Jane, his wife, 170; Wm., and Mary, his wife, 227
Smithson, Smythson, Ann, 189, 189 n.; Calvert, esq., 203; Chr.; 190; family of, 203 n.; Sir Jerome, 190 n.; Jeremy, 131, 131 n.; John, 171, 181, 183; Julian, wife of, 171, 183; Major, 160 n.;
———, 169; Rob, 171, 183; Grace, wife of, 171, 183; Wm., 171, 183
Smorthwaite, Jane, 122
Smythworth, alias Smurfitt, John, 227
Snaith, Thos., 168
Snell, Wm., and wife, 170
Snow, Rich., 269 n., 272
Snowball, Wm., 207
Snowden, Snawden, Chr., 207; Grace, 206, 227; Peter, 206; Rob., 155, 156, 157, 239 n.; Roger, 239 n
Softley, Cuth., 206
Sole, Henry, 131, 132
Solsby, Soulsby, Matt., 173, 174; Wm., 206
Somersides, Dorothy, 171
Sommerset, Sumerset, Godfrey. 43; Duke of, 277, 277 n
Sotheby, Suddeby, Sutheby, Sowthebie, Sowtheby, Lieut., 89 n., 90, 91, 92; Mary, 166
Sowerbies, John, 292
Sparke, Robt., 34, 35
Sparlinge, Hen., 262, 275 n.; Wm., 111, 111 n
Sparrow, John, 170
Spavild, Nich., 24, 24 n., 25
Speight, Spight, John, 126 n,; Rich., 133, 167
Spence, Jane, 170, 180, 183; Marmaduke, 181; Eliz., wife of, 181; Thos., 169, 180; Cecily, wife of, 169
Spenceley, Anth., 239 n
Spencer, John, 87 n., 88 n., 169; Wm., 117
Spicer, Rich., 121; Mary, wife of, 121
Spinke, Thos., Mary, wife of, 139
Spivy, Hester, 51
Sprotts, Ann, 121
Sprowston, Henry, 20
Squire, Squires, Alex., 223, 224; Bess, 224; Chr., 167; Eliza, wife of, 167; John, 241, 256; Mary, 138; Thos., and wife, 169, 179; Wm., 249 n
Stabler, Anne, 121
Stableton, Laird of, 299
Stacke, Mark, 121; Jane, wife of, 121
Stackhouse, Thos., 138
Stafford, Thos., 3
Stainthrop, Ann, 120
Stamadin, Alice, 167

Stamper, Robt., 78 n
Stancliffe, Jas., 287, 288, 290
Standfield, Thos., 122
Standley, John, 285 n
Stanes, Dr., 33
Stanhope, Dr. George, 4, 4 n.; John, 31, 38
Stanke, Laird of, 299
Stanley, Bridget, 122; Chr., 180
Stansey, Edw., 207; Anne, wife of, 207
Stansfeilde, Josias, 158
Stapleton, Mr. Jo., 234; Sir Miles, 240 n., 243, 243 n., 246, 251, 251 n
Starkey, Rich., 175
Staunton (Stenton), John, 95
Staveley, Simon, 171, 180
Stead, Steed, Hen., 122; Margt., wife of, 122; Mary, 121
Stearson, Francis, 182; John, 182
Stebin, Eliz., 137
Steele, Jane, 179
Steere, Wm., 87 n
Stephenson, Stevenson, Clement, 133, 167; Dorothy, 267; Frances, 120; Jas., 120; Rich., 274; Robt., 206; Uscella, 56
Stewart, Barbara, 227
Stevens, Mr. John, 298
Stileman, Alex, 20
Stiring, Styringe, Thos., 39, 53
Stobart, Stobbart, Geo., 196; Simon, 188 n
Stockdale, Stocktell, Ellinor, 131, 171; Thos., 50, 59; Wm, 136, 171; Anne, wife of, 136, 171
Stockton, Jane, 181; Hellen, 183; Mary, 120; Wm., 183
Stonecliffe, Matt., 137
Stones, John, 9
Story, Storie, Mr. Geo., 274 n.; Isabella, 122; John, 122, 294
Stote, Sir Rich., 191, 193, 199, 245
Strafford, Earl of, 1 n., 13 n., 15 n., 119; Lady, 278 n., 279
Stranger, Strangers, Dan., 112; Dorothy, 112, 113, 114; Eliz., 114
Strangewayes, Strangways, Jas., 90, 91, 178, 178 n
Strawhin, Anne, 207
Streater, J., 187 n
Strickland, Mr. Robt., 163; Sir Thos., 259, 259 n.; Mr. Wm., 259; Sir Wm., 53
Stringer, Mr., 74; Thomas, esq., 97; Wm., 121; Anne, wife of, 121
Strother, Struther, Edw., 206, 227, 239 n.; Mary, wife of, 206; James, 207

330 INDEX OF NAMES.

Stuart, Stuarde, Sturde, Stewart; Prince Charles, 51, 79, 80, 81; family of, 176
Stubbs, Stubbes, Anne, 170, 183; Bridget, 181; Jas., Anne, wife of, 136; Nich., 136, 171; Margt., wife of, 136, 171
Studdart, John, 110
Studholme, Studham, Capt., 104, 108
Sugden, John, 123
Summerside, Dorothy, 137
Sumner, Jas., 121; Frances, wife of, 121
Surtees, Robt., esq., 102 n., 111 n., 188 n
Suttell, Anne, 180; Ralph, 180; Anne, wife of, 180
Sutton, Anne, 140; Robt., 283 n.; Thos., 87, 87 n., 106
Suttrice, Jas., (alias Clarkeson,) 283
Swaile, Henry, and wife, 169
Swailes, Philip, 183; Isabel, wife of, 183
Swainson, Geo., 179
Swallow, Josias, 291
Swan, Swann, Mr. John. 89 n.; Thos., 239 n
Swayne, Sam., 157; Wm., 117
Swinburn, Swinburne, Allan, 228; Sir John, 227; Mr. 286; Wm., 196
Swinhoe, Swincho, Swinhowe, Gilbert, 187, 187 n., 188; Jas., 187, 187 n., 188, 189; John, 239 n
Sykes, Mr. C., 15 n.; Mary, 28, 28 n., 29, 30.; Moses, 166; Rich., 254 n.; Wm., 54, 54 n., 55
Sympson, Kath., 227

T

Tallentyre, Wm., 162 n
Tanckard, Tankard, Tankered, Tankerd, Mr., 220, 221; Sir Rich., 97, 112; Thos., 260, 261
Tanfield, Capt. 36 n.; Sir Wm., 182; Eliz., wife of, 182
Tarlett, Margt., 207
Tatham, John, 16, 18, 20; Mary, wife of, 18, 138, 167, 184; Wm., 20
Tattersall, Jonathan, 11
Tatterson, John, 64, 65; Thos., 65
Tailor, Tayler, Taylor, Abigail, 263; Andrew, 262, 262 n., 263, 263 n.; Anthony, 206; Geo., 94, 192, 196, 200, 201, 206; John, 42, 139, 166, 181; Mary, wife of, 139; John, and Eliz., his wife, 167; John, and Jane his wife, 217; Michael, 167; Philip, 207; Eliz., wife of, 207; Rich., 16, 19, 182, 283; Thos., 79, 87, 87 n., 181; Wm., 206
Teale, Thos., 181
Teasdale, Teasdle, Eliz., 163; Margt., 197
Telfare, Geo., 155
Tempest, ——, 49, 49 n., 50; Henry, 28, 30, 32, 38, 51, 52; John, 99, 106, 108, 138
Tempest, Lady, 232 n., 233, 235, 235 n., 236, 237, 243, 244 n., 246, 246 n.; Rich., 138; Eliz., wife of, 138; Mr. Stephen, 243 n.; Sir Stephen, 119, 140, 235 n.; Anne, wife of, 119, 140; Thos., esq., 138; Eliz., wife of, 138
Tenant, Tennant, Easter, 133; Eliz., 133; Jas., 133; Margery, 182
Tendall, Thos., 207
Tenison, Eliz., 122; Ralph, 122
Tenney, Tenny, Geo., 122, 139; Frances, wife of, 122, 139
Terry, Chr., 69
Thackwray, Anne, 169, 180; Mary, 180; Thos., 87 n
Theakeston, Theakston, Edw., Eliz., wife of, 180; Eliz., 171; Ellen, 171; John, Elianor, wife of, 138; Michael, 284, 285
Thewlis, Rich., 290
Thewson, David, 121; Anne, wife of, 121
Thimleby, Anne, 184; Charles, 184; Ellinor, 184
Thirlewall, Thirlwall, John, 188 n., 227
Thistlewood, Mary, 122
Thomas, Thos., 225
Thompson, Thomson, Tompson, Tomson; Alice, 124 n.; Anne, 170, 181; Edw., 169, 179, 207; Eleanor, wife of, 169, 179, 207; Edw., jun., and Eliz., his wife, 207; Eliz., 171, 207; Ellinor, 124 n.; Francis, 137, 276, 277; Anne, wife of, 137; Geo., 274; Hannah, 263; Henry, and wife, 96, 96 n., 97, 189 n., 190; Sir Henry, 175 n., 190, 219; Isab., 197, 201; James, 180; Jane, 120, 170; John, 47, 48, 129, 135, 135 n., 136, 172 n., 174, 179, 206, 259 n., 275 n; John, and Alice, his wife, 136, 184; John, and Eleanor, his wife, 207; John, and Eliz. his wife, 171; John, and Kath., his wife, 120; Joseph, 168; Kath., 127 n; Levett, 265; Lucy, 191, 192, 193, 195, 196; Margt., 169, 179; Mr., 45; Mrs., 174; Ralph, 190 n.;

INDEX OF NAMES.

Rob., 120, 217, 217 n., 218, 248 ; Stephen, 99, 257, 257 n., 258 ; Thos., 121, 274 n. ; Wm., 47 n., 124 n., 179
Thoresby, Thursby, Geo., and wife, 172 n., 174 ; Jeremiah, 263 n. ; John, 263 n. ; Ralph, esq., 15 n., 146 n., 174 n., 215. n., 224 n., 241 n., 251 n., 254 n., 255 n
Thorley, Geo., 121
Thornburrow, Rob., 124
Thorne, Geo., 39 n
Thorncley, Francis, 122, 166
Thornes, Sam., 263 n
Thornhill, Francis, 95 n. ; Geo., 278 ; Joseph, 140 ; Mrs., 147 ; Thos., 6, 164 n. ; ———, 147 n
Thornton, Henry, 54 n., 227, 239, 249 n.; Henry, jun., 249 n. ; Jas., 171, 269n. ; Nich., 249 n. ; Wm., 227, 228, 239, 249 n. ; Capt. Will., 41 n
Thorpe, Tharpe, Baron, 14 n., 34, 35, 35 n., 36, 46, 46 n., 52 ; Francis, 180 ; Jane, wife of, 123, 180 ; John, and Jane, his wife, 121, 168, 169, 181 ; John, and Eliz. his wife, 121 ; John, jun., 121 ; Lancelott, 90, 91 ; Anne, wife of, 91 ; Thos., 123 ; Dorothy, wife of, 123 ; Wm., 121
Threlkelde, Nich., 104
Thun, M. de, 272
Thwaite, Thwaites, Thwayte, Ann, 122 ; Chr., 163 n. ; Geo., 270 ; Mary, wife of, 270 ; Marmaduke, 182 ; Eliz., wife of, 182 ; Wm., 122
Thweng, Thwinge, Alphonso, 270, 270 n.; Edw., and wife, 137 ; family of, 232 n.; Geo., 270 ; Mr., 240 n., 241, 241 n.; Thos., 270 n.; Wm., and wife, 137
Tiplady, John, 137 ; Alice, wife of, 137 ; Stephen, 120 ; Wm., 120
Tislay, Margt., 168
Todd, Anne, 181 ; Capt. 20 ; Geo., 239n ; John, 183 ; Mary, 167, 171 ; Matth., 181, 183 ; Eliz., wife of, 181 ; Ralph, 139 ; Anne, wife of, 139 ; Rich., 181; Isab., wife of, 181 ; Rob., 206 ; Margt. wife of, 206
Tolson, Thos., 163 n. ; Wm., 111
Toman, Eliza, 122
Tomlinson, Thomlinson, Tomlynson, Francis, 262 ; Gabriel, 122 ; Isab. ; 122 ; Margt., 122 ; T., 14 n
Tonge, Humphrey, 175, 175 n., 176
Topham, John, 133 ; Mary, wife of, 133
Torneholme, Eliz., 166
Towle, Wm., 87 n
Towler, Thos., 44

Treese, Judith, 169, 180 ; Wm., 169, 180 ; Jane, wife of, 169, 180
Trewren, Trueren, Thos., 135, 135 n., 136
Trollop, Mr. 47
Trott, Edw., 167
Trotter, Edw., 131, 133, 232 n.; Wm., 238, 239
Troutbeck, John, 4, 5
Trumbell, Trumble, Anne, 207 ; Isab., 269 ; Rob., and wife, 207 ; Thos., 207
Tuadon, Philip, 122
Tubman, Hen., 265 n
Tullie, Tulley, John, 169, 179 ; Eliz., wife of, 169, 179 ; Mr., 96 n
Tunstall, Tonstall, Anne, 183 ; family of, 218 n.; Francis, 137, 171, 269 n., 284 ; Anne, wife of, 137, 171 ; George, 173, 173 n.; Thos., 44 n.; Wm., 137
Turner, Abigail, 269 ; Baron, 165 n.; Chr., 121 ; Edmond, 138, 166, 181 ; Eliz., 184 ; Geo., 137, 207 ; John, 98, 182, 184 ; Merrill, wife of, 184 ; Jonas, 166, 181 ; Joseph, 214 ; Margt., 184 ; Saml., 182 ; Thos., 138 ; Agnes, wife of, 138 ; Valentine, 137
Turpin, Jas., 284 ; Dick, 1 n
Tyndall, Tyndale, Bradwardine, 229 ; Mary, 170 ; Rob., 133 ; Thos., 169 ;
Tyrconnell, ———, 290, 290 n
Tyson, Rob., 40
Tysycke, Zachariah, 206

U V

Ullithorne, Wm., 123 n
Ushard, Joseph, 180
Usher, Anne, 191, 194, 196
Usherwood, Edw., 180
Utley, Jonas, 7
Vadcoe, ———, 182
Vanvalkenburghs, Vanvaulconburghe, Volkenburgh, Mark Van, 12, 13, 174 n., 175 n.; Sir Mat., 12 n
Vasey, Matth., 78, 78 n., 79
Vaughan, Thos., 40 n
Vaux, Andrew, 139 ; Jane, wife of, 139
Vavasour, Vavasor, John, 122, 237, 237 n.; Julian, wife of, 122 ; Peter, 48, 49 n., 121, 243 n., 244, 244 n.; Sir Thos., 244 n.; Sir Walter, 49, 243, 243 n., 244 n
Verity, John, 166
Vernat, Sir Gabriel, 174 n
Verner, Thos., 275 n
Vermuyden, Sir Cornelius, 12 n.

INDEX OF NAMES.

Vernon, Wm., 89
Vevers, Wm., 140
Villiers, Capt. 273
Vittie, Kath., 181

W

Wade, Waide, Wayde, Anthony, 122, 169; Jane, wife of, 122, 169; Chr., 136, 171, 183; Isab., wife of, 136, 171; Cuth., 115; Eliz., 65; Francis, 122; Izrael, 81; Lawrence, 6; Margt., 65; Mary, 75, 75 n., 76, 77; Mr., 126; Philip, 210; Wm., 75, 75 n., 76, 77
Waddington, John, 145 n
Wadsworth, Abraham, 88; Henry, 138; Timothy, 138
Waikefeild, Thos , 4
Waine, Wayne. Timothy, 169, 182
Wainewright, Rich., 142, 143
Waite, Wayte, Geo., 181, 272, 272 n.; Mary, wife of, 181; Jane, 207; Mary, 269 n., 272
Wake, John, 131 n
Walbancke, Welbancke, Alice, 167, 184; Geo., 137, 181; Anne, wife of, 137, 181; Robt,, 138; Elleanor, wife of, 138
Walbran, Mr., 76 n
Wales, Prince of, 24, 291 n
Walker, Anne, 163, 183; Ellioner, 136; Geo., 120; Anne, wife of, 120; Henry, 31; Jane, 179; James, 122, 136, 165 n.; Margery, wife of, 136; John, 32, 78 n., 110, 123, 166, 168, 176, 183, 210, 291; Dorothy, wife of, 123; Margt., 139, 179, 181; Mary, 181; Matthew, and wife, 136, 183; Michael, 120; Anne, wife of, 120; Oswald, Sarah, wife of, 90; Ralph, 9, 284; Rich., 116, 117; Robt., 136, 137, 181, 183, 283; Anne, wife of, 136; Robt. jun., 181; Thos., 181; Eliz., wife of, 181; Wm., 78 n., 139, 184, 283 ; Cecily, wife of, 184
Wall, Eliz., 119
Waller, John, 102 n., 103, 104, 106, 107 n., 108; Robt., 109, 262; Thos., 72; Sir W., 33
Wallis, Wallas, Jane, 299; Jas., 296 n.; John, 137, 171; Eliz., wife of, 137, 171, 183
Walne, Jane, 138; Jane, jun., 138
Walsh, Wm., 123 n
Walters, Robt., 59, 63 n
Walton, John, 226; Lionell, 226; Thos., 226

Walworth, Wm., 137; Wm. jun., 137
Wamesley, Chrysis, 180
Wandesford, Sir Chr., 89 n., 190 n.; John, 82 n
Wannope, Wannoppe, Chr., 151, 152, 153
Ward, Warde, Waude, Anne, 122, 169; Eliz., 122; Ellen, 67; Ellinor, 183; Francis, 263; Humphrey, 71 n.; Isaac, 248; Isab., 169, 180; Jane, 169; John, 38, 48, 74, 108, 109, 122, 169, 174, 182, 273; Joseph, 166; Mary, 263; Mr. 258, 262 n., 263; Ralph, 263, 263 n.; Robt., 122, 169, 182; Sam., Master of Sidney Coll., 84 n.; Thos., 122, 182; Wm., 172, 180
Wardell, Rich., 239 n
Wardeman, Alice, 169, 179; Eliz., 169, 179; John, 169, 179
Warler, Thos., Anne wife of, 5
Warren, Warunn, John, 13; Mark, 89n.; Wm., 72 n., 165
Warriner, Warryner, Simon, 59; Thos., 59
Warton, Dr., 159, 160
Wasse, Ellinor, 160, 160 n
Wastell, Mary. 182
Waterhouse, Chas., 263; Jonas, 116, 117
Waterloe, Andrew, 175 n
Waters, Watters, Col., 104; Robt., 62, 62 n., 63, 63 n
Waterson, Watterson, John, 102, 104, 106
Watkin, Nicholas, 123; Alice, wife of, 123
Watkinson, Dr., 211 n., 213 n.; Geo., 87, 169; Anne, wife of, 169; John, 179; Anne, wife of, 179; Thos., 169, 179
Watson, Alex., 227; Corporal, 103, 106; Edw., 197; Thomasine, wife of, 197; Eliz., 68 n.; Ellen, 180; Geo., 136; Ellen, wife of, 136; Jane, 92, 92 n., 93, 206; James, 68 n.; John, and Anne, his wife, 123; John, and Eliz., his wife, 206; Margt., 179; Mary, 83 n., 136, 180, 184; Matth., 123; Rich., Mary, wife of, 171; Sam., 87, 138; Walter, 207; Wm., 57, 207
Watterton, Anne, 184; Mr., 184, 298 n.; Thos., 45, 167
Waugh, Geo., 174
Wayborne, Wiburn, Robt., 175, 175 n
Wearing, John, 133
Webster, Anth., 172 n.; Hester, 253;

INDEX OF NAMES. 333

Jo., 82 n.; Margt., 121; Sarah, 167; Thos., 255
Weddall, John, 117; Ralph, 207
Wedrell, John, and wife, 180; Mary, 180
Weeke, Sicily, 123
Welborne, Welburne, Anne, 123; Henry, 88 n
Welch, Welsh, Welse, Jos., 141; Mr., 275 n.; Thos., 25, 26
Welken, Wm., 227
Wells, Henry, 168, 182
Wenington, Henry, 168; Alice, wife of, 168
Wentworth, Col., 1, 1 n., 2; Darcy, 1, 1 n., 5, 6, 208; Sir Geo., 1; John, 117; Sir Thos., 249 n
West, Anth., 170; Mary, wife of, 170; Wm., 5
Westerdale, Ralph, 169; Constance, wife of, 169
Westmerland, Earl of, 161 n
Westwood, Margt., 139
Wetherhead, Luke, 150 151
Wetherell, Wetherill, Isab., 183; Jas., Ellen, wife of, 120; John, 171; Mary, wife of, 171; Joseph, 101 n.; Stephen, 104
Whales, Henry, 263
Whaley, Whaely, Whally, Col., 33; John, 166; Wm., 8
Wharfe, Rich., 138
Wharter, Jane, 181
Wharton, Edw., 218; Ursula, wife of, 218; Eliz., 219; John, 218, 236; Lord, 3, 103 n., 108; Mr., 234, 235, 236; Rob., 104; Thos., 104
Wheatley, Lieut., 2
Wheelas, Kath., 169; Wm., and wife, 179
Wheelhouse, Francis, and wife, 179; James, 179; Mary, wife of, 179
Wheldin, Thos., 138; Frances, wife of, 138
Whitaker, Dr., 102 n., 111 n., 254 n
White, Whyte, Col., 283, 283 n.; Cuthbert, 207; Francis, 97, 178, 291; Matth., 275 n.; Rich., 207
Whiteheele, Whitheele, Whitehead, Thos., 148, 148 n., 149
Whitfield, Ann, 194; John, 194; Utrick, 248
Whitnell, Mr., 236
Whittell, John, Eliz., wife of, 168
Whittie, Rich., 167
Whitton, Chr., 111; Thos., 170; Kath., wife of, 170
Wickett, ——, 170; Mary, 182

Wickham, Dr., Dean of York, 281; Wm., 147
Wickliffe, Wicliffe, Wycliffe, Ralph, 135 n., 136; Wm., 135 n., 136
Widdows, Wm., 251
Widdrington, Widrington, Withrington, Lady Bridget, 228; Dame Christiana, 227; Edw., 227, 249 n.; Francis, 206 n., 227, 239 n.; Dorothy, wife of, 206, 227; Henry, 227; Lady, 245, 227; Rob., 187; Wm., esq, 180, 228, 239 n.; Wm., Lord, 101 n., 228
Wier, Mary, 137
Wiggin, Wiggins, John, 298; Robt., Lucy, wife of, 181
Wigglesworth, Wiglesworth, Thos., 80 n., 138
Wiggoner, Mr., 41, 41 n
Wilberfosse, Edw., 120; Frances, wife of, 120
Wilbore, Thos., 260
Wilde, Welde, Wylde, Jane, 138, 171; John, 135, 135 n., 136
Wilding, Wylding, Thos, 135 n., 136; Isabel, 167, 184
Wildiman, Wyldeman, Jeffrey, 133; Ann, wife of, 133; Math., 133, 167; Mary, his wife, 167
Wildsmith, Thos., 142, 143, 144
Wilford, Wilsford, Buckley, 143. 144
Wilkes, Wilks, 47 n.; John, 116
Wilkin, Dorothy, 170
Wilkinson, Agnes, 78; Anne, 176, 177, 218; Edw., 87 n.; Eliz., 170, 183; Francis, and wife, 169; John, 104, 108, 117; Mary, 180; Rich., 120; Anne, wife of, 120; Robt., 174; Stephen, 120; Merial, wife of, 120; Thos., 133; Wm., 100, 174
Willans, Rich. 275 n
William the Conqueror, 218 n
William III., King, 85 n., 286 n., 290, 290 n., 293, 294, 296 n., 298, 299, 300
Williams, Jas., 48; William, 87 n
Williamson, Anne, 123, 170; Eliz., 64; John, 40, 64; 99, 99 n., 100; L., 257 n.; Sarah, 99, 100; Thos., 110, 285 n
Willis, Wyllis, Charles, 168; John, 181; Ellen, wife of, 181
Willman, Jonas, 166
Willoughby, Willughby, Mr., 178; Rich., 179 n
Wilson, Anne, 206; Cath., 272; Chr., 87 n., 137; Anne, wife of, 137; Eliz., 121, 139, 170, 182; Faith, 206; Geo., 89 n., 168, 268; Jane, 168; John,

70 n., 87 n., 122, 241; Eliz., wife of, 122; Margt., 121, 206; Marm., 136, 170, 183; Kath., wife of, 136, 170, 183; Mary, 75; Peter, 207; Prudence, 121, 168; Rich., 98 n., 227; Rich., and Eliz., his wife, 186; Rich., and Margt., his wife, 177; Robt., 269 n., 271; Thos., 87 n., 135, 135 n., 139, 207; Jane, wife of, 139; Wm., 26, 98, 98 n
Wiltshire, Lord, 253
Wiley, Thos., 219, 219 n
Winchester, Marquis of, 258, 258 n
Wincopp, ——, 169; Ellen, 169
Winigates, Mich., 207; Isabel, wife of, 207
Winne, Kath., 255
Winter, John, 123
Wintrees, Bartholomew, 227
Wintrup, Barth., 206
Wiseman, Anne, 284; Francis, 136; Margt., wife of 136; John, 170; Margt., wife of, 170; Michael, 183
Witham, Geo., 137; Grace, wife of, 137; Kath., 269 n
Witty, Dr. 173 n
Witwan, Wetwan, Francis, 129 n.; John, 129 n.; Wm., 122
Wolf, Capt., 299
Wolmesley, Womesley, Womersley, ——, 180, 184; Anne, 167; Eliz., 167; Francis, 167; Wm., 87 n.; Wm., and wife, 180
Wolsingden, Jas., 138; Eliz., wife of, 138; Stephen, 138
Wombwell, Capt., 1.
Wood, ——, 82, 126 n.; Ann, 120; Chr., 133; Francis, 175; Geo., 175 n.; Isabel, 121; Jas., 39, 97; John, 121, 183, 269; Eliz., wife of, 183; Martha, 9 n.; Mary, 137; Rich., 8; Robt., 122, 129 n.; Anne, wife of, 122; Ruth, 125 n.; Sam., 125 n.; Thos., 117
Woodell, Rich., 123
Woodhouse, John, 167
Woodroffe, Thos., 46

Woodward, ——, and Jane, wife of, 139
Woother, Alice, 166
Wormall, John, 166
Worsley, John, 40
Wortley, Sam., 142, 143, 144
Wouldhave, Robt. 93
Wray, Eliz., 137, 169, 171; James, 181; Dorothy, wife of, 181; John, 181; John, and Eliz., wife of, 123, 169, 182; Walter, 174 n
Wren, Mrs., 158 n
Wright, Wreight, Anthony, 57; Chr., 46; Dorothy, 122; Eliz., 172; Jas., 94 n., John, 58; Laurence, 120; Jane, wife of, 120; Mary, 122; Matt., 166; Michael, 179; Ursula, wife of, 179; Mr., 221; Peter, 139; Robt., 122, 138; Joan, wife of, 122; Thos., 107; Wm., 191
Wrightson, Fran., 168; Geo., 177; John, 168; Mich., 168
Wyndham, Hugh, 70
Wythes, Ralph, Frances, wife of, 145 n

Y

Yarbroughe, Yarburgh, Thos., 117; Sir Thos., 251 n
Yeates, John, 121, 210; Wm., 121; Jane, wife of, 121
Yong, Young, Andrew, 276 n.; Anne, 169, 180; Dr., 241; Edw., 168, 182; Henry, 121; John, 14 n., 169, 180; Mary, wife of, 169, 180; Margaret, 168; Robt., 120, 169, 179; Anne, wife of, 169, 179; Thos., 120, 168, 182; Anne, wife of, 120; Tomisin, 127; William, 121, 122, 168, 182; Mary, wife of, 121, 122, 168, 182
York, Dean of, 278; Duke of, 243, 265, 277; Duchess of, 235; John, 138, 171; Eliz., wife of, 138; Mr., 243 n.; Recorder of, 81 n
Younger, Matt., 227
Yowart, Thos., 130

INDEX OF PLACES.

N. B. *The letter* n *after the Number of the page refers to the Note.*

A

Abberwick, 207
Aberdeen, University of, 85 n
Abergavenny, 241
Ackley, Great, 111
Ackworth, 1 n
Aclam-cum-Leavening, 133
Acton, 81 n., 248
Agnes-Burton, 221
Aislaby, 140
Aldbrough, 75 n., 137, 181
Aldfeild-cum-Studly, 179
Aldstone-Moore, 226
Allandaile, 197
Allanton, 227
Allensford, 197
Allergarth, 267
Allerston, 79
Allerton, 181, 203; Mauleverer, 46 n., 70 n.; cum-Wilsden, 138
Almondbury, 23, 86, 89 n
Alne, 63 n., 176, 177
Alnwick, Alnewicke, 85, 85 n., 134 n., 150, 206, 227; Abbey of, 227
Altofts, 123 n
Alwoodley, Alwoodleyes, 139, 170
Ampleford, 130
Amyens, 241
Andfield, 164 n
Antofts, 130
Antwerp, 245 n
Appleby, Apleby, Applebie, Appulby, 64 n., 79, 102 n., 103, 103 n., 104, 105, 106 n., 108, 109, 124, 124 n., 147 n., 277, 285 n
Appleby Castle, 103 n
Appleton, 101 n., 111, 119, 160 n
Ardesley West, 32
Arkendall, 168, 179
Arksey, 133
Armaugh, 286
Armine, 139
Arnold, 123
Arpatrick, 286
Arras, 241

Arrathorne, 180
Arundell, 70 n
Ash-on-Blakesmoor, 222 n
Ashorton, 267
Ashly, 236
Ashwell in Rutlandshire, 43
Askew, Aiskew, 36
Askrigg, 147 n
Attercliffe, 117, 118
Auckland, 158 n
Aughton, 121
Austwicke, 133
Awkley, co. Notts, 95 n
Awsbers, 122
Ayton, East, 55, 88 n
Ayton, Little, 111, 120
Azerley, 169, 179

B

Baghill, 19
Baildon, 170
Bainbrigg, 218
Bardsey, 35 n
Barford, 136, 171, 183, 184
Barforth, 98 n
Barkisland, 86, 166, 181
Barmiston, Barmston, 123, 131 n., 259
Barmoor, 207
Barnard-Castle, 103, 104
Barnbow, Barnbo, 235, 236, 240 n., 241 n., 242 n., 244, 245, 262, 270 n
Barnby Dun, 175, 175 n
Barnby-super-Moram, 139
Barneby, 122
Barningham, 168
Barnoldswicke, 138, 184, 296 n
Barnsley, Barnesley, 6, 142, 142 n., 143, 144, 168, 219 n., 262
Barnsley, Old, 144
Barrasford, 191
Barwick, (Berwick-on-Tweed,) 156, 191
Barwick-in-Elmet, 119, 141, 134, 139, 240
Basing-house, 42

INDEX OF PLACES.

Batley, 83 n., 178 n., 291
Bawtry, 24 n., 25
Beaufront, 227
Beckwith, 169
Bedale, Beadall, Beedall, 36, 36 n., 122, 169, 182, 203, 203 n., 214, 218
Bedlington, Bedlinton, 203, 229
Beeforth, 123
Bees, Beose, St., 298, 298 n
Beeston, 253 n., 254, 254 n
Beilby, 80 n
Belford, 207
Bellerby, 171
Belton, 175 n
Benfullside, 248
Beningbrough, 259 n
Bensley, 174 n
Bentham, 107
Berehall, 227
Berehow Cragg, 207
Berwick, Berwicke, 197, 245 n
Beverley, 46, 47, 50, 52, 53, 53 n., 63, 63 n., 67, 67 n., 128, 144 n., 172 n., 233
Bewcastle, 151 n., 152 n., 153, 155 n., 294
Bewerley, Buerley, 123, 179, 217, 217 n
Bewhall-super-Nunkeeling, 123
Bickarton, Bickerton, 206, 227
Billington, Long, 261
Bilsdale, 130
Bilton, 168, 182
Binchester, 158 n
Bingley, Morton Banks par., 100
Birdsall, 133, 141, 142
Birge, 241
Birka, Birkey, Birkett, 66, 102 n., 103, 104, 105, 107, 138
Birkhill, 207
Birkside, Birkenside, 194, 196, 201
Birkside-nooke, Birchen-nooke, Birksnooke, Birksnuke, 191, 192, 193, 199, 200
Birstall, 14 n
Bishopbridge, Byshopbridge, (The county of Durham,) 37
Bishop Warmouth, 27
Bishop-Wilton, 3 n
Biskerton, 157
Bittleston, 227
Blackstone, Blaxton, 95
Blaydon, 93
Blyth, 49 ; Blyth-Nook, 229, 229 n
Boldon, 135 n
Bolling, Bowling, 28, 29, 30, 180
Bolton, 68 n., 207 ; New, 253
Bolton-hill, 138
Booth-Ferry, 49 n., 50

Bootland, 228
Boroughbridge, Burrowbridge, 169, 180, 218, 290 n., 297 n
Boston, Boaston, 20, 34
Bothal, Bothel, Bothwell, 135 n., 189 n., 190 ; Castle of, 189, 189 n
Botterill, 221
Bothwell-Bridge, 239 n
Boulton, 139, 181 ; Boulton juxta-Bolland, 184
Bowes, 168
Bowland, 184
Bowness, 124 n
Boynton, 258, 259, 259 n
Bradfeild, 167
Bradford, 51, 51 n., 86 n., 107, 109, 116, 116 n., 117, 118, 118 n., 130 n., 137, 138, 146 n., 166, 205 n., 207, 291
Bradford, Waddington-in, 184
Bradley, 227
Braithwaite, Little, 110
Bramham, 11 n., 298 ; Bramham-Moore, 214
Brandesburton, Brandsburton, 43, 88 n., 123
Bransby, 27, 28, 137
Brearley, 167
Brecon-hill, 300
Bretton, 249 n
Brettonby, 203 n
Bridlington, Burlington, 41 n., 42, 79, 144, 144 n., 222, 291 n
Brigg, 35
Brigham-baulke-end, 221
Brighton, 84
Brinkburn, Brinkburne, 126 n., 206
Bristol, 27, 33, 258 ; Kings' Roads, at, 33
Brodsworth, 1 n
Bromeley, 206
Bromerigg, 184
Brompton, 138, 230 ; Super-Swale, 100 n., 139, 225
Broom Park, 207
Brotherton, 45, 229, 294
Brough, 72, 73, 123, 153, 182, 207
Broughton, 115, 138, 234 ; Hall, 232 n., 233, 235, 236
Brownelston, 292
Bruges, 241
Brumfeild. co. Cumb., 291
Brussels, 286
Bubwith, 121
Buckden, 88 n
Bulmer, 137
Burgh, 170
Burley, 170

INDEX OF PLACES.

Burnby, 50
Burneston, Burniston, 224 n., 225
Burnsall, 6 n
Burrell-cum-Coolinge, 182
Burstwick, 122, 166
Burton, 121, 180; Agnes, 43, 221; Cherry, 53; Leonard, 145 n., 169, 179; Super-Ure, 122, 169
Busby, 120
Butterwicke, 27
Byerley, 30; Byreley-North, 166, 181
Byland, Old, 25
Bywell, 196, 199, 228, 297

C.

Calais, Calice, 241
Caldwell, Caudwill, 136, 171, 183
Callaly, Calliley, Callolee, 207, 228, 248 n
Calverley, 138, 166, 180
Cambridge, 9 n., 224 n.; St. John Coll., 165 n.; Sidney Coll., 253 n
Camerton, 121
Campsall, 167
Canterbury, 172 n
Cantley, 139
Capheaton, 227
Cardew, 291
Carleton, Carlton, 48, 82 n., 136, 243, 251 n.; Miniott. 59, 59 n., 60
Carleton-Thwaite, 292
Carlinghow, 291
Carlisle, Carlile, 95, 95 n., 96, 97, 97 n., 98, 104, 105, 106, 108, 124 n., 150 n., 151, 151 n., 152 n., 154, 162 n., 286 n., 292, 299, 300
Carnonley, 291
Cartington, 227
Casterton, 35
Castleford, 1 n., 167
Cathorp, 70 n
Catterick, Cathericke, 160, 160 n., 182, 218, 218 n
Cavers (Scotland,) 208, 208 n
Cawthorne, 142
Cawood, Cawwood, 154, 154 n
Chatton, 187 n., 207
Chepstow, 42
Chester, 81 n., 190, 190 n., 270 n., 281 n
Chillingham, 187
Chipchase, 75 n
Cissenbury-craggs, 294
Clackheaton, Cleckheaton, 138, 166, 181
Clapham, 133, 167
Clayton, 208
Cleaburne (Westmerland), 73
Cleasby, 139

Clenell, Clennall, 159, 227
Clide, The, 273
Cliffe, 137
Clifton, 82 n., 123, 169, 181, 277
Cloughton, 257 n
Coategill, 104
Cockermouth, 94, 290 n
Cockerton, 110, 111
Coftley, 206
Colden, 123
Coldhil, 23
Coley Hall, par. Halifax, 86, 86 n., 157
Collingham, 134 n
Coniescote, 180
Connondell, 46 n
Copgrove, Copgrave, 67, 67 n., 68 n
Corbridge, 150 n., 191, 197, 227
Corby, 152 n., 162 n., 286
Cotherstone, 168
Cottingwith, 122
Coulburne, Coulburne, 170, 182
Coverham-cum-Oglethorpe, 171, 181
Cowton, North, 80
Craister, 188 n
Cramb, 65
Craven, 115, 115 n., 217, 223 n., 232 n., 235, 236
Crawhall, 226
Cray, 88 n
Creswell, 229, 229 n
Cridling-stubbs, 139
Crockesam, Crocksom, 34
Crofton, 85 n.; Hepworth, par., 166
Cronkley, 248
Crosby, Crosbie, 151 n.; -Garrat, 103; -Ravenside. -Ravensworth, 72, 163 n.,
Crosland, South, 86
Crosthwaite, 110
Croston, 8
Crumlin, 299
Cudworth, 167
Cundall, 63 n.

D

Dalston, 292, 293
Dalton, 171, 183, 289; -cum Gailes, 136; North, 26
Danby, 298 n
Danthorpe, 121, 168, 181
Darder, 155
Darfield, 83
Darlington, Darnton, 5 n., 94 n., 106
Darrington, 98 n., 146 n
Deighton, North, 70 n
Denbigh, Denby, 209, 210
Denham, 227

Z

INDEX OF PLACES.

Denmark, 286
Dent, 133
Denton, 238
Derby, 70 n
Derwentwater, Island on, 286
Develstone, 228
Dewsbury, Dewisbury, 215, 215 n., 216, 216 n., 282, 286, 286 n., 287, 288, 290
Dilston, 300 ; -Hall, 300 n
Dinnington, 167
Dolbank, Dolbanck, 232 n., 240 n., 242, 242 n., 246.
Don, The, 12 n
Doncaster, 12 n., 14 n., 16, 16 n., 17, 17 n., 22, 23, 24, 25, 33, 33 n., 34, 35, 95 n., 117, 225 n., 249, 249 n., 256, 279 n
Dortres, Dartrees, 206, 207, 227
Douay, Doway, Coll. of, 44, 231 n., 241.
Dover, 45
Downeholme, Downham, 181, 207
Driffield, 167 ; Little, 56 ; South, 167
Drighlington, 166, 181
Dringoe, 123
Dublin, 254, 298 n., 299
Duggleby, 133
Dumfrees, 106
Dunbar, 11 n
Dundalk, 285
Dunham-Massey, 81 n
Dunkirke, 26, 31
Durdar, 292, 293
Durham, 11 n., 37 n., 46 n., 68 n., 70 n., 85 n., 94 n., 99 n., 102 n., 104, 105, 106, 106 n., 107, 107 n., 108, 111 n., 157 n., 194, 237 n., 248 n., 271 n., 277 n., B'pric of, 47, 72, 104, 109, 111, 135 n., St. Mary in South Bailey, 135 n., St. Nicholas in, 27 n

E

Eadlethorpe, 141
Ealand, 182
Easby, 137
Easington, 26
Ecclesfield, 5, 5 n., 128
Eccleshill, 181
Edderston, 207
Edinburgh, 85 n,, 165
Edgebridge, Edgebrigg, 196, 199, 200, 201
Edlington, 207, 261
Edmondbyers, Edmondshyers, Edenbyers, 194, 199, 201
Eglingham, 135 n

Egremont, 285 n
Egton, 39 n., 147, 147 n., 230 n., 232 n
Ellerton, 134, 160, 181
Ellerstring, 122
Ellington, 122, 169, 182
Elmsall, 14 n
Elsdon, Ellesden, 84, 85 n., 206
Elsternwick, 121, 182
Elswick, 75 n., 229
Elton, 53
Emley, 126 n
Eppleby, Appleby, 136, 163, 184
Errinden, Erringdon, 138, 166
Escrick, Eskirk, 46 n
Esdale, 147
Esk, 292
Eslington, 207, 228
Esper-sheilds, 248
Everingham, 244 n., 271
Everley, 55
Everton, (co. Notts.) 95

F

Fairly-May, 194, 196
Farburne, 45, 294
Farlam, 151 n
Farlington, 137
Farmanby, 170
Farnaby, 111
Farneham, 61, 62, 169, 227
Farneley, nr. Leeds, 82 n., 102 n., 111 n., 112, 116, 141, 141 n., 146 n., 216 n., 254 n
Farneworth, 63 n
Fawdon, 277
Fearby, 122, 169
Featherstone, 167
Felton, Fellton, 52, 206, 227, 249 n
Fencote, Great, 203 n.
Fenham, 227, 238, 245, 245 n., 246, 249 n
Ferry-bridge, Ferry-briggs, Ferribriggs, 16, 17, 20
Filingdales, 140
Finghall, 180
Finningley, 95 n
Firby, 57, 182
Fishlake, Fislake, 31, 87 n
Fitling, Fittlinge, 121, 168, 182
Fixby, Fekisby, 147, 147 n., 164 n., 166
Flamborough-Head, 41
Flanders, 26, 45, 286
Flinton, 121, 168
Florence, Florrence, 233
Forcett, 136, 170, 183
Ford, 184

INDEX OF PLACES.

Foston, 39
Foulforth, 263
Fountains-Abbey, 123; Castle, 179
Foxholes, 43
France, 146, 285
Froddingham, North, 123
Fylcy Bay, 41

G

Gainsborough, Gansebrough, 98, 221, 260
Gallow-hill, 227
Galtres, 161 n
Ganstead, 121, 168
Garford, 262
Garforth, 126 n
Gargoe, 300
Gargrave, Gargreave, 64, 65, 115, 126 n
Gariston, Garistown, 299, 300, 300 n
Garton-cum-Grimston, 168
Gateshead, Gateside, 10 n., 135 n., 145 n., 226
Gawthorpe, 152 n
Germany, 230
Gilling, 137, 171, 183
Gisburne, 83 n
Glanton, 277
Glasgow, Univ. of, 85 n
Gomersall, 138
Goodmadam, 122
Goswick, 187 n
Gowle, 139
Grange, 206
Grantham, 260
Graystocke, Greystocke, 106, 166
Greatland, 166
Greene Leyton, 155
Greenhill, co. Derby, 161
Greenes-burne, 153
Greta Bridge, 163 n., 190 n
Grewillthorpe, 179
Gristropp, 122
Grosmont-Bridge, 230 n
Guernsey, Garncey, Garnsey, 32, 34
Gumpton, 180
Gunnerby, 261
Gunnerton, 294, 294 n., 295

H

Hackness, 140, 188 n
Haggerston, Haggerstown, 245 n., 246, 292
Hagthorpe, 48
Halifax, Hallifax, Halyfax, Hallyfax, 7 n.,
11, 11 n., 52, 52 n., 86 n., 93 n., 126 n.,
137, 146 n., 147, 147 n., 157 n., 165,
166, 224 n., 276 n.; Brears-Chapel,
par. 83 n
Halletrome, 123
Hallikeld, 182
Halsam, Halsham, 122, 139, 166
Haltwhistle, Witchells par., 188 n
Hambleton, Hamblton, 165; Black, 47
Hamton, 45
Hampton Court, 95 n
Hansworth, 139
Hardger, church of, 165 n
Harker, 97
Harla-Hill, 135
Harnby, 181
Harrogate, Harrigate, The Spa, The Wells, 99 n., 102 n., 104, 107, 108, 160, 179, 252 n
Harrow, 135 n
Harshead, 166
Harsley East, 116 n
Hartforth, 218
Hartlepool, 208 n
Hartley, 105, 147, 148 n
Harup, 207
Harwood, 139; Dale, 140
Haslewood, Hazlewood, Heslewood, 48, 243 n., 244 n
Hatfield, 69 n., 123, 174 n., 175, 175 n.; Chase, 12 n., 174 n.; House, 128
Havercroft, 167
Hawkinge-Bower, 148 n
Hawksworth, 89 n., 91, 92
Haworth, 137, 166
Haxby, 39
Haydon, 197
Hayholme, 123
Heale, Healle, 206, 227
Healey-cum-Sutton, 122, 169
Heapall, 227
Heaton, 181; -cum-Clayton, 138, 166
Hebden, 138
Heckmondwicke, Heckmondwike, Heckmondwyke, Heckmondyke, 138, 166, 181, 278, 291
Helagh, 148 n
Helgrainge, 87 n
Helmesley, Helmsley, Hemsley, 25 n, 48, 129, 129 n, 130
Hempholme, 123
Heptenstall, Heptonstall, 6, 7, 8, 9, 138
Herbert, St., Island of, 286, 286 n
Hesle, 28
Heslerigg, 207
Hesleyside, Heslysyde, Hesslyside, 228, 296 n., 297, 297 n
Heslington, 10 n., 41 n

340   INDEX OF PLACES.

Hessay Moor, 270, 272
Hewby, Huby, 138, 228, 228 n., 229
Heworth, 137, 181, 232 n., 241 n., 270 n
Hexham, 155 n., 188 n., 206, 227, 228, 297, 298; -shire, 228
High House (Cumb.), 159
Highlands, The, 297, 300
Highley, 161, 162
Hillam, 221
Hilton, 120
Hinderskelfe, 56, 137
Hinderthwaite, 168
Hindley-sheale, 207
Hingham, 293
Hipperholme, 164, 166, 181
Holbeck-Moor, 255 n
Holbeck, 103, 263 n
Holborn, (White Swan, nr.) 33
Holdon, (Hayle Mill, nr.) 219
Holderness, 129 n., 233, 234
Holland, 6, 34, 45, 165, 257, 259, 273, 298
Holling-hall, 223, 223 n
Hollisfeild, 197
Hollow Mill, 148, 148 n
Holme, Hollam, Hollen, Holleym, Hollim, Hollym, 122, 128 n., 129, 171; The, 152; Beacon, 120; in Spaldingmore, 89 n., 120
Hooke, 139
Hopperton, 46 n
Hopton, 146
Horbury, 85 n., 166
Horneby, 138
Hornsey, 129 n.; cum-Barton, 123
Horsley, 206; Long, 206
Horton, 130 n., 133, 166, 167, 180, 205 n
Housesteads, 227
Houghton, Howton, 167, 183
Howden, 49, 49 n., 219 n., 220, 221; Panns, 206
Howe, 59 n
Howley Park, 111
Hoyland, 166
Huddersfield, Hothersfeilde, 51, 52, 286, 287 n., 289, 290
Hull, 43, 46 n., 125 n., 129 n., 208 n., 275 n., 278, 283 n
Humber, The, 26, 27
․․․, 121, 168, 182, 207
.unbre

Offerton, 135 n
Ogle, 188 n

188 n.; upon-Darwent, 56; John, 66, 66 n.; Pannell, 133, 167; Robert, 139; Rudby, 120

I J

Idle, 137, 166, 181
Ilkley, 223, 224
Ilton-cum-Pottoe, 122, 169, 182
Ingleton, 70, 95, 133, 167
Ipres, Ypres, 241
Ireland, Ierland, 14 n., 33, 45, 164 n., 165, 190 n., 230, 232 n., 254, 255, 255 n., 265 n., 293, 297
Islip, co. Derby, 190
Jedburgh, 208 n
Jersey, 32 n
Jerusalem, Hierusalem, 161 n

K

Kabar, Kaber, Kabur, Caber-rigg, 96, 102 n., 103, 104, 105, 107, 111 n
Kendall, 63, 64, 94, 104
Kestron, 227
Keswick, 94 n., 110; -East, 140
Kighley, 78, 114, 126
Kildwick, 134 n
Kilham, Kelham, 94, 207
Killen, 285
Killerby, 225
Killinghall, 169, 179; -Moor, 99
Killnsey, 129
Kirkby, Kirby, 120; Grindelythe, 133; Hill, 136, 170, 184, 219; Malzard, 179; Moorside, 53 n.; Ravensworth, 126 n., 284; Stephen, 105, 147 n., 149; Usborne, 63; Wiske, 78 n
Kirke Smeaton, 167
Kirkham, 40 n
Kirk-heaton, 281, 288, 289
Kirklees, 164 n
Kirklington, 82 n., 89 n
Kirkethorpe, Kirkethorpp, 38
Kilvington, 44, 45, 231 n., 266
Kintir, 297
Kirstall, 141
Kipling, 203
Kippax, 140, 178 n
Klint, 179
Knaresborough, Knaseborough, Knaseborough, 4, 5 n., 46 n., 47 n., 169, 179, 216, 252, 297 n.
Knapton, 263
․․ ․ttingley, 22, 54 n., 55
․nowlestones, 138

INDEX OF PLACES.

L

Labourne, Laborne, Layburn, 80, 180, 272 n
Lamesley, 135, 135 n
Lanches, 207
Lanckaster, 27 n
Langfoild. 166
Langley, 17, 123
Lanton, 207, 227
Larcon, 179
Lartington, 168
Larton, 169
Laton, 170, 183
Laughton-en-le-Morthen, 69 n
Laytons Ambo, 136
Leathey, 234
Leeds, 12, 15 n., 46, 67, 68, 81, 87 n., 88, 100 n., 102 n., 103, 141, 146 n., 214, 215, 215 n., 216, 216 n., 220, 224, 244 n., 246, 253 n, 254, 255 n., 257 n., 263, 263 n., 290, 290 n
Leeming, 37
Lee-Ryden, 206
Lelley, Lelly, 121, 168, 182
Lemmonton, 207
Lesbury, 207
Lotbury, 1, 1 n
Lincolne, Lyncolne, 20, 24 n., 25, 98, 161 n., 261
Linnells, The, 295
Linton-cum-Youlton, 139
Lisle, Lyle, 241
Liverseige, Leversedge, 88 n., 181
London, 28, 33, 34, 35, 36, 42, 46, 59 n., 60, 64 n., 89, 99, 104, 111, 134, 134 n., 146, 146 n., 164 n., 165 n., 174 n., 187 n., 219, 220 n., 230, 234, 235, 237, 237 n., 239, 239 n., 251, 251 n., 254, 254 n., 262, 283 n., 285, 293 ; Charing Cross, in, 234 ; Cripplegate, 134 n., 290 ; Gray's Inn, 271 n. ; Lincoln's Inn, 90 ; St. Martin's-in-the-Fields, 164 ; Newgate, 28, 241 n. ; Pye Corner, in, 240 n. ; Tower of, 37 n., Whitehall, in, 34, 62, 141, 146, 296 n., 297 n., 298
Longtown, 292
Longwitton, 155, 247
Louth, 285
Lowe, The, 272 n
Lowesk, 207
Loweswater, 94, 94 n. ; Baryet (pat.), 94 n
Luddendon, 276 n
Lupset, 81, 81 n
Lyham, 207
Lynn, 26

M

Mackworth, 81 n
Malham, 184
Maltby, Maultby, 120, 260
Mallerston, Mallerstone, Mallerstang, 106, 107, 108, 147 n
Malton, 44, 45, 47 n., 55 n., 89 n., New, 9, 40, 40 n., 53 n., 55, 56, 57, 90, 91 ; Old, 9, 47 n., 90
Man, Isle of, 97 n
Manchester, 225
Manningham, 86 n., 116
Mansfeild, 260 n., 261
Markingfield Park, 69, 70 n
Marrick, Marwick, 49 n., 168
Marseilles, Marcellis, 233
Marshland, 58 n
Marske, 168, 258 n
Marston, 270 n ; Moor, 4 n., 20 n., 270 n
Marton, 46 n., 223 n
Maryland, 125 n
Masham, Massam, 122, 182
Matfen, 228
Mayneby, 78 n
Melborne-cum-Storthwaite, 121
Melmerby, 81
Melsonby, 136, 171, 184
Menston, 170
Metham, 89 n., 270, 270 n
Methley, 5, 178, 178 n
Mickley, 192, 193, 195
Middleton, 81 n. ; One-Row, 271 n. ; Quarnehow, 182 ; South, 227
Midgeley, 166, 182
Midlam, 225
Midlins, 12, 12 n., 13
Milford, 43
Minskip, 179
Mirfield, 31, 32, 146, 146 n., 147, 287, 288, 289
Misterton, 95 n
Mitton, 184 ; cum Bashall, 168
Monmouth, Munmouth, 283
Mooretoune, 214
Morcarre, 70 n
Morley, 112
Morpeth, 189 n., 191, 193, 194, 195, 198, 202, 248, 264
Morton, 208 ; Hart, 170
Mountgrace, 111
Mowshoms, 6
Mugg..
19.
Mul..
Murton
Mu...
My...

342   INDEX OF PLACES.

N

Nabbock, 227
Naborn, Naburne, 167, 263
Naddall, 110
Nafferton, Naferton, 228, 286
Namur, 297 n
Naples, 175 n
Naseby, Nazeby, 33
Nateby, 148 n
Naworth, 269 n
Netherhaye, 206
Netherwitton, 227, 249 n
Newark, Newarke, 49 n., 260, 261
Newband, 218
Newbiggin, 108, 153, 188 n., 227, 292
Newby, 292; Park, 164, 164 n
Newcastle-on-Tyne, 20, 74 n., 83, 85 n., 88, 92, 92 n., 93 n., 99, 112, 112 n., 116, 124, 124 n., 127, 135, 143, 145 n., 152 n., 154, 158 n., 165, 172, 172 n., 173 n., 174 n., 189 n., 190, 192, 195, 198, 204, 208, 208 n., 237, 238, 239 n., 240 n., 241, 242, 245, 245 n., 251 n., 253, 268, 268 n., 273, 273 n., 274, 274 n., 275, 275 n., 276, 286, 293 296, 296 n., 297; All Saints Church, 173 n., 174 n.; Bigg Market, 158; St. John's Church, 173 n., 174 n.; Sandgate, in, 88, 154, 275; Pipergate, in, 208 n
Newfeild, 196
Newhall, 16, 17
Newlands, 227
Newlathes, 249
Newless, 25
Newmarket, 252
Newport, 241
Newsham, Newsam, Newsholme, 78 n., 121, 138, 167, 171, 183, 184, 225
Newton, 66, 122, 138, 139, 156; -hall, 206; Kime, 72; -super-Derwent, 139; West, 121, 207
Nitherdaile, 48
Norfolk, 293
Normanby, 27
Northallerton, 104, 220 n., 240
Northwick, 81 n
Nortoft, 174 n
Norway, 286
Nottingham, 236, 260
Nunappleton, 119
N....ok, 164 n

Okenshaw, 138
Oldstead, 130
Ollerton, 15, 20
Omer, St., 241
Ormskirk, 245 n
Orton, 104, 108
Osmotherley, 45, 111, 138
Ossett, 166, 184
Oswald-Kirk, 153
Otley, 170
Ottringham, 122
Otterburn, 206
Owram, North, 93 n., 166; South, 138, 180
Ouse, The, 270 n
Ouseburn, Useburn, Usburn, 62, 71, 71 n.; Great, 71; Little, 46 n., 71
Ovenden, 86, 138, 181
Overacres, 297 n
Ovingham, 135 n., 228; Spittal par., 228
Ovington, 171, 183
Owstwick, 129 n
Oxford, 262

P

Pannell, 179
Paris, 45, 233, 236, 241, 248 n
Parke, 227
Parlington, 298 n
Pateley Briggs, 140
Pattericke-cum-Brumpton, 170
Pattrington, 121, 166
Pawston, 188 n
Peglesworth, 135
Pendragon Castle, 107
Penrith, 106, 110, 159
Peterborough, 34
Pewill Hill, 262
Pickall, 182
Pickering, Pickring, 24, 43, 46, 47 n., 90, 140, 170, 178 n., 186; Thornton in, 140
Piercebridge, 163 n
Plumpton, 46 n
Pocklington, 24, 45, 80 n., 87 n
Poole, 170
Pontefract, Pomfreit, 6, 13, 15 n., 16, 17, 18, 19, 20, 20 n., 23, 23 n., 43, 98 n., 100, 101, 126 n., 146 n., 165 n., 221, 253 n.; Castle of, 5 n., 13 n., 14 n., 16 n., 18 n., 19, 20, 21, 22, 23, 270 n
Pont-island, 237, 275
Portinscale, Portinshail, 110
Portugal, Portingale, 42, 106
Preston, 167

INDEX OF PLACES.

Prudhoe, Pruddoe, Pruddow, 192, 194, 195
Pudsey, 138, 166, 181

Q

Quokit, 297

R

Ragnall, 221
Raichell-foot, 206'
Rastricke, 138, 181
Ravenstondale, 103, 105, 108
Ravensworth, 137, 183
Rawden, Rawdon, 99, 139
Reath, Reeth, 10 n., 168
Redesdale, 297 n
Redhouse, 298 n
Reednes, 58
Reins, in Champagne, 285
Remington, Rimington, 167, 184
Richmond, 81, 99 n., 100 n., 110, 126 n., 145, 146, 160 n., 214, 218, 224 n
Rickerby, 153
Riding Mill, 156, 191, 192, 193, 194, 195, 198
Ridley, New, 194, 196
Rimside, Rimpside, 155, 156; -Moor, 165
Ripley, 232 n., 242, 242 n., 246
Ripon, Rippon, 43, 45, 59, 59 n., 60, 69, 75 n., 76 n., 77, 99, 164 n., 211, 217, 217 n., 283, 284, 284 n., 285
Risam, 129
Rishworth, 138, 166, 181
Ritton, 227
Riveling Forest, 70 n
Rivis, 25
Rochdale, Ratchdale, 43, 126 n , 216
Rocke, 134 n.
Rockliffe, Rocliffe, Rowcliffe, 14 n., 97, 169, 180, 300
Rodbury, 157
Rodwell, 115 ; Rhodes, par. 69
Rokeby, 11 n., 163
Romanby, Rummonby, 240, 241
Rome, Roome, 45, 233, 236, 266
Rookwith, 169; -cum-Therne, 123, 182
Rossington, 256, 256 n., 257
Rothberry, 227
Rotherham, 31, 53 n., 96, 125, 125 n., 128, 239, 239 n., 260, 261
Rothwell, 85 n., 134
Rotterdam, 258
Roundhay, 119
Rownton, West, 138

Rouse, 169
Royston, Roistone, 34, 261
Rukton, 248
Russia, 152 n
Rushton, Ruston, 47, 47 n., 123
Ryall, 121
Ryton, 90

S

Sandal, 260 n
Sandford, 277
Sandhutton, 59 n., 215 n
Santoft, 174, 175, 175 n
Sawley, 217
Saxton, 243 n., 276
Scaleby, 173 n
Scarborough, Scarbrough, Scardbrough, 26 n., 27, 30, 30n., 31, 41, 41 n., 47n., 80 n.. 101 n., 257, 257 n., 283 ; Castle of, 22 ; Spa, 173 n
Scarcroft, 119, 140
Scargill, 44 n., 168
Scarthingwell, Scardingwellgate, 89n., 276
Scarwick, 141 n
Scotland, Scottlande, 33, 34, 39, 86, 98, 101, 103, 106, 150 n., 239, 241, 242, 263 n., 297
Scotton, 4 n., 169, 179, 252
Screwton, 182
Seacroft, 119, 140 ; Moor, 11, 11 n
Seamer, 120
Seaton, 123
Sedberge, Sedbergh, 80, 133, 167
Sedgemoor, 277 n
Seine, 248 n
Selby, 54, 54 n., 67, 89 n
Sepulchres near Hedon, 43
Shadwell, 123 n
Sharlston, 74, 81 n
Sheffield, 69 n., 128, 139, 161, 261 ; Park, 70 n
Shelfe, 181
Sheriffe-button, 137
Shields, Sheilds, 84, 264, 268, 286 ; North, 237 n., 264, 268, 268 n., 275 n
Shieldfield, 208 n
Shippen, Shippon, 262 ; Hall, 240
Shipton, 120
Shire-oak, Scarwick, Scyrack, 14 n
Shitlington, 166
Siena, 233
Siglesthorne, 123
Skamston, 91
Skeeby, 183
Skerne, 133

INDEX OF PLACES.

Skewsby, 137, 271 n
Skidby, 43
Skipsey, 38 n., 121
Skipton, 114, 138, 217, 232, 232 n., 233, 234, 236
Skipwith, 130 n
Skircoate, 138, 180
Skirley, North, 123 ; South, 121
Skriven, 169
Slaidburne, 66, 80 n., 138, 283 n
Slealy, 197, 201
Sledmere, 15 n., 23 n
Sleights, 230
Smeaton, 140; Great, 139; Parva, 139
Snainton, 10 n
Snaith, 78 n., 85 n
Snape cum-Thorpe, 182
Snow-hill, 75
Southburne, 133
Sowerby, 157, 157 n
Spain, 45
Spaldington, 48
Spenithorne, 181
Spennhouse, 149
Spinnelston, 207
Spittle, 103
Spofforth, 70 n
Sprotley, 121, 168, 182
Stacksby, 124 n
Stafford, 28, 45
Staindrop, Staindropp, 68 n., 161 n
Stainemore, 72, 73
Stainforth, 138
Stainland, 166, 182
Stainley, 189 ; -cum-Caton, 169
Stamford, 260
Standwicke, 183
Stangrave, 47
Stanhope, 277 n
Stannering-End, 157
Stanners, The, (Morpeth,) 202
Stannington, 82 n., 277
Stansfield-cum-Langfield, 138
Stanton, 207
Stanwick, Stanig, Stanwix, 131, 131 n., 190
Staynton-dale, 283
Stappleton, 139
Staveley, 179, 190
Steanbecke, 169, 179; Steanbeck-downe, 169, 180
Steeton, Steeton, 114, 126, 134 n
Stella, 116 n
Stiford, 198
Stillington, 139
Stilton, 34, 261
Stirling, 300
Stokes, 207

Stocksfield, 192, 194, 195 ; Stockfield Hall, 228
Stockhill Hall, (Stokeld) 243
Stokesley, Stoxley, 111, 120
Stonecroft, 228
Stonegarth-side, 263 n
Stonesdales, West, 147 n
Stratforth, 168
Studley, 75, 76 n., 77 ; Magna, 77 ; Roger, 123 ; Royal, 210 n., 211
Sugdell, 184
Sunderlande, 27, 88 n
Sunderlandwicke, 94
Sutton Howgrave, 217 n
Sutton-super-Derwent, 171
Swaledale, Swailedale, 147 n., 149, 258
Swarland, 206
Sweden, 286
Swillinton, 262
Swine, 168
Swinfleet, 139
Swinton, 182; -cum-Wartherin kc, 122
Syddell, Little, 116 n
Sykehouse, Sikehouse, 87 n., 98, 176

T

Tadcaster, 72 n., 214
Tanfield, Marmion Chantry at, 37 n. ; West, 182
Tangier, 190, 220 n
Tankersley Park, 70 n
Tanston, 121
Tees, The, 41
Thickett, Thicket, 25, 130 n., 219 n
Thirsk, 36 n., 215 n
Thoralby, 217 n
Thornaby, Thorneby, 89 n., 116 n., 135 n
Thorne, 49 n., 87 n., 88 n., 98, 99 n., 175 n
Thorneton, Thornton, 133, 138, 166, 170, 171, 181 ; -in-le-Beanes, 138 ; in-Craven, 80 n.; -in-Pickering, 140 ; Risebrough, 47 n.; Steward, 59 n., 180 ; Watlas, 123
Thorngrafton, 188 n
Thornington, 207
Thorpe, 10 n., 14 n., 163
Threlkeld, 124
Thropton, 227
Thurleston, 6
Thurne, 169
Thwaite, 121; -in-Swaledale, 148 n
Tickhill, Castle of, 68 n
Tollerton, 177
Tong, Touge, 29, 130 n., 166, 181, 225
Topcliffe, 59 n., 60

INDEX OF PLACES.

Tote Hill, 147
Townhead (in Jedburgh), 206, 208, 208 n
Towthrop, 39
Treason field, 80
Tunstall, 170, 182
Turnebrigg, 20
Tursdale, 271 n
Turvelawes, 187 n
Turvin, Valley of, 126 n
Tuxford, 221
Twisleton, 70
Tyburn, 286 n
Tyno, The, 296 n
Tynemouth, Tinmouth, 20 n., 82, 84, 84 n., 264, 264 n.; Castle of, 20, 20 n., 240 n., 245 n., 273

U V

Ugthorpe, 230 n
Ullock, 83 n., 290 n.
Ulrom, 121
Unthanke, 228, 248, 248 n
Upsall, 44
Upton, 34, 123
Usfleet, 139
Virginia, 214

W

Waddington-cum-Bradforth, 167
Wadsworth, Waddsworth, 7, 138, 166
Wadworth, 178 n., 181
Waitwith, 179
Wakefield, 38, 74, 81, 88 n., 97, 97 n., 146 n., 184, 216, 220 n., 263 n., 276 n
Walden, 93 n
Wales, 270
Walkington, 144
Wall, the Roman, 150 n
Wallicke-Grainge, 228
Walsend, 206
Walton, 45, 298 n.; -cum-Bretton, 184
Waltowne, 227
Walworth, 215 n
Wapping, Wappen, 36, 164 n.; Chapel at, 17 n
Warder, 235, 236
Warlaby, 139
Warley, Wareley, 138, 166, 181
Warmfield, 38; -cum-Heath, 166
Warter, 87 n., 234
Warwick-Briggs, 292
Wascow-Shield, 155
Watton, 133, 166
Waune, Waghen, 121

Wawton, 50
Welburne, 137
Welburg, 95 n
Wells, 33
Welmarch, 123
Wonsidaile, 218
Wensley, 181
Wentbridge, 221
Wentworth, 15 n
Westharle, 227
Westminster, 60; Abbey of, 281 n.; St. Margaret's in, 9 n
Westow, Westowe, 40, 40 n., 57
Wetherby, 45, 99 n
Wetwood, 227
Whalton, 173 n
Wharlow, 70 n
Whashton, 284
Wheldrake, 4, 4 n, 78 n
Whenby, 137
Whingate-Wood, 72
Whitby, 41, 41 n., 46, 126, 147 n., 230, 257 n
Whitehaven, Whithaven, 265 n., 277, 286
Whitgift, Whitguift, 139, 219
Whitley-Knoake, 295
Whittingeshaw, 194
Whittingstall, 196
Whitton, 206; hill, 140
Whitwell, 40 n
Whixley, 71
Whorlton in Cleveland, 120
Widrington, 228
Wigan Lane, 16 n
Wigton, 95
Wilberfosse, 122
Williamontswick, 227
Willoughby, Willoughbie, 20, 20 n., 270
Wilsden, 166
Winlington, 92, 93
Winnington-bridge, 81 n
Wintersett, 167
Winton, 103 n
Witherneseey, 121
Withernwicke, 123
Witton, 182, 228; East, 180; Shields, Shells, 207, 227, 249 n
Wolsingham, 277 n
Wolverhampton, Wollerhampton, 236
Wombwell, 126 n
Woodam Moor, 111
Woodchurch, 32, 111
Woodend, 124
Woodhall, 43
Woodsome, 86
Wooler, Woolaw, 155, 165, 206, 207, 227, 277

2 A

Woolley, 208
Worcester, 51, 51 n., 52, 52 n
Workington, 265
Worsall, Woorsall, 111 ; High, 138
Wressell, 122
Wycliffe, 44 n., 218 n
Wyke, Wike, 88, 138

Y.

Yarm, Yarme, 47, 111
Yeadon, 139
Yeddingham, 43
York city, *passim;* All Saints Pavement in, 3 n.; the Bederne in, 282; Bishophill the newer, 9; Buckingham House in, 210 n.; Blake Street in, 188 n.; Blue Boar in Castlegate, 1 n.; Bootham, Bowtham, in, 85, 101 ; Boulen Bar, 211 n. ; Castle of, 1, 10, 19, 20, 23, 27, 27 n., 41, 41 n., 42 n., 44 n., 47 n., 97 n., 146 n., 216 n., 230 n., 238, 244 n., 251, 252, 252 n., 269 n., 281 n., 282, 298 n.; Castlegate, 1 ; Friars' Garden in, 234; St. Helen's, 10 n.; St. Mary's-in-Castlegate, 241 n., Merchants' Hall, 11, 11 n.; Micklegate, 185, 262 n., 278 n., 279; Micklegate Bar, 263; Minster of, 165 n., 215 n., 278, 278 n., 279, 280, 281 n., 282.; Monckbarr in, 212; Ousebridge in, 126 n., 262 n., 269; Peasholme Green in, 243 ; Penley Croft in, 212, 213 ; St. Saviourgate in, 262 n., 263 n., Swinegate in 282 , Walmgate Bar in, 41 n,; Weavers' Company, of, 10
Youlthorpe, 3, 3 n

N.B. The names and places in the Preface are not indexed.

www.ingramcontent.com/pod-product-compliance
Lightning Source LLC
Chambersburg PA
CBHW021337300426
44114CB00012B/979